Fifth
Edition

Criminal Investigation

THE ART AND THE SCIENCE

Michael D. Lyman

Columbia College of Missouri

PEARSON

Prentice
Hall

Upper Saddle River, New Jersey 07458

Library of Congress Cataloging-in-Publication Data

Lyman, Michael D.
    Criminal investigation : the art and the science / Michael D. Lyman.—5th ed.
    p. cm.
    Includes index.
    ISBN 0-13-613306-1
    1. Criminal investigation.   I. Title.

HV8073.L94 2008
363.25—dc22

2006052537

Editor-in-Chief: Vernon R. Anthony
Senior Acquisitions Editor: Tim Peyton
Associate Editor: Sarah Holle
Marketing Manager: Adam Kloza
Production Editor: Janet Bolton, Milford Publishing Services
Project Manager: Barbara Marttine Cappuccio
Managing Editor: Mary Carnis
Manufacturing Manager: Ilene Sanford
Manufacturing Buyer: Cathleen Petersen
Senior Design Coordinator: Miguel Ortiz
Interior and Cover Design: Wanda España
Cover Images: Crime scene tape: Arthur Turner/Alamy Images; Crime scene unit: Mary Altaffer/AP Wide World Photos; Hands/magnifying glass: Mikael Karlsson/Arresting Images; Car/lasers demo: AP Wide World Photos
Composition: Pine Tree Composition
Printing and Binding: Courier Kendallville
Copyediting and Proofreading: Maine Proofreading Services

Part and Chapter Opening Photo Credits

Part 1: Arthur Turner, Alamy Images; Chapter 1: City of New York Police Department Photo Unit; Chapter 2: Kathy McLaughlin, The Image Works; Part 2: Mikael Karlsson, Arresting Images; Chapter 3: AP Wide World Photos; Chapter 4: © Ron Sachs, Corbis Sygma; Chapter 5: AP Wide World Photos; Chapter 6: Dr. Michael D. Lyman; Chapter 7: Dr. Michael D. Lyman; Chapter 8: A. Ramey, PhotoEdit Inc.; Chapter 9: Dwayne Newton, PhotoEdit Inc.; Chapter 10: Jason Cohn; Part 3: Dana Fisher, AP Wide World Photos; Chapter 11: Marc D. Longwood, Pearson Education/PH College; Chapter 12: Bushnell/Soifer, Getty Images Inc.-Stone Allstock; Chapter 13: Bill Aron, PhotoEdit Inc.; Chapter 14: Rhoda Sidney, The Image Works; Chapter 15: Jeff Roberson, AP Wide World Photos; Chapter 16: Michael Newman, PhotoEdit Inc.; Part 4: Pictor, Image State/International Stock Photography Ltd.; Chapter 17: Dr. Michael D. Lyman; Chapter 18: Reed Saxon, AP Wide World Photos; Chapter 19: Michael Newman, PhotoEdit Inc.; Chapter 20: James Shaffer, PhotoEdit Inc.; Part 5: Getty Images-Stockbyte; Chapter 21: Wes Pope/Aurora; Chapter 22: Getty Images, Inc.; Part 6: David R. Frazier Photolibrary, Inc.; Chapter 23: Bob Daemmrich, The Image Works.

Pearson Education LTD.
Pearson Education Singapore, Pte. Ltd
Pearson Education, Canada, Ltd
Pearson Education–Japan
Pearson Education Australia PTY, Limited
Pearson Education North Asia Ltd
Pearson Educación de Mexico, S.A. de C.V.
Pearson Education Malaysia, Pte. Ltd
Pearson Education Upper Saddle River, New Jersey

10 9 8 7 6 5

ISBN 13: 978-0-13-613306-3
ISBN 10:   0-13-613306-1

This book is dedicated to the most important people in my life, my wife, Julie, and my daughter, Kelsey, who have offered their continual and ongoing support of me in the painstaking preparation of this book. Their support played no small role in this book's successful completion, and for that I am deeply grateful.

Brief Contents

Contents

► **CHAPTER 2**

Processing the Crime Scene   25

PART 2 # The Investigative Process   51

► **CHAPTER 3**

The Crime Scene: Field Notes, Documenting, and Reporting   53

▶ **CHAPTER 4**

Search and Seizure   81

▶ CHAPTER 5

Identification of Criminal Suspects:
Field and Laboratory Processes   125

► **CHAPTER 8**

Making an Arrest   215

► **CHAPTER 9**

Interviews and Interrogations   233

► **CHAPTER 10**

Development and Management of Informants   257

PART 3   # Interpersonal Violence   271

► **CHAPTER 11**

Wrongful Death   273

► **CHAPTER 12**

Robbery   305

► **CHAPTER 13**

Assault and Related Offenses   321

► **CHAPTER 14**

Sexual Assault   339

▶ **CHAPTER 15**

Missing and Abducted Persons   363

▶ **CHAPTER 16**

Child Abuse and Neglect   387

PART 4 **Property Crimes   413**

▶ **CHAPTER 17**

Burglary   415

▶ **CHAPTER 18**

Larceny–Theft   429

▶ CHAPTER 19

Motor Vehicle Theft   455

▶ CHAPTER 20

Arson and Bombings   477

PART 5   Vice Crimes and Related Offenses   501

▶ CHAPTER 21
Drug Offenses   503

▶ CHAPTER 22

White-Collar Crime   541

PART 6   # Prosecution   567

▶ **CHAPTER 23**

Preparation for Court   569

Preface

Criminal investigation represents a timeless and dynamic field of scientific study. This book, now in its fifth edition, was written with the perception that crime detection is a field that relies heavily on the past experiences of investigators as well as recent practical, forensic, and technological innovations. The investigator's success in crime detection can be influenced by several external variables. For example, increased pressure by public interest groups and courts of law has caused police supervisors to place greater emphasis on case management and officer accountability. In addition, because of increased social problems associated with drug abuse, criminal violence, and related gang activity, the public spotlight has focused more than ever before on methods of crime detection and successful prosecution of lawbreakers. Finally, because of the rising incidence of mass and serial murders in the last decade, more people are realizing the importance of a thoroughly investigated case and the reasons behind the occurrence of such crimes.

This book is intended to meet the needs of students and others interested in criminal justice by presenting information in a logical flow, paralleling the steps and considerations observed in an actual criminal investigation. Additionally, it is designed to fulfill an ongoing need for a book that explains clearly and thoughtfully the fundamentals of criminal investigation as practiced by police officers on the job.

The book is written with several observations in mind. First, as its title indicates, it is designed to blend scientific theories of crime detection with a practical approach to criminal investigation. It has been drafted on the assumption that sound criminal investigations depend on an understanding of the science of crime detection procedures and the art of anticipating human behavior. There is yet another critical observation made in the book: It recognizes that both the uniformed officer and the criminal investigator play important roles in the field of criminal investigation. The duties of each are outlined throughout the book, recognizing that there is a fundamental need for both to work in tandem throughout many aspects of the criminal investigation process.

One underlying theme of the book is that as with all police endeavors, criminal investigation is a law enforcement responsibility that must be conducted within the framework of the U.S. Constitution and the practices of a democratic society. Consequently, court decisions and case studies have been quoted extensively for clarification of issues and general reader information.

In summary, I am hopeful that this book will prove to be an engaging textbook that is descriptive of the duties of modern-day crime detection and police professionalism. For more efficient use, this book has been designed to follow closely standard curriculum format. Accordingly, each chapter contains key terms and ends with discussion questions to aid in the instructional process.

Michael D. Lyman

Acknowledgments

No book can be written entirely as a solo effort, and this project was no exception. The preparation of this book represents hundreds of painstaking hours maintaining continuous contact with criminal justice agencies, federal information clearinghouses, police practitioners, and colleagues in the field of criminal justice. In addition, to offer the reader the most up-to-date and relevant information, it was important to consult libraries, police journals, periodicals, newspapers, government publications, and other sources of literature germane to the field of crime detection on an ongoing basis.

Many persons were helpful in the preparation of this book, including practitioners in the field as well as experts in academe. Among these, the contributions of certain persons deserve special recognition. Included are Chief Randy Boehm and the men and women of the Columbia Police Department; the Missouri State Highway Patrol; agents from the Federal Bureau of Investigation and Drug Enforcement Administration; contributors from the Department of Homeland Security; and the International Association of Chiefs of Police.

A special debt of gratitude goes to Detective Michael Himmel of the Columbia Police Department (ret.) and Brian Hoey of the Missouri State Highway Patrol Crime Laboratory who provided a great number of crime scene and laboratory photos for this new edition. Without the cooperation and guidance of these persons and organizations, this book would not have been possible.

A special thank-you is also well deserved for Sarah Holle, Tim Peyton, and the many other dedicated publishing professionals at Prentice Hall for their hard work and support for the new edition of this text. Finally, I would like to extend special thanks to those criminal justice academics and practitioners who painstakingly reviewed the manuscript of this book. These persons include: James T. Burnett, Rockland County Community College, Suffern, NY; David Graff, Kent State University–Tuscarawas Campus, New Philadelphia, Ohio; Harold Frossard, Moraine Valley Community College, Palos Hills, IL; Mark McCoy, University of Central Oklahoma, Edmond, OK; Elvage Murphy, Edinboro University, Erie, PA; and Gary Yoshonis, Grossmont Community College, San Diego, CA.

Without the support and assistance of all these people, and many more, this book would not have become a reality. Thank you all.

Michael D. Lyman

About the Author

Michael D. Lyman is a Professor of Criminal Justice at Columbia College of Missouri, located in Columbia, MO. In addition to being a teaching faculty member, he serves as the program director for the Master of Science of Criminal Justice Program and is the founder and director of the college's Forensic Science Program. Prior to entering the field of college teaching, he was employed as a criminal investigator for state police organizations in Kansas and Oklahoma and has taught literally hundreds of law enforcement officers in the techniques of proper and professional criminal investigation. Dr. Lyman has authored numerous textbooks in criminal justice dealing with the areas of criminal investigation, policing, organized crime, drug enforcement, and drug trafficking. He received both his bachelor's and master's degrees from Wichita State University and his Ph.D. from the University of Missouri–Columbia. He has been called upon on over 100 occasions by law enforcement and the legal communities to review criminal investigations and render the results of his evaluations and his opinions in federal court proceedings nationwide.

Textbooks such as this are an ongoing work in progress, and the author welcomes communication and correspondence about his work. Dr. Lyman can be contacted at Columbia College, 1001 Rogers Street, Columbia, MO 65216 or at mlyman@ccis.edu. Thank you for using this textbook.

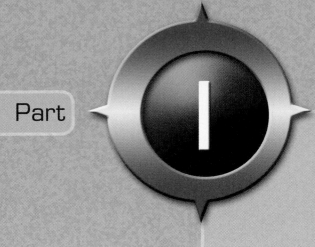

Part I

Fundamentals of Criminal Investigation

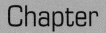

Chapter

Criminal Investigation

An Overview

Key Terms

- ▶ abduction
- ▶ ballistics
- ▶ Bertillon system
- ▶ bobbies
- ▶ Bow Street Runners
- ▶ data mining
- ▶ deductive reasoning
- ▶ expert systems
- ▶ forensic dentistry
- ▶ inductive reasoning
- ▶ major case squads
- ▶ preventive response
- ▶ proactive response
- ▶ Prohibition
- ▶ reactive response
- ▶ relational databases
- ▶ rogues' gallery
- ▶ Scotland Yard
- ▶ serology
- ▶ thief catchers

This chapter will enable you to:

- Understand the myths of crime solving and the criminal investigation process.

- Realize modern developments in science and crime detection.

- Consider recent research in criminal investigation.

- Define the objectives of criminal investigations.

- Understand the various types of investigations.

- Identify the most desirable characteristics of criminal investigators.

INTRODUCTION

The study of criminal investigation involves probing several different fields at once and is therefore a difficult task about which to write. For example, it is important for an investigator to understand basic techniques of collection and preservation of evidence, but to do so, a fundamental understanding of criminalistics or forensic science is often required. In addition to technical competence, modern-day investigators must be well versed in the law. Legal skills include a working knowledge of criminal law, constitutional law, and rules of evidence, all of which are essential for successful prosecution of a criminal case. This chapter is designed to give the reader the underlying essentials of this field of policing, which is both rewarding and challenging.

THE ROMANCE AND REALITY OF CRIME SOLVING

Throughout modern history, people have harbored a fascination with cops and criminals—crime and crime fighting. Whenever there is a public crime scene, large groups of people gather to watch crime scene investigators in action. For the average citizen, police cars and emergency units with their screaming sirens and flashing lights spark an insatiable curiosity. Fueling people's interest and imagination are newspapers and periodicals that sensationalize criminal investigations, which often involve both heinous and interesting aspects. For example, in 2003, a number of high-visibility cases surfaced in the national media calling attention to techniques of criminal investigation. These included the case of pop singer Michael Jackson, who was charged with sexual abuse, and the case of Scott Peterson, on trial for the murder of his wife and unborn child.

Adults aren't the only ones who show an interest in crime detection; children visualize the clashing forces of good and evil in vividly illustrated children's books, comic books, and early morning television cartoons. In the twenty-first century, the Teenage Mutant Ninja Turtles represent a teenage version of crime fighters, while J. K. Rowling's Harry Potter children's book series portrays the classic clash between good and evil. Children's movies also portray fictional crime fighters such as Batman and his sidekick Robin in confrontations with evil foes. Indeed, American pop culture typically portrays the conflict between the forces of good and evil in movies, novels, and television cartoons.

Notorious outlaw gangs of the Old West have also interested people for decades. Gangs active on the western frontier, such as the Younger brothers and the Dalton gang, represent the colorful heritage of the antihero. Another outlaw, Jesse James, was one of the most famous of the American West. During his time, he acquired a Robin Hood reputation. With brother Frank and several other men, the James gang gained national notoriety by robbing banks, trains, and stagecoaches.

Detective magazines, books, and movies pitting the shrewd criminal against his or her persevering police counterpart have also perpetuated the detective mystique. For generations, fabled yarns featuring sleuths such as Sherlock Holmes and Hercule Poirot have presented readers with a menagerie of farfetched tales filled with unlikely clues and colorful suspects. In fact, part of the allure of the classic detective novels of the early twentieth century was the introduction of the private eye. Mickey Spillane's Mike Hammer, for example, had a

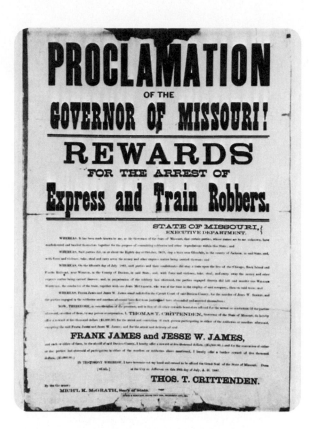

Figure 1.1 During the settlement of the western frontier, wanted posters were used to identify persons wanted by law enforcement. *State Historical Society of Missouri*

remorseless desire to punish wrongdoers who managed to escape an impotent criminal justice system while walking a fine legal line himself.

As with the private eye, the spy of the 1960s enlivened espionage stories featuring such heroes as James Bond, whose popularity rivaled even that of Sherlock Holmes. In reading the material, however, readers would gain little practical insight into the mind of the criminal, the nature of crime, the science of detection, the techniques of law enforcement officers, or courtroom procedures where one is found either guilty or innocent. Although entertaining, such stories bear little resemblance to the real world of criminal investigation.

CRIMINAL INVESTIGATION AND OUR ENGLISH HERITAGE

The history of criminal investigation is vast, and over the years many writers have attempted to engage the topic. In this section, we focus on the roots of our criminal justice heritage in Great Britain as it pertains to the field of criminal investigation. We begin our story during the era of Europe's Industrial Revolution, which attracted the peasant class from the countryside into the towns and cities. The ensuing crime wave forced law enforcement officials to take drastic measures. As a result, **thief catchers** were recruited from the riffraff of the streets to aid law enforcement officials in locating criminals. Two classes of thief catchers were identified: (1) hirelings, whose motivations were mercenary in nature, and (2) social climbers, who would implicate their accomplices in order to move up the social ladder.

Figure 1.2 Jesse James, the elusive outlaw of the Wild West, helped to establish the mystique of the antihero.
State Historical Society of Missouri

One hireling, Jonathan Wild, gained fame in eighteenth-century England for operating a London brothel which also served as headquarters for thieves and thugs, with whom he was well acquainted. Coining the phrase "set a thief to catch a thief," Wild operated simultaneously as an undercover operative for London's authorities and as a criminal in London's underworld. It soon became clear, however, that he could profit more from arranging the return of stolen goods to the police than from selling the goods at outrageous discounts to the local fence. So while he acted as the receiver of stolen goods masquerading as the "recoverer" of lost property, he also served as the middleman, taking his cut for finding stolen goods while hiding and protecting thieves in his employ.

In England, the first police worked only at night and were originally called the Watch of London. They soon developed into the Old Charleys, who were paid by the residents they served. These parish constables originated in London in 1253 and lasted until 1829. Soon after the hanging of Jonathan Wild, Henry Fielding was appointed magistrate in Westminster, a city adjacent to central London. Fielding, a writer known for his novel *Tom Jones,* located himself in a house on Bow Street that served as both home and office, and soon began what is credited as England's first police force.

The Bow Street Runners

During the 1750s, crimes such as burglary and street robbery were rampant in England. Fielding took on the challenge of reducing the profits realized by criminals. Working relationships were established with local business owners, in particular pawnbrokers, who were provided with lists of stolen property. Fielding encouraged them to contact him should any stolen property come to their attention. Fielding took seriously his new duties as crime fighter and promptly employed new crime-fighting methods. One such method was the appointment of a handful of parish constables acclimated to night watchman duties. These trackers soon began performing criminal investigation functions and became well known as successful thief takers by using their ties with London's criminal underworld. Originally called "Mr. Fielding's People," they soon became known as the **Bow Street Runners,** the first well-known investigative body in England. Fielding's runners were not paid as police officers but rather, in terms of thief-taker rewards, a percentage of all fines resulting from successful prosecution of thieves. Shortly after his appointment as magistrate, Fielding's health deteriorated and he was confined to a wheelchair. As a result, his half-brother, John Fielding, was appointed to share his magistracy. Because of his blindness, John Fielding was soon dubbed the "blind beak" (*beak* meaning magistrate) to the criminal underworld in London.

The Bow Street Runners were forerunners of a trend in policing for specialization within the police force. In fact, by 1800, the Bow Street Police Office was considered by many to be the leading law enforcement organization in the area. Johnson adds: "Even if the evils of the justice/constable system had been eliminated from Bow Street Office operations, no local jurisdiction could combat the rising crime wave throughout London."[1] Between 1760 and 1800, Fielding was given authority to organize a horse patrol, which was later followed by a permanent foot patrol. The patrol officers, smartly outfitted in red vests and blue jackets and trousers, became the pioneers of England's uniformed police.

The London Metropolitan Police

The great watershed in British police development occurred in 1829 with the establishment of the London Metropolitan Police Department. Officers of the department were dubbed **bobbies** after the department's founder, Home Secretary Sir Robert Peel. The "new" police were England's first paid, full-time police force, consisting of about 1,000 uniformed officers. In addition, they replaced the old constables, such as the Bow Street Runners, who had ultimately gained a reputation of incompetency and inefficiency. Indeed, the bobbies were required to meet rigid standards of professionalism. Minimum standards included minimum weight and height requirements and standards of literacy and character. A detective bureau was created in the police force in 1842 but was not publicly acknowledged until some 35 years later for fear that the specter of French-style repression would be remembered.

Technology in crime detection began to flourish during the nineteenth century with the creation of a personal identification system by Alphonse Bertillon, the director of the criminal identification section of the Paris Police Department. The **Bertillon system** was based on the idea that certain aspects of the human body, such as skeletal size, ear shaping, and eye color, remained the same after a person had reached full physical maturity. It used a combination of photographs with standardized physical measurements. In the mid-1840s, the study of fingerprint patterns became a popular means to identify suspects in crime. Although the use of fingerprints is commonplace today, it wasn't until the late nineteenth century that it was learned that a person's fingerprints could act as a unique, unchangeable method of personal identification. Such discoveries have been credited to the Englishmen William J. Herschel and Henry Faulds, who were working in Asia at the time. The use of fingerprints was refined by Sir Francis Galton and was adopted by Scotland Yard in 1901.

The Creation of Scotland Yard

For many people, much misunderstanding has existed about the function and role of **Scotland Yard.** Some believe that it represents a single police authority in Great Britain. In fact, it is the headquarters of London's Metropolitan Police and has never exerted any authority over other police organizations in Great Britain. Although London's Metropolitan Police was founded in 1829, it took more than 10 years to organize a detective branch. Even then, however, "the Yard" was only a small division within the department. The strength of the force was increased in 1867 after an incident in which an explosion occurred when a small group of Irishmen were trying to free a prisoner from the Clerkenwell House of Detention. Several citizens were killed. A decade later another reorganization occurred when several senior detectives of Scotland Yard were convicted of corruption charges.

A strengthened Criminal Investigation Division (CID) was then set up and has endured to the present. In fact, the phrase "Call in Scotland Yard" refers entirely to the investigative section of the force. CID officers of the Yard are selected from candidates who have served as uniformed constables. To avoid the problem of complacency within the force, officers are regularly rotated from the uniformed division to the detective division and back again.

CRIMINAL INVESTIGATION IN AMERICA

As the American frontier moved westward during the nineteenth century, outlaws posed serious problems in newly settled areas. Mining camps and cattle towns seemed to experience more violence than other areas. The movement west had moved men and women far from the institutions that had served them previously. Law enforcement agencies and criminal courts, if present at all, made only minor strides in protecting the vast areas under their jurisdictions. Indeed, it was in these areas that criminals could easily hide and witnesses would often move away, making detection and apprehension of criminals a discouraging task.

Following the lead of London's police force, the first professional police forces were established in the United States in Boston in 1837, New York in 1844, and Philadelphia in 1854. By the 1870s, almost all major U.S. cities had municipal police departments. As in England, criminal investigation by public law enforcement was viewed as politically hazardous since it favored only those who could pay. But the rapid growth of cities produced violence, crime, and vice activities that demonstrated a breakdown of social order in small communities. Growing incidents of mob violence between Protestants and Catholics, immigrants and Native Americans, and abolitionists and pro-slavery groups were probably the most crucial catalysts for expanded police functions. During the middle of the nineteenth century, three significant elements emerged that had an impact on criminal investigation:

1. Municipal police were supplemented by the county sheriff in rural areas.
2. Establishment of the Texas Rangers (established before Texas became a state).
3. Expansion of police functions with establishment of the U.S. Marshal's Service and the Secret Service, formed during the Civil War to investigate counterfeiters.

In the 1890s, criminal investigators became an important part of the U.S. Post Office and the Bureau of Immigration and Naturalization. Because of the lack of effective law enforcement in rural areas, however, people banded together on their own to investigate crimes and apprehend perpetrators. Vigilantes in the mining camps would conduct trials and even execute some of the most dangerous offenders. Cattle ranchers would often hire range detectives to capture rustlers. As a result, some business firms emerged, such as the famed Pinkerton's Detective Agency, which offered to protect property and pursue offenders for a fee.

The Pinkerton National Detective Agency

Pinkerton's National Detective Agency, founded in 1850 by Scottish immigrant Allan Pinkerton, was the first organization of its type in the United States (Figure 1.3). In fact, its organizational structure was later adopted by the Federal Bureau of Investigation (FBI). The Pinkerton Agency was called on by communities to handle cases that local law enforcement officers were unable to investigate due to incompetence or limited resources. Pinkerton offered the field of criminal investigation several innovations in crime detection. For example, he was the first to devise a **rogues' gallery,** which was a compilation of descriptions, methods of operation, hiding places, and the names of associates of known criminals.

Pinkerton gained national fame when he uncovered a plot to kill Abraham Lincoln during the 1860s. The plot was designed to kill Lincoln on a train while enroute to give his first inauguration speech in Washington. Pinkerton outwitted the assassins by putting Lincoln on an earlier train. Soon after, Pinkerton was placed in charge of the secret service operations during the Civil War. After Pinkerton's death in 1884, agency detectives gained a reputation for the use of violence to undermine unions as well as to frame and convict their leaders. Among the more notable Pinkerton cases were those in which dozens of union spies were used by the infamous Jay Gould to break a strike against the Texas and Pacific Railroads and when Pinkerton detectives were used in 1905 to

Figure 1.3 Allan Pinkerton, President Abraham Lincoln, and General McClellan at Antietam, Maryland, about October 3, 1866. *Courtesy of the Library of Congress*

Figure 1.4 "We Never Sleep." The famous Pinkerton "private eye" became the logo of Allan Pinkerton's National Detective Agency. *Printed with permission of Pinkerton's, Inc.*

involve labor leaders in the murder of ex-Governor Frank Steunenberg of Idaho. After Congress declared labor spying unconstitutional in 1937, the industrial division of the Pinkerton agency was officially dissolved.

Prohibition

Prohibition (1920–1933) represented another significant period in which criminal investigation underwent change. Unlike the drug trade of later years, the Volstead Act of the Prohibition period failed to criminalize the purchase or consumption of alcohol—only its manufacture, transportation, and sale. Because liquor was legal in other countries, smuggling (bootlegging) was a major criminal enterprise. Prohibition criminals avoided the federal law against alcohol by creating a cottage industry, manufacturing beer and wine at home. By 1924 rival gangs organized themselves for control of "speakeasy" operations, prostitution rings, and virtually any other source of illegal income. Police corruption flourished as many law enforcement officers accepted bribes from mobsters. During this time, the FBI had no jurisdiction in enforcing the Volstead Act. Instead, enforcement responsibility was given to the Treasury Department.

The Creation of the FBI

Probably the single most significant development in criminal investigation in the United States was the establishment of the FBI in 1924. Originating as the Justice Department's Bureau of Investigation in 1907, the FBI originally had very few responsibilities. When new federal laws governing interstate transportation of stolen automobiles were passed, however, the bureau gained much notoriety. J. Edgar Hoover, the bureau's newly named director, announced in 1924 that he would strive to eliminate corruption and get the agency out of politics. In doing so, he raised the qualifications of agent personnel, reduced the number of agents nationwide, and closed some field offices. It was only after Hoover's death in 1972 that many of his abuses of power surfaced. For example, it became widely known that the FBI kept files on certain persons, such as politicians and adversaries of the FBI. Today, the FBI is one of many federal investigative agencies that have made great strides in professionalizing the field of criminal investigation.

THE INCREASE OF FORENSIC SCIENCE IN CRIME DETECTION

The seeds of modern forensic science were sown in the last quarter of the nineteenth century. Progress from that time has been slow but steady. The American Academy of Forensic Sciences (AAFS), a professional organization of forensic scientists in America, was established in 1948. Specific areas of expertise of AAFS members include pathology and biology, toxicology, criminalistics, questioned documents, and forensic odontology and anthropology.

In addition to the development of fingerprinting as an aid to criminal detection, several other forensic advances were either being developed or had already been placed into service by the late nineteenth century. Historic strides in criminal investigation included study in serology, forensic dentistry, and ballistics. For example, research into human blood was vastly expanded during the early twentieth century by Paul Uhlenhuth, a German physician. Uhlenhuth's work created serums that enabled one to distinguish one species of animal blood from another. Consequently, **serology** was a procedure that was established to study human blood stains and distinguish them from the blood of most other animals.

Forensic dentistry was widely studied during the mid-nineteenth century as a means to identify teeth marks in victims. Because bite marks are so distinctive, they are now commonly used as evidence. Whether on the body of a suspect or victim, such evidence can implicate suspects in crimes such as assault, rape, and murder. **Ballistics** is yet another critical area of investigative detection. In 1835, the use of ballistics to solve a murder was first conducted by Bow Street Runner Henry Goddard. Since then, evidence such as powder burns and markings on bullets and casings is accepted as valuable evidence to connect suspects with both victims and weapons used.

Today, increases in the demand for scientific techniques by investigators have created special financial burdens on law enforcement agencies. Techniques such as these call for people with a high degree of formal education in areas such as chemistry, forensic science, and physiology.

CRIMINAL INVESTIGATION RESEARCH

As with other aspects of criminal justice, research plays an important role in helping us to understand how criminal investigations can be more effective. Early studies by both the RAND Corporation and the Police Executive Research Forum challenged long-held opinions about criminal investigation and made some practical recommendations.

The RAND Corporation Study

In the late 1970s, the National Institute of Law Enforcement and Criminal Justice awarded a grant to the RAND Corporation to undertake a nationwide study of criminal investigations by police agencies in major U.S. cities. The goals of the study were to determine how police investigations were organized and managed, as well as to assess various activities as they relate to the effectiveness of overall police functioning. Until this study, police investigators had not been placed under as much scrutiny as those in patrol functions or other areas of policing.

Design of the Study. The focus of the RAND study was the investigation of "index" offenses: serious crimes such as murder, robbery, and rape. Other less serious crimes, such as drug violations, gambling, and prostitution, were not considered in the study. A national survey was conducted that assessed investigative practices of all municipal and county police agencies employing over 150 sworn personnel or serving a jurisdiction with a population over 100,000. Observations and interviews were conducted in more than twenty-five departments, which were chosen to represent various investigative methods.

The *Uniform Crime Reports* (UCRs), administered by the FBI, were used to determine the outcome of investigations. Data on the allocation of investigative endeavors were obtained from a computerized network operated by the Kansas City Police Department. In addition, information from the National Crime Victimization Survey and the UCRs were linked to identify the effectiveness of arrest and the overall relationships between departments. Finally, the study analyzed case samples to determine how specific cases were solved.

Recommendations of the Study. A number of policy recommendations were made as a result of the study. First, it was recommended that postarrest activities be coordinated more closely with the prosecutor's office. This could be accomplished by assigning an investigator to the prosecutor's office or by permitting prosecutors discretionary guidance over the practices of investigators, thus increasing the number of prosecutable cases. The second recommendation was that patrol officers be afforded greater responsibilities in conducting preliminary investigations, providing greater case-screening capabilities for investigators while eliminating redundancy. The study suggests that many cases can be closed at the preliminary investigation stage. Therefore, patrol officers should be trained to perform such duties. The third recommendation was to increase forensic resources for processing latent prints and to develop a system to organize and search fingerprint files more effectively. Finally, the study recommended that with regard to investigations of cases that the agency chose to pursue, a distinction should be made between those cases that require routine clerical skills and those that require special investigative abilities. Those investigations falling into the second category should be handled through a specialized investigation section.

In addition to the RAND Corporation's study, several others have offered support for its findings. Block and Weidman's study of the New York Police Department and Greenberg et al.'s decision-making model for felony investigations both support the idea that patrol officers make the majority of arrests during preliminary investigations and can provide excellent case-screening benefits for investigations.[2]

The PERF Study

In one important study, the Police Executive Research Forum (PERF) considered the roles played by detectives and patrol officers in the course of burglary and robbery investigations. The study examined three areas: DeKalb County, Georgia; St.

Recommendations of the Rand Study

- Coordinate police investigations more closely with prosecutors.
- Expand the investigative role of patrol officers.
- Provide additional resources to process, organize, and search for latent prints.
- Distinguish between cases that can be handled clerically and those that require specially trained investigators.

Petersburg, Florida; and Wichita, Kansas. Of the major findings of the study, several observations were made.[3] For example, PERF concluded that detectives and patrol officers contributed equally to the resolution of burglary and robbery cases. However, it was determined that in most cases, a period of four hours (stretched over several days) was sufficient to close cases and that 75 percent of burglary and robbery cases were suspended in less than two days, due to a lack of leads. In the remainder of cases, detectives played a major role in follow-up work conducted to identify and arrest suspects. It was determined, however, that both detectives and patrol personnel are too reliant on victim information for identification purposes, as opposed to checking leads from sources such as informants, witnesses, and other information sources in the police department.

The implications of the PERF study suggest that there is not as much waste or mismanagement in investigations as earlier thought as a result of similar studies. The value of follow-up investigations by detectives in identifying and arresting suspects is also thought to be much greater than indicated by earlier studies.

Other Recommendations. The PERF study also recommended that greater emphasis be placed on the collection and use of physical evidence when applicable. Although physical evidence is seldom used in identifying suspects, it can be effective in corroborating other evidence of suspect identification, indicating that although not all police departments use extensive training of evidence technicians, many have established policies regulating situations in which they should be used. In the past, many departments overused the services of evidence technicians on cases where physical evidence was minimal, resulting in the collection of more evidence than required. As a result, another recommendation by the PERF study is that police departments develop policies and guidelines regulating the use of evidence technicians in routine cases such as burglary and robbery where there is no physical injury to victims. This policy should be based on the assumption that if the suspects can be found through other means of identification, physical evidence is not likely to be useful.

Yet another recommendation of the PERF study is that officers dedicate greater effort to locating witnesses through the use of a neighborhood canvass. This was not found to be common practice by patrol officers in the cities studied because initial information was commonly learned via interviews with witnesses and victims. It was suggested that patrol officers seek additional witnesses and victims through a neighborhood canvass, in order to expand the scope of their investigation. Finally, PERF recommended that patrol officers make more extensive use of department records and informants to develop and identify suspects. Although checking department records would be a relatively easy task, the skills needed to develop and interview informants are not common among patrol officers. Supervisors in the patrol area could make a greater effort to provide such training to street officers to help them develop informants.

COMPUTER-AIDED INVESTIGATIONS

The application of science and technology is evident in the use of large computer databases by some police departments that can cross-reference specific information about crimes to determine patterns and to identify suspects. One of the earliest of these programs was HITMAN, developed by the Hollywood, California, Police Department in 1985. HITMAN has since evolved into a department-wide database that assists detectives in the Los Angeles Police Department (LAPD) in solving violent crimes. The LAPD uses a similar computer program to track a target population of approximately 60,000 gang members.[4]

Computers use artificial intelligence to make inferences based on available information and to draw conclusions or make recommendations to the systems operators. **Expert systems,** as these computer models are often called, depend on three components:

1. The user interface or terminal,
2. A knowledge base containing information already known in the area of investigation, and
3. A computer program, known as an inference engine, that compares user input and stores information according to established decision-making rules.

Numerous expert systems exist today. For example, one is used by the FBI's National Center for the Analysis of Violent Crime (NCAVC) in a project designed to profile violent serial criminals. The NCAVC PC system depends on computer models of criminal profiling to provide a theoretical basis for the development of investigative strategies. A number of other systems have been developed that specifically focus on serological (blood serum) analysis, narcotics interdiction, serial murder and rape, and counterterrorism.[5]

Similar to expert systems are **relational databases,** which permit fast and easy sorting of large records. Perhaps the best-known early criminal justice database was called Big Floyd. It was developed in the 1980s by the FBI in conjunction with the Institute for Defense Analyses. Big Floyd was designed to access the more than 3 million records in the FBI's organized crime information system and to allow investigators to decide which federal statutes apply in a given situation and whether investigators have enough evidence for a successful prosecution. In the years since Big Floyd, other relational databases targeting offenders of various types have been created, including computer systems to track deadbeat parents and quack physicians. In 1996, President Bill Clinton ordered the Department of Justice to create a computerized national registry of sex offenders. The national sex offender registry, developed as part of an overhaul of the FBI's computer systems, went online in 1999.

Some systems are even more problem specific. For example, ImAger, a product of Face Software, Inc., uses computer technology to artificially age photographs of missing children. The program has been used successfully to identify and recover a number of children. In one case, an abducted six-month-old was found after ImAger depicted what the child would look like at age five. The child was recognized by viewers who called the police.[6] Another composite imaging program, by Visatex Corp., is used by police artists to create simulated photographs of criminal suspects.

The most advanced computer-aided investigation systems are being touted by agencies such as NASA and the Defense Advanced Research Projects Agency (DARPA) as having the ability to prevent crime. DARPA, for example, announced its new Total Information Awareness (TIA) program in 2003.[7] The five-year development project uses information-sorting and pattern-matching software to sift through vast numbers of business and government databases in an effort to identify possible terrorist threats. The software attempts to detect suspicious patterns of activity, identify the people involved, and locate them so that investigations can be conducted.

Suspected insurgents might be identified when the software detects a series of credit card and official transactions that form a pattern that resembles preparation for an insurgency attack. The process, known as **data mining,** will generate computer models in an attempt to predict terrorists' actions. Privacy advocates have raised concerns about DARPA's initiatives, but the agency has tried to defuse concerns by assuring the public that the project is not an attempt to build a supercomputer to snoop into the private lives or track the everyday activities of American citizens. The agency claims that all TIA research complies with all privacy laws, without exception.

Another DARPA project that could aid law enforcement but is currently being developed for military use overseas is called Combat Zones That See (CZTS).[8] The CZTS program will build a huge surveillance system by networking existing cameras from department stores, subway platforms, parking lots, and other points of surveillance and feeding images to supercomputer-like processors capable of recognizing suspects by face, gait, and mannerisms as they move from one place to another. The data can be fed via satellite to remote locations across the globe, allowing the agency to track suspects on the move—either within cities or between countries. CZTS is being introduced gradually in selected locations beginning in areas in and around American military bases. Future uses of CZTS include nano-cameras equipped with micro-miniaturized transmitters that can be spread over a city like particles of dust which communicate relatively detailed information to local cellular-like installations for entry into the CZTS network.

THE OBJECTIVES OF CRIMINAL INVESTIGATION

Because of the changing nature of criminal activity and the role of the investigator, the objectives of the criminal investigation may be more complex than people imagine. The objectives of criminal investigations are to:

- Detect crime.
- Locate and identify suspects in crimes.
- Locate, document, and preserve evidence in crimes.
- Arrest suspects in crimes.
- Recover stolen property.
- Prepare sound criminal cases for prosecution.

The premise behind the criminal investigation field is that people make mistakes while committing crimes. For example, a burglar may leave behind broken glass or clothing fibers; a rapist may leave fingerprints, skin tissue, semen, or blood. As a result of these oversights, evidence of who they are is also left behind. It is the job of the criminal investigator to know how, when, and where to look for such evidence. In doing so, he or she must be able to draw on various resources, such as:

- Witnesses and informants, for firsthand information about the crime.
- Technological advances in evidence collection and preservation.
- Their own training and experience in investigative techniques.

Criminal investigation involves a process of inductive and deductive reasoning. The distinctions are as follows:

- **Inductive reasoning** is statistical reasoning toward a probable conclusion based on the frequency of certain things occurring. For example, all of John Wayne Gacy's victims found to date were male—so Gacy did not kill females.
- **Deductive reasoning** is reasoning based on specific pieces of evidence to establish proof that a suspect is guilty of an offense, for example, identifying muddy footprints outside a window where a burglary has occurred. An issue would be whether the footprints belonged to an occupant of the house or to the burglar. Criminal investigators must anticipate all possible scenarios and know what evidence is needed to support prosecution of the case, as each issue in dispute must be supported by evidence. The more evidence an investigator collects, the stronger the case and the proof of guilt. Conversely, the criminal investigator must also consider what evidence is available to exonerate innocent parties.

In 2002, Jon J. Nordby questioned the processes of inductive and deductive reasoning in his book *Dead Reckoning: The Art of Forensic Detection*. Nordby suggested that it's not enough to just collect and analyze evidence, but rather, investigators also need a guiding theory that's flexible enough to accommodate new information and sufficiently logical to show a clear pattern of cause and effect.[9]

For example, Nordby states that a homicide investigation could show that the killer did not need to break in to a residence because he had a key. This theory would significantly narrow the possibilities. It is important for investigators to not only have a theory that guides the investigation but that any theory that is contradicted be discarded. In other words, it is important for investigators to understand how logic and science work together.

Abduction is the process, therefore, of proposing a likely explanation for an event that must then be tested. For example, the killer had a key to the victim's home. Nordby suggests,

> "Induction is the wrong way of looking at science . . . because the classic problem of induction is the contrary instance [something that contradicts the claim].
>
> Let us consider the notion that once a crime scene investigator observes a hair or piece of fiber, he or she now has their evidence. The reality is that many if not most crime scenes exist in dirty, debris-filled rooms. Such places are abundant with hair and fibers. So what is the investigator actually looking for? Which of all of those hairs and fibers is actually evidence? Unless the criminal investigator has an idea or theory that will make one object relevant and another irrelevant, the evidence-collection process will be overwhelming. In order to have purpose in what is being done, the investigator must have something in mind. That comes from abduction."

Developing an explanation that can be tested moves the investigation forward and guides the accumulation of knowledge, giving way only when contradicted. Abduction helps to make links among events, and the development of the overall theory of a crime depends on adding new links. Nordby suggests that abduction keeps guessing to a minimum.

THE EMERGENCE OF THE POLICE SPECIALIST

The process of investigating criminals in the United States is structured very differently from the process followed in England. A division exists within law enforcement agencies between officers whose responsibility it is to maintain order and those who investigate crimes. In larger departments, specialized squads typically perform the investigative function in law enforcement agencies. In fact, many such departments have several detective divisions within, each dealing with different categories of crime, such as crimes against persons (e.g., rape, assault, robbery), crimes against property (e.g., burglary, larceny, auto theft), and vice (e.g., drug violations, gambling, prostitution). Smaller rural departments often lack financial resources to specialize, so patrol officers often conduct criminal investigations in addition to their patrol duties.

In some types of crime, such as homicide, investigators must develop leads through interviews with friends, family, and associates of the victim as well as witnesses to the crime. In other cases, investigative leads are developed by sifting through files and prior police records and establishing the suspect's mode of operation (MO). In all cases, the investigative process uses traditional and historical methods of detection through the use of official records, photographs, fingerprints, and so on, as opposed to daily face-to-face contacts with the citizenry, such as with the patrol division. The investigative specialist is generally an older person who has had considerable experience in police work. Most detectives are former patrol personnel who have worked up through the ranks, due to the common practice of promoting from within.

TYPES OF INVESTIGATIONS

The mission of law enforcement is complex and demanding but contains some fundamental components, including the maintenance of peace in our communities and the protection of lives and property. When people choose to violate laws that provide for these essentials, the perpetrators must be identified and brought before a court. It is the task of identifying such offenders that is the quintessence of criminal investigation. Criminal investigators will confront investigations in several areas in the regular course of their duties:

- Personal background, to determine a person's suitability for appointment to sensitive public trust positions.
- Suspected violations of criminal law.
- Infractions of civil law.
- Vice (drug and organized crime activity).

CRIME SCENE INVESTIGATORS

The popular television show *CSI* has brought the role of the crime scene investigator (CSI) to the public, creating considerable interest in forensic science. Of course, CSIs require very specific training with regard to crime scene protection

Figure 1.5 The television show *CSI: Crime Scene Investigation* has generated considerable interest in the field of forensic science. *Picture Desk, Inc./Kobal Collection*

and the identification and preservation of evidence, and not every law enforcement agency is able to support a dedicated CSI unit. A description of the crime scene unit (CSU) is provided by Michael Weisberg (2001):[10]

> The CSU provides support services in the form of crime processing, fingerprint identification, and forensic photography. The CSU responds to major crime scenes to detect, preserve, document, impound and collect physical evidence. The unit assists in the identification of unknown subjects, witnesses and victims involved in criminal investigations. . . . The CSU will work closely in conjunction with the Detective Bureau in providing assistance in follow-up investigations, as well as subject apprehension and arrest. Members of the CSU may be either sworn or non-sworn.

MAJOR CASE TASK FORCES

A multidisciplinary approach to case investigation uses specialists in various fields from within a particular jurisdiction. A multi-jurisdictional investigation, in contrast, uses personnel from different police agencies. Many larger municipalities consist of twenty or more municipalities that surround a core city. In many metropolitan areas, multi-jurisdictional **major case squads,** or metro crime teams, have organized, drawing the most talented investigative personnel from all jurisdictions. In addition, federal, state, or county police personnel may be used.

In some major cases—for example, homicides involving multi-jurisdictional problems, serial killers and rapists, police officer killings, or multiple sex offenses—it is advisable to form a major case squad from the jurisdictions that have a vested interest in the case. Evidence located from the joint investigation is sent to the same laboratory for continuity and consistency.

MODES OF INVESTIGATION

Criminal investigations are conducted through the use of three different responses: reactive, proactive, and preventive. The **reactive response** addresses crimes that have already occurred, such as murder, robbery, and burglary. In this case, investigators typically respond to a crime, collect evidence, locate and interview witnesses, and identify and arrest a suspected perpetrator. Investigations are also conducted as a **proactive response** to anticipated criminal activity, as with many vice and organized crime investigations. Proactive investigations differ from reactive investigations in two major regards: (1) the investigation is conducted before the crime is committed (rather than after), and (2) the suspect is identified before he or she commits the crime. Finally, investigations are sometimes conducted as a **preventive response.** Prevention through deterrence is sometimes achieved by arresting the criminal and by aggressive prosecution.

THE ROLE OF THE CRIMINAL INVESTIGATOR

As indicated earlier, many myths exist regarding the role of the criminal investigator. Perhaps these were best summarized by Herman Goldstein, who wrote:[11]

> Part of the mystique of detective operations is the impression that a detective has difficult-to-come-by qualifications and skills; that investigating crime is a real science; that a detective does much more important work than other police officers; that all detective work is exciting; and that a good detective can solve any crime. It borders on heresy to point out that, in fact, much of what detectives do consists of very routine and very elementary chores, including much paper processing; that a good deal of their work is not only not exciting but downright boring; that the situations they confront are often less demanding and challenging than those handled by patrol officers; that it is arguable whether special skills and knowledge are required for detective work; that a considerable amount of detective work is usually undertaken on a hit-or-miss basis; and that the capacity of detectives to solve crimes is greatly exaggerated.

Indeed, some studies have suggested that the role played by investigators is overrated and that their time could probably be spent more productively by focusing on those crimes with the best likelihood of clearance.[12] Other researchers suggest that the investigative process is a valid utility in crime detection but should be augmented by the use of proactive patrol programs.

Characteristics of the Investigator

What characteristics best define a professional criminal investigator? Certainly, standards vary from one law enforcement agency to the next, but certain commonalities can be identified. To recognize these qualities, many police agencies implement a supervisory performance appraisal system to evaluate suitability for appointment to investigator. Once taken, the police manager can choose from candidates who possess the most sought-after qualities. According to a study by the National Institute of Justice (NIJ), investigative traits most commonly desired include:[13]

Motivation	Persistence
Intuition	Reliability
Stability	Intelligence
Judgment	Dedication
Street knowledge	Integrity
Teamwork	

Investigators are specialists. They undertake activities related primarily to law enforcement, whereas the patrol officer routinely spends his or her time on order maintenance and the provision of general services (e.g., emergency aid, finding lost children, traffic control). Despite the diversity of tasks performed by patrol officers, the investigator also assumes many substantial duties. For example, detectives gather crime information, effect arrests, and prepare cases for prosecution and trial.

Gathering Information

Many criminal investigations are initiated with a call to the police dispatcher, where a crime is reported. Some of the most critical tasks performed by detectives include rapid arrival at crime scenes; searching the area; and identifying, collecting, and preserving evidence. In addition, the investigator must be familiar with the department's computer and manual records, which contain such information as mug shots, fingerprints, intelligence, and stolen property files. Depending on the assignment, detectives must be able to follow up on leads through the use of various methods and procedures. These include visits to pawn shops, suspected fencing locations, taverns, and other places thought to be frequented by criminals.

Field Operations

The best investigators have demonstrated ability to function in field operations such as patrol and surveillance functions (stakeouts). At times an investigator may even be required to perform in an undercover capacity to procure information on illegal activities such as drug trafficking, fencing operations, prostitution, or corruption. In addition, such investigations require the investigator to know how to operate technical and complicated electronic surveillance equipment, such as hidden-body transmitters, night-viewing devices, and photography equipment. Along with these skills, stamina and a willingness to work long hours are prerequisites.

Arrests

One of the basic functions of law enforcement is to arrest violators of the law. Accordingly, making arrests is a significant objective for investigators because they spend so much time collecting and evaluating information on criminal activity. The quality of arrests is also an important variable, as the officer who has a reputation for making many poor-quality arrests will probably not be considered for the position of detective. Because a major purpose of an arrest is to secure a conviction, the quality and number of prosecutions and convictions are critical elements in assessing the performance of investigators.

Qualities Involved in Investigative Performance

Gathering Information	Intelligence	**Prosecutions**
Crime scene management	Perseverance	Quantity
Communication skills	Initiative	Presentation of testimony
Field Operations	Judgment	Percent of convictions
Stakeouts	Teamwork	**Personnel Performance**
Patrol	Involvement	Absenteeism
Crime pattern analysis	Dedication	Complaints
Developing informants	**Arrests**	Awards
Street knowledge	Quantity	Dedication
Personal Traits	Quality	**Qualifications**
Motivation	**Public–Victim Satisfaction**	Education
Stability	Crime reduction	Training
Persistence	Diminution of fear	Previous assignments in department

Patrol Investigations

In recent years, due to financial and practical considerations, the role of the patrol officer has been extended to include certain investigatory functions. Many of the responsibilities previously assumed by investigators are now shared with members of the patrol division. This practice not only serves the need for both a patrol officer and a criminal investigator but provides those officers in patrol work some variety in their assigned duties. Patrol–investigatory functions include:

Figure 1.6 The 9-1-1 emergency calls received by the communications center of any law enforcement agency are typically where the criminal investigative process begins.

Figure 1.7 Many criminal investigations are initiated through routine traffic stops.

- Patrol officers are usually the first officers to arrive at a crime scene. Often, they conduct the original interview of the victim and witnesses.
- In small departments, patrol officers may assume full responsibility for all criminal investigations.
- Patrol officers are often authorized to conduct investigations of certain categories of crimes, such as misdemeanors, which would only keep investigators from more specialized investigation.
- Crimes that require a greater commitment of time are left to the investigator; others may be handled by the patrol officer.

The expanded role of patrol officers in recent years has meant increased efficiency and effectiveness in policing in general and criminal investigation in specific. It has also served to enlighten those who serve the community in the capacity as patrol officers and to make them more aware of their important role as first responders to crime scenes and as the police department's eyes and ears on the street.

DISCUSSION QUESTIONS

1. In what ways have our historic roots affected the manner in which criminal investigations are conducted in the United States today?

2. Discuss ways in which the media have affected our perceptions of the reality of criminal investigation.

3. Discuss the role of the FBI and how it has changed criminal investigation over the years.

4. List and discuss promising developments in criminal investigation technology that have emerged in recent years.

5. Explain the differences between proactive and reactive investigations.

6. Discuss the various types of criminal investigations.

NOTES

1. JOHNSON, H. A. (1988). *History of criminal justice.* Cincinnati, OH: Anderson.
2. BLOCK, P., and D. WEIDMAN (1975). *Managing criminal investigations: Perspective package.* Washington, DC: U.S. Government Printing Office. GREENBERG, B., C. V. ELLION, L. P. KRAFT, and H. S. PROCTOR (1977). *Felony decision model: An analysis of investigative elements of information.* Washington, DC: U.S. Government Printing Office.
3. ECK, J. (1983). *Solving crimes: The investigation of burglary and robbery.* Washington, DC: Police Executive Research Forum.
4. WILLIAM S. SESSIONS. Criminal justice information services: Gearing up for the future, *FBI Law Enforcement Bulletin,* February 1993, pp. 181-188.
5. OFFICE OF TECHNOLOGY ASSESSMENT. *Criminal justice: New technologies and the constitution—A special report.* Washington DC: U.S. Government Printing Office, 1988.
6. "Saving face," *PC Computing,* December 1998, p. 60.
7. Security or Privacy/ DARPA's Total Information and Awareness Program Tests the Boundaries. InformationWeek.com
8. Information in this paragraph comes from U.S. Sensors Could Track Any Car. All Passengers in Foreign Cities. Worldtribune.com, July 30, 2003.
9. NORDBY, J. J. (2002). *Dead reckoning: The art of forensic detection.* Boca Raton, FL: CRC Press.
10. WEISBERG, M. W. (2001). Recent directions in crime scene investigations. *The Law Enforcement Trainer,* March/April 2001, pp. 44–48.
11. GOLDSTEIN, H. (1977). *Policing a free society.* Cambridge, MA: Ballinger, p. 1.
12. MORE, H. (1988). *Critical issues in law enforcement,* 4th ed. Cincinnati, OH: Anderson.
13. NATIONAL INSTITUTE OF JUSTICE (1987). *Investigators who perform well.* Washington, DC: U.S. Department of Justice, September.

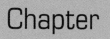

2 Processing the Crime Scene

Key Terms

▶ associative evidence

▶ corpus delicti

▶ crime scene

▶ electronic evidence

▶ flash description

▶ follow-up investigation

▶ latent evidence

▶ medical examiner

▶ neighborhood canvass

▶ preliminary investigation

▶ trace evidence

This chapter will enable you to:

- Understand the function of the preliminary investigation.

- Realize the significance of crime scene evidence.

- Identify the duties of the first responding officer.

- Deal with witnesses at the crime scene.

- Understand the procedures for dealing with a suspect on the scene.

- Identify the procedures to protect the crime scene.

- Understand the follow-up investigation procedures.

INTRODUCTION

The actions taken by patrol and investigative personnel at a crime scene often determine the success or failure of a criminal investigation. The survival of victims, the apprehension of the perpetrator, and the ultimate outcome of any resulting criminal prosecution may depend entirely upon prompt and proper responses by the officers at the scene. All personnel must understand, and be prepared to carry out correctly, the operational procedures established by the department for the management of crime scenes. Police officers responding to a crime scene have several very important responsibilities. They must:

- Be prepared to inform superiors of their findings.
- Assist victims.
- Secure and protect the crime scene.
- Apprehend the perpetrator.
- Collect and preserve evidence.
- Interview witnesses.
- Perform other necessary operational functions.

Even though some of these tasks may be the responsibility of departmental specialists, every officer in the department should be able to conduct any of these functions properly if called upon to do so. Above all, the patrol officers initially responding to the scene must understand that they have a heavy responsibility to ensure that the appropriate actions are taken to protect life and property, preserve evidence, and make it possible for subsequent investigative work to be successful.

Any officer responding to a crime scene must understand that the proper management of a crime scene has at least three distinct aspects: administrative, operational, and legal. The officer must comply with the administrative requirements of the officer's department as to procedures to be followed en route to the scene, while at the scene, and after departure from the scene (such as investigative follow-up and submission of reports). From an operational standpoint, the officer must be aware of all applicable departmental policies (assisting victims, securing the crime scene, collecting evidence, or preserving it in place for collection by others, and so on), and must be able to carry out these functions effectively. Furthermore, the officer must be aware of the legal constraints applicable to the conduct of officers regarding crime scenes (i.e., authority to enter a suspected scene, authority to search the scene, authority to arrest or otherwise detain persons found there, and so on). This three-fold responsibility can be carried out properly only if the department provides adequate guidance through well-crafted crime scene policies and the necessary training to ensure that all officers understand what is expected of them and what they are and are not permitted to do.

THE PRELIMINARY INVESTIGATION

Evidence of one type or another exists in all crimes. A logical procedure for identifying, collecting, and preserving evidence is therefore essential. The practice of following prescribed steps in the identification and collection of evidence is critical in making an arrest and in subsequent prosecution of the offender. The evidence collection process begins immediately after the discovery of a crime. In most situations this precursory investigative phase is known as the **preliminary investigation.** Generally, the term *preliminary investigation* is defined as an initial inquiry by officers to establish facts and circumstances of a suspected crime and to preserve any evidence related to that crime. Preliminary investigation includes:

- Securing the crime scene.
- Considering the possible arrest of a suspect.
- Locating and questioning witnesses and victims.
- Documenting the crime scene.
- Identifying and collecting evidence.

The function of the preliminary investigation is closely linked with the duties of the first officer to arrive at the crime scene (discussed later), who, in most cases, is a respondent from the patrol division. As with any crime scene, the first officer and investigators should consider the scene itself as evidence. This is because much valuable information can be learned from items left on the scene, provided that it has not been tampered with or altered in any way.

The crime scene represents the ultimate situation that places many responsibilities on the first officer arriving at the scene. These include making an arrest, rendering first aid to injured parties, and protecting evidence on the scene. The latter responsibility includes preservation of trace evidence, firearms, and blood or other bodily fluids.

THE ROLE OF EVIDENCE AT THE CRIME SCENE

Crime scene evidence is dynamic. Protection and preservation of the scene are therefore crucial, as both will avert the possibility of contamination, loss, or unnecessary movement of physical evidence. In the evidence collection process, contamination of evidence occurs most commonly when evidence is not properly secured, is wrongfully mixed with other types of evidence, or altered significantly from its original condition at the **crime scene.** When this occurs, the evidence is usually rendered inadmissible or "incompetent" by the court.

The transfer of evidence theory states that when one object touches another, a transfer of material occurs from one object to the other. This theory presumes that no one can enter a crime scene without bringing evidence to it or leave the scene without depositing some type of evidence behind. Material transferred in this fashion is usually referred to as **trace evidence,** which generally refers to minute or even microscopic bits of matter that are not immediately apparent to the naked eye. Consequently, such evidence is extremely difficult to locate at the crime scene. Because of its microscopic nature, the criminal may be far less likely to eliminate it purposely than with more telltale evidence such as blood splattering or fingerprints. As a reminder of the significance of trace evidence, one should remember that serial killers such as Wayne Williams, John Gacy, and Gary Ridgeway (the "Green River Killer") were apprehended as a result of trace evidence or implements of their crimes being found in their possession.[1] Hence, the first officer at the scene bears the critical responsibility of protecting such evidence from contamination.

In criminal investigations, the utility of physical evidence should be clearly understood. Some types of physical evidence are more obvious in nature than others. For example:

- Physical evidence can prove the elements of a crime or reveal that a crime has been committed. *Case example:* A search warrant served on the residence of a suspected drug dealer revealed a quantity of cocaine, scales, paraphernalia, business records showing drug dealing, and large amounts of cash concealed in shoeboxes.

- Physical evidence may be used to place the suspect at the scene. *Case example:* Shoe impressions found in the mud outside a burglary victim's residence were found to match those of a known burglar in the community.

- Physical evidence can be used to eliminate innocent persons. *Case example:* A murderer was careful not to leave fingerprints at the crime scene. However, blood samples taken from the scene later revealed, through DNA typing, the true identity of the perpetrator.

- Suspects confronted with physical evidence may confess to a crime. *Case example:* Although a convenience store robbery suspect was wearing a ski mask at the time of the robbery, he admitted his role in the crime when a hidden-camera shot of him during the crime revealed a recognizable torn edge on the corner of his jacket.

- Witness testimony can be supported with physical evidence. *Case example:* A neighbor told the police that she heard glass breaking at about 1:30 A.M. Investigators later located a broken pane of glass in a nearby house and through use of the witness's statement was able to determine the time of the offense.

- Physical evidence can have a powerful positive impact on juries in criminal cases. *Case example:* As the nickel-plated .38-caliber handgun was handed to the first jury member for inspection, fellow jurists leaned forward and watched while anticipating their chance to touch and hold the weapon that the prosecutor claimed was used in the crime.

Types of Evidence

Evidence can also be classified in several distinct ways. Classifications can be considered either individually or in combination with other classes of evidence. In general, there are two commonly used classifications: corpus delicti and associative evidence. The term **corpus delicti** simply refers to evidence which establishes that a crime has been committed, such as pry marks on a doorjamb. Conversely, **associative evidence** links a suspect with a crime, such as fingerprints, footprints, bloodstains, and fibers. Examples of evidence are:

- *Physical evidence.* As a practical matter, physical evidence could be considered as a classification of its own. Physical evidence is self-explanatory in nature and generally speaks for itself in a court of law. Examples are weapons, fingerprints, blood, and drugs. (See Appendix A for a list of types of physical evidence.)

- *Direct or prima facie evidence.* Prima facie evidence can be defined as evidence established by law which at face value proves a fact in dispute. For

Figure 2.1 Evidence being documented at a homicide crime scene.

example, states establish the minimum blood alcohol content to show that a person is under the influence.

- *Indirect or circumstantial evidence.* Circumstantial evidence merely tends to incriminate a person without offering conclusive proof. For example, although a person's footprint located outside a burglary victim's residence doesn't show that the person who left the print was the burglar, it does suggest that he or she could be.

- *Testimonial evidence.* As the term implies, testimonial evidence consists of a verbal statement offered by a witness while under oath or affirmation. It may also be evidence offered by way of a sworn pretrial deposition. Although many people define testimony in the same way as evidence, they are clearly distinct. Simply, testimony is evidence offered in an oral manner and is used most commonly to explain some form of physical evidence (e.g., gunpowder residue, fingerprints).

- *Trace evidence.* Trace evidence consists of extremely small items of evidence, such as hair or clothing fibers. With the aid of modern forensic analysis, trace evidence plays a greater role today than ever before in solving capital cases.

- *Demonstrative evidence.* Demonstrative evidence is evidence used to demonstrate or clarify an issue rather than to prove something. An example is the use of anatomical dolls to aid in the testimony of children in a sexual molestation case.

Legal Considerations

Officers collecting evidence, or "evidence custodians," must have a good working knowledge of state and federal laws governing the handling and disposition of evidence under their control. As custodians of evidence, they are often called upon to testify concerning their evidence management practices in general and their control over specific items of evidence in particular. As such, evidence custodians should be familiar with the following general federal restrictions on the gathering, preserving, and disposing of evidence, as well as state law and court rulings that may affect their responsibilities.

Search Warrants. The Fourth Amendment to the U.S. Constitution is the primary constraint on the seizure of property by government agents. A search warrant, designating the specific premises to be searched and the specific items to be seized, is the basic requirement in order for law enforcement officers to seize property. The types of property subject to seizure include stolen property, property unlawfully possessed or contraband, property used or possessed for the purpose of being used to commit or conceal the commission of an offense, or property constituting evidence or tending to demonstrate that an offense was committed.

There are circumstances in which a warrant to search or seize property need not be obtained. Included are searches conducted incident to arrest and those conducted with consent of the individual having authority over the premises, property in "plain view" of the officer making a lawful search even though the property was not named on the search warrant, property uncovered during the lawful "stop and frisk" of a subject, property seized in hot pursuit of a criminal in order to safeguard the officer, and property seized under exigent circumstances where there is likelihood that it will be destroyed or removed if time is taken to obtain a search warrant.

Continuity of Evidence. A fundamental rule to remember is that evidence in support of an arrest must be preserved untainted by the passage of time. This requirement mandates that the "chain of custody" of the evidence be documented during custody and storage. Innumerable criminal cases have been lost or their prosecution inhibited by failure to observe commonly accepted procedures for the preservation of evidence and maintenance of records regarding personal custody. Because of the singular importance of this aspect of evidence control, it is examined in depth.

Custody and Disposition. Normally, evidence must be held in custody of the law enforcement agency until a prosecutor or similar authority formally issues a release allowing it to be returned to its owner or otherwise disposed of. In certain jurisdictions, release of evidence is guided by statute or case law.

Under other circumstances, however, the custody and release of evidence may be guided by other regulations. Even when no longer needed as evidence in a criminal proceeding, items may be held pursuant to civil forfeiture proceedings under state or federal law. Under the federal Comprehensive Drug Abuse Prevention and Control Act of 1970, Section 511 (a)(6), as amended, 21 U.S.C.A. Section 881 (a)(6), the federal government may seize property for forfeiture as long as there is a substantial connection between the property and illegal drug transactions. Most state forfeiture laws are more restrictive than their federal counterparts.

Evidence in custody may also be subject to other federal or state laws. For example, reacting to public health concerns over the dumping of potentially harmful biological wastes, Congress enacted the 1988 Medical Waste Tracking Act. While this act addresses the management and tracking of medical wastes in

particular, in certain states it also has present and future implications for the disposal of certain biologically contaminated wastes under law enforcement control. This is particularly the case with regard to blood, blood products, and other bodily secretions in vitro, materials contaminated by such fluids, as well as sharp implements such as knives or IV needles that may also have been contaminated. Law enforcement officers, laboratory technicians, and evidence custodians should be aware of the risks of exposure to HIV and hepatitis B infections through these and related sources, and take those steps necessary to protect themselves and others from exposure. Disposal of these and related waste products should conform to state and federal laws and to procedures set forth by the Centers for Disease Control.[2]

Evidence custodians should also be familiar with federal and any state regulations relating to the handling, storage, transportation, and disposal of chemical wastes. Chemicals seized during drug raids, particularly with regard to clandestine laboratories, can individually or in combination be explosive, toxic, and/or carcinogenic. At the federal level, the handling of these materials from an employee health and safety standpoint is regulated by provisions of standards CFR 1910.1200 of the Occupational Safety and Health Administration (OSHA). Included in these provisions are requirements that employees be trained in the recognition of chemical health hazards, safe chemical-handling techniques, and first aid. OSHA has also set standards for clothing, equipment, and working conditions in clandestine laboratory dismantling operations.

The Department of Transportation (DOT), under CFR 49, regulates the carriers of hazardous materials, while the Environmental Protection Agency (EPA), pursuant to CFR Title 40, controls the handling and destruction of hazardous wastes. Law enforcement agencies that are inexperienced with handling these types of chemical wastes should consult their regional office of the Drug Enforcement Administration (DEA) and/or appropriate state or federal agencies for guidance.

Records Maintenance. There are a variety of records related to the control and management of evidence in custody, many of which vary by state law or local custom. In all cases, however, evidence custodians must take those steps necessary to ensure that these records are properly compiled, organized, and preserved. In so doing, the fulfillment of legally prescribed procedures can be fully documented and referenced as necessary, potential questions concerning the chain of custody and related matters can be readily answered, and cumulative information can be compiled concerning the volume and flow of evidence through the agency's evidence control operation.

THE FIRST OFFICER'S RESPONSIBILITIES

The initial response to a call by the responding officer is a critical phase of any criminal investigation. This response is usually made by patrol officers who must be prepared to initiate a preliminary investigation and carry out the functions discussed below until such time as they are relieved by superior officers or specialists (such as detectives or crime scene specialists) who will then assume responsibility for their specific functions at the scene. Unfortunately, improper actions by responding patrol officers can cause the loss of evidence or otherwise so prejudice an investigation that a subsequent successful criminal prosecution becomes impossible. Further, in some instances improper initial actions may result in aggravation of injuries to victims, endangerment of other officers, even loss of life. Therefore, the responding officers must be prepared to carry out the following initial actions promptly and correctly.

In certain situations, it may not be possible to perform the actions described below in the order in which they are listed. However, all of the actions discussed below, where appropriate, should be taken as soon as circumstances permit.

1. *Actions while en route to the crime scene.* While en route to the location, officers must be alert to the possible presence of perpetrators or perpetrators' vehicles fleeing from the scene. While actions taken to detain suspicious vehicles or persons must comply with legal requirements for investigative detention and/or arrest, the information furnished to the responding units by the dispatcher or by other officers will normally provide sufficient "reasonable suspicion" to justify detention of persons or vehicles found in or leaving the crime scene area. In addition, the suspects' own conduct (suspicious appearance or behavior, traffic violations, and so on) may provide grounds for an investigatory stop. Although the opportunity to apprehend a perpetrator while en route to the crime scene may not arise in a large percentage of cases, officers while en route to the location of a crime should always be alert for such possibilities.

2. *Initial actions upon arrival.* Upon arrival at the location, officers should, if possible, first verify that a crime has been committed. In many instances, it will be obvious that a crime has been committed or that, at the very least, there is sufficient evidence to justify further investigation. However, officers

should be aware that, unless the circumstances are sufficient to justify a reasonable belief that a major crime has occurred or is occurring within a dwelling, or that some other exigent situation exists, they may not enter that dwelling without a warrant. To do so risks subsequent suppression of evidence and possible civil liability. Even when circumstances do not justify an immediate entry, officers may remain outside to protect the premises while additional information or a warrant is obtained. Reasonable belief that a crime has been or is being committed may be based upon such various factors as information from dispatchers, statements provided by neighbors upon arrival, physical aspects of the scene (e.g., broken windows or doors), or sounds from the premises indicating that a crime is in progress within (e.g., screams, gun shots).

Deciding whether or not to enter premises where a crime may have been committed is often difficult. Such entries are considered "searches," and often the police on the scene must make an on-the-spot decision under borderline circumstances. While each case will be different, and state or local law may vary, in general it may be said that under "exigent" (i.e., emergency) circumstances officers are permitted to enter any premises, even using force if necessary, without a warrant and conduct a "protective" search of the premises when the officers have reasonable grounds to believe that (1) a person within the premises is in immediate need of assistance, or (2) a perpetrator is present.[3]

Officers entering premises under these circumstances are not permitted to search the premises for evidence. The "protective search" is limited by law to a "sweep" of the premises to discover victims or perpetrators. Any search beyond the scope of a protective sweep requires a search warrant. However, if in the course of the protective sweep, evidence is discovered in plain view, it may be seized without a warrant or noted for later removal once a warrant is obtained.

Wherever possible, verification of a crime at the location, or the responding officers' reasonable suspicion thereof, should be communicated immediately to the dispatcher or to superiors so that decisions can be made regarding backup, entry into the structure, dispatch of medical assistance or crime scene specialists to the location, and so on. Failing to communicate promptly may endanger victims, the responding officers, and all subsequent aspects of the investigation.[4]

In many instances, circumstances do not permit transmission of complete information at the time of the initial arrival at the scene. In that event, follow-up communications should be made to provide the necessary additional information. See "Follow-up Communications" on the next page.

3. *Assistance to victims and protection of witnesses and bystanders.* Administering first aid to, and summoning medical assistance for, any victims present must be a top priority of responding officers. If the victim(s) is still in danger, either from the perpetrator or from other circumstances (such as fire), immediate steps must be taken to ensure the victim's safety. Similar protection must be rendered to witnesses and other bystanders. However, unless the bystanders are in danger or circumstances otherwise make it necessary, officers should avoid ordering bystanders from the scene until it has been determined which, if any, of the bystanders is also a witness or potential witness to some aspect of the crime.

4. *Arrest of the perpetrator.* If the perpetrator is at the scene and probable cause for arrest exists or an arrest warrant has been issued, the perpetrator should be arrested in accordance with departmental policy and local law. If officers need to leave the scene in order to effect the arrest (e.g., the perpetrator is fleeing from the scene and must be pursued by officers), the officers must determine whether it is appropriate to leave the crime scene at that time. Conflicting considerations will often be present in such circumstances. For example, the officers must balance the need to remain on the scene to render assistance to victims or to protect others from harm against the risk to the public if the perpetrator should escape. Ideally, sufficient personnel will be available to perform both functions simultaneously; if not, officers must decide where the priorities lie. Circumstances will dictate the decision, but, in general, protecting the crime scene, any victims present, and the witnesses and bystanders will be the first consideration. Other units may then be alerted to pursue the fleeing perpetrator.

5. *Follow-up communications.* As noted above, initial communication at the time of the officers' arrival at the crime scene is essential. However, circumstances may not permit the responding officers to furnish complete information to their headquarters at that point. Further communications should be made to provide, at a minimum, the following information:

Superiors must be informed of the apparent nature of the offense discovered by the officers. Where possible, reports should be factual in nature. When it is necessary to state opinions or conclusions in such transmissions, these opinions or conclusions should be supported by the known facts. Approved departmental codes may be employed where appropriate.[5] If the exact nature or seriousness of the crime cannot yet be determined, the possibility of the more serious offense should be made clear in the transmission.

If the perpetrator has fled the scene, a full description of the perpetrator, together with any information regarding the perpetrator's mode and direction of flight, should be communicated as soon as possible. If there were accomplices, similar information about them should be included. Likewise, if a vehicle was involved either in the commission of the crime or in the flight of the perpetrators from the scene, this information should also be communicated.

If the perpetrators are known or believed to be armed, it is especially important that this information be transmitted as soon as possible. Any information available regarding the number and nature of the weapons possessed by the perpetrators should be provided. This will permit other officers who may encounter the perpetrators to assess the threat level and proceed appropriately.

If not already requested during the initial transmission, support units may be requested during follow-up communications.

6. *Identification of witnesses and vehicles.* The identification and preliminary interviewing of witnesses are extremely important considerations for officers arriving at a crime scene. These functions are discussed in detail below.

License numbers and descriptions of vehicles parked in the area should be noted. In addition, the license number and description of any vehicle moving through the area in a slow, repeated, or otherwise suspicious manner should be recorded.

Officers should also be alert for suspicious persons who, though not present in the immediate vicinity of the crime scene, are observed in the general area. Such persons should be approached, identified, and, if circumstances justify it, detained for further investigation.

7. *Briefing investigators and superiors.* Officers should be prepared to brief investigators and other authorized personnel when they arrive on the scene. All information gathered, together with a summary of the actions taken by the responding officers up to that time, should be provided. Unfortunately, experience shows that in many instances valuable information known to the officers making the initial response is not communicated to detectives, superiors, or other personnel. Responding officers should therefore make it a point to communicate all known facts accurately and completely to investigators or other authorized persons arriving on the scene.

Broadcasting a Flash Description

Additional preliminary duties may include the broadcasting of a **flash description** of the suspect and the suspect's vehicle (also called a BOLO—"be on the lookout"). If able to determine certain facts about possible suspects, weapons, and vehicles, the responding officer should put out a flash description to other officers in case the suspects are still in the vicinity. Flash descriptions vary in nature, depending on the specific law enforcement agency. Generally, they should be precise and to the point. The flash description consists of the following information:

1. Type of crime, location of crime, and time of occurrence.
2. Number of suspects involved in the crime.
3. The physical description of those involved:
   - Gender
   - Race
   - Age
   - Height
   - Weight
   - Eye color
   - Hair color
   - Style or type of hair
   - Length of hair
   - Facial hair, if any
   - Clothing description
   - Other outstanding physical characteristics (e.g., tattoos, scars)
4. Weapons used.
5. Direction in which suspect was last observed proceeding and how long ago.
6. Means of escape (mention any possible route that suspects may take).
7. If anyone was wounded.
8. Any vehicle used. When broadcasting flash descriptions of vehicles, remember the CYMBL rule:

C: color
Y: year
M: make, model
B: body style
L: license number

Managing Emergency Situations

Unless a life-threatening situation or other exigent circumstances exist, the responding officer must attend to any injured party. Because the preservation of human life is a fundamental premise of public safety, this responsibility should take priority over apprehension of the suspect. If the situation calls for summoning emergency personnel, it should be done immediately. Once emergency personnel arrive on the scene, the officer should instruct them carefully on how to enter the scene without causing damage to the evidence on the scene. This must be done in a manner that does not impede the responsibilities of emergency personnel.

SECURING THE SCENE

One of the more important functions of responding officers is to ensure that neither their actions nor the actions of others will disturb the crime scene unnecessarily. Much too often, criminal evidence and many criminal cases have been lost because the crime scene was not adequately secured and protected. Protecting the crime scene has always been essential to good police work, and this is doubly true today since scientific evidence analysis techniques are becoming an increasingly important part of criminal investigations. Unnecessary or improper entry into the crime scene may:

Figure 2.3 A New York City police officer with the crime scene unit collects evidence in front of a building where two small makeshift grenades exploded. *Mary Altaffer, AP Wide World Photos*

- Destroy or contaminate important evidence.
- Introduce items or substances into the crime scene that may mislead investigators.
- Provide defense attorneys with a basis for discrediting the investigators or the findings of a crime laboratory.

For these reasons, the following principles should be observed.

The responding officers should enter the crime scene only for the limited purposes of:

- Determining that a crime has been committed.
- Aiding victims.
- Apprehending perpetrators.
- Securing the area.

Unless circumstances or departmental policies dictate otherwise, after these initial functions have been performed, the responding officers should thereafter avoid entering the crime scene and prevent others from doing so until superiors, detectives, or crime scene specialists relieve the responding officers of that responsibility.

Although, as mentioned above, responding officers often must enter the crime scene to perform their essential preliminary functions, every entry into a crime scene area has the potential to destroy evidence or introduce irrelevant substances into the scene. Therefore, even when entering the crime scene to perform necessary actions as described above, responding officers should, to the greatest extent possible, avoid touching or moving objects at the scene or entering areas where entry is unnecessary to accomplish the above-stated purposes. In addition, wherever possible the crime scene should be entered only by one narrowly defined route, to avoid the destruction of evidence, the contamination of possible scent trails, and so on.

In addition to keeping their encroachment upon the crime scene to a minimum, officers should also carefully note the portions of the scene through which they have passed, the routes taken, the objects that they have touched, and any other actions that they have taken that may have altered or tainted the scene. This information will assist investigators in determining the original state of the crime scene and will enable them to disregard matters that are not relevant to the crime itself.

Once the responding officers have completed their preliminary examination of the scene, the scene should be secured to protect it from encroachment by unauthorized persons. This is not always a simple task, and circumstances may dictate what can and cannot be done. However, in general the following actions should be taken:

1. *The area to be declared a crime scene must be defined.* This will include any portion of the premises that may reasonably be anticipated to contain useful evidence. While it is often impossible to cordon off all of the surrounding areas that might conceivably hold such evidence, the area designated as a crime scene should be as large as the circumstances require or permit. The seriousness of the crime, the location of the crime, the nature of the surrounding environment, the amount of manpower available to maintain a perimeter, and similar factors will determine the definition and extent of the

crime scene in a given case. The specific nature of the suspected crime may also dictate the definition of the crime scene. For example, in a homicide case, the place where the body is found is obviously considered the crime scene, even though the actual death may later be determined to have occurred elsewhere, whereas in the case of a suspected kidnapping, the place where the victim was last seen should be regarded as a crime scene and treated accordingly. If the perpetrator has fled or a victim or other significant person is believed to be missing from the scene, the widest possible area should be protected in order to preserve any evidence present, including any possible scent trails leading away from the immediate scene.

2. *Backup should be requested to help restrict access to the defined crime scene and control onlookers.* Only rarely will one or two responding officers be able to maintain complete control of a crime scene by themselves. Assistance should be obtained quickly, before others encroach upon the scene and evidence is lost.

3. *The interior of the crime scene area should be cleared.* Persons other than law enforcement officers or other officials actively engaged in crime scene duties should be removed from the premises.[6]

The crime scene should be secured by the use of tape, rope, barricades, locks, or other appropriate measures. Once the crime scene has been secured, access to the scene should be restricted to authorized personnel.

4. *Record actions previously taken at the scene.* Responding officers should note and record any alterations that may have occurred to the crime scene due to their own activities or the activities of personnel rendering emergency assistance to victims. In addition, officers should determine what (if any) actions of the persons reporting the crime, or of other persons present on the scene prior to the arrival of the officers, may have altered or tainted the crime scene in any way. In particular, actions involving moving or otherwise disturbing the victim's body should be noted. All of this information should be communicated to investigators and/or superiors at the earliest possible opportunity.

5. *Restrict access to the scene.* After the crime scene has been defined, cleared, and secured, access to the scene should be limited to authorized personnel directly involved in the investigation. In the case of major crimes, the identities of all persons entering the perimeter should be recorded, and, if possible, the times at which they entered and left the scene should be noted. Attempts by news media personnel, nonessential city or county officials, and others to gain access to the scene should be referred to the supervisor in charge of the scene or other officer designated to handle requests for entry.[7] Where a decision is made to allow any such persons to have access to the scene, they should be escorted by an officer during the period of their entry, to prevent their taking any action that might result in the loss of evidence or otherwise endanger the investigation.[8]

HANDLING SPECIAL SITUATIONS AT THE SCENE

Myriad situations may present themselves to officers at a crime scene, so they should be able to adapt to different circumstances. The key in the preliminary investigation is for the responding officer to maintain control.

Dead Body

In the event that a body is located on the scene, the officer must make a precursory determination of the cause of death or injury. In an obvious cause of death, certain signs may be evident. Such indications may include odor or early stages of decomposition of the body. Other signs include postmortem lividity or rigor mortis. In any case, the body should not be touched, moved, or tampered with until investigators arrive. On discovery of a dead body, supervisors should be notified immediately as to the nature of the scene.

Hanging Victim

In the case of a person found hanging, the body should generally not be moved at all. Careful attention to protect the knot on the noose is important, as many investigative leads may be developed from rope or other materials used as a ligature. If, however, the responding officer finds it necessary to cut down the deceased, the rope should be cut far above the knot so that the knot can be preserved for examination. In this case, care should be taken to support the body as best as possible so that there is no additional damage to the body upon impact with the floor or ground. Critical attention should be given to all evidence in hanging cases because the appearance of suicide may in fact be a cover-up for a murder.

Firearms

Generally speaking, all objects at the crime scene should remain untouched, in particular, firearms, bullets, or shell casings. Additionally, the first officer at the scene must remember that he or she, too, can be a valuable source of physical evidence. For example, ballistics experts commonly testify that shells found at the scene of a homicide match the corresponding markings on a shell test-fired from the defendant's revolver.

Accordingly, experts may also testify that an empty shotgun shell casing found at the scene of a homicide was fired from the defendant's shotgun. Such a statement can be made based on breech-face markings on the shell developed through macrophotography. In many cases, however, such evidence is difficult to find and may not be discovered until after the body or other evidence has been removed. Officers searching for firearms should remember that shell casings should be nearby. Both types of evidence are extremely valuable. Fingerprints, for example, may exist on a weapon in the oils present on the weapon. Great care should be exercised in this case to preserve such evidence.

When seizing a handgun as evidence, officers should never attempt to pick up the weapon by inserting a pen or pencil into the barrel. This could damage or destroy valuable evidence such as blood or fibers deposited inside the barrel, which could later be retrieved by specialists. Generally, the prescribed way for officers to move a handgun is to pick it up using two fingers on the textured part of the grip where no fingerprints can be removed.

Other considerations are that officers must never adjust the safety catch, unload, or alter the condition of the weapon in any fashion until a complete examination has been performed. Only after investigators inspect and properly mark the position of the cylinder can the weapon be unloaded. Officers should remember that the weapon and all related objects must remain in exactly the same condition as they were found. Weapons, of course, should always be properly documented through photos and sketching before they are moved.

Collecting Electronic Evidence

The Internet, computer networks, and automated data systems present many new opportunities for committing criminal activity.[9] Computers and other electronic devices are increasingly used to commit, enable, or support crimes perpetrated against people, organizations, money, and property. Whether the crime involves attacks against computer systems—or the information they contain—or more traditional offenses like murder, laundering, drug trafficking, or fraud, **electronic evidence** is increasingly important.

Electronic evidence is "information and data of investigative value that is stored in or transmitted by an electronic device." Such evidence is often required when physical items such as computers, removable disks, CDs, DVDs, magnetic tape, flash memory chips, cellular telephones, personal digital assistants, and other electronic devices are collected from a crime scene or are obtained from a suspect.

Electronic evidence has special characteristics: (1) it is latent; (2) it can transcend national and state borders quickly and easily; (3) it is fragile and can easily be altered, damaged, compromised, or destroyed by improper handling or improper examination; and (4) it *may not be* time sensitive. Like DNA or fingerprints, electronic surveillance is **latent evidence,** because it is not readily visible to the human eye under normal conditions. Special equipment and software are required to "see" and evaluate electronic evidence. In the courtroom, expert testimony may be needed to explain the acquisition of electronic evidence and the examination process used to interpret it.

In 2002, in recognition of the special challenges posed by electronic evidence, the Computer Crime and Intellectual Property section of the Criminal Division of the U.S. Department of Justice released a how-to manual for law enforcement officers called *Searching and Seizing Computers and Obtaining Electronic Evidence in Criminal Investigations.*

About the same time, the Technical Working Group for Electronic Crime Scene Investigation (TWGECSI) released a detailed guide for law enforcement officers to use in gathering electronic evidence. The manual, *Electronic Crime Scene Investigation: A Guide for First Responders,* grew out of a partnership formed in 1998 between the National Cybercrime Training Partnership, the Office of Law Enforcement Standards, and the National Institute of Justice. The working

---

Investigator's Checklist: Crime Scene Equipment

- *Surveillance equipment:* Night vision equipment, listening devices.
- *Cameras:* The digital camera has surpassed the 35-mm camera as the photographic tool of choice for crime scene documentation. Both cameras and editing software have now become affordable for even the smallest departments. Digital video cameras are another recent innovation in crime scene documentation, offering the best evidence of crimes in progress and fresh crime scene evidence. Camera accessories such as lenses, tripods, and lighting attachments might be required for unusual crime scenes.
- *Lights:* Handheld flashlight (e.g., Streamlight), emergency flashing strobes instead of vehicle fog lights, handheld floodlights for crime scenes.
- *Notebook:* Sketching material for producing rough sketches while on the scene. Writing utensils such as pencils, pens, and markers must be available.
- *Other materials:* Tape measures (both cloth and metal), evidence tape, carpenter-type ruler, eraser, chalk, tweezers, scissors, labels, tongue depressors, clipboard, and outdoor and indoor templates.
- *Containers:* Envelopes, boxes, plastic and paper bags, and glass bottles of all sizes and shapes.
- *First-aid kit:* To treat injured parties at the scene.
- *Casting material:* Plaster or dental stone to make casts (e.g., pry marks, footprints).

group was asked to identify, define, and establish basic criteria to assist federal and state agencies in handling electronic investigations and related prosecutions.

TWGECSI guidelines specify that law enforcement must take special precautions when documenting, collecting, preserving, and examining electronic evidence to maintain its integrity. The guidelines also note that the first law enforcement officer on the scene should take steps to ensure the safety of everyone at the scene and to protect the integrity of all evidence, both traditional and electronic.

Biohazardous Materials

All crime evidence rooms must be equipped to maintain evidence from crimes contaminated by bodily secretions such as blood, semen, urine, or feces. In addition, evidence rooms are generally required to secure laboratory samples and similar items that have been or will be tested. Wherever blood is apparent, there is the potential for infection by the HIV (AIDS) and hepatitis B viruses as well as other blood-borne diseases. In order to ensure the highest degree of safety, one should assume that all items contaminated with human or other animal secretions are potential sources of infection and should take those steps necessary to protect themselves and others who may come into contact with the items.

Under normal circumstances, evidence custodians should not allow contaminated materials to be brought into the evidence room unless they have been adequately packaged beforehand. Evidence custodians should retain the prerogative of refusing to accept materials that are not properly packaged. Any biohazardous materials should be double-bagged in secure plastic bags, taped, or secured by adhesives (never stapled) and labeled as a biohazardous material. In an effort not to reduce its evidentiary value, soaked clothing should be air-dried before being bagged. As noted, however, organic matter containing moisture to any degree may be subject to decay if sealed in a nonporous container. Such items should be packaged in porous containers so that they can breathe.

In those cases where items must be inventoried at or following intake at the evidence room, "universal precautions"—as prescribed by the Centers for Disease Control (CDC) for prevention of exposure to HIV and hepatitis B viruses should be closely followed.[10] At a minimum during inventories, disposable rubber gloves should be worn; cuts or abrasions covered by bandages or dressing; hand contact with the mouth, eyes, or nose should be avoided; and smoking, eating, drinking, or the application of makeup should not be permitted. The handling of needles or other sharp objects should require the wearing of leather gloves over disposable rubber gloves. Cleanup of any areas, such as counters, tabletops, or equipment that may have come in contact with contaminated items should be performed using a diluted chlorine bleach solution of one part chlorine to 10 parts water. In all cases after dealing with such materials, one should thoroughly wash any exposed skin surfaces with hot running water and soap for at least 15 seconds before drying. Any contaminated clothing should be carefully removed as soon as practicable, separated from noncontaminated linens, and laundered in water at least 160° F for 25 minutes. Latex gloves should be rinsed before removal, and hands and arms should then be cleansed in the prescribed manner. All sharp instruments such as knives, razors, scissors, or broken glass should be encased before being enclosed in the evidence envelope, and the exterior of the envelope should indicate that a sharp object is enclosed. In most cases, contaminated samples that may require laboratory analysis should not be encased directly in plastic because of the possibility of contaminating the evidence. Other packaging material is often required, and laboratory technicians should be consulted for instructions.

Evidence samples that may be subject to DNA testing must be kept in a frozen state to avoid deterioration, and samples destined for blood typing and certain other forensic tests should be refrigerated. A freezer and a refrigerator are required in nearly all evidence rooms for this type of evidence as well as for any perishable products that must be stored for evidentiary purposes.

The handling and packaging of hypodermic needles and syringes have become common tasks for many officers and evidence custodians in the wake of increased narcotics use on the street. Most plastic or paper evidence containers are not puncture-proof, so particular care must be taken to avoid needle sticks. Some agencies use flexible plastic tubes with screw-on or pressure tops for this purpose, although some of these have been subject to leakage. Puncture-resistant containers for used syringes and needles can be purchased from medical supply distributors or local hospitals. A special device has recently been introduced into the market that is a tube constructed of seamless, heavy-gauge transparent

DNA Evidence

Evidence suitable for DNA analysis can be found at many crime scenes and is a powerful investigative tool for linking suspects to crimes, eliminating suspects, and identifying victims. All officers shall be aware of common sources of DNA evidence, ways to protect against contamination of samples, and basic collection and packaging guidelines.

   a. Wear a mask to avoid contamination through talking, sneezing, or coughing over evidence.
   b. Blood and semen are the two most common sources of DNA evidence. However, other body tissues and fluids can be used for analysis even in microscopic quantities.
   c. DNA is particularly sensitive and subject to contamination. Therefore, first responders in particular must be familiar with situations that will degrade, destroy, or contaminate DNA evidence and shall observe the following precautions:

Change gloves between collections of samples in different areas.

Use disposable instruments, or clean them thoroughly with a 10 percent bleach-to-water ratio before and after handling each sample.

Avoid touching the area where you believe DNA may exist.

Air-dry evidence thoroughly before packaging. If it cannot be air-dried, refrigerate and submit to the laboratory in not more than seven days.

Put evidence into new paper bags or envelopes, not into plastic bags.

Sterile swabs shall be used to collect liquid blood. Vials containing blood samples should be refrigerated as soon as possible but for no longer than seven days.

Bloodstains shall be photographed, then packaged or wrapped carefully in paper so that the bloodstain is not dislodged or disturbed. Smaller objects can be placed in envelopes or cardboard boxes.

Wet bloodstained materials must be dried prior to submission to a laboratory. Officers shall not use heaters, freestanding room fans, or intense light to facilitate drying as this may destroy the evidentiary value of the samples. Low-humidity, cold environments that are well ventilated are suitable for this purpose.

If exigent circumstances dictate immediate action to prevent destruction of evidence, wet bloodstained materials may be rolled or folded in paper or placed in a brown paper bag or box, sealed, and labeled. Avoid folding garments through stains.

Bloodstained articles and blood samples shall be transported as soon as possible and should never be stored in patrol vehicles or otherwise exposed to heat.

Use a cotton Q-tip or swab lightly moistened with saline solution to collect dried bloodstains on fixed objects that are too large to transport or are on porous surfaces. If saline is not available, tap water may be used as long as a control standard of the water is collected for comparison.

As in the case of blood samples, clothing and bedding that may retain semen evidence shall be air-dried if wet, packaged separately in paper containers, and labeled.

polypropylene in two parts with a mechanical seal joining the two halves. It is long enough to accommodate most syringes even with plungers extended, comes in a small plastic bag with instructions for use, and is affixed with a label for recording the officer's name, assignment, and case number.

Biohazardous materials should be housed in a segregated area within the evidence room that is clearly marked "Biohazardous Material Only." Care must be taken to package items separately so as to avoid cross-contamination of other evidence.

All contaminated evidence that is ready for disposal, as well as all disposable equipment or cleaning materials contaminated with bodily fluids, should be bagged in accordance with state and federal laws as discussed earlier in this document. The CDC recommends that, in general, infective waste should be either incinerated or decontaminated before disposal in a sanitary landfill. Bulk blood or other bodily fluids may be carefully poured down a drain connected to a sanitary sewer. Sanitary sewers may also be used to dispose of other infectious wastes capable of being ground and flushed into the sewer. In all cases, departments should be familiar with state and local laws governing such disposal.

Chemical and Other Hazardous Wastes

Most chemical agents are seized by law enforcement officers in connection with clandestine drug manufacturing operations. Enforcement actions against these operations require specialized training and equipment in order to avoid the dangers of fire, explosions, and contact with caustic, corrosive, toxic, or carcinogenic substances. As discussed earlier, the occupational and environmental dangers associated with these chemicals have caused federal and state regulatory agencies to impose strict standards for the handling, transportation, storage, and disposal of these substances. The DEA requires that all its agents, chemists, and task force officers who deal with clandestine laboratories be certified by a special safety school. State and local law enforcement officers should not conduct raids on or make arrests within suspected clandestine laboratories without proper training and equipment. Officers without this training and equipment should, prior to conducting any such raid, consult the regional office of the DEA or a properly trained and outfitted enforcement unit of their state or local government.

A chemist or other qualified individual should always be available when conducting enforcement operations on clandestine laboratories. These are the appropriate individuals for making decisions on the packaging, transportation, and storage of all chemical substances. Normally, chemicals should not be housed in evidence storage rooms and require specialized off-site storage facilities. Chemicals seized during the investigation of environmental crimes or under other circumstances should also not be moved or otherwise handled until assistance can be obtained from a hazardous materials (HAZMAT) or similarly qualified unit. The same precautions should be followed for the handling, transportation, or storage of potentially explosive or other dangerous substances.

ASSESSING THE CRIME SCENE

To the extent practical, the investigator in charge should develop a plan for processing the crime scene. The plan should include information learned from any responding officers as well as observations and information known to the investigator. Crime scene assessment includes the following steps:

Figure 2.4 Spotsylvania County Police search the scene along Route 1 near I-95 where a man was shot dead at an Exxon Station October 11, 2002. Police suspected this shooting was connected with the "Beltway Sniper" attacks that terrorized the Washington, DC, area.
© Ron Sachs, Corbis Sygma

1. Evaluate measures and steps that have been taken, to include safety procedures, perimeter security and access control, the adequacy of investigative resources, whether witnesses and suspects have been identified, and the degree to which preliminary documentation of the crime scene has been made.

2. Conduct a crime scene walk-through in cooperation with the first responder and individuals responsible for processing the crime scene to identify any threats to crime scene integrity, and begin an initial identification of evidence.

3. Determine the need for a search warrant prior to collection of evidence.

4. Assess the overall crime scene prior to evidence collection in order to develop a plan for working within the crime scene without unnecessarily destroying or contaminating evidence.

5. Identify evidence collection, and document team members, including specialists such as odontologists, bomb technicians, arson investigators, entomologists, fingerprint technicians, or others.

6. Identify protective equipment and clothing that are required to safely process the crime scene.

7. Identify a separate area if necessary for equipment and personnel staging and for gathering and sanitizing tools, equipment, and personal protective gear between evidence collections.

8. Assign one officer whose primary responsibility is recording and collecting items of evidence. This will increase efficiency, establish the chain of custody, help prevent loss, and reduce the number of officers who must appear in court.

9. Determine the evidence search method to be used and the point(s) at which the search will begin, and establish a working route around the scene to minimize disruption and contamination.

10. Develop, in cooperation with crime scene technician(s) or other trained personnel, a collection plan for identified items of evidence detailing the process and the order of collection.

    a. Focus initially on easily accessible areas in open view and work outward.
    b. Select a systematic search pattern (e.g., grid search or spiral search; see Chapter 4).
    c. Select the best progression of processing and collection so as not to compromise subsequent processing and evidence collection efforts.

Collecting Evidence

1. *Collection of evidence by responding officers: Limitations.* The collection of evidence at a crime has always involved significant operational and legal considerations. Today, because scientific analysis techniques (e.g., DNA testing) have become such a major part of criminal investigations, it is vital that trained specialists collect, preserve, and transmit evidence. Therefore, officers initially responding to a crime scene should not collect evidence unless: (1) exigent circumstances exist that make it necessary to collect the evidence immediately to prevent its contamination or destruction, or (2) authorization has been received from a supervisor to engage in collection activities.

2. Unless one or both of the foregoing circumstances exist, responding officers should limit their activities to securing the scene and preventing unauthorized persons from taking any action that might cause the alteration, loss, or destruction of evidence.

3. *Collection of evidence by responding officers under exigent circumstances.* If it appears that evidence will be altered, lost, or destroyed unless the responding officers secure the evidence, the evidence may be collected. However, such emergency actions should be taken in accordance with proper procedures, and, even in an emergency, the authorization of a supervisor should be obtained whenever possible. Even when undertaken, emergency collection of evidence should be limited to the least interference needed to preserve the evidence from loss. Supervisory or specialized assistance should be obtained as soon as possible to minimize any adverse effects on the evidence or its admissibility due to the emergency collection.

4. *Collection of evidence by responding officers under direction of the officer in charge (OIC) of the crime scene.* Where so directed by the crime scene OIC, officers may search the crime scene for the purpose of finding and collecting items that may establish how and by whom the crime was committed. This may include, but is not limited to, the following:

   • Weapons, tools, clothing, stains, blood spatters, fingerprints, footprints, tire or tool marks, broken glass, hair, fibers, soil.
   • Any unusual objects or objects found in unexpected or unusual locations.
   • Any other object or substance that the police officer feels may be relevant to the investigation.

In conducting the search, officers will comply with the directions of the crime scene OIC and all applicable departmental directives. In particular, the officers will comply with the department's policy and procedures regarding evidence control, photographing evidence before and/or after collection, and preserving, packaging, and labeling criminal evidence. Officers should be aware that failure to follow these procedures may result in the loss of the evidentiary value of the item or substance collected and/or suppression of the evidence at trial. (For example, the incorrect collection and packaging of a wet blood sample or stain may result in the deterioration of the sample to the point that its unique characteristics can no longer be identified by a crime laboratory, or the failure to mark or label any item of evidence correctly may lead the criminal defense to seek its subsequent suppression at a trial on the grounds that it cannot be adequately identified.)

Officers collecting evidence shall preserve the chain of possession or chain of custody of all evidence collected. Departmental directives regarding initial collection, packaging, labeling, transporting, and maintaining custody of such evidence shall be scrupulously observed. Normally, this involves a series of written receipts that document the location of and access to the evidence at all times following its initial discovery by police. Any inability to present written documentation covering any period following this initial discovery of the evidence may result in suppression of the evidence at trial.

INTERVIEWING WITNESSES

As noted earlier, persons at the crime scene who are or may be witnesses to the crime, or who may have information that may be relevant to the crime, should be identified, and preliminary interviews of these persons should be conducted as soon as possible. Promptness is vital in this regard. Often, the arrival of police will lead persons who have witnessed the crime or have information about it to leave the scene to avoid becoming involved. Therefore, potential witnesses must be identified before this occurs.

Witnesses' full identities, including addresses and phone numbers, should be obtained immediately. Witnesses who have been identified as such should be requested to remain on the scene until they can be interviewed more fully. Even persons who are present but who deny having witnessed the crime or having any information about it should be identified for further reference. Officers should also attempt to obtain information from those present about other persons who may have been witnesses but who have left the scene.

In addition, those present on the scene should be asked to provide the names of persons who are not present at the scene but who are known to live in the vicinity or who are known to be present in the area on a regular basis.

When circumstances permit, the neighborhood surrounding the crime scene should be canvassed to identify additional witnesses or other persons who may have information bearing upon the crime.[11] Even though detectives or other investigative personnel may conduct the follow-up on the information taken above, the officers who make the initial response must gather as much of this data as possible, since crowds may disperse quickly, vehicles may be removed from the area, and so on, before investigators arrive. Quick action by responding officers may preserve information that would otherwise be lost.

Figure 2.5 Identifying and interviewing a witness is an essential part in all criminal investigations.

CONTACTING THE MEDICAL EXAMINER

The responding law enforcement agency's standard operating procedure (SOP) should dictate the circumstances in which the **medical examiner** or county coroner should be contacted. Some police organizations wait to call the medical examiner until after the crime scene technicians have conducted preliminary investigations on the crime scene. Investigators must realize that in almost all jurisdictions, the medical examiner will have jurisdiction over the body, so police without proper authorization may not move it.

In the event that the responding officer must move the body, its position should be documented through the use of both photographs and sketching. Additionally, tape or chalk should be placed on the floor to indicate to crime scene investigators how the head, arms, and legs of the body were positioned. If possible, officers must take care to see that the body remains in exactly the same position in which it was found. Specifically, limbs that are bent should not be straightened; if the body was discovered lying face down, it should be returned to the same position to avoid any shifting of the blood and subsequent altering of lividity.

CONDUCTING A NEIGHBORHOOD CANVASS

A **neighborhood canvass** may also be in order during the early phases of an investigation. Although investigators may perform this function, the first officer on the scene might be directed to conduct a neighborhood or door-to-door canvass of the area to identify witnesses. This could focus not only on residents but also on employees of stores, delivery personnel, utility personnel, bus and taxi drivers, and so on.

PREPARING CRIME SCENE REPORTS

Both responding officers and those conducting follow-up investigations should prepare reports in accordance with departmental policy. At a minimum, crime scene reports should include the following information:

- The date and time at which the officers arrived on the scene.
- Relevant conditions at the time of arrival at the crime scene, including the weather and other observations.
- The manner in which the crime was discovered and reported, and the identity of the reporting individuals, if known, including their relationship to the victim or other persons involved.
- Identity of any police officers or emergency personnel who were present at the time of arrival of the reporting officer, or who arrived thereafter.
- Physical evidence collected and the identities of those who collected it. (Special note should be made of any valuables discovered or collected, such as currency or jewelry.)
- Full identification, including name, address, telephone number, and other identifying data, regarding witnesses to the crime.
- The results of interviews with victims and witnesses, including identity and/or description of suspects, the method of operation and other actions of the suspects, the means and route of escape employed by the suspects, etc.
- Diagrams, sketches, photographs, videotapes, or other information prepared at the scene or afterward, including the identity of the persons, whether officers or civilians, who recorded or prepared these items.

Recommendations that may be helpful to the follow-up investigation (e.g., the names of witnesses or other persons who may be able to provide additional information).

PERFORMING THE FOLLOW-UP INVESTIGATION

The investigator's duties don't end at the crime scene. Indeed, they may very well extend into the community to virtually any source of information that may be of value in the investigation. Accordingly, officers should not construe the **follow-up investigation** as a negative reflection on their investigative abilities. Conversely, it demonstrates that officers are conscientious enough to follow up on leads even after the preliminary investigation has long been concluded. The investigator should remember that the follow-up investigation should build on what is learned in the preliminary investigation. Double-checking addresses, possible escape routes, and other leads may provide the investigator with priceless new information. Tasks required of the follow-up investigator include:

- Analyzing reports of officers conducting the preliminary phases of the investigation.
- Reviewing official departmental records and MO files.
- Gathering information on friends and associates of suspects.
- Examining the victim's background.
- Checking police intelligence files to develop potential suspects.
- Organizing police actions, such as neighborhood canvassing, raids, and search warrants.

In summary, the investigator must possess organizational skills that enable him or her to sift through detailed and fragmented pieces of information. As with organizational skills, personality traits can aid in communicating with people in the community who may possess valuable information.

Figure 2.6 A neighborhood canvass is a useful and important step in the investigative process. Here, two police officers jot down notes while interviewing a woman about a crime occurring in the area. *Michael Newman, PhotoEdit Inc.*

DISCUSSION QUESTIONS

1. Define the term *preliminary investigation* and discuss how it applies to a crime scene.

2. What is meant by the term *contamination of evidence*?

3. Is there a "typical" size for a crime scene? Provide a rationale for your answer.

4. Discuss some of the concerns and priorities of a responding officer when entering a crime scene.

5. How should firearms found on the scene be protected during the preliminary investigation?

6. Discuss some hazards that may be encountered when entering certain crime scenes.

7. List and discuss the preliminary duties of the responding officer at a crime scene.

8. What measures must be taken to ensure that a crime scene is secured?

9. With the exception of any unusual circumstances, explain why evidence at a crime scene should be recorded before any objects are collected or removed.

10. Discuss the reasons for conducting a neighborhood canvass.

11. Discuss the reasons for follow-up investigation.

NOTES

1. KEPPEL, R. D., and J. G. WEIS (1993). HITS: Catching criminals in the Northwest. *FBI Law Enforcement Bulletin*, April, pp. 14–19.

2. THEODORE M. HAMMETT, "1988 Update: AIDS in correctional facilities," U.S. Department of Justice, National Institute of Justice, Issues and Practices, June 1989.

3. The purpose of the entry by the officers affects the courts' views as to whether or not the entry was lawful. Courts have typically upheld an entry and protective sweep if the officers had any substantial reason to believe that there were victims within the premises who might be in need of help. In contrast, courts are much more likely to hold a warrantless entry unlawful where the entry was made primarily or solely for the purpose of apprehending a perpetrator thought to be inside.

4. In emergencies, entry to protect victims may have to take priority over communication with superiors. Even in emergency circumstances, however, whenever possible, communication should be simultaneous with emergency entries or the taking of other emergency measures, or, if sufficient manpower is on the scene, one officer should communicate while other officers are performing emergency functions.

5. Note that police frequencies are often monitored by persons other than law enforcement officers or agencies. News media, curious citizens, or even the perpetrators themselves may be listening. This may require the use of discretion as to what is said on the radio. However, even when transmissions are subject to such monitoring, sufficient information must be provided by the responding officers to enable superiors to take appropriate action. The codes used must not be so cryptic that they fail to convey the information necessary to ensure an appropriate response from headquarters or other officers.

6. Persons who are or may be witnesses or have relevant information should not be allowed to leave the scene completely. They should, however, be moved out of areas in which their presence may result in loss or destruction of evidence. If the persons present at the scene include relatives of a victim or other persons who have a legal right to be on the premises, the clearing of the area must be accomplished with tact and, in some cases, may be subject to considerations of the welfare of the persons involved.

7. Local officials may, for various reasons not directly connected with the investigation of the crime, come to the scene of a major crime. Dealing with such persons requires tact. The officer in charge or some other experienced person should be designated to handle such situations.

8. The entry of any nonessential person into the crime scene area threatens the integrity of the case. In any subsequent legal proceeding, the criminal defense may claim that the entry of such persons into the area compromised the scene and cast doubt upon the validity of the prosecution's case.

9. Adapted from Technical Working Group for Electronic Crime Scene Investigation, *Electronic crime scene investigation: A guide for first responders*; Washington, DC: National Institute of Justice, 2001, from which much of the information in this section is taken.

10. THEODORE M. HAMMETT, "1988 Update: AIDS in correctional facilities," U.S. Department of Justice, National Institute of Justice, Issues and Practices, June 1989.

11. Some departments prefer that development of this type of information be left to detectives or other investigators.

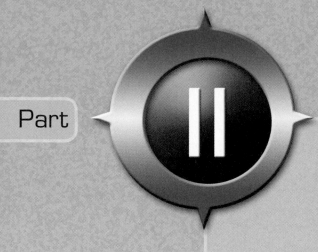

Part **II**

The Investigative Process

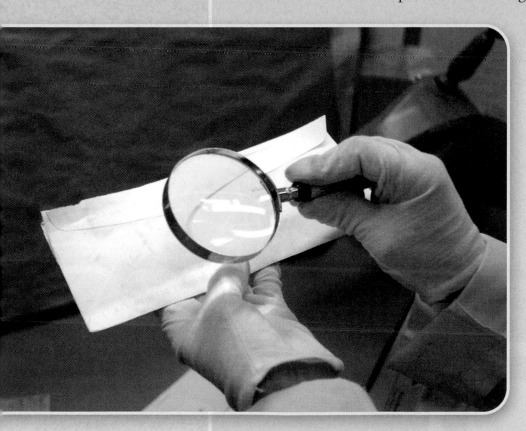

3

The Crime Scene

Field Notes, Documenting, and Reporting

Key Terms

▶ baseline technique
▶ chain of custody
▶ coordinate method
▶ cross-projection method
▶ field interview cards
▶ field notes
▶ finished sketch
▶ markers
▶ rough sketch
▶ surveillance
▶ triangulation method

This chapter will enable you to:

- Understand the role and importance of field notes.

- Discuss the role and importance of the written police report.

- Describe the advantages and disadvantages of crime scene photography.

- Understand various techniques of crime scene sketching.

- List and discuss the differences between rough and finished crime scene sketches.

INTRODUCTION

A fundamental premise of criminal investigation is that investigators have the ability to reconstruct the facts and circumstances surrounding each case. This is generally accomplished through well-written reports, photographs, and crime scene sketches. Accompanying such evidence is the ever-important laboratory testing of objects seized from the scene and supportive testimony by investigators and laboratory technicians. With the exception of unusual circumstances, such as the removal of injured parties or inclement weather at a crime scene, all evidence at the scene is properly recorded before any objects are collected or removed.

FIELD NOTES AND REPORTS

Many law enforcement organizations place a high value on an officer's ability to document information through note taking and report writing. Indeed, good report writing skills are one consideration in both an officer's qualifications for promotion and in his or her ability to present a thoroughly investigated and understandable case to a prosecutor (Figure 3.1). The practice of taking notes is one that is common in many professions. For example, physicians take notes regarding the physical and psychological condition of their patients; attorneys commonly interview witnesses in criminal and civil cases as well as victims and suspects in crimes; and police officers are certainly in need of accurate notes to record conversations, events, and observations. A good investigator should develop the ability to write down information as it is learned, not later. Failure to do this could result in information being forgotten or confused. In many cases, it will be difficult or even impossible to locate witnesses or victims of crimes for a second interview, as they may relocate or even die. Most departments will furnish officers with a notebook in which field notes can be made. It is usually up to the officer what type of notebook he or she carries. Most typically, a small spiral-bound notebook is used. In any case, it should be accessible to the officer at all times.

The Role of Field Notes

When one thinks of a police officer taking field notes, the Hollywood portrayal of an officer writing down bits and pieces of information on the inside of a matchbook cover may come to mind. Unfortunately, in some cases this is a reality, but it is not the prescribed method of note taking. **Field notes** have many benefits for both the officer and the department. Most notes result from interviews, but there are other uses as well. For example, notes may be the most important step in documenting a crime scene initially. An investigator's field notes are his or her most personal and readily available record of the crime scene search. It is difficult, if not impossible, to recommend a particular form of field note taking, as most officers usually adopt their own style. However, one objective of this process remains clear: The notes taken at a crime scene must adequately reflect the condition and state of the location at the time of the crime scene search.

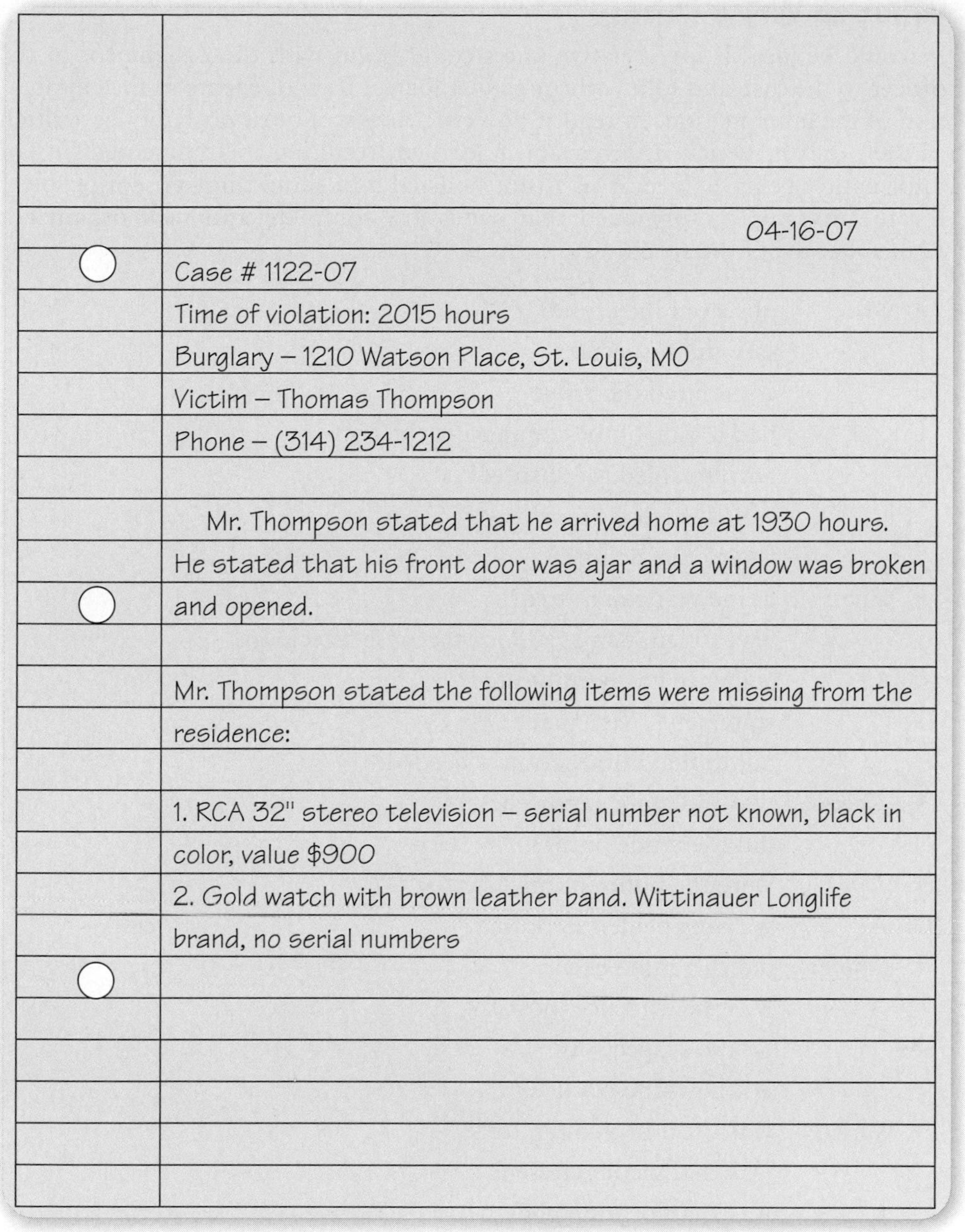

Figure 3.1 Sample crime scene field notes.

04-16-07

Case # 1122-07

Time of violation: 2015 hours

Burglary – 1210 Watson Place, St. Louis, MO

Victim – Thomas Thompson

Phone – (314) 234-1212

Mr. Thompson stated that he arrived home at 1930 hours. He stated that his front door was ajar and a window was broken and opened.

Mr. Thompson stated the following items were missing from the residence:

1. RCA 32" stereo television – serial number not known, black in color, value $900
2. Gold watch with brown leather band. Wittinauer Longlife brand, no serial numbers

When to Take Notes

The investigative process begins as soon as an officer gets a call to the scene of a crime. Accordingly, the note-taking process begins at this time. Officers should remember that note taking is a continual process that occurs throughout the duration of an officer's involvement in an investigation. Some victims or witnesses may be intimidated by an officer taking down what is said during an interview. If it appears that this is the case, the investigator should take time to explain the importance of brief notes and how they will benefit the overall investigation. If a subject simply refuses to talk while comments are being recorded, the officer can wait and make the required notes immediately after the interview.

What to Write Down

It would be ideal if investigative notes could begin with the assignment of the officer to the case and follow through in a logical flow of events to the culmination of the investigation. In reality, however, they will most probably be written in the order in which information is learned, resulting in fragmented bits of information being logged. This is not unusual and should not pose a problem for the investigator provided that notes are complete and well organized. Remember to get the specifics.

- Who: observed the crime?

    saw the suspects?

    committed the crime?

    had a motive for committing the crime?

    accompanied the suspect?

    called the police?

    is/was the victim?

- What: crime was committed?

    was stolen, damaged, or otherwise affected?

    evidence has been located?

    statements were made?

    additional information is needed?

- When: was the crime reported?

    did the crime occur?

    were the police notified?

    was any evidence located?

- Where: did the crime occur?

    was the evidence located?

    do the suspects live?

    do the witnesses live?

- Why: was the crime committed?

    was that victim chosen?

    was that location chosen?

    was that specific property taken?

- How: did the suspects get in?

    was the crime committed?

    was evidence discovered?

Certain specifics should be included in the note-taking process. The following are some examples of essential topics of information:

- *Dates, times, and locations.* To begin, the date and time of the investigator's assignment to the case should be well recorded in his or her notes. Additionally, officers should include from whom they received the assignment. Supplementary information should include the exact time of arrival at the crime scene, the location of the scene, lighting and weather conditions, and the names of other officers contacted and other persons present at the scene.

- *Description of victim.* This information should include all identifiers of the victim, including name, age, social security number, height, weight, color of hair and eyes, and so on. In addition, clothing should be noted as to style (if possible) and color of garment. Special attention should be given to extemporaneous identifiers such as complexion, tattoos, and scars.

- *Wounds on the victim.* Notes regarding the type and location of wounds should be documented carefully. It is important to emphasize descriptions of the wound, and if it is a bruise, its color should be noted. For example, notes of a gunshot wound might read: "Gunshot wound approximately ¼ inch in diameter to the left temple and approximately 1½ inches from the left eye. A dark gray circle about ¼ inch in diameter surrounds the entire wound."

- *Overall description of the crime scene.* Investigators must note anything unusual at the crime scene. This includes items damaged or in disarray, items that seem misplaced or that don't seem to belong in the scene, open (or closed) doors or windows, and so on.

- *Notes on photographs taken on the scene.* For every photograph taken of the scene (and there should be many), the F-stop, shutter speed, distance, and direction of the photo should be logged in an officer's notes. Also included should be the time and location of each photograph. In the event that a video camera is used to document the scene, an officer's notes should include the type of camera and any special attachments that may have been used.

- *Type and location of each piece of evidence.* An investigator should be careful to document adequately the location of each piece of evidence found at the crime scene. This includes its description, location, the time it was discovered and by whom, the type of container in which it was placed, how the container was sealed and marked, and the disposition of the item after it was collected. For example:

  > 9mm cal. S & W model 669 semiautomatic handgun, nickel plated with wooden grips, Serial #36348. 71 inches from the S.W. corner of the master bedroom, 16 inches E. of S. edge of W. door. Marked "WT" on evidence tag placed on trigger guard. Placed in manila evidence envelope, sealed with tape, and marked #11 WT 7-21-01 at 03:25 hrs. Released to Officer Mary Schultz, laboratory firearms examiner, 09:35 hrs. 7-21-01 WT.

- *Absence of items.* This notation includes the documentation of items not at the crime scene that probably should be such as certain articles of clothing missing from the deceased or certain home furnishings absent from the scene.

Developing a Note-Taking System

It is advisable for a system of note taking to be developed to allow an officer greater swiftness in his or her interview. For example, initials can be used in place of complete names. This can be illustrated by using S for suspect, V for victim, W-1 for witness number 1, C for complainant, and so on. When adopting this system, officers should be careful not to move into "shorthand," making it difficult for others to interpret what the notes are trying to say. Remember that field notes may be required later as evidence in court.

Field Interview Cards

One unique and successful method of documenting information on the street is through the use of **field interview** (FI) **cards.** These are used when patrol officers happen on people or circumstances that appear suspicious but there is not sufficient cause for arrest. The FI card is used to document the name(s), address(es), and other pertinent information. At the end of the officer's watch, he or she turns the FI cards in, and they are filed for future reference.

PUTTING FIELD NOTES TO WORK

As much as we have emphasized the importance of field notes on the crime scene, it should be stressed that notes are only a means to aid an investigator's recall at the time that he or she prepares the official detailed investigative report. The officer should be prepared to testify in court as to the findings of the investigation. The notes taken on the crime scene as well as the investigative report will be needed for review by the officer before testifying.

Storage of Field Notes

Once crime scene notes have been compiled, they must be stored in a safe place to avoid loss or tampering. This should remain the rule of thumb even after the suspect is convicted and the case is subsequently closed. This is performed in anticipation of a future appeal of the case, retrial, or possible civil action brought against the department or officer by the defendant.

Using a Tape Recorder

In many cases investigators choose to use a small tape recorder in lieu of a notebook pad for note taking. Aside from the convenience of using a small tape recorder, investigators can also make more detailed memos about the scene. A drawback to the use of such a device is the difficulty on the part of the officer to review his or her notes on short notice. In the event that a tape recorder is used, however, transcripts should be made of the information contained on the tape, and great effort must be made to protect the tapes as evidence and to ensure that they do not become inadvertently erased or damaged during transportation or storage.

Using Field Notes in the Courtroom

As with many other types of evidence, notes are an important item of evidence in the case and can be required by the court. It is acceptable for a person who didn't prepare the field notes to testify about their reliability provided that the person was present at the time they were written. It is also acceptable for officers to use their notes to refresh their memory before testifying in court. Doing so, however, will enable the defense council to take possession of them and examine them if he or she wishes. Typically, the defense will attack the validity of the notes based on the conditions under which they were taken or attack the notes on their face value (e.g., poor weather conditions, poor lighting conditions, spelling errors).

Recalling the matchbook example cited at the beginning of this chapter, at times the type of notebook used by investigators has become an issue in a courtroom. Because the notes taken at a crime scene may be designated as evidence by the court, officers should be careful not to use one notebook for more than one investigation. This will eliminate the embarrassment of disclosure of sensitive information regarding a case different from the one at hand. Therefore, officers should either use a different notebook for every investigation or a loose-leaf notebook so that pages can easily be removed and filed.

As a provision of the best evidence rule (*Cheadle* v. *Barwell*, 1933), the original notes must be provided in court whenever possible. In a legal sense, original notes are the archetype from which other documents are copied or duplicated (*Arenson* v. *Jackson*, 1916). In the event that the original notes cannot be located, photocopies may be used pursuant to a reasonable explanation to the court. In any case, however, it is important for the officer to protect his or her original notes by storing or filing them where they can easily be retrieved for court.

WRITING THE OFFICIAL POLICE REPORT

Many police officers write mediocre reports. A poorly prepared report can easily become evident when one officer tries to read another officer's reports and tries to interpret what is being said. If an official report is difficult to understand, the complaint-issuing process will be bogged down and it will be difficult for the prosecutor to decipher the facts and circumstances of the case. In addition, a poorly written report gives the defense attorney a tool to use during trial to confuse the officer's testimony and to muddle the issue.

Investigators should remember that the official police report is the backbone of the criminal prosecution process. It is a permanent record of the complaint and of the facts and events leading up to the arrest of the suspect. An important three-pronged rule of thumb to remember is that official reports should be factual, thorough, and to the point, as they will be under close scrutiny when the case goes to court.

Factuality

The police report must be prepared carefully so that it accurately reflects all pertinent facts learned by investigators. Special attention should be given to dates, times, and other details of the investigation. In addition, these facts must be written in such a manner that the reader of the report easily understands them. It is important that the police report be factual and not contain hearsay information, speculation, or opinions of the investigator. Facts are generally defined

---

Steps in Report Writing

1. Collect information about the crime scene, informants, and witnesses.
2. Take complete notes.
3. Organize the information.
4. Prepare the report.
5. Proofread and evaluate the report.

as information learned personally by the investigator and not conclusions presumed by him or her. For example, if an informant tells the investigator that a suspect is a heroin addict, this information should be verified before stating it as fact in the official report.

Once the information has been verified, the investigator should include in the report how the information was validated. For example, were undercover officers used to converse with the suspect, or were court orders obtained for disclosure of medical records? In the event that verification is not possible, the investigator should mention that the information was "alleged" to be true by the source (e.g., confidential informant, witness, newspaper article).

Thoroughness

All facts learned pertaining to the investigation should be included in the official report. This practice is necessary for completeness of the report and also for credibility of the investigation. For example, if an undercover officer was offered illegal drugs and declined to purchase them, the offer should be documented in the event that the dealer later claims to have sold the drugs to the officer. In addition to the narrative aspect of the report, attached to every report should be copies of related documentation. For example, if investigators are looking at a check-kiting ring, copies of the suspect's checks should be attached to the report. Additionally, if surveillance photos are taken, they become part of the official report.

The report should also reflect the **chain of custody** of all evidence in the case. For example, in a drug case, the report should reflect how the drugs were collected, who handled them after seizure, where and how they were stored, and who now has possession of them (e.g., the crime laboratory).

Figure 3.2 Careful preparation of the police report and related documents is an essential part of documenting the investigation.

Getting to the Point

The best investigative report is one that is not only thorough but is concise as well. In preparing such a report, the investigator must be aware that although details and completeness are important, excess information can bog down the report and possibly confuse the reader. For example, if the investigation involves an informant with the assigned number CI-01-28, this should be referred to the first time the informant is mentioned in the report but not every time thereafter. Subsequent references to the informant should simply be "CI," which will result in a more readable document.

Word Choice

Investigators need not worry about choosing complicated words to "officialize" their written reports or appear more professional. Instead, they should simply use everyday language that is readable to the average person. Some words seem to have special appeal to police officers when preparing their reports. Ironically, many of these words are among the most ambiguous in the English language. An example is use of the word *indicate*. A person can indicate something by making a verbal statement, nodding his or her head, pointing to an object, using a facial expression, and so on. Use of the word is not very helpful for the prosecutor, judge, or jury. In fact, they will then be forced to ask the officer specific questions to learn the details of what occurred.

Consider the following example: *Poor word choice:* "Johnson said that he did not desire to submit to custody." *Better word choice:* "Johnson said 'there's no way you're taking me in, pig!'" Another poor word choice is *contact*. A person can be contacted by phone, mail, e-mail, cellular phone, messenger, telegram, and so on. Each of these methods of communication presents different problems of proof. Instead of saying that a person was "contacted," the officer should say "who" made "what" specific statement to "whom." For example, the report should read: "My partner and I went to the suspect's house and advised her that she was under arrest."

THE STRUCTURE OF THE REPORT

The report should be structured so that the reader is able to learn pertinent information quickly and succinctly. To best accomplish this, the effective organization of information on the report is critical. As a rule, the two types of reports are initial complaint (the face sheet) and supplemental reports (describing new findings).

Elements of the Report

- Who the officer was met by at the crime scene.
- What the officer found at the scene.
- What the officer did at the scene (e.g., administered first aid, notified immediate supervisor).
- Description of injuries to victim or suspect.
- Type of weapon used.
- Description of all evidence.
- Names and identifiers of all suspects arrested.
- Names of all witnesses.
- Copies of written statements given by witnesses.

The Initial Complaint

Also called the *face sheet* or *initial page,* the complaint depicts an "at-a-glance" summary of the investigation (Figure 3.3). This information includes the suspect's name and related identifiers as well as a brief summary of the facts and circumstances surrounding the case (i.e., times, dates, locations, who did what, who saw what, what evidence was collected, and so on). The initial complaint is the first report seen by anyone examining the file of the investigation, so it is important to keep it direct and to the point. Although individual departmental policies will dictate the precise manner in which the reports are organized, the following sections are usually included:

- *Type of crime.* Depending on the department, crimes will generally be designated either as crimes against property, crimes against persons, or vice crimes. In addition, they will be indexed according to the specific act that is being alleged, such as robbery, burglary, or drug distribution.
- *Date.* The date of the offense.
- *Case number.* Before any paperwork is filed at the department, it must have a case number assigned by the records division. This number will be used on all subsequent reports in the investigation.
- *Officer's name.* The investigator's full legal name (no nicknames), rank, and badge number.
- *Suspect's name/address.* The suspect's full legal name, monikers, addresses, date of birth, social security number, and any other pertinent information known about the suspect.
- *Victim.* The name of the victim(s) and address(es). No additional identifiers are required. If this is a vice case, the victim part of the report will either remain blank or reflect the jurisdiction in which the offense occurred (e.g., the state of Washington).
- *Witnesses.* Names and addresses of witnesses of the crime.
- *Synopsis of crime/investigation.* This section should be no longer than one paragraph and should contain all general details of the case.
- *Details of crime/investigation.* This section is much longer than the synopsis, as it encompasses all pertinent details of the investigation in a logical progression.
- *Attachments.* This section includes a list of all evidence relating to the case. Included are drugs, weapons, statements by victims or witnesses, references to videotapes used by investigators, photos, and so on.

Supplemental Reports

As the case progresses, investigators will undoubtedly develop new sources of information, such as new witnesses, physical evidence, and documents. As this information is learned, a supplemental report is generated to update the case. The supplemental report is considerably longer than the initial complaint, as it goes into much greater detail on pertinent aspects of the case. In fact, it is the supplemental report that incorporates the who, what, when, where, how, and sometimes, why of the case.

The report begins with a brief synopsis of the subject of the report, which gives the reader an overall view of the body of the report. The main portion is

COMPLAINT FORM

Note: Hand print names legibly: handwriting satisfactory for remainder.

Subject's name and aliases	Address of subject	Character of case
Baker, Shawn Willis	1234 Cutter Ct. St. Louis, MO 65203	Burglary

Complaint	Complainant's address and telephone number	Complaint received
Officer William O'Shay	City Police Department (555) 456-7899	☒ Personal ☐ Telephonic Date April 14, 2007 Time 7:35 pm

Race W	Sex ☒ Male	Birth date and birthplace	Hair Brn.	Build Avg.	Height 6' 0"
Age 25	☐ Female	9/18/85	Eyes Blu.	Complexion Med.	Weight 190

Scars, marks, or other data

Tattoo on left forearm: "Ride to Live — Live to Ride"

Facts of complaint

Advised by radio at 1930 hours that a prowler was in the vicinity of 309 Watson Place in the city limits. Proceeded to the area and observed a white, older model Ford van parked on Watson Place in front of the residence at 309. Summoned backup and proceeded on foot to inspect the residence and discovered an open window on the north side. Paint chips and pry marks were visible on the window and on the ground.

Standing to the side of the house, suspect Baker exited the dwelling at approx. 1935 hrs. as he was apprehended. In his possession were two bags, one a canvas bag containing a screwdriver, slim jim, and pry bar. In the second bag, which was a brown paper bag, a gold watch and three gold and diamond rings were found.

Suspect was read his rights under *Miranda* in the presence of officers Larry White and Sandra Winslow. Baker then admitted illegally entering the residence and stealing the jewelry. Baker was transported by this officer to the city police department for processing and field notes were turned over to Detective Samuel Ramone for follow-up investigation.

Baker's van, which was registered to him, was towed to the city impound lot.

Action recommended

(Signature)
(Agent)

Figure 3.3 Sample complaint form.

the details section. As the investigator formulates this section, events are prepared in paragraphs and in chronological order. For example, a report of a drug purchase by an undercover agent should contain the following information in the details section of the report:

- Type of offense (e.g., possession, distribution).
- Date and time of offense.
- Location of violation (e.g., suspect's residence, parking lot).
- Description of suspect's vehicle.
- Description of weapons possessed by suspect.
- Description of how the violation was discovered (e.g., through informant information, undercover agents, search warrants).
- Who (undercover agent or informant) was wearing concealed transmitters and names of officers monitoring the conversation, if relevant.
- Description of evidence in the case (e.g., drugs, weapons, videotape of transaction, statement of informant).
- Field test results of drugs seized.

Each report must also reflect additional details of the case, such as:

- Chain of custody of evidence.
- Statements made by suspects (before and after arrest).
- How the suspect was identified.
- Names of all witnesses in the case (e.g., officers, informant [identify by number, not name]).
- List of property seized (e.g., cars, guns).

Copies of legal documents should be attached (e.g., search warrants, search warrant returns, vehicle seizure forms, informant statements).

PHOTOGRAPHING THE CRIME SCENE

As with the use of the crime scene sketch (discussed later), the use of the photograph in crime scene investigations has been fundamental for decades. It is important to note that both photos and sketches are necessary in criminal investigations, as photos may distort distance, color, and so on. Today, the practice of crime scene photography has been extended to digital recorders to depict crime scenes. In this section, the term *photograph* (or *photo*) will allude to either or both forms of audiovisual reproduction.

Although the adage "a picture is worth a thousand words" might seem unrealistic, clearly a visual portrayal of the crime scene adds a dimension to both the investigation and prosecution of the case that no other medium can emulate. In fact, without the benefit of pictures, a witness or juror may be influenced by past experiences, preconceptions, stereotypes, and biases in making decisions about a crime scene. Indeed, photos and videotapes may convey information to the court more accurately than a verbal description of the crime.

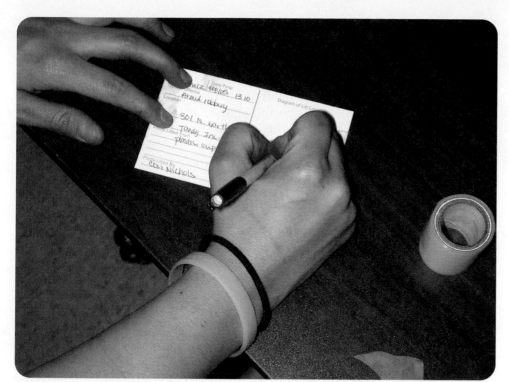

Figure 3.4 Investigators must take time to properly document every piece of evidence.

The New Age of Digital Imaging

A key challenge today in law enforcement is the switch from film to digital imaging technology for criminal investigations. On a global basis, digital technology is becoming state-of-the-art. Not only are many law enforcement agencies going digital, but many camera manufacturers are abandoning their 35-mm lines in favor of digital technology. Some police administrators are resisting the digital trend arguing that silver-based film (35 mm) is still the best because it cannot be manipulated and or changed. However, with today's low-cost computer software, even photos taken with the older 35-mm film are subject to some manipulation.

While some departments continue to resist the switch, many have gone totally digital. For example, in 2004 the Miami-Dade Police Department adopted digital imaging and had begun to phase out instant-film technology (e.g., Polaroid), initially as a cost-cutting measure.[1] Other departments have been more reluctant to move away from 35 mm but have adopted some form of digital imaging technology. For example, some departments have almost completely stopped using 35-mm film in capturing latent fingerprint evidence in the laboratory. This is now accomplished through digital imaging. Laboratory technicians are using software packages that enable them to make enhancements to the fingerprints. Such enhancements can make identification easier and in some cases make identification possible where before it was not.

Making the switch to digital is not an easy commitment for a department. Much thought must be given to what must be done before the transition is made. This includes consideration of legal, technical, training, and hardware/software issues to name only a few. Proper planning will help a law enforcement organization avoid unnecessary expenses and duplication of efforts.

Photographs as Evidence

The principal requirements to admit a photograph into evidence are relevance and authentication. In general, a photograph will be admitted into evidence at the discretion of the trial judge. In rare cases, a chain of custody will be required, or the best evidence rule may be invoked if the photograph is offered for its truth and is the basis of a controlling issue in the case.

The most important requirement is authentication. Specifically, the party seeking to introduce the photograph into evidence must be prepared to present testimony that the photograph is accurate and correct. In most cases, the testimony need not be from the photographer; a qualified witness who has knowledge of the scene and can testify that the photograph accurately portrays the scene will suffice. Some courts will rule that a photograph is self-authenticating or presumptively authentic. If the authenticity of the photograph is challenged, it is usually a question for the trier of fact (e.g., the jury).[2]

An inquiry into relevancy assures the trial court will at least consider whether a photograph, even if probative, might unduly confuse or deceive the trier of fact. The authentication requirement serves as a check against outright fraud, and a chain of custody requirement applied in particular instances provides additional insurance. Lastly, although federal laws allow the introduction of a print made from a negative as an original (rather than a duplicate), in those few cases involving the best evidence rule, even this relaxed application provides some protection. At a minimum, it indicates official recognition that there is (or was) a negative—a "super original," which, in accordance with the laws of physics, must bear some logical relationship to any duplicates.

Due to the recent advances in digital imaging technology, it has become necessary for police organizations to develop a procedure that supports the use of digital images as evidence in criminal investigations.

Preserving Digital Images

From an evidentiary standpoint, digital images must be handled with special care and consideration in order to preserve their integrity as evidence. As a rule, digital images are stored on removable media such as Secure Digital (SD) cards, CompactFlash (CF) cards, and Memory Sticks. Images saved to these storage media must be immediately stored, or as soon as reasonable, on a compact disc (CD) or other protected medium to create the "master disc." Digital images contained on this master disc must not be altered or manipulated in any way. Of course, the master disc must then be properly stored and protected so images can be viewed in the future. Once the master disc is successfully made, the original medium contained in the camera may be erased and reused for subsequent investigations.

A "working copy" of the master disc can then be made for investigative purposes while protecting original images contained on the master disc. Images contained on the working copy can be manipulated for investigative purposes. However, any changes or adjustments must be properly documented. Finally, the master disc must be safely maintained until such time as there is an official determination that there will be no future need for the images.[3]

What to Photograph

Extensive expertise in photography and audio electronics is always a clear benefit to a crime scene investigator, but such training is not always required for good pictures of the scene. Any camera is better than no camera at all, and many relatively low-cost cameras come equipped with auto focus and rewind features. In any case, one important point to remember is that when photographing a crime scene, there can never be too many pictures. Depending on the crime scene, 100 to 200 photos may be typical for proper documentation. When using digital technology, it is vital for the investigator to back up crime scene photos/digital video (as discussed above).

Because digital media are relatively inexpensive, most departments can afford to take numerous photographs. In doing so, mistakes or problems encountered with one photo can usually be circumvented through the choice of others depicting the same scene or item. Photographs of the crime scene are usually taken in three stages: from the general view to the medium-range view to the close-up view. This approach enables a picture of all circumstances to be painted for jurors while leading up to the most critical part of the crime scene.

General Views. The general photograph is a sweeping view of the crime scene area (i.e., an overall scene, such as the neighborhood, including angles from all streets leading up to the crime scene). It demonstrates what the scene looks like in its own environment. Examples are:

- Photo of a bank that was robbed.
- Photo of a house that was burglarized.
- Abandoned "getaway" car in a wooded area.

Photos depicting such scenes should be taken at a distance to reveal the natural surroundings of the location. In the case of a bank robbery, the bank should be photographed from across the street and from both sides of the building. This will give jurors a perspective of where the structure was situated and the location of possible escape routes.

Medium-Range Views. As we move in closer to the subject of the crime scene, additional photos should be taken. These photos should be taken at a distance no greater than 20 feet away from the subject or item being photographed. The intent of the medium-range photo is to depict specific items or objects in the crime scene. Some examples are blood splatters on the walls or an open window that served as the entry point for an intruder. Different lenses can be used to accomplish this phase of photography. For example, a wide-angle digital lens should be considered for a broad panoramic view of the scene. The purpose of the medium-range photography process is to allow jurors to link each print with the general crime scene photos.

Crime Scene Photographs

Benefits
- Provide easy storage and retrieval of data on the crime scene.
- Remove many inferences by practically placing the judge and jury at the crime scene.
- Give the investigator a source of reference as to the location of evidence at the scene.

Disadvantages
- Do not show true or actual distances.
- Can distort color and perceptions.
- Can be ruined by mechanical errors in processing.

Figure 3.5 Photo of jawbone of murder victim located as a result of a cold case murder investigation 15 years after the victim's disappearance.

Close-up Views. Moving from the broad to the specific, the last phase in photographing the crime scene is the close-up. These photos are taken at a distance of less than 5 feet using the zoom feature on the digital camera, and should focus on small segments of a larger surface or on specific objects in the scene. Examples are bullet holes in the walls, weapons, blood-splatter stains, latent fingerprints, and so on. As with the medium-range photo, these photographs should include some identifiable item from the medium-range photos to link object(s) being photographed with the general crime scene.

Other Hints

Because many types of evidence undergo significant changes at the crime scene, it is important for investigators to photograph the crime scene in a timely fashion. This will typically precede most other tasks of the crime scene processing, as objects cannot be examined adequately until after they are photographed from every angle. Accordingly, it is important that all camera angles and settings be recorded on the crime scene sketch.

Photos of the interior scenes should be conducted to depict the entire area. This is accomplished by overlapping photos from one scene to the next and working in one direction around the room. In the use of video, a slow panorama of the crime scene is necessary. It is usually advisable to use either a tripod or to attempt to keep the camera at eye level for all the photos. Fox and Cunningham offer several other considerations that crime scene photographers should consider:[4]

- Approaches to and from the scene.
- Surrounding areas (e.g., the yard of a house in which the homicide occurred, the general area surrounding an outdoor crime scene).
- Close-up photographs of the entrance and exit to the scene, or if these are not obvious, those most likely to have been used.

- A general scenario shot showing the location of the body and its position in relation to the room or area in which it was found.
- At least two photographs of the dead body at 90-degree angles to each other, with the camera placed as high as possible, pointing downward toward the body.

As many close-ups of the dead body should be taken as needed to show wounds or injuries, weapons lying near the body, and the immediate surroundings. After the body is removed, and after the removal of each item of evidence, the area underneath should be photographed if there is any mark, stain, or other apparent change. All fingerprints that do not need further development or cannot be lifted should be photographed. Areas in which fingerprints were discovered are photographed to show the locations if these areas were not included in other photographs. Bloodstains should always be photographed, including locations. Today, color digital images are considered the norm and, almost without exception, are accepted by courts as the best photographic evidence.

Perspective. It is important that the crime scene photographer show the relationship between one item of evidence and another. This is accomplished by showing the location of the articles in accordance with recognizable backgrounds. In the event that an item to be photographed is smaller than 6 inches, two photos should be taken. The first should be taken at close range, and the second should be taken from at least 6 feet away. This will portray the object in proper perspective.

Suitable Lighting. As a rule, the crime scene photographer will find that natural light at the scene is inadequate for good-quality photos and that artificial lighting is required. Investigators must therefore select the proper equipment for this task. Whether a flash is used or a more elaborate lighting system, it is of utmost importance to avoid unnecessary shadows. Shadows tend to hide details, some of which might be of grave significance to the investigation. In addition, the part of the photo that is closest to the flash may become washed out, and details might be lost. A good solution to this problem is the strategic use of floodlights to ensure consistent illumination.

Use of Markers. A generally accepted practice in crime scene photography is the use of measuring or other identifying devices in photos. These include rulers, tapes, coins, and so on. **Markers** such as these are included in the finished photograph and call attention to specific objects or enable the viewer of the photo to get a sense of the size of the object or the distance between objects. Some markings can be made with chalk to show specific locations of objects such as dead bodies, footprints, or weapons. Other markers include ink markings made on the surface of photographs after they have been printed.

Because the use of a marker introduces something foreign into the crime scene, investigators should take a photo of the area before placement of the marker, then a second photo of the same setting after the marker is in place. Another marking technique is to place over the photo a transparent overlay containing all necessary arrows, circles, and so on to depict relevant information. This technique preserves the original photo and allows for comparison between the two.

Figure 3.6 A bloody shoeprint is photographed using a marker to show perspective.

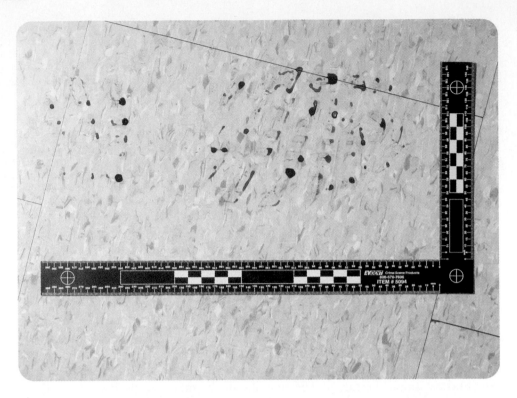

ADMISSIBILITY OF PHOTOGRAPHIC EVIDENCE

Trial courts bear the responsibility of admissibility of photographs as evidence in court. Such determinations have been based on several legal precedents:

1. *Materiality.* The object portrayed in the photo must be material and relevant to the case at hand. All photographs, provided that they serve to prove a particular point in the issue, should be admitted into evidence.
   a. A *material photograph* is one that relates to and makes a substantive contribution to the specific case in question.
   b. A *relevant photograph* also applies to the matter in question and is used to support testimony. It is representative of the evidence that relates it to the matter in question to determine the truth of the circumstances (*Barnett* v. *State*, 1922).

2. *Prejudicial images.* Any photograph or image admitted must not prejudice, or appeal unfairly, to the emotions of the jury. Some judges have suppressed photos depicting unusually gruesome crime scenes. In one recent case, photos were taken of a defendant immediately after his arrest, showing him as dirty and unkempt. The photos were offered as evidence to contrast the defendant's clean and polished image in the courtroom. The judge refused to admit the image into evidence on the basis that it was prejudicial.

3. *Distorted photos.* Photographs must be kept free of distortion. Three types of distortion have generally been common in crime scene photographs: (1) incorrect point of view, (2) perspective, and (3) misrepresentation of tone or color. These problems commonly occur through improper use of angles of the photo. For example, a handgun lying next to a dead body may be

photographed to appear much larger in size than it actually is, thus distorting the perception of the scene. Another example would be bruises on a body, which might indicate the extent of the wound or even the time it was inflicted. Therefore, if the tone of a bruise is shown in a photo as greenish in color rather than bluish, a different conclusion may be made as to the extent of the injuries. Because of this, the photographer or laboratory technician may be subjected to rigorous cross-examination regarding his or her expertise in the processing of digital images. Such distortions must be avoided, as they will taint the case and will probably be excluded as evidence.

Additionally, photos and physical evidence have different requirements regarding the chain of custody. For example, it is not necessary for the person taking the photograph to be the one to testify about it in court. In *State* v. *Fournier* (1963), however, the court held that evidence must be offered to show that the photograph is an accurate representation of the object(s) portrayed (as mentioned above). Such evidence is usually given by an officer who was present on the crime scene and who can vouch for the validity of the photo.

Since the late 1960s, there has been an avalanche of cases regarding the admissibility of videotape recordings in criminal trials. Generally, the courts have held that such evidence is admissible on the same basis as motion picture films with sound and is subject to the same rules of evidence as motion pictures and photographic evidence. Many courts have even admitted videotapes that had inferior-quality sound but permitted the sound track to be "cleaned up" electronically.

IDENTIFICATION OF PHOTOGRAPHS

It is of critical importance for investigators to log their photos carefully as to date, time, and sequence number (Figure 3.7). Also included should be the following:

- Type of case.
- Description of subject of photo.
- Location.
- Names of persons handling evidence.
- Assigned case number.
- Any other relevant information.

This technique will reduce hours of sorting out finished photos and trying to determine what picture goes where.

SURVEILLANCE PHOTOGRAPHS

Surveillance photography is used covertly in establishing identities or in documenting criminal behavior. Photography of this nature is selective and can have many benefits. For example, it can aid officers in identifying the physical locations of criminal activity or in formulating a raid plan for serving a search warrant. The covert use of **surveillance** is now used commonly in banks and convenience stores as a deterrent for would-be robbers and as an aid in prosecution. Some systems use single-reflex cameras with telephoto lenses, whereas others use infrared film.

PHOTOGRAPHIC LOG

PAGE __1__ of __1__

LOCATION __Living Room__

DATE __04-16-07__

CASE # __0211-07__

OFFICERS __Lt. Johnson, Officer Watson, Officer Smith__

CAMERA __#31__

CAMERA TYPE __Nikon Coolpix__

__P-1 digital__

COMMENTS __SD Disk #14__

Photo #	Description of Subject Photographed	Scale	Misc. Comments	Sketch (if required)
1	Long-range shot — living room		Photos from top	
2	Close-up — defense wound			
3	Medium-range shot — knife			
4	Close-up — powder burns		↓	
5	Long-range shot — hallway		From left side	
6	Medium-range shot — handgun		From right side	
7	Close-up — handgun			
8	Close-up — knife		↓	

Figure 3.7 Sample photographic log.

Most investigations using surveillance photography are vice and organized crime operations, and a specially outfitted van or truck is usually employed by investigators. In these operations, illegal transactions are made discreetly among criminals, and thorough documentation is necessary to establish proof beyond a reasonable doubt. Such photography can be problematic, however, in that proper lighting is sometimes difficult to come by. In response, many police agencies have purchased night-vision devices that affix to surveillance cameras. This device uses natural light emitted by stars or the moon and usually produces an identifiable image.

CAPTURING THE CRIME SCENE ON DIGITAL VIDEO

In addition to the use of digital photography at crime scenes, the use of digital video of the crime scene is becoming commonplace. There are many benefits to the use of digital video cameras at the crime scene. They are easy to use, relatively inexpensive, faster than photographs, and, in many ways, offer jurors a more complete reproduction of the crime scene.

Several distinct advantages exist in using digital video at crime scenes. For example, officers are able to begin recording at the extreme perimeters of the crime scene (i.e., point of entry) and walk closer and closer to the specific objects in question. Such evidence lends great perspective to photographs, which can depict minute details of the same objects. For example, a panoramic video view of a dead body lying near a handgun can show proportional distance between the two. In conjunction with the video, a close-up photograph can further depict details of bloodstains, possible powder burns, and wounds on the victim.

Another advantage is that digital video can easily be used in the courtroom, as many players can play back digital tapes. In addition, because digital media are "developed" instantly, prosecutors can view the evidence moments after recording. Another benefit of digital video recording at the crime scene is the use of the freeze-frame feature in most video systems. This enables the viewer to stop the tape at any critical point for a closer view of the subject being recorded. Many photo and video stores also have the capability to make individual photographs directly from digital video, which can be useful in the investigation or prosecution of the case.

THE CRIME SCENE SKETCH

The task of sketching the crime has endured as one of the hallmarks of crime scene investigations. If properly prepared, the sketch can be used in questioning suspects and witnesses, preparing the investigative report, and aiding the investigator's testimony in court. In addition, the sketch complements the photos and notes of the crime scene search.

Reasons to Sketch

With increased use of video cameras on the crime scene, one might argue that preparation of the sketch is no longer required. In actuality, photos and videos may at times tend to distort the dimensions of the crime scene. In such a case, one can glance at the detailed sketch and make determinations as to distances and locations of important evidence on the scene.

Putting It Together

Several methods have been developed over the years to best conduct a detailed sketch of the scene. One should remember that the objective of the crime scene sketch is to portray the scene accurately, not artistically: Too much detail in a crime scene sketch will remove the advantage of a sketch over a photograph. Thus, most officers can be expected to produce a sketch successfully.

In each crime scene sketch, there are some items that are considered essential. As with note taking, however, such items should not be considered the only items needed for complete documentation of the scene. The crime scene sketch should include the following information:

- The investigator's complete name and rank.
- The date, time, type of crime, and assigned case number.
- The complete names of other officers assisting in the making of the sketch.
- The address of the crime scene, its position in a building, landmarks, and so on.

- The scale of the drawing (if no scale, indicate by printing "not to scale").
- The primary items of physical evidence and other critical features of the crime scene, located by detailed measurements from at least two fixed points of reference.
- A key or legend identifying the symbols or points of reference used in the sketch.

Measurement

One general rule of sketching is that the sketch should reflect as accurately as possible the important details of the scene. Such information must be recorded uniformly. For example, if the dimensions of a dead body in a field are recorded accurately but the location of a handgun found near the body is estimated only roughly, the sketch is virtually useless. Accordingly, all measures of distance must be conducted by using the same method. Specifically, one part of the scene should not be paced off and another area of the scene measured with a tape measure.

Once the case goes to court and a measurement error is discovered, the explanation of such an error may prove embarrassing and difficult. Use of a tape measure is therefore considered the most effective method of measuring the scene. Other tools for crime scene sketching include:

- Paper for the sketch (preferably graph paper)
- Clipboard
- Colored pencils (if necessary)
- Fifty-foot steel tape
- Thumbtacks to hold down one end of the tape if the investigator is alone
- Straightedge ruler
- Eight- to 12-foot tape for measuring from the baseline

Rough and Finished Sketches

There are generally two sketches for every crime scene: a rough sketch and a finished sketch. The **rough sketch** is the one drawn by officers on the crime scene. Generally, it is not drawn to scale but should reflect accurate dimensions and distances between objects of importance. At times it might be necessary to draw more than one rough crime scene sketch. For example, one sketch might portray the overall scene, and a second sketch could show only the body and its immediate surroundings. Alterations to the rough sketch should not be made after the investigator leaves the scene.

The **finished sketch** is simply a completed sketch drawn to scale. This is drawn from information contained on the rough sketch and should accurately reflect all measurements indicated on the rough sketch. With the finished sketch being drawn to scale, however, it won't be necessary to include the specific measurements on the sketch itself. If the finished sketch is not drawn to scale, measurements are required. Finished sketches need not be prepared by the crime scene investigator, although in court the investigator will be required to affirm that the finished sketch is an accurate portrayal of the scene. In many cases, the finished sketch is prepared by a professional draftsperson or is made with the use of specially designed computerized programs.

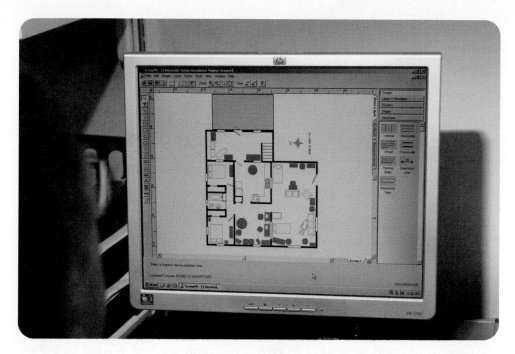

Figure 3.8 Final sketches must depict precise measurements and can be accomplished using computerized programs.

Figure 3.9 In the absence of a computerized program, investigators can rely on a hand-written diagram of the scene. Finalized sketches should be drawn to scale.

Choosing the Best Method

Different crime scenes present different sketching problems. Let's now consider three of the most widely used sketching methods:

1. *Coordinate method.* The **coordinate method** employs the practice of measuring an object from two fixed points of reference. One such procedure is the **baseline technique,** in which a line is drawn between two known points (Figure 3.10). The baseline could also be a wall or a mathematically derived point along a designated area where exact measurements can be determined. The measurements of a particular item are then taken from left to right along the baseline to a point at right angles to the object that is to be plotted. This distance is noted in the legend with a circled number following the name of the object.

2. *Triangulation method.* The **triangulation method** is a bird's-eye view of the scene, utilizing fixed objects from which to measure. This is particularly useful for sketching outdoor crime scenes where there are no easily identifiable points of reference. In this procedure, two or more widely separated points of reference are required. The item of interest is then located by measuring along a straight line from the reference points (Figure 3.11).

3. *Cross-projection method.* The **cross-projection method** is used in indoor crime scenes. It is basically a top-down view of the crime scene, with the walls of the room "folded" down to reveal locations of bullet holes, blood-

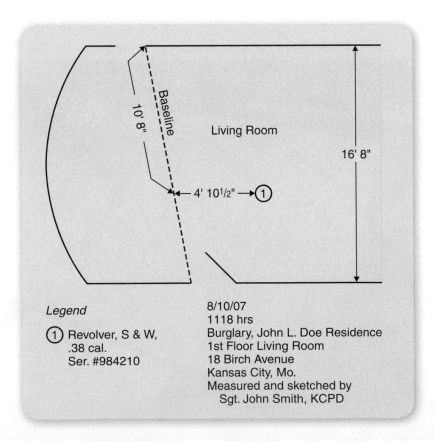

Figure 3.10 Baseline or coordinate sketching method.

Figure 3.11 Triangulation sketching method.

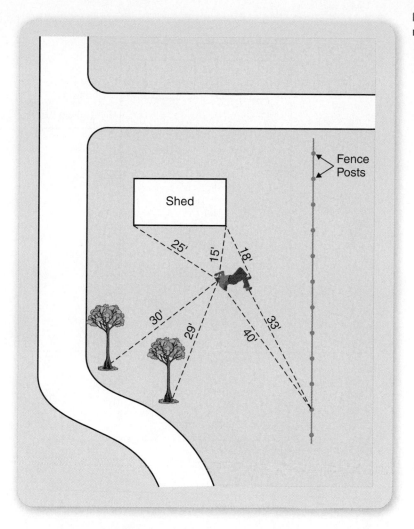

spatter evidence, and so on, which would not be apparent otherwise. Measurements are then made from a designated point on the floor to the area on the wall in question (Figure 3.12).

On completion of the sketch, the investigator should be prepared to do two things: (1) photocopy the sketch and attach the copy to the officer's report, and (2) file the original sketch in a secure location so that it is ready for presentation in court at a later date. The officer should remember that both the rough and finished sketches are admissible in court if they are prepared or witnessed by the investigator, provided that they both portray the crime scene accurately.

In summary, the crime scene sketch is an integral part of the crime scene investigation, as it gives perspective to what happened at the time of the crime. Jurors, typically, can relate to a well-drafted sketch depicting all important areas of the crime scene location, and thus investigators must take appropriate measures to ensure an accurate and meaningful crime scene sketch.

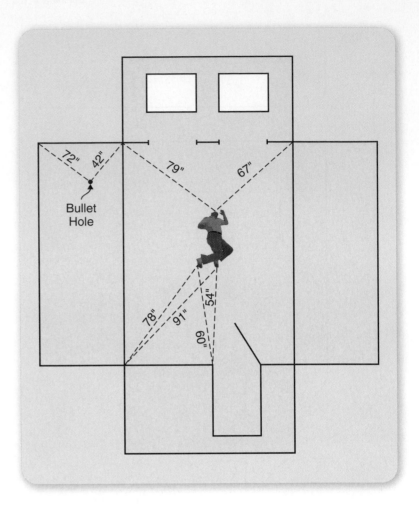

Figure 3.12 Cross-projection sketching method. Note that in this type of sketch the walls are drawn as if folded flat.

DISCUSSION QUESTIONS

1. Describe the twofold process of documentation in a criminal investigation.

2. Discuss the types of information that should be included in the note-taking process at a crime scene.

3. Explain the primary purpose of the official police report.

4. What is the three-pronged rule of thumb that investigators should remember when writing official reports?

5. Discuss and compare the differences between the initial complaint and supplemental reports in a criminal investigation.

6. Discuss the benefits and disadvantages of crime scene photography.

7. In what ways can the perspective of a crime scene be distorted through photography?

8. When considering crime scene photography, discuss the various media most commonly used to record the scene.

9. Discuss the role of surveillance photography in criminal investigation.

10. What benefits does a digital video recorder offer the criminal investigator?

11. With the exception of any unusual circumstances, explain why evidence at a crime scene should be recorded before objects are collected or removed.

NOTES

1. SANFILIPPO, PHILIP J. "Tips on managing the switch from conventional film to digital" *Evidence Technology Magazine*, Vol. 2, no. 5 (September-October 2004), pp. 18–21.

2. TYLER, P. B. (1995). The Kelly-Frye "general acceptance" standard remains the rule for admissibility of novel scientific evidence: *People* v. *Leahy.*

3. SCIENTIFIC WORKING GROUP IMAGING TECHNOLOGY (SWGIT). *Definitions and guidelines for the use of imaging technologies in the criminal justice system,* Federal Bureau of Investigation; June 8, 1999; INTERNATIONAL ASSOCIATION OF IDENTIFICATION (1997), *1997 Resolution and legislative committee, resolution 97-9.*

4. FOX, R. H., and C. L. CUNNINGHAM (1989).*Crime scene search and physical evidence handbook.* Washington, DC: U.S. Department of Justice.

Key Terms

▶ affidavit
▶ Bill of Rights
▶ body packing
▶ chain of custody
▶ consent search
▶ due process
▶ exclusionary rule
▶ exigent circumstances
▶ plain-view doctrine
▶ probable cause
▶ scope of the search
▶ search warrant
▶ search warrant return
▶ stop and frisk
▶ triggering condition

This chapter will enable you to:

• Understand the legal guidelines of searching for evidence.

• Discuss relevant U.S. Supreme Court precedents relating to police searches.

• Understand warrantless searches.

• Structure a search warrant.

• Describe the various methods of executing a search warrant.

• List various searching techniques.

• Explain the importance of marking and preserving physical evidence.

INTRODUCTION

The body of constitutional law addressing searches and seizures by police is immense and includes thousands of case decisions from courts in virtually all levels of government. Of paramount importance in criminal investigations is the officer's ability to be aware of and work within constitutional (and departmental) guidelines. Issues such as what to search, when to search, and how to conduct the search play a vital role in determining what is fair in the eyes of the U.S. Supreme Court. In this chapter, we examine some of the more crucial principles of searches and seizures and how officers must conduct themselves to present a legally sound criminal case.

DUE PROCESS AND THE CONSTITUTION

In addition to affording protection by ensuring a separation of powers within the government, the U.S. Constitution safeguards operations of the criminal justice system. One means of power was granting individual freedoms in what is called the Bill of Rights, added to the Constitution in 1791. Initially, the **Bill of Rights** applied only to the manner in which the federal government operated within the justice system. However, in 1868 the Fourteenth Amendment was passed extending due process to each of the states as well. Under this amendment, citizens are basically guaranteed three classes of rights:

1. Privileges and immunities of citizens of the United States.
2. Due process of law.
3. Equal protection under the law.

For more than 30 years, the U.S. Supreme Court's interpretation of the Constitution has served as the basis for the establishment of legal rights of the accused. The fundamental principles that govern criminal procedure are required by the Bill of Rights. Therefore, it is here that we consider the implications of the Fourth, Fifth, and Sixth Amendments, which limit and control the manner in which government officials operate in our justice system.

1. *Fourth Amendment.* Two clauses of this amendment are significant in the realm of criminal investigation:
   - *Unreasonable searches and seizures clause.* "The right of the people to be secure in their persons, houses, papers, and effects, against unreasonable searches and seizures, shall not be violated."
   - *Warrants clause.* "No warrants shall issue, but upon probable cause, supported by oath or affirmation, and particularly describing the place to be searched and the persons or things to be seized."
2. *Fifth Amendment.* The principal component of this amendment is the self-incrimination clause:
   - *Privilege against self-incrimination clause.* "No person . . . shall be compelled in any criminal case to be a witness against himself."
3. *Sixth Amendment.* This amendment guarantees people the right to confront their accuser and to have legal representation.

- *Right of confrontation clause.* "In all criminal prosecutions, the accused shall enjoy the right . . . to be confronted with the witness against him."
- *Right to counsel clause.* ". . . to have the assistance of counsel for his defense."

The Fourth, Fifth, and Sixth Amendments limit and control the manner in which government officials operate in the justice system.

LEGAL GUIDELINES FOR SEARCHES

Investigators must remember that they not only must have legal grounds to begin a search but that while conducting the search, they not contaminate any evidence. Doing so will result in the dismissal of such evidence in the courtroom. Additionally, searches must first be justified under law. In the past, officers have not always followed the rules, as the case histories discussed in this chapter show.

The Probable Cause Requirement

For the last three decades, courts have scrutinized virtually every aspect of the Fourth Amendment. The probable cause requirement is one of the most important components of the Fourth Amendment because it lies at the heart of the police officer's authority to search, seize, and make arrests. Simply put, **probable cause** is the minimum amount of information necessary to warrant a reasonable person to believe that a crime has been or is being committed by a person who is about to be arrested. Officers generally establish probable cause through their own observations. For example:

- Did the suspect attempt to run away when approached by the officer?
- Did the suspect admit to any part of the alleged crime?
- Did the suspect behave furtively, as if he or she were trying to hide something?

It is unlikely that a single fact or circumstance will establish probable cause, but several such facts put together might. Probable cause is the minimum amount of information necessary to cause a reasonable person to believe that a crime has been or is being committed by a person who is about to be arrested.

It is also common for probable cause to be established through hearsay information provided by third-party sources, typically informants. Here, officers must be careful that the information is reliable, verifiable, and is not based on rumor or suspicion, as such information is not sufficient to establish probable cause.

THE EXCLUSIONARY RULE

The **exclusionary rule** relates primarily to cases involving issues of search and seizure, arrests, interrogations, and stop-and-frisk violations. In addition, it pertains to any evidence obtained illegally, even though it may be both relevant and material. The exclusionary rule states that courts will exclude any evidence that was illegally obtained even though it may be relevant and material.

The exclusionary rule originated with the 1914 case of *Weeks* v. *United States* but was geared to apply to federal, not state, governments. Although the

Weeks case was virtually ignored by the courts, the subsequent *Mapp* decision (*Mapp* v. *Ohio*, 1961) expanded the scope of the exclusionary rule by applying it to both federal and state courts. In 1957, Cleveland police officers went to the residence of Dolree Mapp while acting on information that a fugitive was in hiding there. Mapp refused to admit officers to the residence without a search warrant. The officers left but maintained surveillance on the residence. Three hours later, more officers arrived and forced their way into the Mapp residence. By this time, Mapp's attorney had arrived, but officers ignored him. Mapp then demanded to see a search warrant, at which time one of the officers held up a piece of paper, claiming that it was a search warrant. Mapp grabbed the piece of paper and stashed it in her blouse. A struggle ensued and officers retrieved the paper and arrested Mapp for being "belligerent." The officers then began to search the entire home. Although they never located the fugitive they were looking for, they ran across some obscene material for which Mapp was subsequently arrested and convicted. The U.S. Supreme Court overturned the conviction, stating that the methods used by officers to obtain the evidence were a violation of her constitutional rights.

The question in the *Mapp* case was whether or not the illegally seized evidence was in violation of the Fourth Amendment's search and seizure provisions, which would render it inadmissible in the state trial, in which Ms. Mapp was found guilty. Although the state supreme court in Ohio upheld the conviction, the U.S. Supreme Court overturned it. In addition to imposing federal constitutional standards on state law enforcement personnel, the Court pointed out that there was a relationship between the Fourth and Fifth Amendments which makes up the legal basis for the exclusionary rule.

Since the early days of the exclusionary rule, other decisions have highlighted the fact that the Fourth Amendment protects people, not places. Stated differently, while the old saying "a person's home is his castle" has a great deal of validity within the context of constitutional law, people have a reasonable expectation to privacy in "homes" of many descriptions: apartments, duplexes,

Figure 4.1 Justices of the Supreme Court of the United States pose for a 2006 class photo inside the Supreme Court in Washington, March 3, 2006. Standing from left to right are: Justice Stephen Breyer, Justice Clarence Thomas, Justice Ruth Bader Ginsburg, and Justice Samuel Alito. Seated from left to right are: Justice Anthony Kennedy, Justice John Paul Stevens, Chief Justice John Roberts Jr., Justice Antonio Scalia, and Justice David Souter.
Larry Dowing, Landov LLC

motel rooms, even cardboard boxes or otherwise makeshift dwellings of the homeless. Indeed, all of these places can become protected under the Fourth Amendment. For example, in *Minnesota* v. *Olson* (1990), the U.S. Supreme Court extended the protection against warrantless searches to overnight guests residing in the home of another. The deciding factor in one's capacity to claim the protection of the Fourth Amendment depends on whether the person who makes that claim has a legitimate expectation of privacy in the place searched.

The Fruit of the Poisonous Tree Doctrine

With its ruling in *Silverthorne Lumber Co.* v. *United States* (1918), the Court built further on the rules of evidence. The Silverthorne case articulated a new, far-reaching principle of **due process** which has become known as the fruit of the poisonous tree doctrine. Complicated police cases may be jeopardized if criminal lawyers are able to show that the prosecution's case was based originally on a search or seizure that violated due process. In such cases, it is likely that all evidence will be declared "tainted" and thrown out of court. But prior to the Warren Court era, most U.S. Supreme Court decisions were regarded as applicable only to federal law enforcement agencies.

Search Incident to Lawful Arrest

The legal considerations of what constitutes an arrest are discussed in Chapter 7, but as this chapter deals with search and seizure, we will now consider a search immediately following an arrest. *Chimel* v. *California* (1969) dealt with areas that are not in plain view searched without a warrant. The case also addresses arrest activities by police. Ted Chimel was approached in his home by police officers who possessed a valid arrest warrant for him. The officers then advised Chimel that they wanted to "look around" and proceeded to search the premises without Chimel's permission. After a one-hour search, some coins were located and seized as evidence in a crime. Although initially convicted, Chimel later appealed the case, which was reversed by the U.S. Supreme Court because the coins were not found lawfully. Although the coins were found "incident to a lawful arrest," the evidence was excluded because it was not in plain view and the officers did not have a search warrant to search Chimel's residence, only an arrest warrant. The *Chimel* decision established that a search made incidental to a lawful arrest must be confined to the area around the suspect's immediate control.

The point in the *Chimel* case is that the officers who searched Chimel's house went far beyond any area where he might have either hidden a weapon or been able to destroy any evidence. Therefore, there was no constitutional basis for an extended search of the house. The *Chimel* case is important, as it relates to criminal investigation, because it changed the policy with regard to the **scope of the search** as it relates to an officer's authority to search incident to an arrest. Prior to *Chimel*, officers had more leeway to search the area around an arrested suspect. Since *Chimel*, however, officers can search only the arrested person and the immediate physical surroundings under the defendant's control (i.e., within arm's length of the defendant). Such searches are for weapons or to safeguard against the destruction of evidence. To search further, officers must obtain a search warrant.

In 1990, the U.S. Supreme Court further defined the circumstances under which officers may conduct a limited search in the home of an arrested person.

In *Maryland* v. *Buie* (1990), the Court held that a protective sweep during an arrest in a home is allowed if justified. Of course, this case authorized only a "protective" warrantless sweep for additional suspects who might be located in the residence.

In 1989, the U.S. Supreme Court clarified the basis on which law enforcement, lacking probable cause to believe that a crime has occurred, may stop and detain a person for investigative purposes. In *United States* v. *Sokolow* (1989), the Court ruled that the legitimacy of such a stop must be evaluated according to a "totality of the circumstances" criterion, in which the defendant's entire behavior is taken collectively to provide the basis for a legitimate stop. In this case, the defendant, Sokolow, appeared to be suspicious to police because while traveling under an alias from Honolulu he paid $2,100 in $20 bills (taken from a larger sum of money) for a round-trip airline ticket to Miami, where he spent a very short period. Sokolow was noticeably nervous and had checked no luggage. A warrantless airport investigation by DEA agents revealed more than 1,000 grams of cocaine on the defendant. Upon appeal, the Court ruled that although no single activity was proof of illegal activity, taken together they created circumstances under which suspicion of illegal activity was justified.

EXCEPTIONS TO THE EXCLUSIONARY RULE

Since the *Mapp* and *Chimel* cases, the U.S. Supreme Court has developed several exceptions to the exclusionary rule. These play a considerable role in shaping the manner in which police officers are allowed to behave before, during, and after a search and seizure of evidence.

The Good Faith Exception

In the years since the *Weeks* and *Silverthorne* cases, some people have criticized the U.S. Supreme Court for a "chipping away" of the exclusionary rule. One such case emerged in the summer of 1984 when the laws dealing with search and seizure changed dramatically in *United States* v. *Leon* (1984), when the first good faith exception to the exclusionary rule was decided. During the course of a drug trafficking investigation by the Burbank, California Police Department, officers secured a search warrant for the residence of Alberto Leon. The warrant was reviewed by three prosecutors prior to its being issued by a state court judge. The subsequent search netted large quantities of drugs, and Leon was arrested and charged with drug trafficking. The defense challenged the validity of the warrant based on the unreliability of the informant and moved to suppress the evidence. The district court and the U.S. Court of Appeals both held that the affidavit was insufficient, but the U.S. Supreme Court supported the prosecution, holding that the exclusionary rule was designed only as a deterrent for the abuse of police authority. The Court specified that evidence might be excluded if (1) police officers were dishonest in preparing the affidavit, and (2) if the warrant was deficient on its face (e.g., a wrong or missing description of the place to be searched) such that no officer could reasonably serve it, or (3) if the magistrate was not found to be neutral.

The practical effect of the *Leon* case is that any evidence seized through a search warrant is immune from suppression even if the judge signing the warrant was wrong and there was not probable cause to believe that contraband or other evidence would be discovered under the warrant. The *Leon* case allows the use of evidence obtained by officers acting in reasonable reliance on a search warrant issued by a neutral magistrate but that is ultimately found invalid.

Another case decided by the U.S. Supreme Court that same year was *Massachusetts* v. *Sheppard* (1984), which reinforced the concept of good faith. In the *Sheppard* case, officers served a search warrant that failed to describe accurately the property to be seized. Although they were aware of the error, they were assured by the magistrate that the warrant was valid. After conviction of the defendant, the Massachusetts Supreme Court reversed the conviction of the trial court. But upon review, the U.S. Supreme Court supported the good faith exception and allowed the original conviction to stand. The scope of the exclusionary rule was diminished further in yet another case, *Illinois* v. *Rodriguez* (1990). In the *Rodriguez* case, Gail Fischer, who was badly beaten, complained that she had been assaulted in a Chicago apartment. She led police to the apartment, which she claimed she was sharing with the defendant, and produced a key and opened the door. The defendant, Edward Rodriguez, was found inside asleep on a bed with cocaine and drug paraphernalia spread around him. Rodriguez was arrested and charged with assault and possession of drug paraphernalia and cocaine.

After his conviction, Rodriguez demonstrated that Fischer had not lived with him for at least one month and argued that she no longer had legal control over the apartment. So the defense claimed that Fischer had no authority to give police warrantless access to the apartment. But the U.S. Supreme Court disagreed by stating that there was no Fourth Amendment violation because the police "reasonably believed" at the time of their entry that Fisher had authority for consent.

The Inevitable Discovery Doctrine

The inevitable discovery exception to the exclusionary rule was developed in the 1984 *Nix* v. *Williams* case. This exception states that evidence that has been seized illegally or evidence stemming from illegally seized evidence (e.g., fruit of the poisonous tree) (*Wong Sun* v. *United States,* 1963) is admissible if the police can prove that they would have inevitably discovered it anyway by lawful means. On Christmas Eve, a 10-year-old girl disappeared from the YMCA in Des Moines, Iowa. Shortly thereafter, Williams was seen leaving the YMCA carrying a large bundle wrapped in a blanket. A young boy who had helped Williams carry the bundle reported that he saw skinny white legs in it.

The next day Williams' car was located near Davenport, some 160 miles away. The police assumed that the girl's body would be located somewhere between the YMCA and Williams' car and began conducting a massive search. In the meantime, Williams was located and arrested in the town where the car was located. Williams' lawyer was told that Williams would be transported back to Des Moines without being interrogated. During the trip back, however, the officer had a conversation with Williams in which he suggested that it would be nice if the girl could be located before a predicted snowstorm, and have a Christian burial. As Williams and the officer neared the town where the body was hidden, Williams directed the officer to the body, a location about two miles from one of the search teams.

At the trial, the motion to suppress the evidence was denied and Williams was convicted of first-degree murder. On appeal, the U.S. District Court declared that the evidence was wrongfully admitted at Williams' trial. At his second trial, the prosecution did not offer Williams' statements into evidence and did not attempt to show that Williams led officers to the body. The trial court held that if Williams had not led police to the body, it would have been found by searchers anyway. Williams was convicted of murder a second time.

So, because the *Miranda* warnings were not read to the defendant before he confessed, evidence that was seized was excluded at the first trial. However, because the evidence would have been discovered anyway as a result of the police search, the court admitted the evidence.

The Computer Errors Exception

In the 1995 *Arizona* v. *Evans* case, the Court created a computer errors exception to the exclusionary rule. The exception held that a traffic stop, which led to the seizure of marijuana, was legal even though officers conducted the stop based on an arrest warrant stored improperly in their computer. The case was initiated in 1991 when Issac Evans was stopped in Phoenix, Arizona, for driving the wrong way on a one-way street in front of a police station. A routine computer check revealed an outstanding warrant for Evans, who was taken into custody. Police then found marijuana in Evans' car, and he was later convicted on drug charges. After the arrest, however, police learned that the arrest warrant reported to them by their computer had actually been quashed a few weeks earlier but had not been removed from the computer. The court upheld Evans' conviction by reasoning that officers should not be held responsible for a clerical error made by a court worker and concluded that the arresting officers were acting in good faith based on the information available to them at the time of the arrest.

SEARCHES WITH A WARRANT

Over the years, the **search warrant** has proved to be one of the most valuable tools in criminal investigation. It authorizes the search of homes, businesses, and vehicles of suspects; typically results in the arrest of multiple suspects; and expedites investigation and subsequent case closure.

When Are Search Warrants Necessary?

If the warrant specifies a certain person to be searched, the police can search only that person unless they have independent probable cause to search other persons who happen to be present at the scene of a search. However, if an officer has a reasonable suspicion that an onlooker is engaged in criminal activity, the officer can question the onlooker and, if necessary for the officer's safety, can frisk for weapons.

Technically, a person may require the police to produce a warrant before admitting them into his or her home for a search. However, people sometimes run into trouble when they "stand on their rights" in this way. A warrant is not always legally necessary, and a police officer may have information of which a person is unaware that allows the officer to make a warrantless entry. If an officer announces an intention to enter without a warrant, a person should not risk injury or a separate charge of "interfering with a police officer." Rather, the person should stand aside, let the officer proceed, and allow a court to decide later

Figure 4.2 Briefing officers prior to serving a search warrant.

whether the officer's actions were proper. At the same time, the person should make it clear that he or she does not consent to the search.

When Search Warrants Aren't Required

Most searches occur without warrants being issued. Over the years, the courts have defined a number of situations in which a search warrant is not necessary, either because the search is per se reasonable under the circumstances or because, due to a lack of a reasonable expectation of privacy, the Fourth Amendment doesn't apply at all. Later on in this chapter, we will discuss some circumstances under which a search warrant is not required under law.

Advantages of Searching with a Search Warrant

Among the many tools afforded the criminal investigator, the search warrant has proved to be of substantial worth. It represents an authorization by the court for officers to enter a designated location or structure and search for specific items. It can be useful to a criminal investigator in many situations. The search warrant can be used to:

- Recover stolen property.
- Seize drugs or other contraband.
- Seize any other type of property used in the commission of a crime.

The search warrant must contain specifics about the location to be searched, the objects being sought, the probable cause which indicates that there is property to seize, and a signature of the judge authorizing the search. Evidence obtained through the use of a search warrant may also be more readily accepted by courts than if seized without a warrant or incident to arrest. In

Figure 4.3 Tactical unit being utilized to serve search warrant.

addition, the officer is protected from civil liability when a warrant is obtained. A search warrant also benefits the prosecutor by shifting the legal burden to the defendant. Instead of the prosecutor having to justify a presumably unreasonable search, it becomes the burden of the defendant to show that the evidence was seized illegally. This factor alone has encouraged officers to obtain search warrants when possible.

Structuring the Warrant

A search warrant cannot be issued unless it meets with constitutional guidelines. In addition, for the warrant to be legal, it must meet specific legal requirements. The legal requirements for a search warrant are:

- It must be authorized by the proper official.
- It must be issued only for specifically authorized objects.
- It must be issued on probable cause.

The search warrant **affidavit** (Figure 4.4) presents facts that the officer believes constitute probable cause to justify the issuance of a warrant. Authorization of the warrant is through the judicial branch of government. If a magistrate agrees that probable cause exists, he or she signs the affidavit and issues the warrant. The warrant must contain the following information:

Figure 4.4 Sample search warrant affidavit.

**IN THE DISTRICT COURT OF THE FIFTH JUDICIAL DISTRICT
IN AND FOR:
JACKSON COUNTY, MISSOURI**

Before _____ Judge, District Court of
Jackson County, Missouri

State of Missouri ⎫ ss.
Jackson County ⎭

Affidavit for Search Warrant

On this ____ day of _____, 07, _Agent Brian Johnson_ being first sworn, upon oath deposes and says:

That a certain _Residence_ within said County and State, located and described as follows, to wit:

2304 N.W. 38th Place, Kansas City, Missouri located in Jackson County being a single family wood frame dwelling facing South, and under the control of Lance T. Anderson, and wife Chelsea. The garage area of the house is to the West end of the South side. The house is on the North side of the street with tan colored brick along the lower third of the front, while being fenced in, with a chain link fence, around the back yard area.

the same being the _residence_ of _Lance and Chelsea Anderson_ whose more full, true and correct name is unknown to the affiant, there is located certain property particularly described as follows, to-wit:

Controlled substances to include marijuana, Schedule I, LSD, Schedule I, Cocaine, Schedule II, and one fifty dollar bill ($50.00) U.S. currency bearing serial number JO3744496B, and any other records or documents showing illicit business dealings in controlled drugs.

which said property is subject to search and seizure as set out by the laws of Missouri for the following grounds, to-wit:

Violation of the state criminal code controlled substances section RsMo 195.233.

and that the probable cause of the affiant believing such facts exist as follows, to-wit:

1) Your affiant is a sworn police officer with the Kansas City Police Department, who has been a full time narcotics investigator for three years and seven months. 2) On April 30, 2007 at approximately 1630 hours, Officer Johnson purchased one (1) kilo of marijuana for $2500 from Chelsea Anderson which was contained in a black trunk located in the hallway of the residence. 3) On April 30, 2007 at approx. 1945 hours Officer Johnson purchased 100 units of LSD for $4350 from Lance Anderson which he acquired from the freezer area of the kitchen. 4) On April 30, 2007 Lance Anderson also displayed approx. one (1) ounce of white powder claiming it to be cocaine which was also kept in the refrigerator area of the kitchen.

_____
Affiant

Subscribed and sworn before me this ___ day of ____ 2007

_____
Judge, District Court of
Jackson County, Missouri

- Reasons to request the search.
- Name of the officer requesting the warrant.
- Items to be seized.
- Specific place to be searched.
- Signature of the issuing judge.

Once issued, all warrants should be executed promptly. During the course of a search, other items of contraband should not be sought unless they are specified in the search warrant. The seizure of items other than those listed in the warrant is not considered "within the scope of the search" and will probably be excluded from the trial as evidence obtained illegally. The search warrant process consists basically of three stages: the affidavit, the search warrant, and the search warrant return.

The Affidavit

A search warrant affidavit must be prepared before obtaining a search warrant. The affidavit tells the judge three things:

1. What is being searched for.
   - Contraband
   - Instrumentation of crime
   - Weapons
   - Fruits of crime

2. Where the search is to occur.
   - Residence
   - Business
   - Vehicle

3. Why the search is to be conducted.
   - Probable cause adequately outlined
   - Facts establishing probable cause

The Search Warrant

Basically, the search warrant (Figure 4.5) sets forth the same facts as outlined in the affidavit. Prior to signing the affidavit, the affiant (the officer) must be certain that he or she is first sworn in by a judge. The judge must then sign and date all pages of the affidavit and warrant.

The Search Warrant Return

The **search warrant return** (Figure 4.6) is an itemized inventory of all property and material seized by officers at the location of the search. A copy is left with the defendant, and the return itself is returned to the issuing judge. In most cases, the officer who executes the warrant is the one to return it, and this must be accomplished within 24 hours after the search. The search warrant return should include the following information:

- The name of the officer serving the warrant.
- The date the warrant was served.
- An itemized list of all property seized.
- The name of the owner of the place searched.

Figure 4.5 Sample search warrant.

**IN THE DISTRICT COURT OF THE FIFTH JUDICIAL DISTRICT
IN AND FOR:
JACKSON COUNTY, MISSOURI**

BEFORE _____ JUDGE, DISTRICT COURT OF
JACKSON COUNTY, MISSOURI

State of Missouri ⎱ ss. **SEARCH WARRANT**
Jackson County ⎰

In the name of the State of Missouri, to any sheriff, constable, marshal, policeman, or peace officer in the County of Jackson, State of Missouri.

Proof by affidavit having been this day made before me, by _Agent Brian Johnson_ that there is probable cause for believing that in the herein described _residence_ is located the following property particularly described as follows, to-wit:

Controlled substances to include marijuana, Schedule I, LSD, Schedule I, and Cocaine, Schedule II, and one fifty dollar bill U.S. currency bearing serial number: JO3744496B

and that the herein described _residence_ should be searched by reason of the following grounds to-wit:

Possession of the above described controlled dangerous substances and currency is evidence of violation of the state criminal code controlled substances section RsMo 195.233.

YOU ARE THEREFORE COMMANDED at any time of day or night to make immediate search of the _residence_ of _2304 N.W. 38th Place, Kansas City, Missouri_ whose more full, true and correct name is unknown, located and described as follows, to-wit:

a single family wood frame dwelling facing South, and under the control of Lance Thomas Anderson, and wife Chelsea. The garage area of the house is to the West end of the south side. The house is on the north side of the street with tan colored brick along the lower third front, while being fenced in, with a chain link fence, around the back yard area.

for the said property above described, and, if you find the same or any part thereof to bring it forthwith before me at my office in Kansas City, Jackson County, Missouri.

Dated this _1st_ day of _May_, 2007.

_____
Judge, District Court of
Jackson County, Missouri

- The signature of the officer who served the warrant (usually signed in the presence of the judge).
- The signature of the issuing judge and the date of the return.

Execution of the Warrant

Once issued, the search warrant is basically an order by the court to execute it. The officer has no choice but to do so. If the warrant is valid on its face, has been authorized by the proper official, and is executed correctly, the officer is protected from both civil liability and criminal prosecution. Certain procedures

Figure 4.6 Sample search warrant return.

SEARCH WARRANT RETURN

Received this writ _____ day of _____, 2007

Executed the same on the _____ day of _____, 2007 by going to the within designated place where I found and seized the following property, to-wit:
_____
_____
_____ *(ITEMIZE PROPERTY HERE)* _____
_____
_____

and brought the same before the within named court.

_____
Sheriff - Peace Officer
Marshall - Policeman

Executed the same day on the _____ day of _____, 2007 by searching the within designated place, where I could find none of the above described property.

_____
Sheriff - Peace Officer
Marshall - Policeman

OFFICER'S FEES

Executing writ _____ $ _____

Mileage _____ Miles $ _____

Total: $ _____

_____
Sheriff - Peace Officer
Marshall - Policeman

should be adhered to carefully when executing the search warrant. Search warrant execution guidelines include:

- A search warrant may authorize a specific officer (the affiant) to execute it. Typically, however, a class of officers will be authorized to execute the warrant, so that anyone within that class may do so.

- Time limitations must be adhered to. Although the word *reasonable* has not been defined by the courts, execution of a warrant must be within what a rational person would consider reasonable. To deal with this issue, many states have outlined a specific period in which the warrant must be issued. Periods may range from 48 to 96 hours. If the warrant cannot be executed within that designated period, it is invalid.

Figure 4.7 Investigator preparing search warrant affidavit.

- Only necessary force can be used in executing a search warrant. The U.S. Code requires that officers announce their purpose and authority, and if refused admittance, break both outer and inner doors to gain entry. Denial need not be specific, or even be inferred, such as the occupants refusing to answer the door.

- Some states may authorize a "no-knock warrant." If such a warrant is obtained, specific information must be contained in the affidavit justifying why the no-knock warrant is necessary.

Anticipatory Search Warrants

An anticipatory search warrant is a warrant based on an affidavit showing probable cause to believe that at some future time, particular evidence of a crime will be located at a particular place. Anticipatory warrants may not be executed until some specific event (other than the passage of time) has occurred. The specified events are called triggering conditions, and even though the warrant has been issued and it is in the hands of the police, until the **triggering condition** has arisen, the search may not be carried out.

Anticipatory search warrants have been the subject of a great deal of litigation, much of that based on the argument that all anticipatory warrants are unconstitutional because they violate the Fourth Amendment requirement of probable cause. The contention of many defendants has been because, by definition, anticipatory search warrant affidavits show only that there will be probable cause to search the premises at some later time—not that there is at present probable cause to search—the Fourth Amendment requirement is not satisfied. Although this argument has been repeatedly rejected by various federal courts of appeals, the issue has recently come before the Supreme Court of the United States in the case of *United States* v. *Grubbs,* 377 F.3d 1072 (2004). Even though the case involved a warrant obtained by federal officers for a federal crime, the Supreme Court's opinion in that case is of value to all law enforcement officers and agencies in understanding anticipatory search warrants and their use.

United States* v. *Grubbs. Respondent Jeffrey Grubbs purchased a videotape containing child pornography from a Web site operated by an undercover postal inspector. Officers from the postal inspection service arranged a controlled delivery of a package containing a videotape to Grubbs' residence. A postal inspector submitted a search warrant application to a magistrate judge for the Eastern District of California, a copy of an affidavit describing the proposed operation in detail. The affidavit stated:

> "Execution of the search warrant will not occur unless and until the parcel has been received by a person(s) and has been physically taken into the residence . . . at that time, and not before, the search warrant will be executed by me and other United States Postal Service inspectors, with appropriate assistance from other law enforcement officers in accordance with this warrant's command."

In addition to describing this triggering condition, the affidavit referred to two attachments, which describe Grubbs' residence and the items officers would seize. These attachments, but not the body of the affidavit, were incorporated into the requested warrant.

The magistrate judge issued the warrant as requested. Two days later, an undercover postal inspector delivered the package. Grubbs' wife signed for it and took the unopened package inside. The inspectors detained Grubbs as he left his home a few minutes later, then entered the house and commenced the search. Approximately 30 minutes into the search, Grubbs was provided with a copy of the warrant, which included both attachments but not the supporting affidavit that explained when the warrant would be executed. Grubbs consented to interrogation by the postal inspectors and admitted ordering the videotape. He was placed under arrest, and various items were seized, including the videotape. Grubbs subsequently pleaded guilty but reserved his right to appeal the denial of his earlier motion to suppress the evidence.

The Triggering Condition

In order to understand both the *Grubbs* case and the use of anticipatory search warrants in general, it is essential that the concept of the triggering condition be kept clearly in mind. The triggering condition is the anticipated future event that, when it occurs, gives rise to the necessary probable cause to search the premises. Even though the anticipatory search warrant has been issued, if the triggering condition has not yet occurred, the probable cause requirement of the Fourth Amendment has not yet been satisfied and the search is invalid.

The U.S. Supreme Court's decision in *Grubbs* upholds the constitutionality of anticipatory search warrants, provided that the following prerequisites are satisfied:

1. It must be true that if the triggering condition occurs "there is a fair probability that contraband or evidence of a crime will be found in a particular place."
2. There is probable cause to believe that the triggering condition will occur.

3. The affidavit supporting the warrant provides that the magistrate was given sufficient information to evaluate both aspects of the probable cause determination.

It is apparent in the *Grubbs* decision, however, that it is not essential that the defendant be presented with a copy of the affidavit at the time that the search warrant is instituted nor that the defendant be told at the time of the search what the triggering condition was.

WARRANTLESS SEARCHES

Officers must remember that the rules that apply to searches differ from those applying to arrests. An arrest and a search are two completely separate and distinct law enforcement procedures. For example, depending on certain statutory restraints, an officer might be empowered to make an arrest without an arrest warrant, provided that probable cause exists. In addition, arrests are permissible even when there is time for the officer to get a warrant. For searches, the rules are different. The Fourth Amendment says that all searches must be preceded by the officer obtaining a search warrant. Regardless of how much probable cause an officer may have, if he or she searches without a search warrant, there is a legal presumption that the search is unconstitutional. Several exceptions have been developed in which a warrantless search is authorized under law:

- Consent searches
- Searches under exigent circumstances
- Searches incident to lawful arrest
- Stop-and-frisk searches
- Plain-view searches
- Automobile searches
- Open-field searches

Search by Consent

Police can search without a warrant when a suspect gives them permission to do so. Searches in this instance must, of course, be subsequent to an initial detention that was lawful. As a case in point, *Florida* v. *Royer* (1983) held that evidence obtained as a result of a **consent search** when the detention was made without probable cause is a violation of the defendant's Fourth Amendment rights and will be excluded.

The consent search can be especially useful in cases in which officers have no legal basis for obtaining a search warrant. It is important to remember, however, that a consent search must be authorized voluntarily, with no coercion from officers. This was affirmed in *Bumper* v. *North Carolina* (1968) in a decision in which the U.S. Supreme Court held that a search is not justified on the basis of consent when consent was given only after the officer conducting the search asserted possession of a warrant. Although it is legal for officers to search on the word of the suspect, it is a better idea to have the person sign a consent-to-search waiver authorizing the search in writing (Figure 4.8). For the consent to be valid, officers must first establish that the person giving consent has legal authority to do so. Just because a suspect is present in a particular residence, he

CITY POLICE DEPARTMENT
CONSENT TO SEARCH

DATE _____

LOCATION _____

I, _____, having been informed of my constitutional right
not to have a search made of the premises hereinafter described without a search warrant and of my
right to refuse to consent to such a search, hereby authorize _____
_____, officers of the City Police Department, to conduct a complete
search of my:

Premises ___

Curtilage ___

Vehicles ___

These officers are authorized by me to take from my premises any letters, papers, materials, or other
property which they may desire, after receipting me for same. I further state that I am the proper
person to give the consent and authorization referred to herein.

This written permission is being given by me to the above named officers(s) voluntarily and without
threats or promises of any kind.

_____
Signature

WITNESSES:

_____

_____

_____

or she may not have legal authority to grant a search. Dominion and control can
be verified through the seizing of utility bills, for example, that bear the name of
the suspect and the associated address.

One interesting aspect of a consent search is that the suspect does not have
to be given the *Miranda* warning or told that he or she has the right to withhold
consent for the search to be valid (*Schneckloth* v. *Bustamonte,* 1973). In the
event that the suspect changes his or her mind about the search, officers must
cease searching or obtain a search warrant to continue.

Another problem with consent searches is that the person giving permission to search can limit the scope of the search. Permission to search can be withdrawn at any time, and any area or container within the search area can be specifically exempted. What if an area or container that might reasonably hold the object of the search isn't specifically exempted? In the case of *Florida* v. *Jimeno* (1991), the Court held that a person's general consent to search the interior of a car includes, unless otherwise specified, all containers in the car that might reasonably hold the object of the search. In this case a Dade County police officer began following a car after overhearing the driver, Enio Jimeno, make arrangements for a drug transaction over a pay phone.

When Jimeno failed to come to a complete stop before turning right at a stoplight, the officer pulled him over. The officer advised Jimeno that he was going to receive a traffic citation for failure to stop at the red light. Next, since he had reason to believe that Jimeno was involved with a drug transaction, the officer asked for permission to search the automobile. Jimeno agreed, claiming that he had nothing to hide. As a result of the search, the officer found 1 kilo of cocaine in a brown paper bag located under the passenger side floorboard. Jimeno was arrested and charged.

The issue here is that because Jimeno had not given specific permission to search the bag, the Florida courts ordered the cocaine suppressed as evidence. The courts claimed that although the officer was proper in asking for permission to search the vehicle, permission was not extended to the bag under the floorboard or any other containers in the car. The U.S. Supreme Court didn't agree. In his delivery of the majority opinion, Chief Justice William Rehnquist stated: "The scope of a search is generally defined by its expressed object. [The officer] had informed Jimeno that he . . . would be looking for narcotics in the area. We think that it was . . . reasonable for the police to conclude that the general consent to search [the] car included consent to search containers within that car which might bear drugs." Rehnquist further explained that a different degree of privacy should attach to a paper bag than to a locked suitcase and that it is probably unreasonable for an officer to think that a person who gives consent for a search of his vehicle has also given consent to pry open a locked bag inside the car. But it probably isn't unreasonable for the officer to open a paper bag under the same circumstances. Rehnquist went on to say that "a suspect may of course delimit as he chooses the scope of the search to which he consents . . . but if his consent would reasonably be understood to extend to a particular container, the Fourth Amendment provides no grounds for requiring a more explicit authorization."

In a related case, *Florida* v. *Bostick* (1991), the U.S. Supreme Court permitted warrantless sweeps of inner-city buses. In *Bostick,* the Court ruled that law enforcement officers who approach a seated bus passenger and request consent to search the passenger's luggage do not necessarily "seize" the passenger under the Fourth Amendment. The test applied in such situations is whether or not a reasonable passenger would feel free to decline the request or otherwise terminate the encounter. In the *Bostick* case, the defendant was traveling from Miami, Florida to Atlanta, Georgia. When the bus stopped in Ft. Lauderdale, two police officers involved in drug interdiction efforts boarded the bus and, lacking reasonable suspicion, approached the defendant. After asking to inspect his ticket and identification, they then requested and were given consent to search the defendant's luggage for drugs. Cocaine was found as a result of the search.

The Florida Supreme Court ruled that the cocaine had been seized in violation of the Fourth Amendment. In doing so, the court noted that the defendant had been illegally seized without reasonable suspicion and that an impermissible seizure necessarily results any time that police board a bus, approach passengers without reasonable suspicion, and request consent to search luggage. The U.S. Supreme Court reversed the Florida court's decision and held that this type of drug interdiction effort may be permissible as long as officers do not convey the message that compliance with their request is required.

The Court noted that previous cases have permitted the police, without reasonable suspicion, to approach people in an airport for the purpose of asking questions, verifying identification, and requesting consent to search luggage.

Emergency Searches

In the case of an emergency or **exigent circumstances,** a search may also be conducted without a warrant provided that probable cause exists. As a general rule, the police are authorized to make an emergency warrantless search when the time it would take to get a warrant would jeopardize public safety or lead to the loss of important evidence. Here are some situations in which judges would most likely uphold a warrantless search:

- A threat of the removal or destruction of evidence. *Case example:* Following a street drug arrest, an officer enters the house after the suspect shouts into the house, "Eddie, quick, flush our stash down the toilet." The officer arrests Eddie and seizes the stash.

- A danger to life. *Case example:* A police officer on routine patrol hears shouts and screams coming from a residence, rushes in, and arrests a suspect for spousal abuse.

- The threat of a suspect escaping.

Any one of these circumstances may create an exception to the Fourth Amendment's warrant requirement. It is incumbent on investigating officers to demonstrate that a dire situation existed that justified their actions. Failure to do so will result in the evidence seized being deemed illegal. However, if a judge decides that an officer had time to obtain a search warrant without risking injury to people or the loss of evidence, the judge should refuse to allow into evidence whatever was seized in the course of the warrantless search. Judges always have the final word on whether police officers should have obtained warrants.

The need for emergency searches was first recognized by the U.S. Supreme Court in *Ker* v. *California* (1963) and *Cupp* v. *Murphy* (1973) when it decided that police may enter a dwelling unannounced in cases in which a delay in the search would result in the destruction of evidence. In a related decision, the court held that it was lawful for police to enter a residence without a warrant if they were in pursuit of a fleeing robber (*Warden* v. *Hayden,* 1967). In another case, *Mincey* v. *Arizona* (1978), the Supreme Court held that the "Fourth Amendment does not require police officers to delay in the course of an investigation if doing so would gravely endanger their lives or the lives of others." Finally, in the 1995 case of *Wilson* v. *Arkansas,* the Supreme Court ruled that police officers generally must knock and announce their identity before entering a dwelling or other premises with a search warrant. However, in certain emergencies, officers armed with a search warrant need not knock or identify themselves.

Searches Incident to Arrest

As we learned earlier, the *Chimel* decision authorized a search of an arrested suspect and the immediate area around him or her. This is justified by an officer's right to search a suspect for weapons before transporting him or her to jail. The area around the suspect is searched because it is considered lunging distance, where a suspect could conceivably acquire a weapon. When the suspect is arrested in a vehicle, the immediate area is defined as the entire passenger compartment of the vehicle, including closed but not locked containers (*New York* v. *Belton,* 1981). In circumstances in which a thorough search is desired pursuant to an arrest, a search warrant should be obtained.

Stop-and-Frisk Searches

In 1968, the Supreme Court of the United States declared in the case of *Terry* v. *Ohio* (1968)[1] that a police officer may stop a person for questioning if the officer reasonably suspects that the person has committed, is committing, or is about to commit a crime. It is not necessary that the officer have probable cause to arrest the individual at the time that the stop is made. All that is required is that the officer has a reasonable suspicion that the individual is involved in criminal activity. However, to be reasonable, this suspicion must be based on articulable facts that would lead a reasonable person to suspect that the individual is involved in criminal activity.

The Supreme Court further declared in *Terry* v. *Ohio* that an officer who has stopped a suspect may ". . . search for weapons for the protection of the police officer, where he has reason to believe that he is dealing with an armed and dangerous individual."[2] This case is the landmark legal decision that grants officers the authority to conduct field interviews (also called "investigative detentions" or *Terry* stops) and pat-down searches (an investigative detention is commonly referred to as a **"stop and frisk"**). Numerous federal and state court decisions have interpreted and applied the principles of *Terry.* In addition, many states have enacted statutes dealing with field interviews and pat-down searches.[3]

Field Interviews versus "Consensual Encounters." The principles discussed here apply to field interviews only. They do not apply to so-called consensual or voluntary encounters. As noted earlier, an officer may conduct a field interview as defined in the policy (an investigative detention or *Terry* stop) only when he or she has a reasonable suspicion, based on objective facts, that the individual to be interviewed is engaged in criminal activity. Conversely, an officer who lacks "reasonable suspicion" as defined above may nevertheless approach a suspect and ask questions designed to produce evidence of criminal activity as long as the encounter is voluntary or "consensual."

The distinction is a critical one. Field interviews are "seizures" of the person within the meaning of the Fourth Amendment, and the discovery of any physical evidence during such an interview is valid only if Fourth Amendment considerations are met. On the other hand, consensual encounters are not seizures of the person. Should the officer discover evidence during the consensual encounter, it will normally be admissible in a trial even though there was no basis for "reasonable suspicion" at the time that the officer initiated the

Figure 4.9 A police officer "covers" his partner as he conducts a pat-down search of a teen suspect beside their squad car. *Spencer Grant, PhotoEdit Inc.*

encounter. Thus, it will often be desirable for the officer to approach a suspect in a manner that will make the initial contact a consensual encounter rather than a field interview.

Factors Defining a Field Interview. The U.S. Supreme Court has held that a police–citizen encounter is consensual (i.e., does not amount to a seizure of the person) as long as the circumstances of the encounter are such that a reasonable person would feel that he or she was "free to leave," that is, to terminate the encounter and depart at any time.[4] The following factors, among others, may be considered by a court in determining whether the contact was a consensual encounter or a field interview (hereafter sometimes referred to as an "investigative stop"):

1. Interference with the suspect's freedom of movement. *Case example:* If officers position themselves or their vehicles in such a manner as to block the suspect's path, this indicates that the suspect is not free to leave and may render the encounter an investigative stop.

2. Number of officers and their behavior. *Case example:* Confrontation of the suspect by more than one officer may create an atmosphere of intimidation that will cause the courts to consider the contact an investigative stop. Excessive display of weapons, such as drawn or pointed firearms, will have the same effect. Even the prolonged or repeated display of badges or other

police identification may be considered intimidating.[5] A threatening or bullying manner may lead to the same result.

3. Physical contact with the suspect. *Case example:* Any physical contact with the suspect for purposes of stopping or holding the individual or to search for weapons or evidence will almost certainly cause the contact to be considered a nonconsensual (i.e., an investigative) stop or even a full-fledged arrest.

4. Retaining personal property of the suspect. *Case example:* If the officer wishes the contact to be regarded as consensual, any personal property taken from the suspect, such as a driver's license or other identification, should be returned promptly to the suspect. Prolonged retention by the officer of such items may lead a court to conclude that the suspect was not free to leave.

An officer may ask the suspect to move to another area during the encounter without altering the consensual nature of the contact if it is made clear to the suspect that the request to move to another location is just that—a request only—and that the suspect is free to refuse the request.

One method of emphasizing the consensual nature of the encounter is for the officer to advise the suspect that the suspect has the right to refuse to answer questions, the right to refuse to consent to a search, and so forth. Such warnings may not be legally required under the existing circumstances, but if given, they will often persuade a court that any continuation of the encounter beyond that point was still voluntary on the part of the suspect. Even if the contact is not a consensual contact, it is still perfectly lawful if conducted in accordance with the principles applicable to investigative stops.

Initiation/Conduct of Field Interviews. The initiation of a field interview is justified only when an officer has reasonable suspicion that a suspect is engaged in criminal activity. This suspicion must be based on specific facts known to or observed by the officer that the officer can later articulate in detail to a court. Such facts may include the demeanor of a person (furtive behavior); the time of day or night; the area in which the encounter occurs; the inappropriateness of the suspect's presence in that area at that time; the fact that the suspect is carrying suspicious objects; objective evidence that the suspect may be armed (bulge in the clothing); and knowledge of the officer that a crime has recently been committed in that area, especially if the suspect matches the description of the perpetrator of the crime.[6]

In addition to the above, on January 12, 2000, the U.S. Supreme Court decided the case of *Illinois* v. *Wardlow* ((98-1036) 183 Ill. 2nd 306, 701 N.E. 2d 484), which provides officers with an additional criterion for establishing reasonable suspicion to initiate a field interview. *Wardlow* deals with the common scenario in which a person notices police approaching and runs away to avoid them. In the past, it has generally been held by the courts that the act of fleeing from police does not, in and of itself, justify officers pursuing and stopping the individual concerned. The *Wardlow* decision does not alter that basic fact, but it does permit officers to include fleeing as one more element that police may consider in determining whether reasonable suspicion exists sufficient to justify a *Terry* stop.

Officers must conduct the field interview in such a manner that the courts will not consider it an unlawful arrest. It must be remembered that in the view of the courts, an arrest may occur even though the actual words "you're under arrest" have not been uttered by the officer. Therefore, unless the stop produces probable cause to arrest the suspect, the officer should still conduct the field interview in a manner that will not convey the impression that the suspect is under arrest. For this reason, the officer should:

- Exercise reasonable courtesy and avoid intimidating or threatening behavior.
- Minimize physical contact which may induce a court to treat the encounter as an arrest.
- Avoid detaining the suspect any longer than is absolutely necessary. One of the more common bases for judicial rulings that a stop has become an arrest is detention of the suspect for an excessive period of time.

In addition, any movement of the suspect from the point of initial contact, such as to an area where there is more light, should be limited to that which is reasonably necessary for officer safety and the determination of criminal involvement. However, it should be clearly understood here that notwithstanding cautions regarding the legal requirements for a field interview, officer safety should remain a paramount consideration and should be emphasized in any departmental policy.

Pat-Down Searches. As noted earlier, *Terry* v. *Ohio*, other court decisions, and various state statutes give officers the authority to conduct a pat-down[7] search or "frisk" of a suspect who has been the subject of a valid investigative stop if the officer reasonably believes that the suspect may possess a weapon.

The following points are vital when conducting a valid pat-down search:

- If the stop is invalid, the pat-down search is also invalid. Only a valid investigative stop based on reasonable suspicion of criminal activity justifies a pat-down search.
- The right to stop the suspect for questioning does not automatically give the officer the right to conduct the pat-down search. The erroneous belief that the right to stop automatically gives the officer the right to frisk is one of the more common errors made by police officers. In reality, even if the stop is valid, before a pat-down search may be conducted, there must be a separate basis for believing that the person who has been stopped may possess a weapon and may be a threat to the officer.
- Factors that may justify an officer reaching the conclusion that a suspect who has been validly stopped may possess a weapon include the type of crime suspected;[8] the circumstances of the stop (number of suspects, number of officers present, and time of day and location of the stop); the behavior of the suspect (belligerence); any visual indication that the suspect may be carrying a weapon (such as a bulge in the clothing); and any prior knowledge that the officer may have that this particular individual is or may be prone to violence.
- The pat-down search is limited to a "frisk" of the suspect's outer clothing only. It is not a full-scale search such as might be conducted following a valid arrest.[9] An officer may not reach into the suspect's clothing or pockets unless and until the presence of a weapon has been detected by the pat-down.[10]

The officer's belief that the suspect may be armed and dangerous must be both reasonable and actual. In order for the frisk to be valid, the officer's fear for his or her safety must be objectively reasonable and must actually exist. A federal circuit court has pointed out that an officer "cannot have a reasonable suspicion that a person is armed and dangerous when he in fact has no such suspicion."[11] Therefore, if the officer was not actually concerned for his or her own safety but frisked the suspect anyway, the frisk is illegal. When called on to justify the frisk, the officer must be prepared to make it clear that he or she was both reasonably and actually apprehensive for his or her safety.

Pat-down searches should, if possible, be conducted by officers of the same gender as the suspect. The fact that a male officer pats down a female suspect does not necessarily invalidate the pat-down, but it may lead to contentions of civil rights violations and hence to civil liability.

Frequently, the person who has been stopped for a field interview will have in his or her possession containers such as sacks, briefcases, or bags. Although "frisks" of such containers have sometimes been upheld by the courts, officers should not attempt to open them. Rather, the officer is instructed to place such items out of reach of the suspect during the field interview. This ensures the officer's safety while avoiding the risk of an unlawful search.[12]

State Court Decisions and Statutes. As noted earlier, the primary legal basis for field interviews and pat-down searches arises from the U.S. Supreme Court case of *Terry* v. *Ohio*. However, many states, including Illinois, New York, and Virginia, have statutes that govern these activities. These statutes may place restrictions on officers that are more stringent than those imposed by the U.S. Supreme Court. In addition, state constitutions may also place limits on an officer's authority to detain and frisk suspects that are more restrictive than those announced by the U.S. Supreme Court.

Plain-View Searches

Police officers have the opportunity to begin investigations or confiscate evidence, without a warrant, based on what they find in plain view and open to public inspection. This has become known as the **plain-view doctrine,** a doctrine first stated in the Supreme Court ruling in *Harris* v. *United States* (1968). A police officer found evidence of a robbery while inventorying an impounded vehicle. The court ruled that "objects falling in the plain view of an officer who has a right to be in the position to have that view are subject to seizure and may be used as evidence." This doctrine has been widely used by investigators in such cases as crimes in progress, accidents, and fires. An officer might enter an apartment, for example, while responding to a domestic disturbance and find drugs on a living room table. He or she would be within his or her rights to seize the drugs as evidence without having a search warrant. The criteria for a valid plain-view search were identified in *Coolidge* v. *New Hampshire* (1971). In that decision, the court identified three criteria that must be present:

1. The officer must be present lawfully at the location to be searched.
2. The item seized must have been found inadvertently.
3. The item is contraband or would be useful as evidence of a crime.

Prior to 1990, the courts required that all items found in plain view be found inadvertently, but in *Horton* v. *California* (1990), the Court ruled that "inadvertent discovery" of evidence is no longer a necessary element of the plain-view doctrine. Other cases supporting the plain-view doctrine include the 1958 *United States* v. *Henry* decision, in which the Court ruled that if an officer discovers evidence of another crime "unexpectedly," that evidence can be seized. In 1978, coinciding cases *Michigan* v. *Tyler* and *Mincey* v. *Arizona* concluded that while officers are present on a person's premises carrying out legitimate emergency responsibilities, any evidence in plain view is seizeable. In another case, the Court held that the officer needn't know that the evidence is even contraband, only that it is associated with a crime (*Texas* v. *Brown*, 1983). In this case, the officer's personal knowledge that heroin was transported in balloons was sufficient to seize a balloon without knowing exactly what it contained.

The plain-view doctrine has, however, been restricted by more recent court decisions, such as the case of *United States* v. *Irizarry* (1982), where the court held that officers cannot move objects to gain a better view of evidence otherwise hidden from view. This view was affirmed in the case *Arizona* v. *Hicks* (1987), which stated that evidence seized must be in plain view without the need for officers to move or dislodge it. In *Hicks,* officers responded to a shooting in a second-floor apartment where a bullet had been fired through the floor, injuring a man in the apartment below. The premises of James Hicks were in considerable disarray when investigating officers entered.

As the officers looked for the person who might have fired the weapon, they discovered a number of guns and a stocking mask that might have been used in some local robberies. The items were seized. But in one corner, officers noticed two expensive stereo sets. One of the officers approached the equipment, suspecting that it might be stolen, and read a few of the serial numbers from where it sat. But in order to read the remaining serial numbers, the equipment was moved away from the wall. After calling in the serial number, the officer learned that the equipment had, in fact, been stolen.

Hicks was then arrested and later convicted of armed robbery, through use of the seized property. On appeal the U.S. Supreme Court decided that the search of Hicks's apartment became illegal when the officer moved the stereo set away from the wall to record the serial numbers. The Court explained that Hicks had a reasonable expectation of privacy, which means that the officers, although invited into the apartment, must act more like guests than inquisitors.

Automobile Searches

The precedent established for warrantless searches of automobiles is the automobile exception, or *Carroll doctrine* (*Carroll* v. *United States,* 1925). This decision established that the right to search a vehicle does not depend on the right to arrest the driver but on the premise that the contents of the vehicle contain evidence of a crime. In this case, George Carroll, a bootlegger, was convicted for transporting intoxicating liquor in a vehicle, a violation of the National Prohibition Act. At the trial, Carroll's attorneys contended that the liquor need not be admitted into evidence, because the search and seizure of the vehicle were unlawful and violated the Fourth Amendment. Because of the mobility of the automobile, the warrantless search under Carroll is justified. Following the

Carroll decision, there existed some uncertainty about the moving vehicle doctrine. Much of this doubt was laid to rest in 1970, however, when the U.S. Supreme Court reaffirmed the right of officers to search a vehicle that is moving or about to be moved out of their jurisdiction, provided that probable cause exists that the vehicle contains items that officers are entitled to seize.

Since the ruling of the *Carroll* doctrine, related cases have raised the question of whether officers searching under *Carroll* also have the right to search closed containers in a car. In a 1981 decision, the U.S. Supreme Court held that warrantless seizures of evidence in the passenger compartments of a car, after a lawful arrest, are valid (*New York* v. *Belton,* 1981). Before this decision, there was some confusion about the authority of police to search within the vehicle but outside the driver's "wingspan." The Court authorized a search of the entire passenger compartment of the vehicle, including the backseat. It also authorized the opening of containers in the vehicle that might contain the object sought. The following year, the Court held that after a lawful arrest, police may open the trunk of a car and containers found therein without a warrant, even in the absence of exigent circumstances (*United States* v. *Ross,* 1982). This case further defined the scope of police search-and-seizure authority in vehicle searches. The Ross case therefore has expanded the scope of warrantless searches only to what is "reasonable." It should be noted, however, that police may not open large containers taken from the car, such as footlockers, without a warrant, provided that there is time to obtain one.

In a high-impact case, *California* v. *Acevedo* (1991), much of the confusion about vehicle searches was eliminated. Federal agents in Hawaii intercepted a package of marijuana being sent via Federal Express to Santa Ana, California. At that time officers staked out the Santa Ana Federal Express office. The man who claimed the package was then followed to his apartment, where he went inside and came back out a few minutes later with an empty carton, which he pitched into a dumpster. At that time, one officer left the area to obtain a search warrant while the other officers maintained surveillance on the residence.

Before the officer returned with the warrant, Acevedo drove up and entered the apartment. In about 10 minutes, he exited the apartment with an object in a paper bag that was about the same size as a brick of marijuana. Acevedo placed the bag in his vehicle trunk and began to drive away. In an effort to stop Acevedo before he would be lost, the officers stopped him and searched his trunk. The bag was discovered and was found to contain marijuana. Although the trial court found Acevedo guilty, on appeal the California Court of Appeals ruled that the officer's probable cause was attached to the bag and not the vehicle: therefore, they should have obtained a warrant pursuant to the Chadwick rule. The U.S. Supreme Court didn't agree. Its response included a statement by Justice Harry A. Blackmun, who wrote: "The [Chadwick] rule not only has failed to protect privacy but it has also confused courts and police officers and impeded effective law enforcement." He continued, "We conclude that it is better to adopt one clear-cut rule to govern automobile searches and eliminate the warrant requirement for closed containers. We therefore interpret Carroll as providing one rule to govern all automobile searches—the police may search an automobile and containers within it where they have probable cause to believe contraband or evidence is contained." Stated simply, the *Acevedo* case holds that if an officer has probable cause to believe that a container in an automobile holds contraband, the officer may open the container and seize the evidence,

Case in Point

The Case Against O. J. Simpson

Early morning on June 13, 1994, two dead bodies were dis-covered at a West Los Angeles home. Dead was the attrac-tive wife of football great O. J. Simpson, Nicole, and an aspiring young actor and waiter, Ronald Goldman. The murders were discovered at 875 South Bundy Drive in the exclusive Brent-wood area of the city. Police discovered sufficient physical evi-dence along with a history of spousal abuse to charge Simpson with the murders. In a CBS television interview, lead detective Philip Vannatter commented that he had never, in 30 years of investigating crimes, seen so much conclusive evidence in a case.

But this case was unlike others seen by prosecutors and police. Both victims were white, whereas the defendant, Simp-son, was black. In addition, he was a wealthy and famous sports hero with considerable public recognition and a nationwide base of adoring fans. To mount a defense, Simpson quickly hired a team of the best-known trial lawyers in the country. Included on this "dream team" were attorneys F. Lee Bailey, Johnnie Cochran, Alan Dershowitz, and Robert Shapiro. Each attorney brought with him special expertise in different aspects of the case, and all were well known for their consider-able success in defending celebrities. The prosecution team was headed by veteran prosecutors Marcia Clark, Christopher Darden, and William Hodgman, and at their disposal were more than 800 deputy district attorneys available to help, including experts on DNA evidence. Long before the trial began, the case was receiving considerable media attention. As the case came

to its conclusion, media analysts declared that the Simpson trial received more coverage than any other event in the history of television, with literally thousands of hours of television cover-age of the proceedings being offered by network television and cable channels, accompanied by expert commentary from key legal personnel.

Evidence presented at the trial, which lasted nearly a year, was examined closely in detail by defense lawyers, and prose-cution witnesses were all rigorously cross-examined. The trial ended in late 1995 with a "not guilty" verdict and cost California taxpayers in excess of $7 million.

Evidence in the Case

- Bloodstains found on a pair of socks in Simpson's bed-room: one spot of blood matched Simpson's blood, another matched Nicole Simpson's.

- A total of 11 bloodstains were found in Simpson's Ford Bronco: four were Simpson's blood, one matched Nicole Simpson's, and two were a mixture of Simpson, Nicole Brown Simpson, and Ronald Goldman.

- The glove found on the grounds of Simpson's estate con-tained a mixture of blood consistent with the mixture of blood of Simpson, Nicole Brown Simpson, and Ronald Gold-man. The glove also contained hair matching Nicole Brown Simpson and Ronald Goldman, fibers similar to those found in the Bronco carpeting, and fibers from Goldman's shirt.

provided that the evidence is in fact contraband. Two subsequent cases further clarified the authority in which police officers may search vehicles.

The law on vehicle searches has changed dramatically over the past 15 years, enabling police officers more latitude in their search and seizure authority. For example, in *Pennsylvania* v. *Labron* (1993), the Supreme Court ruled that there is no need for a search warrant in vehicle searches if the vehicle is readily mobile, even if there is time to obtain a warrant. In a related case, the Court held that police officers with probable cause to search a car may inspect passengers' belongings found in the car that are capable of concealing the object of the search (*Wyoming* v. *Houghton*, 1999)[13].

Vehicle Inventory Search. In 1970, the U.S. Supreme Court reaffirmed the right of officers to search a vehicle that is moving or is about to be moved,

- Blood drops at the crime scene leading away from the bodies: five drops matched O.J. Simpson's blood.

- The ski cap found at the crime scene contained "unusual" fibers like those from the carpet of the Bronco and also contained 12 hairs like those of O.J. Simpson.

- Goldman's shirt contained hairs like those of O.J. Simpson.

- Two bloodstains in O.J. Simpson's driveway matched his blood.

- Bloodstains found in O.J. Simpson's house matched O.J. Simpson's own blood, and these were seen by Kato Kaelin and several police officers while O.J. Simpson was in Chicago, before the police had a sample of O.J. Simpson's blood.

BLOOD DROPS
- *Prosecution:* Argued that DNA tests on blood at the scene and in Simpson's Bronco and estate positively identified Simpson as the killer.

- *Defense:* Attacked DNA tests as unreliable, tried to cast doubt about DNA science, and argued that Simpson's blood at the scene and estate could be old.

BLOODY GLOVES
- *Prosecution:* Called Detective Mark Furman to testify that he found the bloody glove at Simpson's estate that matched a glove found at the crime scene.

- *Defense:* Attempted to impeach Furman's testimony, arguing that he was a racist who set up Simpson.

HAIR SAMPLES
- *Prosecution:* Argued that hair found on Goldman's body and a knit cap at Simpson's estate were those of a black man, and placed Simpson at the scene.

- *Defense:* Argued that hair could belong to any black man, including investigating officers.

OPPORTUNITY
- *Prosecution:* Argued that Simpson had more than enough time between 9:45 and 10:56 p.m. to kill the victims, get rid of the knife, and return to his estate about a mile away.

- *Defense:* Insisted that Simpson did not have enough time to kill two people and get back home.

MOTIVE
- *Prosecution:* Introduced evidence that Simpson abused his ex-wife at least 19 times, and argued that escalating violence led to murder.

- *Defense:* Argued that all of the abuse allegations were isolated incidents and irrelevant to the murder charges.

provided that there is probable cause to believe that the vehicle contains items that are legally seizeable. In the *Chambers* v. *Maroney* (1970) case, the Court referred to the earlier case of *Carroll* v. *United States* and determined that a search warrant is unnecessary provided that probable cause exists that contraband is contained in the vehicle, that the vehicle is movable, and that a search warrant is not readily obtainable. This doctrine applies even if the vehicle has been driven to the police station by a police officer and there was time to secure a search warrant.

In the *Chambers* case, officers received a report that a service station had been robbed. After receiving a description of the station wagon the robbers were driving and a partial description of the suspects, officers stopped a vehicle matching the vehicle description and arrested the occupants. After the suspects were arrested, the officers took the vehicle down to headquarters to be searched.

Although a search warrant could have been obtained, one was not. During the search, officers located two .38-caliber handguns concealed under the dashboard, some small change, and credit cards belonging to a service station attendant who had been robbed previously.

At the trial, the court rejected the search incident to lawful arrest because the search was made at the police station some time after the arrest. On appeal, however, the U.S. Supreme Court stated that there were alternative grounds for the search. When a vehicle is seized, its contents are routinely inventoried to prevent subsequent claims by the defendant that items were taken. The search and the inventory are, however, two separate processes under law but can be conducted simultaneously, as was the case in *Chambers*. Evidence located as a result of the inventory search is admissible in court. It has been recommended, however, that in the case of an automobile that is rendered immobile or one that has been transported to the police station, a search warrant should be obtained as a precautionary matter.

Open-Field Searches

In *Oliver* v. *United States* (1984), the U.S. Supreme Court reaffirmed its position that open fields are not protected by the Fourth Amendment. This differs from constitutional protection over buildings, houses, and the area surrounding them, known as *curtilage*. It is the curtilage that is considered one's yard; thus both the house and yard are protected and cannot be searched without a warrant or one of the exceptions mentioned. Open fields and pastures outside the curtilage are not protected by the Constitution; thus searches made by the government of those areas are not considered "unreasonable."

In the *Oliver* case, police officers, acting on reports that marijuana was growing on Oliver's farm, proceeded to investigate, but without a warrant or probable cause. They drove past a locked gate with a sign that read "No Trespassing." However, a path was also observed leading around the side of the property. After following the path around the gate, officers found a field of marijuana located over a mile from the house. Oliver was subsequently charged and convicted of manufacturing a controlled substance.

This case is significant because the Court essentially stated that a person's "reasonable expectation of privacy" under the Fourth Amendment does not apply when the property involved is an open field.

Defining Curtilage. In a 1987 decision, *United States* v. *Dunn*, the Supreme Court ruled that the warrantless search of a barn that is not part of the curtilage is valid. From this decision came four factors that laid out whether an area is considered a part of the curtilage:

1. The proximity of the area to the home
2. Whether the area is within an enclosure surrounding the home
3. The nature and uses of the area
4. The steps taken to conceal the area from public view

The *Dunn* decision, while still subject to imprecise application, is helpful because it narrows the definition of what buildings should be considered curtilage of the main residence.

BEGINNING THE SEARCH

Once an investigator has documented a crime scene, the actual search must begin. Generally speaking, evidence discovered at the crime scene will serve four objectives: (1) to determine the facts of the crime, (2) to identify the lawbreaker, (3) to aid in his or her arrest, and (4) to aid in the criminal prosecution of the perpetrator. History has shown that there are many different ways to search a crime scene for evidence. Indeed, methods for crime scene searching vary according to the types of crime scenes and evidence at hand. Varieties of crime scene evidence include firearm evidence, trace material collection, tool mark evidence, collection of bodily fluids, standards of evidence, fire and explosion evidence, outdoor crime scenes, vehicle searches, and interior and victim searches. The search of the crime scene consists of several distinct phases:

- Surveying the crime scene.
- Documenting the crime scene through sketches and photographs.
- Recording all physical evidence.
- Searching for fingerprints.

Search Patterns

Regardless of the method used, the search of the scene should be conducted in a systematic way. Of the most employed methods of searching, several have been most commonly used over time. The most common search patterns include the spiral search method, grid method, strip- or line-search method, and quadrant- or zone-search method (Figure 4.10). Some methods of searching are best suited for indoor scenes, whereas others are more applicable to outdoor crime scenes. Other scenes present unique problems and are discussed next. Whichever method is adopted, the rule to remember is that the search must be thorough.

Indoor Crime Scene Searches. It is generally recommended that at least two officers search an indoor crime scene. This may best be accomplished by dividing the room in half and having each investigator search half (also known as the quadrant or zone-search method). At the conclusion of the search, the investigators switch halves. In this fashion, each half of the room is searched twice.

Outdoor Crime Scene Searches. In most cases, the outdoor crime scene covers a broader area than those that are indoor. If this is the case, more investigators will be required. Accordingly, with the increased size of the scene, a more systematic searching method must be employed. One way is to rope off the scene into a grid. Each square, averaging about 6 square feet, represents a specific search area that is a manageable size for each investigator (also known as the grid search method).

Nighttime Crime Scene Searches. If possible, investigators should wait until daylight to search a crime scene. Obviously, circumstances can require investigators to proceed with the search at night. These may include inclement weather or other emergency circumstances. In the event that such a search is to be conducted, lighting generators should be employed to provide sufficient illumination for the search.

Figure 4.10 Search patterns.

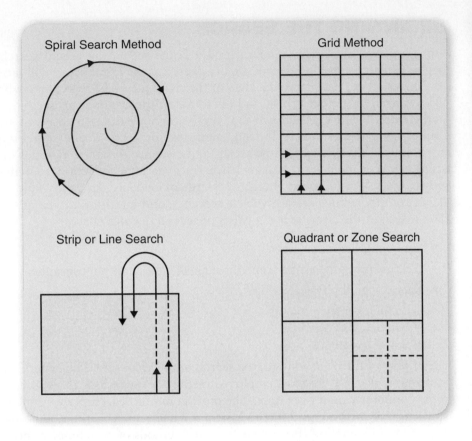

Vehicle Searches.   The search of a vehicle requires the same degree of attention as indoor and outdoor searches. Obviously, the nature of the crime will dictate the area of the vehicle to be searched. For example, a drug smuggling or murder case will require closer examination of the interior of the vehicle, whereas a hit-and-run investigation will necessitate examination of the exterior of the vehicle. Like an interior search, a vehicle should also be searched for fingerprints. This should be done after other trace evidence has been sought.

Strip Searches

A strip search must be conducted in a private and controlled environment. This technique requires the suspect to undress completely, and all clothing is searched. In some cases, the suspect's body cavities may need to be searched. Officers are allowed to search the ears, mouth, and nose visually, but the vaginal and rectal areas may be searched only by authorized medical personnel. It is also recommended that investigators communicate with the prosecutor before conducting a strip search of any suspect, to safeguard against possible procedural errors.

Body Cavity Searches

In early 2005, officers of the Suffolk County (New York) Police Department arrested 36-year-old Terrance Haynes and charged him with marijuana possession. After placing him in the back of a patrol car, officers noted that Haynes appeared to choke and have difficulty breathing. Soon his breathing stopped, prompting officers to use the Heimlich maneuver, which dislodged a plastic bag from Haynes' windpipe. The bag contained 11 packets of cocaine. Although Haynes survived the ordeal, he now faces up to 25 years in prison.

While some suspects may literally "cough up" evidence, some are more successful at hiding it in their bodies. Body cavity searches are among the most problematic types of searches for police today. "Strip" searches of convicts in prison, including the search of body cavities, have generally been held to be permissible.

The 1985 Supreme Court case of *U.S.* v. *Montoya de Hernandez* focused on the issue of "alimentary canal smuggling," in which the offender typically swallows condoms filled with cocaine or heroin and waits for nature to take its course to recover the substance.[14] In the *Montoya* case, a woman known to be a "balloon swallower" arrived in the United States on a flight from Colombia. She was detained by customs officials and given a pat-down search by a female agent. The agent reported that the woman's abdomen was firm and suggested that x-rays be taken. The suspect refused and was given a choice of submitting to further tests or taking the next flight back to Columbia. No flight was immediately available, however, and the suspect was placed in a room for 16 hours, where she refused all food and drink. Finally, a court order for an x-ray was obtained. The procedure revealed "balloons," and the woman was detained another four days, during which time she passed numerous cocaine-filled plastic condoms. The Court ruled that the woman's confinement was not unreasonable, based as it was on the supportable suspicion that she was **body-packing"** cocaine. Any discomfort she experienced, the court ruled, "resulted solely from the method that she chose to smuggle illicit drugs."

SEARCHING THE SCENE

Evidence of crimes is dynamic. That is, it is unique, often fragile, and may constantly be undergoing change. Experience indicates that there is usually only one chance to search a crime scene properly, so for this reason it is a good idea to survey the scene carefully before embarking on the search process itself.

There are two approaches to crime scene searches. As a first step, the investigator should consider all information provided to him or her by officers who arrived earlier on the scene. Such information includes the officers' perceptions of what occurred and the nature of the evidence. Next, investigators should rationalize which evidence items seem to play the greatest role in the alleged crime. In brief, the principal concern at this point is to observe and document the scene rather than take action.

Of specific importance in the observation phase is the relative distance of any object to the victim. The distance between an object and a victim may play a greater role in the evidence collection phase than the item itself. For example, if the crime scene consists of a dead person who has apparently been shot and a 9mm handgun, the locations of spent shell casings could indicate the angle of the weapon or the position of the victim at the time the gun was discharged. Such a determination could point to either suicide or homicide, and may subsequently alter the character of the investigation. As indicated, while observations are being carried out, notes should be taken to organize the sequence of events. Witness statements should be taken as well, regarding the victim(s) or related information. Additionally, videotapes and photographs should be made during this phase to document the scene adequately for future reference. Both of these considerations are discussed in greater detail later in the book.

RULES FOR COLLECTING EVIDENCE

There is a tendency on the part of many investigators to rush the evidence collection process and focus attention on the obvious. Understandably, the task of observing firsthand the scene of another's misfortune is a difficult one for many, and one might appreciate the desire for expeditiousness on the part of the investigator. It is a fact, however, that much critical evidence, often seemingly unimportant, can be located in and around the scene of almost every crime. As discussed in the earlier section on crime scene searches, investigators must choose which method of searching is best suited for the crime in question. Regardless of the method used, evidence must be collected in a comprehensive, nondestructive manner; within a reasonable period; and with a minimum of unnecessary movement about the scene. Although every criminal case is unique and should be evaluated on an individual basis, experience has shown that the following general recommendations are beneficial in organizing the search and preventing errors.

Gathering And Preserving Evidence

Once the initial crime scene search has been completed, and following the sketching and photographing of the scene, evidence should be collected. The manner in which evidence is collected must be consistent with each law enforcement agency's policy and procedure and should be in keeping with accepted

Figure 4.11 A crime scene search in a rural area.

rules of evidence. The evidence collected first is usually that which is most frag-ile. Therefore, fingerprints should be lifted as a priority. Next, other fragile evi-dence, such as blood and other trace evidence, should be collected. It is important for officers to search the crime scene a second time after the evidence has been collected. This should uncover any evidence overlooked accidentally. When possible, one investigator should serve as the evidence collector. This des-ignation ensures that all evidence gets recorded and processed at the scene in a uniform and correct manner. It also ensures that evidence will be moved only when the collector decides that it can be moved.

When the case goes to court, both the investigator who discovered the evi-dence and the collector will usually be required to testify. The greatest advan-tage to using this system is that all evidence is collected in a uniform manner, and one officer is responsible for packaging and marking the evidence and filling out necessary paperwork. This reduces the need to tie up additional officers back at the office for such a task.

The Chain of Custody

Evidence that has been collected must be safeguarded until the case goes to court. During the trial, if it is determined that labels are missing and evidence is not properly initialed or is otherwise missing or altered, the evidence may be considered inadmissible and the case thrown out. The total accounting of evi-dence is known as the **chain of custody**. This is made up of all persons (usually, law enforcement personnel) who have taken custody of the evidence since its collection and who are therefore responsible for its protection and storage. The chain of custody is established by adhering to certain guidelines:

- The number of persons handling evidence from the time that it is safely stored should be limited. If the evidence leaves the possession of an officer, he or she should record to whom the evidence was given, the date and time, and the reason it was turned over.

- Anyone who handles evidence should affix his or her name and badge number to the package containing evidence.

General Rules of Crime Scene Searching[15]

If there is an indication that evidence is deteriorating significantly with time or by the elements, these have first priority. Crime scene investigators should always wear protective clothing to protect evidence from contamination and to safeguard themselves as well.

All major items are examined, photographed, recorded, and collected, as appropriate, taking them in the order that is most logical, considering the requirement to conserve movement. Making casts and lifting latent prints from objects to be moved from the scene are done as necessary. Items should not be moved until they have been examined for trace evidence. Fingerprints should be taken, or at least developed and covered with tape, before the object is moved. When an (obviously) deceased person is involved, the evidence items lying between the point of entry to the scene and point of exit from the scene and the body are processed; then the detailed search of the deceased is conducted. After that search, the body should be removed and the processing of obvious evidence continued as noted earlier.

After processing the obvious evidence, the search for and collection of additional trace material is begun. Trace evidence should be searched for and collected before dusting for fingerprints. After the trace materials have been collected, other latent prints are lifted. When sweeping or vacuuming, surface areas should be segmented, the sweepings from each area packaged separately, and the location of their point of recovery noted. Normally, elimination fingerprints and physical evidence standards are collected after the preceding actions have been completed.

Proper Sealing of Evidence

The method shown below permits access to the invoice letter without breaking the inner seal. This allows the person entitled to receive the evidence to receive it in a sealed condition just as it was packed by the sender.

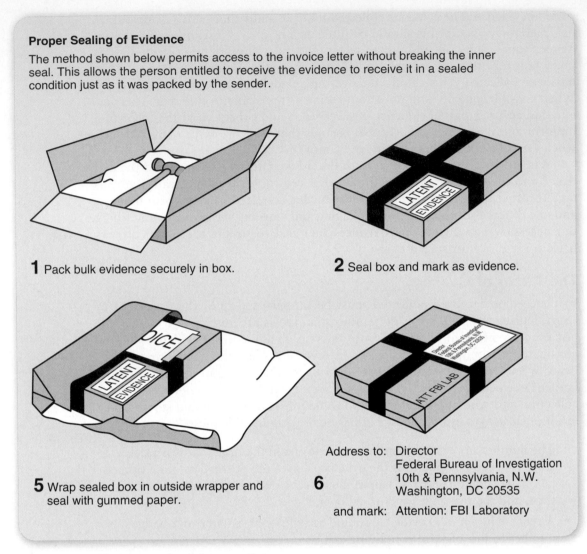

1 Pack bulk evidence securely in box.

2 Seal box and mark as evidence.

5 Wrap sealed box in outside wrapper and seal with gummed paper.

6

Address to: Director
                   Federal Bureau of Investigation
                   10th & Pennsylvania, N.W.
                   Washington, DC 20535

and mark: Attention: FBI Laboratory

Figure 4.12 Method for the proper sealing of crime scene evidence.

- A signed receipt should be obtained from the person accepting the evidence. In turn, the investigator should sign a receipt or log when the item is returned.

- When a piece of evidence is turned in, the investigator should check his or her identification mark on it to ensure that it is the same item.

- After an item is returned to the investigator, he or she should determine if the item is in the same condition as when it was discovered. Any change in the physical appearance of the evidence should be called to the attention of the court.

Evidence can be stored in vehicle trunks, strongboxes, property rooms, locked file cabinets, evidence lockers, or vaults. The only stipulation is that it be marked properly and protected from tampering or destruction. Most evidence is

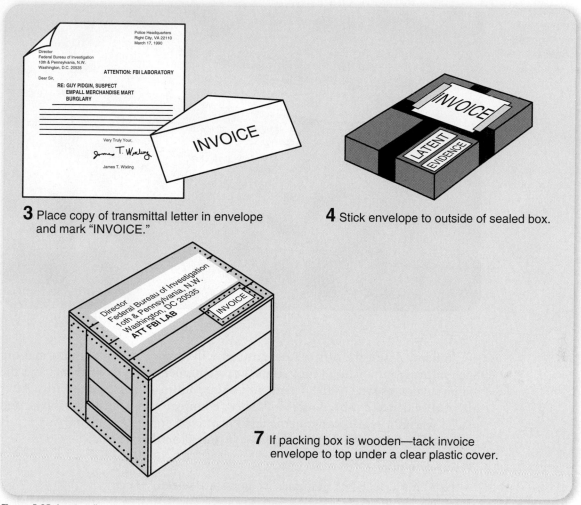

3 Place copy of transmittal letter in envelope and mark "INVOICE."

4 Stick envelope to outside of sealed box.

7 If packing box is wooden—tack invoice envelope to top under a clear plastic cover.

Figure 4.12 (*continued*)

turned over to an evidence custodian, who is usually an employee of the crime lab. This person will sign off on an evidence form as the recipient of the evidence. The seizing officer can then indicate in his or her investigative report the person to whom the evidence was given.

Marking the Evidence

Another important rule to remember during the evidence collection process is that all evidence must be marked immediately upon seizure to ensure proper identification later, as it is common for the officer who seizes evidence to identify it at trial. Such testimony ensures the integrity of the chain of custody. Proper marking of each piece of evidence also ensures organization of all items of evidence for restructuring the events of the crime and the questioning of witnesses. Generally, it does not matter how the officer marks evidence as long as the initials of the seizing officer and the date of the seizure are clearly indicated on the seized item and on any container used to enclose the object, such as an envelope or cardboard box (Figure 4.12).

Figure 4.13 Proper marking of evidence is vital to protect its integrity for court. Here, a brown paper bag containing evidence has been sealed and marked "Do Not Open". *Mikael Karlsson, Arresting Images*

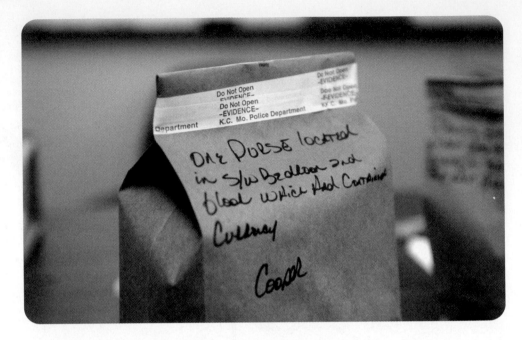

In many cases, the officer's department will require additional information. Such information includes the assigned case number, the type of crime, and the victim's name as well as the defendant's name, address, and date of birth. After physical evidence has been marked, sealed, counted, weighed (if necessary), and placed within a sealed container, a label is affixed containing identifying information. The following details should be included on the evidence label:

- Case number
- Exhibit number (when numerous items are seized)
- Date and time of seizure
- Name and description of articles
- Location at time of discovery
- Signature or initials of officer making the discovery
- Name or initials of others witnessing the discovery

SPECIAL CASES IN EVIDENCE HANDLING

Just as evidence can be damaged or destroyed in the mishandling of a crime scene, improperly collected and managed evidence can sabotage an otherwise successful investigation. For example, improperly handled evidence, if contaminated, may either result in investigators reaching inaccurate conclusions or wasting time trying to correct the problem. The question commonly arises as to whether or not an object is or is not evidence. The decision is based on the officer's ability to consider the facts and circumstances at the crime scene, as well as his or her good judgment, common sense, and past experience. When any doubt exists, the object should be collected and processed as evidence; the object can be reevaluated later. Let's now examine some ways that certain types of critical evidence should be dealt with on the crime scene.

Infected Evidence

Among the many dangers encountered by law enforcement officers in the performance of their duties is the threat of street violence and even death. The rising specter of acquired immunodeficiency syndrome (AIDS) has created a health concern for criminal investigators charged with collection and preservation of crime scene evidence. Problems in collection of suspected infected evidence arise out of the fact that unlike many health care professionals, crime scene investigators are operating in an uncontrolled environment and often under extremely adverse conditions. Even the use of protective devices such as gloves and masks may not provide the investigator with adequate protection from communicable diseases such as AIDS, tuberculosis, and hepatitis B.

This is partly due to the fact that such protective measures often fail to protect against cutting or puncturing, allowing the transmission of disease and infection through blood or other bodily fluids. Implements such as weapons, drug paraphernalia, razor blades, and hypodermic needles, which can be secreted in pockets, drawers, and in automobiles, all pose a threat to crime scene technicians.

An unfortunate side effect of the AIDS epidemic is that it is likely that officers who either lack adequate protective equipment or are uneasy about the prospect of contracting certain diseases, or who lack training on how best to deal with such problems, might tend to limit their searches, intentionally or inadvertently, for fear of contracting an infecting organism. This could result in the attitude "it's just not worth it," which could have many negative side effects for the overall investigative process, including inadequately seized evidence, resulting in a poorly investigated case, which would, in turn, result in weak prosecution of the defendant. The National Institute of Justice has offered a list of recommendations on how best to deal with the problem of infected evidence.[16]

Hepatitis B: A Greater Threat

Much has been written about HIV (human immunodeficiency virus), and the Centers for Disease Control's (CDC) "universal precautions" have been widely advocated for controlling the risk of HIV infection. HIV is primarily a sexually transmitted disease, even though it may be contracted through other means such as needlesticks or other contaminated items with sharpened ends. This latter form of transmission has been well documented among health care workers. While the concern over possible HIV infection among law enforcement officers remains legitimate, relatively little attention has been directed to the risks posed by hepatitis B infection. HBV (hepatitis B virus) is far more easily contracted than HIV and can have serious medical consequences for those infected, including long-term disability or death. Considering that nearly all officers serving in enforcement and investigative capacities are potentially exposed to blood and other bodily fluids, the risks of contracting the virus are a great concern. For example, patrol officers, investigators, crime scene technicians, and laboratory specialists are all commonly called to the scene of automobile accidents, required to intervene in fights, aid injured persons, investigate violent crimes, and deal with a multitude of situations where blood and other potentially infectious bodily fluids are present. Under these conditions, universal precautions and related safeguards must be followed.

Health care workers are the only occupational group for which hepatitis B infection rates are known. Among this group, the CDC estimates about 8,700 cases annually to include about 200 deaths. Nationwide, there are about 280,000 cases of HBV infection annually, about 5 to 10 percent of which become chronic carriers of the virus.

Hepatitis means "inflammation of the liver." While there are several forms of the hepatitis virus, hepatitis B (formerly called "serum" hepatitis) is the major threat to public safety workers. HBV attacks and replicates in liver cells. Presence of the virus in an infected person is readily detectable through laboratory testing of blood samples.

An otherwise healthy HBV-infected individual most often develops what is referred to as "self-limited acute hepatitis." The infected individual produces an antibody that destroys the liver cells containing the virus, which eliminates the virus from the body and serves to immunize the person from any reinfection for life. About one-third of those infected in this way have no symptoms; another third have relatively mild flu-like reactions; another third have more acute reactions that may include jaundice—a yellowing of the eyes and skin—dark urine, extreme fatigue, anorexia, nausea, abdominal pain, and sometimes joint pain, rash, and fever. About 20 percent of these more severe sufferers require hospitalization and often several weeks or months of work loss for purposes of treatment.

Another form of response to HBV is chronic HBV infection, which has greater long-term consequences for the infected individual. Under these conditions, the infected person cannot clear the virus from the liver and becomes a chronic HBV carrier. Such persons are at high risk of developing chronic persistent hepatitis, which is a relatively mild, nonprogressive form of the disease, or chronic active hepatitis, which is a progressive form of liver disease that often leads to cirrhosis of the liver and death after some years.

Transmission of HBV in the workplace takes place through introduction of infected blood or blood-derived bodily fluids. Exposure to the virus most often occurs in the eyes, mouth, or mucous membranes or through lesions of the skin from needlesticks or other sharp objects. Preexisting lesions in the recipient's hands, caused by injuries or dermatitis, for example, have been demonstrated as a prime route of entry for the virus whether dealing with contaminated blood or contaminated objects or work surfaces. Splashes of blood or serum into an individual's eyes or mouth should be considered particularly serious exposures. Exposure to extremely small samples of HBV-positive blood may be sufficient to transmit infection. Fortunately, sterilization or disinfection procedures using fresh mixtures of household bleach in a solution of one part bleach to ten parts water are relatively easy and effective.

Firearms

Extreme care should be taken when handling firearms because of the types of trace evidence typically found on such evidence. The guidelines are as follows:

- The firearm should be handled carefully by the grip or the sides of the trigger guard.
- Never stick anything, such as a pencil, into the barrel of a firearm; this could destroy valuable trace evidence.
- There should be no attempt to fire the gun, dismantle it, or to interfere with the mechanism in any way.

Recommendations for Dealing with Infected Evidence

- *Human bites.* Viral transmission through saliva is unlikely; however, if bitten, after milking the wound, rinse well and seek medical attention.
- *Spitting/urine/feces.* Viral transmission through saliva is unlikely. In urine, the virus is isolated in very low concentrations and nonexistent in feces. No AIDS cases have been associated with urine or feces.
- *Cuts/puncture wounds.* When searching areas hidden from view, use extreme caution to avoid sharp objects. Cases involving needlesticks are very rare.
- *CPR/first aid.* Minimal risk is associated with CPR, but it is a good idea to employ the use of masks/airways and gloves when in contact with bleeding wounds.
- *Body removal.* As with all crime scenes, when in contact with a dead body, always wear protective gloves.
- *Casual contact.* No AIDS cases or infections have been associated with casual contact.
- *Any contact with bodily fluids or blood.* Wear protective gloves if contact with blood or bodily fluids is likely. If contact is made, wash the area thoroughly with soap and water. Clean up spills with one part water and ten parts household bleach.
- *Contact with dried blood.* No cases of infection have been traced to exposure to dried blood. The drying process itself seems to deactivate any viruses in blood. However, it is still a good idea to wear protective clothing such as gloves.

If the weapon is a revolver, mark empty cases or live cartridges and the rear edge of the cylinder with a code to show the chambers in which each empty case or live cartridge rested at the time of its removal.

Bullets, Cartridges, and Empty Cases

Bullets, cartridges, and empty cases should be handled with particular attention paid to the portions used in identification. Such evidence can be beneficial in determining the type of weapon used by a criminal. A more exact laboratory analysis may also determine the exact caliber of weapon. Investigations have revealed instances in which criminals have purposely used one gun for the commission of a crime and a second gun to fire rounds into walls or the floor to confuse investigators. Certain areas of cartridges are typically used for identification: (1) the base and (2) the rim or cannelure (just above the base of the case).

The exact location of spent cases should be noted. Bullets must be removed carefully from their point of impact, and the location they were found must be recorded accurately. In many cases, it is not advisable for a crime scene investigator to attempt to remove spent bullets. If possible, try to remove the material encasing a spent bullet (part of a door, wall, etc.) and transport it to the laboratory to be examined there. A spent bullet can be ruined by attempting to dig it out of an enclosure with a pocketknife. Care must be taken so that a drill, saw, or other cutting instrument does not damage the bullet. Bullets should be handled minimally and packaged to prevent movement and protect the side portions used in ballistic comparison and identification. Rather than attempting to mark a bullet directly, it should be packaged individually and the container marked appropriately.

Stains

Many crimes result in some type of characteristic stain being left on the crime scene. Blood is the stain most commonly found and can provide an investigator with much valuable evidence. Investigators should remember that not all bloodstains found at a crime scene belong to the victim. Indeed, a bloodstain may belong to the perpetrator, who might have been injured while committing the crime. It is usually a good idea in any case to adhere to the following guidelines when considering the collection of blood:

- Good photos and videos should be taken of bloodstains.
- Samples should be taken from all locations where blood is found.
- Blood samples can easily rot so they should be swabbed and air-dried prior to storage.

Glass

Glass fragments can result from many circumstances. For example, a bullet can shatter glass by passing through it; glass purposely broken will leave behind fragments in the crime scene and on the perpetrator. When collected, glass could be used to:

- Show the direction of travel of a projectile.
- Show the sequence of impact of a projectile.
- Match other broken glass.

Impressions

Many crimes result in the formation of impression marks. Such crimes include burglary and rape, but almost any crime could produce such evidence. In all cases, impression evidence should be regarded as valuable and must be protected. Examples of impression evidence include:

- Tool marks (usually found on metal doors or window frames and on locked metal desks, cabinets, and safes)
- Tire impressions
- Foot impressions
- Teeth impressions (sometimes located on partly eaten food at crime scenes)

Investigators should locate the object that made the impression so that a comparison can be made in court.

Drugs

Studies have revealed that drug abuse is the greatest contributor to the commission of crime. Many illicit drugs exist and may appear quite different from one another in form. Therefore, great care must be practiced by evidence collectors to (1) preserve such substances for court, (2) transport the substances, and (3) protect themselves from the possible harmful effects of certain drugs. Most illicit drugs come in one of several forms: plant, powder, liquid, and tablet or capsule. Each requires specific attention from the evidence officer to avoid danger. For example, some drugs, such as liquid PCP and liquid LSD, may be absorbed accidentally through the skin. Others, such as marijuana, are more benign in nature and don't pose such a notable physical threat from handling. However, certain general considerations apply in any collection process.

Plant Material

Because plant material is organic, it will decompose in time. To best preserve plant evidence, it should be placed in a porous container such as a paper bag. For large amounts of plant material, such as evidence collected at a marijuana-

---

Precautionary Rules for Collecting Drug Substances

If an illicit laboratory is encountered and a chemist from the crime laboratory is not present, do not attempt to shut down the operation. Ventilate the area, call for assistance, and wait outside. If an illicit laboratory operation is anticipated, include a chemist from the crime lab as a member of the raid team. Never taste or smell any material suspected of being a controlled substance. Do not handle controlled drugs more than absolutely necessary. After drugs have been handled, wash hands thoroughly as soon as possible.

All chemical materials must be handled with care. They may be highly flammable, corrosive, or susceptible to explosion. Care should be practiced when searching a drug suspect, an automobile containing drugs, or any area believed to contain drugs. Investigators might encounter hypodermic needles which could be contaminated with drugs or even with the AIDS virus.

---

growing site, samples of the material should be collected and the remainder destroyed after weighing (in metric units). This is only done, of course, after authorization of such action is obtained from the prosecutor expected to handle the case.

Powdered Material

Powdered material such as heroin, cocaine, and methamphetamine can generally be packaged in sealed plastic envelopes to prevent loss of powder. Officers should also compute the net weight of the powder seized. This is done by weighing the entire exhibit to obtain a gross weight. The actual weight of the container should then be determined and subtracted from the weight of the exhibit.

Liquid Material

Depending on its composition, liquid material may be stored effectively in a glass bottle. Caution should be exercised, in that many liquids are explosive, corrosive, or dangerous because of their composition. A chemist should be consulted for advice. Liquid evidence should also be weighed for content in metric units.

Tablets or Capsules

This type of evidence is typically packaged in a clear plastic envelope, sealed, and properly marked. Investigators must also remember to weigh this evidence as well as count each dosage unit. The resulting weight should then be recorded in the police report as an "approximate" weight.

Actions taken by the crime scene investigators often have a vital effect on subsequent investigation and prosecution of the case. Indeed, the success or failure of any criminal investigation could hinge on the competency of the crime scene investigator and on his or her treatment of the crime scene.

IMPORTANT CASES TO REMEMBER

California v. *Acevedo*

Carroll v. *United States*

Chambers v. *Maroney*

Chimel v. *California*

Coolidge v. *New Hampshire*

Florida v. *Bostick*

Florida v. *Jimeno*

Illinois v. *Rodriguez*

Mapp v. *Ohio*

Massachusetts v. *Sheppard*

Nix v. *Williams*

Oliver v. *United States*

Silverthorne Lumber Co. v. *United States*

Terry v. *Ohio*

United States v. *Grubbs*

United States v. *Leon*

United States v. *Sokolow*

U.S. v. *Montoya de Hernandez*

Weeks v. *United States*

DISCUSSION QUESTIONS

1. Discuss the significance of the Fourteenth Amendment as it pertains to criminal investigation.

2. Explain the role played by the Fourth, Fifth, and Sixth Amendments in searches and seizures by police.

3. Explain what is meant by probable cause and how it is used as a basis to make arrests and searches.

4. Discuss why the inevitable discovery doctrine is an exception to the exclusionary rule.

5. List and discuss the advantages of searching with a search warrant.

6. Under what conditions may a search be conducted without a search warrant?

7. List and discuss the three criteria that must be present in a plain-view search.

8. List and discuss the four most popular methods of searching a crime scene.

9. Explain the chain of custody and how evidence should be protected and stored.

10. Explain the manner in which firearms, bullets, and cartridges should be handled.

NOTES

1. *Terry* v. *Ohio*, 392 U.S. 1 (1968).
2. Ibid.
3. State courts' decisions and statutes may place restrictions on officers not imposed by the Supreme Court of the United States.
4. See, e.g., *United States* v. *Mendenhall*, 446 U.S. 544 (1980); *Michigan* v. *Chesternut*, 486 U.S. 567 (1988).
5. Officers must, for reasons of both legality and personal safety, adequately identify themselves as police officers. Proper identification as a police officer does not render an encounter nonconsensual. It is only the excessive, unnecessary, or deliberately intimidating display of authority that affects the consensual nature of the encounter.
6. Knowledge by the officer that this particular individual has a prior criminal history or has been involved in criminal activity may also be considered. However, knowledge of a suspect's prior record shouldn't be the sole basis for the stop.
7. It should be noted that the term "pat-down" does not necessarily describe the proper technique for searching a suspect for weapons. It is a legal term, not a descriptive one. It refers to the fact that the search must be confined to contact with the suspect's outer clothing unless and until the presence of a weapon is detected.
8. Crimes involving violence or the use of weapons (such as murder or armed robbery) or crimes whose perpetrators often carry weapons (such as distribution of narcotics) may alone be sufficient to justify a pat-down search of any individual reasonably suspected of involvement in the crime. See,

e.g., *Landsdown* v. *Commonwealth*, 226 Va. 204, 308 S.E.2d 106 (1983).

9. A search is a full-scale attempt to locate evidence—that is, contraband or fruits, instrumentalities, or other evidence of a crime. It may include a complete examination of the suspect's clothing, including interior clothing, pockets, and the like. By contrast, a pat-down is a limited frisk of a suspect's outer clothing or a brief inspection of an object, vehicle, or area for the sole purpose of detecting weapons that may be used to harm the officer.

10. Once the officer has detected the presence of a weapon, or what the officer reasonably believes to be a weapon, the officer may reach into the clothing to remove the object. If the object proves to be a weapon or contraband or other evidence that would justify an arrest, the officer may then place the individual under arrest and conduct a full-scale search of the person.

11. *U.S.* v. *Lott*, 870 F.2d 778 (1st Cir. 1989).

12. Should the officer detect the presence of a weapon in the container, seizure of the weapon would be justified.

13. DEL CARMEN R. V., and J. T. WALKER (2000). *Briefs of leading cases*. Cincinnati, OH: Anderson.

14. *U.S.* v. *Montoya de Hernandez*, 473 U.S. 531, 105 S. Ct. 3304 (1985).

15. FOX, R. H., and C. L. CUNNINGHAM (1985). *Crime scene search and physical evidence handbook*. Washington, DC: U.S. Department of Justice.

16. NATIONAL INSTITUTE OF JUSTICE (1987). *Investigators who perform well*. Washington, DC: U.S. Department of Justice, September.

Key Terms

▶ composite
▶ DNA technology
▶ exemplars
▶ Frye test
▶ Identi-kit
▶ latent fingerprint
▶ lineup
▶ personality profile
▶ plastic fingerprint
▶ relevancy test
▶ suggestiveness
▶ visible fingerprint

This chapter will enable you to:

- Understand the fundamentals of fingerprint science.

- Identify the different types of fingerprint patterns.

- Comprehend the various techniques of developing fingerprints.

- Understand the significance of DNA analysis in the criminal investigation process.

- Understand the importance of handwriting analysis in suspect development.

- Learn the legalities of police lineups in suspect identification.

INTRODUCTION

Although many investigative techniques used in suspect identification involve forensic procedures, forensics is not the primary focus of this book. Rather, the intent is to provide the reader with a basic understanding of some of the technological advances in suspect identification through brief offerings of some of the most innovative and effective techniques in this area.

Of paramount importance to any criminal investigation is establishment of the identity of the perpetrator or victim. This can be accomplished through numerous investigative techniques. *Fact:* When criminals are at work, they cannot avoid leaving behind clues as to their true identity. Such clues include fingerprints, bloodstains, and handwriting specimens. Today, such evidence may be a clear indicator of the identity of the criminal and can help expedite criminal prosecutions. In this chapter, we examine the role of the crime laboratory as well as some of the most critical techniques used in criminal investigation.

THE ROLE OF THE CRIME LABORATORY

The crime laboratory plays a pivotal role in criminal investigation. Thus, criminalists are major contributors to the investigative process. The duties and qualifications of criminalists vary greatly from one position to the next. For example, positions in crime labs include specialists in DNA (blood), trace evidence, handwriting analysis, toxicology, and ballistics, to name only a few. Students interested in becoming criminalists must be mindful of the very different job requirements and specific college coursework required to successfully compete. Let's now look at a few of the investigative functions performed by the crime laboratory.

Figure 5.1 Criminalist working on DNA results.

Trace Evidence

The Trace Evidence Unit identifies and compares specific types of trace materials that could be transferred during the commission of a violent crime. These trace materials include human hair, animal hair, textile fibers and fabric, ropes, and wood. Physical contact between a suspect and a victim can result in the transfer of trace materials such as hairs and fibers. The identification and comparison of these materials can often link a suspect to a crime scene or to physical contact with another individual. Torn pieces of fabric can be positively associated with a damaged garment, and broken pieces of wood can be fit together. Odontology (forensic dentistry) and physical anthropology (skeletal remains) examinations assist in the identification of human remains.

Questioned Documents

The Questioned Documents Unit examines and compares data appearing on paper and other evidentiary materials. These surface data include handwriting, hand printing, typewriting, printing, erasures, alterations, and obliterations. Impressions in the surface of paper, such as those from indented writing or use of a check writer or dry seal, are also routinely evaluated by unit examiners, as are shoeprint and tire tread impressions.

In addition to data contained on the surface of documentary evidence, data *within* paper or other surfaces—watermarks, safety fibers, and other integral features—may be components of document examinations. Unit examiners also match the torn or perforated edges of items such as paper, stamps, or matches.

Other unit examinations include analyses of typewriter ribbons, photocopiers, facsimiles, graphic arts, and plastic bags.

Forensic Chemistry

A crime laboratory's chemistry section is typically divided into three subunits whose analyses and functions include the following:

GENERAL CHEMISTRY SUBUNIT

- Identifies specific dyes and chemicals used in bank security devices. Analyzes items such as clothing or currency for the presence of these dyes and chemicals.

- Analyzes controlled substances to determine identity and quantity.

- Compares stains or markings to suspected sources. Detects presence of lubricants and compares to suspected sources.

- Compares the formulations of known and questioned ink (e.g., pens, typewriters, stamp pads).

- Conducts chemical analysis of unknown solids or liquids.

- Performs pharmaceutical identification of constituent composition, active ingredients, quantity, and weight.

TOXICOLOGY SUBUNIT

- Conducts toxicological analyses of biological specimens or food products for drugs, drug metabolites, and poisons.

- Investigates claims of product tampering.

Figure 5.2 Crime Lab workstation.

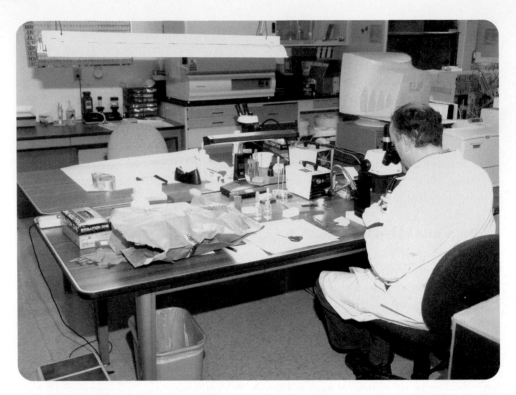

PAINTS AND POLYMERS SUBUNIT

- Analyzes paint chips for comparison to suspected sources.
- Conducts automotive make, model, and year determinations from suspected paint samples.
- Compares plastics to suspected sources.
- Determines tape composition, construction, and color for comparison to suspected sources. Determines manufacturer of suspected duct tape. Performs tape identifications with the torn or cut end of the tape and a roll of suspected tape.
- Compares caulks, sealants, and adhesives by color and composition to suspected sources.

DNA Analysis

A crime laboratory's DNA Analysis Unit analyzes bodily fluids and bodily fluid stains recovered as evidence in violent crimes. Examinations include the indentification and characterization of blood, semen, saliva, and other bodily fluids using traditional serological techniques and related biochemical analysis. Once the stain is identified, it is characterized by DNA analysis using the restriction fragment length polymorphism (RFLP) and/or polymerase chain reaction (PCR) techniques. The results of the analyses are compared to results obtained from known blood and/or saliva samples submitted from the victims and/or suspects.

In 1996, a number of DNA crime laboratory analysis units began using mitochondrial DNA (mtDNA) analysis, which is applied to evidence containing small or degraded quantities of DNA from hair, bones, teeth, and bodily fluids. The results of mtDNA analysis are compared to blood and/or saliva submitted

Figure 5.3 Blood examined and collected from the crime scene.

from the victims and/or suspects. The unit examines evidence that may not have been suitable for significant comparison purposes prior to the development of this technique.

The Mitochondrial DNA Population Database is comprised of complete nucleotide sequences of the first and second hypervariable segments of the control region of the human mitochondrial genome and consists of two main data sets. The first data set contains individuals from populations of forensic relevance and is contributed mostly by the Scientific Working Group on DNA Analysis Methods and forensic laboratories. The second data set, based on mtDNA concordance, contains nucleotide sequences from ethnic groups around the world.

Mitochondrial DNA Analysis. Both data sets are bundled in MitoSearch, a software package specifically designed for the compilation and analysis of mtDNA databases. MitoSearch estimates the relative frequency of specific sequences for the various populations represented within the database and assesses the relative relatedness of each population with reference to the size of each database.

Ballistics

Forensic Ballistics Unit receives and examines evidence related to firearms, firearm components, ammunition, ammunition components, tools, and tool marks. Evidence in a typical case may include a number of recovered rifles, pistols, shotguns, silencers and other muzzle attachments, magazines, holsters, and a variety of fired and unfired cartridges. Lead and other metal fragments, shot wads, shot cups, and bullets removed from bodies at autopsy are also frequently received items in firearms-related casework. Evidence submitted in tool mark

Figure 5.4 Straw (grass) closeup—dried grass on the roadside had blood on it. The blood trail on the grass led investigators to a body deposited several feet away from the roadside. The DNA matched the body. This evidence helped investigators theorize that the body had been dragged to its location.
Missouri State Highway Patrol Crime Laboratory

cases may include screwdrivers, scissors, knives, pliers, wrenches, crowbars, hammers, saws, wire, sections of sheet metal, chains, safety-deposit boxes, human bone or cartilage, plates, locks, doorknobs, bolts, and screens.

Forensic firearms examinations are based on firearms identification, which involves the identification of a bullet, cartridge case, or other ammunition component as having been fired by or in a particular firearm. Firearms examiners microscopically compare bullets and ammunition components to each other as well as to any number of firearms to determine whether an association exists between or among items submitted as evidence and items whose origins are known. Similarly, forensic tool mark identifications involve the identification of a tool mark as having been produced by a particular tool to the exclusion of all others. Examiners compare the micro- and macroscopic features of tool-marked items with known and questioned tools that may have produced them.

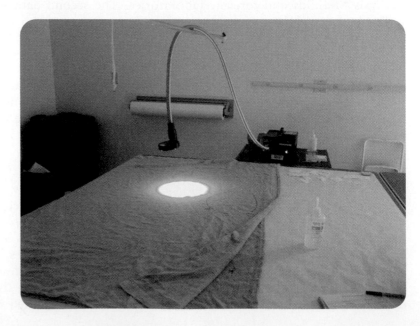

Figure 5.5 DNA analysis—search for bloodstains.

Tests and examinations routinely performed by laboratory ballistic criminalists include:

- Trigger pull tests
- Function tests
- Full-auto conversion tests
- Accidental discharge tests
- Shot pattern examinations
- Gunshot residue examinations
- Ejection pattern testing
- Trajectory analysis examinations
- Silencer (flash suppressor) testing
- Serial number restorations

Latent Prints

The Latent Print Unit conducts all work pertaining to the examination of latent prints on evidence submitted to the FBI laboratory. Latent prints are impressions produced by the ridged skin on human fingers, palms, and soles of the feet. Unit examiners analyze and compare latent prints to known prints of individuals in an effort to make identifications or exclusions. The uniqueness, permanence, and arrangement of the friction ridges allow unit examiners to positively match two prints and to determine whether an area of a friction ridge impression originated from one source to the exclusion of all others.

Figure 5.6 Ballistics section in crime lab.

Figure 5.7 Pistols commonly encountered in criminal investigations:

(1) 9mm caliber Smith & Wesson model 5906
(2) 9mm caliber Taurus model PT 99
(3) .40 caliber Glock model 22
(4) .45 auto caliber Colt model M1911A1
(5) 9mm caliber Sturm & Ruger model P89DC
(6) .25 auto caliber Beretta model 21A
(7) .22 caliber Beretta model 21A
(8) .380 auto caliber Walther model PPK/S

A variety of techniques, including use of chemicals, powders, lasers, alternate light sources, and other physical means, are employed in the detection and development of latent prints. In instances where a latent print has limited quality and quantity of detail, unit personnel may perform microscopic examinations in order to effect conclusive comparisons.

In 1999, the FBI developed and implemented a new automated fingerprint system known as the Automated Fingerprint Identification System (AFIS), which has since been adopted by most state crime laboratories as well. Although AFIS is primarily a ten-print system for searching an individual's fingerprints to determine whether a prior arrest record exists and then maintaining a criminal arrest record history for each individual, the system also offers significant latent print capabilities. Using AFIS, a latent print specialist can digitally capture latent print and ten-print images and perform several functions with each. These include:

- Enhancement to improve image quality.
- Comparison of latent fingerprints against suspect ten-print records retrieved from the criminal fingerprint repository.
- Searches of latent fingerprints against the ten-print fingerprint repository when no suspects have been developed.
- Automatic searches of new arrest ten-print records against an unsolved latent fingerprint repository.
- Creation of special files of ten-print records in support of major criminal investigations.

Using the AFIS fingerprint search capability against data from the FBI Criminal Justice Information Services (CJIS) Division, which maintains one of the largest repositories of fingerprint records, identifications are made in cases for which no known suspects have been named for comparison purposes and in cases in which latent prints on crime scene-related evidence were not identified with suspects named in the investigation.

Personnel from a crime laboratory's Latent Print Unit may also form the nucleus of the local or state disaster squad, which renders assistance in identifying victims at disaster scenes.

Forensic Photography

A crime lab's Forensic Photography Unit is responsible for imaging operations. This unit captures, processes, produces, analyzes, archives, and disseminates images using traditional silver-based photographic processes and digital-imaging technologies. The unit is typically responsible for the following:

- Crime scene and evidentiary photography
- Forensic photography
- Surveillance photography
- Aerial photography
- Venue photography
- Tactical imaging
- Photographic scanners
- Field photographic equipment
- Regional color photographic processing mini-laboratories
- Silver-based and digital darkrooms
- Digital-imaging technologies
- Courtroom presentations and exhibits

SPECIALIZED LABORATORY EQUIPMENT

The use of specialized laboratory equipment is one of the hallmarks of the modern crime lab. For example, the spectrograph is used to identify minute samples of a substance by burning the material and interpreting the light emitted from the burning process. Another device, the spectrophotometer, is used to analyze coloring agents in small samples such as those found in paint and cloth. The gas chromatograph is most commonly used for isolating gases or liquids from complex solutions or mixtures, generally in the analysis of illicit drugs, plastics, and explosives. Another crucial instrument, the mass spectrometer, is used to separate and record ions according to their characteristic masses. It is most commonly used in detection of trace elements in glass, ashes, and other inorganic material. Throughout the remainder of this chapter, other important instruments used by the crime lab will be featured and discussed according to their particular purpose.

Figure 5.8 DNA analysis equipment.

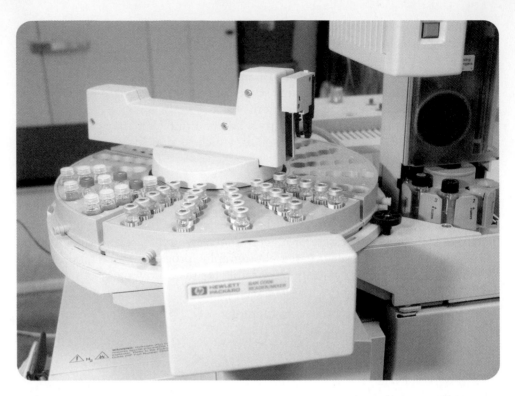

FINGERPRINTING

Identifying criminal suspects through the use of fingerprinting has proved to be one of the most effective methods for apprehending persons who might otherwise go undetected and continue their criminal activities. In addition to identifying criminal suspects, the use of fingerprinting also makes it possible to learn accurately the number (and type) of previous arrests and convictions. This, of course, often results in more appropriate sentences being handed down to repeat or career criminals. Early on, fingerprinting, because of its peculiar adaptability to the field, has been associated in the layperson's mind almost exclusively with criminal identification. Interestingly, the civil fingerprint file of the FBI contains three times as many fingerprints as the criminal file. Such files also provide a humanitarian benefit to society in general by identifying missing persons, amnesia victims, and unknown deceased.

In the latter case, victims of major disasters can be identified quickly and positively if their fingerprints are on file. The background and history of the science of fingerprints constitute an eloquent drama of human lives of good versus evil. Few developments in crime solving have played a more exciting role than that dramatized by the fascinating loops, whorls, and arches etched on the fingers and palms of a human being. Although faults have been found with earlier identification systems, to date no two fingerprints have been found to be identical.

The History of Fingerprinting

In earlier times, branding, maiming, distinctive clothing, and photography were used to distinguish the criminal for the crime that he or she committed. Thieves, for example, were sometimes deprived of the hand that committed a criminal act. Romans employed the tattoo needle for identifying and preventing desertion of military soldiers. In more recent times, law enforcement officers relied heavily on identification of criminals by sight, or what was known as the "camera eye." In using this system, photography lessened the burden on memory but was not the answer to the criminal identification problem—for personal appearances change. Throughout history, people have been aware of the friction ridges on the tips of fingers and palms. Although the precise origin of the science of personal identification is somewhat unclear, records show its application extending back to ancient civilizations.

For example, on the face of a cliff in Nova Scotia, a prehistoric Indian picture writing exists of a hand with ridge patterns crudely marked. Other examples include references to fingerprinting in clay tablets of recorded business transactions in ancient Babylon and to ancient Chinese documents identified with the eighth-century A.D. T'ang Dynasty, which refers to fingerprints being impressed on business contracts.

Such instances are common in history, but earlier accounts of the use of fingerprinting as an invaluable aid in identifying people lacked scientific verification. In 1686, Marcello Malpighi, professor of anatomy at the University of Bologna, contrived some new uses of the newly invented microscope. He observed "certain elevated ridges" on the palmar surfaces, which he perceived to be "drawn out into loops and spirals" at the ends of the fingers. It was more than 100 years before additional study was conducted on fingerprinting. In 1823, John Evangelist Purkinje, professor of anatomy at the University of Breslau, published a thesis in which he commented on the diversity of ridge patterns, "especially in the last phalanx of each finger." He then specified a vague differentiation of these patterns into nine varieties.

The first official use of fingerprinting was in 1858 by Sir William Herschel, British chief administrative officer for the Hooghly district, Bengal, India. He required natives to affix their fingerprints as well as their signatures to contracts. Although there is no evidence to suggest that Herschel was aware that fingerprints were individualized, he believed that to the native mind, this procedure would be impressive enough to discourage dishonesty.

Herschel continued his study of fingerprinting and in 1877 submitted a report to his superiors asking permission to identify prisoners through fingerprinting. Also around 1870, the French anthropologist Alphonse Bertillon developed a system to measure and record the dimensions of certain bony parts of the body. These measurements were reduced to a formula that, theoretically, would apply to only one person and would not change during his or her adult life. This system, called the Bertillon system, was generally accepted for more than 30 years but was pronounced as fallible as a result of the Will West case of 1903.

The value of fingerprints as a means of detecting the fallibility of the Bertillon system and establishing the value and reliability of individualized identification for criminal suspects was therefore established.

Between 1875 and the turn of the century, several new developments were documented regarding fingerprinting. For example, an article published in 1880 by Henry Faulds of the Tsukiji Hospital in Tokyo, Japan, discussed future possibilities of fingerprint science. He recommended the use of a thin film of printer's ink as a transfer medium, as is generally used today. He also discussed the potentialities of identification of criminals by their fingerprints left at the scene of crimes. The first documented use of fingerprinting in the United States was in

A Closer Look
The Will West Case

When William (Will) West was received at Leavenworth Penitentiary, he denied previous imprisonment there. The record clerk, however, ran the Bertillon (body measurements) instruments over him anyway, as he was aware of the reluctance of many criminals to admit previous crimes. Sure enough, when the clerk referred to the formula derived from West's Bertillon measurements, he located the file of one William West, whose measurements were almost identical and whose photograph appeared to be that of the new prisoner. Indeed, Will West was not being coy about a previous visit to Leavenworth, for another William West was already at the prison and serving a life sentence for murder. Subsequently, the fingerprints of both William Wests were compared, and it was found that they bore no resemblance.

1882. Gilbert Thompson of the U.S. Geological Survey, while in charge of a field project in New Mexico, used his own fingerprint on commissary orders to prevent their forgery. Later that year, Sir Francis Galton, a noted British anthropologist, published his book *Fingerprints*. He also contributed to the field by devising the first scientific method of classifying fingerprint patterns.

In 1891, the first files for fingerprint identification were installed as a means of identifying criminals. Juan Vuchetich, an Argentinean police official, based this system on pattern types by Sir Francis Galton. The Vuchetich system is the basis of systems presently used in many Spanish-speaking countries. Between 1890 and 1924, the official use of fingerprinting escalated in the United States. The New York Civil Service Commission implemented the use of fingerprints to prevent applicants from having better qualified persons take their tests for them (1902). The New York State prison system also adopted the first practical use of fingerprints in the United States for the identification of criminals (1903).

As the use of fingerprints became more accepted throughout the United States, the penitentiary in Leavenworth, Kansas, and the St. Louis, Missouri, Police Department both implemented fingerprint bureaus. The St. Louis system was activated through the assistance of a sergeant associated with London's Scotland Yard. As more and more police departments established identification bureaus, many sent copies of their files to the National Bureau of Criminal Identification, established by the International Association of Chiefs of Police. In 1924, the fingerprint records of both the National Bureau of Criminal Identification and the Leavenworth Penitentiary, totaling 810,188, were consolidated to form the nucleus of the FBI Identification Division. Between 1924 and 1954 alone, more than 130 million fingerprint cards had been received by the FBI. It has since become renowned as the world's largest repository of fingerprints.

Types of Prints

Among the most valuable clues for the investigator at the crime scene are fingerprints and palm prints. Once such prints have been collected by investigators and evaluated by classification experts, a definitive determination can be made as to the exact identity of the suspect(s). Generally, fingerprints can be divided into three main groups: (1) latent, (2) plastic, and (3) visible.

A **latent fingerprint** (also called a *patent fingerprint*) is one that occurs when the entire pattern of whorls on the finger, which contain small amounts of grease, oil, perspiration, or dirt, for example, is transferred to an object when it is touched. The grease and oil are usually natural and are transferred to the fingers when the person touches other areas of his or her body containing various bodily excretions. Latent prints include those not only visible to the naked eye but also those that can be examined properly only after development. Those are usually found on paper and smooth surfaces.

A **plastic fingerprint** results when a finger presses against plastic material and leaves a negative impression of friction ridges. Typically, these are found on recently painted surfaces, wax, grease, tar, putty, in the gum on stamps or envelopes, and on adhesive tape.

A **visible fingerprint** (also called a *dust print*) is a print that has been adulterated with foreign matter. If a finger is placed in a thin layer of dust, for example, the dust may cover the friction ridges. If the finger subsequently touches a clean surface, a visible fingerprint may result. A visible fingerprint may also develop as a result of touching other substances such as blood, flour, ink, or oil.

Types of Patterns

The use of fingerprints for identification purposes is based on distinctive ridge outlines that appear on the bulbs on the inside of the end joints of the fingers and thumbs (Figure 5.9). These ridges have definite contours and appear in several general pattern types. Each type has general and specific variations of the

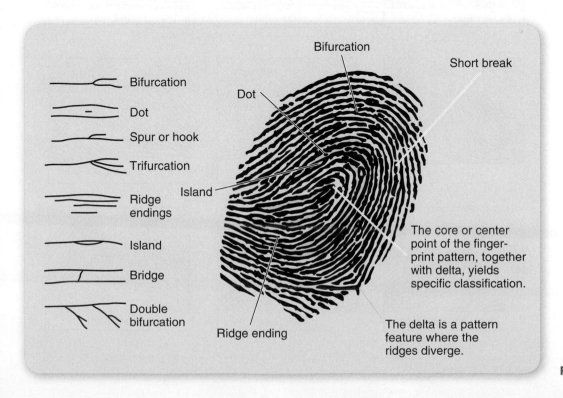

Figure 5.9 Basic fingerprint.

pattern, depending on the shape and relationship of the ridges. The ridge outlines appear most clearly when inked impressions are taken on paper, so that the ridges are black against a white background. This results from the ink adhering to the friction ridges. Impressions can be made by a variety of substances, including blood, dirt, grease, or any other foreign matter present on the ridges, or the saline substance emitted by the glands through the ducts or pores that constitute their outlets. The background or medium may be paper, glass, porcelain, wood, cloth, wax, putty, silverware, or any smooth, nonporous material.

Fingerprints may be resolved into three large general groups of patterns: the arch, the loop, and the whorl (Figure 5.10). Each group bears the same general characteristics. Patterns can be further subdivided by means of the smaller differences existing between patterns in the same general group. Patterns are divided as follows:

- Arch loop
- Whorl
- Plain radial

Plain Arch	Tented Arch	Plain Loop
Plain Loop	Whorl	Central Pocket Loop
Lateral Pocket Loop	Twinned Loop	Accidental

Figure 5.10 Basic fingerprint patterns.

- Plain tented
- Ulnar
- Accidental double
- Central pocket

Before pattern definition can be understood, it is necessary to understand the meaning of a few technical terms used in fingerprint work. As far as classification is concerned, the pattern area is the only part of the finger impression worth focusing on. It is present in all patterns, of course, but in many arches and tented arches it is impossible to define. This is not important, however, as the only patterns in which one needs to define pattern areas for classification purposes are loops and whorls. The U.S. Department of Justice defines the pattern area as follows: the part of a loop or whorl in which appear the cores, deltas, and ridges with which we are concerned when classifying.[1] Type lines enclose the pattern areas of loops and whorls. *Type lines* may be defined as the two innermost ridges, which start parallel, diverge, and surround or tend to surround the pattern area. Fingerprint impressions can be made from blood, dirt, grease, or the saline substance emitted by the glands through ducts or pores in the skin.

Searching for Prints

Investigators must be judicious in their search for fingerprints, as such evidence may be located in not-so-obvious places at the crime scene. In a burglary case, for example, the search for prints should begin at the place of entry by the criminal. Investigators should be able, at that point, to determine whether or not the burglar's hands were protected. If a door has been forced open, prints may be located on the lock or its immediate surroundings or in the general area of entry. When entry is gained through windows, broken glass should be searched for and documented. Generally, this method of entry involves the criminal breaking a piece of glass just large enough for a hand to reach through and open the latch.

Broken pieces of glass don't always fall inside a residence. Indeed, they may or may not be in the structure at all, or the burglar might pick up the pieces and throw them outside, out of the way. When attempting to climb through the window, the burglar may leave fingerprints on a window jamb, frame, or sill. The search for fingerprints should begin at the place of entry by the criminal.

Some burglars have been known to eat food or drink something while in a residence. The investigator must anticipate this and take care to preserve any fingerprints left on glassware (including liquor bottles) and even on some types of food (detectable by superglue fuming, discussed later). Electric light switches, circuit breakers, and lightbulbs should also be examined closely for prints. If it has been determined that the burglar was wearing gloves, places where gloves would be awkward to wear should be examined, as the burglar may have removed the gloves to accomplish a particular task. Experience shows that this is common and that it typically occurs early in the commission of a crime. Many police officers have grown accustomed to wearing gloves during their crime scene search. Today, this has become a recommended practice for the investigator's safety as well as to safeguard against contaminating the evidence.

Another technique used for recognizing fingerprints on a crime scene is shining a flashlight at an oblique angle at the suspected area. Although using this technique on some porous surfaces does not work well, it is effective on surfaces such as tile floors, glass surfaces, and countertops.

DEVELOPING LATENT FINGERPRINTS

The sole purpose of developing, or lifting, a latent fingerprint impression is to make it visible so that it can be preserved and compared. Several powders and chemicals are used for this purpose in addition to several techniques designed to develop such evidence.

Powders

When a latent print is clearly visible, it should be photographed before attempts are made to develop it. Accordingly, wet fingerprints should be allowed to dry before any attempt is made to develop them. Failure to do so will probably result in the print being destroyed. The powder method is used to develop fingerprints by making them show up on a surface where they would otherwise go unnoticed. To develop a latent fingerprint with powder, the powder used should contrast with the color of the surface of the print. The powder is lightly brushed over the print so that it will adhere to the oils on the surface of the print pattern.

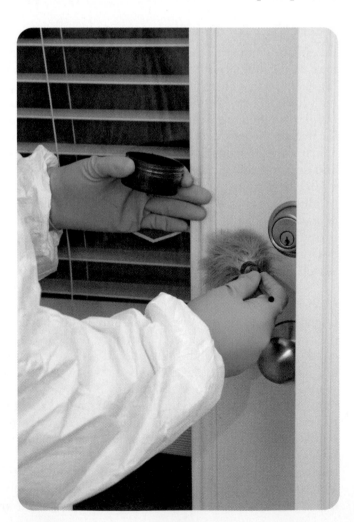

Figure 5.11 Great care must go into searching and dusting for fingerprints.

Generally, gray and black powder are best for latent fingerprint development: gray for dark backgrounds and black for light backgrounds.

Usually, a small camel hair, fiberglass, or nylon brush is used in dusting for latent prints. The brush must be kept dry to be effective. A small amount of powder is first placed on the brush for application to the surface being powdered. Some investigators prefer use of the Magna-Brush®, a magnetic brush that is used with magnetic powder. When the particles of the magnetic powder come into contact with the latent surface, the print becomes apparent. The sole purpose of developing, or lifting, a latent fingerprint impression is to make it visible so that it can be preserved and compared.

When brushing, the investigator should try to identify the contour of the ridges of the print so that brush strokes can go the same direction. Powder particles will then affix themselves to the oily ridges of the fingerprint, and the print will become visible. Typically, beginners tend to use too much powder and too little brushing, thus making the print unidentifiable.

Many investigators have adopted the use of fluorescent powders as an investigative alternative. Available in both powder and aerosol form, these are typically used to dust currency or other documents that may be handled by criminals. This technique differs from traditional fingerprinting in that these powders are used "before" the fingerprint is deposited. Once the criminal touches the dusted object, the area is examined by the use of an ultraviolet light which will display any fingerprints clearly. These are then photographed and classified.

Attempting to develop fingerprints on absorbent surfaces such as paper, cardboard, unpainted wood, and so on requires the use of more complicated procedures than the simple use of fingerprint powder, but positive results are worth the effort. Often, because powders cannot be removed from paper surfaces, it is best not to employ them, as the powder may interfere with writings on the document. In the next few paragraphs, we discuss the use of chemical developers. The first three, iodine, ninhydrin, and silver nitrate, are the most commonly used.

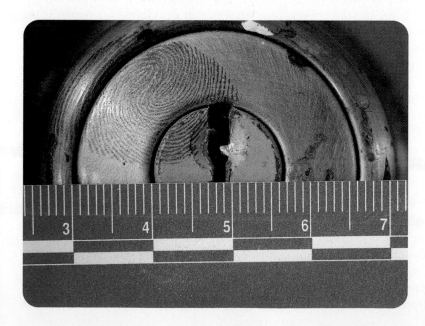

Figure 5.12 Latent fingerprints developed on a doorknob.

Iodine

Iodine is used on the premise that it attacks the object and changes its color. The grease and oils naturally produced by the skin discolor very easily and naturally become good candidates for development with iodine. Iodine prints, generally used on paper and wood, are temporary and will begin to fade once the fuming has stopped. It is therefore necessary for the investigator to be prepared to photograph the prints immediately.

Iodine fumes are controlled through the use of an iodine gun for smaller specimens or a fuming cabinet for larger objects. The gun consists essentially of two parts: one tube (through which the breath is blown) containing a drying agent such as calcium chloride to remove moisture from the breath, and a second tube containing a small number of iodine crystals that are vaporized by the heat of breath and the warm hand cupped around the tube containing the iodine. The vapor is blown on the specimen.

When an iodine cabinet is used, several pieces can be developed at a time and the investigator can observe the process. The cabinet is constructed of wood or plastic with glass sides. Fumes are generated by placing a small glass dish containing the iodine crystals in a hole cut in the bottom of the cabinet. As soon as the fumes begin to appear in sufficient amounts, the burner is removed. Specimens can be hung in the cabinet by wooden clothespins fastened to a removable strip. The top of the cabinet is hinged to permit access.

Iodine fumes can be removed by placing the specimen in a current of air from a fan, blow-dryer, or other device. The process should be carried out in a well-ventilated area, as fumes can cause respiratory damage if inhaled in large amounts.

Ninhydrin

A second process, involving the development of prints using amino acids present as a result of perspiration, is generally the most common method of fingerprint development for latent prints. Solutions of ninhydrin in powder or aerosol form can be acquired from fingerprint supply companies. Like chlorides, amino acids permeate the friction ridges of the fingerprint and remain unchanged for an extremely long time. In some cases, prints have been developed on paper 30 or 40 years after they were deposited. One fundamental requirement is that the paper must have been stored under dry conditions from the time deposited to the time developed.

A ninhydrin solution can be applied to the surface of an object by spraying, dipping, or brushing, with spraying being the method preferred. After treatment, prints should develop within 24 hours but will probably appear within an hour or two. Development can be expedited through the use of heat. Generally, a blow-dryer can accomplish this, but investigators should take care not to scorch the material being printed.

Silver Nitrate

Latent impressions developed by the use of silver nitrate are caused by the reaction of sodium chloride present in perspiration. When a person touches a surface with a sweaty finger, sodium chloride remains (almost indefinitely) while the other chemical compounds decompose. If a solution of silver nitrate is used on the impression, a chemical reaction occurs between the sodium chloride and the silver nitrate, resulting in the appearance of two new chemicals: sodium

A Closer Look
The FBI's National DNA Database: CODIS

When scientists James Watson and Francis Crick first mapped the structure of the DNA double helix a half century ago, little did they know that they were also unleashing a powerful weapon in the fight against crime and terrorism. DNA can uniquely identify an individual in ways that even fingerprints can't. DNA is found in virtually every human cell. It can be extracted from hair, teeth, bones, and body fluids (blood, saliva, semen, even sweat!). It leaves traces on everything from cigarette butts to postage stamps, from shirt collars to napkins. And it lasts for years—even in harsh conditions, even when there's little left of human remains. For example, following the 9/11/01 attacks, investigators were able to find traces of DNA in the rubble of the World Trade Center that identified victims and brought some measure of closure and relief to their devastated families.

In 1990, the FBI began a pilot project called the Combined DNA Index System, or CODIS—which became fully operational in 1998. CODIS is a three-hitter:

1. computer technology (a database program and software),
2. forensic science (DNA profiles rigorously measured and maintained), and
3. telecommunications (the ability of local, state, and federal labs to share information and communicate electronically) all rolled into one system.

Simply put, CODIS stores DNA profiles from around the country in a series of local, state, and national databases, all linked via computers, enabling crime labs at every level to share and compare DNA profiles electronically. Lightning fast searches using CODIS can link DNA found at one crime to other crime scenes and to convicted criminals whose DNA is already on file.

The overwhelming majority—more than 1.5 million DNA profiles—come from convicted felons. Depending on the state, the felons include those serving time for rape, murder, crimes against children, robbery, burglary, kidnapping, and assault and battery. The National DNA Index System (NDIS) also includes more than 78,000 DNA samples collected from crime scenes, more than 100 from missing persons and another 300 from relatives of missing persons, and some 150 from unidentified human remains. DNA samples from suspected terrorists are also collected today, but not uploaded to NDIS. When you add it all up, there are more than 1.6 million DNA profiles in the national system.

A total of 175 crime labs in all 50 states and Puerto Rico . . . as well as the FBI Lab and the U.S. Army Crime Lab. And, in a sign of how effective the system is, 31 labs in 18 nations worldwide also use CODIS, but they are not connected to any DNA databases here in the U.S. They simply borrow the FBI's technology to help investigations in their own countries, much as we do here.

The success of CODIS is measured primarily by keeping tabs on the number of investigations helped by CODIS through a hit or match that wouldn't have otherwise been developed. In December 2003, that total passed the 10,000 threshold. As of 2005, it stands at 10,770. "Forensic hits" are also measured when two or more DNA samples from a crime scene are linked in local, state, or national databases. "Offender hits" are measured when one or more DNA profiles from a crime scene are linked to a convicted felon. Between 1998 and 2005, there were over 3,000 forensic hits and over 7,000 offender hits.

nitrate and silver chloride. Through the use of ultraviolet radiation or sunlight, the silver chloride is reduced to metallic silver, bringing out a brownish print. One commonly used procedure is to prepare a 5 percent silver nitrate solution in distilled water. The solution is either brushed on the paper or the paper is dipped in the solution. After it dries, the paper is exposed to sunlight or ultraviolet light to bring out the latent prints. Because the entire paper will soon darken, prints must be photographed immediately.

Superglue Fuming

Cyanoacrylate resin, or superglue, was developed in the late 1950s as a bonding adhesive for metals and plastics. The substance was first used in fingerprinting, however, by the Japanese national police in 1978. Since then the process has been refined and accepted as valuable for developing latent fingerprints on various types of surfaces. The use of superglue fuming is a relatively simple procedure and is particularly valuable in developing prints on plastic bags, metal foil, waxed paper, lacquered wood, leather, and almost all hard surfaces. Even fruits, vegetables, and dinner rolls have been processed successfully with this procedure. The process occurs as the fumes adhere to the friction ridges, then harden as ridge detail is built up on the print.

The vapor is controlled through the use of an airtight container such as a tropical fish aquarium or other glass or plastic container. To begin, a small amount of glue is recommended, usually a 1- to 2-inch-diameter pool for approximately 8 cubic feet of container space. The glue can be placed on a disposable receptacle made of aluminum foil. The glue is then heated to emit the fumes. This can be accomplished easily by placing a hot plate or lightbulb under the receptacle. Objects to be printed are placed in the container, usually by suspending them with wooden clothespins or spring-loaded clips, allowing maximum exposure to fumes. Exposure time may vary, so periodic inspection of the objects is necessary to check progress. The investigator must remember that because the flashpoint of the glue may vary, great care should be given to maintain a desired temperature level. After the procedure, all prints are photographed and the specimens should be powdered.

Lasers

The detection and development of latent fingerprints left at crime scenes have taken a quantum leap forward with the use of laser technology. Since its development in 1976, this technique has been used to develop prints that could not have been developed through the use of powders, iodine, ninhydrin, silver nitrate, or superglue fuming. The laser procedure is a clean, relatively easy method to develop prints, and pretreatment of the specimen is not required.

As with the ninhydrin method, the age of the print is of no importance. Additionally, there is no alteration of the evidence; therefore, it is generally used before other methods are employed. In this process, an expanded laser beam is used to luminesce certain properties of perspiration, body oils, or other foreign substances found on a latent print. Three types of lasers are currently operational in the development of fingerprints: the argon ion laser, the copper vapor laser, and the neodymium:YAG laser. Because laser light is extremely bright, eye protection must be worn by equipment operators. Special light-filtering goggles can be worn to illuminate latent prints with greater clarity.

Preservation of Fingerprints

Because of the importance of latent fingerprints in any criminal investigation, great care must be taken to preserve them for later examination and use in court. Fingerprints remain on affected areas for varying amounts of time, depending on whether they are plastic, visible, or latent. Generally, plastic and latent prints may remain for years, depending on the type of surface on which they are located. Methods of fingerprint preservation include photography of the print and lifting techniques.

Often, fingerprints are left on a surface that can be transported to the crime laboratory for examination. Undoubtedly, this is the preferred way to facilitate classification of the print. Unfortunately, however, many prints must be processed on the crime scene, as they are found on surfaces too large to transport. In general, plastic and latent prints can remain for years, depending on the type of surface on which they are located.

Fingerprint lifters are used to remove the print from surfaces that are curved or otherwise difficult to photograph. For surfaces such as these, rubber lifters are recommended. Rubber lifters are available at fingerprint supply houses and consist of a thin black or white flexible material coated with an adhesive. The adhesive side is guarded by a thin cover that is removed just before placing it on the print and then replaced just after use. As a general rule, the latent fingerprint is dusted with print powder. The adhesive side of the lifter is then placed against the print and slowly pulled away. The print is preserved by the fingerprint powder being pressed against the lifter. Once the print is lifted, the lifter cover is replaced.

Lifting tape is also a commonly used medium for fingerprint preservation. This is a special transparent tape supplied in rolls 1 to 2 inches wide. The procedure is to dust the print with fingerprint powder and then place the tape over the print, thus removing it. The investigator must take care to avoid air pockets in the tape while it is being applied, as these will show up as void areas on the print impression. Once applied, the tape will adhere to the powder particles and transfer the fingerprint impression.

Prints from Gloves

The notoriety of the success of fingerprinting has resulted in the use of gloves by many criminals as a protective measure. Investigators may discover "smearing" from gloves on a crime scene but may give the matter little consideration. Indeed, such gloves, if located, may produce valuable evidence in locating the perpetrator. The glove itself may have a unique, identifiable pattern, as with a fingerprint.

Leather gloves, for example, may contain fatty material, and fabric gloves are often contaminated with soil or other foreign matter. In both cases, ridge patterns may be left behind. A leather glove may possess certain pattern characteristics that make it distinguishable. This is because animal hide possesses friction ridge skin similar to that of human beings, and its characteristics can readily be identified. Fabric gloves don't offer as identifiable a pattern as that of leather gloves, but certain features may still be identifiable. After wearing gloves for a period, certain wrinkles or cracks in the material may create distinguishable markings. Sometimes, a fingerprint can be recovered from a glove, in particular if it is made of latex material.

INTEGRATED AUTOMATED FINGERPRINT IDENTIFICATION SYSTEM (IAFIS)

The Integrated Automated Fingerprint Identification System, more commonly known as IAFIS, is a national fingerprint and criminal history database maintained by the Federal Bureau of Investigation (FBI), Criminal Justice Information

Services (CJIS) Division. The IAFIS provides automated fingerprint search capabilities, latent searching capability, electronic image storage, and electronic exchange of fingerprints and responses, 24 hours a day, 365 days a year. It combines with criminal histories, mugshots, scar/tattoo photos, height, weight, hair and eye color, and aliases to help match evidence with identities. As a result of submitting fingerprints electronically, agencies receive electronic responses to criminal ten-print fingerprint submissions within two hours and within 24 hours for civil fingerprint submissions.

The IAFIS maintains the largest biometric database in the world, containing the fingerprints and corresponding criminal history information for more than 47 million subjects in the Criminal Master File. The fingerprints and corresponding criminal history information are submitted voluntarily by state, local, and federal law enforcement agencies.

Just a few years ago, substantial delays were a normal part of the fingerprint identification process, because fingerprint cards had to be physically transported and processed. A fingerprint check could often take three months to complete. The FBI formed a partnership with the law enforcement community to revitalize the fingerprint identification process, leading to the development of the IAFIS. The IAFIS became operational in July 1999.

Since its implementation, the IAFIS has been responsible for the successful identification of suspects in hundreds of cases. Examples are as follows:

1. *The case of the cocaine murderer:* In April 2004, a man was arrested in Connecticut by a drug task force for possession of cocaine. He was fingerprinted, and his electronic prints were sent to IAFIS. Ten minutes later there was a match. Turns out he'd been wanted in Miami since September 2002 for fleeing the state to avoid being prosecuted for homicide . . . and he'd

Figure 5.13 The IAFIS fingerprint identification has revolutionized suspect identification.

been wanted in Fort Lauderdale since October 2003 on homicide charges. In no time he was picked up and extradited to Florida for prosecution.

2. *The case of the vicious rapist:* In June 2004, a man was arrested by police in New Jersey for simple assault and endangering the welfare of children. That turned out to be the tip of the iceberg. When officers fingerprinted the man and sent his prints to IAFIS . . . 13 minutes later, MATCH! Turns out he'd been wanted in Norfolk, Virginia, since October 2000 for rape and sexual abduction . . . and he'd been wanted in Yorktown, Virginia, since May 2001 for kidnapping/sexual assault. In no time he was facing charges in New Jersey before being shipped off to Virginia to face charges there.

3. *The case of the Christmas murderer:* In September 2004, a 57-year-old man was arrested in Massachusetts for slashing another man with a pocket knife. They'd been on a public bus, words were exchanged, and out came the knife. Fingerprints were taken at the booking station and sent to IAFIS. Turns out he was the man accused of a horrific crime in Baltimore in 1974. It was Christmas eve 30 years ago when police department employee McKinley Johnson was helping put together food baskets for the poor. Suddenly a young man approached and stole a can of lunch meat from one of the baskets. Johnson ran after him—and the thief shot him point blank. Before dying, Johnson identified his alleged assailant from photographs . . . and the hunt had been on ever since.

   Since that time, the suspect had lived in different places, assumed 10 different identities, and been arrested five times in Boston in the 1980s for charges from shoplifting to weapon possession. In the meantime, though, IAFIS was created, allowing matches of fingerprints nationwide. And so, with the slash of a pocket knife, 30 years on the run came to an end.[2]

THE GENETIC FINGERPRINT: DNA

Because of its success in identifying suspects, fingerprinting has proven to be one of the most effective methods in law enforcement. However, a dramatic advance in forensic science may now overshadow the technique of fingerprinting: **DNA technology.** DNA has given scientists the means with which to detect the remarkable variability existing between individuals. The results of this technology hold great promise in aiding the criminal justice system in making positive determinations of criminal identity.

What Is DNA?

In all life forms, from viruses to human beings, the basis for difference lies in the genetic material known as deoxyribonucleic acid (DNA). In every living organism, with the exception of certain viruses that possess ribonucleic acid (RNA), DNA represents a genetic facsimile, or "blueprint," of that organism. Additionally, in every cell within each human body, the DNA is identical. This applies whether the cell is a white or a red blood cell, a piece of skin, spermatozoa, or even a follicle of hair (Figure 5.14).

Although DNA is extremely complex chemically, it consists of only five basic elements: carbon, hydrogen, oxygen, nitrogen, and phosphorus. These five elements combine to form certain molecules known as nucleotides. The four bases that code genetic information in the polynucleotide chain of DNA are

Figure 5.14 Sources of DNA evidence.

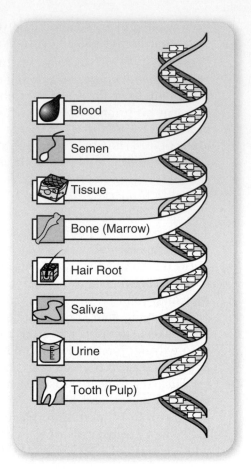

thymine, cytosine, adenine, and guanine (T, C, A, and G, respectively). Although just four letters exist in this short alphabet, a variety of different sequences of nucleotides exist. A single strand of DNA can be millions of nucleotides long. For example, 6 billion nucleotides constitute the DNA in one human being.

In human beings, 23 pairs of chromosomes originate from each parent: one of each pair from the mother and one from the father at the time of conception. Therefore, when a person is born, his or her genes are made up of a combination of maternal and paternal genes. Because of this, no two persons are exactly alike except identical twins.

DNA's History

The discovery of DNA and the ability to decode its complex network of information is considered a turning point in an understanding of human ancestry. This technology was not considered as meaningful earlier on as it is today. In 1985, a routine investigation showed scientists that "portions of the DNA structure of certain genes are as unique to each human being as fingerprints."[3] Let's go back to the early 1980s and review a murder case in England that was the first to use DNA technology in criminal investigation. (See page 150.)

Since the Narborough murders, the DNA technique has often been used successfully in the United States, beginning in 1987 in the *Florida* v. *Andrews* case, involving a sexual assault. Although it has been used successfully in many criminal trials, future issues will probably focus on the admissibility of DNA test results.

In the *Florida* v. *Andrews* case, police in Orlando, Florida, suspected that one man was involved in over 20 cases of prowling, breaking and entering, and attempted sexual assault. In every case, the modus operandi was similar: The man would stalk his victim for weeks, prowling around her house and peeping through windows. When attacked, she had little or no opportunity to make a visual identification. Until Tommie Lee Andrews was arrested, all police had to go on were composite drawings and several calls about a prowler. After his arrest, one rape victim (who had seen her assailant for only about six seconds while being attacked) picked Andrews out of a photo lineup.

When attorney Hal Uhrig was appointed to be the defense attorney for Tommie Lee Andrews, his concern was not about DNA evidence. Instead, he was worried about the amount of time and effort that would be required for him and his small law firm to defend Andrews against multiple rape charges. It was not until later, after prosecutor Jeffrey Ashton read an advertisement in a legal publication about DNA testing and employed the services of Lifecodes, Inc., that Uhrig discovered he was involved in the first-known DNA criminal case in the United States.

At Andrews's first trial, prosecutors successfully introduced results from the test by Lifecodes. The defense, however, successfully challenged the introduction of any testimony regarding the statistical probabilities resulting from the test. The trial ended in a hung jury. At the retrial, DNA evidence was again admitted. This time, the prosecution was prepared to argue that the statistical probabilities of the test be introduced. Using a relevance standard similar to that in the federal rules of evidence, the court admitted the statistical data. Andrews was subsequently convicted.

Prosecutor Ashton said that he was unaware at the outset that this was the first case to use DNA testing in the United States but that he felt it would be a powerful tool in future cases, especially when the suspect is a serial rapist who is careful not to leave much evidence. Defense attorney Uhrig said that he came away from his experience in defending against DNA evidence most concerned about the use of statistical data, which he felt carries inordinate weight in the minds of the jury. As more population data are collected, the numbers could become much smaller and lose "real-world meaning" to juries.

Hypothetically, said Uhrig, odds of 10 billion to 1 could be introduced into court. But if the defendant in such a case had an identical twin (and hence identical DNA patterns), the odds of a random match would be 5 billion to 1 but still a 50 percent probability that the DNA in question would not belong to the defendant. DNA typing, Uhrig said, might well result in more rape defenses that center on consent rather than on alibi or denial defenses.

Analyzing DNA

Genetic patterns found in blood or semen can be just as distinctive as fingerprints. Traditional serology tests on bodily fluids often do not discriminate enough to either exclude or include a suspect in a crime. DNA analysis provides much more conclusive analysis. The unique genetic patterns found in each person's DNA make it possible, with a high degree of accuracy, to associate a

A Closer Look

DNA's First Case: The Narborough Murders[4]

The November 1983 discovery of a murdered 15-year-old girl in the English village of Narborough ultimately had an enormous impact on international criminal investigation. Before the four-year murder investigation was completed, a scientific discovery was applied that not only solved a double criminal homicide but completely revolutionized forensic identification: the mapping of DNA fragments. At first, the murder of Lynda Mann was barely noticed outside the area known as Leicestershire, but it soon launched one of the biggest homicide investigations in English history. A squad of more than 150 detectives was formed and exhausted every lead in the case. So thorough was the investigation that every male between the ages of 13 and 34 living in the area of the murder was noted and in many cases questioned. Nonetheless, no murder suspect was apprehended.

Then, in July 1986, 15-year-old Dawn Ashworth, also of Leicestershire, was found brutally raped and strangled. The modus operandi (MO) indicated the same killer and alerted authorities to the possibility of a serial killer. This time, more than 200 investigators from all across the country were placed on the case. Word of the killings began to be cause for concern in almost all of England, but investigators were still unable to develop significant indicators as to who the killer might be. At last, a case against one suspect was developed. A 17-year-old hospital kitchen porter linked to the murder through circumstantial evidence was arrested. After interrogation, the suspect admitted the second killing but denied the first, despite the belief by the police that both victims were murdered by the same person.

The ultimate solution to the problem was found only a short distance away, at Leicester University. Alec J. Jeffreys, a university scientist working in the field of genetic research since the early 1980s, had recently discovered a process of human identification based on the DNA molecule. Whether the suspect's father or the British police first initiated contact with Jeffreys is still under dispute, but the scientist was well known for his work in a paternity lawsuit in which DNA technology established the identity of the father. In the Narborough murders, Jeffreys analyzed a semen sample from the body of Lynda Mann and then analyzed a sample from the Dawn Ashworth crime scene. The technique yielded a DNA image that was identical for both murders. Then, from the suspect's blood sample, Jeffreys obtained a comparison DNA fingerprint. Alarmingly, the suspect's DNA failed to match up with either murder, including the murder in which the suspect already confessed. The suspect was then released from custody.

Certain of one fact—that the same person had killed both teenagers—investigators decided to single out the perpetrator through genetic fingerprinting. Accordingly, in January 1987, all males 17 to 40 years of age living in the village were asked to submit blood samples. Over 4,500 samples were examined before the police, in September 1987, arrested a local baker, Colin Pitchfork, and charged him with the murders. Pitchfork had a long history of sexual assault and indecent exposure, and an informant had alerted police that he had cheated on his blood examination by persuading a co-worker to submit a blood sample for him. When a legitimate test of the suspect's blood was conducted, an identical match was made with fingerprints found at both murder scenes. Based solely on DNA fingerprinting and the resulting confession, Pitchfork was convicted of both murders.

suspect with (or exclude a suspect from) a crime. Except in the case of identical twins, every person's DNA and resulting DNA pattern are different. The process of analyzing, or "typing," DNA begins with DNA source material such as blood or semen. After the DNA is removed from the sample chemically, restriction enzymes known as endonucleases are added that cut the DNA into particles or fragments (Figure 5.15). The particles are then mixed with a sieving gel and sorted out according to size by a process called electrophoresis. In this process,

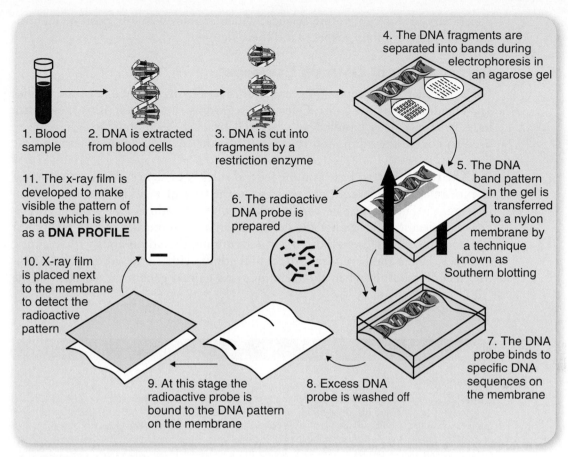

1. Blood sample
2. DNA is extracted from blood cells
3. DNA is cut into fragments by a restriction enzyme
4. The DNA fragments are separated into bands during electrophoresis in an agarose gel
5. The DNA band pattern in the gel is transferred to a nylon membrane by a technique known as Southern blotting
6. The radioactive DNA probe is prepared
7. The DNA probe binds to specific DNA sequences on the membrane
8. Excess DNA probe is washed off
9. At this stage the radioactive probe is bound to the DNA pattern on the membrane
10. X-ray film is placed next to the membrane to detect the radioactive pattern
11. The x-ray film is developed to make visible the pattern of bands which is known as a **DNA PROFILE**

Figure 5.15 DNA profiling method.

the DNA moves along the gel-coated plate, some faster than others. At the completion of the process, the double-stranded fragments of DNA are treated so that the strands separate from each other.

Next, a transfer method developed by Edward Southern, called Southern blotting, occurs. In this process, the DNA is transferred to a nylon membrane in much the same way that ink is transferred to a blotter. The nylon sheet is then treated with radioactively labeled DNA probes, single-stranded pieces of DNA that can bind through complementary base pairing with target DNA. A single-locus probe "looks" for only one field, whereas a multilocus probe looks for numerous fields simultaneously. The radioactive probe then merges with the specific DNA sequences found on the membrane fragments. The images that result from x-ray film placed in contact with the membrane to detect the probe configuration look like the price bar codes used on supermarket products.

These images are analyzed visually or by computer. Although not yet considered a routine procedure for all police agencies, it is clear that DNA will prove to be one of the most exciting and valuable investigative tools developed in recent decades, possibly even more significant than that of fingerprinting technology. As time goes on, there will undoubtedly be significant legal and scientific challenges to the application of DNA technology in crime solving. Certainly, however, as the "bugs" are worked out, society as a whole will be the beneficiary of this captivating science, which enables virtually positive identification of both criminal suspects and their victims.

Admissibility of DNA as Evidence

For evidence to be accepted into court, it must be offered by one of the parties and be admitted by the court. Questions regarding the admissibility of evidence have generally been handled at a pretrial hearing. Two standards have been used to govern the admission of scientific evidence: the relevancy test and the Frye test.

The **relevancy test,** based on the federal rules of evidence, permits the admission of relevant evidence that is helpful to the trier of fact. The second pretrial hearing, the **Frye test,** or **Frye standard,** involves the admission of scientific evidence. This test, named after the defendant in a 1923 murder case, is the oldest test and the one used most often for determining the admissibility of scientific evidence. Under the Frye standard, courts admit evidence based on novel scientific techniques only when the technique has gained general acceptance in the

DNA Evidence

Advantages

DNA can be used to test any DNA-containing biological trace evidence. The composition of the DNA molecule does not vary essentially from cell to cell; therefore, the DNA in blood is identical to that found in other biological material, such as hair, skin, and bone marrow. Because DNA testing is so sensitive, only a trace amount of biological material is needed for identification purposes. DNA evidence can identify probative physical evidence in some cases. For example, semen left at the scene of a rape is more closely related to the commission of the crime of rape than is the presence of a fingerprint. DNA is especially useful in crimes of violence that yield little useful evidence. Testing is potentially very helpful in identifying perpetrators of sexual assault in cases where, although biological evidence is found, witnesses are often lacking and identification of the assailant by the victim is unreliable or nonexistent.

Using DNA test results, a crime laboratory can establish data banks that could identify serial criminals. For example, law enforcement agencies could determine that the same rapist is responsible for a series of assaults in several different jurisdictions. As suspects were identified by investigators through DNA data banks, investigators could redirect and narrow their search for the perpetrator. DNA testing provides crime labs and forensic scientists with a new tool that can be used for investigatory purposes (e.g., identifying remains), which in coordination with other types of evidence could lead to more arrests and convictions.

Criticisms and Limitations

Some critics argue that the development of DNA data banking poses an invasion of civil liberties, particularly due process (the taking of a sample without establishing a foundation of probable cause) and privacy (since DNA can reveal more information than identity alone). Testing may involve the use of expert witnesses from private companies whose primary goal is to get into court first in order to achieve a judicial imprimatur of acceptability. DNA has been rushed into court without agreement being reached in the scientific community regarding standards that ensure the reliability of the evidence and guidelines for the interpretation of the results. The probability of a sample having come from someone other than the defendant can be so infinitesimal, according to statistical data, as to hold inordinate weight with a jury, thus obscuring other evidence.

Many defendants will not be able to afford the cost of rebutting state-induced DNA evidence. Additional costs incurred in cases involving DNA evidence include testing, the cost of expert witnesses, and legal fees. If defendants cannot afford these costs, the difference between defense and prosecutorial resources, already large, could increase further.[5]

scientific community to which it belongs. General acceptance under the Frye test appears to require a two-step analysis:

1. Identifying the field in which the underlying theory falls (i.e., in determining whether the technique meets the test of acceptance in the scientific community, defining what community is relevant).
2. Determining whether the principle has been accepted by most members of the field identified.

The Frye test has several perceived advantages and disadvantages. Its proponents note that the test guarantees a minimal amount of support by experts for a scientific test or procedure in its introduction in a court of law. As noted by one court, the experts "form a kind of technical jury, which must first pass on the scientific status of a procedure before the lay jury utilizes it in making its findings of fact." Following the pretrial Frye or evidentiary hearing, a court rules whether DNA testing will be admitted into evidence and, if so, under what conditions. At trial, any party may offer expert testimony. It is the obligation of the party calling expert witnesses to lay the foundation for such testimony. The foundation includes the qualifications and experience of the witness, details on how DNA testing works, what procedures were followed, the results of the test, and facts and opinions that can be drawn from the test results.

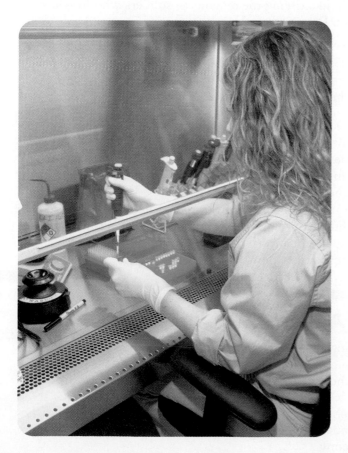

Figure 5.16 Crime lab biologist working on the analysis of DNA.

> **DNA at Work[6]**
>
> - In one amazing success, investigators linked the DNA in the saliva used to lick an envelope to one of the World Trade Center bombers.
> - DNA matches have kept families united by allowing immigrants to stay in the United States legally when the genetic study proved they were related to a resident.
> - DNA studies have freed persons wrongfully convicted of murder or rape. The Innocence Project at Yeshiva University in New York, founded in 1992 by Barry Scheck, has helped release 144 prisoners as of July 2, 2004, when DNA tests proved they were innocent.
> - Paternity suits are commonly settled by DNA testing. Former mayor Coleman Young of Detroit agreed to child support payments in 1992 after testing resolved a dispute.

Other Uses of DNA

In addition to its utility in criminal investigations, DNA blood typing can be put to use in other ways. For example, with the use of a new process called polymerase chain reaction (PCR), cells producing billions of DNA strips can be reproduced rapidly in a test tube, a feat that would take a dividing cancer cell at least a month to perform. The PCR technique has recently been used to perform the following examinations:

- To compare the DNA of extinct animals with that of their closest living relatives.
- To assist the military in identifying the remains of soldiers who fought in wars such as Operation Desert Storm.
- To help physicians detect small numbers of cancer cells circulating in the bloodstream and to make prenatal diagnosis of genetic diseases such as sickle-cell anemia.
- To ensure better matches between organ donors and transplant recipients.

In January 1992, the Defense Department announced that it would establish a repository of genetic information on all U.S. service members as a way of identifying future war casualties. The Armed Forces Institute of Pathology will collect samples of DNA from blood and oral swabs and add the information to fingerprint, dental, and other records.

DNA profiling may be the most significant breakthrough in forensic science since the development of fingerprinting. Federal, state, and local crime laboratories are currently working to enhance profiling techniques and to establish a national DNA index. In addition, a uniform approach to DNA testing is being sought to ensure an effective and secure system.

HANDWRITING ANALYSIS

Like skills acquired in piloting an aircraft or interpreting a polygraph, accurate handwriting analysis requires many years of study and practice. From our earliest years in elementary school, we are taught how to sculpt letters of the alphabet meticulously to form words and sentences. People often adopt unique styles of their own, frequently characteristic only of that person. Such characteristics are identifiable to the handwriting expert, who must be knowledgeable in both photography and microscopy.

Writings may occur in many forms, including that on personal correspondence, desks, walls, and even dead bodies. In all cases, they may offer the investigator valuable evidence in identifying suspects. To understand how best to proceed with the handwriting analysis process, we should first consider that the average handwriting specimen has 500 to 1,000 characters, including elements such as form, movement, connections, alignment, punctuation, slant, spacings, and embellishments. Any object containing handwritten or typewritten markings and whose source or authenticity is in doubt may be referred to as a questioned document.[7]

Collection of Exemplars

Cases involving questioned documents require a comparison between the suspect document and a sample or exemplar (also known as a *standard*). Two types of **exemplars** exist: the requested and the collected. In either case, its origin must be well documented before analysis, to ensure genuineness.

Requested Exemplars. A requested handwriting standard is obtained from a suspect at the formal request of a law enforcement officer and is performed solely as a means to acquire a comparison document. It is logical to assume that no two samples of a suspect's handwriting are identical. Therefore, a sufficient number of exemplars must be collected to demonstrate to the examiner the range of natural variations in a suspect's writing peculiarities. In the event that investigators might not be successful in obtaining exemplars of a suspect's handwriting, an exemplar may be obtained directly from the suspect.

In a 1967 case, *Gilbert* v. *California,* the court held that requiring a suspect to give a handwriting sample does not violate a person's Fifth Amendment protection against self-incrimination. Therefore, he or she cannot refuse. Exemplars requested by the police are a means to acquire a comparison document from a suspect.

Collected Exemplars. A collected handwriting exemplar is a sample of the suspect's handwriting that was not written for the purpose of examination and is not evidence in the crime under investigation. The obvious reason for this is that the sample document must be one that the suspect has not prepared or altered deliberately to match a suspect document.

The most valuable collected document is one that has been acquired close to the time the suspect document was produced. For example, if the document questioned was produced on a typewriter, an exemplar of the suspected typewriter would be collected. Accordingly, if the suspect's signature is in question, a standard of his or her handwriting must be collected. Typically, collected exemplars can be acquired from such documents as insurance policies, credit card receipts, canceled checks, and personal letters. Collected exemplars are samples of the suspect's handwriting that were not specially written for the purpose of examination that are used as comparison documents.

The Writing Medium

The process of collecting handwriting exemplars includes being sure that the writing instruments (e.g., paper, pencils) used in the sample are the same as those used in the suspect document. Things to look for in selection of paper include its size, thickness, color, and condition. In short, the sample paper should match, as closely as possible, that used by the suspect.

If more than one sample document is being acquired from the suspect, they should not be stacked on top of one another. This is because writing impressions might press through one page to another and hinder the examination of them. Additionally, each handwriting sample should be taken from the suspect's sight as soon as it is obtained. This will prevent the suspect from attempting to compare his writing from one exemplar to another.

The same type of instrument used for the document questioned should be furnished to the suspect for the control exemplar. This includes the pencil, pen, felt-tip marker, and so on. Special attention should also be given to matching the lead number of a pencil, the color of an ink pen, and the width of a felt-tip marker to that used on the questioned document.

The Writing Area

The suspect should be afforded a comfortable writing area. The backseat of a police car, for example, will prove to be a waste of time. The investigator must make sure that the suspect is writing in the same general style as in the suspect document: block letters for block letters, cursive writing for cursive writing, and so on. It might also be advisable to obtain a sample of writing in the suspect's opposite hand in the event that the suspect used this technique as a deception. In addition, the investigator will have to observe as the suspect writes the sample document, as his or her testimony will be required in court. The investigator must make sure that the suspect is writing in the same general style as in the suspect document.

CRIMINAL COMPOSITES

One method of developing an idea of the suspect's general description is to have the witness provide information to a police artist so that a **composite** can be generated. The drawing can be freehand or developed through use of computer-generated composite programs. For example, **Identi-kit,** requires initial information on a suspect's build, gender, race, and hairstyle. Then personal characteristics such as eyes, nose, lips, mustache or beard, and chin are added. A composite sketch can aid investigators in unearthing a physical description of a criminal suspect.

PERSONALITY PROFILING

A **personality profile** is a means of identifying the type of person responsible for a particular crime. This is accomplished by identifying psychological and social characteristics surrounding the crime as well as the manner in which it was committed. An example is the Unabomber case, where mail bombs killed four people in a period spanning 15 years. Forensic investigators subsequently determined that the bomber chose his postage carefully, using Frederick Douglass stamps when he wanted to injure his targets and stamps of playwright Eugene O'Neill when he intended to kill. O'Neill's plays were known for their dark themes.

One play, *Dynamo*, was highly critical of America's growing reliance on machinery and industrialization, a theme echoed in the Unabomber's manifesto. The profiling technique can be advantageous in illuminating certain clues at the crime scene that may not be apparent upon first examination. For example,

Figure 5.17 The composite sketch can be an important component to the identification process.

hate, passion, fear, and confusion may all have certain indicators somewhere at the scene, such as postmortem slashing or cutting, rapes, lust and mutilation murders, and so on.

The practice of profiling was developed during World War II by government psychologist William Langer to predict Adolph Hitler's future actions. As it relates to criminal investigation, profiling is based on the notion that crime is, directly or indirectly, based on the personality of the person committing it. Profilers typically scrutinize evidence found on the crime scene and attempt to re-create the circumstances surrounding the crime and to predict the offender's frame of mind. The profile is then used to narrow down the list of suspects as it develops. From a practical standpoint, profiling can be helpful in investigating any crime in which the evidence suggests that the suspect is irrational or mentally or emotionally unstable.

Profiling gained popularity during the 1980s, when the FBI became heavily involved in the profiling of violent sex offenders and arsonists. More recently, caregivers suffering from a disorder called Munchhausen syndrome by proxy (MSBP) have become the subject of profilers. The disorder involves offenders who injure or cause illnesses in their children in order to gain attention and sympathy for themselves. Past cases have revealed that most suspects are women who victimize their children so as to become the center of attention by police, doctors, family members, and others. MSBP is thought to be a serial offense usually affecting families with more than one child. Characteristics of offenders include a history of self-inflicted wounds, past psychiatric treatment, past attempted suicides, a middle- to upper-class background, a better-than-average education, and knowledge of the medical field and related procedures.

The field of psychological profiling continues to grow as new areas are developed. Two of the newest areas include hostage negotiation and terrorism.[8] The psychological profiling technique was used successfully by the FBI in the investigation of Theodore (Ted) Bundy, the serial murderer responsible for the murders of 30 young women in the northwestern United States between 1973 and 1978.

According to John Douglas and Robert Ressler of the FBI, most (normal) persons have personality traits that are more or less identifiable. However, an abnormal person tends to become more ritualized and tends to display a "pattern" to his or her behavior. Often, the suspect's personality will be reflected in both the crime scene and in the furnishings of his or her home. Because of the nature of such evidence, the profiling procedure has its limitations and should be used in conjunction with other investigative techniques. The profiling technique requires the collection of certain types of information:

- *Photographs:* focused on the extent and depth of wounds
- *Neighborhood information:* racial, ethnic, and social data
- *Medical examiner's report:* photos of damage to body, such as stabs, gunshots, bruises, and lividity; includes information regarding toxicology, postmortem wounds, and personal observations of the medical examiner
- *Map of the victim's travel before death:* residence and employment information, where last seen, and crime scene location
- *Complete investigation report of the incident:* date, time, location, type of weapon used, and detailed interviews of witnesses
- *Background of victim:* age, race, gender, physical description, marital status, lifestyle, sexual preference, medical history (physical and mental), personal habits, use of alcohol or drugs, and friends or enemies

The psychological profiling technique recognizes that hate, passion, fear, and confusion may all have certain indicators somewhere at the scene. These can include postmortem slashing or cutting, rapes, lust and mutilation murders, and so on.

Once the information is collected, the investigator analyzes the information and attempts to reconstruct the event. Techniques used are brainstorming to critique the case, use of intuition to follow hunches, and educated guessing. Profiling factors do not consist of clinical observations solely but rather a collection of investigative data from which to draw inferences about the suspect, victim, and motive of the crime.

SAFEGUARDING AGAINST MISIDENTIFICATIONS

It is common in criminal investigations for investigators to rely on eyewitness identifications. Experience and research have shown that civilian eyewitnesses can frequently prove to be unreliable observers, and erroneous identifications are often the result. A number of factors can contribute to misidentifications by eyewitnesses. For example, human perception tends to be inaccurate, especially under stress. The average citizen, untrained in observation and subjected to the stress of being a victim of or witness to a crime, is seldom able to describe a perpetrator accurately even in some cases after coming face-to-face with the individual. Also, a witness, especially one who is unsure what the perpetrator actually looked like, may be easily influenced by suggestions conveyed to him or her during the identification process. This fact was recognized in *United States v. Wade,* where the Supreme Court of the United States stated:

"The influence of improper suggestions upon identifying witnesses probably accounts for more miscarriages of justice than any other single factor. Perhaps it is responsible for more such errors than all other factors combined."[9]

Law enforcement officers can also cause misidentifications by suggestive words or conduct. The average witness, anxious to make an identification and influenced by the police officer's image as an authority figure, tends to be very sensitive to any suggestion made by the police regarding the identity of the perpetrator. Officers may, intentionally or unintentionally, convey to the witness by words or conduct that a particular person being viewed is the perpetrator.

As a result, great care must be taken by officers conducting identification sessions of any type to avoid any action that might lead to an erroneous identification. Carefully adhering to the proper identification procedures will help avoid misidentifications that may lead to unjust accusations or even erroneous convictions of innocent persons and divert the investigation away from the actual offender. In addition, even if the actual offender is caught and brought to trial, using improper identification procedures during the investigation will often cause the suppression of identification evidence at trial, resulting in dismissal of the charges or otherwise making it difficult or even impossible to convict the guilty party.

If a court determines that an identification procedure was excessively suggestive, the court may prohibit introduction of the evidence in question. It may rule that any in-court identification of the accused by the victim is inadmissible and/or suppress other evidence that was obtained as a result of an improper pre-trial identification procedure. Of course, any of these actions may result in prosecution being thwarted.

Today, in evaluating proper identification procedure, the courts will generally be concerned with whether it was suggestive. If the court finds that the procedure was suggestive, the court will then proceed to determine whether, despite the suggestiveness, the identification was reliable when considering the "totality of the circumstances."[10] The court will consider the following six factors:

1. The opportunity of the witness to view the criminal at the time of the crime.
2. The witness's degree of attention.
3. The accuracy of the witness's prior description of the criminal.
4. The level of certainty demonstrated by the witness at the confrontation.
5. The length of time between the crime and the confrontation.
6. Whether the witness was a "casual observer" or the victim of the crime.

If in view of these various factors, it appears that the identification was reliable despite the suggestiveness of the procedure, evidence of the identification will be admissible to bolster a subsequent in-court identification.

Procedures for Identification

For purposes of this chapter, identification procedures may be categorized as photo identifications, lineups, or showups. Photo identification procedures may involve the showing of one or several photographs to a witness for the purpose of obtaining an identification. In a **lineup,** eyewitnesses are presented simultaneously with a number of individuals. By contrast, in a show-up, witnesses are confronted with one suspect only.

Photo Identifications. Photo identifications may take a number of forms. If a single photo is shown to the witness, the photo identification has all of the shortcomings of the show-up (discussed below) and is generally regarded by the courts as improper and suggestive. Consequently, multiple-photo procedures are preferable. In such procedures, the photos may be shown individually, one at a time, or displayed simultaneously in a book or array. This procedure is similar to a lineup (discussed below), and virtually all of the cautions set forth for line-ups in the preceding discussion apply to multiple-photo identification procedures as well.

Specifically, the following recommendations are made regarding photo identifications in whatever fashion they are presented:

1. There should be at least six photographs.
2. The photographs should be of people who are reasonably uniform in age, height, weight, and general appearance, and of the same sex and race.
3. The photographs themselves should be similar. For example, color photographs and black-and-white photographs should not be mixed; they should be of approximately the same size and composition.
4. Mug shots should not be mixed with snapshots since they are generally recognizable as such and have an immediate tendency to "brand" an individual.
5. If mug shots are used or if the photographs otherwise include any identifying information regarding the subject of the photograph, this information should be covered so that it cannot be seen by the witness. If only some of the photos have such information, the corresponding portions of photos should be covered so that none of the photos will look different.
6. The array should not include more than one photo of the same suspect.
7. The photo array should be shown to only one witness at a time.
8. As with show-ups and lineups, no suggestive statements should be made. For example, witnesses should not be told that the suspect's photo is in the group or that someone else has already picked out one of the photos as being the criminal. Similarly, nothing should be said or done to direct the witness's attention to any particular photograph. For example, pointing to a particular photo and saying "Is this the guy?" is improper and may lead to the identification being excluded.
9. If possible, the photo array should be preserved for future reference. In fact, in some states, failure to preserve the array will lead to suppression of the identification process. Additionally, full details about the identification process should be recorded and preserved. Assuming that the photo identification has been properly conducted and that the array itself was not in any way suggestive, preserving this information helps the prosecution refute any claims by the defense to the contrary.

The proper use of photographs to obtain identification of a perpetrator has been approved by the courts.[11] However, the courts appear to prefer that photo

Figure 5.18 The photo "lineup" must be conducted to avoid any suggestiveness.

identification procedures be used only to develop investigative leads. Some courts have criticized the practice of using photo identifications once the suspect has been arrested, preferring that once the suspect is in custody, and therefore readily available, a lineup be employed for eyewitness identification.[12]

Lineups.   The lineup, if properly conducted, is significantly less suggestive than the show-up and hence is generally far preferable. Nevertheless, police officers conducting a lineup must use caution to avoid suggestive influences. Studies of witness psychology reveal that lineup witnesses tend to believe that the guilty party must be one of the individuals in the lineup. Consequently, witnesses tend to pick out the person in the lineup who most closely resembles their perception of the perpetrator, even though the perpetrator is not in fact present.

In addition, it is possible that witnesses, in an effort to please the police officers conducting the lineup, feel obligated to pick out someone from the lineup rather than "disappoint" the officers.[13]Such witnesses are often sensitive to, and strongly influenced by, clever clues conveyed by the officers that may indicate to the witness that the officer believes that a particular individual in the lineup is the perpetrator. This makes it even more important that officers conduct the lineup—and their own behavior—in a nonsuggestive manner.

Preparing for a lineup may be as important to the validity of the procedure as actually conducting it. Selecting individuals for the lineup is a particularly important issue. In determining which individuals are to be presented to the witnesses in a lineup, the following principles should be observed:

1. *The lineup should consist of individuals of similar physical characteristics.*
   Witnesses tend to pick out anyone who stands out from the rest of the group

in any significant way. Therefore, the individuals who appear in the lineup should be reasonably similar with respect to age; height; weight; hair color, length and style; facial hair; clothing; and other characteristics such as glasses. Of course, the individuals must be of the same race and sex. Absolute uniformity of the lineup participants is obviously unattainable and is not procedurally necessary.[14]

2. *The lineup should consist of at least five or six persons.* The smaller the lineup, the less objective it is. A lineup with only two or three persons is little better than a show-up, and suggestive factors become excessively influential. As a result, most authorities recommend that at least five, preferably six, persons be in the lineup. In addition, some authorities caution against the use of plainclothes police officers in lineups because they do not naturally look or act like suspects, a factor that causes witnesses to reject them as possibilities.

Preparing a witness for viewing the lineup is another important consideration. Preparation should be limited to nonsuggestive statements, such as explaining the procedure that will be used and making it clear that the individuals in the lineup will be unable to see him or her. Officers should avoid taking any action or making any statement that will adversely affect the validity of the lineup. In particular, before a lineup, officers should avoid:

1. Showing the witness any photos of the suspect.[15]

2. Conducting a show-up with the suspect or allowing the witness—accidentally or otherwise—to see the suspect, such as in an office or holding cell, prior to the lineup.

3. Making suggestive statements to the witness, such as telling the witness that the person whom the police suspect will be in the lineup. It is even desirable to tell the witness that the perpetrator may not be among those in the lineup. Other common errors that should be avoided include telling the witness that another witness has identified someone in the same lineup, advising the witness to take special notice of some particular individual in the lineup, or making any other statement or action which may cause the witness to focus on a particular individual or to feel that the witness must pick out somebody.

Finally, if more than one witness is to view a lineup, the witnesses should be kept separated prior to the lineup and should not be permitted to discuss the case with each other, compare descriptions, and so forth.

In conducting the lineup, officers who are not assigned to that case should handle the procedure if possible. This helps to minimize the possibility that the officers who are conducting the investigation will, in their zeal to solve the case, convey (inadvertently or otherwise) clues to the witness as to which person to pick out or put pressure on the witness to pick out somebody. The following should also be observed in conducting lineups:

1. *Statements that put pressure on the witness to make an identification should be avoided.* Witnesses are anxious to please the officers conducting the lineup, so they should not be made to feel that they are expected to pick out someone. For example, telling a witness that the person the police suspect is in the lineup or urging the hesitant witness to make an identification or to "try harder" would be improper.

2. *Statements that may cause the witness to focus on a particular individual should be avoided.* The same sort of statements discussed in regard to witness preparation should be avoided during the actual conduct of the lineup. Officers are often tempted to prompt a witness when someone in the lineup is a prime suspect and the witness is hesitant to make an identification. Statements such as "What about the second guy from the right?" or "Take another look at the one in the middle" are so suggestive that they will, if challenged by the defense attorney, almost certainly result in any subsequent identification being suppressed by the court.

3. *The lineup should be presented to one witness at a time.* The common practice of having a group of witnesses view a lineup simultaneously should not be permitted. Courts, including the U.S. Supreme Court,[16] have disapproved multiple-witness lineups. If for some reason, more than one witness must be present simultaneously, witnesses should be required to make their identifications silently, in writing, and should not be permitted to discuss the identification aloud with each other or with the officers present.

4. *If possible, conduct a "blank" lineup.* Conducting two or more lineups, where one lineup includes the suspect and the others do not, assists the prosecution in later refuting any claim by the defense that the lineup was too small or was suggestive.

5. *If multiple lineups are to be conducted for the same witnesses, do not put the suspect in more than one.* Seeing the same face in a second lineup may cause the witness to erroneously "recognize" the person as the perpetrator, merely because the face is familiar from the first lineup. Because of this, the courts have disapproved this practice.[17]

In another context, the U.S. Supreme Court has held that requiring a suspect participating in a lineup to speak, even to the extent of uttering the same words used by the criminal, does not violate the Fifth Amendment, since it is not "testimonial self-incrimination." Other actions, such as standing, walking, gesturing, and the like, are similarly not self-incrimination within the meaning of the Fifth Amendment. Similarly, requiring the suspect to wear certain clothing has been held to be outside of the coverage of the Fifth Amendment.

Following the lineup, certain precautions should be taken. For example, where more than one witness has viewed a lineup, witnesses should be kept separate after the lineup procedure has been completed. While discussions between witnesses following a lineup will presumably not render any previously made identification invalid, it may affect the admissibility of a subsequent in-court identification of the defendant by these witnesses during the trial itself.

Additionally, witnesses should not be praised or congratulated for picking out the suspect. This may serve to reinforce a shaky identification, convincing the witness that he or she has picked out the actual perpetrator when the witness is in some doubt. In addition to increasing the chances of a miscarriage of justice, this may lead to suppression of a later in-court identification of the perpetrator by the same witness.

Show-ups. The show-up has been widely condemned by the courts and by experts in law, law enforcement, and law enforcement identification procedures.[18] Whereas the courts have not held show-ups to be categorically improper, they have ruled that the determination of whether a specific show-up was excessively suggestive will be made based on the "totality of the circumstances" attending that particular show-up. In practice, evidence deriving from show-ups is frequently suppressed because the show-up is so inherently suggestive that it is virtually impossible to eliminate suggestion from the procedure.

Consequently, the use of show-ups should be avoided whenever possible. Only where exigent circumstances make it absolutely necessary should this technique be employed. Where it must be employed, certain guidelines should be followed to minimize the **suggestiveness** of the procedure and the risk of suppression of any resultant identification evidence.

Show-ups conducted in the station house or jail are the most unreliable and hence the most objectionable. When used, station house show-ups should, at a minimum, be subject to the following guidelines:

1. Show-ups should not be conducted when the suspect is in a cell, manacled, or dressed in jail clothing.

2. Show-ups should not be conducted at a late hour.

3. Show-ups should not be conducted with more than one witness present at a time. If show-ups are conducted separately for multiple witnesses, the witnesses should not be permitted to communicate before or after the show-up regarding the identification of the suspect.

4. The same suspect should not be presented to the same witness more than once.

5. Show-up suspects should not be required to put on clothing worn by the perpetrator, to speak words uttered by the perpetrator, or to perform other actions mimicking those performed by the actual perpetrator.[19]

6. Words or conduct by the police that may suggest to the witness that the individual is or may be the perpetrator should be scrupulously avoided. For example, one should never tell the witness that the individual was apprehended near the crime scene, that the evidence points to the individual as the perpetrator, or that other witnesses have identified the individual as the perpetrator. Unfortunately, the mere fact that the individual has been presented to the witness for identification strongly suggests that the officers believe him to be the guilty party.

Even when these guidelines are followed, it is entirely possible that a court may suppress the resulting evidence on the grounds that no amount of care can eliminate suggestion, and hence unreliability, from the procedure.

Yet, exigent circumstances may justify the use of show-ups in certain instances. For example, in certain instances, a station house show-up may be tolerated by the courts if it can be demonstrated that time or other factors prevented the police from arranging a proper lineup. However, the reasons for not taking the time to prepare and conduct a lineup must be substantial and reasonably explained. Even then, they may not be accepted by the courts.

Exigent circumstances may also justify a show-up in the field. A show-up conducted shortly after the commission of the offense and in reasonable proximity to the crime scene may be tolerated by courts. The court may recognize that the realities of the situation often make it vital that a witness view a suspect immediately, at or near the scene. Courts have noted that this procedure has potential advantages both for the suspect and for the police. If the identification is negative, it will result in the freeing of the suspect and permit the officers to devote their time and attention to other leads. If the identification is positive, the police can focus their attention on the identified suspect. Consequently, some courts are more willing to tolerate this type of show-up.

The Right to Counsel at Eyewitness Identifications

In 1967, the Supreme Court of the United States held that a suspect has a right to counsel at a postindictment lineup.[20]Subsequently, the Court expanded this ruling to provide for a right to counsel at any lineup conducted after formal adversary proceedings have been initiated against the suspect, whether by way of formal charge, preliminary hearing, indictment, information, or arraignment.[21] There is, however, no right to have counsel present at a lineup conducted before such adversary proceedings have been initiated. These same rules apply to show-ups. However, there is no right to counsel at photo identification sessions.[22]The purpose of having counsel present at the identification is to enable counsel to detect any suggestiveness or other irregularities in the procedure. It should be recognized, however, that the presence-of-counsel requirement may actually help the police in certain instances. First, the department's goal should be to avoid any possibility of an erroneous identification and a resultant miscarriage of justice. Therefore, the presence of counsel may be regarded as a positive step in preventing any such occurrence. In addition, if counsel is present and acquiesces in the procedure being employed, this may preclude any subsequent defense contention that suggestiveness or other impropriety occurred. This will strengthen the prosecution's case. Therefore, to the extent that defense counsel is responsible and objective, cooperation with counsel in constructing and conducting a nonsuggestive and otherwise proper identification procedure may benefit all concerned.

Of all investigative procedures employed by police in criminal cases, probably none is less reliable than the eyewitness identification. Erroneous identifications create more injustice and cause more suffering to innocent persons than perhaps any other aspect of police work. Proper precautions must be followed by officers if they are to use eyewitness identifications effectively and accurately.

DISCUSSION QUESTIONS

1. In what ways were fingerprints historically first used?

2. Discuss the three types of fingerprints and how they differ.

3. Review the various ways of locating and identifying fingerprints at a crime scene.

4. Discuss the new role that IAFIS fingerprinting technology offers the field of criminal investigation and identification.

5. To what extent has DNA technology improved methods of criminal identification?

6. Discuss the significance of recent court rulings addressing the admissibility of DNA evidence in the courtroom.

7. Explain the procedure recommended for collecting a handwriting sample from a suspect.

8. Discuss the value of the composite sketch in identifying a criminal suspect.

9. Discuss the method of conducting a photo lineup.

NOTES

1. U.S. DEPARTMENT OF JUSTICE DRUG ENFORCEMENT ADMINISTRATION (1987). *Intelligence collection and analytical methods. Training manual.* Washington, DC: U.S. Government Printing Office.
2. Source: FBI.gov (2006).
3. SAFERSTEIN, R. (1990). *Criminalistics: An introduction to forensic science.* Upper Saddle River, NJ: Prentice Hall.
4. Ibid.
5. U.S. OFFICE OF TECHNOLOGY ASSESSMENT (1990). *Genetic witness: Forensic use of DNA tests.* Washington, DC: U.S. Congress.
6. SCHEFTER, J. (1994). DNA fingerprints on trial. *Popular Science,* November, p. 64.
7. SAFERSTEIN, R. (1990). *Criminalistics: An introduction to forensic science.* Upper Saddle River, NJ: Prentice Hall.
8. STRENTZ, T. (1988). A terrorist psychological profile: Past and present. *FBI Law Enforcement Bulletin,* April, pp. 13–19.
9. *United States v. Wade,* 388 U.S. 218, 229 (1967).
10. *Neil v. Biggers,* 409 U.S. 188 (1972). See also *Manson v. Brathwaite,* 432 U.S. 98 (1977). (*Biggers* test applied to photo identifications).
11. *Simmons v. United States,* 390 U.S. 377 (1968).
12. Once a witness has identified a photo, subsequent identifications may be influenced. The contention is that the witness thereafter is really only recognizing the previously seen photograph, not the actual criminal. For this reason, the practice of showing a witness a photograph of the defendant just prior to trial to "refresh the witness's memory" should be avoided.
13. Although it may surprise many officers to hear it, the average citizen still sees the police officer as a benevolent "father-figure" (or perhaps, in the case of a female officer, a "mother-figure"), with the result that the lineup witness is often extremely anxious to please the officer by making an identification—even though the citizen is not at all certain that the person chosen is the guilty party.
14. *U.S. v. Lewis,* 547 F.2d 1030, 1035 (8th Cir. 1976).
15. Even a photo array should be avoided. This is especially true if the suspect is the only person in the photo array who is also in the lineup.
16. See *Gilbert v. California,* 388 U.S. 263 (1967).
17. See *Foster v. California,* 394 U.S. 440 (1969).
18. See *Stovall v. Denno,* 388 U.S. 293 (1967).
19. Although such requirements sometimes may properly be imposed during a lineup, the show-up is so inherently suggestive that the same court that would approve their use in a lineup may find them excessively suggestive when employed during a show-up.
20. *United States v. Wade,* 388 U.S. 218 (1967), *Gilbert v. California,* 388 U.S. 263 (1967).
21. *Kirby v. Illinois,* 406 U.S. 682, 688-89 (1972).
22. *U.S. v. Ask,* 413 U.S. 300 (1973). At least one state supreme court has held that where simulated lineups are filmed or videotaped for later exhibition, there is no right to have counsel present when the film or videotape is subsequently shown to witnesses, *People v. Lawrence,* 481 P.2d 212 (1971). Showing witnesses a film or tape of a previously recorded simulated lineup has become known as a "Lawrence lineup."

6 The Criminal Intelligence Function

Key Terms

▶ analysis
▶ closed files
▶ collation
▶ covert information collection
▶ dissemination
▶ flowcharting
▶ intelligence gathering
▶ link analysis
▶ open files
▶ overt information collection
▶ RISS projects
▶ strategic intelligence
▶ tactical intelligence

This chapter will enable you to:

- Understand the role of criminal intelligence.
- Learn about the various types of intelligence.
- Consider the role of the police intelligence unit.
- Identify the procedures of intelligence collection.
- Understand the different types of criminal activity focused on in the intelligence investigation.
- Explain the types of flowcharting used in intelligence-gathering operations.
- Learn the role of the federally funded Regional Information Sharing Systems (RISS) projects.

INTRODUCTION

The collection of criminal intelligence is another important function of the criminal investigative process, and one that has resulted in significant identification and arrest of major crime figures. Illustrating the importance of the intelligence function, leading expert in the field of terrorism and counterterrorist tactics Brian Jenkins made an argument regarding the need for developing criminal intelligence when he notes that:

> [P]hysical measures don't reduce terrorism—they only move the threat along. Society cannot invest enough resources to protect everything, everywhere, all the time. Someone wanting to set off a bomb in Manhattan to kill scores of people can do it. And reducing terrorism has nothing to do with access control or how thick you make the concrete wall. It requires going after the terrorists and taking their groups apart.[1]

Unfortunately, from a national level, the United States apparently lacks the intelligence capabilities necessary to adequately combat terrorism according to a major interagency study of federal capabilities and defenses. The 73-page report, commissioned by the U.S. Justice Department, pinpoints a lack of intelligence sharing on domestic terrorists as a significant problem and added that

> the single most significant deficiency in the nation's ability to combat terrorism is a lack of information, particularly regarding domestic terrorism.[2]

While the above deals specifically with domestic and international terrorism, the same observations hold true with regard to the prevention and interdiction of many other serious crimes. An effort to identify criminal groups and the persons who participate in and control them requires a systematic approach to information collection and analysis. Intelligence within the law enforcement context, whether of a tactical or strategic nature, refers to the collection, collation, evaluation, analysis, and dissemination for use of information relating to criminal or suspected criminal activities of a wide variety. Development of a systematic approach to this function within police agencies is essential in order to put what may otherwise be scattered—or even unrecorded—information and data to use in a constructive and concerted manner.

The History of Intelligence Collection

The collection of information for intelligence purposes has a long history. For hundreds of years, governments and their military forces have engaged in various activities to obtain intelligence about individuals and groups viewed as threatening. Although the origins of intelligence gathering by the police in the United States are difficult to determine, it appears that the intelligence function was first carried out by large-city police departments when immigrants first concentrated in urban centers of this country. Nationality groups thought to be threatening by virtue of their suspected involvement in vice, narcotics, racketeering, and organized criminal activities were singled out as the primary target of police intelligence efforts.

The intelligence operations of federal, state, and local police agencies shifted focus over the decades based on perceived needs and threats. For example, during Prohibition, intelligence operations concentrated on crimes directly and indirectly related to alcohol smuggling and sales and its connections to organized crime. In the post–World War II era, intelligence was used to gather information on suspected Communist organizations, and during the Vietnam War period, it shifted more toward information gathering on political activists and dissidents, civil rights demonstrators, and antiwar protesters. Intelligence operations have long been used to aid in monitoring and building information on organized crime operations and are still widely used in this manner, although their focus has expanded to include the involvement of international conspiracies involved in drug trafficking. Most recently, intelligence operations have been directed at countering the threat of domestic and international terrorism. Considering the bombings of the World Trade Center (2001) and the federal building in Oklahoma City (1995), and the continued threat of terrorist activities, the need for law enforcement intelligence operations has become even more apparent.

Pitfalls of Intelligence Gathering

While intelligence plays a key role in law enforcement operations, history tells us that it can also be the instrument of abuse if such operations are not properly organized, focused, and directed. Aggressive intelligence gathering operations that resemble fishing expeditions have been employed improperly in the past to garner sensitive or confidential information on individuals for whom there is no reasonable suspicion of criminal activity. Once documented, such information can develop a life of its own if sufficient safeguards are not built into screening, reviewing, and managing intelligence files. If passed on to other law enforcement agencies as intelligence, it can form the basis for abuse of civil liberties and potential civil liability.

In the same manner, intelligence operations are misguided that directly or indirectly gather information on persons based solely on their dissident political activities or views, because they espouse positions or philosophies that are perceived to threaten conventional social or political doctrines, traditionally accepted social mores, or similar societal values or institutions. Use of law enforcement intelligence resources to intimidate, inhibit, or suppress such activities under the pretext of legitimate police concern for maintaining social order is at best misguided and, in the worst case scenario, constitutes a threat to the principles of law enforcement in a democratic society.

The Usefulness of Intelligence

It is important to have an understanding and appreciation of potential abuses of criminal intelligence operations in order that intelligence gathering can be properly directed and information thus collected properly controlled and managed. That said, it is also important to reemphasize the indispensable role that criminal intelligence plays in support of law enforcement and the ultimate protection of society. Even though the Justice Department report is no doubt accurate in its assessment that this nation's intelligence resources are lacking in many regards, particularly with respect to the new threats of chemical, biological, and nuclear terrorists, it tends to overlook many of its successes.

This is probably nowhere better illustrated than in the efforts of local, state, and federal agencies in thwarting international and domestic terrorism in the United States. Though the World Trade Center bombing and the Oklahoma City bombing stand out in our collective memories, they are exceptions to the norm. It is worth noting that as devastating as these were, we often miss the fact that many attacks of a similar or even a potentially more devastating nature have been thwarted largely through the development and use of criminal intelligence.

The United States has been fortunate to avoid serious terrorist attacks within its borders, but much of that is attributable to the efforts of intelligence resources. The vast majority of such incidents against the United States have been limited to attacks against U.S. interests abroad. The largest percentage of terrorist attacks in this country are bombings by special interest groups perpetrated against commercial establishments located in urban areas, such as the Animal Liberation Front, Up the IRS, and the Earth Night Action Group. Organizations such as these and right-wing groups such as the Aryan Nation, the Order, and Posse Comitatus are among the more threatening. At the same time, left-wing terrorist groups, such as the Marxist-oriented United Freedom Front, have been generally inactive since the 1980s due in part to the extensive number of arrests of group leaders during the last decade, largely serving as a credit to good intelligence operations.

Organized crime that has traditionally occupied a great deal of the focus of intelligence operations, while still a prominent threat, has experienced serious setbacks over recent years due largely to effective intelligence gathering operations and aggressive prosecution.

But domestic and international terrorism and organized crime are certainly not the only focus of criminal intelligence operations for state and local law enforcement agencies. State and local law enforcement share in the responsibility to counter these threats. Their input into regional and national intelligence databases is essential to this effort.

But state and local law enforcement agencies also are concerned with more provincial criminal matters. Defining these local criminal enforcement objectives and priorities forms the basis for needed information required to drive the intelligence function of individual agencies. Information gathering by individual officers is at the heart of any intelligence operation. Without the input of the officer on the beat, the generation of intelligence that can be returned to these officers for strategic and tactical purposes is not possible. Support of the agency's intelligence function is, therefore, the responsibility of every law enforcement officer who provides necessary information to fuel the process. And, if raw information provides the indispensable material to fuel the intelligence function, a professionally organized system of information evaluation, collation, analysis, and dissemination is the refinement process that turns this raw information into useful products in support of law enforcement operations.

Intelligence, even the best of intelligence, does not produce decisions. Decisions on the use of law enforcement manpower and resources are made by command personnel who use intelligence constructively within the context of their professional experience. But, without good intelligence to point the way and weigh the options, law enforcement executives are at a serious disadvantage.

OVERT AND COVERT INTELLIGENCE COLLECTION

Overt information collection includes personal interaction with people, many of whom are witnesses to crimes, victims of crimes, or the suspects themselves. To best facilitate the overt collection process, agency administrators should require officers from all divisions to document any information on suspected criminal activity and to pass such information on to intelligence officers. The patrol division can be especially instrumental in the overt intelligence collection process by noting any activity around residences or businesses operated by major criminals in the area. Findings should be reported on a special intelligence report form and forwarded to the proper investigators.

Covert information collection is the most common and includes a process known as **intelligence gathering.** This is a process of data collection on criminal acts that have not yet occurred but for which the investigator must prepare. Covert intelligence collection methods employ the use of physical surveillance, electronic surveillance, informants, and undercover officers. In this chapter, we discuss both the intelligence collection functions of criminal investigation and techniques for obtaining information through interviews and interrogation.

CRIMINAL INTELLIGENCE AND CRIMINAL INVESTIGATION

The process of intelligence gathering originated as a function of the military but has now expanded to include "criminal" intelligence as it applies to domestic law enforcement. Despite its technological and scientific advancements, criminal intelligence gathering is one of the least understood aspects of criminal investigation. Additionally, it is probably one of the most valuable (yet underused) resources of the police function.

Defining Criminal Intelligence

To set the pace for this chapter, we should first attempt to define the term *criminal intelligence.* According to the federally funded RISS projects (discussed later in this chapter), criminal intelligence is defined as knowledge of past, present, or future criminal activity that results from the collection of information which, when evaluated, provides the user with a basis for rational decision making.[3] Many law enforcement agencies assign sworn personnel to the criminal intelligence division. However, many departments have difficulty adequately defining the mission of the intelligence unit or the tasks of officers working within it, and therefore officers often conduct multiple duties within the unit. Some of these duties are not relevant to the intelligence collection objective. In a practical sense, because it serves the department by delivering information to line personnel, the role of intelligence personnel is more of a staff than a line function. Officers may therefore experience difficulty adjusting to their staff-related duties.

Technically, the role of intelligence personnel is to deliver information to line personnel. To absolve any confusion about the differences between the criminal intelligence function and the criminal investigation function, the four fundamental differences between the two are discussed next.

1. Criminal investigations are usually reactive in nature. Intelligence gathering, conversely, is a proactive function.
2. Criminal investigators generally work with deductive logic. This works by a logical progression through a sequence of events—the general to the specific. An example would be collecting evidence from the crime scene, interviewing any witnesses, checking a suspect's criminal records, and so on.

Figure 6.1 Intelligence files should only be accessed on a "need to know" basis.

Intelligence unit personnel, conversely, exercise inductive logic. This affords them the luxury of beginning with the specific and expanding to the general.

3. Investigation case files are generally considered **open files.** They contain information developed for the purpose of eventually making an arrest and gaining a conviction in a court of law.

    In comparison, intelligence files are **closed files.** They contain information regarding ongoing criminal activity, but much of this information has not been verified as factual (Figure 6.1).

4. Intelligence files must therefore be maintained apart from criminal investigation files to prevent unauthorized inspection of data. The successful culmination of a criminal investigation is the arrest or conviction of a suspect in a crime. Successful intelligence operations are gauged by the cataloging of an intelligence product.

Types of Intelligence

The distinction between the different types of intelligence is often unclear, as various methods are commonly employed by different departments. To understand best the most common types of intelligence—strategic and tactical—the following definitions will be considered:

1. **Strategic intelligence** plays a role in the investigation of crimes by providing the investigator with a tool for long-range planning. Simply stated, it provides the investigator with information as to the capabilities and intentions of target subjects. Strategic intelligence has proved most useful in organizing long-range plans for interdiction in areas of criminal activity over extended periods.

| CITY POLICE DEPARTMENT | File: |
| **INTELLIGENCE REPORT** | Date: |

SUBJECT: (Name and any identifying numbers)

SOURCE IDENTIFICATION:
Private Citizen ☐   (Name or Number) _____
Criminal Source ☐
Govt. Agency   ☐   Personal Knowledge☐ Documents☐ Hearsay/Rumor☐ Hypothesis☐
Law Officer   ☐   Other _____

EVALUATION OF SOURCE:
Highly Reliable ☐   Usually Reliable ☐   Reliability Questionable ☐   Unevaluated ☐

BY:

INFORMATION CONTENT: **INFORMATION FILES CHECKED:**
Partially Verified ☐   State Criminal Record ☐   Similar Info.
Unverified ☐   State Driver's License ☐   In File No. _____
Verified ☐   NCIC ☐
                              Other _____

RECOMMENDED FOLLOW-UP:
Investigator to Verify ☐   Source to Verify ☐   Analyst to Research ☐   File Only ☐

DISSEMINATION:

Figure 6.2 Intelligence report.

2. **Tactical intelligence** targets criminal activity considered to be of immediate importance to the investigator. Specifically, tactical intelligence furnishes the police agency with specifics about individuals, organizations, and different types of criminal activity.

PROCEDURES FOR INTELLIGENCE GATHERING

The intelligence collection process should be thought of as a process of connecting a series of interrelated components of information. Failure on the part of the investigator to connect any of these components adequately could jeopardize the success of the investigation. Therefore, everyone associated with the collection process must have a keen understanding of the entire intelligence function and its various components. The intelligence function includes target selection, data collection, data collation and analysis, and dissemination.

Phase 1: Target Selection

Target selection is the first phase of the process (Figure 6.3). To obtain the greatest success, intelligence targets must be selected in a systematic manner. They may be based entirely on the utility, or size, of the target or available resources of the department. Factors for investigators to consider in selection of a suitable target include the following:

- Does this target conform to the unit's goals and objectives?
- Does the department (unit) have sufficient resources for the operation?
- What is the expected value of the target?

FACTORS TO CONSIDER IN SELECTION OF SUITABLE INTELLIGENCE TARGETS

1. *Utility.* This is the worth of the successful result. If the desired information is collected, how valuable is the result? In determining target utility, consider the following:

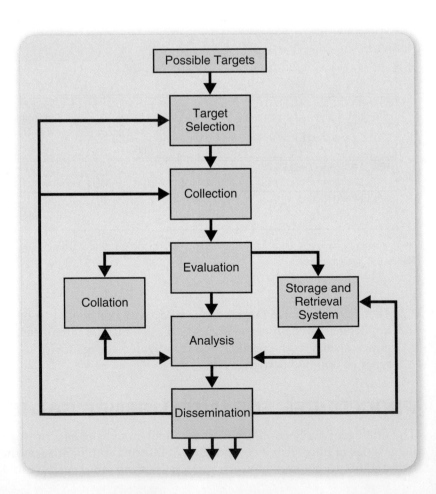

Figure 6.3 Intelligence target selection.

- Type of criminal activity
- Amount and frequency of criminal activity
- Impact of criminal activity

2. *Probability of success.* What are the chances of success with this target? In determining probability of success, consider:
   - Amount of effort to be expended
   - Experience and expertise of the intelligence unit personnel
   - Past success rate in similar operations
   - Availability of sources of information

3. *Required resources.* What resources are required to collect the desired information? When determining resources, consider the following:
   - Personnel hours—the primary required resource
   - Equipment
   - Confidential funds
   - Travel expenses
   - Amount of time required

4. *Objective.* The primary objective of selecting a target is to guarantee that intelligence efforts are focused toward targets that are an acceptable balance to merit or value, probability of a successful result, and resources used.

Phase 2: Data Collection

Collection of criminal information is the hallmark of the intelligence function and may be done either overtly, covertly, or as a combination of both. Written policy should dictate exactly what types of information may or may not be gathered. Because the collection of both personal and sensitive information on individuals could be a high-liability issue for some communities, great care is warranted by the police agency. Generally, intelligence information regarding any suspected criminal activity can be gathered, such as the following:

- Drug trafficking
- Extortion
- Pornography
- Fraud
- Bribery
- Robbery
- Murder
- Gambling
- Prostitution
- Labor racketeering
- Fencing
- Burglary
- Forgery

In addition:

- Organizations that advocate the use of violence or other unlawful means to affect any unit of government.
- Organizations that possess or attempt to control shipments of arms, explosives, or controlled chemicals or biological weapons for unlawful purposes.
- Organizations that finance violent or unlawful activity.

- Organizations whose actions constitute unlawful activity targeted toward other organizations or individuals.
- Leaders of organizations such as those above.

Information should not be gathered merely because of a person's membership in organizations unless such organizations meet the criteria set forth previously and are found to present a clear and present danger to society. Under no circumstances should information be gathered solely on the basis of race, creed, color, national origin, sexual preference, or political or religious beliefs. Once information is obtained, intelligence units are faced with the problem of maintaining a storage and retrieval system so that the information can become available when needed. Generally, this is done with a computer, but many departments prefer to rely on index cards as a simplified and more secure system. Information to be cataloged may originate from many different sources:

1. Information from investigators assigned to the intelligence unit.
2. Information from nonintelligence departments of the agency. For example:
   - Offense reports
   - Arrest records
   - Field interrogation reports
   - Identification photographs
   - Fingerprint files
   - Warrant files
   - Traffic records
3. Information from other federal, state, and local jurisdictions.
4. Information from sources other than law enforcement organizations. For example:
   - Newspapers
   - Trial records
   - Telephone companies
   - Public utilities
   - Credit agencies
   - Banks
   - Professional associations
   - Insurance companies

Phase 3: Data Collation and Analysis

The third phase in the procedure is the information collation process. *Webster's Dictionary* defines **collation** as "the process of comparing texts carefully" to clarify or give meaning to information. One example of collation is taking a deck of playing cards and arranging them into four piles, one pile for each suit, and in numerical order. Many different techniques are used by intelligence analysts to accomplish this function. These include linked data charts, different types of flowcharts, frequency distribution charts, and so on. Many of these are discussed later in the chapter. Following the collation of raw information is the analysis chase. This is the heart of any intelligence system, the procedure in which meaning is given to all of the otherwise fragmented parts of data collected. The analytical process involves data integration and clarification, inference development, inference testing, and finalizing inferences that are relevant and meaningful to the user (the intelligence product).

Phase 4: Dissemination

The **dissemination** stage of the intelligence process is the final stage, in which the process most commonly breaks down. As one intelligence analyst once remarked: "Possessing good intelligence information is like possessing gold nuggets because everybody wants as much as they can get but nobody wants to share what they have." Unless intelligence is shared through the law enforcement community in an interagency fashion, all of the effort and expense of collecting it could become meaningless. Most law enforcement agencies have strict guidelines, however, as to the release of information (e.g., who gets what information).

ANALYZING THE INFORMATION

The purpose of **analysis** is to make fragmented information flow in a logical sequence to make it purposeful to the user, such as taking a group of surveillance reports and arranging them in the order in which they occurred, to determine primary suspects, locations most frequented, vehicles driven, and so on. Intelligence gathering can be problematic in and of itself. For example, when officers are working with large amounts of information regarding individuals and organizations, the sources of that information may be varied and unorganized and can include confidential informants, surveillance reports, police reports, investigative reports, and so on.

Link Analysis

To make sense out of the multitudes of information, a process known as *data description and integration* is used. Accordingly, one of the most common methods of data description and integration is link analysis. **Link analysis** charting is a technique designed to show relationships between individuals and organizations using a graphical visual design (Figure 6.4). It is used to show graphically transactions or relationships that are too large and confusing for one to assimilate through the reading of reports.

There are several ways to illustrate this type of collation technique suitably. In all cases, the investigator must follow certain mechanical rules for the structure of the diagram. These include:

- Assembly of raw data (usually from a report).
- Selection of certain data points, such as names of individuals or organizations.
- Construction of a collation matrix showing the data points.
- Entry of the association points on the matrix.
- Tabulation of the number of association points on the matrix.
- Designation of the types of relationships by drawing different types of lines from one association point to another (usually accomplished by drawing dotted lines, solid lines, etc.).
- Relationship of individuals to organizations by constructing circles for individuals and boxes for businesses.

The Role of the Intelligence Analyst

- To guide data collection
- To suggest operational recommendations
- To provide information to decision makers
- To assume a position of noninvolvement in policy formation

Figure 6.4 Hypothetical link analysis chart.

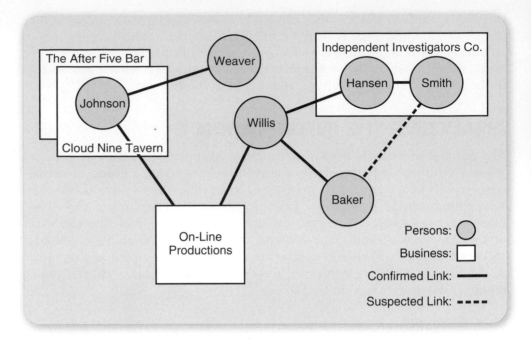

- Examination of final diagram and recommendation(s) regarding a course of action.

To illustrate the process of link analysis, consider the following scenario as if it were information from a surveillance report. The objective should be to determine the most appropriate target. Johnson and Taylor are longtime close associates and were cell mates in the Missouri State Prison in 1996. Every Tuesday during the month of October, Johnson met with Stephens at the Playboy Lounge for lunch. Public records reveal that Johnson is the sole owner of Equity Auto Sales. Taylor and Mullen are both employed at Tiger Beverage Company and have been observed on numerous occasions riding to work together.

On November 3, Johnson met Washington in the South Park Shopping Center parking lot at 3:00 P.M. and both sat in Washington's car for approximately 1 1/2 hours. After Johnson left, Washington drove to Anderson's residence. There, Anderson entered Washington's vehicle and they drove away. The surveillance team lost them approximately two miles from Anderson's residence, due to heavy traffic. Two hours later, Washington and Anderson returned to Anderson's residence and both went inside. On three separate occasions, Taylor has been seen with an unidentified male believed to be Stephens. "Pen register" records from Mullen's telephone reveal that several calls were made each day to Equity Auto Sales. The relationships in which each of the suspects is involved may reveal who is the most appropriate target. One can see how the method of link analysis can aid in an understanding of complex raw criminal information.

Flowcharting

Flowcharting is another common technique used in the data description and integration phase. Unlike the "frozen" nature of the link analysis diagram, the flowchart demonstrates a chain of events or activities over a period. Although use of flowcharts is not as common as link analysis, two types of flowcharts have emerged as the most useful in criminal intelligence collection: *event flow analysis* and *commodity flow analysis*. Both types of analysis give investigators a graphic display of a series of events that might be too complex if read in a report. There are no hard-and-fast rules regarding the construction of flow-charts; therefore, the analyst should try to maintain a degree of consistency throughout the chart regarding the symbols used.

Event Flow Analysis. Event flow analysis is usually conducted early in an investigation. Examples of flow analysis include charting a brief description of an event enclosed in a symbolic area such as a circle or rectangle (Figure 6.5). As different events are documented, they are connected by arrows to indicate the direction of the sequence. Consider the following scenario and observe how the information from a reliable informant can best be portrayed by using the event flowchart: Kevin Johnson is a local businessman in town and owns three small businesses. On August 12, Johnson's Deli burned to the ground and another of his stores, the Barbecue Shack, was vandalized. Later that night Johnson's convenience store was bombed. Although Johnson couldn't say for sure who the perpetrator might be, he noted that he had recently fired a 34-year-old part-time employee who had threatened Johnson as he left the property. This firing took place one week prior to the problems with the stores.

Commodity Flow Analysis. Commodity flow analysis may greatly simplify the investigative process by charting the logical flow of such commodities as drugs, money, and illegal arms shipments (Figure 6.6). For example, in a drug distribution network, if money can be traced from its origin to certain key individuals, an investigation will probably result in an arrest and conviction. This is particularly useful when the main drug kingpins don't typically possess the drugs themselves.

The structure of a commodity flowchart is generally the same as that of the event flowchart except that rather than descriptions of events being placed in circles or rectangles, persons or businesses are used. A scenario follows in which commodity flowcharting might best be used. Study this information from an investigation report and observe how the resulting flowchart illustrates and clarifies the facts and circumstances of the case.

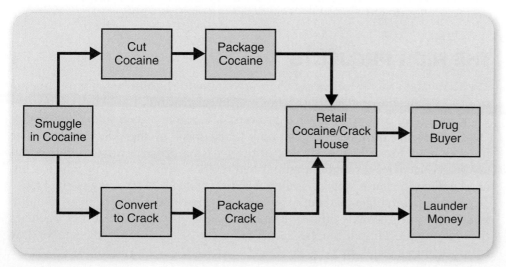

Figure 6.5 Hypothetical event flow analysis chart.

Figure 6.6 Hypothetical commodity flowchart.

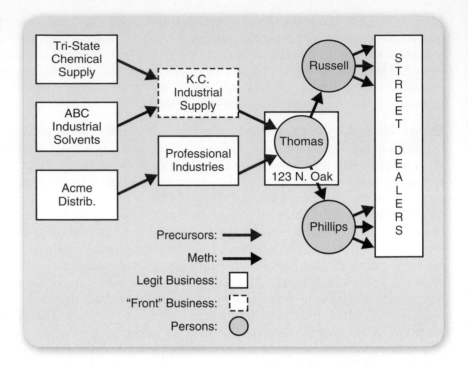

Eddie Jaso purchased cocaine weekly from Sharon Martin. Jaso paid Martin about $20,000 per week on average. Undercover narcotics agents observed Jaso, along with Mario Barbisca and Timothy Freisen, selling cocaine to several known drug users at a local mall video arcade on several occasions over a period of a month. Records seized during a search of room 32 of the Bradford Hotel showed this location to be a trafficking site for drugs. The hotel's catering department served as a cover for the cocaine distribution network. Seized records also showed payments of about $40,000 per week each from Barbisca and Freisen to the catering department. Records revealed a monthly average of $300,000 in payments to Leonard Smith for various "supplies." Smith, a close associate of Freisen for the past two years, makes monthly deposits of about $500,000 to his accounts at Central Savings and Loan. He also makes large withdrawals on occasion. Both Smith and Freisen have records for drug trafficking.

THE RISS PROJECTS

The RISS (Regional Information Sharing Systems) Program began with funding from the Law Enforcement Assistance Administration (LEAA) discretionary grant program. Since 1980, **RISS projects** have been placed under the Justice Department and have been funded on a yearly basis by the U.S. Congress. The primary basis for the establishment of the six RISS projects is to provide criminal justice agencies throughout established regions with a means by which criminal intelligence can be shared among member agencies. According to the Justice Department, intelligence-related services are provided to more than 150,000 sworn law enforcement officers in more than 1,700 criminal justice agencies throughout the United States. Specifically, the services offered member law enforcement agencies are:

- A centralized database
- Analysis of intelligence and investigative data
- Specialized equipment on loan
- Confidential funds
- Technical assistance
- Specialized training
- Access to telecommunications systems

All states throughout the country are placed in one of the six RISS regions:

1. *Western States Information Network:* Alaska, California, Hawaii, Oregon, Washington
2. *Rocky Mountain Information Network:* Arizona, Colorado, Idaho, Montana, Nevada, New Mexico, Utah, Wyoming
3. *Mid-State Organized Crime Information Center:* Illinois, Iowa, Kansas, Minnesota, Missouri, Nebraska, North Dakota, South Dakota, Wisconsin
4. *Regional Organized Crime Information Center:* Alabama, Arkansas, Florida, Georgia, Kentucky, Louisiana, Mississippi, North Carolina, Oklahoma, South Carolina, Tennessee, Texas, Virginia, West Virginia
5. *Middle Atlantic-Great Lakes Organized Crime Law Enforcement Network:* Delaware, District of Columbia, Indiana, Maryland, Michigan, New Jersey, New York, Ohio, Pennsylvania
6. *New England State Police Information Network:* Connecticut, Maine, Massachusetts, New Hampshire, Rhode Island, Vermont

The goal of the RISS projects is to aid state and local law enforcement agencies in the organizing and sharing of criminal intelligence. The very existence of the massive project illustrates the importance of criminal intelligence information in the field of criminal investigation.

AUDITING AND PURGING FILES

Intelligence files that are no longer accurate, are not relevant to the mission of the unit, do not pertain to investigative interests and activities, or contain insufficient supporting documentation are among those that should be purged. When files are deficient in one or more of these areas, consideration may be given to updating or improving them through validation and other means. However, when the basic information contained in these files is of such an age or of such poor quality as to make these efforts either too costly or unproductive, a decision should be made to purge the file. A record of any purged files should be maintained by the department.

Use of a qualified outside auditor is typically the best approach to purging intelligence files. This is because independent third parties remove much of the bias or the appearance of bias that may be evident when using in-house intelligence personnel. While a yearly review of the files for purposes of purging useless materials is recommended, this does not preclude the destruction of files on an ad hoc basis where appropriate and with approval of the intelligence or investigative unit.

DISCUSSION QUESTIONS

1. Define the goal of the intelligence function as it pertains to the collection of criminal information.

2. List and discuss the four fundamental differences between criminal investigation and criminal intelligence gathering.

3. Discuss the two categories of criminal intelligence.

4. List examples of the type of activity that may be documented by police intelligence units.

5. According to the text, what are four variables to consider in selecting an intelligence target?

6. List and discuss the four phases of the intelligence process.

7. Discuss the general premises of the right to know and the need to know in intelligence information dissemination.

8. What are the most common methods of data description and integration, and how do these contribute to the overall process of criminal investigation and apprehension?

9. Discuss the basic differences between event and commodity flowcharting.

10. Discuss the function of the federally funded RISS projects and address their contribution to the field of criminal investigation.

NOTES

1. "Interview with Brian Michael Jenkins," *Omni,* November, 1994, Vol. 17, No. 2, p. 77.

2. ROBERT SURO, "U.S. lacking in terrorism defenses: Study cites a need to share intelligence," *The Washington Post,* Friday, April 24, 1998, p. A-18.

3. U.S. DEPARTMENT OF JUSTICE (1988). *Intelligence collection and analytical methods training manual.* Drug Enforcement Administration.

7

Undercover and Surveillance Operations

Key Terms

▶ burned
▶ buy-bust
▶ buy-walk
▶ cover story
▶ deep cover
▶ entrapment
▶ forward-looking infrared
▶ Global Positioning System (GPS)
▶ inside team
▶ mobile surveillance
▶ outside team
▶ seed money
▶ stakeout
▶ stationary surveillance
▶ support officer
▶ undercover (UC) officer

This chapter will enable you to:

- Understand the usefulness of undercover investigations.
- Describe the steps to properly implement an undercover investigation.
- Understand the resources required for a successful undercover investigation.
- Explain the benefits of surveillance in criminal investigation.
- Identify the different types of surveillance operations.

INTRODUCTION

Undercover operations are an important part of the criminal investigation function but one that is highly specialized and not practiced by all law enforcement agencies. Investigators require specialized training to successfully perform this function. Stories abound regarding both investigative successes and failures in this area. From a practical standpoint, undercover work and surveillance are viable options for the police investigator, as they provide considerable information not otherwise available through traditional investigative methods.

For example, in January 2004, drug enforcement agents from federal, state, and local jurisdictions concluded what was called "Operation Streamline," an investigation into a Cali, Colombia–based heroin trafficking organization in Florida. The undercover investigation, focused on the Orlando Ospina trafficking organization that was known to smuggle more than 990 pounds of high-grade heroin a year into Miami for distribution to New York, Philadelphia, and Newark, resulted in the arrests of 17 persons. During the course of the operation, investigators discovered that the traffickers used both traditional and nontraditional smuggling routes and methods. For example, they smuggled approximately 220 pounds of heroin over three months from Cali to Nicaragua by secreting the drugs in drinking straws and placing them in boxes of seafood. The organization also used internal body couriers to transport drugs from Cali, Bogotá, and Buenos Aires to major east coast cities.

This case revealed that traffickers also used both traditional and nontraditional methods to transport the money earned by drug sales from the United States back to Colombia. In the nontraditional method, $100 bills were rolled into a cylinder shape, pressed, and then swallowed by couriers. Most of the couriers were able to swallow 1,000 bills and thus could smuggle $100,000 per trip (also see Chapter 4). The organization also operated a check-cashing business in Cali that could launder approximately $25,000 a day in proceeds. Additionally, the organization used Western Union wire transfers to send drug proceeds in $1,000 increments from the United States to Colombia.

The subjects of undercover operations and surveillance are discussed in this chapter because of their close relationship with one another and because of their importance to the investigative function. Typically, undercover work has been associated with drug enforcement, but it is a tool that can be useful in the investigation of a number of criminal activities.

OVERVIEW

Undercover operations have been used by police agencies for decades. However, they present many problems and concerns for the department because of the delicate nature of undercover work and the officer's role in determining whether someone is committing criminal violations.[1] Undercover work forces the officer to assume a different identity and, sometimes, a lifestyle that thrusts him into the criminal subculture, where he can be tempted to do things that would otherwise be immoral or even illegal (such as using illegal drugs). This has the potential to exact a heavy price from individual officers as, depending on the nature of the assignment, they may be separated from family, friends, and other department members for extended periods of time.

Undercover work is street-level work at its best (or worst, however you wish to view it). Officers are required to participate in undesirable activities, and those who remain in undercover positions for too long a period may begin to adopt the very behaviors of the criminals they are investigating, including undesirable mannerisms and foul language at the least. Even worse, the department can become involved in illegal activities during the course of an investigation. For example, New York City undercover officers ran a pornographic bookstore as part of an undercover sting operation. Officers, as part of their undercover investigation, purchased 1,200 pornographic films and resold them for considerable profit. After eight months, officers finally arrested several film distributors.

Langworthy observes that some undercover operations result in additional criminal activities.[2] As a result of his analysis of a Birmingham undercover antifencing operation, he concluded that the operation caused a substantial amount of crime by creating a market for stolen goods. If the police operation had not existed, no market would have existed and criminals would have stolen less.

Any undercover operation is subject to claims of **entrapment**. Officers are permitted to do things that provide the opportunity for a suspect to commit a crime, but they may not induce someone to commit a crime. Because undercover operations generally may be initiated without prior judicial authorization, the results are subject to strict scrutiny by the courts. Allowing police to make the decision to initiate an undercover operation based on mere suspicion has been the subject of much criticism.[3] Recognizing the magnitude of the problem, the FBI now requires that large-scale undercover operations first be reviewed by their Criminal Undercover Operations Review Committee.

Informants, discussed in Chapter 10, are particularly useful and often necessary in the investigation of vice crimes. They can be problematic, however, because police sometimes overlook illegal acts committed by informers in order to pursue their investigations. For example, narcotics users or lower-level dealers may be allowed to continue violating the law in order to make cases against their suppliers. Consequently, in order to move up the distribution network, undercover officers may find it necessary to cooperate with dealers who are selling a significant amount of drugs.

A 1989 informant management case in Cleveland resulted in disastrous consequences for the department.[4] Officers of the narcotics unit enlisted the help of Arthur Feckner, one of the city's major wholesalers, to arrest his supplier. The investigation, which resulted in the seizure of more than 100 pounds of cocaine, caused enormous problems for the department. Allegations surfaced that the police allowed Feckner to continue to sell drugs in a housing project to finance their drug investigation. Detectives maintained that they believed the money came from the sale of his assets and collection of debts from past drug sales. However, Feckner says he sold $20 million worth of drugs with the knowledge of the police.

Undercover operations require a number of decisions. Administrative discretion is exercised in determining what activities will be pursued; operational discretion is exercised in determining who will be targeted for investigation. Because police do not have the resources to investigate every crime, they engage in selective enforcement, enforcing only particular types of violations or targeting specific types of offenders. The decision-making process for vice crimes is subject to the factors previously discussed. The most important criterion for officers is the seriousness of the offense.[5] Most forms of vice, when considered alone, could be viewed as relatively minor crimes. However, in the current political climate, which emphasizes "zero tolerance," possession of even small amounts of drugs is viewed as serious. Officers are therefore much less likely to use size discretion in their decision to arrest in drug cases.

UNDERCOVER OPERATIONS

The use of undercover agents is not recommended for every police organization because of resources required for a successful undercover operation. These resources include manpower, training, funding, specialized equipment, and other unique resources.

Police administrators must be careful in the selection of the proper candidate(s) for undercover work. Not every police officer can function properly and professionally in an undercover capacity. Typically, the undercover officer works with minimal direct supervision.[6] As such, officers can be exposed to a number of enticements, which could result in the compromising of the officer's integrity or the investigation. Because of this, the undercover officer must have considerable personal integrity.

One of the greatest challenges to undercover officers is the development of skills that maximize their efforts to match wits with some of the most intelligent and artful criminals on the street. Undercover assignments are either performed in the short term or long term (or "deep cover"). Short-term undercover operations are normally considerably safer for the officer than those that are **deep cover.** Short-term operations permit the help of surveillance officers and protection that undercover agents working in a deep-cover capacity do not have. However, the benefits of working a deep-cover undercover operation allow an undercover agent time to gain total trust of the criminal suspect to the point of openly discussing criminal operations. This is a great advantage to an undercover agent because as a rule, criminals are very suspicious about meeting new "clients" who could be (and sometimes are) police informers or undercover officers.

While no two cases are exactly the same, Motto and June point out that there are certain elements common to each undercover operation: (1) the introduction, (2) the acceptance, (3) the buy, (4) the arrest, (5) covering the informant, and (6) the "after action."[7]

The informant typically makes the "introduction" of the undercover operative to the suspect. This is the initiation of the case. From this point on, the "acceptance" phase takes over when the undercover agent is either accepted or not. In the event the suspect does not accept the officer, it might be necessary for the informant to meet the suspect at a later time without the undercover officer to determine why the suspect was suspicious. In the event the officer is not accepted, the informant can bring in a second officer with a different cover story. This time, both the officer and informant will try to overcome the difficulties experienced during the first contact.

After the introduction, there is a short period of "bobbing, weaving, and circling": The suspect gets to know or feel if he can trust the undercover officer. If a feeling of trust is established, conversation will quickly turn to the criminal activities in which the suspect is involved.

Figure 7.1 Undercover work sometimes involves working prostitution and other "general vice" activities.

In the case of an undercover drug operation, for example, this conversation will generally result in the undercover agent asking for or obtaining samples, and the suspect will quote the purchase price. After the samples have been delivered and the undercover agent has had an opportunity to examine them, the purchase price is discussed.

This purchase, or the "buy," may or may not go through. In other words, a decision must be made whether or not to arrest a suspect when he delivers the contraband (also known as a **"buy-bust"**) or to take that action after subsequent deliveries (known as a **"buy-walk"**). If it is determined that the investigation should continue, no arrests should be made and nothing should be done to arouse the suspect's suspicion or to identify accidentally the true role of the undercover operative. This is known as *covering the informant.*

In drug investigations, the first buy is usually a small one whereby the agency doesn't mind losing its **seed money** so that the undercover officer can make a bigger purchase at a later time. Subsequent purchases of contraband are known as the "after action." As a rule, the second purchase or, if necessary, several subsequent purchases are large enough to warrant not only the appearance of a suspect but also some of the people connected with him. These individuals could be present in several capacities: countersurveillance, protection, main participants, or equal partners, perhaps even higher-ups. Sometimes it is necessary because of the development of circumstances surrounding the case to arrest a suspect when an initial delivery is made.

PREPARING FOR UNDERCOVER ASSIGNMENTS

Undercover work can be defined as assuming a fictitious identity and associating with known or suspected criminals for the purpose of collecting information or evidence on criminal activity. All undercover work has the potential for considerable danger. It requires that officers establish a cover story (which may or may not be blown at any time during the investigation) and that they associate closely with individuals who may be armed, unpredictable, under the influence of drugs, or mentally unstable.

Personnel Considerations

Given the inherent dangers of undercover work, the selection and training of personnel must be meticulous. Consideration must be given to the particular goals and resources of the unit, the officers' personalities, their professional backgrounds, and their physical and mental conditions. In addition, an officer's proficiency with firearms, good reporting skills, and the ability to keep a cool head and use common sense under stressful conditions must be carefully weighed by police supervisors. Because of concern for officer safety and the increasing potential for agency liability, the days of the undercover officers working the streets in deep cover and under minimal supervision are becoming less common.

Those being considered for undercover assignments should be disabused of any myths created by television and popular media stereotypes. Undercover work is not a glamorous job providing the agent with expensive meals, luxurious sports cars, and unheard-of electronic gadgetry. Conversely, it is also not a duty that requires an officer to isolate him or herself from family and friends and become a drug-using martyr.

Most undercover work consists of a brief meeting between the agent and a suspect, an exchange of dialogue, and a transaction—usually a purchase of contraband such as a quantity of illegal drugs, stolen property, or illegal weapons. Deep-cover assignments, that is, assignments that require agents to operate with minimal protection over extended periods of time, are not as widely used and require specialized training.

Although required to work one-on-one with a suspected drug dealer, undercover officers must also realize that both their safety and the overall success of the investigation require equal participation by all unit members. Each officer's role (undercover contact, surveillance officer, radar officer, and officers assisting in arrest) is of equal importance. Even though every officer within the unit must maintain his or her caseload, each should regard the overall mission of the unit as an effort of a team rather than of one individual.

Functions of Undercover Officers

There are two general functions for officers within the undercover unit. The **undercover (UC) officer** contacts individuals or infiltrates establishments or organizations suspected of being involved in criminal activity. Usually, such contacts are possible because the officer's appearance, mannerisms, dress, and overall demeanor are similar to those of the suspect. Considerable time and money are spent in carefully cultivating the officer's ability to function effectively in this capacity, so the true identity of the undercover officer should be protected at all times.

The **support officer** (sometimes called an intelligence, cover, or tactical officer) is a plainclothes officer who works with the undercover unit but not in an undercover capacity. Support officers assist undercover officers by observing the illicit transactions (e.g., an illegal drug transaction) in which they, or their informers, are involved. Support officers also participate in drug raids at the culmination of an investigation, interview arrestees, and perform other functions within the unit that would otherwise jeopardize or expose the identity of the undercover agent.

Because criminal enterprises differ in their resources, methods, procedures, and philosophies, the operational distinctions between undercover and support officers may not be feasible in some agencies. In such circumstances, officers may be required at different times to perform both functions.

EQUIPMENT

To approach any covert investigation effectively, one of the first orders of business is to determine what equipment is necessary. The choice of equipment will, of course, vary according to the agency's financial resources, the size of the unit, the mission, and the type of assignment at hand. However, when considering an equipment purchase, careful thought should be given to its purpose and user, its usefulness, and its durability.

Undercover investigators require equipment different from that given to support officers. In addition, equipment assigned to a criminal investigator might be regularly carried with him or her in an assigned vehicle. Therefore, it may experience much wear and tear from moving around in the trunk of a car or the back of the van, or it may suffer from drastic changes in weather conditions due to changing humidity, temperature, or dust particles, for example.

VEHICLES

As a rule, each vehicle owned by the agency should be assigned a separate number, and a maintenance and repair file should be kept on each vehicle. The kinds of vehicles the agency should own and the equipment the vehicles should contain depend on how they will be used. Following are some examples.

Support Officer Vehicles

Vehicles for a support officer should generally be nondescript: two-door sedans or commonly observed SUVs, in plain colors such as white, tan, gray, or dark blue. Exotic or expensive sports cars might be advantageous in short-term undercover assignments, but they will also be easily remembered, or identified as police vehicles (**"burned"**) by nervous or attentive suspects during any moving surveillance.

Vehicles should also be assigned to match the driver. For example, a more expensive car should be assigned to an appropriately dressed agent; a sports car should be assigned to an investigator who fits the role of someone who would typically drive one. If local laws permit, seized vehicles, if in good condition, are good assets and can provide a constant source of plausible vehicles for the undercover unit. Undercover personnel should not use vehicles assigned to support officers. Support officers' vehicles need to be outfitted differently from those assigned to undercover officers. These vehicles should have more standard "police-type" electronics that benefit them but would identify, or "burn," an undercover investigator. Support officer vehicles are sometimes equipped with "kill switches." These are standard toggle switches, usually concealed in the glove box and wired so that a single headlight, the tail lights, or brake lights can be turned off. This is beneficial in nighttime surveillance, to change the appearance of the vehicle when a suspect is looking for surveillance through their rearview mirror (see the section on surveillance methods).

Undercover Officer Vehicles

Those vehicles used by undercover investigators should not be equipped like support officer vehicles. Undercover vehicles must be kept "clean." Criminal suspects will often be inside the undercover vehicle, and it is common for them to examine the vehicle for possible police radio or hidden wires to microphones, or even to check vehicle registration. Consequently, anything the suspect discovers in the vehicle should be placed there purposely to support the officer's cover story.

THE UNDERCOVER WORKING ENVIRONMENT

While undercover operations have unique benefits, they also have a serious downside. On one hand, undercover is an investigative method by which the officer can see firsthand the inner workings of criminal organizations. Officers can converse and strategize with their criminal targets and learn the ways criminal minds work. Conversely, this close interaction may place the officer in jeopardy, as he or she might inadvertently reveal something inconsistent with their cover story. Furthermore, exposure to criminal elements in a close, undercover capacity for extended periods of time might result in the undercover officer acting and speaking in a manner other than they are accustomed, even when off duty, reflecting poorly on the officer's credibility.

To minimize problems associated with undercover operations, a certain degree of preparation is imperative. This includes establishing a sound cover story and understanding specialized infiltration techniques.

The Cover Story

A prerequisite for assuming an undercover role is to establish a **cover story.** Simply defined, the cover story is a fictitious story that the agent will convey to suspects concerning his or her background: name, address, hometown (or area), and employment, if applicable. Other details may be included, but it is a good idea to keep the cover story simple in case an agent must deal with inquisitive criminal suspects.

The cover story should fit with the area and people involved with the investigation. When an officer chooses to associate him- or herself with a particular town or area, it should be one with which the officer is already familiar, in case he or she later meets someone from that area. Officers should remember that mixing a partial truth with the cover story makes an officer more believable to the suspect.

When claiming a place of employment, the officer should choose one that cannot be easily checked out by suspects. This is more of a problem in rural areas because people are more likely to know one another. It may be desirable to choose an out-of-town place of employment that requires a lot of travel or to present a fictitious job in which the officer is self-employed, thus harder for criminal suspects to verify. Whatever story is chosen, the officer should be provided with business cards, customized stationery, credit cards, checking and savings account books, and other supporting credentials to corroborate the cover story. Moreover, the officer should be familiar with the profession chosen for the cover story for the same reasons he/she should be familiar with the purported hometown.

The officer's appearance and mannerisms should also fit the cover story. If the officer claims to be an oil field worker, for example, it might be out of character for the officer to be seen by the suspect in an expensive business suit. On the other hand, if the officer's cover story is that of financier for a big money deal, then expensive clothing might be more appropriate. It might also be necessary for an undercover officer to wear expensive jewelry to help convince sellers of his or her cover story. Depending on the nature of the investigation, expensive jewelry can sometimes be borrowed from local stores for short periods; however, the safety and security of the jewelry are the responsibility of the undercover officer.

Protecting the Undercover Officer's Cover

Once the cover story has been established, the undercover officer is committed to it. Certainly the basics—name, hometown, and location—cannot easily be changed without jeopardizing the officer's safety and the integrity of the investigation. Even if changes are not necessary, however, the undercover officer must be able to detect and withstand attempts by suspects or their associates to test and invalidate the officer's cover story.

Typically, suspects will barrage the officer with questions in an attempt to catch any inconsistency in the cover story. If they are successful, or believe that they are, suspects usually attempt to frighten or intimidate the officer into admitting he/she is a law enforcement agent or into abandoning the investigation out of fear for their personal safety.

Panic is the undercover officer's worst enemy. Officers must realize two important things: (1) paranoia is common among drug dealers, and (2) no matter what suspects say they know about the agent, many times they're just attempting to lock the officer into an admission for which they have no proof. If the officer keeps the cover story general, most questioning and suspicion should be easily overcome. Moreover, if the officer has been properly trained and responds to the suspects according to his or her training, a bond of trust may develop between the officer and suspects, which can pave the way to a successful investigation.

Different criminals use different methods to expose undercover police agents. Even though good field training should prepare undercover personnel for most of these obstacles, not every confrontation can be anticipated. Undercover personnel should remember that most questions about their cover story are bluffs, and they should remain calm and confident, discounting the challenges presented without appearing scared, intimidated, or paranoid.

An investigator should also be aware that criminals can be quite tricky and cunning when trying to expose possible police infiltration. For example, they may:

- Attempt to intoxicate the officer in the hope that he or she will say something inconsistent with the cover story while under the influence of alcohol.
- Use prostitutes, girlfriends or boyfriends, or associates to attempt to seduce the officer; in doing so, the upper torso will be felt for body mikes, the waist area for weapons, and pockets for police credentials or anything else indicating an association with police work.
- Ask the officer questions about his or her cover story when the suspects already know the answer; the suspects hope to observe nervousness on the part of the officer.
- Ask the officer to furnish drugs to a friend or an associate knowing that it is against regulations for a law enforcement officer to do so.
- Ask the officer to consume drugs furnished by the suspect.
- Attempt to learn information about the officer's family (spouse, children, other relatives, or friends) so that an officer's story can be more easily verified.
- Ask the officer to perform various illegal acts.
- Attempt to rummage through the officer's car or personal belongings in order to locate police-related material or information showing that the officer was lying about his or her cover story.
- Ask the undercover officer excessive questions to see how many he or she is willing to answer before becoming suspicious or angry.

Infiltration

Once a cover story is established, a methodical process of infiltration must take place to uncover criminal wrongdoing and its associated evidence. During infiltration, a relationship is established between the officer and a suspect. Frequently, an officer finds it difficult to meet or establish any rapport with the suspect without the help of an informant (see Chapter 10). In some cases, however, informants may cause more trouble for the officer and the investigation than they are worth; therefore, their use should be carefully considered. Infiltration requires inventiveness and originality on the officer's part because he or she might have to create their own opportunity to speak with the suspect.

Once contact is made between the officer and the suspect, the suspect's confidence must be gained as soon as possible. An officer can best accomplish this by learning the interests of the suspects, which the officer can then discuss: jobs, the opposite sex, local bars, motorcycles, cars, drugs, and so on. Context must be regularly attempted throughout the investigation to maintain rapport with the suspect.

When working without an informant, it might be necessary to canvass a target area. The undercover officer can expedite the investigation by revealing intelligence on target suspects and locations, concentrating on areas with high levels of crime that might provide investigative leads. Typical starting places might be bars, nightclubs, or taverns, which can be excellent sources of intelligence for undercover officers. Much can be learned just by being present at these

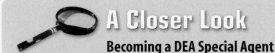

A Closer Look

Becoming a DEA Special Agent

Drug Enforcement Special Agents are a select group of men and women from diverse backgrounds whose experience and commitment make them the premier federal drug law enforcement agents in the world. Applicants must be at least 21 years of age and no older than 36 at the time of their appointment.

Education.   The most competitive candidates possess a bachelor's or master's degree, along with a grade point average (GPA) of 2.95 or higher. Special consideration is given to candidates with degrees in Criminal Justice/Police Science or related disciplines; Finance, Accounting, or Economics; foreign languages (with fluency verified) in Spanish, Russian, Hebrew, Arabic, dialects of Nigerian languages, Chinese, Japanese; computer Science/Information Systems; and Telecommunications/Electrical/Mechanical Engineering.

Depending on scheduling and candidate availability, DEA's hiring process may take 12 months or longer. Hiring involves a multi-step process that includes the following phases:

- Qualifications Review
- Written and Oral Assessment and Panel Interview
- Urinalysis Drug Test
- Medical Examination
- Physical Task Test
- Polygraph Examination
- Psychological Assessment
- Background Investigation
- Final Hiring Decision

Training.   All applicants must successfully complete all phases of the hiring process and remain most competitive to receive a final offer of employment. For more information, please contact your nearest DEA field division recruitment office. Scheduling times and locations are handled by the local Recruitment Coordinators. Special Agent candidates are required to successfully complete a 16-week Basic Agent Training (BAT) program at the DEA Training Academy in Quantico, Virginia.

Through this program, instruction and hands-on training are provided in undercover, surveillance, and arrest techniques, defensive tactics and firearms training, as well as the basics of report writing, law, and drug identification and recognition. In addition, you will participate in a rigorous physical fitness program.

Duty Station.   Between the 8th and 12th weeks of your training, you will be provided with your final duty station. Mobility is a condition of employment. Assignments are made based upon DEA's current operational needs.

Mobility.   Mobility is a condition of employment. Special Agents are subject to transfer throughout their career, based upon the needs of the agency.

Salary.   DEA Special Agents are generally hired at the GS-7 or GS-9 level, depending on education and experience. The salary includes federal Law Enforcement Officer base pay plus a locality payment, depending on your duty station. Upon successful graduation from the DEA Training Academy, 25% Availability Pay will be added to your base and locality pay. After graduation, the starting salaries are approximately $49,746 for a GS-7, and $55,483 for a GS-9. After four years of service Special Agents are eligible to progress to the GS-13 level and can earn approximately $92,592 or more per year.

Drug Use Policy.   DEA is charged with enforcement of the Federal Controlled Substances Act; therefore, all applicants must fully disclose any drug use history during the

(continued)

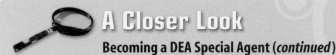

A Closer Look

Becoming a DEA Special Agent (*continued*)

application process. Applicants whose drug use history is outside of acceptable parameters will not be considered for employment. All DEA employees are subject to random urinalysis drug testing throughout their careers.

The Physical Task (PT) Test.   The PT test determines if potential candidates can withstand the rigors of Special Agent training. Candidates must be in excellent physical condition in order to pass this test.

If a candidate fails the first PT test, administered in the field, a second test must be successfully taken within 30 days. A second failure will cause the candidate's application process to be discontinued. Candidates are encouraged to train to ensure that they are prepared to successfully complete this test.

Background Investigation.   A background investigation (BI) is one of the final steps in the application process that seeks to discern a comprehensive snapshot of you. The investigation provides information on personal history, education and work experience, personal and professional references, as well as other necessary checks. The time it takes to complete the BI is dependent on the type and scope of investigation being conducted.

SOURCE: http://www.dea.gov/job/agent/faqs.html#question002

locations; generally people do not have a reasonable expectation of privacy when "openly" conversing in public in such places as a bar. The undercover agent can simply overhear otherwise private or guarded information about their suspects' names, types of criminal activities, places of employment, and vehicles they drive. Once the officer learns such information and it appears that the information might be useful in showing criminal activity, it should be properly documented in intelligence reports. The lack of such properly generated intelligence reports accounts for the loss of much valuable criminal information to the unit.

It should be noted that although bars, nightclubs, and taverns can be lucrative sources of information, officer safety is greatly reduced in these settings. If two undercover officers are available, it is a good idea to assign both of them to a particular tavern, working independently of one another. This accomplishes two goals: It gives both officers additional backup, and it provides each officer the chance to identify different suspects in criminal groups operating within the tavern.

If a tavern is to be infiltrated, the undercover officer has several potentially good targets to consider. The first people contacted may not be offenders but might know those who are. Without being too aggressive, the undercover officer might consider befriending one of the following people in the bar:

- *Bartender:* Bartenders may or may not be involved in criminal activity, but they will most likely know of any criminal activity occurring and who is responsible.

- *Waitresses:* Waitresses are also frequently aware of an array of criminal activity taking place within the bar.

- *Bar customers* (regulars): Regular customers in a tavern might also be good players to befriend; they, too, often know who might be involved in criminal activity.

Sometimes an informant will arrange a transaction for the purchase of contraband and a first-time meeting between a contraband dealer and the undercover officer. In this case, the seller will have some degree of suspicion about the officer, and some initial questioning should be anticipated. At this point in the investigation, the officer should remember a few guidelines.

First, the officer should not let the suspect question him any more than if the roles were reversed. Some questioning is understandable and justifiable, but it can become excessive. If this occurs, the officer should deal with that the best way possible, perhaps by acting angry, advising the seller that he's too inquisitive and that the deal is either on or it is not. This should help convince the seller that the officer is aware of what the suspect is attempting to do and that he or she is being manipulated. Undercover officers will find that subsequent transactions are usually much easier because the dealer feels confident since he has not been arrested as a result of dealing with the officer.

Second, while working in a bar, an officer might purchase drinks or pay for pool or video games in order to start a conversation with a suspect. However, officers must be careful to abide by established police policy regarding the consumption of alcoholic beverages while on duty. Most law enforcement agencies permit officers to consume liquor while working undercover, but because an officer's judgment may be impaired and because he or she might become less likely to remember necessary facts, this must be done with considerable discretion. Furthermore, in case it becomes an issue in court later, the officer should drink as little as possible in order to avoid attacks on the officer's credibility by defense attorneys once the case goes to trial.

Third, if the undercover assignment takes the officer to the suspect's house, in addition to taking additional safety precautions, officers must recognize that this is a good opportunity to learn new information about the suspect. The officer should mentally map out all entrances, exits, and windows that the suspect may use for escape during a possible future raid. The officer should mentally note the number on the telephone, which might furnish a lead to the name of a new associate later. Discreetly observing mail lying out in the open may also reveal the names of associates or roommates. Finally, noting the presence of controlled substances and their hiding places, in addition to any weapons, may be useful later when obtaining a search warrant or conducting a raid.

Fourth, officers should remember that the practice of lying and deceiving is common for drug dealers. If the officer gets caught in a lie, he or she should never become prematurely paranoid and fear that his or her cover has been blown. The officer should react with disinterest or perhaps even laugh it off for the suspect's benefit. It is best to try to justify the line by claiming that he or she doesn't "want too many people knowing too much about my personal business." The suspect will most likely identify with and respect such an explanation.

SURVEILLANCE OPERATIONS

Similar to undercover operations, conducting surveillance requires using the team concept. The considerable resources required for surveillance draw personnel away from other investigative functions. The potential also exists for alerting the subject of the investigation to law enforcement's interest, which conceivably could compromise the covertness of not only the surveillance but the entire investigation. Proper preparation at the onset can make the difference between a productive surveillance and expending considerable resources without any results.[8] Perhaps the most challenging task in criminal investigation is to keep a suspect under surveillance without arousing his suspicions. Surveillance is a process that may take place under a variety of conditions for which the officer must be prepared. The teamwork concept is usually necessary since most surveillance operations involve more than one officer, one mode of travel, and one location.

A surveillance operation may be directed toward a person, a vehicle, or location for the purpose of bringing an investigation into sharp focus. By identifying individuals in obtaining detailed information about their activities, the criminal investigator can accomplish the following:

- Obtain evidence of a crime.
- Prevent the commission of an act or apprehend a suspect in the commission of an act.
- Locate persons or watch their hangouts and associates.
- Obtain probable cause for obtaining search warrants.
- Obtain information for later use in an interrogation.
- Develop leads and information received from other sources.
- Obtain admissible legal evidence for use in court.
- Protect undercover officers or corroborate their testimony.

Preparing for the Surveillance

Before initiation of the surveillance, a study should be made of all files relating to the suspects, their activities in crimes, their working and neighborhood environments, and the vehicles involved in the case. In studying information relating to the suspects, the officer should focus on names and aliases used by suspects and detailed physical descriptions, including photographs when available. When possible, the suspect should be pointed out to the surveillance officers.

Identifying characteristics and mannerisms of the suspect should also be studied by the officers. The habits and normal routines of the suspects should be examined, as well as their probable suspicion of, and ability to elude, the surveillance operation. The identities and descriptions of known or suspected contacts or associates should be known, and the officer should be knowledgeable about the scope and extent of crimes and activities in which the suspects are involved.

Officers must also familiarize themselves with the type of neighborhood in which the operation will take place, concentrating on such aspects as the type of inhabitants, their dress, and their use of language. This information will assist the officers in blending in with the neighborhood.

The types of equipment employed by surveillance officers are limited only by the improvisational ability of the officers themselves. For example, on a short-term surveillance of a building, the surveillance officers may use utility belts with tools and hard hats to adopt the appearance of public utility employees, or utilize some other type of "cover" equipment.

A physical reconnaissance should study the areas where the surveillance will take place and identify vantage points suitable for the officers. Similarly, traffic conditions should be observed, and the officers should become familiar with the names and locations of streets in the area, including locations of dead-end streets that may be used by the suspect to spot surveillance officers. The reconnaissance will also yield information on the neighborhood and its inhabitants that would not be in the police files.

The officer must mentally and physically prepare himself for surveillance operations. The officer needs to realize that he must be patient and possess endurance. Perseverance is needed while waiting for the suspect to appear or to doggedly follow a suspect through the same routine day after day.

The officer must be alert and resourceful, because regardless of careful planning, there are always many unanticipated occurrences in surveillance work. The officer must develop keen powers of observation and memory for often he or she is unable to write down all events, descriptions of contacts, or times as they occur. Furthermore, the officer must prepare a logical explanation for being in a particular place at a particular time in the eventuality that he or she is approached by the subject and accused of following him.

The officer must address and adopt the demeanor of local inhabitants in order to blend into the setting. The type of clothing to be worn will determine whether concealment of weapons or use of personal radios jeopardizes the operation. Ideally, the officer should have an ordinary appearance since he must avoid attracting the suspect's attention. Doing so will better ensure that the officer is able to blend in to the target's environment. He must have the ability to act naturally under all circumstances as if he belongs at that scene.

Officers should also have such items as caps, jackets, and glasses available to quicky change appearance if needed. Flexibility and versatility are the keys to any surveillance. The change of clothing may suffice for one individual, while another may use clothing to suggest a trade or service. The clothing and behavior should be coordinated to communicate some cover or excuse for being in a neighborhood.

Foot Surveillance

Generally, the foot surveillance technique is used only during relatively short distances or to maintain contact with a suspect after he has left a vehicle. There are four principal methods for conducting a moving surveillance on foot:

Surveillance Kit Checklist

- Department two-way radio
- Handheld portable radio with spare battery
- Cellular phone
- Digital camera with telephoto lens (if available) with extra storage media and spare battery
- Digital video camera
- Stabilizing device such as a tripod
- Binoculars and/or thermal-imaging device
- Detailed road maps / compass / GPS navigation device
- Flashlight with extra batteries
- Change of clothing including hat and toiletries
- Food and water
- Cash, including coins for toll lanes
- Extra set of car keys
- Towels and glass cleaner
- Equipment bag to contain above items

one-man surveillance, two-man surveillance, ABC method, and progressive, or leapfrog, method.

One-Man Surveillance. The single-officer technique is extremely difficult to conduct because the suspect must be kept in view at all times and close contact is required to enable the officer to immediately observe the suspect if he enters a building, turns a corner, or makes other sudden moves.

Two-Man Surveillance. This method affords greater security against detection and reduces the risk of losing the suspect. On streets that are crowded with pedestrian or vehicular traffic, both officers should normally remain on the same side of the street as the suspect. The first officer trails the suspect fairly closely. The second officer remains some distance behind the first. On a less crowded street, one officer should walk on the opposite side of the street nearly abreast of the suspect. In order to avoid detection, the two officers should make periodic changes in their positions relative to the suspect.

ABC Method. By utilizing a three-man surveillance team in this technique, the risk of losing the suspect is further reduced. Under most conditions, this method provides greater security against detection. The ABC method also permits a greater variation in the position of the officers and also allows an officer who suspects he has been spotted by the suspect to drop out of close contact. Under normal traffic conditions, officer "A" keeps a reasonable distance behind the suspect. Officer "B" follows "A" and concentrates on keeping "A" in view. He also checks if an associate of the subject is being used to detect the surveillance (countersurveillance). Officer "C" walks on the opposite side of the street slightly behind the suspect. On streets with little or no traffic, officers "B" and "C" may be on the opposite side of the street, or officer "C" may be in front of the suspect. On crowded streets, however, all three officers should generally be on the same side of the street. The lead officer should follow closely to observe the suspect at intersections or if he enters a building. As with the two-man method, the officers should frequently alter their positions relative to the suspect to avoid detection.

When the suspect approaches an intersection and there is a probability that he might turn, officer "C" across the street should reach the intersection first. By pausing at the corner, officer "C" can watch the suspect and signal his actions to officers "A" and "B." If "C" signals that the suspect has turned the corner and stopped, both "A" and "B" may have to cross the intersection and proceed to a point out of the suspect's view and rely on "C" to signal them when the suspect continues on his way. Whether or not the suspect stops, turning the corner provides an opportunity to rotate the positions of the officers.

In order to communicate with each other, surveillance officers must have agreed on some basic hand signals. These hand signals must be simple and given in such a manner as not to attract attention. When possible, small, easily concealed personal radios can be used by the team.

Progressive, or Leapfrog, Method. In the progressive, or leapfrog, method of surveillance, the suspect is observed intermittently as he moves along a certain habitual route. The surveillance officer stations himself at a fixed point until the suspect disappears from view. If a suspect follows the same route each day, his destination may be determined without constant surveillance. The officer should station himself each day where the suspect disappeared from view the previous day. More than one officer can be used to extend the period of observation. This method may be of value in locating hideouts or meeting places when the risk of trailing a suspect is too great.

Use of this method is not common because of the time involved and the probability of obtaining poor results. There is no assurance that the suspect will either go to the same destination or take the same route each day. However, a modified version may be useful when a suspect's rounds are routine or his contacts are known but his source or base of operation is unknown. The suspect can be followed until the risk of detection is too great. The surveillance can then be canceled for that day and reinstituted the next day at the location where the previous day's surveillance was called off.

Difficulties in Surveillance Operations

Problems that may be encountered when conducting a foot surveillance are infinite, but there are certain common difficulties that preplanning may help to resolve. For example, if the suspect enters a building, at least one officer should follow the suspect inside unless the building is a private home or small shop or if entry would expose the officer. In the case of a large public building with many exits, all officers should follow the suspect into the building. It is prudent for one officer to remain in the lobby or at the door to spot the suspect if he leaves the building.

In instances where a suspect enters a restaurant, at least one officer should enter behind the suspect to note any contacts made inside. If possible, the officer should pay his check before the suspect so that he can be prepared to leave with him. In some cases, it is desirable for the officer to leave shortly before the suspect and wait for him outside. Doing so could give the suspect the impression that he is not being observed by the surveillance officer.

Should the suspect register in a hotel, the room number and length of anticipated stay may be obtained from a manager or desk clerk. However, these employees should not be asked for information until it is determined that they can be trusted. If the hotel management is cooperative, it may be possible to obtain a room near the suspect, which can be used as a surveillance base. All in-room outgoing telephone numbers dialed by the suspect are normally recorded by the hotel switchboard operator. These records should be examined for leads. Trash from the suspect's room should not be overlooked, although trespassing to retrieve this or any other possible evidence without a search warrant is not permitted.

A clever suspect, discovering that he is under surveillance, may not reveal this knowledge but may attempt to lose his followers by means of false contacts or decoys. For example, when attempting a surveillance on a suspected illicit drug exchange, the suspect may leave a package full of worthless papers or materials with the contact, thereby causing unwary officers to redirect or discontinue their surveillance, leaving him free to make his real contacts unobserved. Similarly, the suspect may attempt to lead the officer into a trap. A thorough knowledge of the locality, tempered with good judgment and alertness to realize when trailing becomes too easy, is a good defense against such traps. If a suspect resorts to trickery, it is good policy to change surveillance officers. Some common methods that a suspect may use to detect foot surveillance are:

- Stopping to tie a shoelace, meanwhile looking for followers.
- Stopping abruptly and looking at people to the rear, or reversing course and retracing his steps.

- Stopping abruptly after turning the corner, or alternately walking slowly and rapidly.

- Arranging with a friend in a shop or other place to watch for surveillants behind him.

- Riding short distances on buses and taxis, or circling the block in a taxi.

- Entering a building and leaving immediately via another exit.

- Watching in lobby and restaurant mirrors to see who is coming and going.

- Starting to leave a location quickly then suddenly turning around to see if anyone else also suddenly rises.

- Opening and closing his hotel door to indicate that he has left the room and then waiting inside the room with the door slightly ajar to see if anyone leaves an adjacent room.

Vehicle Surveillance

As is the case with foot surveillance, there are four types of vehicular surveillance (or **mobile surveillance**): the one-, two-, and three-car surveillance and the leapfrog method. If only one car is available for surveillance, its position should be behind the suspect car, the distance varying with the amount of traffic in the area. In city traffic, no more than two vehicles should be permitted between the suspect car and the surveillance vehicle. In rural areas, it is advisable to give the suspect a good lead. If intersections and road forks are far between, the lead can be extended to a point where the suspect car may be even temporarily lost from view over hills or around curves. When possible, there should be another car between the surveillance vehicle and the suspect car. At night, the surveillance vehicle should not have its headlights on high beam unless absolutely necessary to maintain contact. Similarly, all other unnecessary lights on the car should be off.

Whenever possible, the surveillant's car should be occupied by two officers—one driver and one observer to take notes. The second officer can also take over surveillance on foot if necessary. Seating arrangements and appearance of these two officers should be changed periodically to avoid recognition by suspects. The officers should prepare for emergencies by carrying food, raincoats, tire chains, and any other items appropriate for the circumstances of the surveillance. Many agencies install switches (kill switches) on surveillance cars to enable the officers to darken lights, shut off running lights, or to shut off individual lights needed to change the vehicle's appearance.

When conducting a two-car surveillance in city areas during daylight hours, both cars should be behind the suspect's car. Occasionally, one car may operate on a parallel route, timing itself to arrive at intersections just before the suspect in order to observe his route at the intersection. This method is also highly suitable for use at night in suburban areas.

In a three-car surveillance, parallel routes can be more readily utilized, and the positions of the cars can be changed frequently enough to prevent discovery of the surveillance. One car may be used to lead the suspect vehicle while observing it through the rearview mirror.

The leapfrog surveillance with cars is very similar to leapfrog surveillance on foot. In this type of surveillance, for example, the suspect vehicle may be

Figure 7.2 Detective conducting a "moving" or vehicle surveillance.

observed intermittently as it proceeds along its suspected route. From a fixed position, the officers watch the suspect vehicle disappear from view. After a number of such surveillances, the suspect's final destination is finally determined. This particular approach of the leapfrog surveillance is often impractical due to the greater distances that can be covered by car. For this reason, it would be more beneficial if the surveillance officers followed the suspect's car until the risk of detection is too great, whereupon the surveillance is called off for that day. The next time the suspect makes his scheduled trip, the officers can initiate their surveillance at the geographical point the previous surveillance was ended.

As with foot surveillance, the suspect who believes he may be being followed can resort to various techniques to detect the surveillance automobile. Some of the most common techniques include:

- Alternating fast and slow driving or parking frequently.
- Stopping suddenly around curves or corners or speeding up a hill, then coasting slowly downhill.
- Driving into dead-end streets or pulling into driveways.

Once a suspect has confirmed his suspicion, he can use a variety of techniques to elude automobile surveillance. Some examples are:

- Committing flagrant traffic violations such as making U-turns, driving against traffic on one-way streets, and running through red lights.
- Using double entrances to driveways—in one entrance and out the other.

- Cutting through parking lots.
- Driving through congested areas.
- Deserting the vehicle beyond the blind curve or corner.

Stakeouts, or "Stationary Surveillance"

When a **stakeout** is utilized, officers watch from a **stationary surveillance** vantage point such as a room, house, or camouflaged outdoor fixture located near the premises being observed. A stakeout is the tactical deployment of police officers in anticipation of the commission of a crime at a specific location. The anticipated perpetrators may be known individuals or may be suspects known only by their mode of operation or "MO." The purpose of the stakeout is to arrest the suspect(s) during the attempted or actual commission of a crime.

Stakeouts almost always involve enforcement actions against armed criminal suspects. Therefore, the safety of officers and bystanders should always be of primary concern. The objectives of criminal arrest should never supersede the need to protect officers and civilians against unreasonable risks.

Figure 7.3 Detective conducting a "stakeout" or fixed surveillance.

Briefings

The briefings preceding deployment of a stakeout should be of two types:

1. The first type is the dissemination of information by detective personnel. The detectives in charge of the case should provide the assigned officers with all information concerning the suspect(s) and his MO. This should include, when available, photos or composites, suspect armament, and the suspect's potential for violence based on previous crimes. Is the suspect armed? Has the suspect used his weapon? Has he taken hostages? Does the suspect appear to be in control, or is he under the influence of alcohol or drugs? Does he run after committing the crime or calmly exit the location? Is there a getaway car with a driver? What is the possibility of outside accomplices? Does there appear to be inside help? Are the suspects "counter jumpers," or do they position or station themselves in a particular area or manner? As these and related issues are discussed, one can begin to formulate the tactical actions that officers must take.

2. The second type of briefing is provided by those officers who surveyed, or "advanced," the assigned location. An *advance* consists of assessing a potential stakeout location and developing an initial tactical plan. The advance should be the responsibility of the stakeout supervisor or senior officer(s) with stakeout experience. Organization, manpower deployment, and related concerns should be the responsibility of supervisors with tactical knowledge.

Investigative Procedures

Generally, a stakeout consists of an inside team and an outside team of two officers each. The **outside team** is normally designated as the arrest team. Enforcement action should not be taken by the inside team unless a life-threatening situation develops. Once the subjects have exited the stakeout location, the inside team is also responsible for securing the location to ensure that the suspects do not reenter and possibly create a barricade or hostage situation.

While the outside team is normally the arrest team, assignment of this responsibility will ultimately be based on factors associated with the specific stakeout location. For example, normally crowded public stores are not generally the best location for an arrest confrontation. On the other hand, less trafficked locations, such as exclusive jewelry stores that use controlled public access, would be preferable over a busy public street. These and related factors concerning the stakeout location should be addressed during the stakeout advance, and a decision made on team responsibilities by the detail supervisor.

The **inside team** is responsible for briefing officers concerning their actions if a crime occurs. They should ensure that employees do not initiate any independent action and should remove any privately owned weapons. All employees must understand that they should not inform anyone that police are present, nor should they seek assistance from the stakeout team for crimes such as shoplifting. If necessary, uniformed officers may respond as usual to handle these offenses. Such incidents should be handled as quickly as possible, and uniformed officers should exit the area once the call for service has been handled. Investigators must conduct themselves in a normal and inconspicuous manner at all times. They should also be cautioned to lie prone on the floor should gunfire develop.

If the inside team is not going to observe from a concealed position, employees must be inconspicuous in their particular setting. If employees wear a distinctive attire, then so must the inside team. There is always a possibility that the suspects may inspect a location before committing the crime, so stakeout officers must appear to be part of the local operation. All police equipment must be concealed, and radios must be turned off. Any private security should be dismissed and should leave the area. If the absence of private security would be obvious, security personnel may be permitted to stay, but they should not be armed and should be thoroughly briefed as to their role.

Investigators should be informed that no police action will be taken inside, with the exception of actions necessary to save lives, so as to relieve any unnecessary anxiety on the part of employees. Employees must also ensure that there is nothing on the premises, such as a scanner, that would reveal the stakeout operation. If any employee displays obvious signs of stress, serious consideration should be given to removing that employee with the cooperation of the location's management personnel.

If there is any suspicion that an officer may be involved with the suspects, an inside team should not be deployed and no one outside of the police agency should be notified of the stakeout operation. In such instances, assigned officers should conduct the stakeout from a covert observation post outside the location.

Concealment of the outside team is a concern that officers sometimes overlook. Just as suspects survey prospective target locations from inside, they also frequently survey the surrounding area. Stakeouts that do not adhere to good concealment practices risk detection. There is simply no way, for example, that two officers can sit in a vehicle or use the same disguise for an extended period of time without being conspicuous.

A sedan is frequently used but may not be the best available option for the outside team. If a sedan is preferred, however, one officer should sit in the front seat and one in the right rear seat. The officer in the rear seat should position himself so he has a clear view of activities to the rear of the vehicle. This positioning is necessary, since there are cases in which officers have been fatally wounded while seated together in the front of their vehicle and unable to see suspects approaching from the rear.

Underground parking, carports, and residential driveways also provide concealment and allow officers some freedom of movement. Vans and other businesses or residences are also frequently used. Whatever the location, the observation post should be selected with the understanding that it could be in place for an extended period of time.

Response of the outside team to the stakeout location should be tested taking into account changing traffic patterns at different times of the day. Experience has shown that 30 seconds should be considered the maximum allowable response time for the outside team to get to the stakeout. To reduce response time, outside teams should not situate themselves on the opposite side of major thoroughfares and either minimize the number of intersections that must be crossed or eliminate them altogether.

Entry and exit of the inside team to the stakeout location are extremely important. All equipment, particularly weapons, must be concealed, and officers should not arrive at the location at the same time. Once inside, the first officer should contact the designated manager or person in charge. Officers should seek a private area to brief the manager on stakeout procedures and then reevaluate the situation for safety. If circumstances that could affect safety have sufficiently changed since the advance was conducted, officers should contact a supervisor immediately and, if necessary, redeploy until the problem(s) can be resolved.

The physical environment of a stakeout is one of the most problematic issues should the use of firearms be needed. Regardless of whether an officer is stationed inside or outside the location, all officers must visually inspect the entire location with background in mind. For example, plateglass windows from floor to ceiling or plasterboard walls are unacceptable background materials should the use of firearms become necessary by the inside team.

Officers should be positioned to minimize interior backgrounds. A standard procedure in this regard is to station one officer undercover, at a point in the facility well above eye level. This positioning provides several advantages. If the use of firearms is required, this officer will be firing downward, thus minimizing or eliminating background problems. It also provides for greater visibility and strategic advantage. With one officer in this position providing cover, the second inside officer can be used to collect the suspect's weapons and frisk and handcuff the subject if an arrest must be made inside the stakeout location.

The inside team should alert the arrest team as soon as anything unusual is suspected. Radio contact with the arrest team should be maintained as long as

Figure 7.4 Photo of a crack cocaine transaction taken via stationary surveillance one-half block away.

possible to describe the suspects and the types of weapons being carried, anticipated exit route, and other pertinent information that would assist the arrest team and promote their safety.

Weapon readiness is also an important consideration. When shotguns are used, a round should be chambered with the safety on. Shotguns should never be leaned against a wall, table, or other object, but laid flat when not being held. Semi-automatic handguns should also be in a ready condition with the safety on. There is no time to chamber a round when needed instantly in a tactical situation. In addition, when disengaging the safety in such instances, it should be done as quietly as possible. Placing a finger on each side of the safety release when disengaging is a good way to ensure silence.

Exiting a location is as critical as entering. Officers should exercise the same caution in leaving the location as they did when entering. As a stakeout continues, fatigue may become a factor. Officers and supervisors should be alert to signs of fatigue, and personnel should be rotated as necessary. This is particularly the case with inside team officers whose level of preparedness and stress is greatest. Rotation can help to alleviate this constant tension as well as allow other officers to become knowledgeable about other duties of the stakeout operation.

Post-Stakeout Procedures

The potential for the use of deadly force is a part of nearly all stakeouts. However, this potentiality does not constitute grounds for an exception to existing policies and procedures that govern the use of deadly force in individual agencies. The safety of officers and citizens alike and overall reverence for human life remain important issues. As in other circumstances, officers should use deadly force only as a last resort after all other reasonable alternatives are exhausted.

Should a suspect be shot, he should be disarmed and handcuffed immediately. Officers should not diagnose the condition of the suspect to determine whether handcuffs are required. Instances exist in which presumably dead or incapacitated suspects have inflicted serious injuries on unsuspecting officers. The suspect's weapon should also be secured. If the officer is not familiar with the weapon, he should handle it only to the degree necessary until it can be rendered safe.

Following the arrest, the surrounding area should be checked for accomplices and getaway cars and the immediate area secured as a crime scene as soon as possible. In addition to ambulances, a call should be made for assistance from uniformed support personnel. These calls should be made by telephone since police radio communications are frequently monitored by the news media and the public.

All plainclothes officers should display proper ID and be easily identified as police officers since responding officers may not be aware that the location was a stakeout. Raid jackets are relatively inexpensive, easily obtainable, and easily recognized.

Once the location is secured, standard procedures for handling a crime scene should be employed. The area should be roped off or isolated, evidence should be preserved, and witnesses should be located and identified. Information to be released should be channeled only to assigned press relations officers. Officers involved in the incident should not be subjected to press interviews and should not make public statements.

ELECTRONIC SURVEILLANCE AND WIRETAPS

With the growing use of high technology to investigate crime and uncover violations of criminal law, courts throughout the nation are evaluating the applicability of constitutional guarantees with regard to high-tech surveillance. Recent technology makes possible increasingly complex forms of communication. One of the first Supreme Court decisions involving electronic communications was the 1928 case of *Olmstead* v. *United States*. In *Olmstead,* bootleggers used their home telephones to discuss and transact business.[9] Agents tapped the lines and based their investigation and ensuing arrests on conversations they overheard. The defendants were convicted and eventually appealed to the high court, arguing that the agents had in effect seized information illegally without a search warrant in violation of the defendant's Fourth Amendment right to be secure in their homes. The Court ruled, however, that telephone lines are not an extension of the defendant's home and therefore are not protected by the constitutional guarantee of security. However, subsequent federal statutes have substantially modified the significance of the *Olmstead* decision.

Recording devices carried on the body of another cover agent or informant were ruled to produce admissible evidence in *On Lee* v. *U.S.* (1952) and *Lopez* v. *U.S.* (1963).[10] The 1967 case of *Berger* v. *New York* permitted wiretaps and "bugs" in instances where state law provided for the use of such devices and officers had obtained a warrant based on probable cause.[11]

The Court appeared to undertake a significant change of direction in the area of electronic eavesdropping when it decided the case of *Katz* v. *U.S.* (1967). Federal agents had monitored a number of Katz's telephone calls from a public phone using a device separate from the phone lines and attached to the glass of a phone booth. The Court, in this case, stated that a warrant is required to unveil what a person makes an effort to keep private, even in a public place. In the words of the Court, "the government's activities in electronically listening to and recording the petitioner's words violated the privacy upon which he justifiably relied while using a telephone booth and thus constituted a search and seizure within the meaning of the Fourth Amendment."

In *Lee* v. *Florida* (1968), the Court applied the Federal Communications Act to telephone conversations that might be the object of police investigation and held that evidence obtained without a warrant could not be used in state proceedings if it resulted from a wiretap.[12] The only person who has the authority to permit eaves dropping, according to that act, is the sender of the message.

The Federal Communications Act, originally passed in 1934, does not specifically mention the potential interest of law enforcement agencies in monitoring communications. Title III of the Omnibus Crime Control and Safe Streets Act of 1968, however, mostly prohibits wiretaps but does allow officers to listen to electronic communications when (1) an officer is one of the parties involved in the communication, (2) one of the parties is not the officer but willingly decides to share the communication with the officer, or (3) officers obtain a warrant based on probable cause. In the 1971 case of *U.S.* v. *White,* the Court held that law enforcement officers may intercept electronic information when one of the parties involved in the communication gives her consent, even without a warrant.[13]

In 1984, the Supreme Court decided the case of *U.S.* v. *Karo,* in which DEA agents had arrested James Karo for cocaine importation.[14] Officers placed a radio transmitter inside a 50-gallon drum of ether purchased by Karo for use in processing the cocaine. The device was placed inside the drum with the consent of the seller of the ether but without a search warrant. The shipment of ether was followed to the Karo house, and Karo was arrested and convicted of cocaine trafficking charges. Karo appealed to the U.S. Supreme Court, claiming that the radio beeper had violated his reasonable expectation of privacy inside his premises and that, without a warrant, the evidence it produced was tainted. The Court agreed and overturned his conviction.

Minimization Requirements for Electronic Surveillance

The Supreme Court established a minimization requirement pertinent to electronic surveillance in the 1978 case of *U.S.* v. *Scott*.[15] Minimization refers to the requirement that officers take every reasonable effort to monitor only those conversations, through the use of phone taps, body bugs, and the like, that are specifically related to the criminal activity under investigation. As soon as it becomes obvious that a conversation is innocent, the monitoring personnel are required to cease listening. Problems arise if the conversation occurs in a foreign language, if it is "coded," or if it is ambiguous. For example, in one wiretap operation heroin traffickers referred to a pound quantity of product as an "elbow" or "LB." Investigators were aware of this street term and were able to continue monitoring the conversation. It has been suggested that investigators involved in electronic surveillance maintain logbooks of their activities that specifically show monitor conversations as well as efforts made to minimize noncriminal conversations.

The Electronic Communications Privacy Act of 1986

In 1986, Congress passed the Electronic Communications Privacy Act (ECPA) that brought major changes in the requirements law enforcement officers must meet to intercept wire communications (involving the human voice). The ECPA deals specifically with three areas of communication: (1) wiretaps and bugs, which enable officers to listen to criminal conversations; (2) pen registers, which record numbers dialed from a telephone; and (3) tracing devices, which determine the number from which a call emanates. The act also addresses the procedures to be followed by officers in obtaining records relating to communication services, and it establishes requirements for gaining access to stored electronic communications and records of those communications. The ECPA basically requires that investigating officers obtain wiretap-type court orders to eavesdrop on ongoing communications. The use of pen registers and recording devices, however, is specifically excluded by law from court order requirements.[16]

A related measure, the Communications Assistance for Law Enforcement Act (CALEA) of 1994, appropriated $500 million to modify the U.S. phone system to allow for continued wiretapping by law enforcement agencies. The law also specifies a standard-setting process for the redesign of existing equipment that would permit effective wiretapping in the face of coming technological advances. The law essentially requires telecommunication carriers, as defined by the act, to ensure law enforcement's ability, pursuant to a lawful court order, to intercept communications notwithstanding advanced telecommunications technologies. In 2003, federal and state judges approved 1,442 wiretap requests, and approximately 4.3 million conversations were intercepted by law enforcement agencies throughout the country. Approximately one-third of all intercepted conversations were classified as "incriminating."[17]

The Telecommunications Act of 1996

Title V of the Telecommunications Act of 1996 made it a federal offense for anyone engaged in interstate or international communications to knowingly use a telecommunications device "to create, solicit, or initiate the transmission of any comment, request, suggestion, proposal, image, or other communication which is at the scene lewd, mischievous, filthy, or indecent, with intent to annoy, abuse, threaten, or harass another person." The law also provides special penalties for anyone who "makes a telephone call . . . without disclosing his identity and with intent to annoy, abuse, threaten, or harass any person at the called number who receives the communication" or who "makes or causes the telephone of another repeatedly or continuously to ring, with the intent to harass any person at the called number; or makes repeated phone calls" for the purpose of harassing a person at the called number.[18]

A section of the law, known as the communications decency act (CDA), criminalize the transmission to minors of "patently offensive" obscene materials over the Internet or other computer communications devices. Portions of the CDA, however, were invalidated by the U.S. Supreme Court in the case of *Reno* v. *ACLU* (1997).[19]

THERMAL IMAGING

In 1996, the California appellate court decision in *People* v. *Deutsch* identified the kinds of issues that are likely to be encountered as America and law enforcement expand its use of high technology.[20] In this case, judges faced the question of whether a warrantless scan of a private dwelling using a thermal imaging device constitutes an unreasonable search within the meaning of the Fourth Amendment. These devices, also known as **forward-looking infrared** (FLIR) systems measure radiant heat energy and display their readings as thermographs. Images that a thermal imager produces can be used (as in the case of Dorian Deutsch) to reveal unusually warm areas or rooms that might be associated with the cultivation of drug-bearing plants, such as marijuana. Two hundred cannabis plants, which were being grown hydroponically under high-wattage lights in walled-off portions of Deutsch's home, were seized following the exterior thermal scan of her home by a police officer who drove by the residence at 1:30 in the morning.

Satellite-Assisted Surveillance

Shortly after Laci Peterson disappeared in Modesto, California, on Christmas Eve 2002, her husband, Scott, assured police that he had nothing to do with it. The police, however, were suspicious. Without Peterson's knowledge, they received court permission to attach **global positioning system (GPS)** tracking devices to the undersides of three vehicles he was known to drive. The devices, which use cell phone networks and signals from orbiting satellites to pinpoint land locations, indicated that twice in January 2003, Peterson drove to a San Francisco Bay marina near where the bodies of his wife and unborn son washed ashore three months later.

A Closer Look

The Mechanics of Thermal Imaging

In its simplest terms, thermal imagers operate like the human eye, but are much more powerful. Energy from the environment passes through a lens and is registered on a detector. In the case of the thermal imager, that energy is in the form of heat. By measuring very small relative temperature differences, invisible heat patterns are converted by the thermal imager into clear, visible images that can be viewed by the operator through a viewfinder or monitor. Thermal imagers are usually very sensitive and can detect temperature variations smaller then 0.1°C.

Thermal imagers "see" nothing more than the heat emitted by all objects in the camera's field of view. They do not see visible light, nor do they see rays or beams of energy. Thermal imagers are completely passive and non-intrusive. Because these devices see heat and not light, they can be used for both daytime and nighttime operations.

Thermal imagers can be compared to image intensifiers, which are another type of night vision technology and one that has been used by law enforcement and the military for years. In contrast to image intensifiers, thermal imagers are unaffected by the amount of light in a scene and will "bloom" or shut down indirect light. Unlike image intensifiers, thermal imagers can see through dust, smoke, light fog, clouds, haze, and light rain because infrared wavelengths are longer than visible wavelengths of light.

Because the officer had not anticipated entering the house, he proceded without a search warrant. The California court ruled that the scan was an illegal search because "society accepts reasonable expectation of privacy" surrounding "non-disclosed activities within the home."

In a similar case, *Kryllo* v. *U.S.* (2001), the U.S. Supreme Court reached much the same conclusion. Based on the results of a warrantless search conducted by the officers using a forward imaging device, investigators applied for a search warrant of Kryllo home.[21] The subsequent search uncovered more than 100 marijuana plants that were being grown under bright lights. The Court held, "where, as here, the government uses a device that is not in general public use, to explore details of a private home that would previously have been unknowable without physical intrusion, the surveillance is a Fourth Amendment search, and is presumptively unreasonable without a warrant."

Scott Peterson was subsequently arrested and charged with the murder of his wife and unborn child. Prosecutors in the case used data gathered by the GPS devices as part of a body of evidence suggesting that Peterson was guilty.

The use of GPS in the Peterson case reflects how police across the nation are turning to such devices for surveillance, eavesdropping, and other tasks that traditionally have been performed by uniformed officers and detectives. Recent improvements in cell phone technology and in the quality of satellite signals allow investigators to track and record a vehicle's movements in real time and display the information on a map displayed on a laptop computer.

A typical GPS tracking device is about the size of a paperback book and can be affixed to a car's undercarriage with a magnet. The cost for such a device is minimal, at about $1,000. As of the writing of this text, questions over whether police need a court's permission (a court order) to use GPS devices in investigations have become the subject of concern in state and federal courts across the nation.

Wiretaps and property searches ordinarily must be authorized by a state or federal judge, who determines whether such tactics are needed to investigate a crime. The surveillance on public roads ordinarily does not require such court orders. Because GPS devices are a substitute for ordinary visual surveillance, many police departments believe it can be used without a court order. Civil rights advocates are concerned that the technology has advanced to where police can track thousands of people anywhere, anytime, and police don't have to give a reason.

As of the preparation of this text, there are no records of how often GPS is being used nationally in criminal investigations. However, an examination of recent criminal investigations has revealed that its use is somewhat common. For example:

1. In May 2004, a Honolulu police unit that locates stolen automobiles parked a car with a GPS tracker in a high-crime area. The "bait" car was stolen and located quickly. Police arrested the driver.

2. In 2002, criminal investigators in Nassau County, New York, used two GPS devices to track a car driven by burglary suspect Richard Lacey. Prosecutors utilized GPS records to show that the car was in the vicinity of several homes at the time they were burglarized.

3. In 2000, the FBI in Las Vegas used two GPS devices that had been built into a car to eavesdrop on the targets of an investigation into organized crime. The device, offered as a safety accessory by some carmakers, allows lost or endangered drivers to be located quickly if they are calling for help.

4. In 1999, in Spokane, Washington, GPS devices on the Ford pickup and the Honda Accord driven by murder suspect William Bradley Jackson led police to the grave of his missing nine-year-old daughter, Valiree. The GPS data indicated that Jackson made two trips to the site in the three weeks after he reported the girl missing. He was convicted of murder and sentenced to 56 years in prison.

The first GPS devices were developed by the military in the 1980s and read signals transmitted by a network of 24 satellites. The device calculates its location based on its distance from each satellite. A built-in modem and antenna transmit information similar to a cell phone call (see Figure 7.5). Experts suggest that the system can be accurate, down to a nanosecond and within 20 feet. Criminal investigators claim GPS devices have distinct advantages over human trackers in that they can operate around-the-clock without a break and they're less likely to lose track of the targets or to be noticed.

Courts are just beginning to address issues raised by GPS use in criminal investigations. In the *Jackson* case in Washington State, police argued that the devices do not require a court order because they provide the same information as a visual search. The state's court of appeals agreed, finding that the GPS devices used to track Jackson were "merely sense augmenting" and revealed information open to "public view" as Jackson traveled county roads. However, the state supreme court disagreed stating that under Washington's state constitution, GPS surveillance requires a court order because it amounts to a search. In September 2003, Justice Barbara Madsen wrote in an opinion joined by all nine of the court's justices: "the intrusion into private affairs made possible with

Figure 7.5 How GPS tracking works in criminal investigation. USA Today. *Copyright 2004, USA Today. Reprinted with permission.*

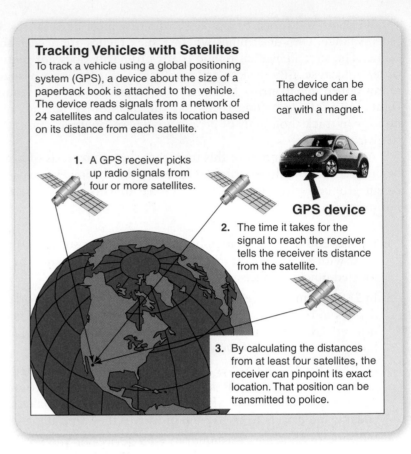

Tracking Vehicles with Satellites

To track a vehicle using a global positioning system (GPS), a device about the size of a paperback book is attached to the vehicle. The device reads signals from a network of 24 satellites and calculates its location based on its distance from each satellite.

The device can be attached under a car with a magnet.

GPS device

1. A GPS receiver picks up radio signals from four or more satellites.

2. The time it takes for the signal to reach the receiver tells the receiver its distance from the satellite.

3. By calculating the distances from at least four satellites, the receiver can pinpoint its exact location. That position can be transmitted to police.

the GPS devices is quite extensive . . . vehicles are used to take people to a vast number of places; they can reveal preferences, associations, personal habits and foibles." She continued to say that "GPS can provide a detailed picture of one's life."

However, the murder conviction in the Jackson case was upheld because Spokane County investigators took the precaution of getting a court order, even as they argued that it wasn't needed. It is possible that federal courts could reach a different conclusion because the U.S. Supreme Court, for over 20 years, has authorized law enforcement to plant electronic transmitters on vehicles without a warrant and to track them, as long as the vehicles do not enter private property.

In addition to tracking criminal suspects, some law enforcement agencies are also using GPS devices to check on the activities of their own employees. For example, between 1999 and 2003, law enforcement agencies in Des Moines, Iowa; Omaha, Nebraska; Orlando, Florida; and other cities have used GPS devices on police cars to track the cars' whereabouts during duty hours. In one case, in Clinton Township, New Jersey, in 2001, five officers were let go after their handwritten activity logs conflicted with information collected by GPS devices. In this case, one night shift officer reported that he had spent about two hours checking the security of a residence and several local businesses. The global positioning data indicated that his cruiser had been parked at a McDonald's restaurant the entire time.

DISCUSSION QUESTIONS

1. Explain the ways in which a cover story can be established and the various concerns in doing so.

2. Compare and contrast deep-cover operations with those that are short term. What are the advantages and disadvantages of each?

3. Describe the buy-bust and buy-walk procedures for undercover drug purchases, and explain the advantages and disadvantages of each.

4. Explain the relationship and role of the undercover officer and the support officer.

5. Explain some of the tactical and legal concerns of undercover operations.

6. Describe the various personnel considerations in choosing individuals for undercover assignments.

7. Explain the role and function of surveillance operations.

8. Compare and contrast the different types of surveillance methods.

9. Identify the different problems that may arise in surveillance operations, and describe how best to overcome them.

10. Distinguish between the duties of an inside and outside team in a stakeout operation.

NOTES

1. ADAMS, T. (2001). *Police field operations*, 5th ed. Upper Saddle River, NJ: Prentice Hall.

2. LANGWORTHY, R. (1989). Do stings control crime? An evaluation of a police fencing operation. *Justice Quarterly*, 6:28–45.

3. SCHOEMAN, F. (1986). Undercover operations: Some moral questions. *Criminal Justice Ethics*, 5 (2):16–22.

4. TURQUE, B. and J. STOFFEL (1989 May 8). Fury over an unholy alliance: How Cleveland cops teamed up with a drug dealer. *Newsweek*, p. 26.

5. BLACK, D. (1971). The social organization of arrest. *Stanford Law Review*, 23:1087–1111; LAFAVE, W. (1965). *The decision to take a suspect into custody*. Boston, MA: Little, Brown and Company; SMITH, D. A. and C. VISHER (1981). Street-level justice: Situational determinants of police arrest decisions. *Social Problems*, 29:167–178.

6. LYMAN, M. D. (2007). *Practical drug enforcement*, 3rd ed. Boca Raton, FL: CRC Press.

7. MOTTO, C. J. and D. L. JUNE (2000). *Undercover*, 2nd ed. Boca Raton, FL: CRC Press.

8. NASON, J. (2004). Conducting surveillance operations: how to get the most out of them. *FBI Law Enforcement Bulletin*, May.

9. *Olmstead v. U.S.*, 277 U.S. 438 (1928).

10. *On Lee v. U.S.*, 343 U.S. 747 (1952); *Lopez v. U.S.*, 373 U.S. 427 (1963).

11. *Berger v. New York*, 388 U.S. 41 (1967).

12. *Lee v. Florida*, 392 U.S. 378 (1968).

13. *U.S. v. White*, 401 U.S. 745 (1971).

14. *U.S. v. Karo*, 468 U.S. 705 (1984).

15. *U.S. v. Scott*, 436 U.S. 128 (1978).

16. For more information on the ECPA, see Robert A. Fiatal, "The Electronic Communications Privacy Act: Addressing Today's Technology," *FBI Law Enforcement Bulletin*, April 1988, p. 24-30.

17. THE ADMINISTRATIVE OFFICE FOR THE UNITED STATES COURTS (2003). Wiretap Report; posted at uscourts.com.

18. Telecommunications Act of 1996, Public Law 104, 110 Statute 56.

19. *Reno v. ACLU*, 117 S. Ct. 2329 (1997).

20. *People v. Deutsch*, 96 C.D.O.S. 2827 (1996).

21. *Kyllo v. U.S.*, 533 U.S. 27 (2001).

8 Making an Arrest

Key Terms

▶ arrest
▶ assault
▶ battery
▶ deadly force
▶ detention
▶ fleeing-felon rule
▶ reasonable force
▶ *Terry* stop

This chapter will enable you to:

- Understand the process of using force in effecting an arrest.

- Define the term *arrest*.

- Describe the elements of a lawful arrest.

- Distinguish between detainment and arrest.

- Understand the reasonable application of use of force.

- Explain the significance of the *Tennessee* v. *Garner* decision.

- Appreciate the importance of the various levels of use of force.

INTRODUCTION

The Fourth Amendment reads: "The right of the people to be secure in their persons, houses, papers, and effects, against unreasonable searches and seizures, shall not be violated, and no warrants shall issue, but upon probable cause, supported by Oath or affirmation, and particularly describing the place to be searched, and the persons or things to be seized." It has been said that an estimated 80 percent of a criminal investigator's duties are uneventful, routine, and unglamorous. But the successful completion of an investigation will end in the arrest of a suspect, who will then be prosecuted. This process is far from routine. It is the arrest that is one of the most critical aspects of an investigator's responsibilities. Arrests are always dangerous and often result in injury or even death of the arresting officer. Therefore, certain considerations must be kept in mind by the professional investigator before exercising this important police function.

DEFINING ARREST

One of the fundamental charges of criminal investigation is to identify a suspect in a crime and take him or her into custody. Indeed, when a suspect has been arrested pursuant to the filing of criminal charges, or when an officer invokes the criminal process pursuant to the filing of charges, the officer must be familiar with certain critical legal guidelines.

What Is an Arrest?

The term **arrest** may take on many different interpretations. For example, it is the official interaction between a peace officer and a suspected lawbreaker when the suspect is captured and delivered before the court. It may also be construed as the simple restriction of one's freedom by an agent of the government. There may not be the announcement "You're under arrest" by the arresting officer, nor may *Miranda* warnings be given. In some cases, the suspect may not even consider himself or herself to be under arrest. When a person is arrested, he or she forfeits many constitutional rights. Consequently, because of the severe legal implications, the arresting officer must ensure fair and lawful treatment of the arrestee and the legal process of criminal apprehension.

The Legal Arrest

The general test the courts consider to determine whether probable cause exists for an arrest is whether facts and circumstances within the officer's knowledge are sufficient to warrant a prudent person to believe a suspect has committed, is committing, or is about to commit a crime.[1] Laws of arrest will vary from one jurisdiction to another, but peace officers are generally authorized to make an arrest on the authority of an arrest warrant for either a misdemeanor or a felony offense. In many cases, the only restriction placed on the officer in these circumstances is the time of day that the arrest is authorized. As a general rule, misdemeanor arrest warrants are authorized only during the daytime hours, whereas felony warrants are typically authorized for daytime or nighttime service. Under the strictest interpretation of the U.S. Constitution, a warrant should be required for all arrests. However, the courts have loosely interpreted this

Figure 8.1 Patrol officers often assist investigators in making arrests.

requirement in allowing officers to arrest without a warrant if they personally observe any violation of the law.

Realistically speaking, arrests result after a situation between the officer and suspect develops, whereupon the officer requests information from the suspect. Only when the suspect attempts to leave and tests the limits of the officer's response may the suspect realize that he or she is really under arrest. The "free to leave" test was created in 1994 in *Stansbury* v. *California* in an effort to create a test to determine the point at which an arrest had been made. The *Stansbury* case involved the interrogation of a suspected child molester and murderer, and the court attempted to clarify the issue of arrest. It held that "when determining when a person is in custody, the court must examine all of the circumstances surrounding the interrogation, but the ultimate inquiry is simply whether there [was] a formal arrest or restraint on freedom of movement of the degree associated with a formal arrest."

The most common type of arrest is that which follows the questioning of a suspect. Once a decision to arrest is reached, the officer must come to the conclusion that a crime has been committed and that the suspect is probably the one who committed it. The presence of these elements constitutes the probable cause needed for a legal arrest. Under any circumstance, probable cause is the minimum requirement for arrest, and where a suspect is caught in the process of committing a crime, the officer has the immediate probable cause required for arrest. Most jurisdictions permit a felony arrest without a warrant when a crime is not in progress, provided that probable cause has been established. In the case of *Payton* v. *New York* (1980), the U.S. Supreme Court ruled that unless the suspect gives permission or an emergency exists, an arrest warrant is necessary if an arrest requires entry into a suspect's private residence.

In a related Supreme Court ruling, *County of Riverside* v. *McLaughlin* (1991), a person arrested without a warrant must generally be provided with a judicial determination of probable cause within 48 hours after arrest. Arrests are authorized under the following conditions:

- When the officer has probable cause to believe that the person to be arrested has committed a violation of the law "in his or her presence."
- When the officer has probable cause to believe that the person to be arrested has committed a felony but "not in his or her presence."
- When the officer has probable cause to believe that the person to be arrested has committed a felony whether or not a crime has been committed.

The in-presence requirement generally refers to the context of sight, but court rulings have supported prudent use of all five senses to support probable cause for a warrantless arrest. Other cases also have addressed the significance of the probable cause requirement. For example, *Draper* v. *United States* (1959) found that specific information as to the location of a suspect, when provided by a reliable informant, can also constitute probable cause for an arrest. In *Brinegar* v. *United States* (1949), the courts underscored the importance of the probable cause requirement as it relates to arrests by stating that a relaxation of the requirement would leave law-abiding citizens at the mercy of the personal whims of police officers.

Detention versus Arrest

What constitutes an arrest? How does an arrest differ from an investigative **detention?** There are many different types of situations in which it might appear that an officer has arrested someone but has not. Adams states that police intervention may be classified as a contact, a consensual encounter, an investigative detention, or an arrest:[2]

- *Contact.* In this situation, the subject is free to walk away if he or she so desires. It is the sole decision of the subject whether or not to cooperate with an officer.
- *Consensual encounter.* In this situation, the officer may not exert any authority over the subject. Officers can continue to seek the subject's cooperation but cannot demand it.

Probable Cause

- An officer has probable cause to make an arrest whenever the totality of facts and circumstances known to the officer creates a fair probability that a particular person is guilty of a crime.
- Probable cause is analogous to reasonable suspicion in all ways but one: Probable cause requires evidence that establishes a higher probability of guilt.
- The Fourth Amendment requires probable cause for four different purposes: (1) a warrantless arrest, (2) issuance of an arrest warrant, (3) issuance of a search warrant, and (4) warrantless search and seizure.

- *Investigative detention.* This is defined as something less than an arrest but more than a consensual encounter. Generally, this is when a person thinks that he or she cannot just walk away (*Terry* v. *Ohio*).
- *Arrest.* Act of placing a person in custody for a suspected violation of criminal law.

Investigatory Stops

Terry v. *Ohio* (1968) is the seminal case that recognized investigative stops (the investigative detention) as a separate category of seizures allowed on a lower degree of suspicion. Three constitutional requirements exist for a **Terry stop** to be lawful:

1. The officer must be able to point to objective facts and circumstances that would warrant a reasonable police officer to link the detainee's conduct with possible criminal activity.
2. The officer must proceed with the investigation as expeditiously as possible, to avoid unnecessarily prolonging the period of involuntary detention.
3. The officer must stay within the narrow investigative boundaries allowed for reasonable suspicion in *Terry* stop situations.

To satisfy the reasonable suspicion standard, the officer must possess objective grounds for suspecting that the person detained has committed, is committing, or is about to commit a crime. To satisfy this standard, the officer must be able to point to specific facts that, taken together with irrational inferences that arise from them, provide a rational basis for suspecting the detainees of criminal activity.

Whether the facts known to the officer provided an objective basis for reasonable suspicion is determined from the vantage point of a trained police officer. Courts consider "rational inferences that arise from the facts," as well as the facts themselves, in deciding whether the officer's information was sufficient to satisfy the reasonable suspicion standard. Examples of how reasonable suspicion may affect criminal investigators are:

- *Criminal profiles.* Criminal profiles are groupings of behavioral characteristics commonly seen in a particular class of offenders. While police are allowed to consider criminal profiles in evaluating the evidentiary significance of things they observe, the fact that a suspect exhibits characteristics included in the criminal profile is not a guarantee that a court will find that the officer possessed sufficient reasonable suspicion.
- *Tips from the public.* Police officers may not act on information received from members of the public without independent corroboration unless they have a rational basis for believing this information to be reliable.
- *Officer-to-officer information.* An officer who makes an investigatory stop (or an arrest) at the direction of another police department or officer need not be informed of the evidence that supports the action. However, if the officer making the stop lacks grounds to support the action, the stop will be constitutional only if the department or officer requesting the action had grounds to support it.

Investigatory stops are allowed on a lower degree of suspicion than arrests because they are designed to be less intrusive than arrests. When the police overstep the lawful boundaries of an investigatory stop, the stop automatically escalates into an arrest, resulting in a violation of the detainee's Fourth Amendment rights unless probable cause for an arrest has already been established.

Some investigatory techniques are too intrusive and too much like an arrest to be validated by reasonable suspicion alone. The police should never do the following unless they have probable cause for an arrest:

- Take a suspect against his or her will to the police station (*Hayes* v. *Florida,* 1985).
- Search the suspect for nondangerous contraband without his or her consent.

Police should also avoid doing the following during a *Terry* stop:

- Give *Miranda* warnings before police have developed grounds for an arrest unless highly intrusive safety measures become necessary during the stop.
- Perform a weapons frisk without a reasonable suspicion that the detainees may be armed or dangerous.
- Transport detainees to a second location unless this action is necessary for officer safety or to further the investigation.
- Display weapons, use handcuffs, place detainees in a patrol car, or perform other acts traditionally associated with an arrest unless these precautions appear reasonably necessary for officer safety or to further the investigation.

WHEN IS A PERSON UNDER ARREST?

In most cases, it is easy to determine when a person is under arrest: A suspect is taken into custody based on a warrant or probable cause. Handcuffs are applied and the suspect is read his or her *Miranda* warning and transported off to jail. However, is a person under arrest simply when an officer displays his or her "authority" to arrest (e.g., turning on the red lights on a police car, ordering a person to stop)? The answer is that such actions may, indeed, not constitute a legal arrest.

The courts have held that a suspect is seized within the meaning of the Fourth Amendment whenever a law enforcement officer restricts their freedom to leave. This occurs when the suspect's liberty is restrained and brought under an officer's control, either through submission to a show of legal authority or physical restraint. For example:

- *Seizure by submission to a show of legal authority.* The test for whether there has been a show of authority is objective—whether a reasonable person in the suspect's shoes would feel that he or she was not free to ignore an officer's request and walk away.
- *Seizure by physical restraint.* If the suspect does not submit to an officer's show of legal authority, no seizure occurs until the suspect is actually brought under the officer's control. The free to leave "test" has been repeatedly adopted by the court as the test for a seizure.[3]

Figure 8.2 In 2005, police made over 14 million arrests. Here, a police officer guides an arrested man through a parking lot toward his squad car.

David Kennedy, Creative Eye, MIRA.com

This issue was considered in the *California* v. *Hodari* (1991) case, where the court ruled that a Fourth Amendment seizure does not occur when law enforcement officers are chasing a fleeing suspect unless the officers apply physical force or the suspect submits to the officer's show of authority. A juvenile named Hodari was standing with three other youths on a street corner in downtown Oakland, California. When an unmarked police car was observed approaching, the youths ran in different directions. An officer exited the police car, pursued, and finally caught up with Hodari. Just before being tackled, Hodari tossed away a bag containing crack cocaine that was later used as evidence to convict Hodari of possession of cocaine.

On appeal, the California Court of Appeal held that Hodari had been constructively seized as soon as the chase began; therefore, an arrest had taken place. The officer's display of authority was sufficient to place him under arrest. Consequently, since there was no probable cause for the arrest before the cocaine was discovered, it was inadmissible as evidence. The conviction was overturned.

A *Terry* Stop Must Be:

1. Brief (90 minutes maximum).
2. Conducted efficiently so as to avoid unnecessarily prolonging the period of involuntary detention.
3. Confined to investigating the suspicion that prompted the stop unless clear grounds for reasonable suspicion of unrelated criminal activity developed during the stop.

Upon review by the U.S. Supreme Court, the justices considered the issue of whether or not an arrest had been made. There was no doubt that the officer had displayed his authority, that he wanted Hodari to stop, and that the suspect recognized all of this. However, even though the suspect had not submitted to arrest, was an arrest made? In a majority decision, Justice Antonin Scalia said: "An arrest requires either physical force . . . or, where that is absent, submission to the assertion of authority." He later added: "Neither usage nor common-law tradition makes an attempted seizure a seizure." The conviction was reaffirmed.

When there is no physical contact between an officer and a suspect, the totality of the circumstances must be considered when deciding if an arrest has been made. It must be shown that the officer's words or actions would have led a reasonable person to believe that he or she was not free to leave before attempting seizure of the person. Also, the person must somehow show his submission to the officer's authority before the seizure actually occurs. Other factors affecting the legality of an arrest include the following:

- The officer must have the appropriate legal authority to do so (e.g., jurisdiction).
- Arresting officers must be sure that persons arrested fall under the authority of the law (e.g., being physically placed into custody by the officer or submitting to the assertion of authority).

Related U.S. Supreme Court decisions include the following:

- *County of Riverside* v. *McLaughlin* (1991). Detention of a suspect for 48 hours is presumptively reasonable. If the time-to-hearing is longer, the burden of proof shifts to the police to prove reasonableness. If the time-to-hearing is shorter, the burden of proof of unreasonable delay shifts to the suspect.
- *Florida* v. *Bostick* (1991). The test to determine whether a police–citizen encounter on a bus is a seizure is whether, taking into account all the circumstances, a reasonable passenger would feel free to decline the officer's requests or otherwise terminate the encounter.

USE OF FORCE

Police are granted specific legal authority to use force under certain conditions. But the authority of officers to use force is limited. Penalties for abuse of authority can be severe, so police officers must be clear as to what they can and cannot do. The management of force by police officers is a constant challenge facing law enforcement managers. Balancing issues of a violent society with the safety concerns of police personnel creates many obstacles and concerns in developing departmental policies and procedures. The prevailing police perspective is based on a serious concern for the welfare of officers who must cope with the constant threat of a violent society. In contrast, citizens are fearful that police officers may exceed their legal bounds and use force as a means of punishment rather than control.

Public awareness of police brutality was sparked by an unfortunate incident that occurred in Brooklyn, New York, during the summer of 1997. On Saturday, August 9, a fight between two women broke out in a bar and the police were called. Haitian immigrant Abner Louima, a 30-year-old bank security guard, was taken into custody in connection with the incident. As Louima was being driven to the station house, he was beaten and upon arrival he was stripped, searched, and sodomized with a wooden stick attached to a toilet plunger. Doctors examining Louima discovered he suffered a ruptured bladder, a punctured lower intestine, and several broken front teeth. Louima claimed that during the assault the two arresting officers taunted him by saying, "That's yours, nigger" and "We're going to teach you niggers to respect police officers" and "This is Giuliani time, not Dinkens time." (The latter comment was an apparent reference to the mayor's zero-tolerance policy, as well as his law-and-order approach to crime control.)

Police officers deal every day with persons who are violent, under the influence of drugs or alcohol, mentally deranged, or just desperate to avoid arrest. To cope, officers are granted specific legal authority to use force under constitutional law and the laws of most states. However, the authority of officers to use force is limited. Those limitations may be enforced through the use of criminal prosecution, civil lawsuits, and disciplinary actions. Our society recognizes three legitimate and responsive forms of force:[4]

1. The right of self-defense, including the valid taking of another person's life to protect oneself.
2. The power to control those for whom some responsibility for care and custody has been granted an authority figure, such as a prison guard.
3. The institution of a police group that has relatively unrestricted authority to use force as required.

Police officers are taught that the penalties for abusing their authority to use force can be severe. To avoid harsh penalties, police officers must be aware of the rules that govern the use of force. Such rules are included in state law, federal law, and department policy. The federal standard for police use of force was established by the U.S. Supreme Court in *Graham* v. *Connor* (1989). In that case, the Court recognized that the police officer's duty to make arrests and to conduct searches and investigatory stops carries with it the authority to use force reasonably or to threaten the use of force. The *Graham* decision allows officers to use

---

Fourth Amendment Requirements for a Constitutional Arrest

There are two types of arrests: (1) formal (i.e., intentional) arrests, and (2) detentions that last too long or are too invasive to constitute a *Terry* stop.

• The Fourth Amendment requires probable cause for an arrest.
• An arrest warrant is mandatory under the Fourth Amendment only when the police make a nonconsensual entry into a private residence to arrest someone inside (*Payton* v. *New York*, 1980).

   An arrest warrant has two advantages over an arrest without a warrant.

• It ensures that evidence seized during an arrest will be admissible.
• It immunizes the officer from a civil suit.

   However, both of the advantages above will be lost if the officer:

• Deliberately or recklessly includes false information in his or her affidavit, or
• Fails to include enough factual information to enable a magistrate to make an independent determination as to whether probable cause exists for the arrest.

   A defendant who is arrested without a warrant and not released on bail is entitled to a judicial determination of probable cause without undue delay after the arrest. Absent extraordinary circumstances, this detention must take place within 48 hours after a warrantless arrest.

force for two reasons only: defense and control, not punishment. One must remember that the Fourth Amendment protects the "right of the people to be secure in their persons . . . against unreasonable searches and seizures and shall not be violated." Because a police officer's use of force constitutes a seizure, using excessive force is a violation of a citizen's rights under the Fourth Amendment.

Based on the totality of the circumstances, three key factors can be used to evaluate the extent of an officer's use of force:

1. The severity of the crime committed.
2. Whether the suspect poses an immediate threat to the safety of the officer or others.
3. Whether the suspect actively resisted arrest or attempted to evade arrest.

When police are compelled to use force, a court will use the following standard to determine whether such force was reasonable. First, the officer's conduct will be compared to that of a "reasonable officer" confronted by similar circumstances. Second, when the judge and jury evaluate the officer's actions, they must do so from the "standing in your shoes" standard. This means that they can only make use of information the officer had at the time that he or she exerted force; 20/20 hindsight cannot be considered in this analysis.

One of the confusing aspects about the use of force is that there are no clear-cut answers regarding how it is applied. Worse yet, there are many severe penalties for police officers who take the wrong course of action on the street. We know that numerous dangerous situations confront police officers every day. From time to time officers are required to use force—it's inevitable. After a police officer makes a decision to use force, his or her department and the courts will take considerable time scrutinizing the situation to determine if such actions were appropriate.

Remember, the modern-day police officer must not only know how to use force techniques, such as the swinging of a baton, but when to apply those techniques. The use of force by police officers stems from the premise that in a modern democratic society, citizens are discouraged by law from employing force to solve personal disputes. Instead, they are expected to rely on the justice system to arbitrate and resolve conflicts. With few exceptions, such as cases involving self-defense, this restriction applies to most situations.

Defining Use of Force

The authority to use force carries with it awesome responsibilities. The fear of criticism can cause officers to second-guess themselves and hesitate, which could be dangerous. People have different ideas about just what constitutes force and police brutality. Police officers, in particular, have specific ideas of what justifies the use of force. Generally speaking, force is defined through the concepts of assault and battery.

Battery is generally defined as an intentional, nonconsensual bodily contact that a reasonable person would consider harmful. Certainly, hitting someone with our fists or with a baton or shooting someone would be considered offensive, harmful, and forceful by a reasonable person. However, battery also includes any intentional, nonconsensual contact associated with the body. For the most part, battery and assault are often used together. However, under most criminal statutes, there is a significant difference between them.

Use of Force in Making an Arrest or Other Seizure

Use of excessive force is regulated by three provisions of the Constitution: the Fourth, Eighth, and Fourteenth Amendments.

- The Fourth Amendment standard used to evaluate whether unconstitutional force has been used in making a seizure is whether a reasonable police officer on the scene would have considered this amount of force necessary. This is called the *objective reasonableness standard*.
- Physical force may be used for the following three purposes only:
  1. To protect the officer or others from danger.
  2. To overcome resistance.
  3. To prevent escape.

Assault means to intentionally put someone in fear of immediate battery or to threaten someone while having the apparent ability to carry out that threat. So although battery requires actual contact, the legal concept of assault doesn't necessarily include actual bodily contact. It's wrong to think that an officer uses force only when striking someone. In other words, an officer who displays his or her weapon while shouting "Stop or I'll shoot!" fits within the definition of assault. So even though the officer doesn't fire in that situation, force was used. Acting in any manner that implies a threat, such as raising fists, mace, weapons, or batons, constitutes the use of force.

Understanding Reasonableness

Under the *Graham* decision, the Court identified three key factors based on the totality of the circumstances to use in evaluating an officer's use of **reasonable force:**

1. The severity of the crime committed.
2. Whether the suspect posed an immediate threat to the safety of officers or others.
3. Whether the suspect actively resisted arrest or attempted to evade arrest by flight.

According to the *Graham* decision, active resistance to arrest includes any physical actions by the suspect that make the arrest physically more difficult to accomplish. Active resistance to arrest includes pushes and shoves as well as more obscure actions, such as holding on to the steering wheel while being removed from a car. An interesting finding of the *Graham* decision was an explanation of the standards under which officers' conduct should be judged by a jury and trial judge. First, the actions of the officer(s) will be compared to actions of a "reasonable officer" involved in a similar situation. Second, the Court said that when the judge and jury evaluate the officer from within the "shoes" of the officer under review, they must make their decision based on the information the officer had at the time that he or she took action. Thus, hindsight cannot be used to consider the behavior of the officers in question.

Levels of Force

In 1991, the Christopher Commission, which investigated the behavior of the Los Angeles Police Department in the Rodney King beating incident, found that there were a significant number of officers who regularly used force against the public and who often ignored department guidelines for the use of force. Under department guidelines, officers were required to exercise the minimum amount of force necessary to control a suspect. The Commission set forth guidelines that identify levels of force and the permissible use-of-force techniques within each level (Figure 8.3):

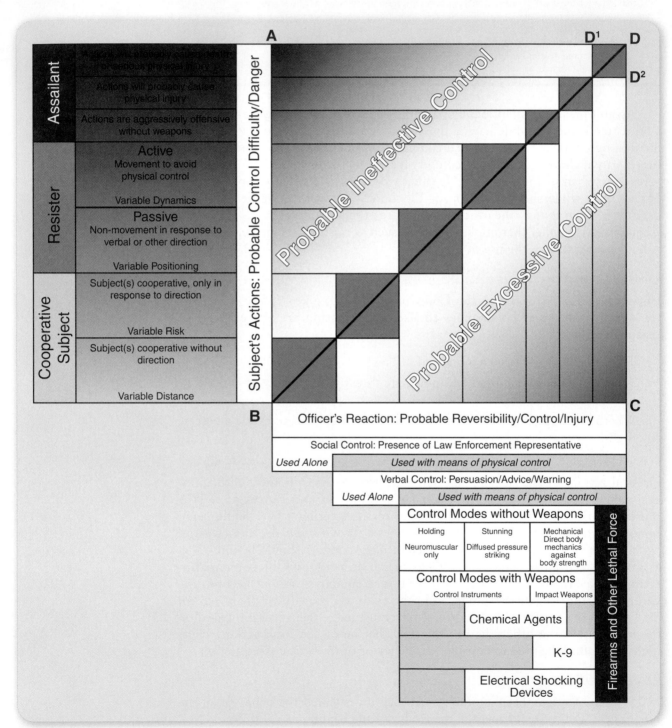

Figure 8.3 Use-of-force continuum.

Proactive Safety Systems, Inc.

1. Social control (uniformed presence)

2. Verbal control

3. Weaponless control techniques (including pressure/pain holds, starting at "hands-on" with no pain, stunning (diffused impact with soft striking surfaces), and mechanical (skeletal)

4. Electrical shocking devices (roughly equivalent to weaponless pressure compliance methods)

5. Chemical agents

6. Control instruments (equivalent to weaponless pressure/pain holds)

7. Impact weapons (equivalent to weaponless mechanical modes)

8. Firearms (and other means of force that could cause death or serious bodily damage when utilized)

Although it is important to consider this continuum in determining the various levels of force, it is also important to consider operational basics that apply to all police officers regarding the use of force. For example, experience tells us that while modern aerosol sprays can cause considerable discomfort, they seldom (if ever) result in bodily injury. In comparison, use of a baton can result in serious tissue damage, depending on the area targeted by the officer. So since aerosol spray has a lower propensity for causing pain or injury, it has a low level of force.

Another example is the use of impact weapons, such as a baton or a flashlight. The flashlight has a greater propensity to create damage than the baton, and although the flashlight is commonly used as an impact weapon, it is not designed for this use. In comparing the two, it is easy to see that a flashlight would be on a higher level of force than a baton. Officers should constantly consider their options when approaching what they perceive to be a dangerous situation. In doing so, if the need to use force becomes a reality, proper application of force will be available quickly.

DEADLY FORCE

In 1967, the President's Commission on Law Enforcement and the Administration of Justice noted that most police departments had no policy to guide them on the use of **deadly force.** At the time, most state laws were extremely broad in defining the circumstances under which officers could employ deadly force. In its most commonly used parlance, the term *deadly force* refers to actions of police officers that result in the killing of a person. As mentioned above, police officers are legally authorized to use deadly force under certain circumstances.

As a rule, such actions result from situations in which persons are fleeing the police, assaulting someone, or attempting to use lethal force against another person (including a police officer). If deadly force is used improperly or illegally, the officers responsible may be criminally liable and both the officers and the police department may be sued in a civil action. Most rules regarding the use of deadly force come from federal statutes and case law and, as a rule, are concerned with police use of deadly force to arrest fleeing felons engaged in nonviolent felonies. These cases are different from those pertaining to suspects committing violent felonies, such as murder, assault, rape, robbery, or other types of behavior that represent a substantial risk of bodily harm or death.

The Fleeing-Felon Rule

Until the mid-1980s, the shooting of a suspect by police was tolerated by many police agencies. Although this is currently not the case, it was prevalent in the early development of policing when most felonies were punishable by death and there was an assumption that all felons would avoid arrest at any cost. Therefore, the **fleeing-felon rule** was developed during a time when apprehension of felons was considered more dangerous than it is today. Police officers in those early days often worked alone and lacked sophisticated communications technology with which to track suspects who were wanted by police.

The concern was that felons would escape arrest and retreat to another community where they could begin a new life of crime. As time went by and more efficient means were developed for apprehension, arrests became easier for law enforcement officials. For a period of time, police still relied on the ability to use deadly force even though some felons were not considered dangerous and posed no particular threat to the officer or the community. Prior to 1985, police officers were legally authorized by most states to employ the use of deadly force in apprehending fleeing felons.

Over the years, many states had modified the fleeing-felon rule, but some still allowed rather broad discretion about when to use deadly force. In a watershed decision by the U.S. Supreme Court in March 1985, it was determined that Tennessee's fleeing-felon law was unconstitutional. *Tennessee* v. *Garner* (1985) involved the police shooting and subsequent killing of an unarmed boy as the youth fled from an unoccupied house. In this case, the officer could see that the suspect was a youth and that he was unarmed. The officer argued, however, that if the youngster were able to leap a fence, he would be able to escape. The state statute in Tennessee at the time permitted officers to shoot fleeing felons to prevent escape. Pursuant to *Garner,* the Court ruled that for the employment of deadly force by police to be lawful, it must be "reasonable." Reasonable deadly force is authorized under three circumstances:

1. To prevent an escape when the suspect has threatened an officer with a weapon.
2. When there is a threat of death or serious physical injury to the officer or others.
3. If there is probable cause to believe that the suspect has committed a crime involving the infliction or threatened infliction of serious physical injury and, when practical, some warning has been given by the officer.

In some instances, the Tennessee statute allowing an officer to shoot a fleeing felon may be constitutional. However, the special circumstances in the *Garner* case, in which the suspect was an unarmed juvenile involved in a nonviolent crime, made the shooting both unreasonable and unlawful. The use of force by police is necessary and appropriate but only when used properly. Otherwise, it violates the rights of others and can result in serious injury or death as well as a loss of confidence in the police department.

The Deadly Force Triangle

One way to help officers decide when to use deadly force is by referring to the deadly force triangle. This is a time-tested model that enhances an officer's ability to respond to a deadly force encounter while at the same time keeps him or her within the limits of the law and department policy. The three sides of an

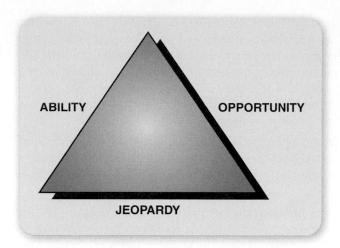

Figure 8.4 Decision model: the deadly force triangle. All three factors must be present to justify deadly force. *D.T. Olson, Improving deadly force decision making.* FBI Law Enforcement Bulletin, *February 1998, p. 1–8.*

equilateral triangle represent three factors: ability, opportunity, and jeopardy. All three factors must be present to justify deadly force (Figure 8.4).[5]

According to this model, *ability* means the suspect's physical capacity to harm an officer or another innocent person. This is widely interpreted as a suspect's being armed with a weapon, such as a firearm, knife, or club, capable of inflicting death or serious physical injury. Ability also includes personal physical capabilities, such as those possessed by martial arts practitioners, agitated suspects under the influence of drugs, or a powerfully built person.

Opportunity is described as the suspect's potential to use his or her ability to kill or seriously injure. An unarmed but large and powerfully built suspect might have the ability to kill or injure a smaller person who is not in comparable physical shape. However, opportunity does not exist as a rule if the suspect is more than 50 yards away. Accordingly, a suspect armed with a knife has the ability to kill or seriously injure but might lack opportunity if he or she is too far away to make use of the weapon.

Jeopardy exists when suspects take advantage of their ability and opportunity to place an officer or another person in imminent physical danger. For example, a situation in which, after a foot pursuit, an armed robbery suspect refuses to drop a weapon when ordered would constitute jeopardy.

OFF-DUTY ARRESTS

Policing is generally considered a 24-hour-a-day responsibility, and officers, whether on or off duty, are expected to respond when necessary and departmentally authorized to potential or actual violations of the law and to provide assistance, as necessary, to citizens under emergency conditions. In most cases, while off duty, police officers are responsible for reporting any observed criminal activities to on-duty authorities. As a rule, off-duty police officers should not enforce minor violations such as harassment, disorderly conduct, minor traffic violations, or other "nuisance" offenses. As a general matter of practice, when off duty, a police officer should make an arrest only when:

1. *The officer is not personally involved in the incident underlying the arrest.* This precaution is geared primarily toward ascertaining whether, for liability purposes, the officer was acting within the scope of his employment. An

example of this would be an off-duty officer who is drinking in a bar with a friend. The officer's friend becomes involved in a dispute with other patrons, all of whom have also been drinking. A brawl ensues, and the off-duty officer arrests a person who punched his friend. The officer is later sued for false arrest. In situations like this, off-duty officers who are personally involved in a situation should summon on-duty personnel. Effective police work requires dispassionate, objective analysis of the facts.

2. *There is an immediate need to prevent a crime or apprehend a suspect.* In all instances of true emergencies, where a serious crime is being committed or lives or property are endangered, immediate action by an off-duty officer may be warranted.

3. *The crime would require a full custodial arrest. Case example:* An off-duty officer sees someone breaking into a neighbor's house and the suspect flees immediately thereafter. The officer chases the suspect and apprehends him. This would be a permissible arrest, as the officer acted properly to prevent the immediate escape of a fleeing suspect of a serious crime.

4. *The arresting officer possesses appropriate police identification and equipment.* Before making a permitted off-duty arrest, an officer should have complete police identification, such as a badge and police photo identification, and should be armed. This will greatly reduce the possibility that the officer will be mistaken as a perpetrator when on-duty officers arrive at the scene. Actual police identification will also forestall situations where the off-duty officer intervenes in an altercation or other situation and is mistaken as another assailant.

Off-duty police officers must be aware of state laws, local ordinances, and case laws that govern the limit of their off-duty authority. These requirements will most likely vary from jurisdiction to jurisdiction. In some cases, the increasing amount of civil litigation focusing on off-duty law enforcement actions has resulted in many officers taking a grim view of their role as Good Samaritans. For example, an article in the *Washington Post* questioned the advisability of an off-duty arrest based on the following incident. An off-duty Washington, D.C., police officer, jogging near his Rockville, Maryland, home, responded to shouts and what he thought was a cry of "rape." He arrived at the scene and saw a person lying on the ground and several other persons with their shirts off. The officer immediately acted to stop what he perceived to be a potential rape. As it turned out, no rape was occurring. It was merely a group of teenagers from a party. The officer was sued for assault, battery, and false imprisonment of the teenagers, charging that the officer overstepped his authority. Thus, civil litigation has added several new factors to be considered in the cost-benefit calculus of off-duty enforcement powers. Recognizing these risks, many police agencies are adopting policies designed to reduce the exposure of off-duty police officers, both to physical danger and to the increased likelihood of civil or criminal liability lawsuits.

In summary, police officers should not make off-duty arrests when:

• The arresting officer is personally involved in the incident underlying the arrest; or

• Engaged in off-duty employment of a nonpolice nature and the officer's actions are only in furtherance of the interests of the private employer; or

- The arrest is made solely as enforcement of a minor traffic regulation. Despite the fact that a police officer has police powers and responsibilities 24 hours a day throughout his or her jurisdiction, the off-duty officer should not enforce minor traffic regulations.

POSTARREST PROCEDURES

In addition to making a proper and lawful arrest, officers are also responsible for the safety of the arrestee(s). For example, officers should not allow victims or other bystanders to come into close proximity with the arrestee. In addition, they should not allow the arrestee out of their immediate presence for any reason until he is properly secured and transported. An example would include permitting the arrested person to leave the immediate area of the arrest to gather personal items or to perform other tasks prior to being transported. In the event such a request is granted, the arrestee should first be searched for weapons and then be accompanied and closely monitored by the arresting officer or other officers.

Once the arrestee is completely secured and out of reach from both victims and the public, officers should (if not already done so) conduct a thorough search of the person for weapons and contraband. Whenever possible, all searches that are conducted incident to arrest should be performed by an officer of the same gender as the arrestee. Any criminal evidence discovered during the search of the arrestee's person should be seized and preserved in accordance with accepted procedures (see Chapter 4). Furthermore, the search incident to arrest can and should include not only the person of the arrestee but also areas within the reach and control of the arrestee.

Strip searches should not be conducted in the field except under the most extreme circumstances and normally only with approval of a supervisor. Any officer who chooses to conduct a strip search in the field must be prepared to justify the exceptional reasons for the search and must document those reasons in a subsequent written report. In order for a strip search to be valid at a jail or similar holding facility, it must be justified under existing circumstances and conducted in a reasonable manner. Failure to conform to either of these requirements will invariably make the search illegal. Moreover, body cavity searches, typically used to search for drugs, may only be performed by health care personnel subsequent to the issuance of a warrant.

DISCUSSION QUESTIONS

1. Define the term *arrest* and state how it relates to the duties of the criminal investigator.

2. Discuss what constitutes a legal arrest.

3. Discuss how detention differs from arrest.

4. Describe under what legal circumstances a person is under arrest.

5. Discuss the impact of the Rodney King incident on the police and their powers of arrest.

6. The U.S. Supreme Court in *Graham* v. *Connor* established the federal standard for police use of force. Discuss the outcome of this decision.

7. List and discuss the Christopher Commission's guidelines for the use of force.

8. Describe the impact of the *Tennessee* v. *Garner* decision on the use of deadly force.

9. List and explain the U.S. Supreme Court decisions that address detaining suspects after arrest.

NOTES

1. *U.S.* v. *Puerta,* 982 F.2d 1297, 1300 (9th Cir. 1992).

2. ADAMS, T. (1990). *Police field operations,* 2nd ed. Upper Saddle River, NJ: Prentice Hall.

3. *Stansbury* v. *California,* 114 S. Ct. 1526, 1529 128 L.Ed2d 293 (1994); *Yarborough* v. *Alvarado,* U.S. Supreme Court No. 02-1684 (decided June 1, 2004).

4. PEAK, K. J. (1993). *Policing America: Methods, issues and challenges.* Upper Saddle River, NJ: Prentice Hall.

5. OLSON, D. T. (1998). Improving deadly force decision making. *FBI Law Enforcement Bulletin,* February, pp. 1–8.

Chapter 9

Interviews and Interrogations

Key Terms

- admission
- coercion
- confession
- custodial interrogation
- duress
- interrogation
- interview
- *Miranda* warning
- polygraph

This chapter will enable you to:

- Perceive distinctions between the interview and interrogation.

- Understand the significance of the *Miranda* decision.

- Appreciate the value of admissions and confessions.

- Recognize the legal requirements of interrogation.

- Understand the process for taking a written statement.

- Realize the investigative utility of the polygraph exam.

INTRODUCTION

Once the suspect in a crime has been arrested, the investigator's job is not finished. The matter of proof and prosecution remain. It is the duty of each investigator to attempt to secure a confession from suspects they have arrested. Once again, legal considerations must always be kept in mind to ensure that any statement is admissible in court. Interviews and interrogations are another fascinating aspect of criminal investigation. It is the phase of the investigation where the investigator wears a different hat so to speak. Putting the officer's psychological talents to work may come into play to enhance the chances of a suspect admitting his or her role in a crime.

INTERVIEW VERSUS INTERROGATION

Investigators must make a clear distinction between the two processes of interviewing and interrogating suspects. An interview should precede every interrogation. Through an interview, investigators learn about the subjects and their needs, fears, concerns, and attitudes. They can then use this information to prepare themes or arguments to use during interrogations.[1]

To be a good interviewer or interrogator, the investigator must apply certain physical and psychological techniques to the person being interviewed to persuade him or her to divulge information. In the case of the interview, it is the investigator's job to create an atmosphere in which the subject can be relaxed enough to recall and explain details of a suspected crime. Conversely, when a criminal suspect is being interrogated, the investigator must gently and skillfully break down the suspect's defenses to gain an admission or confession, and do so while staying within the constraints of constitutional law. In some countries, physical and mental stress are used as ways to coerce information from both witnesses and suspects. It is generally accepted that a person will confess to anything if enough pressure or intimidation is applied. But is a "confession" really a truthful statement under these circumstances? Certainly not!

During the course of an investigation, an investigator will probably conduct many interviews and several interrogations. The distinction between an interview and an interrogation is often blurred, but it can be expressed in terms of the purpose of the contact. An **interview** is a relatively formal conversation conducted for the purpose of obtaining information. Notes are taken and major points are reviewed. Interviews, however, may involve virtually anyone, including informants, witnesses, victims, cooperating citizens, and even the suspect himself or herself. In brief, the interview process occurs either before the case focuses on a particular person or in a place where the suspect can clearly terminate the interview at any time. By comparison, an **interrogation** is the systematic questioning of a person suspected of involvement in a crime for the purpose of obtaining a confession. Legal guidelines affecting the two activities differ considerably as the probability increases that the person being questioned may incriminate himself or herself.

THE INTERVIEW PROCESS

The interview is a form of communication used extensively by law enforcement. It is used in many ways to glean information from the subject being interviewed. For example, interviewing is used to screen job applicants, to extract information from witnesses or victims of a crime, or to obtain a confession from a criminal suspect. Interviews of cooperating citizens and witnesses are often conducted outside the office. More often than not, however, the investigator will have a more productive interview if it can be conducted at a location where the subject is mentally relaxed, such as his or her own home or place of business. Regardless of where the interviews are conducted, investigators should follow certain guidelines due to legal and technical considerations.

Investigators should take time to prepare properly for the interview. Occasionally, this preparation must be done quickly and may consist of no more than a mental review of details of the case, but some type of preparation should precede actual contact with the subject being interviewed. Generally, the most common interviews that investigators will conduct are with witnesses, cooperating citizens, victims, informants, and suspects. Let's look at the fundamentals of each of these.

Interviewing Witnesses, Citizens, and Victims

Investigators must remember that although the interview process is geared toward those believed simply to have information about a crime, witnesses often turn out to be suspects. Sources for interviews include the victim, witnesses, and the complainant. These subjects should be separated before questioning begins. The following considerations should be observed during the interview process.

- *Develop a plan of action.* To begin, the investigator should be familiar with pertinent data about the incident in question before initiating the interview. He or she should take care to develop questions designed to elicit the particular task at hand. For example, questions directed to a witness should be tailored to obtain specific facts for the police report. Questions that are prepared in advance will tend to add to the flow of conversation and give direction to the interview.

- *Conduct the interview in private.* It is sometimes easier to fulfill this requirement than others, depending on the circumstances. In all cases, it is important to provide interviewees with the greatest amount of privacy possible, both to encourage clarity of thought and to protect the confidentiality of the interview.

- *Place the interviewee at ease.* Most interviews involve a great amount of stress and emotional discord for the interviewee. This is usually created by a sense of uncertainty about the expectations of the investigator and the uniqueness of the situation. If a degree of fear develops in the person being interviewed, he or she may withhold information. Indeed, it is during the preliminary phase of the interview that the investigator's personality will be tested rigorously. The investigator should therefore take great care to make the person being interviewed as comfortable as possible and to build rapport. In addition, he or she should attempt to uncover any reasons for the interviewee's reluctance to cooperate. It is also important to relax the person being interviewed, as comments made by a calm person are easier to evaluate than those made by someone who is nervous. This can be accomplished by beginning the interview casually with friendly conversation. Certainly, a strained or awkward initial contact with the subject might convey the message that the investigator doesn't like something about the interviewee. A friendly approach will help defuse any negative feelings in the subject and reinforce positive ones.

- *Be a good listener.* Once the communication barrier is lifted, the investigator must learn to let the interviewee speak freely. Indeed, this is a great shortcoming of many investigators, as many feel the need to interrupt or share their personal opinions with interview subjects. It is the job of the interviewer to listen closely and evaluate not just *what* is being said but *how* it is being said. In short, it is the responsibility of the investigator to control the interview but not to dominate it.

- *Ask the right questions.* Not only is it important to know what questions to ask the subject but how those questions should be asked. During the conversation, the investigator's emotions should be in check at all times, along with an attempt to make the questions easy to comprehend. In addition, the phrasing of questions is critical to the success of the interview. For example, close-ended questions, requiring a simple yes or no response, should be used sparingly. This type of question doesn't elicit personal information from the subject, as it simply permits the person to confirm or deny information being offered. A preferable technique is to ask open-ended questions, which force the interviewee to relate in his or her own words what was observed. Hypothetical questions should also be avoided, as they tend to make the interviewee guess at a certain response or to tell the interviewer what he or she wants to hear. Finally, the interviewer should avoid asking loaded, or leading, questions that contain the answer and require the person being interviewed to choose between the lesser of two evils.

- *Don't dispute the subject's answers.* The emotional reactions of the investigator must be kept under control at all times. Once the subject gives his or her interpretation of what happened, the investigator can later go back and document any discrepancies.

- *Maintain control of the interview.* Frequently during an interview, the subject might try to steer the conversation away from the subject at hand. Again, proper preparation is the key to having a good plan and to staying on track.

- *Take brief notes.* Once the interviewee begins to talk freely, the investigator should avoid interruptions. An attempt to take complete notes while a citizen is narrating a story will probably disrupt the flow of information. This generally occurs because the witness sees the investigator writing profusely and will slow down just to accommodate him or her. In doing so, the witness may become distracted and forget important details. Furthermore, some people are just naturally nervous speaking in the presence of someone recording everything they say. Brief notes are therefore the prescribed method of recording the conversation. These generally consist of names, addresses, and certain phrases that will outline the narrative for review. Most important, however, the investigator should listen carefully and not lose eye contact with the witness.

- *Adjourn the interview properly.* Just as the interview process begins with a proper introduction, it should also end appropriately. Generally, a concluding remark is appropriate, such as: "OK, you may leave—thank you for your time." It might also be advisable to summarize the interview briefly with the witness before dismissal. Such expressions of courtesy during and after the interview create a favorable impression and encourage further cooperation.

THE SUSPECT INTERROGATION PROCESS

During any case it is important for information to be obtained by means of a direct interview with a suspect. As indicated earlier, it is not at all uncommon during the progress of a case for a person who was interviewed as a witness or victim to become a primary suspect at a later date. In that event, as the case progresses, the investigator can use information learned in the earlier interview.

Goals of the Interrogation

The interrogation is designed to match new information with a particular suspect, to secure a confession. The goals of the interrogation process are as follows:[2]

- To learn the truth of the crime and how it happened.
- To obtain an admission of guilt from the suspect.
- To obtain all facts to determine the method of operation and the circumstances of the crime.
- To gather information that enables investigators to arrive at logical conclusions.
- To provide information for use by prosecutors in possible court action.

Legal Requirements of the Interrogation

According to early English Common Law, the confession of a suspect was by far the most important type of evidence against an accused person. In many cases, failure to produce such evidence was equivalent to not having any evidence at all. Therefore, investigators vigorously pursued confessions at all costs, with little regard for the rights of those accused or the fairness of their methods. Techniques for obtaining the confession included submersion in water, stretching, branding, and other types of physical and psychological torture. Today, such tactics have been replaced with legal guarantees of fairness, such as the Bill of Rights, the Constitution, and statutes prohibiting the use of coercion or duress in the interrogation process. Still, the confession reigns as one of the most influential types of evidence in a court proceeding.

SAFEGUARDING AGAINST POLICE MISCONDUCT

Several types of behavior have been identified as improper (even illegal) for police investigators and will result in any confession obtained from the suspect being deemed inadmissible by the courts. These behaviors include coercion or duress, physical constraint, unreasonable delay in arraignment, and refusing legal counsel during interrogation.

Coercion and Duress

Coercion and duress are similar in that they both create an environment of intimidation during the interrogation process. **Coercion** is defined as the use, or threat of use, of illegal physical methods to induce a suspect to make an admission or confession. **Duress** is the imposition of restrictions on physical behavior,

The Laci Peterson Murder Investigation

On the evening of December 24, 2002, Scott Peterson told Modesto, California, police that his 27-year-old wife—7 1/2 months pregnant—was missing. He'd left her around 9:30 that morning to go on a fishing trip to Berkeley Marina (part of San Francisco Bay), 85 miles away. She was about to walk to a nearby park to walk their dog. He tried phoning Laci when he finished, but got no answer. When he got home, Laci was gone, and the dog was in their backyard, its leash still attached.

At first, all police investigation of Scott's story was for the purpose of "eliminating him as a suspect." By mid-January, partly because police learned of Scott's extramarital affair, he became a suspect in Laci's disappearance.

The first week in March, the Modesto PD announced that they were no longer investigating Laci's disappearance as a missing persons case, but as a multiple murder: Laci and her unborn child, Conner. The significance here is that "multiple murder" is one of the special circumstances under California law that allows prosecutors to seek the death penalty.

On April 13, the body of a full-term male fetus was found along the shoreline of Point Isabel Regional Park in Richmond, California, about 80 miles from the Petersons' Modesto home—but only a few miles from where Scott claimed to have been fishing on December 24. During an April 18 press conference, California Attorney General Bill Lockyear announced that the bodies were indeed those of Laci and Conner: Laci was identified by comparing bone samples with DNA samples drawn from her family, while Conner was identified by comparing his DNA to Scott's. This also, of course, silenced speculation that Conner might not have been Scott's baby (which was suggested by some as a possible motive for her murder).

Earlier on April 18, Scott was arrested in San Diego, where he'd been spending much of his time over the previous few weeks. At the time of the arrest, he had $10,000 in cash and his brother's identification in his possession. His arrest was hastened by the fear that he might have been planning to flee to Mexico. (Mexico will not extradite a suspect who faces the death penalty in the United States.) The Stanislaus County District Attorney announced that Scott would be charged with capital murder of both Laci and Conner, making him eligible for the death penalty.

Scott pleaded not guilty on April 21 to two counts of capital murder. The prosecutor listed the Peterson home as the scene of Laci's murder and added that "during the commission of the murder of Laci Denise Peterson, the defendant with knowledge that [she] was pregnant did inflict injury on [her] resulting in the termination of her pregnancy."

Regarding the fact that Laci and Conner were found separately (one day apart), though she was only in her eighth month of pregnancy when she disappeared: Doctors describe a phenomenon known as "coffin birth," by which a fetus can be expelled from a woman's body after death. Peterson was found guilty of Laci's murder and sentenced to death.

A look at the forensic evidence:

- Footprints and tire tracks were found near the spot where Conner's body was found—and police didn't secure the scene or take casts of the footprints or tracks. Police say the taking of casts would have been difficult in the wet surface, but any defense would have certainly brought this up.

- Conner's body was found with no sign of an umbilical cord or placenta, and adhesive tape was wrapped 1 1/2 times around his neck. The tape might have been secured with a knot, which would eliminate the possibility that it became wrapped around him due to random movements in the

such as prolonged interrogation, deprivation of water, food, or sleep. In *Brown* v. *Mississippi* (1936), the U.S. Supreme Court ruled that physical coercion used to obtain a confession was a violation of the Fourteenth Amendment. Following this ruling, the Court focused its attention on cases in which "psychological" rather than physical coercion was used to prompt a confession.

In a related case, *Ashcraft* v. *Tennessee* (1944), a prolonged interrogation resulted in a confession that was overturned because the police used duress, intimidation, and other psychological pressures to invoke a confession. One such measure was not allowing the suspect to phone his wife until after he confessed.

water. What appear to be the remains of a plastic bag were found near Conner, suggesting that he was tied and put in the bag.

- Further evidence suggesting Conner was born alive: Conner appears to have been close to a full-term baby, gestating for 35 to 38 weeks. The defense claimed that as of Laci's December 23 sonogram, Conner was only 31 weeks along. This would indicate that Laci was not killed on either December 23 or 24. Estimations of the length of gestation can be off by up to four weeks, so this would not prove anything—but again, in a case relying on circumstantial evidence, all the defense had to do is introduce reasonable doubt.

- A witness says he saw a verbal altercation on the morning of December 24 between two men and a woman fitting Laci's description—wearing what Scott says she was wearing that day—and accompanied by a dog.

- Scott's hair had, indeed, been professionally dyed before he was taken into custody (despite the defense's claim that the color change had been the result of exposure to swimming pool chlorine).

- The defense seemed inclined to use a "bad boy" defense: Not only did Scott have an affair with Amber Frey, but he'd cheated on Laci repeatedly during their marriage. This means adultery was not something he took seriously, and his relationship with Amber Frey certainly wasn't meaningful enough to him that he'd murder his wife for her.

- The examination of Laci Peterson's body by defense expert Dr. Henry Lee determined that it had not, as the defense had originally suggested, been dismembered

before being dropped into San Francisco Bay. The defense now claimed this worked in their favor: It proved that Scott did not, as some suspect, transport her body in several bags.

False Leads

- A witness reported having seen Laci at a sporting goods store late in the day on December 24. Store security tapes showed that she hadn't been there.

- Early reports that blood and vomit were found in the Peterson home were false.

- The blood traces found in Scott's pickup were his, not Laci's.

- Police believe the break-in at the house across the street from the Peterson home occurred on December 26, and therefore can't be related to Laci's disappearance. A local TV anchor says he and a crew were parked in the street outside the Peterson home on December 26, and he would have seen it.

- Searchers found one body in Berkeley Marina, which was unrelated to the case. They recovered what sonar told them could be another body, but which was in fact an anchor.

- An item spotted on the bottom of a Modesto marina turned out to be a small boat.

The Peterson case illustrates how criminal investigations can produce investigative leads that are both valid and misleading. It is up to the investigator to consider all leads and to qualify them on a timely basis so the investigation can move forward.

Although no physical force was used against the suspect in this case, psychological intimidation was ever-present and was consequently considered illegal.

Unreasonable Delay in Arraignments

Confessions obtained without coercion or duress may still be deemed unconstitutional and inadmissible if the suspect confessed before being allowed to see a magistrate within a reasonable period after arrest. The case of *McNabb* v. *United States* (1943) first illustrated this vital principle. In this case, McNabb was involved in bootlegging, along with several members of his family. After the murder of several federal officers in Tennessee, McNabb was arrested for the crime. After his arrest, he was held in custody and was not taken before a magistrate for a considerable period. Subsequently, he confessed and was convicted. The Court held that the government's failure to take McNabb before a committing officer was a violation of his constitutional rights; therefore, the confession was inadmissible. What made this case particularly significant is that for the first time, a confession, obtained voluntarily and freely, was still considered illegal because officers failed to comply with other constitutional procedures.

A subsequent ruling in *Mallory* v. *United States* (1957) reaffirmed that an officer making an arrest must take the accused, without necessary delay, before the nearest available magistrate and that an official complaint must be filed without delay. These decisions are based on the due process clause of the Fourteenth Amendment of the U.S. Constitution. The U.S. Supreme Court considers whether or not the case in its entirety represents a good picture of the civilized standards expected in this country.

The Suspect's Right to Legal Counsel

The legal guidelines to protect the rights of the accused were defined further by the U.S. Supreme Court in such cases as *Escobedo* v. *Illinois* (1964) and *Miranda* v. *Arizona* (1966). Surprisingly, before 1964 there were no legal rules requiring the presence of an attorney during the interrogation of a criminal suspect. In a ruling in May 1964, the U.S. Supreme Court reversed the conviction of a lower court because prosecutors had used incriminating statements made by the defendant to a friend that were overheard by a federal agent. The remarks were made after the defendant was indicted and while he was out on bail. The Court held that the statement was made by the defendant without the advice of his attorney, whom he had already retained. So, according to the Court, the defendant was deprived of his Sixth Amendment right to an attorney.

In *Escobedo* v. *Illinois* (1964), Escobedo was arrested without a warrant and interrogated in connection with a murder. On the way to the police station, officers told Escobedo that he had been implicated as the murderer and that he should admit to the crime. He then requested to speak to an attorney. After arriving at the police station, his retained lawyer arrived and asked several times to speak with his client. His request was denied on several occasions. In addition, Escobedo requested to speak with his attorney on several occasions and was told that his attorney did not want to speak to him. Subsequently, the defendant made an admission to the crime and was later found guilty.

The legal question here is: Does a suspect have a right to an attorney if he or she requests one during a police station interrogation? The answer is yes. Following this decision, states were directed to require police to advise every person arrested for a felony that they have a constitutional right to counsel and silence. Despite this, the guidelines for police in interrogation settings were still unclear.

The *Miranda* Warning. Two years following the *Escobedo* decision, the U.S. Supreme Court reversed an Arizona court's conviction in a kidnapping and rape case that further defined the *Escobedo* decision and the rights of the accused. In the *Miranda* v. *Arizona* (1966) case, a 23-year-old, Miranda, was arrested and transported from his home to the police station for questioning in connection with a kidnapping and rape. He was poor and uneducated. After two hours of questioning, officers obtained a written confession that was used against him in court. He was found guilty of the kidnapping and rape.

The legal question in this case is: Do the police have a responsibility to inform a subject of an interrogation of his or her constitutional rights involving self-incrimination and a right to counsel before questioning? Again, the answer is yes (Figure 9.1).

In addition to being informed of these rights, the suspect must also agree, freely and voluntarily, to waive them before police can begin questioning (Figure 9.2). Accordingly, the suspect may invoke his or her right to stop answering questions any time during the interrogation. Several court cases have arisen over the years that relate to *Miranda* and custodial interrogations. For example, *Rhode Island* v. *Innis* (1980) interpreted the meaning of interrogation by stating that in addition to direct questioning, interrogation also refers to any actions or remarks made by police that are designed to elicit an incriminating response.

In another case, *California* v. *Prysock* (1981), the U.S. Supreme Court found that **Miranda warnings** do not have to be given in any specific order or with precise wording. Further, in *Edwards* v. *Arizona* (1981), the Court established a "bright line" rule for investigators. The court found that "all" police questioning must be discontinued once a suspect who is in custody has requested an attorney, even if the *Miranda* warning was given a second time. However, in yet another related decision, *Oregon* v. *Bradshaw* (1983), the Court found that the *Edwards* decision doesn't apply if the suspect simply inquires, "What is going to happen to me now?" In this case, police were allowed to continue questioning the suspect. However, in *Minnick* v. *Mississippi* (1990), the Court ruled that once a custodial suspect requests counsel in response to *Miranda* warnings, law enforcement officers may not attempt to reinterrogate the suspect unless the suspect's counsel is present or the suspect initiates the contact with officers.

In related cases, it has been determined that probation officers need not read the *Miranda* warning to clients (*Minnesota* v. *Murphy*, 1984) and that the *Miranda* warning is not required during the issuance of traffic citations (*Berkemer* v. *McCarty*, 1984). The following year, in *Oregon* v. *Elstad* (1985), the Court decided that even though a confession was obtained before the

MIRANDA WARNING

1. **You have the right to remain silent.**
2. **Anything you say can and will be used against you in a court of law.**
3. **You have the right to talk to a lawyer and have him present with you while you are being questioned.**
4. **If you cannot afford to hire a lawyer, one will be appointed to represent you before any questioning, if you wish.**
5. **You can decide at any time to exercise these rights and not answer any questions or make any statements.**

Figure 9.1 Sample of a *Miranda* warning card, carried routinely and used by law enforcement officers in arrest situations.

Figure 9.2 Sample waiver of rights form.

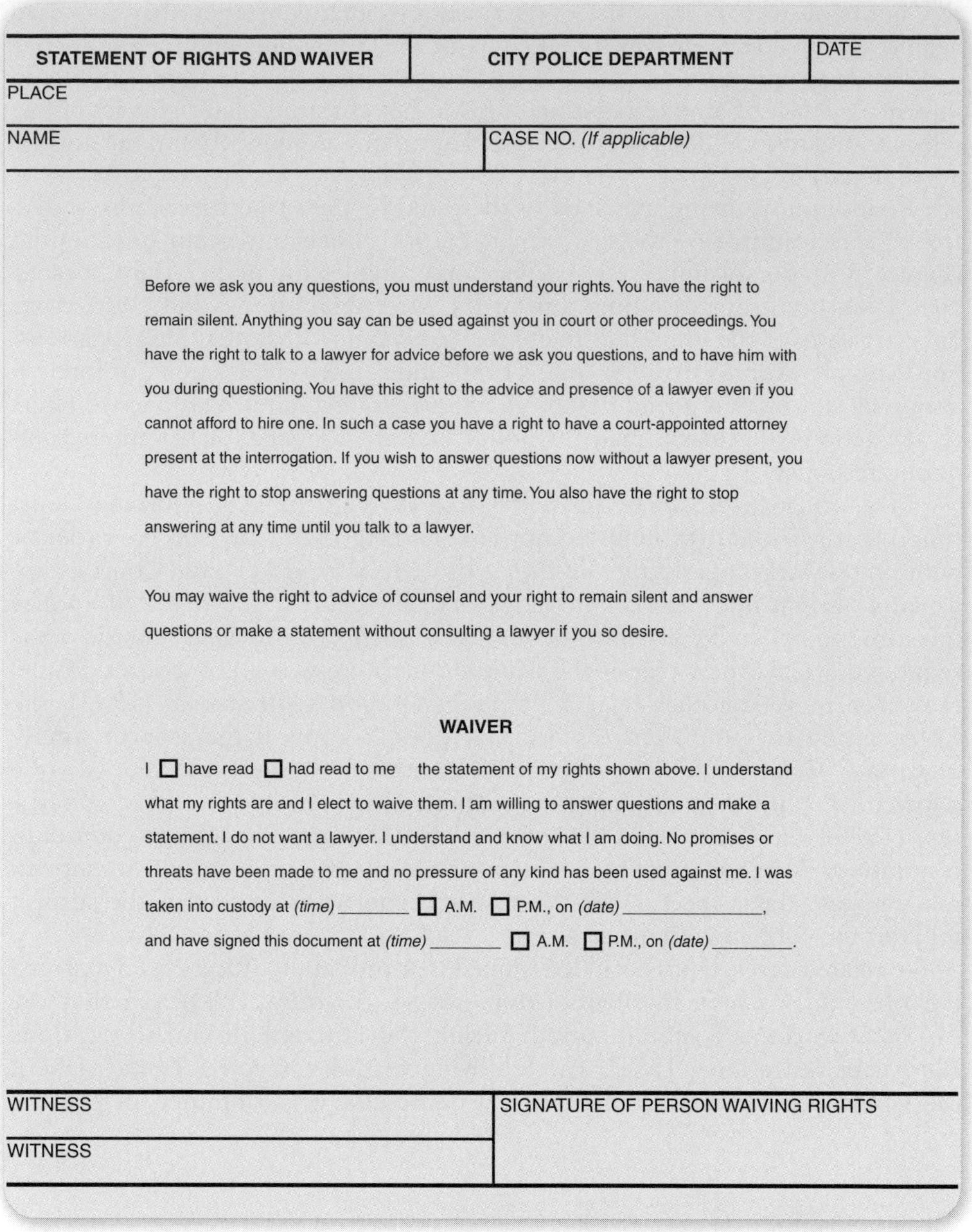

STATEMENT OF RIGHTS AND WAIVER	CITY POLICE DEPARTMENT	DATE

PLACE

NAME | CASE NO. *(If applicable)*

Before we ask you any questions, you must understand your rights. You have the right to remain silent. Anything you say can be used against you in court or other proceedings. You have the right to talk to a lawyer for advice before we ask you questions, and to have him with you during questioning. You have this right to the advice and presence of a lawyer even if you cannot afford to hire one. In such a case you have a right to have a court-appointed attorney present at the interrogation. If you wish to answer questions now without a lawyer present, you have the right to stop answering questions at any time. You also have the right to stop answering at any time until you talk to a lawyer.

You may waive the right to advice of counsel and your right to remain silent and answer questions or make a statement without consulting a lawyer if you so desire.

WAIVER

I ☐ have read ☐ had read to me   the statement of my rights shown above. I understand what my rights are and I elect to waive them. I am willing to answer questions and make a statement. I do not want a lawyer. I understand and know what I am doing. No promises or threats have been made to me and no pressure of any kind has been used against me. I was taken into custody at *(time)* _____ ☐ A.M. ☐ P.M., on *(date)* _____, and have signed this document at *(time)* _____ ☐ A.M. ☐ P.M., on *(date)* _____.

WITNESS | SIGNATURE OF PERSON WAIVING RIGHTS

WITNESS

Miranda warning was given, confessions obtained after it are admissible. In 1994, however, in the case of *Davis* v. *United States,* the Court put the burden on custodial suspects to make unequivocal invocations of the right to counsel. In the *Davis* case, a man being interrogated in the death of a sailor waived his

Miranda Warning

A person being interrogated has the right to remain silent; any statement may be used in a court of law. The person also has the right to have an attorney present during questioning. If the suspect can't afford an attorney, one will be appointed for him or her before questioning.

Miranda rights but later said "Maybe I should talk to a lawyer." Investigators asked the defendant clarifying questions and he responded, "No, I don't want a lawyer." Upon conviction he appealed, claiming that interrogation should have ceased when he mentioned a lawyer. The Court, in affirming the conviction, stated that "it will often be a good police practice for the interviewing officers to clarify whether or not [the defendant] actually wants an attorney."

The Public Safety Exception to *Miranda*. The public safety exception to *Miranda* was ruled on in *New York* v. *Quarles* (1984). This decision found that police officers who are reasonably concerned for public safety may question persons who are in custody and who have not been read the *Miranda* warning. The U.S. Supreme Court also found that subsequent statements are admissible in court. In this case, a woman complained to two officers that an armed man had just raped her. After giving the officers a description of the man, they proceeded to a nearby supermarket, where Benjamin Quarles was located. After a brief chase, the officers frisked Quarles and discovered an empty shoulder holster. Once the suspect was in handcuffs, the officer asked Quarles where the gun was, and he nodded in the direction of some empty cartons and said, "It's over there." The gun was retrieved and Quarles was arrested and read the *Miranda* warning.

When the case went to trial, the court ruled that under the requirements of *Miranda*, the statement "it's over there" and subsequent seizing of the weapon were inadmissible at the defendant's trial. On review, the U.S. Supreme Court acknowledged that Quarles should have been given the *Miranda* warnings. However, the Court recognized that the need to have the suspect talk was more important than the reading of the *Miranda* warning. The Court also ruled that if *Miranda* warnings had deterred the suspect from giving such information, the cost to society would have been much greater than the simple loss of evidence: As long as the gun remained in the pile of cartons, it posed a public safety hazard.

Defining Custody. *Miranda* applies only when testimonial evidence is being sought. In addition, it applies only to **custodial interrogations,** not to circumstances in which the suspect is free to leave. The custodial interrogation rule applies not only when the suspect has been arrested before questioning but also when his or her liberty has been restricted to a degree that is associated with arrest. So the interview itself can also be considered custodial even though no arrest has been made. It depends on the circumstances. For example, if the suspect is being questioned in a relaxed atmosphere at his or her own residence, the *Miranda* warning need not be given. Conversely, if the suspect is approached in his or her own home by officers possessing an arrest warrant, the *Miranda* warning must be given before questioning. In brief, the test is whether the interview is custodial, not whether the investigation has focused on a particular person being interviewed.

PREPARATION FOR THE INTERROGATION

In preparation of the interrogation, the investigator should review all important details in the case and be prepared to seek answers to basic questions such as what, when, why, where, and how In addition, the investigator should give some thought as to what information would be of the most value to the investigation. A series of questions can be drawn up and referred to unobtrusively during the interrogation.

The Interrogation Setting

In addition to the manner in which the interrogator treats the suspect, it is also important to consider the physical surroundings where the questioning occurs (Figure 9.3). Because of pressure from peers and family members who might be present at the scene, it is important to remove the suspect from familiar surroundings and take him or her to a location with a more sterile and less threatening atmosphere. A key psychological factor contributing to successful interrogations is privacy. This encourages the suspect to feel comfortable in unloading the burden of guilt. The structure of the interrogation setting should also be conducive to the obtaining of confessions. Its surroundings should reduce fear and therefore encourage the suspect to discuss his or her role in the crime. Consequently, the interrogation room should reflect a more businesslike atmosphere than a policelike environment.

The interrogation should be conducted in a room specifically designed for that purpose only. It should be isolated from the bustling activity of the rest of the office, the sound of police radios, overhead intercoms, and other interruptions. Ideally, a soundproof room best serves this purpose. The interrogation room should be well lit but not to the extent that its lights are glaring. In addition, it should be protected from interruptions and equipped with some means of communicating with the outside, such as a buzzer or office intercom. Furnishings should be minimal, consisting of chairs, preferably without a desk, and containing pencil and paper but otherwise nondescript, with no distracting decorations.

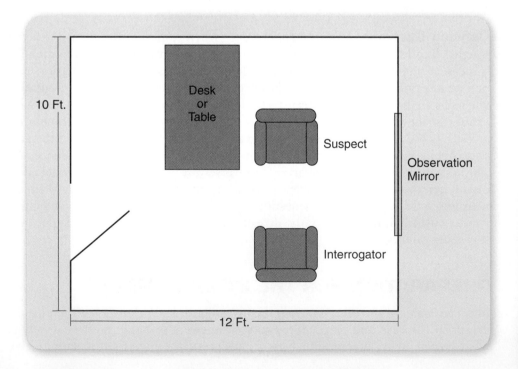

Figure 9.3 Physical layout of a police interrogation room.

Ideally, no obstacles such as tables or desks should block the interviewer's full view of the subject's body. A large portion of nonverbal behavior emanates from the lower body, not just from the hands and face. Feet that fidget or point to the door communicate discomfort. If subjects sit behind a desk or table, the investigator should instruct them to relocate. Deceivers often use soda cans, computer screens, and other objects, both large and small, to form a barrier between themselves—behaviors consistent with dishonesty.[3]

THE INTERROGATION PROCEDURE

As a rule, two investigators handle the interrogation: One actually conducts the questioning, and the second acts as a witness to statements made by the suspect. Obviously, the two investigators should meet before the interrogation to discuss their "roles." Frequently, one investigator will assume one approach to the suspect, whereas the other assumes a different and sometimes contrasting style. The suspect may be more receptive to one approach than the other.

Interrogation Styles

Investigators have developed a variety of interrogation styles and techniques over the years. The decision to choose one style over the other can depend on many factors, including the personality of the suspect, the personality of the interrogator, and the nature of the case. Some of the most common styles of interrogation are described below.

- *Logical style.* In a case in which the evidence seems to be overwhelming, such as a drug trafficking case involving a drug purchase from an undercover agent, the investigator may try to appeal to the suspect's sense of logic. In doing so, the investigator, it is hoped, will persuade the suspect that cooperation is the only way in which the charges against him or her can be lessened. It is important to note here that promises of leniency to the suspect should not be made without direct authorization from the prosecuting attorney. The only promise that can be made is that his or her cooperation will be brought to the attention of the prosecutor for consideration of some kind of leniency.

- *Sympathetic style.* If the investigator thinks that the suspect is easily affected by an emotional appeal, the sympathetic approach might be a good technique. The interrogation is approached by speaking in low tones and will include expressions of concern and understanding for the suspect, his or her spouse, children, business, and so on. The investigator stimulates feelings of self-pity in the suspect when he or she blames others for his or her plight. Ideally, further relief of guilt is achieved by the suspect agreeing to cooperate with the investigator.

- *Indifferent style.* In this technique, the investigator acts as though he or she does not really care if the suspect cooperates or not, but thinks that he or she must go through the motions of making the opportunity available to the suspect. It suggests that the investigator would rather see the suspect punished severely by the court rather than give him or her the opportunity to gain leniency through cooperation.

- *Face-saving style.* In this approach, the investigator will attempt to give the suspect a "way out" that will justify his or her participation in the crime.

By systematically rationalizing the suspect's actions up to the point of the violation, describing them as natural consequences of some other problem, the investigator tries to get the suspect to start talking about his or her actions. Periodically, the investigator interjects comments that tend to diminish the importance of the suspect's own involvement in the crime.

- *Egotistical style.* Here the investigator plays on the suspect's sense of pride and precision in the commission of the crime. It is pointed out how daring and difficult the crime was to implement and that it took a great degree of planning and intelligence to pull it off. This approach encourages the suspect to brag about his or her involvement in the crime and to provide additional details to impress the investigator.

Verbal Symptoms of Deception

Because of certain psychological and cultural differences, a perceptive investigator can sometimes readily identify the manner in which people lie. For example, the trained listener will observe a pattern of evasiveness in the suspect, and after a period will be able to identify these statements as lies or efforts to deceive.

Liars and Lying. Lying requires the deceiver to keep facts straight, make the story believable, and withstand scrutiny. When individuals tell the truth, they often make every effort to ensure that other people understand. In contrast, liars attempt to manage others' perceptions. Consequently, people unwittingly signal deception via nonverbal and verbal cues. Unfortunately, no particular nonverbal or verbal cue demonstrates deception.[4] The ability of an investigator to detect deceptive behavior depends largely on their ability to observe, catalogue, and differentiate human behavior. The more observations investigators make, the greater the probability of detecting deception. Here are some indicators of deceptive behavior:

> Research has shown that vocal changes occur 95 percent of the time when a person lies. A liar's speech rate and voice pitch will also increase 95 percent of the time.[5] In addition, liars will usually stall before giving an answer, to give them time to decide if they should lie or tell the truth, or to decide just how big a lie to tell. Liars will always attempt to con the investigator. They may choose to tell a big lie, a misleading statement, or the complete truth. In most cases, they will attempt to dodge the truth. For example, they may restate the question or ask to have it repeated. They might say "I can't remember" or that they don't understand the question. If the subject stammers, stutters, or has a mental block before answering the question, most of the time he or she is lying.[6]

Lying Techniques. Liars often lie by using *specifics*. For example, the suspect may say, "I don't even own a gun!" Although this could be a true statement at face value, he or she might have borrowed a gun to commit the crime but is relying on the fact that the statement is a true one, and the investigator will, it is hoped, infer that the suspect didn't commit the crime. Liars tend to admit only what the investigator can prove and deny what can't be proved. In addition, they will sometimes make an issue out of trivial things. For example, if a suspect complains about the manner in which the government has treated him in the past, he is probably attempting to sway away from the real issue.

Chapter 9 ▶ Interviews and Interrogations

Physical Characteristics of Lying

Head position

- *Tilted:* cooperative, interested, probably truthful
- *Jutting forward, no tilt, jaw up:* angry, aggressive, stubborn
- *Chin on chest, no tilt:* depressed, bored, probably lying

Eyebrows

- *Both raised with mouth partly open:* surprised, probably truthful
- *One raised:* confused, skeptical, probably truthful
- *Squeezed together and lowered:* angry, worried, confused

Eyes

- *Breaks eye contact* (1 to 2 seconds is common): suddenly tensed, probably lying; may not resume eye contact until new subject is discussed
- *Looks at ceiling and blinks:* just decided to confess
- *Pupils fully dilated:* high degree of emotional arousal, probably lying
- *Closes eyes:* trying to mentally escape, probably lying
- *Narrowed eyes:* looking for trouble, anticipating the worst
- *Rapid blinking:* nervous, probably lying

Hands

- *Covers both eyes:* probably lying
- *Hands over mouth:* probably lying
- *Hand on chin:* probably truthful
- *Touches or rubs nose while talking:* probably lying
- *Hands clasped together, holding back of head:* probably truthful

Legs

- *Men with crossed legs:* probably lying

Feet

- *Moves feet beneath chair:* probably lying
- *One foot tucked beneath the other:* probably truthful

Other lying techniques commonly used include the following:

- The suspect tries to confuse the interviewer by arguing about trivial points rather than addressing the real issues.

- A debating tactic is used in which the suspect tries to discount the investigator's argument in advance. For example, if the investigator makes a statement regarding a piece of evidence, the suspect replies, "You don't really expect anyone to believe that, do you?" The big lie or repeated assertion is based on the assumption that if you say something over and over, people will start to believe it. Repeated denial of the violation only reinforces the suspect's ability to lie.

- The "you don't understand" tactic is used by experienced liars to block an in-depth interrogation. This is attempted by saying, "you wouldn't understand," "you don't know how these things work," or "how would someone like you be expected to know?"

- The "loophole" liar is a dodger who is unsure just how much the investigator knows about the crime. Loophole liars typically respond by saying, "I can't remember" or "to the best of my recollection." This technique gives them a way out in case they are later confronted with contradictory evidence.[7]

WHY SUSPECTS COOPERATE AND CONFESS

When we consider that self-destruction and self-condemnation are not normal human behavioral characteristics, it is perplexing why someone would openly confess to a crime. In addition, one could conclude that when a person is arrested and taken to a police station for questioning, he or she will not readily admit (and even choose to lie about) his or her part in a crime. Many criminals, in particular career criminals, have developed a keen sense of observation over the years. It is likely that this sense has aided them in the past in avoiding detection by police. Such criminals can easily see the direction in which an interrogation is going. Logically, then, one would think that the dialogue between the suspect and investigator would be brief. Strangely, because of complex psychological factors, this is not always the case.

Searching for Information

Depending on the crime in question and the particular suspect, it is logical to assume that many criminals follow the progress of the police through media accounts of the investigation. Still, they really don't have a good sense of exactly what the investigator knows and doesn't know about the suspect. It is the desire of the criminal to want to know exactly what the investigator knows about the crime. This "paranoia" frequently drives the suspect to accompany the investigator willingly to the police station for an interview. Once at the station, however, the suspect not only tries to learn what the investigator knows about the investigation but attempts to lead him or her away from the focus of the investigation.

Closing the Communication Gap

Research indicates that most guilty persons who confess are, from the outset, looking for the proper opening during the interrogation to communicate their guilt to investigators.[8] Suspects also make confessions when they believe that cooperation is the best course of action. Before they talk, they need to be convinced that investigators are willing to listen to all the circumstances surrounding the crimes. Finally, suspects confess when interrogators are able to speculate correctly on why the crimes were committed. They want to know ahead of time that interrogators will believe what they have to say and will understand what motivated them to commit the crime.

Admission versus Confession

Although seemingly alike, there is a notable difference between the admission of a criminal act and the confession of one's complicity in a crime. An **admission** is a self-incriminating statement made by the suspect that falls short of an acknowledgment of guilt. It is, however, an acknowledgment of a certain fact or circumstance from which his or her guilt can be inferred. Conversely, a **confession** is direct acknowledgment by the suspect of his or her guilt in the commission of a specific crime or as being an integral part of a specific crime. For the confession to be lawful, the investigator must be mindful of the constitutional checks governing its admissibility.

WRITTEN STATEMENTS

Because the interrogation will generally produce much more information than is needed for the written statement, the investigator will have to decide what information he or she needs for preparation of the statement. A confession from the suspect should substantiate the elements of the charge or at least contain information related to the investigation. In addition, the statement of the confession should contain any details of extenuating circumstances or explanations offered by the suspect that might be grounds for additional inquiry. Several variables determine what methods are used to take the statement.

These include the intelligence level of the suspect, the amount and nature of information to be recorded, and the availability of stenographic services. In many cases, the suspect will be willing to give a verbal statement about his or her involvement in a crime but might be unwilling to have it written down at the time. If this occurs, the investigator should not interrupt the remarks being made by the suspect just to ask for a signed statement. Instead, after the suspect is finished giving his or her account of what happened, the investigator should ask if the suspect would be willing to sign (or write) a statement to that effect. The suspect should be assured that only the information given to the investigator will be included in the statement and that he or she will have the prerogative of not signing it if it is not accurate. The following techniques can be used if the suspect decides to sign the written statement:

- The suspect may respond orally to the investigator or a stenographer in response to questions. Responses are then written verbatim.

- The suspect may give a statement orally without direction from the investigator. This technique is the most desirable, provided that the end result is a clear and concise statement.

- The investigator could give the suspect a list of the important points to cover during the statement and suggest that he or she include these and other important points.

- The investigator may choose to write the statement according to the information given by the suspect in his or her oral statement.

If these techniques are adopted, the investigator must use the same phrases that were used by the suspect. The completed statement should then be shown to the suspect so that any changes can be made. Once corrections are in order, the statement is signed. The investigator should be careful to make the written statement reflect only one crime, because in a criminal trial the court will ordinarily not permit the introduction of evidence of additional crimes. Exceptions to this are when additional crimes tend to show (1) intent, (2) identity of the defendant, or (3) the scheme used in the commission of the crime in question. So the best policy is to obtain a separate written statement for each crime committed.

Structuring the Written Statement

The statement should begin with the place, date, and identification of the maker and the name of the person who is giving the statement (Figure 9.4). It is acceptable for the body of the statement to be in narrative or expository form. In addition, it should include all the elements of the crime as well as any facts that connect the suspect with the crime. If the investigator or stenographer prepares

Figure 9.4 Sample voluntary statement form.

CITY POLICE DEPARTMENT
VOLUNTARY STATEMENT

_____
         Case #

_____
         Date

I _____ am _____ years of age and
currently reside at _____ which is located in the city
of _____.

Statement:

_____

_____

_____

_____

_____

_____

_____

_____

_____

_____

_____

_____

I have read this statement which consists of _____ page(s) and I affirm that it was given
voluntarily and that all the facts are truthful and accurate.

This statement was given at _____ (location) on the
_____ day of _____, 20__, at _____ (am) (pm).

_____
                                         Signed

_____
         Witness

_____
         Witness

the statement, the suspect should be asked to read and sign each page at the bottom. To ensure that the suspect actually reads the statement, he or she should be asked to correct any typographical errors and to initial any corrections in ink. Finally, each page should be labeled "page _____ of _____ pages." The concluding paragraph should state that the suspect has read the statement consisting of so many pages and that the statement is "true and correct." After the suspect signs the statement in the space provided, two witnesses should sign it under the suspect's signature. Normally, the witnesses are interrogators. Any more than two witnesses could leave the impression with the court that the suspect was intimidated by a large number of police at the time of the statement.

RECORDED STATEMENTS

Frequently, the investigator will choose to record a statement made by a suspect. This can be especially advantageous when the suspect cannot read or write or when he or she is only fluent in a foreign language. One important point to remember is that when the investigator chooses to record the statement, the interrogation should still be conducted first. When it is time to record the statement, the investigator uses his or her notes from the first interrogation to develop the recorded statement. When the recording is complete, the recorded statement is then played back for the suspect to hear so he or she can verify that it is a true and accurate representation of what was said during the interrogation.

The Recording Procedure

The recording should begin with the investigator identifying himself or herself, the suspect, and any other investigators in the room (people entering and leaving the room during the interrogation should also be identified with corresponding times, but at the end of the recording). In addition, the opening remarks should include the location of the statement or interrogation, the time and date of the statement, and a statement by the investigator to the suspect as to why the statement is being recorded. Once the important points of the statement are given, the investigator should ask the suspect if there are any additional comments that he or she would like to make.

Afterwards, the investigator should state that the recorder is now going to be shut off and that the suspect can listen and verify its contents. Once the suspect listens and verifies the recording, it is then turned back on and he or she should verbally acknowledge that (1) the contents accurately represent the statement, and (2) the recorder was not turned off or stopped at any time during the interrogation except for the time when the suspect reviewed the tape. Finally, the investigator states that the session is concluded and repeats the names of the persons in the room and the time and date of the statement. The recording should then be entered into evidence and processed appropriately.

VIDEOTAPED CONFESSIONS

On the basis of a national survey, it is estimated that one-third of all large police and sheriff's departments in the United States videotape at least some interrogations—a practice that is most common in cases of homicide, rape, and aggravated assault.[9] Proponents claim that videotaping has a number of benefits, such as deterring coercive behavior on the part of investigators and providing a more complete and accurate record of the confession for the judge and jury to evaluate the voluntariness and veracity of the defendant's statement.[10]

For evidentiary purposes, videotaped interrogations should provide a complete and objective record of police–suspect interaction. But the question is still raised—what is a complete and accurate record? For example, in an actual police confession in New York, police were convinced that they recorded a confession from a "neutral" camera angle. The camera was positioned behind the investigator and focused directly on the suspect. While this may seem innocent enough, research suggests that it is not. On the basis of studies showing that people make causal attributions to factors that are visually salient, Lassiter and his colleagues taped mock interrogations from three different camera angles so that the suspect, the interrogator, or both were visible to mock jurors. The result was that those who saw only the suspect judged the situation as less coercive than those focused on the investigator. By directing visual attention on the suspect, the camera can lead jurors to underestimate the amount of pressure actually exerted by the "hidden" investigator.[11]

Recap Bias

An important related issue concerns whether jurors are shown a tape of the entire interrogation or merely a recap consisting of only the suspect's final confession. Recaps are common and take an average of 15–45 minutes.[12] On the question of whether they should be admitted into evidence, there are two possible bases for concern. First, the jury sees a final self-incriminating statement but not the circumstances that led up to it, perhaps increasing perceptions of voluntariness. Second, after recounting a story over and over again, a suspect is likely to show less emotion and appear unusually callous. In light of the fact that people are more forgiving of others who express remorse and apologize for their wrongdoings, recaps may bias the jury against the defendant.[13] At this point, empirical research is needed to examine these possible effects.

Framing the Tapes

A suspect often provides the police with a statement that is not a confession but is instead ambiguous (i.e., denying the charges but telling an implausible story). So what is the persuasive impact of an interrogation tape when the suspect maintains his or her innocence and goes to trial? One possibility is for the state to introduce the tape into evidence to highlight inconsistencies in the defendant's story. But another possibility is for the defense to show the tape and focus the jury's attention on the defendant's denials in the face of pressure.

To examine this question, in a 1990 study, Kassin, Reddy, and Tulloch had mock jurors watch a 45-minute "confession" of an actual murder suspect who asserted her innocence but told an implausible story. For some participants, the tape was introduced by the prosecution, who harped on the inconsistencies of the story; for others, it was shown by the defense lawyer, who noted that the defendant maintained her innocence despite pressure to confess (the tape was always followed by the lawyer's argument). Results showed that among participants, those who saw the tape being introduced by the prosecution rather than the defense were more likely to vote guilty.[14] With statements that are ambiguous enough to accommodate opposing interpretations, the adversarial advantage goes to the party that introduces the tape and frames it for the jury.

USE OF THE POLYGRAPH

Of the mechanical devices that have been designed to aid investigators in obtaining information, the **polygraph**, or "lie detector," has proved to be of extreme value. Proper use of this tool can help an investigator determine a suspect's guilt or innocence. However, because of recent court rulings restricting the use of the polygraph in certain settings, the investigator should view this device as an aid only, not as a last resort or panacea. The polygraph is designed simply to measure whether or not the person being tested is being deceptive. As the subject is asked different questions, the graphs observed by the operator will, it is hoped, indicate a truthful or a deceptive response. Indeed, the device does not actually do what its moniker indicates—it will not detect lies. What it does do is measure the physiological responses from the subject, including fear, anxiety, excitation, and other emotions. So the critical consideration in the use of a polygraph is not the machine itself but the operator's ability to interpret its results accurately.

Accuracy of the Polygraph

The criminal justice field is divided as to its acceptance of polygraph results. In fact, most courts will not accept the findings of a polygraph exam as absolute evidence except when stipulated to by all parties. Problems with the use of the polygraph have been in its application. Specifically, the machine should be used to identify statements as being false, not for the purpose of actually detecting a lie. The value of an examination can be looked at in two regards: reliability and validity. *Reliability* refers to the consistency of the examination's results. This can be shown through reproducing the examination repeatedly and obtaining the same results. Indeed, when properly administered, the polygraph can produce very reliable results.

Validity refers to the accuracy of the examination. Validity can be affected by two considerations. First is the ability of the polygraph examiner to interpret the results of the examination accurately. Second, if the measurements that are recorded by the instrument fail to indicate lying directly, it lacks validity.

Administration of the Polygraph Exam

Before the exam occurs, the examiner will request certain information from the investigator. Such information includes the specific offense in question, a copy of the case file, a list of the different types of evidence, specific personal information about the subject, and any physical or psychological data about the subject, if known.

A polygraph examiner then attaches a probe to a person's chest and fingers to record heart rate, respiration, and sweat gland activity during the course of questioning. Responses to questions are charted automatically, and from responses to both innocuous and relevant questions, the examiner can generally determine if the person is being deceptive.

Next, specific questions are structured, usually in a "yes" or "no" format. These questions are reviewed with the subject before he or she takes the test. This is to relax the person taking the test and, it is hoped, to elicit an admission of additional details of the alleged crime. When the test is completed, the subject is generally advised of the results in writing. If deception was detected, the subject might be interviewed about the weak points of the test. Frequently, this part of the process results in the subject admitting to additional complicity in the crime.

Although the polygraph should not be considered a last-resort effort to obtain a suspect's confession, it can save money for the investigating agency. For example, it can weed out suspects in an investigation and let the focus of the investigation fall on specific persons.

Admissibility of Polygraph Results

Over the years, the courts have addressed various aspects of the issue of polygraph results and their admissibility in court. Clearly, the machine can only detect certain changes in the human body, and estimates are that such changes can be detected up to 95 percent of the time. Despite arguments in favor of the use of the polygraph, its results are not currently admissible as absolute evidence in court. One early court case upheld a ruling of a trial court that refused acceptance of the results of the polygraph (*Frye* v. *United States*, 1923). Later that same year, the court in *People* v. *Forts* considered the results of the polygraph inadmissible based on doubts about the instrument's reliability. The *State* v. *Bohner* (1933) case also failed to accept the results of the polygraph but acknowledged its usefulness. Exceptions occur, however, when

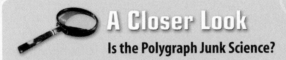

A Closer Look
Is the Polygraph Junk Science?

Although the courts still call it "junk science," the lie detector or polygraph has never been so widely used by criminal justice agencies as a tool for determining the truth. In 1998, the U.S. Supreme Court ruled against the use of polygraph evidence in criminal court, but police agencies still rely on the polygraph exam to make critical personnel decisions from hiring to firing. Over the years, the percentage of police agencies using polygraphs to screen new employees increased from 16 percent in 1962, for example, to 62 percent in 1999, according to a study conducted by Michigan State's School of Criminal Justice. The same survey shows that police are confident of exam results—more than three-fourths believe that polygraphs are 86 to 100 percent reliable.

At the FBI, which employs over 11,000 agents, senior officials have requested permission to administer up to 225 polygraphs per year in investigations of suspected employee misconduct. That figure is in addition to the 3,000 tests given each year to new agents and witnesses and informants in major criminal investigations. The CIA, National Security Agency, Defense Department, Treasury Department, and many large police departments across the nation also depend on the polygraph. Failing a polygraph, as in the case of scientist Wen Ho Lee at Los Alamos National Laboratory in New Mexico, can end a career just as quickly as a guilty verdict. Lee was fired after he failed an FBI-administered polygraph in March 1999 and refused to cooperate with the government's investigation of Chinese espionage at the facility, which is the nation's premier weapons facility.

Fearing unwarranted invasions of individual privacy, Congress passed the *Employee Polygraph Protection Act* of 1988 to curb what had been a growing use of polygraph tests in private business. In 1998, the U.S. Supreme Court expressed concerns about the reliability of polygraphs when it upheld the military's ban on use of them in criminal trials. Yet government agencies still consider polygraphs a valuable personnel tool.

Adapted from Johnson, K. (1999). Government agencies see truth in polygraphs. *USA Today,* April 6, p. 11A.

all parties stipulate to the acceptance of the results before administration of the exam.

THE VOICE STRESS ANALYZER

An investigative tool gaining considerable popularity with law enforcement agencies is the voice stress analyzer (VSA). Unlike the computer polygraph, the VSA requires no wires be attached to the subject being tested. The VSA uses only a microphone plugged into the computer to analyze the subject's responses. As the subject speaks, the computer displays each voice pattern, numbers it, then saves each chart to file. Unlike the polygraph, drugs do not affect the results of the exam and there are no known countermeasures that will cause the ubiquitous "inconclusive" results associated with the polygraph.

Rapidly supplanting the polygraph, the VSA has been used in many investigative situations such as homicide, sex crimes, robbery, white collar, and internal affairs investigations, as well as preemployment examinations for background investigators. The system has been used as an investigative tool for verifying statements of witnesses, denials of suspects, and for determining the validity of allegations made against police officers.

Microtremors are tiny frequency modulations in the human voice. When a test subject is lying, the autonomic, or involuntary, nervous system causes an inaudible increase in the microtremor's frequency. The VSA detects, measures, and displays changes in the voice print frequency.

A laptop computer processes these voice frequencies and graphically displays a picture of the voice patterns. Furthermore, the VSA is not restricted to "yes" and "no" answers and is able to analyze, accurately, tape recordings of unstructured conversations.

Figure 9.5 Voice stress analyzer test.

DISCUSSION QUESTIONS

1. Discuss the differences between the terms *interview* and *interrogation*.
2. Discuss the goals of the interrogation.
3. Discuss the distinction between an admission and a confession.
4. Define *coercion* and *duress,* and discuss how they taint the interrogation process.
5. Discuss how the *Escobedo* and *Miranda* cases affect the interrogation process.
6. Define what is meant by *custodial interrogation.*
7. Discuss the legal implications of the term *in custody.*
8. Explain and discuss the recommended setting for an interrogation.
9. Describe the procedure for recording a suspect's statement.
10. Explain the uses of the polygraph in the interrogation setting.

NOTES

1. Vessel, D. (1998, Oct.). Conducting successful interrogations. *FBI Law Enforcement Bulletin.*
2. Tousignant, D. D. (1991, Mar.). Why suspects confess. *FBI Law Enforcement Bulletin,* pp. 14–18.
3. Navarro, J., and J. Schafer (2001, July). Detecting deception. *FBI Law Enforcement Bulletin.*
4. Ibid.
5. U.S. Department of Justice, Drug Enforcement Administration (1988). *Drug enforcement handbook.* Washington, DC: U.S. Government Printing Office.
6. Ibid.
7. Evans, D. D. (1990, Aug.). 10 Ways to sharpen your interviewing skills. *Law and Order,* pp. 90–95.
8. Coleman, R. (1984, Apr.). Interrogation: The process. *FBI Law Enforcement Bulletin,* p. 27.
9. Geller, W. A. (1983, Mar.). Videotaping interrogations and confessions. National Institute of Justice, *Research in Brief,* Washington, DC.: Department of Justice.
10. Kassin, S. A. (1997). The psychology of confession evidence. *American Psychologist,* 52(3):221–233.
11. Lassiter, G. D., and A. A. Irvine (1986). Videotaped confessions: The impact of camera point-of-view on judgments of coercion. *Journal of Applied Social Psychology,* 16:268–276; Lassiter, G. D., R. D. Slaw, M. A. Briggs, and C. R. Scanlan (1992). The potential for bias in videotaped confessions. *Journal of Applied Social Psychology,* 22:1838–1851.
12. Geller, W. A. (1983). Videotaping interrogations and confessions. National Institute of Justice, *Research in Brief,* Washington, DC: U.S. Department of Justice.
13. Robinson, D. T., L. Smith-Lovin, and O. Tsoudis (1994). Heinous crime or unfortunate accident? The effects of remorse on responses to mock criminal confessions. *Social Forces,* 73:175–190.
14. Kassin, S. M., M. E. Reddy, and W. F. Tulloch (1990). Juror interpretations of ambiguous evidence: The need for recognition, presentation order and persuasion. *Law and Human Behavior,* 14:43–55.

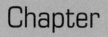 
Development and Management of Informants

Key Terms

▶ credibility
▶ entrapment
▶ informant
▶ motivation
▶ WITSEC program

This chapter will enable you to:

- Describe the types of people used as informants.
- Identify various areas of concern in the use of informants.
- Understand the various motivations of informants.
- Document and process an informant properly.
- Maintain control of an informant during an investigation.
- Protect an informant's identity.
- Understand the problems most commonly associated with the use of informants.

INTRODUCTION

Over a 10-month period, beginning in 2003 motorists in Ohio were terrorized by a sniper firing random shots at vehicles along Interstate 270 that killed at least two persons. The two dozen shootings had struck a variety of targets such as cars, trucks, buses, schools, and homes in the Columbus area. Initially, investigators had little to go on in their investigation and publicly expressed their frustration in not having developed a suspect in the shootings. But finally in early 2004, ballistic tests on a 9mm handgun connected Charles McCoy, Jr., to the Ohio Interstate shootings as well as at least eight other shootings.

In March 2004, McCoy checked into the Budget Suites Hotel in Las Vegas, Nevada, at 3:00 A.M. under his own name. That evening, Conrad Malsom, a 60-year-old unemployed car salesman who lived in Las Vegas, spotted McCoy reading a *USA Today* article about himself in the sports betting parlor of the Stardust Casino. The two even shared a pizza as Malsom got a closer look. As they talked, Malsom learned where McCoy was staying and even took a sheet of paper containing some notes that McCoy was writing down. Malsom called the Las Vegas police, who arrested McCoy outside his hotel at 2:45 A.M. the following day.

The concept of informants in society is nothing new. In fact, both police and civilians attempt from time to time to encourage public participation in solving crime. One well-known program is Crimestoppers, which encourages citizens to engage in "anonymous" informing to assist police in developing suspects in crimes or to catch criminals in the act of committing them. Although some people complain that Crimestoppers makes "snitches" out of law-abiding citizens, others argue that it is simply a system of public responsibility similar to the old days of the "hue and cry," when all citizens assumed responsibility for public order.

Figure 10.1 Suspected sniper Charles McCoy, Jr., was turned in by informer Conrad Malsom in Las Vegas, Nevada, in March 2004. *AP Wide World Photos*

Figure 10.2 Tipster Conrad Malsom notified police of the whereabouts of Charles McCoy, the Ohio Interstate sniper. *Joe Cavaretta, AP Wide World Photos*

In addition to allowing tipsters to call the police anonymously, many receive cash rewards for their cooperation. The amount of the reward depends on the "quality of information" provided by the citizen: that is, information that results in an arrest. All communication between the police and the citizen is accomplished by the assignment of a number to the caller. That number is used in lieu of a name for the remainder of the citizen–police relationship, negating the need for the police ever to know the true name of the tipster.

Along lines similar to Crimestoppers are efforts by victims of crimes to convince the community to become more involved with identifying known criminals and reporting violators to police. One example of this is the well-known television show *America's Most Wanted*. The show has helped track down over 800 fugitives.[1] Other shows, including *Unsolved Mysteries* and *U.S. Customs*, have had similar success.

Another public forum for locating criminals has been around longer than the television shows discussed above: the FBI's Top Ten Most Wanted list. The FBI has maintained its Most Wanted list since 1950, and although it was once a mainstay in crime fighting, it has all but lost its appeal in today's high-tech age of television, computers, and the Internet. Still, it is designed to encourage citizen participation in sharing information with the police about crime and criminals who are wanted. The Most Wanted list was invented by a wire service reporter and later adopted by the publicity-driven director of the FBI, J. Edgar Hoover. As of 1997, 422 of the 449 fugitives who appeared on the list have been captured, a 94 percent success rate.[2]

In its earliest stages, when few Americans owned television sets, the Most Wanted list contained bank robbers, burglars, and car thieves, criminals who dominated the crime scene. Today's Most Wanted list includes cop killers, drug dealers, and international terrorists who aren't even in the country.[3] Skeptics argue that the list has outlived its usefulness because of the age of modern technology: the Internet, electronic billboards, and television. In 1992, the U.S. Post

The Anti-Snitch Movement

It was strange enough for prosecutors and police to see the T-shirt with a traffic-sign message: "STOP SNITCHING," but one of those T-shirts was about to show up in court with matching baseball cap. Worse yet, the wearer was a prosecution witness for Pittsburgh's Prosecutor Lisa Pellegrini.

In March of 2006, Rayco "War" Saunders—ex-con, pro boxer, and walking billboard for an anti-snitch movement—sparked a coast-to-coast debate involving everyone from academics to police to rappers. Pellegrini, while thinking "witness intimidation," told Saunders to lose the hat and reverse the shirt. Saunders, claiming "First Amendment" rights, refused. He left the courthouse, shirt in place. Case dismissed.

The attitude of "don't be a snitch" is common throughout many communities and, in some cases, even condoned. While the Mafia's traditional blood oath of silence, "Omerta," has been broken by turncoat after turncoat, in some inner-city neighborhoods the call to stop snitching is galvanizing. Some say it's an attempt by drug dealers and gangsters to intimidate witnesses, while others say it's a legitimate protest against law enforcement's overreliance on criminal informers.

Take the case of Busta Rhymes, the hip-hop star who refused to cooperate with police investigating the slaying of his bodyguard, Israel Ramirez, on February 5, 2006, outside a Brooklyn studio where Rhymes was recording a video with other rap performers. Police claimed that although Rhymes and as many as 50 others may have witnessed the shooting, no one came forward—reminiscent of the echo of silence that followed the unsolved murders of rappers Tupac Shakur, The Notorious B.I.G., and Run-DMC's Jam Master Jay.

While some argue that it's logical for a witness to a crime to want to talk to the police, others say that due to growing animosities between the police and the public, "not" being an informer is the honorable thing to do.

Informers have always been a key investigative tool but at the same time viewed as a necessary evil. In some cases, if a drug dealer needs to make a deal, he'll tell on friends or family alike if necessary. It may not be right, but it's the only answer for some people. In some cases, criminal informers who are allowed to remain free commit more crimes, return to crime after serving a short prison sentence, frame other people for crimes they didn't commit, or tell prosecutors anything they want to hear.

According to a study by the Northwestern University Law School's Center on Wrongful Convictions, 51 of the 111 wrongful death penalty convictions since the 1970s were based in whole or in part on the testimony of witnesses who had incentives to lie. Based on federal statistics, one of every four black men from 20 to 29 years of age is incarcerated, on probation or parole, and under pressure to snitch.[4] Estimates are that one in 12 of all black men in the highest crime neighborhoods throughout the nation is a criminal informant.

Hence the backlash—"stop snitching." The slogan appeared in Baltimore in 2004 as the title of an underground DVD featuring threatening gun-wielding drug dealers and a brief appearance by NBA star and Baltimore native Carmelo Anthony. Whatever its intent, the stop snitching movement concerns officials who are already enraged about witness reluctance and witness intimidation. State and local governments spend a fraction of what the federal government devotes to witness protection and informant management, although in March 2006, Pennsylvania restored $1,000,000 for that purpose. This move came as more than half a dozen witnesses recanted earlier testimony in the trial of men accused in the Philadelphia street shooting death of a third-grade boy.

The movement has created problems for law enforcement around the country because without informers many cases cannot be properly investigated. "Stop Snitching" T-shirts have been banned from a number of courthouses around the nation. In Boston, Mayor Thomas Menino sent police officers into the stores to remove "Stop Snitching" T-shirts from the shelves. In Maryland, the crime of witness intimidation was elevated from misdemeanor to felony, and in Baltimore, police made a DVD of their own called "Keep Talking."[5]

Office discontinued putting Top 10 posters on its walls. Perhaps it could be argued that the FBI's "list" has become ineffective, especially with the advent of so many different high-tech media showcasing the nation's fugitives. Of late, some victims have taken the initiative to seek help from the public by using their own money and resources.

During August 1997, the parents of murder victim JonBenet Ramsey ran their fourth advertisement in a local newspaper appealing for help from the public. The ad included samples of handwriting from the ransom note and commented that "the killer appears to be obsessed with technocrime movies and phrases from them."[6] In addition, the ad includes quotes from the movies *Dirty Harry* and *Speed* that the family claimed were similar to the ones used in the ransom note.

In any case, whether it be a paid police informant or an anonymous tip, police rely heavily on information from the public to solve crimes. Experience has shown that a primary component of crime control is proactive law enforcement. Proactive investigations include vice cases such as drug trafficking, prostitution, and gambling, in which investigators actually seek out potential crimes and intervene "before" the crimes occur. Accordingly, the use of *informants* as a source of criminal information in such crimes has proved to be invaluable. Consequently, law enforcement officers are insistent in protecting the identity of their sources so that the well-being of the informant will not be jeopardized and so they will continue to be of use to the officer in future criminal investigations. [*Note:* Informants are also commonly called *informers, confidential informers,* or *cooperating individuals* (or *CIs*), but in this book they are referred to as informants.]

One of the most exceptional examples of informant use was the 1963 testimony of Joseph Valachi, a former Mafia soldier. Valachi's highly publicized role as an informant with the FBI resulted in the convictions of several management figures in the American Mafia. This case raised questions and public concern about the appropriateness of law enforcement officers using "criminals to catch criminals." Another high-visibility case involved Tommaso Buscetta, a crime family boss in Palermo, Sicily, who testified against numerous other Mafia bosses during the mid-1980s. His testimony was instrumental in the arrest and subsequent prosecutions of an estimated 450 fellow mafiosos. Nevertheless, many misconceptions still exist about the value and utility of the criminal informant. For example, some think that police officers who are using an informant will be tolerant of that person's criminal lifestyle and might be less willing to report criminal wrongdoing on the part of the informant. Although through the years some improprieties have been documented regarding the use of informants, the value of such persons has proved immense in the prosecution of many high-level crime figures and in aiding law enforcement in understanding the inner workings of sophisticated criminal organizations.

In addition, some people believe that in dealing closely with informants, police officers may themselves become tainted and their positions compromised. In this chapter, we consider the role of informants in criminal investigations and how best to manage the information provided by them.

WHO ARE INFORMANTS?

Although the word **informant** has many negative synonyms, such as snitch and stoolie, the term could best be defined as "anyone who provides information of an investigative nature to law enforcement."[7] Exclusions to this definition, of course, would be victims of crime who have reported specific criminal activity to law enforcement. This makes their role more that of a complainant.

Indeed, the informant is most typically used in cases in which there is no complainant. These typically include vice and victimless crimes such as drug violations, gambling, and prostitution. Because informants can be virtually anyone in a community, the good investigator should consider anybody with whom he or she comes in contact as a potential source of criminal information. That is, the premise of locating a knowledgeable informant is to realize that someone somewhere is aware of various crimes committed. It is therefore the investigator's responsibility to locate and develop relationships with such people.

Generally, people who become informants can be classified into four general groups:

1. *Average citizens.* Although not necessarily a criminal source, those falling into this group may still be an excellent source of information. Most good investigators have several informants of this type who are contacted periodically for leads. Examples of these informants are waitresses, bartenders, dancers, and private investigators.

2. *Fellow law enforcement officers.* On an average day, investigators will exchange valuable information with other investigators many times. Although much of this information is between "friends" who are investigators, a considerable amount is also exchanged by officers working in other units within the department. In addition, investigators who befriend officers with other local, state, or federal agencies can also benefit from useful information about criminals and criminal activity.

3. *Mentally ill persons.* It is unfortunate, but a percentage of informants fall into the category of mentally ill or deranged. The experienced investigator can detect when such persons are simply fabricating information or passing on news stories or gossip. One should also consider, however, that although an informant is deranged, his or her information might still have some validity.

4. *Criminals or their associates.* Without question, the criminal informant has proved to be most valued in many police investigations. This is a person who is currently, or has been, associated with a particular criminal element and is therefore in an excellent position to supply firsthand information about criminal activity. Informants are a dynamic group of people who come from diverse backgrounds and frequently view their role in different ways. For example, one may give information with no reservations about his or her identity becoming known. Conversely, others may have valuable information to render but may do so only with the understanding that their identity remain concealed. Those falling into the latter category typically want their identity to be kept secret for two reasons: (1) for their own protection, and (2) because if their true identities become known, their function as informants would be ended.

Utilizing the Informant

Although a frequent source of valuable information, use of the informant in a criminal investigation can be problematic. Therefore, his or her use should not be considered if similar results could be achieved through other means. Problems that stem from the use of informants are due to three variables. First, informants are often difficult to control; many have been criminals for long periods and are

Figure 10.3 Police informant working as a mechanic relays information to undercover police officer in front of truck, San Rafael, CA.
Bonnie Kamin, PhotoEdit Inc.

very independent by nature. This independence sometimes results in the informant attempting to manipulate the investigator and manage the investigation.

Second, the informant can become a source of public embarrassment for the law enforcement agency. For example, the informant might be arrested for a high-visibility crime during the time that he or she is working with the police. The local media could then make headlines that could jeopardize the investigation in which the informant was involved. Such situations are sometimes unavoidable but can usually be minimized with proper management techniques.

A third area of concern is the informant's questionable **credibility** in court. Depending on the role of the informant in the investigation, he or she might have to testify in court proceedings. A good defense council can expose the criminal background of such people and show that their testimony is not to be believed. If this is accomplished, juries will have difficulty finding the defendant guilty "beyond a reasonable doubt." Once the decision is made to use the services of an informant, they can be used in a number of ways:

- Make observations in areas where strangers would be suspect.
- Furnish information from a source not readily available to the investigator.
- Conduct "controlled" undercover transactions or introduce undercover agents to criminal suspects.
- Collect intelligence information (e.g., determine street prices of drugs, and identify suspects, their associates, and their residences).

The criminal investigator has the responsibility to evaluate every informant used. This will save time and effort if it is determined that the informant's information is unreliable or that the informant harbors a hidden agenda. Thus the motive is extremely important to identify with each informant candidate, as it may directly affect the credibility of the case.

INFORMANT MOTIVATIONS

Successful recruitment and management of informants pivots on the investigator's ability to recognize the **motivation** of the informant. Because the negative stigma of being an informant is so great in the United States, it is sometimes difficult to develop such people successfully. Police occasionally consider average citizens as informants provided that they are willing to offer relevant information in an investigation. The motivation of such people is a sense of civic duty.

As one might guess, the mentally ill informant (depending on his or her illness) is motivated for very different reasons. These reasons are usually very complicated and difficult to determine, and frequently, information furnished by these persons is worthless to the investigator. When the mentally ill informant gives valuable information, however, the person may be motivated by the same reasons as those that motivate the criminal informant. Indeed, the criminal informant is the most valuable of all informant categories. As indicated, these people pose many legal, moral, and ethical considerations not generally associated with the other three categories. Motivations for the criminal informant fall into a number of categories:

- *The fearful informant.* Many persons agree to cooperate with law enforcement when fear is the chief motivator. Fear comes in many forms, such as fear of detection by law enforcement or retribution from criminal associates. Typically, this incentive arises when a person is arrested for an offense and fears being convicted and imprisoned. Given the opportunity, the arrestee may choose to provide information to investigators in exchange for leniency. Investigators must be careful not to make any promises to persons arrested without the consent of the prosecutor, who is generally vested with such authority. The investigator may, however, advise the informant that such a recommendation may be made pending any cooperation.

- *The financially motivated informant.* "Mercenary" informants give information in exchange for a fee. Often, the financially motivated informant will prove to be a valuable contributor to the investigation. Such persons may, however, attempt to manipulate the investigation to prolong payments to them. This is typically done by extending the investigation through providing misleading information or by "setting up" suspects in criminal violations that they are not predisposed to commit (i.e., entrapment).

- *The revengeful informant.* Revenge is not uncommon to the criminal underworld, and wrongs committed by one criminal against another are commonly settled outside the law. Frequently, however, informants motivated by revenge can produce favorable investigative results. Although those motivated by revenge are seldom concerned about revealing their identity in court, investigators must be careful to recognize an exaggerated or embellished story. In addition, such persons frequently have drifting allegiances and may reconcile with their former adversaries midway through the investigation, thus ruining credibility and jeopardizing the well-being of investigators.

- *The egotistical informant.* Many people take great delight in passing on information to others. Informants falling into this category may also be of great value to an investigator. This motivation is sometimes dubbed the *police complex,* because of a person's desire to associate with law enforcement. It is typically characterized by the small-time criminal alleging to have inside information on high-level crime figures.

- *The perversely motivated informant.* People who display a perverse motivation are those who inform with a hidden benefit or advantage to themselves. Sometimes informants with this motivation are (1) trying to eliminate their competition, (2) learning investigative techniques, (3) determining if any of their criminal associates are under investigation by police, or (4) learning the identity of undercover officers. In all cases, the investigator must be aware of such motivations to avoid "setups" or compromising situations.

- *The reformed informant.* Informants characterized by this motivation act out of a sense of guilt from wrongdoing. Such informants are rare but when encountered may provide reliable information to the investigator.

DOCUMENTING YOUR SOURCE

Proper management of informants is essential in avoiding unethical, immoral, or unprofessional allegations later in an investigation (Figure 10.4). The investigator must remember that informants belong to the agency and are not the "personal" resource of the investigator. This understanding will ensure that a system of checks and balances through records and verification of information can be officially maintained.

All candidates for informants should be well documented. They should, therefore, be fingerprinted, photographed, and carefully interviewed by investigators before used as an informant. Interviews should reflect the informant's true name and any aliases, address, employment history, and so on. In addition, criminal records, if any, should be verified through the National Crime Information Center as well as through local and state law enforcement agencies. All such procedures should be contained in an official informant file established specifically for that person. The file should then be indexed by number, not by name, and that number should be used in all subsequent reports referring to the informant.

During the informant interview, the interviewer must be careful to solicit certain information. Some typical questions asked potential informants include:

- What is his or her motivation?
- Has the informer been reliable in the past?
- What is the intelligence of the informant?
- How does he or she know about the violation?
- Does he or she have a personal interest, and if so, what?
- Does he or she have direct knowledge?
- Does he or she have access to additional knowledge?
- Does he or she harbor any vengeance toward the suspect?
- Is he or she withholding some kind of information?
- Has he or she lied about information in the past?
- Is he or she willing to testify in court?

Figure 10.4 Sample informant agreement.

**CITY POLICE DEPARTMENT
COOPERATING INDIVIDUAL AGREEMENT**

I, _____, the undersigned, state that it is my intent to associate myself, of my own free will and without any coercion or duress, with the City Police Department as a cooperating individual.

As a cooperating individual, I understand and agree that I have no police powers under the laws of the state of (____) and have no authority to carry a weapon while performing my activity as a cooperating individual. Further, I understand and agree that my only association with the city of (____) is as a cooperating individual on a case-by-case or time-to-time basis as an independent contractor, and not as an employee of the police department. Any payment I receive from the City Police Department will not be subject to federal or state income tax withholding or social security. I understand that it is my responsibility to report any income and also that I am not entitled to either workmen's compensation or unemployment insurance payments for anything I do as a cooperating individual.

In consideration for being allowed to associate with the City Police Department as a cooperating individual, and in consideration for any payment I may receive, I agree to be bound by the following terms and conditions and procedures while so associated.

1. I agree that under no circumstances will I purchase or possess any controlled substances or suspected controlled substances without the direction and control of a police officer and then will make a purchase only with monies supplied by him.

2. I agree not to use or sell, dispense, or transfer any controlled substance except that I may use any controlled substance prescribed to me by a licensed physician.

3. I agree to maintain a strict accounting of all funds provided to me by the City Police Department and I understand that misuse of city funds could be grounds for criminal prosecution against me.

4. I agree not to divulge to any person, except the officer with whom I am associated, my status as a cooperating individual for the City Police Department unless required to do so in court, and shall not represent myself to others as an employee or representative of the City Police Department nor use the department or any of its officers as personal references or as credit or employment references.

5. I understand that any violation of the above listed provisions may be grounds for my immediate removal as a cooperating individual and that any violation of law may result in my arrest and prosecution.

I understand that association with the City Police Department as a cooperating individual may involve strenuous physical activity and may become hazardous to my physical well-being and safety. Nevertheless, it is my desire to associate myself with the department, on an independent contractor basis, as a cooperating individual. I am associating myself with the department in this status freely and without any coercion or duress. In consideration for being accepted as a cooperating individual, I release and discharge the City of (____), the City Police Department and its elected officials, officers, employees, and agents from all claims, demands, actions, judgments, and executions which I may have or acquire and subsequently claim to have against the City for personal injuries and property damage I may sustain which arises out of or in connection with my association with the city. I make this release for myself, my heirs, executors, and administrators. Also, I agree not to maintain any action against the City of (____), the City Police Department, or its elected officials, officers, employees, or agents for personal injuries and property damage I sustain which arise out of or in connection with my association with the City Police Department.

_____
Cooperating Individual

_____
Date

WITNESSES:

_____
Officer

_____
Officer

After the informant responds to the preceding questions, the investigator should have adequate information to proceed with a final evaluation of the person's potential worth. If the informant poses more of a liability than a benefit, he or she should be eliminated from further consideration.

MAINTAINING CONTROL OF THE INFORMANT

Customarily, the investigator who develops an informer is the one who is assigned to him or her. A cardinal rule in working with informants is for the investigator to command control of the investigation, not the informant. This is sometimes difficult to accomplish, as many informants possess strong, manipulative personalities. Although informants should be asked frequently for their opinions, each suggestion should be considered carefully. Additionally, investigators must be careful not to promise anything that they cannot deliver (e.g., money, a reduced charge, relocation of their family, police protection).

Control of informants is best achieved through frequent personal contacts with them. These interactions are the best method for debriefing informers and maintaining rapport with them. The officer assigned should make most, if not all, contacts with informants. This will reduce additional demands of the informant and ensure the person's allegiance to the control officer. Another critical area of instruction for the informant is **entrapment.** Criminal suspects must be given an "opportunity" for the commission of a crime and not the "motivation" for doing so. If the entrapment issue is not remembered during the course of an investigation, the case may result in the dismissal of charges against the suspect and a soiled reputation for the department.

PROTECTING THE INFORMANT'S IDENTITY

Experience has shown that defendants may attempt to injure, intimidate, or even murder people working with the police. Accordingly, the investigator bears an ethical and professional responsibility to safeguard the identity of informants and their families to the best of his or her ability. During initial interviews, investigators should advise potential informants that it is impossible to guarantee the confidentiality of their identity absolutely, but that all efforts will be made to do so. In fact, the U.S. Supreme Court has ruled that the identity of informants may be kept secret if sources have been explicitly assured of confidentiality by investigating officers or if a reasonably implied assurance of confidentiality has been made. Measures that can be taken by the investigator to protect an informant's identity include:

- Limiting direct contact with the informant to one investigator or the "control" agent (unless the informant is of the opposite sex, in which case, two investigators should be present). Meetings should be brief and held where neither party will be recognized.
- Minimizing telephone conversations between control agents and informants in the event that someone is listening in on the line.
- Selecting different locations to meet.
- Warning informants about discussing their associations with the police to anyone, including their friends and spouses.

The U.S. Supreme Court addressed the issue of protection of the informant's identity in court. In *U.S. Department of Justice* v. *Landano* (1993), the Court required that an informant's identity be revealed through a request made under the federal Freedom of Information Act. In that case, the FBI had not specifically assured the informant of confidentiality and the Court ruled that "the government is not entitled to a presumption that all sources supplying information to the FBI in the course of a criminal investigation are confidential sources."

LEGAL CONSIDERATIONS

Information gathering is a complex process raising many ethical and legal questions regarding the techniques used by investigators. For example, when police pay informants for information, critics argue that the informant might be tempted to entrap persons into committing crimes so that the informant can realize some income. Another common use of informants is *flipping*. This is the procedure where an arrested person is given the choice of providing information to police in exchange for dropping their charges. Flipping is a widely used procedure requiring approval of the local prosecutor, but it still raises questions about the ethical appropriateness of the procedure.

Simply put, the informer's primary role is to provide probable cause to police for arrests and search warrants. The case of *Aguilar* v. *Texas* (1964) established a two-pronged test to the effect that an informant's information could provide probable cause if both of the following criteria are met:

- The source of the information is made clear.
- The police officer has a reasonable belief that the information is reliable.

The two-pronged *Aguilar* test was intended to prevent the issuance of warrants on the basis of false or fabricated information. But two subsequent cases have provided exceptions to the two-pronged test. *Harris* v. *United States* (1968) acknowledged the assumption that when an informant provided information that was damaging to him or her, that information was probably true. In the *Harris* case, an informant told police that he had purchased nontax-paid whiskey from another person.

Since the information actually implicated the informant in a crime, it was taken at face value as being true, even though it failed the second prong of the two-pronged test. In 1969, the case of *Spinelli* v. *United States* created an exception to the requirements of the first prong. In that case, the U.S. Supreme Court ruled that some information can be so highly specific that it must be accurate even if its source is not revealed. Then, in 1983, in *Illinois* v. *Gates,* the Court adopted a totality of circumstances approach, which held that sufficient probable cause for issuing a warrant exists where an informant can reasonably be believed on the basis of everything that is known by the police.

Under the *Gates* decision, however, the Court held that although it is still important to consider the two-pronged test, each part of the test should be viewed separately and independently. The totality of the circumstances approach, therefore, permits any deficiencies of one part of the test to be overcome by the other with available evidence. In their decision, the Court stated:

> For all these reasons we conclude that it is wiser to abandon the two-pronged test established by our decisions under *Aguilar* and *Spinelli*. In its place we reaffirm totality of the circumstances analysis that traditionally has informed probable cause determinations. The task of using the magistrate is simply to make a practical, common-sense decision

whether, given all the circumstances set forth in the affidavit before him, including the "veracity and basis of knowledge" of persons supplying hearsay information, there is a fair probability that contraband or evidence of a crime will be found in a particular place. And the duty of a reviewing court is simply to ensure that the magistrate had a "substantial basis for conclud[ing]" that probable cause existed.

In 1990, the case of *Alabama* v. *White* was reviewed by the Supreme Court, which held that an anonymous tip, even in the absence of other corroborating information about a suspect, could form the basis for an investigatory stop where the informant accurately predicts the "future" behavior of the suspect. The Court reasoned that the ability to predict a suspect's behavior demonstrates a significant degree of familiarity with the suspect's affairs.

FEDERAL PROTECTION OF THE INFORMANT

If the case in which the informant testifies involves organized crime, the informant is eligible to enter the federal Witness Security (**WITSEC**) **program.** The WITSEC program, developed in 1971 and operated under the U.S. Marshal's Service, is designed to relocate government informants, providing them with new names, social security numbers, and other identification. Although a controversial program, it enjoys a 92 percent success rate in convictions of organized crime members by persons entering the program.

OTHER PROBLEMS WITH INFORMANTS

As indicated earlier, working with informants can be problematic. In addition to concerns of entrapment and ethical, moral, and criminal activity on the part of the informant, there are several other areas of concern:

- *Investigators becoming too friendly with informants.* Because investigators and their informers work together closely, it is possible that an officer can become caught up in an informant's personal problems. Certainly, the investigator should lend a sympathetic ear when possible, but investigators should be cautioned that becoming too close to an informant could jeopardize the investigator's level of control over the person.

- *Informants of the opposite sex.* Over the years, many investigators have fallen victim to allegations of sexual misconduct with informants of the opposite sex. Although some have proved truthful, many have had no basis but resulted in disciplinary action against the officer and a termination of the investigation. To avoid such allegations, a second officer should always accompany an investigator. The location of meeting spots with informants should also be considered very carefully, particularly if a second officer is not present.

- *Crimes committed by the informant.* During initial meetings between the investigator and potential informants, officers should stress that any criminal activity on the part of the informant will not be tolerated. History has shown that after being arrested for a crime, informants will sometimes mention the name of their control officer in hopes of being released or of receiving special treatment.

- *Officers who "own" their informants.* Over the years, some corrupt officers have claimed that meetings between themselves and criminals were in fact meetings with informants. Informants should be considered the property of the entire department and should be sufficiently documented. This will avoid any allegations of misconduct on the part of investigators if seen with known criminals.

At times, information provided by informants is of such value that informants are paid for the information they supply. The investigator should be careful not to pay for information that has not been verified or that is not considered useful in the investigation. Accordingly, informant payments should be sufficiently modest as to avoid defense accusations of entrapment. When this occurs, the defense will maintain that the investigator's payment to the informant was so high that the informant was enticed into "setting up" the suspect solely for the monetary reward.

DISCUSSION QUESTIONS

1. Discuss misconceptions commonly held about the role of police informants in criminal investigations.

2. List and describe the four groups of people that most commonly become informants for law enforcement.

3. What are three reasons informants are considered problematic in criminal investigations?

4. List and discuss the advantages and benefits of using informants in criminal investigations.

5. What are the various motivations for becoming involved with law enforcement as an informant?

6. What elements of the initial informant interview are most critical to the possible success of the investigation?

7. Discuss the concept of entrapment and how it relates to the management of informants.

8. Discuss the problem of keeping an informant's identity secret, and describe the two foundational cases addressing this issue.

9. List and discuss other problems that arise in the management of informants.

10. Explain the WITSEC program and how it is useful in managing informants.

NOTES

1. ANON. (1996, May 16). Police upset by cancellation of *America's Most Wanted. USA Today.*
2. PUENTE, M. (1997, July 29). A no longer most wanted list. *USA Today,* p. 3A.
3. Ibid.
4. HAMPSON, R. (2006, March 29). Anti-snitch campaign riles police, prosecutors. *USA Today,* pp. 1A–2A.
5. Ibid.
6. GRAY, P. (1997, Aug. 23). A heart in her hand. *Time,* p. 43.
7. U.S. DEPARTMENT OF JUSTICE, DRUG ENFORCEMENT ADMINISTRATION (1988). *Drug enforcement handbook.* Washington, DC: U.S. Government Printing Office.

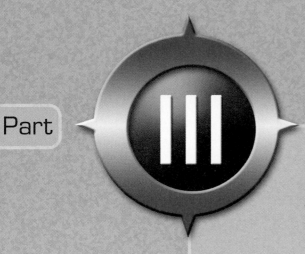

Part **III**

Interpersonal Violence

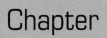

Chapter

Wrongful Death

Key Terms

▶ autoerotic death
▶ dying declaration
▶ homicide
▶ lividity
▶ manslaughter
▶ mass murder
▶ murder
▶ rigor mortis
▶ scene-conscious
▶ sensational murder
▶ serial murder
▶ suicide

This chapter will enable you to:

- Identify the various modes of death.
- Understand the duties of the responding officer.
- Learn the fundamentals of protecting the crime scene.
- Learn techniques used in identifying victims.
- Understand the methods used in estimating time of death.
- Interpret defense wounds.
- Interpret entrance and exit wounds.
- Identify an autoerotic death.

INTRODUCTION

The brutal murder of six-year-old JonBenet Ramsey on Christmas night in 1996 shocked America. Just as the Lindbergh baby kidnapping and murder seven decades earlier had seared the nation's consciousness, this murder—of a beautiful and talented child in a wealthy Boulder, Colo., home—renewed every parent's worst nightmare: No child was truly safe, not even tucked in at home on Christmas night.

JonBenet's murder—particularly as the days went by and no arrests were forthcoming—quickly became a national obsession, featured day after day on network news, television tabloid programs, talk radio, newspapers, and magazines. Her image displayed across television screens countless times, often showing her in a fancy red cowgirl outfit, singing "I want to be a cowboy sweetheart," or dancing across the stage in a glittering Las Vegas showgirl outfit, complete with heavy makeup. Her unusual first name became so well known that like Cher and Madonna, she no longer had need of a last name.

The public's shock at the murder soon spread to dismay at the Boulder Police Department's investigation—a dismay fed by a steady flow of leaks from the Boulder County District Attorney's office about the inept police investigation being conducted. Specifically, it became known that the police had badly botched the initial investigation by failing to seal off the crime scene. It also appeared as though the police were treating the primary suspects—JonBenet's parents—with kid gloves by not only acquiescing to their refusal to be interviewed at police headquarters, but also to being interviewed separately. Fueled with such information, the media, especially tabloid television and talk radio shows, were quick to blame JonBenet's parents, John and Patsy Ramsey. Some in the media began to point the finger directly at her father. Others implied it was her mother who had garroted the girl. Some speculated the crime had to have been committed by both parents. The tabloids even raised the possibility that her brother, Burke, who was just shy of 10 years old at the time, murdered JonBenet.

As of the preparation of this book, this case continues unsolved. A grand jury met for over a year, only to disband in October of 1999 without handing down an indictment or even issuing a report, an option that was open to it. Boulder Police Chief Mark Beckner admitted that the case files have been put in storage, although he said some more "forensic testing" was going on. The then newly elected Boulder district attorney, Mary Keenan, promised to look into the case. Nothing seemed to come of it. In April of 2003, she issued a statement saying she concurred with a federal court in Georgia's contemporaneous finding that JonBenet was most likely murdered by an intruder. Two months later, Keenan shifted responsibility for the case away from the Boulder Police Department to the district attorney's office, and she hired Tom Bennett as lead investigator of the case, directing him to focus his probe on the premise that an intruder killed JonBenet.

During the intervening three years, the case all but dropped from public view. The death of Patsy Ramsey on June 24, 2006—of ovarian cancer at age 49—briefly brought the case back into the spotlight. And then on August 16, 2006, the long-dormant case appeared back in the headlines across the world when a 41-year-old child-sex-offender by the name of John Mark Karr was arrested in Bangkok, Thailand, at the request of the Boulder District Attorney's Office. Karr was extradited back to Boulder at which time DNA results from the JonBenet crime scene failed to link Karr to the crime. As the Boulder District Attorney faced considerable criticism for Karr's premature extradition, his candidacy as JonBenet's killer was dismissed.

In all societies, the instances of assault and homicide have endured as top concerns for law enforcement officials. Considered as one of the gravest social problems, law enforcement plays an important role in investigating the facts and circumstances surrounding each such case. An estimated 15,500 people are murdered every year, and most of these (an estimated 85 percent) involve people who knew each other (e.g., friends, neighbors, family members).

Murder and non-negligent manslaughter, as defined in the Uniform Crime Reporting (UCR) Program, is the willful (non-negligent) killing of one human being by another. The classification of this offense, as for all other offenses that make up the Crime Index, is based solely on police investigation as opposed to the determination of a court, medical examiner, coroner, jury, or other judicial body. The program does not include deaths caused by negligence, suicide, or accident; justifiable **homicides;** and attempts to murder or assaults to murder, which are scored as aggravated assaults.

According to the FBI's Uniform Crime Reports, in 2005 an estimated 16,692 persons were murdered nationwide at a rate of 5.6 per 100,000 people. This is an increase of 3.4 percent from the previous year. Of all the violent crime reported in 2005, murder comprised 1.2 percent.

In terms of race, single victim/single offender incidents showed that 92.6 percent of black victims were murdered by black offenders, and 84.8 percent of white victims were murdered by white offenders.

Of the homicides for which the type of weapon was specified, firearms were the preferred weapon, used in 72.6 percent of the offenses.

Concerning the relationships (if known) of murder victims and offenders, 22.4 percent of victims were slain by family members; 25.4 percent were murdered by strangers. Furthermore, arguments (including romantic triangles) comprised 27.1 percent of reported murder circumstances.[1]

TYPES OF WRONGFUL DEATH

Murders may occur in sprees, which involve killings and two or more locations with almost no time break between murders. John Allen Muhammad, 41, part of the "sniper team" that terrorized the Washington, D.C., area in 2002, was arrested along with 17-year-old Jamaican immigrant Lee Boyd Malvo in the random shootings of 13 people in Maryland, Virginia, and Washington over a three-week period. Ten of the victims died. In 2003, Muhammad and Malvo were convicted of capital murder; Muhammad was sentenced to die. Malvo was

Comparative Rates

Year	Number of Offenses	Rate per 100,000 Inhabitants
2004	15,023	5.5
2005	15,625	5.9
Percent change	+4.0	+0.4

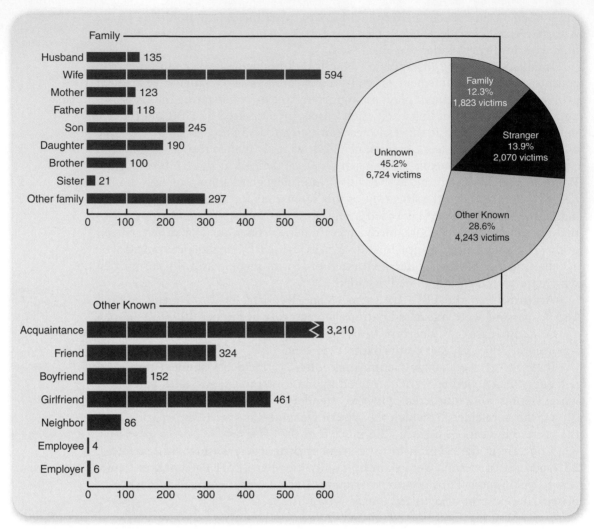

Figure 11.1 Instances of interpersonal violence involving family and other known parties. *FBI, Crime in the United States, 2006.*

given a second sentence of life without the possibility of parole in 2004, after he struck a deal with prosecutors in an effort to avoid the death penalty.

In contrast to spree killing, mass murder entails "the killing of four or more victims at one location, within one event." Recent mass murderers have included Timothy McVeigh (the antigovernment Oklahoma City bomber) and Mohammed Atta and the terrorists he led in the September 11, 2001, attacks against American targets.

Yet another kind of murder, serial murder, happens over time and officially "involves the killing of several victims in three or more separate events." In cases of serial murder, days, months, or even years may lapse between killings. Some of the more infamous serial killers of recent years confessed to are Wichita BTK murderer Dennis Rader; Jeffrey Dahmer, who received 936 years in prison for the murders of 15 young men (and who was himself later murdered in prison); Ted Bundy, who killed numerous college-age women; Henry Lee Lucas, now in a Texas prison, who confessed to 600 murders but later recanted (yet was convicted of 11 murders and linked to at least 140 others); Otis Toole,

Figure 11.2 Homicide crime scene showing considerable blood and trace evidence around the victim.

Lucas's partner in crime; cult leader Charles Manson still serving time for ordering followers to kill seven Californians, including the famed actress Sharon Tate; Andrei Chikatilo, the Russian "Hannibal Lecter," who killed 52 people, mostly schoolchildren; David Berkowitz, also known as the "Son of Sam," who killed six people on lovers' lanes around New York City; Theodore Kaczynski, the Unabomber, who perpetrated a series of bomb attacks on "establishment" figures; Seattle's Green River killer, Gary Leon Ridgway, a 54-year-old painter who in 2003 confessed to killing 48 women in the 1980s; and the infamous "Railroad killer," Angel Maturino Resendiz.

MODES OF DEATH

It is of primary importance that the investigator learn the manner in which the victim died as soon as possible after discovery of the body. Although much of this information is learned from the autopsy, much can also be discovered through careful examination of both the deceased and the crime scene. Modes of death can be divided into four general categories:

1. *Accidental death*. Many types of death are associated with this category: drowning, falling, automobile wrecks, accidental drug overdose, and so on. Often, murders are disguised to appear to be accidental in nature.

2. *Natural death*. Deaths from natural causes include heart attack, stroke, disease, and old age. In many circumstances, the deceased will have been under a doctor's care, but often people are found and their mode of death is questionable. For example, a person might have been forced to consume certain drugs that can cause death, but the symptoms indicate death from "natural" causes (e.g., heart attack).

3. *Suicide.* Methods of committing suicide are numerous and include stabbing, shooting, drug overdose, and carbon monoxide poisoning. As with other modes of death, investigators should be sure that the cause of death was actually suicide and not murder designed to look like suicide.

4. *Murder.* Murder is one person intentionally causing another person to die. Many different situations can result in a person's death. These include:

   - Wounds from handguns and shotguns.
   - Cutting and stabbing wounds.
   - Blunt-force injuries.
   - Extraordinary modes of death such as poisoning and death by asphyxia (strangulation).

LEGAL CHARACTERISTICS OF HOMICIDE

Criminal investigators encounter wrongful death in many ways. Some victims are killed by accident, others in the heat of passion, and still others for profit. Therefore, it is incumbent on the professional investigator to be clear as to what laws best describe the alleged crime. Under law, categories of homicide are generally divided into two distinct classifications: murder and manslaughter. Murder is considered the most serious of all statutory crimes and is defined as the purposeful, premeditated, and unlawful taking of the life of a human being by another person. Persons found guilty of murder will receive the harshest of sentences, which can include life imprisonment or the death penalty. Many states classify murder in different degrees, typically first and second. For example, first-degree murder is considered the most serious and includes, as one of the elements, premeditation and preplanning. Second-degree murder is a lesser offense but requires that the person "attempted" to kill his or her intended victim (e.g., a domestic argument that erupts into a physical altercation resulting in the death of one of the parties).

Figure 11.3 License plate—blood on back matched victim. Victim beat up on trunk of vehicle and subsequently raped and killed. The investigator noticed a small crescent-shaped cut under the victim's eye and theorized that the corner of a license plate could have imparted the cut. When a suspect was developed, investigators took the license plate off his vehicle and found this stain. The DNA matched the victim. *Missouri State Highway Patrol Crime Laboratory*

Manslaughter is the deliberate killing of another person and is typically classified into two subcategories: voluntary and involuntary. *Voluntary manslaughter* generally refers to the killing of another person out of an act of passion but lacks premeditation. For example, a man arrives at his home to find his wife with another man. The husband then loses his temper and immediately shoots the man. The key element here is that the scene must erupt into passion and must be followed immediately by the act of murder without premeditation or "cool reflection" about the incident.

Involuntary manslaughter usually refers to the accidental or nonintentional death of another human being, with severe negligence. Examples of involuntary manslaughter include a motorist who is exceeding the speed limit by 30 miles per hour and hits a child playing in the street. If he were traveling at the speed limit, he would have been able to stop in time to miss the child. Other examples of involuntary manslaughter include the reckless handling of a firearm, resulting in someone's death, and leaving dangerous poisons or drugs in reach of children.

Elements of Homicide

Legal elements of the crime of homicide will vary from one state to another but do exhibit some commonalties.

MURDER

- *First degree.* A person commits the crime if he or she knowingly causes the death of another person after deliberation on the matter.
- *Second degree.* A person commits the crime if he or she knowingly causes the death of another person while committing a criminal act and not acting under the influence of sudden passion.

MANSLAUGHTER

- *Involuntary.* A person commits the crime if he or she recklessly causes another person's death.
- *Voluntary.* A person commits the crime if he or she causes the death of another person by being certain of taking the victim's life and acting in the heat of passion.

THE PRELIMINARY INVESTIGATION

Homicide investigations are usually reactive in nature and are typically initiated by a telephone call to a local law enforcement agency notifying them of some aspect of the offense. Such calls may be a simple request for assistance by an injured person, a call stating "shots fired," or a report of some form of violence that was observed (e.g., a man or woman being beaten). Rarely, however, does this initial call contain enough information to determine exactly what is occurring or what has occurred. Investigators on the scene typically learn such details.

The first officer to respond to a suspected homicide call is generally a patrol officer arriving a short time after the call is received. The actions taken at the time of arrival may have a critical bearing on the subsequent course of the investigation. Some of the most critical of these are featured in this section. Responding officers might encounter:

- A man who directs him or her to the crime scene.
- A crime scene that might be in an isolated place that is untouched and easily safeguarded.
- A crime scene that might be filled with people milling around, acting confused, shouting, or crying.
- A killer who might either still be on the scene or may have just exited.
- A victim who may be dead or may still be alive but in need of medical attention.
- A crime scene in a public place that may be difficult to secure.

In all situations the first officer on the scene has several principal concerns:

- Determine if the victim is dead or alive.
- Contact medical help for the victim if needed.
- Apprehend the perpetrator if still present on the scene.
- Make the appropriate notifications if the perpetrator has left the scene.
- Safeguard the crime scene.
- Detain any witnesses.

After these fundamental steps are dealt with, the officer must become what could be termed **scene-conscious.** That is, he or she must become aware of the crime scene situation and be prepared to take certain immediate actions, the focus being identifying any aspects of the scene that might be subject to chemical change, change by dissipation, or change because something was moved.

PROTECTING THE CRIME SCENE

Once the preliminary duties have been performed, the responding officer must protect the crime scene from unauthorized persons who may move, destroy, or otherwise contaminate evidence. It is important for civilians and unauthorized police personnel alike to be denied entrance to the scene. Experience has shown that probably no aspect of the homicide investigation is more open to error than the preservation and protection of the crime scene.[2] Death scenes can be expected to produce an abundance of evidence. All such evidence will enable the investigator to determine the manner of death, weapons used, time of death, and other pertinent information.

TAKING NOTES AT THE SCENE

Complete notes are critical during the early stages of the homicide crime scene investigation. Because details are of such vital importance, both the investigating and responding officers should take notes. In fact, these notes could later become decisive evidence in the prosecution of the suspect(s). Crime scene notes in a homicide investigation should include the following:

- Names of officers on the scene.
- Names and addresses of witnesses at the scene.
- Name and address of the person notifying the police.

- Manner of entry/exit of the perpetrator to the crime.
- Description of weather conditions.

As indicated earlier, investigators should also be prepared to draft a sketch of the scene. The sketch should show all critical aspects of the homicide crime scene, such as the location/position of the body, location of any weapons, and positions of furniture, clothing, and other types of evidence. The sketch will prove to be of value later in the investigation when reports are being finalized or in preparing for court.

IDENTIFYING THE VICTIM

Homicide crime scenes can vary greatly from one case to the next. For example, in one case, the body might be charred as a result of a fire designed to cover up evidence. In another, the body might have been chopped up and parts distributed over a broad geographical area. In other cases, bodies have been recovered in lakes and rivers and offer little or no immediate clues as to their identity. In all circumstances, the body must be identified.

The Deceased Victim

If the victim is obviously deceased, the officer should not attempt to authorize the removal of the body until after the crime scene has been processed. This will allow valuable time for the identification process. Efforts in identifying the victim may begin with a cursory inspection of the victim's personal effects and clothing. Papers in the possession of the victim may make the identification process easy, in particular if certain items are present (e.g., a driver's license, personal letters).

Witnesses can also provide useful identification information of the victim if known to them. Other people might be able to offer positive identification, such as parents, friends, neighbors, or spouses. A good practice for investigators is to have more than one person identify the remains to avoid a case of mistaken identity. In addition, it is also a sound policy to corroborate positive identifications by additional evidence.

Other identifiers that investigators should look for include:

- *Wounds and blood.* Investigators can also tell if the body has been moved by inspecting wounds or blood around the body. If wounds indicate severe bleeding and little blood is on the scene, the body may have been moved. Blood type and DNA evidence are also options that might be considered by investigators.
- *Fingernail scrapings.* Technicians at the morgue will also look for fingernail scrapings. This evidence might turn up hair, skin, blood, or fibers that might be useful in developing a suspect.
- *Fingerprints of the deceased.* Deceased's fingerprints can be taken by using an ink roller on each finger. Next, while strips of fingerprint paper are placed in a curved holder such as a spoon, each finger is placed against the strip and an impression is taken. Rigid joints can be loosened by working the finger back and forth several times.

Evidence in the JonBenet Ramsey Murder Case

Figure 11.4 is a rough sketch of the Ramsey house and the locations where each piece of evidence was located. Consider the amount of evidence, how it relates to the crime and other pieces of evidence, and the complicated process of investigating wrongful death cases.

1. *The corpse.* The six-year-old JonBenet's 45-pound corpse was found in the basement's wine cellar. According to police reports, John Ramsey said he found the body covered with a white blanket, a Colorado Avalanche sweatshirt, and a pink Barbie nightgown. This last item was JonBenet's favorite possession.

   The dead child's long blonde hair was done up in two loose ponytails. Duct tape covered and sealed her mouth. John Ramsey is said to have ripped this tape off after he removed the coverings from the body. According to information leaked from grand jury hearings, police determined that a fiber found on the sticky part of the tape matched that of a garment Patricia Ramsey was wearing on the night of the killing. However, others point out that the fiber could have become adhered after John Ramsey threw the ripped-off tape on the floor.

   The dead girl was dressed in a crewneck top decorated with a sequined star on the chest and long white underpants, which were extensively stained with urine. Beneath, she wore white panties imprinted with a rosebud pattern. The panties were also stained with urine as well as a small amount of blood. Additional amounts of blood were found around her genitals; her vagina showed signs of penetration and abrasion but no semen was found in, on, or around the body.

   She wore a gold cross and chain around her neck; a gold bracelet on her wrist was inscribed with "JonBenet 12-25-96." On her left palm was a heart drawn in red ink. Two pieces of white synthetic cord were involved in the killing. One was wrapped around the girl's neck and had strands of her hair entangled in its knot. The other was tied around her wrist. The neck cord was also entangled with a broken length of paintbrush handle that is believed to have been used to make a strangulation garrote. Police have matched the wooden handle to a paintbrush found in Patricia Ramsey's oil painting gear.

   According to the Boulder coroner, John E. Meyer, the primary cause of death was strangulation. Based on autopsy information, other medical authorities have suggested that she was hit on the head first and strangled

later. Although the girl had been struck with a blunt object hard enough to open an 8-inch-long skull fracture, the blow did not break the skin, a fact that suggested to police that the object was padded in some manner.

2. *The kitchen flashlight.* During their searches of the Ramsey home, police seized a number of objects that could have been used to inflict the skull-cracking blow. These included a hammer, golf clubs, several baseball bats, and a large rubber-coated flashlight that was found on the kitchen counter on the morning the child's body was discovered. The flashlight has received special attention by police, including analysis at the Colorado Bureau of Investigation laboratory. The results of those forensic tests are not known.

3. *The basement.* The corpse was found in what the family called the wine cellar. The cement-floored space had its own door and contained a collection of bottled wine as well as other household items commonly stored in basements, such as old cans of house paint. Then-Boulder police chief Rick French searched the basement on the morning JonBenet was reported missing but said he did not look in the small wine cellar room.

   Fleet White, a retired oil company executive and neighbor of the Ramsey family, who helped in the morning search for JonBenet, is reported to have told police that prior to the arrival of French, he had inspected the wine cellar room and saw nothing there. Later that day, John Ramsey said he looked in the wine cellar for the first time and saw the body of his daughter lying on the floor.

   Police found the overall basement area to be acoustically well insulated from much of the rest of the house. Tests found that screams in the basement were actually easier to hear outside the building than from the family bedrooms on the second floor. Residents in the vicinity said they heard a child's screams between midnight and 2 A.M. on the night that JonBenet died.

4. *Forensic contamination.* Authorities say that John Ramsey and a police officer disturbed, destroyed, or contaminated important forensic clues when each moved the body shortly after Ramsey said he first discovered it. Ramsey lifted the corpse from the floor of the wine cellar, carried it upstairs, and put it down on the floor of the foyer near the top of the stairs. A short time later, detective Linda Arndt lifted the corpse from that spot and moved it into the living room near the Christmas tree before she called her office to report a homicide. In addition, throughout

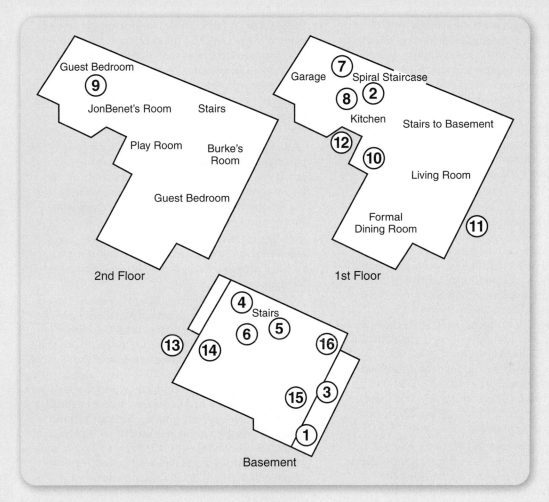

Figure 11.4 Murder of JonBenet: location of evidence in the Ramsey house.

the day, police allowed the Ramseys to host a crowd of friends and neighbors in the house. Dozens of people roamed the rooms, cleaning kitchen counters and appliance surfaces as they prepared to lay out spreads of bagels, coffee, and other snacks for themselves.

5. *The train room.* Another room in the basement was called the train room because it contained a large table for model train setups. The table was covered in artificial grass, traces of which are believed to have been found in JonBenet's hair.

6. *The Swiss army knife.* A Swiss army knife owned by nine-year-old Burke Ramsey was also recovered from an undisclosed spot in the basement. The knife was reported to be one of the young boy's prized possessions.

7. *The ransom note.* One of the most vital and controversial clues of the case is the handwritten ransom note that

(*continued*)

Evidence in the JonBenet Ramsey Murder Case
(*continued*)

Patricia Ramsey says she found on the staircase near the kitchen. The note, which demanded an amount of money that was exactly equal to John Ramsey's Christmas bonus, also contained references to other aspects of the Ramseys' personal lives that would not be known to outsiders. According to police, a rough draft or "practice" version of the note was written on a pad seized from an undisclosed location inside the house. News leaks from both sides of the investigation have indicated that various handwriting experts have reached dramatically different conclusions about whether the writing is similar to Patricia Ramsey's.

8. *The 9-1-1 call.* At 5:51 A.M. on December 26, Patricia Ramsey dialed 9-1-1 and reported her daughter missing, but she failed to put the handset back in its cradle when she hung up. The 9-1-1 connection remained live, continuing to record sounds from within the Ramsey house. The police later turned that 9-1-1 recording over to the Aerospace Corp. in southern California for enhancement. That enhanced tape constitutes one of the most controversial and mysterious aspects of the case. In the recording, Burke Ramsey can reportedly be heard asking his parents, "What did you find?" His father, John Ramsey, can reportedly be heard harshly silencing the boy. Patricia Ramsey reportedly can be heard screaming, "Help me, Jesus, help me, Jesus." Among the reasons the tape is important is because it appears to directly contradict John and Patricia Ramsey's statements to police that Burke was asleep during the early morning commotion.

9. *The victim's bedroom.* JonBenet and her brother, Burke, had separate bedrooms on the second floor near the top of the staircase leading up from the kitchen area. The autopsy reported that the child's bladder was empty when she died.

10. *The pineapple chunks.* The coroner reported finding pineapple in the victim's small intestine, indicating that she had eaten the fruit just hours before she died. It has been reported that pineapple was one of her favorite snacks. But the Ramseys said that JonBenet was asleep when they arrived home from a Christmas party the night before and that they put her right to bed around 10 P.M. after changing her clothes as she continued to sleep.

11. *Unlocked windows and doors.* Police found that six ground-floor windows and the kitchen-area door to the exterior of the Ramsey house were not locked the night of the killing.

12. *Kitchen door pry mark.* An attorney for the Ramseys has pointed to a pry mark on the doorjamb of the kitchen door that leads to the exterior of the building as part of the "substantial evidence" that points toward an intruder as the killer. However, police characterized the mark as a "possible" pry mark, and a locksmith who inspected the house in the wake of the slaying said there was no evidence of a forced entry.

13. *The broken basement window.* The glass of a ground-level basement window at the back of the basement was broken. Police said John Ramsey broke the window months before and didn't repair it. There was dirt at the base of the window that could have resulted from someone squeezing in through the small opening.

14. *The blue suitcase.* Police found a blue suitcase propped below the broken basement window that some suggest could have been used by someone climbing out through the opening.

15. *DNA specimens.* The issue of DNA has been the subject of inaccurate media reports that were later corrected. For instance, shortly after the killing, *Newsweek* magazine reported that semen was found on the dead girl's thigh. That report was later retracted. However, authorities collected blood and hair samples from every member of the Ramsey family as well as a number of people with whom JonBenet was in contact in the days before her death. It is known that DNA experts from the FBI, the Colorado Bureau of Investigation, and several other DNA testing laboratories around the country have been consulted or retained by both sides of the investigation. The exact details of the DNA findings are not known.

16. *A stun gun.* More conjecture than fact is the continuing suggestion (which has not been confirmed) that an electric stun gun may have been involved. The autopsy report made no mention of stun gun marks on the body. However, *New York* magazine reported that among the many videotapes found in the Ramsey house was an instruction program about how to use a stun gun. A rear neighbor to the Ramsey house, Margaret Dillon, was questioned by detectives about stun guns. Another neighbor, Scott Gibbons, reported seeing "strange lights" in the Ramsey home that some have suggested could have been the flash of a stun gun.

The Victim Who Is Still Alive

In cases in which the victim is still alive or conscious, he or she might be willing to give information such as the name of his or her assailant; a description of the assailant's clothing; and the type of automobile the assailant was driving. Once this information is learned, it should be passed on to the communication center for broadcast to other officers and departments.

Obtaining a Dying Declaration

If the victim is badly wounded and believes that he or she is dying, the officer should treat his or her statement as a **dying declaration.** The legal requirements of a dying declaration are that the victim must be rational and competent and must ultimately die of the wounds. The death of the victim is a legal requirement for the admissibility of the statement. Information taken in the statement should include the identity of the suspect and the circumstances surrounding infliction of the mortal wounds.

ESTIMATING THE TIME OF DEATH

If the wrongful death appears to have been a homicide, all areas around the body become important in determining the time of death. The time of death in a homicide case, in particular when there are no witnesses, is one of the most critical variables in its investigation. It can convict a murderer, break an alibi, or even eliminate a suspect. Time may come into play if the deceased had an appointment with someone around the time of his or her death. In addition, in cases of exclusive opportunity, in which only certain persons are present with the victim, husbands or wives, boyfriends or girlfriends, and so on, may become likely suspects.

Changes in the Body

Simply stated, death occurs when vital functions of the body are halted. These include functions of breathing and circulation. In addition, there are other changes that investigators should observe.

Body Color. Once the victim dies, circulation of blood through the arteries and veins ceases. As the body settles, color in the lips and nails will disappear as the blood settles into the lower capillaries of the body. The blood will then change from red to a dark purplish color as it loses its oxygen. This is the beginning of lividity, which we discuss later.

Changes in Eyes. The eyes are the most sensitive part of the human body and, in death, will not react to light, touching, or pressure. In addition, the eyelids may remain open; pupils may become irregular in size and shape and will typically become milky and cloudy in color within 8 to 10 hours of death.

Temperature of the Body. In life, a person's body maintains a body temperature of 98.6 F. Even after death, there may not be a loss of body heat, as the body will tend to adapt to the temperature of its environment. The rate of cooling can, however, be a primary determinant as to the time of death. For example, a corpse will feel cool to the touch from 8 to 12 hours after death and will remain the same temperature as its surroundings for about 24 hours after death.

Figure 11.5 Post mortem lividity located on the back of a murder victim.

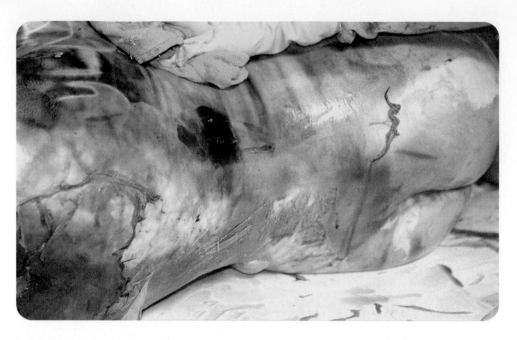

Several factors can contribute to the rate in which a body loses heat. The greater the difference between the body and the environment, the faster the body will cool down.

Water and air temperature are the most important contributing factors. The temperature of the body before death can influence its temperature after death occurs. Predeath conditions such as stroke, sun stroke, and strangulation will generally result in a higher body temperature at the time of death. One reliable method for determining body temperature is to insert a thermometer into the rectum of the deceased (do not insert a thermometer into the wound). The medical examiner will usually place a thermometer in the victim's liver. Body temperature can also be raised by the victim's excessive body fat or heavy clothing worn by the deceased.

The International Association of Chiefs of Police (IACP) offers a working formula to determine the estimated time of death when it is thought to be less than 24 hours:

$$\frac{98.6 \text{ (normal temp.) } 2 \text{ (rectal temp.) no. of hours since death}}{1.5 \text{ (average rate of heat loss)}}$$

Rigor Mortis. **Rigor mortis,** the process of stiffening, or contraction of body muscles after vital functions cease, is generally considered a poor indicator of time of death. As a rule, rigor mortis sets in two to four hours after death, but many variables may contribute to "rigor." Contrary to popular belief, rigor mortis starts at the same time throughout the entire body. However, it is first observed in the jaws and neck.[3] It then tends to progress in the head-to-foot direction. At the time of completion, typically 8 to 12 hours after death, the torso, jaws, neck, and upper/lower extremities are "stiff as a board." Once in this state, the body resists any change in position.

Postmortem Lividity. As indicated earlier, when a body's vital functions cease, blood settles to the bottom side of the body because of gravity. A **lividity**

stain purplish in color will form on the skin of the body closest to the surface on which it is lying. So if a body is lying on its stomach and the lividity stain is on its back, the body has probably been turned over. Postmortem lividity may appear anywhere between one-half hour to four hours after death. It is sometimes valuable in determining whether or not a body has been moved, depending on the state of the lividity. If it is determined that the body has been moved, the officer must ask why—perhaps another police officer turned the body over. Generally speaking, however, after lividity has set in for 12 hours, the body will not diminish in color and will remain unchanged.

Insects

One method of determining the time of death is to examine the larvae of insects found on the body. Investigators should consider contacting an entomologist (insect expert) for advice at this stage of the investigation. This technique studies the various stages of growth of each larvae before it develops into an adult insect. Houseflies, for example, deposit eggs on the remains of the corpse, usually in the area of the eyes, mouth, nostrils, and wounds. The eggs then become maggots and feed on the body. Typically, the time span for the hatching of the maggot is 24 hours.

The developmental stage will depend on the type of insect in question. The entomologist will identify the specific insect and determine an estimated time span for its development as well as the season in which the death occurred. The recommended procedure is for all insects to be placed into alcohol for preservation.

Animals

A body discovered outdoors (and in some cases indoors) will sometimes be mutilated by wild animals. Bodies that have been mutilated will give the appearance of having been grossly injured, but that will not necessarily be evidence of a postmortem attack. Investigators must be careful not to draw false conclusions.

Bodies Found in Water

As described in the preceding section, marine life can also damage and distort dead bodies found in water (floaters). Generally, a forensic pathologist will have to be consulted to distinguish postmortem injuries from those that occurred in life. Experience has shown that bodies found in air will have decomposed twice as fast as those found submerged in water.

GUNSHOT WOUNDS AS EVIDENCE

Several factors can affect the type of wound inflicted by a firearm. Such wounds may resemble a stab wound at first, but certain physical characteristics may vary, depending on (1) the type of caliber weapon used, (2) the distance between the shooter and victim, and (3) whether the lethal bullet had ricocheted off another object. To understand the firearm wound best, let's discuss the effect that a firearm has on the human body. Vernon Geberth states that when a firearm is discharged, several things can occur:[4]

- Fire or flames are emitted from the barrel.
- Smoke follows the flame.

The Investigation of the "BTK" Killer

Dennis Lynn Rader (born March 9, 1945) is a serial killer who murdered at least ten people in Sedgwick County (in and around Wichita), Kansas, between 1974 and 1991. He was known as the BTK killer (or the BTK strangler), which stands for Bind, Torture, and Kill, an apt description of his modus operandi.

The BTK's Modus Operandi, "MO"

Using personal jargon for his killing equipment, Rader casually described his victims as his "projects" and at one point likened the murders of his victims to killing animals by saying he "put them down."

Rader created what he called a "hit kit," a briefcase or bowling bag containing the items he would use during murders: guns, tape, rope, and handcuffs. He also packed what he called "hit clothes" that he would wear for the crimes and then dispose of.

Rader developed a pattern for his murders. He would wander the city until he found a potential victim. At that point, he would stalk the person until he knew the pattern of their life and when would be the best time to strike. He would also get acquainted with his potential victims if they were his co-workers, making them easier to track down and identify. Rader often would stalk multiple victims at a time, so he could continue the hunt if one victim didn't work out. At the time of the murder, Rader would break into the house, cut the phone lines, and hide until his victim came home.

Rader would often calm his victims by pretending to be a rapist who needed to work out some sexual fantasies on them. This caused many of his victims to be more cooperative and even help him, thinking that once the rape was over, he would leave them alone. Instead, Rader would kill them.

The name BTK, chosen by Rader for himself, also dictated his methods. Rader bound, tortured, and killed his victims. Rader would strangle his victims until they lost consciousness, then let them revive, then strangle them again. He would repeat the pattern over and over again, forcing them to experience near-death, becoming sexually aroused at the sight of their struggles. Finally, Rader would strangle them to death.

RADER'S VICTIMS INCLUDED:

- 1974: Four members of one family (Joseph Otero, his wife Julie Otero, and two of their five children: Joseph Otero II and Josephine Otero) and another separate victim, Kathryn Bright

- 1977: Shirley Vian
- 1977: Nancy Fox
- 1985: Marine Hedge
- 1986: Vicki Wegerle
- 1991: Delores Davis

Police officials say there is no reason to believe Rader was responsible for any other murders. He collected items from the scenes of the murders he committed and, reportedly, he had no items that were related to any other killings.

Evidence in the BTK Investigation: Letters

Rader was particularly known for sending taunting letters to police and newspapers. There were several communications from BTK during 1974 to 1979. The first was a letter that had been stashed in an engineering book in the Wichita Public Library in October 1974 that described in detail the killing of the Otero family in January of that year.

In early 1978 he sent another letter to television station KAKE in Wichita claiming responsibility for the murders of the Oteros, Shirley Vian, Nancy Fox, and another unidentified victim assumed to be Kathryn Bright. He suggested a number of possible names for himself, including the one that stuck: BTK. He demanded media attention in this second letter, and it was finally announced that Wichita did indeed have a serial killer at large.

In his 1978 letter, Rader wrote the following (written verbatim):

"I find the newspaper not writing about the poem on Vain unamusing. A little paragraph would have enough. I know it not the media fault. The Police Chief he keep things quiet, and doesn't let the public know there a psycho running around lose strangling mostly women, there 7 in the ground; who will be next?

How many do I have to Kill before I get a name in the paper or some national attention. Do the cop think that all those deaths are not related? Golly -gee, yes the M.O. is different in each, but look a pattern is developing. The victims are tie up-most have been women-phone cut- bring some bondage mater sadist tendencies-no struggle, outside the death spot-no wintness except the Vain's Kids. They were very lucky; a phone call save them. I was going to tape the boys and put plastic bags over there head like I did Joseph, and Shirley. And then hang the girl. God-oh God what a beautiful sexual relief that would been. Josephine, when I hung her really turn me on; her pleading for mercy then the rope took whole, she helpless; staring at me with wide terror fill eyes the rope getting tighter-tighter. You don't understand these things because your not under the influence of factor x. The same thing that made Son of Sam, Jack the Ripper, Havery Glatman, Boston Strangler, Dr. H.H. Holmes Panty Hose Strangler OF Florida, Hillside Strangler, Ted of the West Coast and many more infamous character kill. Which seems senseless, but we cannot help it. There is no help, no cure, except death or being caught and put away. It a terrible nightmare but, you see I don't lose any sleep over it. After a thing like Fox I come home and go about life like anyone else. And I will be like that until the urge hit me again. It not continuous and I don't have a lot of time. It take time to set a kill, one mistake and it all over. Since I about blew it on the phone-handwriting is out-letter guide is to long and typewriter can be traced too. My short poem of death and maybe a drawing; later on real picture and maybe a tape of the sound will come your way. How will you know me. Before a murder or murders you will receive a copy of the initials B.T.K. , you keep that copy the original will show up some day on guess who?

May you not be the unluck one!
P.S.
How about some name for me, its time: 7 down and many more to go. I like the following How about you?
'THE B.T.K. STRANGLER', WICHITA STRANGLER', 'POETIC STRANGLER', 'THE BOND AGE STRANGLER' OR PSYCHO' THE WICHITA HANGMAN THE WICHITA EXECUTIONER, 'THE GAROTE PHATHOM', 'THE ASPHIXIATER'.
B.T.K"

A poem was enclosed entitled "Oh Death to Nancy." In 1979 he sent two identical packages, one to an intended victim who was not at home when he broke into her house and the other to KAKE. These featured another poem, "Oh Anna Why Didn't You Appear," a drawing of what he had intended to do to his victim, as well as some small items he had pilfered from Anna's home. Apparently, Rader had waited for several hours inside the home of Anna Williams on the 600 block of South Pinecrest. Not realizing that she had gone to her sister's house for the evening, he eventually got tired of the long wait and left.

All of Rader's communications were poorly written with many misspellings and incorrect grammar usage. It was theorized at times that the writing style was a ruse to conceal his intelligence, but it turns out Rader really does write that way in his everyday life even though he earned a college degree in 1979.

In 1988, after the murders of three members of the Fager family in Wichita, a letter was received from someone claiming to be the BTK killer in which he denied being the perpetrator of this crime. He did credit the killer with having done admirable work. It was not proven until 2005 that this letter was in fact written by the genuine BTK killer, Rader, although he is not considered by police to have committed this crime.

In March 2004, he began the series of eleven communications from BTK that led directly to his arrest in February 2005. The *Wichita Eagle* newspaper received a letter from someone using the return address Bill Thomas Killman. The writer claimed that he murdered Vicki Wegerle on September 16, 1986, and enclosed photographs of the crime scene and a photocopy of her driver's license, which had been stolen at the time of the crime.

In May 2004, a word puzzle was received by KAKE. In June a package was found taped to a stop sign in Wichita containing graphic descriptions of the Otero murders. In July a package was dropped into the return slot at the downtown public library containing more bizarre material, including the claim that he, BTK, was responsible for the death of 19-year-old Jake Allen in Argonia, Kansas, earlier that same month. This claim was found to be false and the death remains ruled as a suicide.

In October 2004, a manila envelope was dropped into a UPS box in Wichita containing a series of cards with images of terror and bondage of children pasted on them. Also included was a poem threatening the life of lead investigator Lt. Ken Landwehr and a false autobiography giving many details about his life. These details were later released to the public as though possibly factual, but the police were mostly trying to encourage the killer to continue to communicate until making a major mistake.

In December 2004, Wichita police received another package from the BTK killer. This time the package was found in Wichita's Murdock Park. It contained the driver's license of Nancy Fox, which was noted as stolen at the scene of the crime, as well as a doll that was symbolically bound at the hands and feet with a plastic bag tied over its head.

In January 2005, Rader attempted to leave a cereal box in the bed of a pickup truck at a Home Depot in Wichita, but the

(continued)

The Investigation of the "BTK" Killer (*continued*)

box was at first discarded by the owner. It was later retrieved from the trash after Rader himself asked what had become of it in a later message.

Surveillance tape of the parking lot from that date revealed a distant figure driving a black Jeep Cherokee leaving the box in the pickup. In February there were postcards to KAKE, and another cereal box left at a rural location that contained another bound doll symbolizing the murder of 11-year-old Josephine Otero. Rader asked the police that if he put his writings onto a floppy disk if the disk could be traced or not. He received his answer in a newspaper ad posted in the *Wichita Eagle* saying it would be OK.

On February 16, 2005, he sent a floppy disk to Fox TV station KSAS in Wichita. Forensic analysis quickly determined that the disk had been used by the Christ Lutheran Church in Wichita, plus the name Dennis. An Internet search determined that Rader was president of this church. He was arrested on February 25.

After his arrest, Rader stated he chose to resurface in 2004 for various reasons, including the release of the book *Nightmare in Wichita—the Hunt for the BTK Strangler* by Robert Beattie. He wanted the opportunity to tell his story his own way. He also said he was bored because his children had grown up and he had more time on his hands.

Rader's Arrest

The BTK killer's last known communication with the media and police was a padded envelope which arrived at FOX affiliate KSAS-TV in Wichita on February 16, 2005.

- A purple 1.44-MB Memorex floppy disk was enclosed in the package.
- Also enclosed were a letter and a photocopy of the cover of a 1989 novel about a serial killer (*Rules of Prey* ISBN 0-425-19519-8).

- A gold-colored necklace with a large medallion was also in the envelope.
- Police found metadata embedded in a Microsoft Word document on the disk that pointed to Christ Lutheran Church, and the document was marked as last modified by "Dennis."
- A search of the church Web site turned up Dennis Rader as president of the congregation council. Police immediately began surveillance of Rader.

Sometime during this period, police obtained a warrant for the medical records of Rader's daughter, Kerri. A tissue sample seized at this time was tested for DNA and provided a familial match with semen at an earlier BTK crime scene. This, along with other evidence gathered prior to and during the surveillance, gave police probable cause for an arrest.

Rader was stopped while driving near his home and taken into custody shortly after noon on February 25, 2005. Immediately after, law enforcement officials—including a Wichita Police bomb unit truck, two SWAT trucks, and FBI and ATF agents—converged on Rader's residence near the intersection of I-135 and 61st Street North.

Once in custody, Rader talked to investigators for hours, confessing right away. Twelve DVDs were filled with Rader's confession.

Observations

The BTK investigation illustrates the complexity of criminal investigation, evidence, and prosecution. Such cases also show how difficult it is for those who sit as jurors to decipher the truth in a criminal trial.

- The bullet emerges from the barrel.
- Additional smoke and grains of both burned and unburned gunpowder follow the bullet out of the barrel.
- The material spreads outward from the barrel as it is emitted.
- If the firearm is close to the targeted surface, much of this material will be deposited on it.

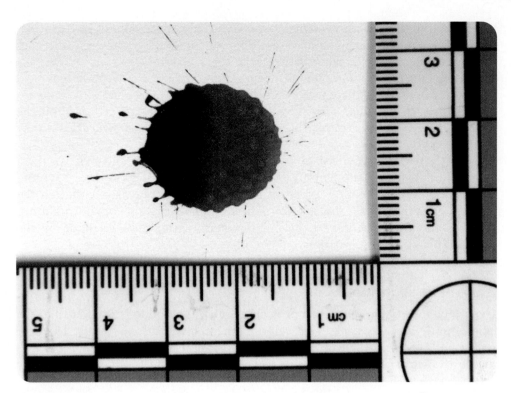

Figure 11.6 Blood drops and spatter are common on violent crime scenes and must be carefully documented.

Figure 11.7 Blood and biological evidence must be properly stored for preservation. This refrigerator is used for storage of blood evidence.

In addition, if the surface is farther away, less of the material will be deposited on it. Depending on the material or clothing present on the body, it is sometimes possible to predict the distance between the firearm and the victim.

In the case of a contact wound, where the muzzle of the weapon was held against the body when discharged, certain residue will be present. Soot is always present in such wounds, with powder particles identified in at least half the cases.[5] These particles are often difficult to readily identify, however, and may require expert analysis.

Gunshot wounds consist of two basic types: entrance and exit wounds. Determining whether the wound in question is an entrance or an exit wound can have an overwhelming effect on the outcome of the case. Although the medical examiner makes this determination, in many cases he or she might not come to the crime scene and the initial determination will be made by the investigator.

Entrance Wounds

Generally, the wound where the projectile entered the body is smaller than the exit wound, but there have been well-documented exceptions to this. The hole will usually be a neat, clean hole with an abrasion mark around it accompanied by a blackish-gray ring around the edges. Minimal bleeding will typically be observed.

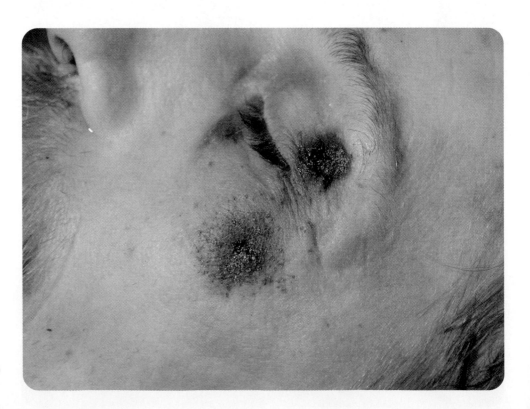

Figure 11.8 Duel gunshot wounds to the head with stippling.

Exit Wounds

An exit wound will usually be a larger wound than the entrance wound, with a ragged or torn appearance. The exit wound will usually have a larger amount of blood around it than the entrance wound.

Smudging

Smudging is usually a ring that results from gunpowder being deposited around the wound. It has a dirty appearance and can usually be wiped off. The significance of smudging is that it indicates that the victim was close to his or her assailant, although the firearm was not actually touching the skin.

Tattooing

Tiny pinpoint hemorrhages may result from the discharge of unburned powder being deposited into the skin. Called tattooing, these marks cannot be wiped away. One issue of critical importance in investigating gunshot wounds is the determination of whether or not the victim was murdered or died from suicide. The presence (or absence) of powder burns will not only help in making this determination but will help the investigator decide the distance between the victim and the firearm.

Defense Wounds

Defense wounds are characteristic of a struggle between the victim and an assailant. Such wounds may appear on the body of the victim and will take many forms. For example, in a fatal stabbing, slashing wounds on the hands of

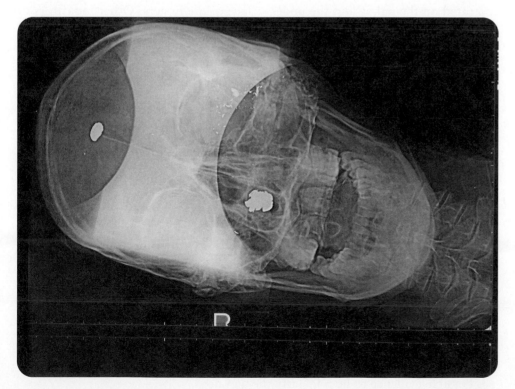

Figure 11.9 X-ray of a shooting victim showing locations of bullets in skull.

Figure 11.10 One of two bullets recovered from the skull of a shooting victim. (*See also* Figures 11.8 and 11.9)

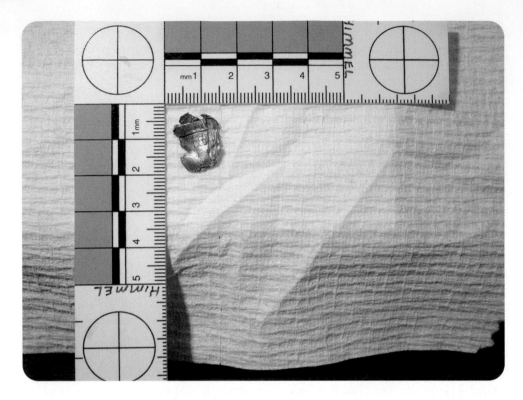

the victim may indicate that the victim grabbed the knife during a struggle, only to have it pulled back by the killer. These wounds will usually be deep and concentrated on the palms and the undersurface of the fingers. Other indicators of a struggle will be bruises on the forearms of the victim of a beating, indicating that they were attempting to defend themselves from attack by the assailant. In addition, a victim of a shotgun killing might have shot from the shotgun blast embedded in their hands or forearms.

Shotgun Wounds

Probably the most common weapon with which officers are confronted is the shotgun. The shotgun shell may project anywhere from 200 small pellets (birdshot) to nine larger (buckshot) to one large lead projectile called a *slug*. The shotgun remains one of the most effective killing weapons because of its capability for massive tissue destruction. It remains a choice of many criminals because all that is required, in many cases, is simply pointing the weapon in the general direction of the victim, and, after discharge, some contact is typically made. In addition, the appearance of the shotgun commands respect from all who face it, making it an effective tool of intimidation. From an evidentiary standpoint, the shotgun wadding usually remains in the skin of the victim if discharged within 10 feet. Shotgun wadding can tell the investigator three things:

1. Type of shot used.
2. Gauge of gun used.
3. Possible evidence to help identify the gun used.

Figure 11.11 Shotgun used in homicide is being tagged as evidence.

PITFALLS IN HOMICIDE INVESTIGATIONS

A recurring theme throughout this book is that the loss of crucial evidence in any criminal case can result in either the guilty party going unpunished or innocent parties being wrongfully incarcerated. This premise certainly applies to wrongful death investigations. In addition, carelessness in the processing of the crime scene can result in undue anguish to families. A study conducted by

Figure 11.12 Homicide investigations must be conducted on a timely basis to avoid missing evidence. Here, a detective is conducting follow-up calls during an investigation.

pathologist Alan Moritz concluded that there are several pitfalls that have been most commonly identified by veteran death investigators in the United States:[6]

SYSTEM ERRORS
- Assumption that the case is not provable.
- Inadequate staffing of the investigative unit.
- Lack of awareness about the objective of the investigation.
- Insufficient training.
- Alteration of the scene before the investigator's arrival.
- Inadequate photographic documentation at the scene.
- Inadequate sketches.
- Inadequate attention to detail.
- Poor documentation.
- Failure to follow up leads on a timely basis.
- Overlooking evidence.

BODY MISTAKES
- Failure to record body information thoroughly at the scene.
- Assumption of identification based on circumstantial evidence.
- Mishandling and mislabeling of bodies.
- Failure to recognize, record, and safeguard personal property.
- Failure to notify next of kin in a timely, humane manner.
- Trace evidence.
- Follow-up errors.
- Failure to report critical facts that determine what examinations need to be performed.
- Failure to complete a timely and accurate death investigation report.
- Failure to develop the victim's family and social history.
- Failure to prepare for courtroom testimony.

PERSONAL PITFALLS
- Fallacy that length of service ensures competence.
- Jumping to conclusions.
- Failure to verify information received from other sources.
- Talking too much and too soon to the wrong people.
- Cutting corners.

Recognizing these (and other) pitfalls will, it is hoped, alert investigators to the possibility that the investigation may be in jeopardy. Once problems are identified, the investigator can plan to avoid these pitfalls and discover solutions to problems rather than create more complications.

SERIAL, MASS, AND SENSATIONAL MURDERS

As mentioned in the beginning of this chapter, serial, mass, and sensational homicide add to the complexity of murder investigations. Such crimes generally have a psychodynamic component that can be very difficult to detect and understand. Because of this component, it is usually a logical decision to incorporate the expertise of psychology professionals in the investigation. For simplicity, let's now define the terms *serial, mass,* and *sensational murder.*[7]

Serial murder is the murder of separate victims with time breaks as short as two days to as much as weeks or even months between victims. Examples of serial murderers are the Hillside Strangler in California and Theodore Bundy, who traveled across the United States leaving a trail of victims. In 1991, serial killer-cannibal Jeffrey Dahmer was arrested in connection with 17 murders in Milwaukee. A search of his apartment revealed 15 dismembered bodies, including a head found in the refrigerator, a heart discovered in the freezer, and a vat of acid for disposing of leftover body parts.

Mass murder consists of four or more murders in a single incident within a short span of time. One classic example of a mass murder is the case of James Oliver Huberty, a 41-year-old security guard who entered a McDonald's fast-food restaurant on July 18, 1984, armed with several different guns and slaughtered 20 people.

Sensational murder is murder that arouses intense public interest. For example, on August 1, 1966, in Austin, Texas, Charles Witman killed his wife and mother. He then went to the University of Texas tower and, with a rifle, shot and killed 14 people. *Lust murders* also commonly attract public interest because of the instances of torture and violence that are typically associated with this type of crime. These types of crimes often involve some type of psychotic motivation, as in the Tylenol poisonings in Chicago, the Atlanta child

Figure 11.13 In October 2006, gunman Charles Carl Roberts (right) shot 10 Amish girls in a schoolhouse in Nickel Mines, PA. Five of the girls died. *AP Wide World Photos (right); Eileen Blass, USA Today. Copyright 2006, USA Today. Reprinted with permission (left).*

Case in Point

The Investigation of the Green River Killer

For 20 years, the bodies of a number of murdered young prostitutes and runaway girls periodically washed up in the Green River, approximately 45 miles from Seattle. By 2004, the total number of victims came to 48 and in addition to the Green River, their remains had shown up in ravines, airports, and freeways, with two of them discovered in Oregon. The victims had been strangled. In time, the killer became known as the Green River Killer.

Over the years, the investigation into the murders produced a considerable amount of evidence but nothing sufficiently conclusive to justify the arrest of a suspect. Finally, in early 2004, 54-year-old Gary Leon Ridgway, a slight man with thick glasses, married three times and the father of a child, was charged with all 48 murders. Ridgway was a long-time painter at Kenworth Truck Co.

Ridgway had been a suspect since 1984, when one of the victim's boyfriends reported that he last saw her getting into a pickup identified as Ridgway's. But Ridgway said he did not know the victim, Marie Malvar, and so told a police investigator in Des Moines who cleared him as a suspect. Later that year, Ridgway contacted the King County Green River Task Force ostensibly to offer information about the case—and passed a polygraph test.

Investigators continued to suspect him, however, and in 1987 searched his house and took a saliva sample. It was 13 years before technology caught up to their suspicions and they could link that saliva sample to DNA taken from the bodies of three of the earliest victims. Ridgway was arrested on November 30, 2001, and later pleaded guilty to seven killings. But facing DNA evidence and the prospect of the death penalty, he began cooperating and trading information for his life.

He confessed to 42 of the 48 listed killings, as well as six not listed. Further, he led investigators to four sets of previously undiscovered human remains. It turned out that the killings had continued long after investigators thought they had stopped. The last victim on the list disappeared in 1984, but one of the cases Ridgway plead to involved a woman killed in 1990 and another in 1998. Ridgway's pleas to the 48 murders gave him the dubious distinction of having more convictions than any other serial killer in the nation's history.

For example, John Wayne Gacy, who preyed on men and boys in Chicago in the 1970s, was convicted of 33 murders; Ted Bundy, whose killing spree began in Washington State, confessed to killing more than 30 women and girls but was convicted of killing only three before he was executed in Florida.

Ridgway's Motives and Method of Operation

Ridgway stated that his motive for the killings was "to kill as many women as I thought were prostitutes as I possibly could." Ridgway continued, "I picked prostitutes as victims because I hate prostitutes and did not want to pay them for sex. I also picked prostitutes because they were easy to pick up without being noticed. I also knew they would not be reported missing right away, and might never be reported missing. I picked prostitutes because I thought I could kill as many of them as I could without getting caught.

"In most cases, when I murdered these women, I did not know their names. Most of them I liked . . . I killed them the first time I met them and do not have a good memory of their faces. I killed so many women that I have a hard time keeping them straight . . . I killed most of them in my house on Military Road, and I killed a lot of them in my truck, not far from where I picked them up . . . I killed some of them outside . . . I remember leaving each woman's body in the place where she was found.

"Another part of my plan was where I put the bodies of these women. Most of the time I took the women's jewelry and their clothes to get rid of any evidence and make them harder to identify. I placed most of the bodies in groups, which I call clusters. I did this because I wanted to keep track of all the women I killed. I liked to drive by the clusters around the country and think about the women I placed there."

Here are Ridgway's accounts of only a few of his murders:

- Wendy Lee Coffield: I picked her up, planning to kill her. After killing her, I placed her body in the Green River.

- Debra Bonner: I picked her up planning to kill her. After strangling her to death, I placed her body in the Green River.

- I strangled Debra Estes to death. I picked her up, planning to kill her. After killing her, I buried her body near the Fox Run Apartments in Federal Way.

- I strangled Carol Christensen to death. I picked her up, planning to kill her. After killing her, I placed her body in a wooded area in Maple Valley.

- I strangled Denise D. Bush to death. I picked her up planning to kill her. After killing her, I left her body just off a dirt road in the neighborhood of Riverton. I later transported some of her remains to a place just off the Bull Mountain Road, near Tigard, Oregon. I left the remains there with the remains of Shirley Sherrill. I did this to throw off police investigators so I could continue killing prostitutes.

Figure 11.14 Gary Ridgway, seated to the left side of his attorney, Mark Prothero, was dubbed the "Green River Killer" almost 20 years ago after the bodies of some of his 48 victims showed up in Washington State's Green River, about 45 miles from Seattle. *Elaine Thompson/AP Wide World Photos*

killings, the California Night Stalker case, and the Son of Sam case in New York.

NATIONAL CENTER FOR THE ANALYSIS OF VIOLENT CRIME

The National Center for the Analysis of Violent Crime (NCAVC) operates from the Behavioral Science Unit of the FBI Academy in Quantico, Virginia. It is a data processing center structured to consolidate training and research for dissemination to law enforcement agencies confronted with vicious or violent crimes. The NCAVC consists of four sections: Research and Development, Violent Criminal Apprehension Program (VI-CAP), Training, and Criminal Personality Profiling. Of these, VI-CAP has proved to be especially valuable in sharing information and tracking violent serial offenders.

VI-CAP

Investigative teams staffed with criminal and forensic psychologists have become an essential component of the apprehension and prosecution of criminals. In 1981, a system specifically designed to identify serial murderers was developed by Pierce Brooks, a retired police chief and former homicide detective of the Los Angeles Police Department. VI-CAP was designed as a computer information clearinghouse for collection and analysis of all aspects of an investigation. The program is operated by the FBI and is staffed by experienced investigators charged with reviewing unsolved violent crimes such as rapes, murders, and child molestations.

These cases are submitted by local law enforcement agencies who fill out a special VI-CAP form. The overall goal is to centralize all information pertaining to cases involving mutilation, dismemberment, torture, or sexual trauma.[8] Proponents of the VI-CAP program have suggested that if the program had been in effect during Ted Bundy's killing spree, he would have been apprehended well before his murder rampage in Florida, where he was finally apprehended.

AUTOEROTIC DEATH

An **autoerotic death** represents one of the most bizarre and complex crime scenes of all. In this type of wrongful death investigation, a body (typically, male) will be discovered in a partially suspended position, nude or clad only in feminine attire. The actual cause of death in this type of case will probably be asphyxia, but until properly investigated, the mode of death could be diagnosed as suicide or homicide when actually it is an "accidental" death.

Vernon Geberth states that most of the literature of autoeroticism focuses on young boys and older men who, through a predetermined ritualistic exercise, gain sexual gratification.[9] Over the years, bodies have been discovered in many different conditions, including being completely nude, partially nude, or dressed in women's attire. Use of a ligature is also common and is designed to restrict the flow of oxygen (hypoxia) to the victim during sexual orgasm. Basically, the sensation of choking is believed to heighten the sexual stimulation of the participant. Rob Hazelwood and his associates have identified three ways in which autoeroticism may result in death:[10]

1. Failure with the physiological mechanism
2. Failure in the self-rescue device
3. Failure on the part of the victim's judgment and ability to control a self-endangering fantasy scenario

When a possible autoerotic death is under investigation, the investigator should ask himself or herself the following:

- Is the victim nude or sexually exposed?
- If male, is he dressed in women's attire?
- Is there evidence of masturbation?
- Is a ligature present?

In the article "Death During Dangerous Autoerotic Practice," Hazelwood suggests several criteria that can be used by the criminal investigator to determine an autoerotic death:[11]

- Evidence of a physiological mechanism for obtaining or enhancing sexual arousal that depends on either a self-rescue mechanism or victim's judgment to discontinue its effect
- Evidence of solo sexual activity
- Evidence of sexual fantasy aids (e.g., pornography, vibrators, mirrors)
- Evidence of prior erotic practice (e.g., photographs)
- No apparent suicidal intent

As indicated, most autoerotic cases involve men, but it is important to realize that women are sometimes involved. For example, what might appear to be a sexual slaying with bondage and suffocation of the victim may actually be an accidental death of a woman who was practicing autoeroticism. One such case involved a 35-year-old woman who was discovered dead by her nine-year-old daughter. The woman was nude and lying on a small-shelved area in the rear of her bedroom closet. She was on her stomach and an electric vibrator with a hard rubber massaging head was between her thighs and in contact with her vulva. The vibrator was still operating when she was discovered. Attached to the nipple of her right breast was a clothespin, which was compressing the nipple. Around the victim's neck was a nylon stocking that was positioned in loop fashion and fastened to a shelf bracket above the victim's head.

The lower portion of her body was supported by the shelf, and her upper body rested on her arms, which were extended downward in a "push-up" fashion. The victim placed clothespins on her nipples to cause discomfort and used the ligature around her neck to reduce the oxygen flow. She obviously intended to support her upper-body weight with her arms, but she lost consciousness, and the weight of her body, hanging from the nylon stocking, caused her to strangle. Investigators should consider any hanging or suffocation crime scene as a possible autoerotic death, especially if the clues described are present. In addition, the investigator may face problems convincing family members that the victim died accidentally (as a result of autoeroticism) rather than as a result of suicide or murder. Therefore, a sympathetic approach when dealing with family members is highly recommended.

SUICIDE

Suicide can be defined as the deliberate taking of one's own life. It has been said that once an apparent suicide has been discovered, the responding officer should question his or her first impression at the scene. Indeed, homicide and suicide appear to have many similarities, and the two are often difficult to distinguish. For example, if the case is actually a suicide but appears to be a murder, the responding officer may waste valuable time processing the scene as though it were a homicide. Conversely, if the scene is processed as a suicide when it is actually a homicide, valuable evidence will be damaged or lost.

Certain questions should present themselves to the officer at a wrongful death crime scene. For example, did there appear to be a struggle? Are defense wounds present on the victim? This situation will call on the investigator's powers of observation and common sense.

Evidence of Suicide

Of primary importance to the investigator is to secure the crime scene to protect evidence of the crime. At least until a complete search of the area has been conducted, individuals should not be allowed to move about the crime scene. This includes police officers and family members of the deceased. From an evidentiary standpoint, most wrongful death crime scenes will produce an abundance of physical evidence. The scene should therefore not be disturbed until the search is complete. All objects left at the scene should be left in their original condition. Such objects include shell casings, weapons, notes, or other items.

The Suicide Note

Although the suicide note has traditionally been the manner in which the victim expresses his or her feelings about his or her death, this should not always be taken as absolute proof of a suicide. The suicide note should be viewed with some suspicion, as elements of it must be scrutinized. For example, if written with a computer or typewriter, an attempt should be made to locate the instrument that processed the note. Comparisons can then be made to see if the note is authentic. Investigators should also try to locate the supply of paper from which the note was taken. Once located, impressions might be identified on the pad to verify that the note was prepared at a certain location. The content of the note might also indicate a motive for the suicide. It may be a confession to a crime, an appeal for understanding, or even a method of placing guilt on those left behind. Because paper is such an excellent preserver of fingerprints, the note should be handled very carefully and protected as valuable evidence. Once collected, it should be delivered to the crime laboratory for handwriting analysis.

Reasons for Concern about Suicides

- The cause of death is an index to society's health.
- Suicides are the largest group of potentially preventable deaths.
- Insurance companies are usually liable for double indemnity in accidental deaths.

Reconstructing the Death

The investigator should attempt to reconstruct the circumstances surrounding the death of a suicide victim. In doing so, the question should be asked: Could the victim logically have killed himself or herself this way? The reconstruction process uses objects found at the crime scene and attempts to make inferences that can, it is hoped, be translated into theories about the commission of the crime. In this process, assumptions should not be made unless supported by some type of evidence. One misconception, for example, is that a gunshot entry wound is always smaller than its exit wound. Another misconception is that suicides by hanging are always accomplished by the total suspension of the victim's body. Again, wrong.

Materials Used

Years of experience have shown that certain self-inflicted wounds happen in a somewhat predictable fashion. Therefore, certain conclusions can be drawn by studying the location and characteristics of specific injuries. Such conclusions may support certain probabilities about the commission of the act. Persons choosing suicide will generally select a method that is as painless as possible. Exceptions to this are cases in which some mentally ill persons purposely inflict immense pain on themselves during the suicide. When completing the act, victims will often "personalize" their actions. For example, they might push aside clothing that tends to get in the way of a knife or gun barrel, enabling the weapon to come in direct contact with the person's skin. In addition, female victims will typically commit the crime while being careful not to disfigure their face. Persons choosing to hang themselves will be careful to place the rope or ligature directly against their skin and not around their shirt collar.

Motives for Suicide

One's behavior can be a good indicator as to why or whether he or she chooses suicide. Indeed, if there is no apparent reason for the victim to consider suicide, homicide should be considered to be the manner of death. Impulses displayed by

---

Checklist: Suicide Shootings and Stabbings

Shootings

- Firearm suicides are common.
- Handguns are used more commonly than rifles.
- An aid such as a string or stick is commonly used.
- A weapon tightly clenched by the victim indicates suicide.
- Gunpowder residue should be located on the "gun hand" of the victim using a firearm. Location of the wound can be used in determining if shooting was self-inflicted. A forensic examination to determine the distance between the gun muzzle and the wound can often distinguish between homicide and suicide.

Stabbings

- Self-inflicted stab wounds are commonly in the chest area.
- When there are a large number of stab wounds in the victim, investigators should be suspicious.
- Generally, the body will be located at the point of the act, indicating no struggle with an assailant.
- Depth of a wound does not necessarily indicate the length of the weapon.
- The instrument, when located, must be well-preserved in its original condition.
- Generally, there will be no "defense wounds" located on the victim of a suicide, but hesitation wounds might be mistaken for defense wounds.

people who commit suicide are complex and difficult to understand. Therefore, investigators will find difficulty in totally understanding this radical course of action and should be satisfied with explanations that might, at least on the surface, appear sketchy. For example, reasons for suicide have included old age, bad health, a failing love affair, marital problems, financial problems, and fear of arrest or imprisonment. When such indicators exist, the investigator should interview friends, family, neighbors, co-workers, or anyone else who might be able to furnish answers to investigators. Other information can be verified through traditional means. For instance, if the apparent reason for suicide is financial problems, such information can be verified through a check of the victim's financial affairs.

During interviews, the investigator should look for comments made by the victim to his or her associates about suicide. For example, the victim might once have remarked to a close friend, "If that ever happened, I'd kill myself." Or, "She would be better off without me." In all cases, however, such remarks should be verified if at all possible, as a false suicide threat might be used to cover up a murder.

DISCUSSION QUESTIONS

1. List and discuss the duties of the responding officer in a homicide case.

2. Define the term *scene-conscious*.

3. What notes should be taken at a wrongful death crime scene?

4. Discuss the advantages of determining the time of death at a homicide crime scene.

5. What is meant by the terms *rigor mortis* and *postmortem lividity*? How is an understanding of these terms important to the investigation of a wrongful death?

6. To what extent do wounds play a role in understanding the facts and circumstances surrounding a wrongful death?

7. Explain what defense wounds are.

8. Explain the problems encountered by investigators in a wrongful death that is believed to be autoerotic.

9. Discuss what evidence should be located in the investigation of a suspected suicide.

10. What are the distinctions among serial, mass, and sensational murders?

NOTES

1. FBI, Crime in the United States, 2005 (2006).
2. GEBERTH, V. (1990). *Practical homicide investigation*, 2nd ed. New York: Elsevier.
3. Ibid.
4. Ibid.
5. DI MAIO, V. J. M. (1985). *Gunshot wounds: Practical aspects of firearms, ballistics, and forensic techniques.* New York: Elsevier.
6. MORTIZ, A. R. (1981). Classical mistakes in forensic pathology. *American Journal of Forensic Medicine and Pathology,* 2(4): 299–308.
7. GEBERTH, V. (1986, Oct.). Mass, serial and sensational homicides. *Law and Order,* pp. 20–22.
8. GEBERTH, V. (1990). *Practical homicide investigation.*
9. Ibid.
10. HAZELWOOD, R. R., A. W. BURGESS, and N. GROTH (1985). Death during dangerous autoerotic practice. In *Social Science and Medicine,* Vol. 15E, pp. 129–133. Elmsford, NY: Pergamon Press.
11. Ibid.

Chapter 12 Robbery

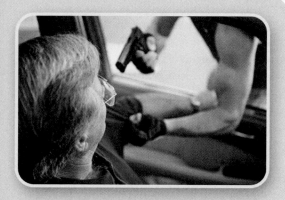

Key Terms

▶ bank robbery
▶ binding material
▶ commercial robbery
▶ method of operation (MO)
▶ neighborhood canvass
▶ residential robbery
▶ school robbery
▶ smash-and-grab robbery
▶ street robbery

This chapter will enable you to:

- Understand the motivations behind the crime of robbery.
- Identify the legal elements of the crime of robbery.
- List the steps to follow in the preliminary investigation of robbery offenses.
- Identify various types of physical evidence found in robberies.
- Appreciate the role of the witness in a robbery investigation.
- Explain the function of the neighborhood canvass during a preliminary investigation.

INTRODUCTION

On Friday, February 28, 1997, two Los Angeles patrol officers were driving by a bank at 9:30 in the morning when one of the officers glanced into a bank window and saw a customer being shoved by someone holding what appeared to be a shotgun. The officers summoned help, and one of the biggest shoot-outs in the city's history ensued. The bank was in fact being robbed, and the two gunmen, clad in bulletproof body armor, exited the bank and began unloading hundreds of rounds from fully automatic AK-47 rifles.

The shoot-out was broadcast live via a news helicopter, and all of America watched in horror as the two robbers, showing little emotion, calmly walked down the street as they emptied and reloaded their weapons over and over again. In a matter of minutes, buildings, police cars, and parked vehicles were permeated with bullet holes. The shoot-out, which drew almost 300 LA police officers, lasted about 30 minutes and ultimately ended with the death of both robbers. Sixteen bystanders and police officers were wounded in the shoot-out, but miraculously, no one other than the robbers was killed.

Robbery ranks among the most serious and feared criminal offenses because it involves both threatened or actual violence and a loss of property to the victim. It is also a particularly significant crime because of the psychological trauma suffered by its victims.

ROBBERY OFFENSES

Robbery, often confused with the crime of burglary, is a personal crime and involves face-to-face contact between victim and offender. Weapons may be used, or strong-arm robbery may occur through intimidation, especially where gangs threaten victims by their sheer numbers. Purse snatching and pick pocketing are not classified as robbery under the Uniform Crime Reporting Program but are included under the category of larceny theft.

Understanding Robbery

The primary motivation for robbery is to obtain money, although some juvenile robbers are also motivated by peer influence and the quest for "thrills." Drug and alcohol use is also common among street criminals and may influence their decisions to choose a particular criminal technique. Indeed, statistics reveal that robbers who use drugs are twice as active as those who do not.[1] Clearly, the distinct advantage of robbery over some other type of crime is that it is quick, easy, and requires little planning or preparation.

Most of what we have learned about robbery is descriptive information about trends and patterns. Statistics show that many robberies do not result in physical harm to the victim or extensive loss, but one in three do involve actual injury. These injuries range from bruises and black eyes to life-threatening gunshot or knife wounds. The statistics, as cited above, are staggering regarding the instance of robbery in the United States.

Defining Robbery

Robbery is defined as the theft or attempted theft, in a direct confrontation with the victim, by force or the threat of force or violence. The range of events commonly associated with robbery is reflected in the vernacular expressions for the crime, including such terms as *holdups, muggings,* and *stickups*. A child "rolled" for his lunch money and a bank teller confronted by a gun-toting gang are also both robbery victims.

Victims of burglary often claim that they were "robbed." Such incidents are not actually robbery unless the burglar encounters someone in the structure and uses force or threatens them as a means of completing the theft. For example, pocket picking and purse snatching are not really robberies unless the victim resists and is overpowered.

The Uniform Crime Reporting Program defines *robbery* as the taking or attempting to take anything of value from the care, custody, or control of a person or persons by force or threat of force or violence and/or by putting the victim in fear.[2]

Trends

Marking the third straight year of a decline in the number of robberies nationwide, the 2005 estimate of 417,122 offenses revealed a 3.9 percent increase from the 2004 estimate. The number of robbery offenses when compared with 2004 statistics declined 22.1 percent in comparison to data from 10 years earlier (1996–2005). (See Figure 12.1.)

Most robberies (44.1 percent) were committed on streets or highways. Firearms were used in 42.1 percent of reported robberies. The average dollar value of property stolen per robbery offense was $1,230. Bank robberies had the highest average dollar value taken: $4,169 per offense.

Consequences of Robbery

In the sense that most robbers are motivated by economic gain, robbery is a property crime. Judged by the value of property taken in robberies, however, it is not a particularly serious crime. The loss sustained in most robberies is less than $100. It is, of course, the violent nature of the crime that makes it a crime against persons and a serious violation of criminal law. Among the other consequences of the crime, robbery creates a sense of widespread anxiety and defensive behavior. For example, an elderly couple was robbed at gunpoint one summer evening in the parking lot of their favorite restaurant. Although less than $75 was taken and no one was physically hurt, they chose not to return to the restaurant, for fear of falling victim to robbers a second time. Other types of defensive behavior include carrying a weapon and moving to the suburbs to avoid the likelihood of becoming a victim of a robbery.

Comparative Rates

Year	Number of Offenses	Rate per 100,000 Inhabitants
2004	401,326	136.7
2005	417,122	140.7
Percent change	+3.9	+4

Figure 12.1 Robbery: Percent Distribution. *FBI, Crime in the United States, 2006.*

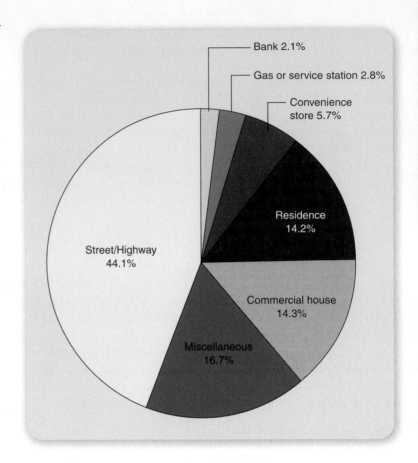

Bank 2.1%

Gas or service station 2.8%

Convenience store 5.7%

Residence 14.2%

Street/Highway 44.1%

Commercial house 14.3%

Miscellaneous 16.7%

Elements of Robbery

State laws are very specific regarding the definition of robbery. As indicated, many people confuse the term *robbery* with *burglary,* but clearly some elements of the crimes differ considerably. For example, an apartment dweller might claim that his apartment was "robbed" when in actuality it was burglarized. Accordingly, a woman might claim that she was the victim of robbery when, in fact, she was the victim of a larceny. The distinction between these offenses is evident in the elements of the crime.

The elements of robbery vary depending on certain attributes of the crime. These attributes can include inflicting serious physical injury on the victim or being accompanied by an accomplice during commission of the crime. Because of these differences, many states have chosen to divide robbery into first, second, and third degrees, depending on the seriousness of the act.

TYPES OF ROBBERY

Attempts have been made to classify and explain the character and dynamics of robbery. In a study conducted in London, McClintock and Gibson found that robbery follows one of five patterns:[3]

1. *Robbery of persons employed in positions placing them in charge of money or goods.* Examples are robberies of banks, stores, offices, jewelry stores, or

Figure 12.2 Robbery is considered a violent crime because it places the victim in fear of death or serious bodily injury as depicted here. *Michael Newman, PhotoEdit Inc.*

other sites where money changes hands. The instance of these types of robberies has decreased in recent years. For example, in 2005, robbery had increased from the previous year by 3.9 percent.[4]

2. *Robbery in open areas.* This includes muggings, street robberies, and purse snatchings. Crimes of this nature constituted an estimated 30 percent of violent crime in 2001.

3. *Robbery on private premises.* This represents crimes in which robbers break into homes and rob residents. The FBI reports that in 2002 this type of incident represented about 12.2 percent of all robberies.[5]

4. *Robbery after preliminary association of short duration.* These types of robberies typically occur as a consequence of a chance meeting in a nightspot, party, or after a sexual encounter.

Legal Elements of Robbery

- Forcibly steal property.
- Using force or threatening the immediate use of physical force against another person.

5. *Robbery after previous association of some duration between victim and offender.* These are considerably less common than stranger-to-stranger robberies, which account for an estimated 75 percent of robberies.[6]

In accordance with the preceding typologies, the following examples of common robberies should be considered. Notice the addition of crimes such as school and vehicle robberies.

Commercial Robberies: Stores and Banks

The **commercial robbery** typically occurs at the end of a workweek and during the evening and very early morning hours. Typical targets of the commercial robber are stores and businesses located close to major thoroughfares, such as main streets, highways, and interstates. Such locations offer the offender a quick and easy means of escape. In addition, stores employing only one or two employees make prime targets for a bandit.

Because many robberies are committed by persons with criminal records, their methods of operation (MOs) can sometimes be established easily. Once identified, the MO can be compared with other robberies with similar MOs, to identify a suspect. Convenience stores represent a growing target for robbers. Convenience stores are the target for an estimated 6 percent of all commercial robberies. The growing numbers of such businesses have contributed to their victimization by robbers. Many stores have a policy of keeping only a minimal amount of cash on the premises to deter would-be robbers. Others employ the use of video cameras to record business transactions and customers in the store.

Bank robbery represents a much greater property loss than other types of robbery but accounts for only an estimated 2 percent of all robberies.[7] Bank robberies are both state and federal crimes; therefore, they fall under the jurisdiction of local, state, and federal law enforcement. The FBI is summoned in these cases because any banking institution federally insured by the Federal Deposit Insurance Corporation (FDIC) falls under federal jurisdiction. These include federal banks, federal credit unions, and federal savings and loan companies. Typically, the investigation of such offenses will involve the collective talents and resources of investigators in each jurisdiction.

The most common method of bank robbery is a threat with a visible firearm, most typically a handgun. Most of the remaining robberies are perpetrated with the use of a demand note passed to the teller. In this case, the note can be a valuable piece of evidence if the robber fails to ask for its return. In addition, in the majority of bank robberies, the perpetrator acts alone in the facility, but accomplices may be waiting in an escape vehicle outside. At times, lookouts are also employed to spot police cruisers.

One of the best tracing clues in a robbery is the vehicle used in the escape. Such clues will vary from one offense to another. For example, the professional robber's getaway vehicle may be rented or stolen and may have stolen license plates. This will enable the suspects to ditch the vehicle or the plates after they have left the area of the robbery. Conversely, the amateur robber will often use his or her own vehicle. The complexion of bank robbery has changed in recent years due to an increase in the number of branch banks, which tend to be located in such a way as to be highly vulnerable to robbers.

Figure 12.3 Thefts from ATM machines can be from crude to sophisticated. *Jasper White, Getty Images— Photonica Amana America, Inc.*

A Closer Look
Brazen Bank Robbers

In 1995, a pair of holdup men who were thought to have robbed at least 18 midwestern banks were also playing a kind of cat-and-mouse game with the FBI. They wore FBI logos during their holdups, used agents' names when they rented their getaway cars, and wrote letters to the newspapers making fun of the FBI. The "Midwestern Bank Bandits," as they called themselves, concentrated on banks in Kansas, Iowa, Wisconsin, Nebraska, Ohio, and Kentucky. The pair adopted a clear method of operation:

- They spent no more than five minutes in a bank.
- They prohibited tellers from touching cash so that the tellers couldn't rig a moneybag with a dye bomb. Instead, they leaned over the counter and grabbed the cash themselves.
- They purchased older used cars before each robbery and signed FBI office chiefs' names on the titles.
- They sometimes wore clothing bearing the logos of the FBI and the ATF.
- They sometimes slowed their pursuers by leaving behind such items as a package they said contained explosives, or a grenade pin or taut string tied to the glove compartment door of their getaway car, giving the appearance of a booby trap.

Street Robberies

The most common type of robbery is the one committed on public streets and alleyways. Most street robberies (also called *muggings*) are committed with a weapon, typically a handgun, usually take place at night, and both the robber and victim are usually on foot. Suspects in street robberies are apt to be teenagers, usually young males. The unarmed **street robbery** is also common in many cities. In this case, the victim is approached by two or more attackers who, through their numbers, intimidate the victim, reducing their willingness to resist. Those who are most likely to become victims of the street mugger are the elderly and those who are drunk in public. Both categories of victims pose no immediate threat to the robber, are slow to react, and will probably not offer resistance. The unarmed robber relies on opportunity rather than a strategic plan in selecting a victim. The most likely victim is one who walks alone on a secluded street after dark.

Residential Robberies

The **residential robbery** is one of the most terrifying, as an armed intruder breaks into a home and holds residents at gun- or knifepoint. Often, these crimes begin as burglaries but "convert" to robberies after the intruder discovers that there is someone home and chooses to use violence as a means of completing the theft. One common type of residential robbery is when someone who has a right to be in the house, such as an invited guest, commits the crime. Indeed, according to the National Institute of Justice, 54 percent of all residential robberies are committed by acquaintances.[8]

School Robberies

The National Institute of Justice concludes that an estimated 3.2 percent of noncommercial robberies occur in schools every year. This averages out to be an estimated one million school-related robberies annually. Accordingly, the victimization rate for youths ages 12 to 19 is about 1 percent per year. **School robberies** fail to meet the stereotypic type of robbery in that they are not stickups or muggings but, for the most part, are instances of petty extortion or "shakedowns" of students or teachers. Ironically, few of these robberies have resulted in property loss. The average dollar loss is typically less than $1.[9]

Characteristics of Robbery

- About 1 in 12 victims experience serious injuries such as rape, knife or gunshot wounds, broken bones, or being knocked unconscious.
- Most robberies are committed by two or more people.
- About half of all completed robberies involve losses of $82 or less; 10 percent involve losses of $800 or more. Most theft losses are never recovered.
- Offenders display weapons in almost half of all robberies.
- Robbers use guns in about 40 percent of robberies.
- Offenders using weapons are more likely to threaten than actually attack their victims.
- In almost 9 out of 10 robbery victimizations, robbers are male.
- More than one-half of all robbery victims are attacked. Female robbery victims are more likely to be attacked than are male victims.
- Victims age 65 and older are more likely to be attacked than younger victims.

Vehicle Robberies

On October 5, 1997, an armored car with $17 million in cash was stolen from its Loomis Wells Fargo and Company warehouse. After a five-month police search, a 28-year-old former Loomis employee, David Scott Ghantt, was arrested in Cozumel, Mexico, together with six others. At the time of Ghantt's arrest, about $14 million was still missing. The police were tipped off because someone noticed that one of the suspects had moved from a trailer park to a $650,000 home, purchased a BMW automobile, and paid for breast implants for his wife—all with cash. One year earlier, the largest armored car heist in U.S. history occurred in Jacksonville, Florida, where an employee pulled a gun on two co-workers and stole $18.8 million in cash. The robber, Philip Noel Johnson, was arrested five months later as he was attempting to cross the Mexican border. In that theft, all but about $186,000 was recovered from a mountain home in North Carolina. The victim of the vehicle robbery is often the driver of the vehicle, as illustrated in the example above. Such vehicles often include delivery vehicles, taxicabs, buses, and so on, while the people involved make easy targets for the robber because they frequently work alone and in sparsely populated areas of town. A delivery vehicle, for example, is most vulnerable when it is arriving for a delivery or after a delivery has been made. Sometimes, the robbers opt for the cash given the driver after delivery has been made.

Taxi drivers are vulnerable because they are required to work alone and cruise all areas of town. The most common MO for a taxi robbery is for the driver to be asked to drive to an address in a secluded part of town, where the robber makes his move. A preventive measure taken by some taxi companies is the placement of a protective shield between the driver and passenger seats. Robberies of buses generally occur during layoff points where there are few passengers. A new trend in vehicle robberies emerged in Miami, Florida, in 1991: the **smash-and-grab robbery.** The robbers stake out streets and exit ramps from airports, and when automobile drivers come to a stop at a street light, the robbers approach the car, break the window, and hold up the driver at gunpoint.

Types of Robbers

Conklin developed a well-known typology of robbers.[10] Rather than focusing on the nature of robbery incidents, Conklin organized robbers into the following types:

- *Professional robber.* The professional robber is characterized as having a long-term commitment to crime as a source of livelihood, planning and organizing crimes before committing them, and pursuing money to support a particular lifestyle. Professionals may be robbers exclusively or may be involved in other types of crime as well. The professional robber recognizes robbery as a type of crime that is quick, direct, and profitable. The "pro" might typically effect three or four "big scores" a year to support himself, all well planned, and sometimes while working in groups with specifically assigned tasks for all group members.

- *Opportunistic robber.* The opportunist will steal to obtain small amounts of money when he or she identifies what seems to be a vulnerable target. Examples of opportunist targets are cab drivers, drunks, and the elderly. The opportunist is typically a younger perpetrator who does not plan the crime well (e.g., use of weapons, getaway car). Typically, he or she operates in the environment of a juvenile gang.

- *Drug addict robber.* The drug addict robber robs to support his or her drug habit. Unlike the professional, he or she has a low commitment to robbery because of its danger but a high commitment to theft because it supplies much-needed funds. Although the addict is less likely to use a weapon, he or she is more cautious than the opportunist. When desperate for funds, however, he or she will be less careful in selecting victims and carrying out the crime.

- *Alcoholic robber.* Excessive consumption of alcohol may cause some persons to enter into robbery as a criminal alternative. Alcoholic robbers plan their crimes randomly and give little consideration to victim selection, escape, or circumstances under which the crime will be committed.

THE FIRST OFFICER ON THE SCENE

After receiving a radio call, the first officer's initial responsibility is to arrive at the scene as quickly and safely as possible. Of the two, safety should be emphasized more so than swiftness. The decision to use equipment such as emergency lights and siren is left to the officer's judgment and may depend on several considerations. Factors influencing the decision to use emergency equipment include:

- Distance to be traveled to the crime scene
- Amount of traffic
- Time of day of the call
- Inability to clear traffic
- Need to halt assault on a victim

Next, the officer should summon assistance and be prepared to wait for backup before attempting to enter the robbery location. When approaching the scene, he or she should be on the lookout for fleeing subjects or persons sitting in parked cars. These might be accomplices or lookouts working with the robber. Police vehicles should be parked a reasonable distance from the robbery location. After removing the keys from the patrol car, the officer should take a shotgun and approach the location cautiously on foot.

The first officer on the scene should cover the most likely exit from the robbery location. After assessing the situation, it is his or her job to direct other responding officers to cover other escape routes. If possible, a determination should be made as to whether or not the robbery is still in progress before officers enter the building.

If the robbery is still in progress, entry into the structure should not be authorized. It is likely that robbers might exit the structure on their own, especially if they are unaware that the police are at the location. If the suspect sees the police, the officer should make every attempt to convince him or her to surrender. If it cannot be determined whether or not a crime is still in progress, officers covering the front should enter together. Under no circumstances should the first-arriving officer enter the location without assistance. Once on the scene, the officer should apprehend the suspect if possible. First aid should then be rendered if victims have been injured. Finally, witnesses should be located and questioned.

THE PRELIMINARY INVESTIGATION

When responding to calls in which the robbers have already left the scene, officers must prioritize the care of any injured parties. In addition, they must keep in mind that the robbery scene is a crime scene, where valuable evidence may be present. Therefore, possible locations of fingerprints and other evidence should be protected. Next, witnesses should be located and statements taken regarding descriptions of the suspects and their vehicles so that a "flash" description can be broadcast.

When obtaining description information from witnesses, officers should first separate them to minimize discussion about the robbery and provide officers with separate suspect description sheets. It is important during this stage of the investigation to get descriptions while the witnesses' recollection of the crime is still fresh. Officers should remember that although speed is crucial at this stage of the preliminary investigation, so is accuracy. A second broadcast is required after further questioning of the witnesses is conducted. The purpose is to correct any errors broadcast in the original transmission and to provide district officers with additional details. The correct form of broadcast is typified by the following example:

> *Robbery.* Seventh Heaven Convenience Store, 308 Granada, at 2330 hours by two suspects.
>
> *Suspect 1.* Male, white, 18 to 25 years of age, 6 feet 2 inches, 210 pounds, long brown hair, full beard, sunglasses, wearing black "Poison" T-shirt and faded blue jeans and white tennis shoes. Suspect in possession of proceeds from robbery: brown paper bag containing approximately $350 cash.
>
> *Suspect 2.* Female, white, 20 to 22 years of age, 5 feet 4 inches, 120 pounds, wearing red tank top and blue jean shorts, dirty white tennis shoes. Suspect has long brown hair pulled back and is armed with a small semiautomatic handgun, possibly .32 caliber.
>
> *Escape.* Both suspects were last seen driving east on Broadway in an older model light tan Ford Mustang, Texas license, with the first two digits believed to be "RW." The paint on the car is faded, and its top is rusted.

The supplemental broadcast should contain as much important information as possible, and when significant information is unavailable, its omission should be so stated. For example, in the preceding scenario, it is not mentioned whether either suspect had a coat. Stating that details are not available at the time of the broadcast will let officers know that there is a possibility that the suspects might, in fact, be wearing coats. The intent here is to eliminate unnecessary inquiries from the field regarding such items.

THE NEIGHBORHOOD CANVASS

Typically, a robbery investigation takes weeks or even months to complete. A logical starting place, however, is a canvass of the area surrounding the location of the robbery. Specifically, investigators should consider the suspect's most likely escape route and question residents and business owners in the area. In addition, while the canvass is in progress, officers should look for evidence

A Closer Look
The "Typical" Robbery

The most common type of robbery is of the individual. And the most common place for it is on your way to and from your car. Nearly half of all robberies occur on the streets and in parking lots. Another 14 percent happening in locations like subway and train stations, indoor ATMS, and other locations. It is always important to recognize when you are entering a "fringe area," where the likelihood of being robbed increases.

There is more than a 60 percent chance that you will be facing a weapon when robbed. That is, however, a statistical norm across all types of robberies. The odds of facing a weapon go up significantly if you are being robbed by only one person. Strong-arm tactics tend to be the domain of the pack; the individual mugger tends to prefer weapons—and guns are the most common.

Weapons

While all robberies are felonies, the use of a weapon tends to bring about stiffer penalties. While all robberies are considered violent crimes, it is not uncommon for states to upgrade the class of felony if a weapon is used in the commission of a robbery. That means the person who is robbing you is risking a much greater prison sentence if he is caught and convicted. And this doesn't bother him.

The weapon of choice is a gun. It is fast, easy to get, and since most robberies happen at point-blank range, requires very little training to hit the target. All the robber has to do is point in the general direction and pull the trigger until either he runs out of bullets or you are on the ground screaming in pain. Guns make up 40 percent of all robberies, with knives and other weapons making up another 20 percent. Again, these numbers are a national average which incorporates every kind of robbery.

Needless to say, guns, knives, and other weapons make up 100 percent of all ARMED robberies. And weapons are the norm for robberies of establishments.

Strong Arm

Many people do not realize that 40 percent of all robberies are committed by strong-arm tactics. That doesn't sound too bad until you realize that this means you are being mugged by a wolfpack. A varying number of individuals surround you and then either threaten or proceed to pilfer your possessions. That means ten or so people proceed to pummel you, and often once you are on the ground, they continue to kick and stomp you.

Furthermore most states recognize both an extreme disparity of force and the shod human foot on a downed individual as legal justification for the victim to use lethal force in order to protect himself from immediate death or serious bodily injury. Both of which can, and often do, occur during a strong-arm robbery. It doesn't matter if they don't have weapons, ten people stomping you can kill or hospitalize you for months just as well as one person with a weapon.

Packs of young criminals roaming or loitering in an area are a serious danger sign, one that should be avoided at all costs. And do NOT walk into their midst. This is literally walking into the lions' jaws.

What makes these kinds of robberies even more difficult is how often they will be explained away as "we were just messin' witcha." And since no weapons have been displayed, it is difficult for prosecutors to prove intent in such cases. Until the robbery has actually occurred, there is no clear-cut crime even if displaying or menacing with a weapon.

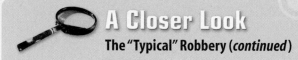

A Closer Look
The "Typical" Robbery (*continued*)

Home Invasion Robbery

Home invasion robberies have become common in the past decade. In areas where automatic garage doors are standard, a tactic often used is to follow the victim home from someplace and then either pull into the garage or jump out of the car and rush the person before the garage door closes.

In other areas, entry through the front door is common. Whether this is achieved by simply ringing the doorbell and crashing the door when the person answers it, through deceit (e.g. "My car broke down; can I use your phone?"), or just kicking in the door depends on the robbers.

While an individual can do a home invasion, these types of robberies tend to be the domain of packs and gangs. And they tend to be armed as well. This is because they expect there to be multiple people at home.

Fortunately, many of the best protections against a home invasion robbery will also keep your home safe from burglars.

discarded by the suspect during his or her escape. Because many citizens are apprehensive about the presence of officers at their residence, investigators should immediately state their intended purpose to place the citizen at ease. It is also important for the officer to stress the significance of all information, regardless of how meaningless it appears to the citizen. Specific questions include whether the citizen observed anyone meeting the description of the suspect or the getaway vehicle. Additionally, it should be determined if anyone heard anything of interest to the officer, such as a car door slamming, gunshots, or tires screeching.

The **neighborhood canvass** is also critical in the event that the robber is hiding somewhere close to the robbery location. Therefore, investigators should look in parked cars, dumpsters, and alleyways for the hidden suspect. In addition, local motels or hotels in surrounding towns and car rental companies should also be checked. When speaking to residents in the area of the robbery, it would be advantageous to have a sketch of what the suspect looks like. The sketch could also be circulated throughout the community along with the establishment of a "tip line" for anonymous information.

THE ROBBER'S METHOD OF OPERATION

Studies have shown that many people who commit a robbery are repeat offenders, or recidivists. Therefore, it is important to document the techniques and **method of operation (MO)** used by the suspect. An MO focuses on the behavior of the criminal during the commission of a crime. For example, the location of the robbery, such as a bank or convenience store, may identify certain groups of suspects. Other factors include the type of weapon used, the dress of the robber(s), and the amount of money, merchandise, drugs, and so on, taken.

Typical MO Information for Robbery

- Type of location robbed
- Time and day of week
- Type of weapon used
- Use or threatened use of force
- Verbal statements made
- Vehicle used
- Object(s) stolen
- Number of suspects
- Use of disguises
- Other peculiarities

In addition to the age, sex, height, and race of a suspect, it is important to document specific behavior during a crime. Such behavior might indicate nervousness (or calmness) or could indicate that a person was under the influence of drugs at the time.

The treatment of the victim(s) could also have a bearing on the investigation. For example, was violence used? If so, what were the injuries? Was the victim kicked, beaten, shot, or struck with the weapon? Other actions might also be significant, such as:

- Did the suspect cut the telephone wires?
- Were the victims locked up?
- Were the victims tied up or gagged?

Investigators should remember that because of a lack of abundant physical evidence, robbery scenes may suggest other types of evidence. MOs in connection with any available physical evidence may help identify the perpetrator and ultimately prove a case.

PHYSICAL EVIDENCE

The crime scene should be processed as soon as possible after physical evidence has been identified. Evidence in robberies may take several forms, including fingerprints, **binding material,** and fired cartridges. The value of fingerprints at a robbery crime scene is immense, so it is essential to conduct a thorough search of all surfaces in or near the scene that the robbers might have touched. These surfaces include countertops, doors and door handles, cash registers and computers, and any furniture encountered by the suspects. In particular, if the robbers handled any paper products (e.g., notes to bank tellers), such surfaces are

---

Physical Evidence in Robberies

- Blood (if applicable)
- Fingerprints
- Notes from the robber
- Binding material
- Fired cartridge

---

particularly good for preserving latent prints and should be protected and processed.

Binding material, if located, can include strips of tape, such as duct or masking tape, cloth strips, wire, rope, or any material used to incapacitate the victim. In the event that rope is used as a restraining device, care should be taken not to destroy any knots. These can be used to link the suspect with any specialized technique of tying knots. Such items can be used as comparison items in the event that similar material is later found in the possession of suspects.

Shell casings or cartridges may also provide important evidence of a robbery. Such items may bear latent prints of perpetrators or identify the type of weapon used for the crime. In fact, rifling (impressions) on the sides of casings might be used in linking a specific gun with a crime.

In the case of bank robberies, some banks might use bait money to aid in capturing the robbery suspect. When used, bait money is placed in a specially designated bin in a teller's cash drawer. This cash has had its serial numbers prerecorded in the event that it is later found in a suspect's possession. In other cases, when bait money is removed from a drawer, a silent alarm will be set off, notifying local police that a robbery is in progress.

THE ROLE OF WITNESSES

Because of the violent nature of the crime of robbery and the imminent threat of injury, witnesses are not likely to remember many specific details of a robbery. It is important, however, that officers attempt to gather as much information as possible from any witnesses. It is vital that witnesses be separated so that their individual perceptions of what happened won't influence other witnesses. Experience has shown that an exchange of dialogue between witnesses might unconsciously alter the way in which some witnesses "recall" an event. Once witnesses have been separated, interviews should be conducted regarding both the event and details about the robber(s).

People at the scene of a robbery will be afraid, confused, and even angry. Because of the emotionally charged environment, officers should expect to receive somewhat different interpretations of what occurred from the witnesses, as no two people will perceive a situation in exactly the same way. In fact, if stories are too similar, the investigator should question the truthfulness of the witnesses' stories. The details regarding perpetrators should be as specific as possible. Information should be sought regarding specifics, such as scars, tattoos, jewelry worn, or other particulars about the suspects. Leading questions asked by the investigator might help draw out these details. Leading questions include:

- What did you notice most about the robber's appearance?
- What were the most noticeable features about the robber's face?
- Was there anything unique or unusual about the robber's manner of speech?

Such questions encourage witnesses to stop and think about specific details regarding a crime.

DISCUSSION QUESTIONS

1. What are the most common motivations for the commission of the crime of robbery?

2. Discuss the distinction between someone who has been robbed and someone who has been burglarized.

3. Discuss how commercial robbery differs from residential robbery.

4. List and discuss the elements of the crime of robbery.

5. Discuss the importance of the flash description during the preliminary investigation phase of a robbery.

6. List and discuss the elements that should be included in the flash description of a robbery suspect.

7. Explain the different types of physical evidence that should be sought in a robbery investigation.

8. Describe the responsibilities of the first officer responding to the scene of a robbery.

9. What is a neighborhood canvass, and how does it relate to a robbery investigation?

10. How is an understanding of the robber's MO valuable in investigating a robbery?

NOTES

1. NATIONAL INSTITUTE OF JUSTICE (1987). *Investigators who perform well.* Washington, DC: U.S. Department of Justice.

2. FBI (2006). Crime in America, 2005. *Uniform Crime Reports.* Washington, DC: U.S. Government Printing Office.

3. MCCLINTOCK, F. H., and E. GIBSON (1961). *Robbery in London.* London: Macmillan, p. 15.

4. FBI (2006). Crime in America, 2005.

5. Ibid.

6. Ibid.

7. Ibid.

8. NATIONAL INSTITUTE OF JUSTICE (1990). *Computer crime: The new crime scene.* Washington, DC: U.S. Department of Justice.

9. NATIONAL INSTITUTE OF JUSTICE (1983). *Robbery in the United States: An analysis of recent trends and patterns.* Washington, DC: U.S. Government Printing Office.

10. CONKLIN, J. (1972). *Robbery and the criminal justice system.* New York: J. B. Lippincott, pp. 1–80.

Key Terms

▶ acquaintance stalking
▶ aggravated assault
▶ cyberstalking
▶ intimate or former intimate stalking
▶ primary physical aggressor
▶ protection order
▶ self-defense
▶ simple assault
▶ stranger stalking

This chapter will enable you to:

- Understand an instance of assault.
- Describe the legal definition of assault.
- Identify various types of assault.
- Understand the problem of domestic violence and recent assault legislation.
- Realize the emerging problem of elder abuse.
- Realize the magnitude of the crime of stalking.
- Explain the methods of investigating stalking cases.
- Identify symptoms of child abuse.
- Cite methods of investigating child abuse.

INTRODUCTION

In December 2004, police charged five Indiana Pacers basketball players and seven Detroit Pistons fans after a mass brawl erupted during a game. The fight, which was aired on national television, was sparked by a dispute over a foul. Pacers teammates Jermaine O'Neal, Ron Artest, David Harrison, Anthony Johnston, and Stephen Jackson were all charged with misdemeanor assault and battery. Detroit fan John Green was charged with two counts of simple assault for throwing cups and ice at Artest, while another fan, Bryant Jackson, was charged with felony assault for throwing a chair into the crowd. In September 2005, Artest, O'Neal, and Jackson were each sentenced to one year probation and ordered to complete 60 hours of community service.

The pattern of assault is similar to that of homicide. One might say that the difference between the two is that the victim survived. Assaults can occur many ways: For example, a rock is thrown by one teen at another, a wife breaks a bottle over her husband's head during a domestic squabble, a drug dealer beats up a customer who steals his drugs. These are all forms of assault. Many "traditional" crimes are also accompanied by assaults against victims. For example, robbery, drug dealing, rape, and loan-sharking all frequently contain some aspect of the crime of assault.

Studies of assault cases have revealed that most victims of assault (two-thirds to three-fourths of cases) are acquainted with their attacker. In addition, it is common for such victims to choose not to file charges against their attackers. If charges are filed, many victims later choose not to follow through with prosecution, particularly if the parties are related or are close friends. Such realities can make investigation of these types of crime difficult and frustrating.

Trends

In 2005, an estimated 862,947 aggravated assaults were reported. Of those, 25.0 percent of aggravated assaults involved a physical (hands, fists, feet, etc.) confrontation. Twenty-one percent of aggravated assaults involved offenders with a firearm. In 2005, the rate of aggravated assaults in the nation was estimated at 291.1 offenses per 100,000 inhabitants. In 2005, the rate of aggravated assault was 16.8 lower than 1996.[1]

Weapons Used

In 2005 the rate of different weapons used in aggravated assaults included the following statistics:

- Firearm: 21%
- Hands, fists, feet: 25%

Comparative Rates

Aggravated Assault Trend

Year	Number of Offenses	Rate per 100,000 Inhabitants
2004	847,381	288.6
2005	862,947	291.1
Percent change	+2.0	+2.5

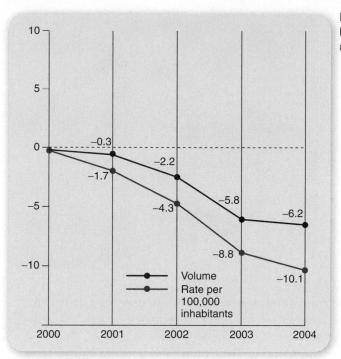

Figure 13.1 Aggravated assault: Percent change from 2000. *FBI, Crime in the United States, 2006.*

- Knife or cutting instrument: 18.9%
- Other weapons: 35.1%

LEGAL CLASSIFICATIONS OF ASSAULT

Although states often define assault differently, some general definitions will be considered. The terms *assault* and *battery* were formerly used to distinguish between threats and actual contact between suspect and victim. Today, many revised state statutes categorize threats and actual physical contact as **simple assault** and **aggravated assault.** These are defined as follows:

Simple Assault

- *Threats by one person to cause bodily harm or death to another.* Investigators must identify evidence to show specific intent to commit bodily injury; an injury received as a result of an accident is not an assault. A suspect's

TABLE 13.1

Aggravated Assault, Types of Weapons Used and Percent Distribution Within Region, 2005

Region	Total All Weapons[1]	Firearms	Knives or Cutting Instruments	Other Weapons (clubs, blunt objects, etc.)	Personal Weapons (hands, fists, feet, etc.)
Total	100.0	21.0	18.9	35.1	25.0
Northeast	100.0	15.6	20.4	33.3	30.7
Midwest	100.0	21.3	17.0	33.1	28.6
South	100.0	22.7	19.9	36.1	21.3
West	100.0	20.0	17.6	35.1	27.3

[1]Because of rounding, the percentages may not add up to 100.0.

Figure 13.2 Bruising on the thigh from assault by blunt instrument.

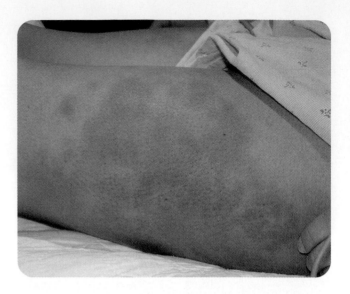

words and actions or any injuries to the victim may demonstrate intent. The injury must be to another party; injury to property or self-inflicted injury, regardless of its seriousness, is not an assault.

- *Purposely inflicting bodily harm on another.* Bodily harm or injury and simple assault need not cause severe physical pain or disability. The degree of force necessary in simple assault may range from a push or a slap to slightly less than that required for the great bodily harm that is characteristic of aggravated assault.

Aggravated Assault

Aggravated assault includes the elements of simple assault plus an element relating to the severity of the attack. Aggravated assault is usually committed with a weapon or by some means likely to produce great bodily harm or death.

- *High probability of death.* The assault is considered aggravated if it is committed by any means so severe that any reasonable person would feel that it would result in a high probability of death. For example, a strike to the head sufficient to cause unconsciousness or coma, a gunshot or knife wound that causes heavy bleeding, or burns inflicted over a large area of a person's body would be considered aggravated assault.

- *Serious, permanent disfigurement.* Permanent disfigurement includes such things as loss of an ear or part of the nose or permanent scarring of the face or other parts of the body that are normally visible. It cannot be a temporary injury that will eventually heal and not be evident.

- *Loss or impairment of body members or organs.* Regardless of the part of the body affected, a charge of aggravated assault is supported by the loss or permanent impairment of body members or organs or by maiming.

Legal Elements of Simple Assault

- Threats by one person to cause bodily harm or death to another
- Purposely inflicting bodily harm on another

Legal Elements of Aggravated Assault
• High probability of death
• Serious, permanent disfigurement
• Permanent or protracted loss or impairment of the function of any body member or organ or other severe bodily harm

Only one of these additional elements is needed to show aggravated assault, although two or all three are sometimes present. Some states do not require that there be permanent or protracted injury or loss if the weapon used in the assault is a dangerous weapon that causes fear of immediate harm or death. As with simple assault, the act must be intentional, not accidental.

SELF-DEFENSE

Under criminal law, persons may defend themselves and their property, and it is not necessary for the victim to wait until he or she has been physically assaulted before acting in **self-defense.** To do so, however, the elements of a threat should at least be present. It is on this point that the law makes a distinction in the interpretation of the word *threat.* For example, derogatory gestures or name calling between two persons does not give one the right to use violence or force against the other (*Naler* v. *State,* 1933). There are many cases, however, in which legal force is permitted under law. For example, the law recognizes that persons are under no legal obligation to retreat from an attack. However, if escape from the attacker is possible without killing him or her, the victim must do so.

Conversely, if in trying to escape, the victim risks further peril, lethal force to defend one's self is allowed. Accordingly, if a situation erupts to the point where force is used by the victim to defend him- or herself, the degree of force should be no more than a reasonable person, under the same circumstances, would be justified in using. Therefore, the type of force used must be only enough to rebuff the attack, and no more. Any display of excessive force used to "punish" the attacker can be interpreted by the courts as an assault in and of itself.

THE PRELIMINARY INVESTIGATION

In the event that an assault has been committed and the suspect is not on the scene, the call turns into an investigation. Experience has shown that most victims of assault know their attackers. After arriving on the scene, either first aid should be administered to the victim, or if necessary, he or she should be transported to the hospital. If this is necessary, an officer should accompany the victim in the event that he or she tries to discard any evidence. If the victim is taken to the hospital, the accompanying officer should question the attending physician to determine if an assault has actually been committed. A brief examination by the physician should disclose whether or not the victim is being truthful about the origin of his or her injuries.

Officers arriving on the scene of an assault should do the following:

- Control and disarm those involved in the altercation.
- Provide medical aid to injured people.

- Separate suspects.
- Protect the crime scene.
- Give the *Miranda* warning if applicable.
- Obtain preliminary statements.
- Photograph any evidence observed.
- Collect and preserve evidence.
- Reconstruct the crime.

Documenting the Elements of Assault

An assault that does not involve a dangerous weapon and results in no serious injury is a relatively minor crime. In comparison, aggravated assault is an extremely serious crime. Investigators can establish intent by determining the events that led up to the assault. The suspect's exact words and actions should be documented, and statements should be taken from the victim and any witnesses.

Responding officers should also establish the severity of the assault by taking photographs and describing all injuries in their notes. The size, location, number, color, depth, and amount of bleeding of any injuries must also be carefully described. Some bruises do not become visible for several hours or even days. Assault victims should also be advised that additional photographs will need to be taken later. An oral or written statement should be obtained from a qualified medical person regarding the severity and permanence of the injuries and any impairment of bodily functioning. Next, the means of the attack and the exact weapon used must be determined (e.g., gun, knife, fists).

Protecting the Crime Scene

The crime scene must be protected to preserve evidence, and photographs should be taken. This is done to document that an altercation actually occurred. It would also be advisable for the investigator to photograph the victim's injuries as soon as possible. If this is not done, medical personnel might bandage the wounds without adequately documenting or describing them beforehand, making a description difficult to obtain.

Initial Questioning

Stating the obvious, the simple task of inquiring about "what happened" is one of the criminal investigator's most important duties. Although many people are reluctant to talk with police officials, others cooperate out of a sense of civic duty, and such statements can make the difference between success and failure of an investigation.

Questioning the Victim.   The victim and any witnesses should now be questioned. When interviewing the victim, the investigator should ask the victim the facts surrounding the incident to determine that an assault actually did occur. Next, investigators should have the victim describe how the weapon was used (if there was one) and if there was any motive for the attack.

Questioning the Witnesses.   It is also important to locate and question any impartial witnesses who can verify or corroborate the victim's story. Such people might be difficult to locate, however, as they may be friends of the attacker or might be afraid of retribution by the suspect. If possible, statements should be taken from anyone who witnessed the assault. Additionally, it might be advisable to canvass the neighborhood to locate residents who might have heard or observed something relevant to the case. The questioning of witnesses might also reveal threats made by either the attacker or the victim that might have fueled the altercation.

Searching the Crime Scene

As with all crime scenes, a thorough search for evidence should be conducted as soon as possible. In many cases, a brief search can even be made while the victim is still on the scene. When searching, the investigator should look for weapons (this can include broken bottles, ashtrays, or other objects), footprints or fingerprints, and trace evidence (e.g., pieces of torn clothing, lost buttons, hair). In the event that the victim cannot accompany the investigator during the search, it would be a good idea to return to the scene at a later time with the victim and have him or her recount the occurrence. The victim might be able to point out evidence that might have been missed during the initial search.

DOMESTIC VIOLENCE

In the 1970s, if a woman telephoned police to complain about being assaulted by her husband, she had little hope of getting him arrested. By the 1980s, a revolution was well under way in the manner that police responded to domestic violence. As of 1984, few arrests were made in domestic violence cases that had no visible injury. In fact, at the time, 22 states barred police from making warrantless arrests in cases they had not personally witnessed. By 1988, many police departments had started treating domestic violence as a crime against the state, as though it had been committed by a stranger.

A growing fear of liability put pressure on police to adopt new policies. For example, in 1984 a jury in Torrington, Connecticut, awarded a $2.3 million judgment against the police department for failing to protect a woman and her son from repeated violence by her husband. One year earlier, he had stabbed her 13 times and broken her neck while the police were at her house responding to her 9-1-1 call.

By 1980, all but six states had adopted some form of domestic violence legislation. The new laws provided for funding for shelters, established more effective procedures, and created "protection orders," to prohibit men from abusing their wives. By 1987, more than half the nation's major police departments had adopted "pro-arrest" policies, which require officers to make an arrest unless they could document a good reason not to do so.

A 1984 study in Minneapolis found that an arrest plus a night in jail cut in half the risk of repeat violence against the victim in the following six months, in comparison to the other two standard approaches: advising the couple to calm down and ordering the suspect to leave his home for six hours. Critics have argued that the mandatory arrest policy may do more to incite violence against women than to cure it.

The Investigative Response to Domestic Violence

Responding to domestic violence calls is one of the most unpleasant duties for police officers. In some cases, officers not trained properly for this type of duty

Figure 13.3 Domestic violence, as portrayed here, has become one of society's greatest concerns. *Michael Newman, PhotoEdit Inc.*

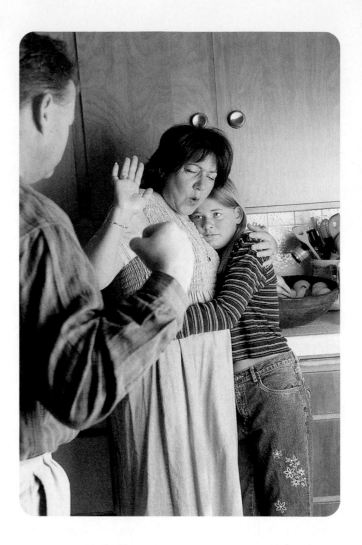

may have preconceptions or biases that it is simply a "family matter" and not a real policing issue. However, domestic assault calls are often dangerous for the police. This is because the highly emotional atmosphere accompanying domestic abuse situations, the raw violence often displayed, the family lives destroyed, and the victim's frequent hesitancy to prosecute or seek shelter all place a heavy burden on the officers sent to such disturbances. Still, an appropriate and effective police response to all domestic calls is warranted.

Response to such calls may be initiated by the dispatcher, who can save hours of leg work by exploring with the victim her frame of mind and that of the potential attacker. From that point on, responding officers' actions are critical. What responding officers do upon arrival will often determine what happens in court, whether an effective arrest will be conducted, and whether or not proper evidence will be collected. Domestic violence calls are complicated in that they may unfold simple battery, assault, kidnapping, trespassing, murder, stalking, terroristic threats, spousal rape, or many other types of criminal violations. Police investigators should never assume that the parties involved in a domestic dispute are merely involved in a minor squabble.

Typically, it is the patrol officer who will respond to a domestic violence call. When that occurs, officers should not park their patrol car within view of

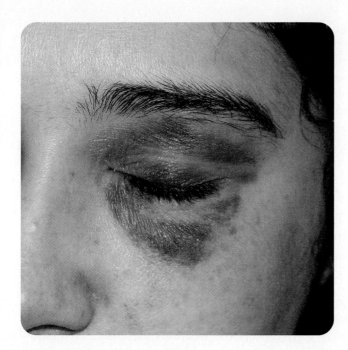

Figure 13.4 Black eye of domestic violence victim.

the location to which they are responding. Doing so may allow the suspect to see the officers coming and to become even more enraged at the thought of going to jail. This could result in the infliction of additional injuries on the victim or provide the suspect with time to gather weapons with which officers could be assaulted.

Once officers have entered the location of the domestic violence call and have secured the area, the investigation begins. The first rule is to interview the suspect and victim separately. Upon first contact with the suspect, the *Miranda* warning should not be read to him or her. At this point, until a determination has been made as to the nature of the dispute and the relationship between the suspect and victim, the suspect is not under arrest for domestic violence. The parties are simply under detention for investigation, since police officers have reasonable suspicion to detain them. This is a critical point in the investigation. Because of their agitated emotional state, many domestic violence suspects will make spontaneous admissible statements that can be used against them later in court. Officers should reduce the level of tension at the scene by separating and talking to the participants. Officers must also consider the safety of the participants and any children present.

Any evidence that would lead an officer to make an arrest in any other situation also applies to spousal abuse situations. Most states allow arrests based on probable cause. In line with the probable cause standard, police officers should arrest all abusers who are not acting in self-defense and issue an arrest warrant even if the offender is absent. Finally, officers should be careful not to detain a potential abuser any longer than other offenders.

Twenty states now mandate police to make an arrest in domestic violence incidents if there is a protective or restraining order against the attacker. A number of states make it mandatory for an officer to make an arrest if there is probable cause, even without an assigned complaint by the victim. In Nevada, for example, if the police have sufficient reason to believe that a person, within the preceding four hours, committed an act of domestic violence or spousal battery, they are required to arrest the person if there are no mitigating circumstances.

Officers should not base their decisions regarding arrest on their perception of the willingness of the victim or witness to testify. The victim need not sign a complaint. If the assault was a mutual assault, that is, both people involved committed assault, officers must try to determine the **primary physical aggressor** and arrest that person. Some factors to consider in making this determination include:

- Prior domestic violence involving either person.
- The relative seriousness of the injuries inflicted upon each person involved.
- The potential for future injury.
- Whether one of the alleged assaults was committed in self-defense.
- Any other factor that helps the officer decide which person was the primary physical aggressor.

As with any criminal investigation, evidence must be collected. In domestic violence cases, evidence includes photographs of injuries, victims' statements, prior police reports, doctor or hospital reports, weapons used, damaged clothing or other property, and statements from neighbors or other witnesses. It should be made clear to the victim that an "order of protection" may be obtained from the court to help prevent further assaults.

Legal Approaches to Domestic Violence

In many cities, a high percentage of female victims request that battery charges be dropped or refuse to testify against their abuser after he has been arrested. In response to this, prosecutors in many cities with vigorous prosecution philosophies are increasingly adopting a controversial policy of "no drop." For example, in San Diego, if the victim won't testify, prosecutors use tapes from the woman's 9-1-1 calls and testimony from neighbors and police to build a case.

Protection Orders.   For many women who have become leery of the criminal justice system but are threatened by their violent partners, **protection orders** have become an option. Now used in all 50 states and the District of Columbia, protection orders are often backed up by the threat of jail. In some cases, judges can establish temporary custody for children, forbid telephone threats or harassment, and make the husband pay financial support or leave his home.

A temporary protection order can be issued the same day the woman requests it and can be put in effect for a year or longer. In comparison, a woman can wait for months for a criminal prosecution to come to trial or years for a property settlement from a divorce decree. On the other hand, in some states protection orders amount to nothing more than a cruel hoax on victims. Husbands or boyfriends have killed women while under protection orders.

ELDER ABUSE

As baby boomers approach retirement, we see the aging population growing larger each year. With this increase in the elder population, a growing concern is that of elder abuse. Some experts characterize it as a "hidden problem" similar to that of spousal abuse 20 years ago.[2] *Abuse* is a general term encompassing emotional, physical, and psychological abuse as well as financial victimization and neglect. Cases involving violence against society's elders include rape and homicide. In one case, a son withheld insulin from his diabetic mother "because it cost too much." In fact, cases have shown that most elder abuse is caused by family members and caregivers rather than strangers. Getz illustrates several of the 1 million typical cases of elder abuse that occur each year:[3]

- A deputy found an elderly man abandoned by his children with no heat or hot water in his home. The bed was saturated with urine, and the man was covered with his own excrement. His body was covered with lesions and sores that were infested with maggots. A foot had to be amputated.

- A home health aide, previously convicted of dealing in stolen property and grand theft, was assigned by a hospital in Sun City, Florida, to care for an 86-year-old man after open heart surgery. The worker and her husband systematically drained his assets to buy cars and gamble, took out a $22,000 mortgage on his home, and attempted to divert his direct-deposit checks to their own use before they were finally caught.

- Officials closed the Riverside Nursing Home in Tampa, Florida, and removed 19 residents on stretchers after administrators ignored repeated citations and scores of deficiencies. One resident restricted to a soft-food diet died from choking on a hot dog. Another was treated for dehydration and malnutrition after not being fed for five days.

It is becoming clear that police need special legal tools with which to deal with elder abuse, especially since so many of the violations against the elderly are not criminal in nature. Methods for investigating elder abuse should follow the standard for other criminal investigations, beginning with the preliminary

A Closer Look

Profiling the Batterer[4]

The profiles of abusive men have been fairly consistent. They tend to be manipulative, persuasive actors. They believe women should be subordinate, although they are often quite dependent on their spouses or girlfriends. They are cons: smart, charming, and cunning. Once they spot vulnerable women, they put on their best behavior and treat women with great respect while the real anger they feel for women is just below the surface. Many batterers don't beat women out of a fit of rage, but after some premeditation. In some cases, men have ripped out the telephone wires just prior to beating their spouses, which prevents the victims from calling 9-1-1 for help. Economic considerations are also a reason why battered women stay with their abusive partners. The cruel choice for battered women is whether to be beaten or to be poor.

Psychologists have likened battering relationships to the Stockholm syndrome, in which hostages, over time, identify with their captors. Entangled in an intimate relationship that often begins as romance, many women come to agree with their partner's view of them as worthless. Often, a batterer goes into a "honeymoon" period just after a beating, persuading his partner that he will reform.

investigation, identification of evidence, documentation of evidence, and location of witnesses to support the evidence.

STALKING

To some, the crime of stalking is a recent social phenomenon, but in actuality, newspapers have featured many stories about stalking over the course of the past two decades. For example, in 1982, movie actress Theresa Saldana was stabbed by a Scottish drifter who believed that he was sending her to heaven. In 1988, TV actress Rebecca Schaefer was shot dead by a stalker as she opened the door of her Hollywood home. She had been followed for months. Such incidents, and the subsequent stalkings of Madonna, David Letterman, and other celebrities have led all 50 states and the District of Columbia to pass antistalking laws since the beginning of the 1990s.

Despite the growing interest in stalking, research on the subject has been limited to studies of small, underrepresentative, or clinical samples of known stalkers; law journal reviews addressing the constitutionality and effectiveness of specific antistalking statutes; and case studies of individual stalkers. Empirical data have been lacking on important questions, which include:

- How much stalking is there in the United States?
- Who stalks whom?
- How often do stalkers overtly threaten their victims?
- How often is stalking reported to the police?
- What are the psychological and social consequences of stalking?

In a 1998 research brief prepared by the National Institute of Justice for the Centers for Disease Control and Prevention, some of these answers were provided. The data are from the National Violence Against Women (NVAW) survey and a nationally representative telephone survey of 8,000 U.S. women and 8,000 U.S. men.[5]

Legal definitions of stalking vary widely from state to state, but the term generally refers to harassing or threatening behavior that a person engages in repeatedly, such as following a person, appearing at a person's home or place of business, making harassing telephone calls, leaving written messages or objects, or vandalizing a person's property. Some states included in their definition such activities as lying in wait, surveillance, nonconsensual communication, telephone harassment, and vandalism. These actions may or may not be accompanied by a credible threat of serious harm, and they may or may not be precursors to an assault or murder.

Most stalking laws require that to qualify as a stalker, the perpetrator must have made a credible threat of violence against the victim; others include in their requirements threats against the victim's immediate family; and still others require only that the alleged stalker's course of conduct constitutes an implied threat.

Using a definition of stalking that requires victims to feel a high level of fear, the NVAW survey found that 8 percent of women and 2 percent of men in the United States have been stalked at some time in their life. Based on U.S. Census estimates of the number of women and men in the United States, one out of every 12 U.S. women (8.2 million) has been stalked at some time in her life, and one out of every 45 U.S. men (2 million) has been stalked at some time in his life.[6]

Who Stalks Whom?

Although stalking is a gender-neutral crime, women are the primary victims of stalking and men the primary perpetrators. Seventy-eight percent of stalking victims identified by the NVAW survey were women and 22 percent were men. Thus, four out of five stalking victims are women. Overall, 87 percent of the stalkers as defined by victims were male.[7]

Although the stereotypical stalking incident has been portrayed in books and movies, such as the movie *Fatal Attraction,* as a male victim pursued by a jealous, obsessive female, many stalking cases involve men stalking men. In 1997, a male stalking case achieved high notoriety, as film producer and director Steven Spielberg was stalked by 31-year-old bodybuilder and would-be screenwriter, Jonathan Norman. Norman was convicted in a Los Angeles court in March 1997. Spielberg, whose studio had turned down an unsolicited script from Norman, could have been targeted both as a celebrity and as an authority figure.

Experts say that the motive can also be romantic jealousy—gay men are the most likely victims of male-on-male stalking. But male stalking is often linked to the high-profile positions that the targets hold in society. For example, students stalk professors, attractive celebrities are pursued by lonely men looking for famous buddies, and business and political leaders can become objects of hate when consumer complaints turn ugly. Researchers say that men stalk other men for primarily the same reasons that they stalk women: a complex mix of mental and personality disorders that can include schizophrenia, drug dependency, narcissism, and antisocial behavior. One of the problems with male stalking is that men are more reluctant than women to report being stalked and can have trouble getting police to take them seriously. Furthermore, public services for stalking victims, such as spouse-abuse shelters, are still oriented to the most frequent targets—women.

While only a small percentage of stalking victims are actually physically attacked, psychological and social consequences are also common. About one-third of women and one-fifth of men who have been stalked sought psychological counseling as a result of their victimization. Over one-fourth of stalking victims said their victimization caused them to lose time from work. This included the attending of court hearings, meeting with a psychologist or other mental health professional, meeting with their attorney, and avoidance of contact with their assailant. For those victims who are stalked, the behavior lasts only a relatively short period of time—about two-thirds of all stalking cases last a year or less.

The crime of stalking generally refers to some form of repeated harassing or threatening behavior. A stalker is someone who intentionally and repeatedly follows and tries to contact, harass, and/or intimidate another person. The Violence Against Women Grants Office adds: "Legal definitions of stalking vary widely from state to state. Though most states define stalking as the willful, malicious, and repeated following and harassing of another person, some states include in their definitions such activities as lying in wait, surveillance, nonconsensual communication, telephone harassment, and vandalism."[8] Other experts have asserted that although statutes vary from one state to another, most define stalking as a course of conduct that would place a reasonable person in fear for his or her safety, and that the stalker attempted and did, in fact, place the victim in fear.

Forms of Stalking

Three broad categories of stalking have been identified, based on the relationship between the stalker and the victim:

1. In **intimate or former intimate stalking,** the stalker and victim may be married or divorced, current or former dating partners, serious or casual sexual partners, or former sexual partners. An estimated 70 to 80 percent of stalking cases fall into this category.

2. In **acquaintance stalking,** the stalker and victim know each other casually. They may be neighbors or co-workers. They may have even dated once or twice but were not sexual partners.

3. In **stranger stalking,** the stalker and victim did not know each other at all. This behavior is characterized by the stalker developing a love obsession or fixation of another person with whom he or she has no personal relationship. Cases involving public figures and celebrities fall into this category.

Brody notes that the growth in popularity of e-mail, along with use of the Internet, has spawned **cyberstalking.**[9] This informal term refers to preying on a victim through his or her computer and is discussed next.

Cyberstalking. Some people say that cyberstalking is the crime of the twenty-first century. Using the Internet to harass, intimidate, and terrorize takes an old problem and adds a diabolically futuristic twist. The types of victims vary: from politicians who get death threats via e-mail to women whose nude photographs, real or doctored, are posted on the Web. Although the average stalking case is serious enough, add the Internet component and it becomes even more frightening, as the stalker could be anyone, anywhere in the world.

Online, stalkers often hide behind false addresses and names and even impersonate their victims. Such a case happened in Los Angeles when a relationship soured and a 51-year-old security guard took to the Internet for revenge. Using his ex-girlfriend's real name, address, and telephone number, the guard went into electronic chat rooms and solicited rough sex during the summer of 1998. He engaged in sexually explicit conversations posing as his ex-girlfriend and introducing the idea of rape. In one instance, he said: "I want you to break down my door and rape me." Six men did in fact show up, and it was simply good fortune that the woman was unharmed. During the summer of 1999, the security guard was sentenced to six years in prison.[10]

The state of California has reacted aggressively to cyberstalking by updating statutes that once applied only to physical or telephonic harassment. Today, it is also illegal to harass or terrorize anyone using devices such as pagers, fax machines, or computers.

The range of sentencing for cyberstalking follows the range for physical stalking, which can be anywhere from no jail time at all to a maximum of four years. Prosecutors are often able to enhance the sentences by adding other charges. However, the U.S. Department of Justice estimates that only about one-third of states have followed California's lead. The department recommends that all states review their statutes to make them technologically neutral. The fact that cybercrime crosses jurisdictional lines is a problem for prosecutors. For example, suppose that a threatening message is sent from a computer in Michigan to a computer in California. Who investigates? Who gets the search warrant? And if evidence is turned up in Michigan, can it be used in California?

The first multi-jurisdictional computer forensic laboratory in the country was established in 1999 in San Diego, California. It aims to identify cyberstalkers, who often operate with little fear of getting caught. Participants include the FBI and the San Diego police, sheriff, and district attorney's office. In 1998, the unit prosecuted Dwayne Comfort, a student at the University of San Diego, who terrorized five female classmates by sending them sexually explicit e-mail that made it clear that he was watching their every move.[11]

The Justice Department released a report in September 1999 that said that based on the number of people who have access to the Internet, there might already have been tens of thousands of victims of cyberstalking.[12] The phenomenon is so new, the report says, that no hard statistics have been compiled. However, experts do know from their experience with ordinary stalking that women are far more likely to be stalked than men.

Some experts predict that the problem is likely to grow because using the Internet to stalk is relatively easy. Technically sophisticated stalkers can generate multiple messages throughout the day without even being present to push the send button. The anonymity they enjoy encourages some who would never have physically stalked a victim to do so with abandon on the Internet. The bad news for victims is that many law enforcement agencies don't have the sophisticated equipment or training that is often needed to track electronic stalkers.

The U.S. Justice Department has noted that all 50 states and the District of Columbia have general stalking laws, some of which can be applied to Internet stalking offenses, and that a number of states have added laws specifically targeting cyberstalking.[13]

Occurrence of Stalking

Research suggests that women are the primary victims of stalking and men the primary perpetrators. Furthermore, stalking is more prevalent than previously thought: 8 percent of women and 2 percent of men surveyed said that they had been stalked at some time in their lives. In addition, 1 million women and 371,000 men are stalked annually in the United States. According to the Department of Justice: "60 percent of women are stalked by spouses, former spouses, live-in partners, or dates, while 70 percent of men are stalked by acquaintances or strangers."[14]

The Investigative Response to Stalking

Typically, the police response to stalkers has been to issue restraining orders. Unfortunately, such orders are often ineffective, as 69 percent of women and 81 percent of men have reported that stalkers violate such orders. Because of the proven ineffectiveness of restraining orders, the perceived inability of the criminal justice system to handle stalkers effectively, and victims' fear of antagonizing stalkers, many stalking incidents go unreported. An estimated one-half of all stalking victims report their stalking cases to the police, and about 12 percent of all stalking cases result in criminal prosecution. Of those offenders convicted for stalking, most were sentenced "for violations of protection orders that had been issued by the court in domestic violence cases."[15]

In dealing with stalkers, an investigator should encourage a victim to make a police report of the incidents and document the harassment. These records can serve as the basis for legal action against the stalker. In many cases, the crime of stalking requires that the victim actually suffers substantial emotional distress because of the stalker's conduct. Consequently, investigators may demonstrate such victim distress through documentation of the victim's response to the harassment. Such documentation can include answers to the following questions. Has the victim:

- Moved to a new location?
- Obtained a new phone number?
- Put a tap on the phone?
- Told friends, co-workers, or family members of the harassment?
- Given photos of the defendant to security?
- Asked to be escorted to the parking lot and work site?
- Changed work schedule or route to work?
- Stopped visiting places previously frequented?
- Taken a self-defense course?
- Purchased pepper spray?
- Bought a gun?
- Installed an alarm system?

Responses to these questions can indicate the victim's state of mind to help prove that element of the crime. In 1996, a federal law prohibiting interstate stalking was also enacted. Such legislation makes stalking a specific crime and empowers law enforcement to combat the stalking problem. Antistalking laws describe specific threatening conduct and hold the suspect responsible for proving that his or her actions were not intended to frighten or intimidate the victim.

DISCUSSION QUESTIONS

1. List and describe various types of assault.
2. Discuss recent statistics as they relate to the problem of assault.
3. Describe the stages of investigation for the crime of assault.
4. Explain in what ways witnesses play a role in an assault investigation.
5. To what extent is the problem of domestic abuse a contemporary problem?
6. Discuss recent models of legislation in which police deal with domestic abuse.
7. Explain the problem of stalking and the investigative response to it.

NOTES

1. FBI. Crime in the United States, 2005 (2005).
2. GETZ, R. J. (1995, Sept.). Protecting our seniors. *Police,* pp. 40–43.
3. Ibid.
4. HEISE, L., and J. ROBERTS (1990). Reflections on a movement: The U.S. battle against women abuse. In M. SCHULER, ed., *Freedom From Violence: Women's Strategies Round the World.* Line Village, NV: Copperhouse Publishing, pp. 5–12.
5. NATIONAL INSTITUTE OF JUSTICE, CENTERS FOR DISEASE CONTROL AND PREVENTION (1998). *Stalking in America: Findings from the National Violence against Women Survey.* Washington, DC: U.S. Department of Justice, Office of Justice Programs.
6. Ibid.
7. Ibid.
8. VIOLENCE AGAINST WOMEN GRANTS OFFICE (1998, July). *Stalking and domestic violence: The third annual report to Congress under the Violence against Women Act.* Washington, DC: U.S. Department of Justice (NCJ-172204).
9. BRODY, J. (1998). Deep disorders drive stalkers, experts say. *Star Tribune* (Minneapolis/St. Paul), August 30, p. E5.
10. NATIONAL INSTITUTE OF JUSTICE, CENTERS FOR DISEASE CONTROL AND PREVENTION (1998). *Stalking in America;* WILLING, R. (1998). Men stalking men: Stalkers often gravitate toward positions of power. *USA Today,* June 17, p. 1A; NATIONAL INSTITUTE OF JUSTICE (1997, Nov.). The crime of stalking: How big is the problem? *Research Preview,* pp. 10–11; ALVORD, V. (1999). Cyberstalkers must beware of the law. *USA Today,* November 8, p. 22A.
11. NATIONAL INSTITUTE OF JUSTICE, CENTERS FOR DISEASE CONTROL AND PREVENTION (1998). *Stalking in America.* (1998).
12. ALVORD, V. (1999). Cyberstalkers must beware of the law. *USA Today,* November 8, p. 22A.
13. Ibid.
14. TJADEN, P., and N. THOENNES (1998). Prevalence, incidence, and consequences of violence against women: Findings from the National Violence against Women Survey. National Institute of Justice, *Research in Brief,* Washington, DC: U.S. Department of Justice.
15. Ibid.

14 Sexual Assault

Key Terms

▶ anger rapist

▶ consent

▶ date rape

▶ power rapist

▶ profile

▶ rape

▶ resistance

This chapter will enable you to:

- Describe the types of rape crimes and their investigative implications.

- Discuss the law as it relates to rape investigations.

- Understand techniques of rape victim interviews.

- Identify evidence in rape cases.

- Appreciate the role of the medical examination in rape investigations.

- Understand the value of the criminal profiling technique in rape cases.

INTRODUCTION

On August 5, 1996, recently released serial rapist Reginald Muldrew struck again, this time breaking into the apartment of a Gary, Indiana, woman, putting a pillow over her face, then raping and threatening to kill her. But this time things went a little awry. As he was leaving his victim's residence, the 48-year-old rapist was chased by and critically beaten by a group of teenagers. The police soon arrived and arrested him. Suspected of over 200 rapes in the Los Angeles area, Muldrew earned himself the nickname of the "pillowcase rapist."

Sadly, cases such as this aren't all that atypical. One doesn't have to look far to read in the newspapers of yet another incident involving criminal sexual misconduct. Because of intense media (and public) interest, such cases tend to raise the consciousness of society regarding the plight of both victims and their perpetrators. Generally speaking, most sex crimes, rape in particular, are thought to be grossly underreported by victims. In fact, an estimated one-half of all rapes are believed to go unreported to authorities. Perhaps this could be attributed to the intense personal nature of such offenses, and that victims are too embarrassed or humiliated to report the incident. Indeed, studies have revealed that many victims would rather just forget such crimes than go through the agony of reliving them through police interviews and in courtroom testimony. In addition, many perpetrators have turned out to be the friends, relatives, and acquaintances of the victims, creating an even greater disincentive for bringing about formal charges.

Although many different types of sex-related crimes exist, this chapter focuses on the crime of rape. Let's take a broader look at some of the most common types of rape that one might consider as an investigative priority. These include forcible rape and acquaintance rape.

THE ROLE OF THE SEX-CRIME INVESTIGATOR

Historically, the police investigator of sexual crimes has faced a somewhat different professional hurdle than that of most investigators. Many officers, including others in his or her own department, may view this job as a sort of "garbage collector" of the street. In fact, those who commit such crimes are also viewed by many as garbage that must be removed immediately.

Conversational topics involving sex are probably the most socially guarded in our society. Accordingly, many sexual disorders are among the most misunderstood in our culture, and those vested with investigating sex offenders are sometimes viewed as being tainted somehow by the very caliber of criminal whom they investigate.

The professional investigator of sexual crimes seeks out opportunities to become more proficient in investigations through reading, attendance at seminars, or job-related courses.[1] This includes staying abreast of recent research on offender typologies and underlying motivations for the various types of offenses encountered and the emotional impact (short and long term) of sexual crimes on victims. Without doubt, he or she must remain current in the field.

FORCIBLE RAPE

In a very broad sense, the term **rape** has been applied to a wide variety of sexual attacks and, in popular terminology, may include same-sex rape and the rape of a male by a female. Use of the term *forcible rape* for statistical reporting

Figure 14.1 Female detective interviewing sexual assault victim.

purposes by law enforcement agencies, however, has a specific and somewhat different meaning. The Uniform Crime Reports (UCR) define a forcible rape as "the carnal knowledge of a female forcibly and against her will." By definition, rapes reported under the UCR Program are always of females. In contrast to what may be an emerging social convention, in which male rape is a recognized form of sexual assault, the latest edition of the *Uniform Crime Reporting Handbook,* which serves as a statistical reporting guide for law enforcement agencies, says: "sex attacks on males are excluded [from the crime of forcible rape] and should be classified as assaults or 'other sex offenses,' depending on the nature of the crime and the extent of the injury." Although not part of the UCR terminology, some jurisdictions refer to same-sex rape as sexual battery. Sexual battery, which is not included in the UCR tally of reported rapes, is intentional and wrongful physical contact with a person without his or her **consent** that entails a sexual component or purpose. Statutory rape, where no force is involved with a female below the age of consent, is not included in rape statistics, but attempts to commit rape by force or the threat of force are included.

Forcible rape is the least reported of all violent offenses. The FBI estimates that only one out of every four forcible rapes are reported to the police. An even lower figure was reported by a 1992 government-sponsored study, which found that only 16 percent of rapes were reported. The victim's fear of embarrassment has been cited as the reason most often given for nonreports. Previously, reports of rape were usually taken by seemingly hardened desk sergeants or male detectives who may not have been sensitive to the needs of a female victim. In addition, the physical examination that victims had to endure was often a traumatizing experience in itself. Finally, many states routinely permitted the women's past sexual history to be revealed in detail in the courtroom if a trial ensued. All these practices contributed to considerable hesitancy on the part of rape victims to report victimizations. The last few decades have seen many changes designed to facilitate accurate reporting of rape and other sex offenses. Trained female detectives often act as victim interviewers, physicians have been better educated in handling the psychological needs of victims, and sexual histories are no longer regarded as relevant in most trials.

Rape is frequently committed by a man known to the victim, as in the case of date rape. Victims may be held captive and subjected to repeated assaults. In the crime of heterosexual rape, any female—regardless of age, appearance, or occupation—is a potential victim. Through personal violation, humiliation, and physical battering, rapists seek a sense of personal fulfillment and dominance. In contrast, victims of rape often experience a diminished sense of personal worth; increased feelings of despair, helplessness, and vulnerability; a misplaced sense of guilt; and a lack of control over their personal lives.

Contemporary research holds that forcible rape is often a planned violent crime, which serves the offender's need for power rather than sexual gratification. Statistically speaking, however, most rapes are committed by acquaintances of the victims and often betray a trust or friendship. Date rape, which falls into this category, appears to be far more common than believed previously. Recently, the growing number of rapes perpetrated with the use of the "date rape drug" Rohypnol has alarmed law enforcement personnel. Rohypnol is an illegal pharmaceutical substance that is virtually tasteless. Available on the black market, it dissolves easily in drinks and can lead anyone who unknowingly consumes it to be unconscious for hours, making the person vulnerable to sexual assault.

Trends

In 2005, there was an estimated 93,934 forcible rapes reported to law enforcement, this was a 1.2 percent decrease compared to 2004 figures. When compared to 2001 data, the number of forcible rapes increased an estimated 3.4 percent but, when compared to 1996 data, the number of forcible rape offenses declined 2.4 percent during the ten year period.

The rate of forcible rapes in 2005 was estimated at 62.5 offenses per 100,000 female inhabitants. Based on rape offenses actually reported to the UCR Program in 2005, rapes by force comprised 91.8 percent of reported rape offenses.

Legal Aspects of Rape

According to common law, there are three elements to the crime of rape when the female is over the age of consent:

1. Carnal knowledge (penetration).
2. Forcible submission.
3. Lack of consent.

Penetration, as an essential element of rape, means generally that the sexual organ of the male entered the sexual organ of the female. Court opinions have held that penetration, however slight, is sufficient to sustain a charge of rape. There need not be an entering of the vagina or rupturing of the hymen; entering of the vulva or labia is usually all that is required. It is important during the victim interview that investigators clearly establish that penetration occurred with the penis. Penetration of a finger is not rape, although it is, of course, another form of assault.

Comparative Rates

Forcible Rape Trend

Year	Number of Offenses	Rate per 100,000 Inhabitants
2004	84,608	32.1
2005	83,312	32.2
Percent change	−1.5	−0.1

In many states, the victim must have resisted the assault and her **resistance** must have been overcome by force. The amount of resistance that the victim is expected to have displayed depends on the specific circumstances of the case. The power and strength of the aggressor and the physical and mental ability of the victim to resist vary in each case. The amount of resistance expected in one case will not necessarily be expected in another situation. It can be expected that one woman would be paralyzed by fear and rendered mute and helpless by circumstances that would inspire another to fierce resistance or that a woman may be rendered incapacitated by drugs such as Rohypnol or GHB (see Chapter 21).[2] For the most part, there must be resistance on the part of the woman before there can be a foundation for a rape charge.

The kind of fear, however, that would render resistance by a woman unnecessary to support a case of rape includes a fear of death or serious bodily harm,

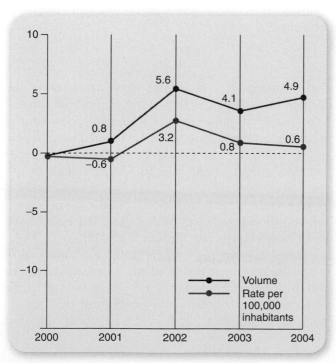

Figure 14.2 Forcible rape: Percent change from 1998. *Crime in the United States: Uniform Crime Reports. FBI, Crime in the United States, 2006.*

a fear so extreme as to preclude resistance, or a fear that would render her incapable of continuing to resist. On the other hand, consent prior to penetration may remove the criminal character of rape from the subsequent intercourse. Of course, it is problematic in some cases whether the consent was voluntary or coerced or whether resistance was possible or even prudent on the part of the victim. As one state ruled, "There is no definite standard fixed for the amount of resistance required in rape cases. Resistance is not necessary where it would endanger the complainant's safety or when she is overcome by superior strength or paralyzed with fear."[3] This ruling may reflect the position of some state courts, although other states require more demonstrable evidence of resistance to rape. In any event, most would recognize that there is a wide difference between consent and submission by force or threat of force: Consent may involve submission, but submission does not necessarily imply consent.

Corroboration

In the absence of a statute requiring corroboration, common law has traditionally held that the unsupported testimony of the victim, if not contradictory, is sufficient to sustain a conviction of rape. Some states, in order to provide safeguards against unfounded accusations of rape, have laws that require corroborative evidence. Corroboration is supportive evidence that tends to prove that a crime was committed. It lends credence to the allegation that the crime occurred and need not be proved beyond doubt.

Investigators should pay close attention to corroborative evidence even if it is not required by statute. Corroboration of a rape offense can take physical forms such as semen stains on clothing, bruises, cuts, and medical evidence of sexual intercourse. Corroborating evidence can also be circumstantial, such as statements and observations of witnesses. Although in some jurisdictions rape can be proved by the sole testimony of the victim, it is not common. Medical and scientific evidence are of prime importance and will often directly influence the successful prosecution of a case.

Date Rape

Typically, people believe that most rapists and victims were strangers to one another. But a disturbing trend in rapes indicates that many victims and offenders were acquainted before the crime was committed. For example, **date rape** is becoming more frequent on college campuses. It has been estimated that 20 percent of all college women are victims of rape or attempted rape. One self-report survey conducted on a midwestern campus found that 100 percent of all rapists knew their victim beforehand.[4]

Another troubling phenomenon is campus gang rape, where a group of men will attack a defenseless or intoxicated woman. Well-publicized rapes have taken place at the University of New Hampshire, Florida State University, Duke University, and Pennsylvania State University.

As the interview progresses, the investigator should encourage the victim to recollect any additional identifying characteristics of the assailant. Such inquiries should be phrased so as not to appear to be probing. If the victim's memory is not jogged through these inquiries, the investigator should proceed with the interview.

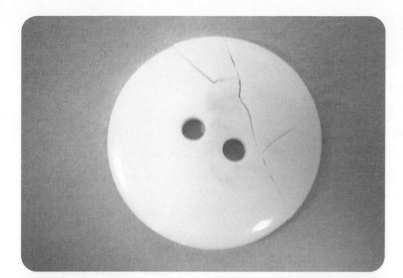

Figure 14.3 Part of the victim's broken button was located at the scene of the sexual assault and part was discovered on the clothing of the suspect. Ballistics comparison made a positive match. *Missouri State Highway Patrol Crime Laboratory*

Victim Interview Checklist

- Interviewers should be sensitive to the needs and concerns of the victim.
- All victims react differently to incidents of sexual assault.
- Police officers react differently to sexual assault victims.
- Interviewer must display a genuine interest in the welfare of the victim.
- Victim interviews demand patience and perseverance.
- Interviewers should ask brief open-ended questions.
- It should be established whether the victim knows the suspect.
- Descriptions of the suspect and his vehicle must be acquired if available.
- Leading questions should not be asked.
- Official police jargon should not be used.
- Victims should be walked through the crime scene to indicate what the suspect may have touched.
- The victim needs to feel that she has regained control of her life.
- Investigators must anticipate what information the victim might want to know.
- Investigative procedures should be explained carefully if the investigator is asked to do so.
- The interview should never be rushed.

EVIDENCE IN RAPE CASES

As with all investigations, identification, collection, and preservation of evidence are the primary responsibility of the investigator. Rape cases are somewhat unique in that evidence may present itself in three general areas:

1. On the crime scene.
2. On the victim.
3. On the suspect (or at locations occupied by the suspect).

Additionally, evidence in rape cases may take many forms. Therefore, after the responding officer has given the rape victim aid, a determination of the circumstances surrounding the attack must be made. When immediate medical attention is required, the officer on the scene may make initial inquiries about the assault while waiting for the ambulance to arrive. The victim should be asked to:

- Describe what happened.
- Describe the assailant.
- Describe the attacker's vehicle.
- Describe the location where the crime occurred.

If the incident was fairly recent, a flash description of the suspect or his vehicle should be given to the dispatcher for possible broadcast. Once the crime scene investigation is under way, the investigator should determine if there is any physical evidence to be collected. Typically, the rape victim will scratch the skin or tear the hair of her attacker, and evidence may be present under her

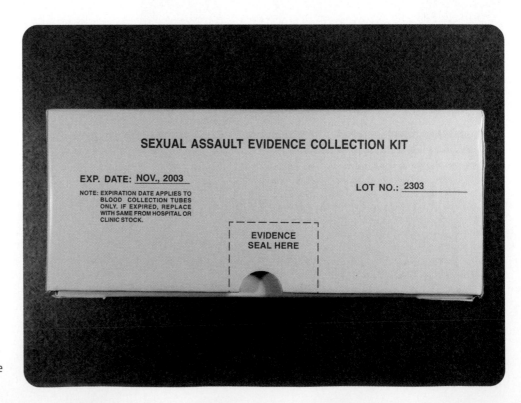

Figure 14.4 Sexual assault evidence collection kit.

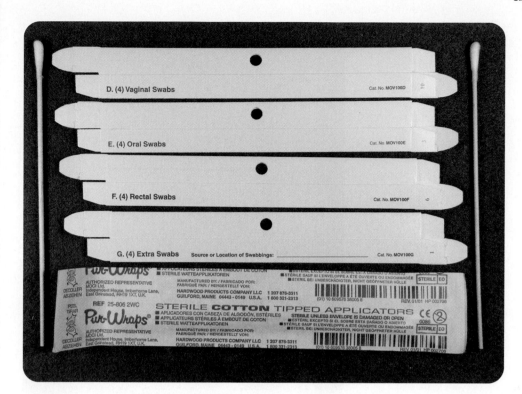

Figure 14.5 Sexual assault evidence kit contents—vaginal, oral, and rectal swabs.

fingernails. For example, a single strand of hair may reveal the gender, race, and age of the attacker. Such evidence is seizable by investigators and extremely valuable in court.[5]

The clothing of the victim can also provide valuable information (e.g., stains, blood, soil, grass stains, trace evidence). As early as possible, clothing should be collected from the victim and preserved for laboratory analysis. Other types of evidence that should be considered are bedsheets, mattress, towels and washrags, discarded facial tissues, robes, and sofa or chair cushions. The investigator is limited only by his or her imagination when considering the types and locations of such articles.

If a suspect is in custody, secure the necessary legal instrument (i.e., court order) to obtain hair and blood standards to compare with those found on the victim.

Rape Evidence Checklist

- Photograph all physical injuries of the victim.
- Note the clothing of the victim (e.g., torn, dirty, missing buttons).
- Examine the hair (both victim and suspect) for foreign fiber, debris, or blood.
- Obtain fingernail scrapings for clothing fibers, skin, blood, hair, and so on.
- Obtain blood samples from the victim.
- Obtain pubic hairs from both the victim and the suspect (this includes standards for comparison).
- Obtain vaginal swabs from the victim (the attending physician should acquire at least two).
- Obtain anal and oral swabs from the victim.
- Allow wet articles to air-dry using fresh air, not heated air.
- Ensure that the victim has a cervical exam by a physician of her choosing.
- Obtain a written report from the examining physician.

Figure 14.6 Sexual assault evidence kit contents—envelopes for hair combings.

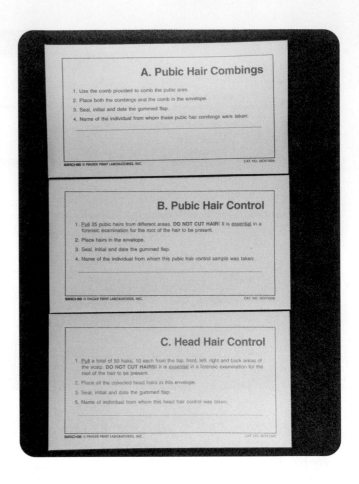

The Rape Evidence Kit

Preassembled kits for rape evidence collection can be found in many different configurations and can be quite useful to the investigator. Typically included are directions for proper use to avoid confusion and error. Hazelwood and Burgess note that commonly included are forms covering (1) medical examination and interview of the victim, (2) consent/release concerning authority to disseminate victim-related information, (3) consent/release regarding evidence obtained from the victim, and (4) chain of custody documentation.[6]

These documents are best constructed as a cooperative effort between local law enforcement and medical professionals who treat sexual assault victims. Many evidence recovery procedures can be incorporated into a rape evidence collection kit. The following is a general list of some essential elements of the kit:

- Head hair brushing comb
- Pubic hair brushing comb
- Packages for head and pubic hairs collected (both known and suspected samples)
- Vaginal swabbings
- Oral swabbings
- Anal swabbings

- Fingernail scrapings
- Miscellaneous debris collection

The acquisition of known biological samples is basically the same for both the victim and the suspect. Accordingly, trace evidence can be collected in a similar fashion. In fact, the components of the victim-oriented assault kit serve as a good guide for kits used on a suspect.

Investigative Procedures: The Crime Scene Investigation

An officer's first duty at the scene of a rape is to aid the victim and obtain medical attention at once if required. If the attack is brutal and the victim is suffering from wounds, briefly question the victim about the attack if she is able to speak. Questions relating to what happened, where the attack took place, and a description of or information about the assailant are pertinent basic facts. This initial attempt to secure information should be made whenever possible while awaiting the arrival of an ambulance or during transport to medical facilities. In turn, the dispatcher should be contacted immediately with this information.

Usually upon arriving at a rape scene, officers will find the victim of a sexual assault under severe emotional stress ranging from hysteria to deep depression. She may be sobbing uncontrollably, excited to the point of incoherence, or in a state of shock. In cases in which the victim was drugged, she may be confused and unsure of what happened to her. When encountering any of these situations, officers must comfort the victim and reassure her that she will be all right and that she has nothing more to fear. A victim in this mental state may best be comforted by another woman: a female officer, a family member, a friend, or a victim advocate. Such individuals should be summoned as quickly as possible if not objectionable to the victim.

The crime scene should be secured and a search for physical evidence begun as soon as possible. Quite often, the victim will pull hair or tear the assailant's clothes or scratch his face and accumulate skin tissue or bloodstains under her fingernails. The victim's clothing can also provide valuable information. This should be collected and forwarded to the crime laboratory with other trace evidence for analysis.

Clothing.   When a rape occurs in the home, the victim should be requested by the complaint taker not to change her clothing, shower, or touch anything in the area until officers arrive at the scene to give her instructions. Responding officers should assume custody of all the clothing worn at the time of the attack, so they may be examined for blood or seminal stains, hair fibers, or other physical trace evidence that may lead to the identification, apprehension, and conviction of a suspect. If the location of the crime makes the immediate recovery of the clothing impractical, the victim should be informed that an officer will collect her garments at the hospital for transfer to the crime laboratory. In these situations, arrangements should be made with a friend or a relative to bring a change of clothing for the victim to the hospital. The number of persons handling the victim's clothing must be restricted. Concerted efforts to protect the integrity of the specimens and to guard the chain of possession also require that evidence be properly marked, packaged, and labeled to facilitate future identification.[7]

The clothing of a rape victim, especially the undergarments, as well as the clothes of a suspect, should be analyzed by crime laboratory technicians for semen stains, bloodstains, hair, and other physical traces, such as soil and grass stains. Scientific analysis of the evidence may link a suspect to the crime, or it may indicate that a suspect is not the person who should be sought.

Recovered clothing should be carefully handled to protect the evidentiary value of the stains it may contain. Seminal traces and bloodstains are highly brittle when dry and may be brushed off the clothing. Clothing should be covered with paper before folding and each item individually placed in an evidence bag.

Semen. Seminal traces may be located by ultraviolet radiation because of their fluorescent qualities. Semen is highly proteinaceous serum normally containing a great number of spermatozoa. These traces are usually found on underclothing of the victim and/or the suspect and may also be located on bedding, mattresses, towels, automobile cushions, and similar types of materials found at or near the crime scene or in the possession of a suspect. Ultraviolet light and/or an acid phosphatase color test is helpful in identifying semen on these and other surfaces. Vaginal secretions and some other material will react to the latter test but not at the same speed as semen. A positive test requires that the material be subjected to microscopic examination for confirmation.

Bloodstains may also be found in similar locations. Both semen and blood samples can be subjected to DNA analysis.

Hair. It is fairly common to find a reciprocal transfer of evidence in crimes involving bodily contact. As such, it is not unusual to find hair of the offender transferred to the body or clothing of the victim and, in turn, to discover some of the victim's hair on the suspect.

Recovered hair is usually subjected to microanalysis at the crime laboratory. The results of this examination can generally narrow the search for a suspect. A single strand of hair may identify the race, sex, approximate age, and the true color of the hair of its host. The analysis can also determine the portion of the body that the hair is from: scalp, chest, arm, leg, or pubic region.

Although the crime laboratory examination leads to general identification characteristics of a suspect, a positive finding may suggest the implication of an individual whereas a negative finding may disprove an erroneous theory. By the same token, hair found on a suspect's clothes can be examined and identified as being similar to that of the victim.

Investigative Procedures: The Medical Examination

Rape victims should receive medical attention and undergo an examination as soon as possible after the incident. This examination and treatment not only are needed for therapeutic and prophylactic reasons, but also are necessary to develop evidence showing penetration, rape, and possible traces of Rohypnol, GHB, or other drugs associated with sexual assault.

The victim has the right to be examined by a physician of her choice. However, for practical reasons, this should be generally discouraged. A private practitioner or a hospital staff physician is often reluctant to be specific in officially reporting findings or to take time from a busy work schedule to testify in court. Gentle persuasion and tact will usually influence an unwilling victim or her parents to allow a physician or sexual assault nurse examiner from a public institution to conduct the examination. A written statement or report should be obtained from the attending physician or nurse after the victim has been examined. This record is extremely important at the trial to sustain the victim's allegation that she was raped.

The medical examination conducted by a licensed physician or a specially trained nurse examiner is necessary to establish proof of penetration. It usually consists of a visual examination of the vaginal area to determine if there is evidence of tissue damage (lacerations, abrasions, contusions) or other indication of physical trauma that is logically connected with the assault. Smears should be obtained from the vaginal passage to determine the presence or the absence of sperm. However, the presence of sperm merely corroborates that the victim had sexual intercourse, not necessarily that she had been raped. In cases in which a drug-facilitated rape is probable, urine and blood samples should be taken.

If the victim dies before the physical examination, she should not be examined by the attending physician. Instead, the body should be examined by the posting physician or the medical examiner. This procedure is followed to reduce the number of persons examining the body. Also, an examination prior to the posting process may destroy or remove important evidence.

The medical examination of a deceased victim should include other body cavities such as the anus, mouth, and ears. Scrapings should also be taken from under the fingernails. A thorough examination is necessary to determine the kind of sexual assault suffered by the victim and to obtain specimens of blood that could possibly be the assailant's. In some instances, assailants insert foreign objects into body cavities before or after the death of the victim. In instances of death, officers should provide the medical examiner with all information surrounding the assault and death of the victim.

Investigative Procedures: The Interview

While the victim interview is one of the key components of a rape investigation, it can also be one of the more difficult functions for a criminal investigator. The difficult and, in many ways, specialized nature of these interviews has been a major reason for the introduction and use of rape crisis specialists to assist in these cases. Most agencies do not have such specialized personnel resources, but many agencies have found it helpful to utilize female officers individually or in conjunction with a male officer for such interviews. Female officers, even without specialized training, are generally effective in mitigating some of the anxiety and apprehension that rape victims have concerning the interview process and related investigatory activities. Significant additional benefits can be realized, for both the victim and the criminal investigation, if the same female officer can be assigned to assist the victim throughout the investigation and prosecution of the case.

Most rape investigations should incorporate a preliminary and subsequent in-depth interview with the victim. The initial interview conducted at the crime scene should be limited to gathering basic facts about the crime sufficient to identify the victim and to describe and locate the offender on a timely basis. The ability of the responding officer or investigator to gather this information will depend greatly on the emotional and physical condition of the victim and the professional and interpersonal skills of the interviewer. However, it is ill advised to attempt to fully explore the events and circumstances surrounding the crime at the scene of the incident. The emotional condition of rape victims generally precludes their ability to clearly focus and to articulate accurate and complete details of the incident. Even in cases in which a victim appears to be under control, officers should be aware that the victim's emotional state may cause her to cloud certain facts, and in cases in which the victim was drugged, she may have blacked out during the assault. Officers should be sure to clarify such information at a later time during an in-depth interview session.

By gathering complete information during the in-depth interview, officers avoid the need to repeatedly question the victim at later dates. Repeated interviews require the victim to relive the experience again and again. A structured interview that will cover all pertinent areas is one of the better means of avoiding such repetitive questioning.

The investigative goal of the police officer in interviewing a rape victim is to determine if and how the crime occurred. It is from the statements made by the victim to the officer that the essential elements of the offense and the direction of the investigation are established. The prosecutor and eventually the court must be given a well-balanced account of the offense describing the actions of the offender, any accomplices, and the victim. It is the investigator's responsibility to provide the court with the explanation and clarification it seeks. Part of the story may be obtained from the analysis of physical evidence, but the eyewitness account of the victim or other persons fills in the missing portions of the picture presented to the court.

Because the interview process may be considered as a routine operation, the police officer may, if not careful, project a feeling of lack of concern for the victim as a person. The danger is that the victim may be left with the impression that she is being treated as an object of physical evidence rather than as a human being. This eventuality must be avoided for its own sake as well as for the good of the investigation. It is by the personal and sensitive communication of the interview that the victim's cooperation is gained and her emotional well-being maintained. If the officer treats the victim impersonally, her confidence will be shattered, the interview will be unsuccessful, and the victim may suffer further emotional stress. The following points should be kept in mind when conducting the in-depth interview.

Officer attitude. When interviewing a rape victim, the officer must realize that, from the victim's viewpoint, what has occurred is a violent and perverted invasion of her "self." Further, the officer must be constantly aware of personal sexual attitudes and prejudices as well as the subtle and not-so-subtle ways in which they emerge. Special care should be exercised so that the rape victim is not placed in the position of perceiving herself as being guilty because of the personal nature of the crime and the social stigma attached to it. Maintaining professionalism throughout the interview will help the officer obtain an accurate report of the crime without causing the victim to experience unnecessary anxiety.

The interviewer's approach should be informal and natural in order to put the victim at ease. Words should be used that are appropriate to the victim's age, intelligence, and social class. Slang or colloquialisms may be appropriate in alluding to matters indirectly related to the offense, but medical terms should be used to refer to the various sexual organs and parts of the body (penis, vagina, vulva, etc.). In some instances, an officer may have to define terms to the victim before the interview. This adds a degree of dignity to the confidential relationship one should establish, indicates respect for the private parts of the body, and helps allay doubt or misgiving about the officer's sincerity and interest.

Physical setting. It is unreasonable to expect a rape victim to respond to detailed questioning while she is uncomfortable or in physical pain. The victim may have been beaten as well as raped. If the rape has occurred outdoors, the victim and her clothing will probably be soiled. Sometimes the victim has been urinated on or has been forced to commit oral sodomy. Under conditions such as these, the preliminary interview should be brief, and the in-depth follow-up interview should be conducted after the victim has been medically examined and treated and her personal needs, such as washing and changing clothes, have been met.

Officers often interview a rape victim at the hospital or other medical facility where the victim is being treated. Most hospitals meet the basic requirements of appropriate physical setting for an interview. The physical surroundings of most hospitals provide desired privacy and a professional care environment that can restore confidence in the victim.

Outside the hospital, the interview should take place in a comfortable setting where there is privacy and freedom from distraction. A crowded office or similar location where the interview is subject to interruption is inappropriate. The reluctance of a rape victim to discuss intimate details of the crime will generally increase if there are other people present. This may include persons who would be close to the victim under otherwise normal conditions, such as a husband or boyfriend.

Opening remarks. Opening remarks represent a critical point at which an officer must gain the victim's confidence and let her know that a major part of the officer's function is to help and to protect her. The officer should make clear his/her sympathy for and interest in the victim. By doing this, the officer contributes to the immediate and long-term emotional health of the victim and lays the foundation of mutual cooperation and respect on which an effective interview is built.

Ventilation period. Following the opening remarks, the officer should allow the victim to direct the conversation into any area of concern to her. This "ventilation" period gives the victim an opportunity to relieve emotional tension. During this time, the officer should listen carefully to the victim and provide answers to questions as appropriate and reassurance when necessary.

Investigative questioning. After a ventilation period, the victim should be allowed to describe what occurred in her own words and without interruption. As the victim provides details about the rape, she will also relate a great deal about herself. Her mood and general reaction, her choice of words, and her comments on unrelated matters can be useful in evaluating the facts of the case. It is important in such an interview that the police officer be humane, sympathetic, and patient. He/she should also be alert to inconsistencies in the victim's statements. If the victim's story differs from the originally reported facts, the officer should point out the discrepancies and ask her to explain them in greater detail. The officer should phrase questions in simple language, making sure that she understands the question. It is best if the questions are presented in a manner that encourages conversation rather than implies interrogation. Often a rape victim will omit embarrassing details from her description of the crime. Officers should expect a certain amount of reluctance on the part of the victim to describe unpleasant facts. The officer should explain that certain information must be discussed to satisfy the legal aspects of rape and pursue the investigation. He/she may add that the same questions will be asked in court if the case results in a trial. In a majority of cases, the attack is premeditated, and in about 80 percent of the cases,[8] the rapist has known or has seen the victim before the assault. Because of this, certain types of questions should be asked. The victim should be asked if, and how long, she has been acquainted with the offender. The circumstances of their meeting and the extent of any previous relationship, including any prior sexual relations, should be explored. Although previous sexual acts with the accused will not absolve the offender at this point in the investigation, knowledge of them helps to establish the nature of the relationship with the offender, as well as prepare for possible prosecutorial problems. Where it is determined that the victim had known the rapist prior to the incident, he should be identified and interviewed. If the offender is unknown, the officer must get a detailed description of him including clothing, speech mannerisms, and related identifying characteristics. The officer should determine whether the offender revealed any personal facts such as area of residence or places he frequented. Questions should be asked related to the presence of any accomplices, use of weapons, and make and model of any vehicle involved, among other pertinent factors.

With the increasing prevalence of date rape drugs such as Rohypnol and GHB, there are new problems that arise during an investigation. The victim may have little or no memory of the assault and may not be sure whether or not an assault took place. The questioning should focus on the events leading up to the incident, beverages ingested, and who provided them. The officer should question the victim as to any unusual side effects she experienced, as well as typical effects on the victim from alcohol and drugs.[9]

Concluding the interview. As a result of having been raped, many victims suffer long-term emotional problems. Because of this, it is appropriate for the officer conducting the interview to determine whether the victim has sought assistance for any such problems. It is generally advisable to inform the victim that emotional reactions to rape are common and that counseling is advisable. Victims who are not familiar with available community resources to assist in these matters should be provided with information on referral agencies.

Actual versus False Complaints

There have been many misconceptions regarding rape, one of which is the prevalence of false reports. Approximately 1 to 6 percent of rape reports are fictitious, no greater than the incidence of false reports for other crimes.[10] A victim's reactions and appearance may lead an officer to question the validity of the complaint, but a victim's reactions can be quite varied. Even a jovial attitude displayed by a rape victim is not abnormal. Another reason officers question the validity of rape reports is the prior sexual involvement a victim may have had with an offender. But this is not conclusive. Even prostitutes are subjected to sexual assault, which includes the humiliation and trauma of the crime.

PROFILING THE RAPIST

As with the investigation of many other types of crimes, one of the best methods for solving rape and sexual assault cases is to understand the offender's motivations. The use of the rapist **profile** can aid the criminal investigator in understanding the behavioral patterns of the suspect. Profiling will not solve rape cases, but will assist in the investigation by focusing on confirming certain events at a crime scene or by eliminating suspects.

Profiles have been of value to law enforcement agencies when investigators review their investigative files and attempt to apply the information to the case. Similarly, profiles can be used to "match" profile characteristics to newly developed suspects who come into only minimal contact with the investigators.

Research by such experts in the field as A. Nicholas Groth, Ann Burgess, and Robert Hazelwood has led to an improved understanding of the rapist and his victim. Groth, a leading expert on sex crimes, describes the role of both the "power" and the "anger" rapist. Groth has developed the main premise behind the rapist profile in his typologies.[11] The **power rapist** has been subdivided into two personality types: the power-reassurance rapist and power-assertive rapist. The **anger rapist** has also been subdivided into two categories: the anger-retaliatory rapist and the anger-excitation rapist.

The Power-Reassurance (Manhood) Rapist

The power-reassurance rapist has the primary motivation of power over his victim. Accounting for an estimated 81 percent of rapes that are reported, the term *power* does not imply that he desires to harm his victim physically in any way; he does not. Indeed, his psychological disorder focuses on how he perceives his manhood or lack of it. The pre-offense behavior of the power-reassurance rapist includes fantasies about having a sexual affair with a member of the opposite sex. Because of his obsession with proving his manhood, his fantasies revolve around "successful" sexual relations with his partner. It is thought that these fantasies center around a relationship that most of the "normal" population enjoys regularly.

Criminal investigations of this type of rapist show that he will usually deploy a particular "plan of attack." If the rapist persists in his attacks, his plan will become more and more refined but also more easily predicted by investigators. In particular, this class of rapist will usually select victims through prior observation

Profile of the Power-Reassurance Rapist[12]

- Rapes between midnight and 5 A.M. every 7 to 20 days.
- Selects victims by watching and window peeping.
- Seeks women about his own age who are living alone and attacks in their home.
- Uses a weapon of opportunity.
- Covers the victim's face or wears a ski mask to prevent identification.
- Asks the victim to remove her clothing
- Performs vaginal sex; may experience premature ejaculation or impotence.
- Asks the victim to say that she likes his sexual performance.
- Is socially inadequate, a loner, lives alone or with parents, has a menial job, frequents porno theaters and shops, has been arrested for window peeping or burglary.
- Has no vehicle; first rapes within walking distance of his home.

A Closer Look
The Disappearance of Dru Sjodin

Twenty-two-year-old University of North Dakota student Dru Sjodin left her job at Victoria's Secret at the Columbia Mall in Grand Forks, North Dakota around 4 P.M. on November 22, 2006. According to her boyfriend, Chris Lang, she was speaking with him on her cell phone around 5 P.M., from the mall parking lot (after doing some shopping), when she said "Oh my God," followed by her phone going dead. He received another call from her phone a few hours later but heard only static. She hasn't been seen since. On December 1, police arrested Alfonso Rodriguez, Jr., a registered Level III sex offender from Minnesota, for abducting her.

DRU SJODIN DISAPPEARANCE TIMELINE

- 4:00: Dru leaves work at Victoria's Secret at Columbia Mall in Grand Forks, North Dakota.

- 4:00: Alfonso Rodriguez, Jr., is seen on a store security camera leaving a Super Target in Grand Forks a few blocks from the Columbia Mall. According to store receipts later found in his home, Rodriguez had been at the Columbia Mall earlier in the day. Evidence shows that Rodriguez returned to the Columbia Mall and was there about the time Dru disappeared.

- 4:30: Rodriguez told police he saw *Once Upon a Time in Mexico* in a Columbia Mall movie theater at this time, which ended between 7:00 and 7:30 (and then ate at a nearby McDonald's and returned home). This film was not playing in any area theater on November 22 and hadn't been playing at any theater in the mall since September.

- 4:55: Dru buys a purse at Marshall Field's in Columbia Mall.

- About 5:00: Dru is seen on a surveillance camera leaving Marshall Field's. She is talking on her cell phone to her boyfriend, Chris Lang, in Minnesota.

- 5:04: The call ends abruptly as Dru says what Lang remembers as "OK, OK" (not "Oh my God" as often reported).

- 7:42: Another phone call from Dru's phone to Lang's, which he describes as being nothing but static and "tones," as if random buttons were being pushed. The call is picked up by a cellular tower in Fisher, Minnesota, about 15 miles from Grand Forks (the phone continued to be logged into that tower for about 24 hours until the evening of November 23, which could mean the phone was nearby until then; the phone has not been recovered). Lang calls Dru's roommate.

- 8:00: Rodriguez returns home (to Crookston, Minnesota), according to his mother (Crookston is a little over 11 miles from Fisher, about a 16-minute drive). She alternately claims he got home around 8:15.

- 9:30: Dru's roommate calls University of North Dakota police to report Dru missing, after Dru doesn't show up for her 9:00 shift at a local bar.

- 11:00: Police find Dru's car in the northeast parking area of the Columbia Mall (she made a habit of parking in the southwest parking area, near both Victoria's Secret and Marshall Field's). The driver's side door was locked, but the passenger side door was not. Inside the car were Dru's pocketbook and the shopping bag containing her new purse, but her keys were gone. Outside of the car, near the passenger's door, was a sheath that matches a knife later found in Rodriguez's car.

A Closer Look

The Disappearance of Dru Sjodin (*continued*)

Forensic Evidence in the Sjodin Case

Suspect Rodriguez, a Level III sex offender living in Crookston, Minnesota, after completing 23 years in prison in May 2003, was spotted by security cameras at a Super Target store in Grand Forks on November 22, about an hour before Dru Sjodin's 5:00 disappearance from the parking lot of the Columbia Mall a few blocks away.

A search of Rodriguez's home turned up receipts from stores in Columbia Mall dated earlier in the afternoon (also taken from the home Rodriguez shared with his mother: two strands of light-colored hair, clothing similar to the clothing he was wearing at the Super Target, and samples of what appeared to be blood from the garage floor).

According to an affidavit, Rodriguez claimed he'd been watching a movie at a nearby theater between about 4:30 and 7:00 or 7:30 and then stopped to eat at a nearby McDonald's before driving home. No theaters in the area were playing that movie that day, and Rodriguez told police he couldn't explain this.

- Grand Forks and Crookston are about 25 miles apart, and the driving time would be about 35 minutes.
- Delores Rodriguez, the suspect's mother, told police he got home around 8:15.
- Grand Forks County Sheriff Dan Hill confirmed that a preliminary DNA match was made between Dru and blood found in Alfonso Rodriguez's car, that a sheath found in the Columbia Mall parking lot near Dru's car was a likely match for a knife found in Rodriguez's car, and that a shoe found near Red Lake River in Crookston, Minnesota, a few days after Dru's disappearance had been identified by Dru's college roommate as probably being Dru's.

There had been talk about harassing phone calls received at the Victoria's Secret store where Dru worked, many of which were supposedly directed at Dru personally. The caller was said to have an accent (though it hasn't been confirmed that the accent matches Rodriguez's). This would suggest that the caller—if he was Rodriguez—had singled out Dru as a victim. But Dru left work about an hour before she was abducted and shopped in the mall before returning to her car. An hour before her abduction (she'd be expected to have been leaving), Rodriguez was seen at the Super Target.

Victim Characteristics of the Power Rapist[13]

- The victim is usually of the same race as the attacker.
- The victim will probably be alone at the time of initial contact.
- The victim will have been evaluated by the attacker as one who probably won't resist attack.
- The attacker considers her to be meek, nonaggressive, or easily dominated.
- Physical size is commonly used in the rapist's consideration of victims.
- The victim is typically attacked through a "surprise" method.
- The rapist hopes that she will yield to his "initial" advance.
- Should the rapist not get the desired initial response from the victim, he will probably flee the scene.

> ## Profile of the Power-Assertive Rapist[14]
>
> - Rapes between 7 P.M. and 1 A.M., every 20 to 25 days.
> - Selects a victim of opportunity; may meet her in a bar or date two or three times.
> - Selects a woman about his own age, uses an overpowering or con approach, dominates victim, rapes indoors or outdoors.
> - Uses a weapon of choice.
> - Uses no mask, may attempt to hide his face, won't let victim look at him.
> - Is a macho type, body-conscious, athletic; frequents singles bars; has a hard-hat job or is a truck driver.
> - Is married or divorced, has been arrested for domestic disturbance or crimes against property.
> - Has a flashy vehicle: sports car or four-wheel-drive pickup.

or stalking. This may be accomplished through prowling, voyeurism, and so on, typically conducted in residential areas. Statistically, attacks occur in the victim's residence after dark and close to the rapist's own neighborhood. Additionally, he will use weapons of opportunity and verbal threats in his attack.

Ironically, studies have shown that after the attack, the offender is likely to apologize to the victim—hence the nickname "gentleman rapist." He may actually view his actions as nonthreatening to the victim and serving only to satisfy his personal needs. Investigations have also revealed that the attacker will sometimes take a personal article from the victim as a souvenir.

The Power-Assertive Rapist

The second profile occurs in an estimated 12 percent of rape attacks and involves the assertive personality of the rapist. It is the desire of this person to demonstrate his manhood to the victim through sexual assault. Research has shown that this type of rapist seldom plans his attacks and is an opportunist by nature. His victims are, however, typically of the same race and age group as the assailant. Many such offenders have chosen the bar scene as their hunting ground and may typically choose a bar close to the place where they live or work.

The power-assertive rapist will probably use the con approach with his victim, and once he gets her in a location where he can make his attack, he will use a moderate degree of force. After the assault, he will probably threaten his victim with retaliation if she reports him. As with the previous type of offender, he will also desire an object from the victim as a souvenir, such as an article of clothing. The power-assertive rapist is also thought to be a repeat offender whose future targets are difficult to predict.

The Anger-Retaliatory Rapist

The anger-retaliatory rapist profile is that of a person who vents his anger and frustration toward the opposite sex by punishing them. The punishment is based on either real or imagined wrongs that they have perpetrated against him (or the male population in general). Sexual assault is the means by which he chooses to humiliate them.

This category of rapist, which accounts for an estimated 5 percent of all rapes, typically includes preoffense behavior that involves a significant stressor that typically relates to women. Studies show that this can usually be traced back to the offender's family or work relationships. For example, a rapist's stressor may be a woman who continually demeaned him in his early home life,

Profile of Anger-Retaliatory Rapist[15]

- Rapes any hour of day or night, at irregular 6- to 12-month intervals, after fight with wife or "put-down" by a woman.
- Selects a victim of opportunity, in his own neighborhood or near work.
- Selects a woman his same age or older, employs "blitz" attack.
- Uses a weapon of opportunity: fists, feet, club; beats victim before, during, and after sexual assault.
- Performs anal, and then oral sex, vaginal sex; has possible retarded ejaculation.
- Employs much profanity and degrading language.
- May have arrests for domestic disturbance, speeding, or fighting on the night of the rape.
- Is a loner, drinker, troublemaker, explosive temper, sports fan, laborer, construction worker.
- Is a married man, abuses wife and children, has been arrested for fighting, family disputes, drinking.
- May have any type of vehicle.

resulting in stress buildup inside. After storming out of his residence, he comes across an unsuspecting woman who he designates as the target of his rage and frustration. Such an assault is usually spontaneous and results from improper management of that stressor.

Victim selection is usually somewhere near the attacker's residence, and she may possess physical characteristics similar to those of the female stressor in his life (e.g., the same age, the same hair style). His characterization of the attack on the victim may sound something like: "She was just in the wrong place at the wrong time." This rapist will typically use a blitz-type attack, with the use of force before, during, and after the attack. Although the actual assault is fairly brief, it is typically violent, as the rapist uses any resistance on the part of the victim to fuel his own anger.

The Anger-Excitation Rapist

Of all of the rapist profiles discussed, the anger-excitation rapist is the most dangerous. The anger-excitation rapist has a strong propensity toward sadism and is prone to severely injure or even murder his victim. In addition, he enjoys the victim's response to the infliction of pain, usually resulting from torture. The planning stage of the attack is done meticulously by this type of rapist, who harbors images and fantasies about sadistic sexual acts with his victims. Typically, every stage of the attack is carefully thought through.

Victims may have certain traits exhibited by women in the rapist's life with whom he has experienced conflict. Research has shown that this type of rapist

Profile of the Anger-Excitation Rapist[16]

- Assaults are extremely well planned.
- His violent fantasies are acted out during the assault.
- Gloves and mask are included in the rape kit.
- The victim's resistance fuels the attacker's rage.
- Victim selection is day or night, at irregular intervals.
- Brutal force is used to control his victim.
- While inflicting pain on the victim, the attacker is usually calm.
- The victim's clothes are usually cut off her.
- Video recordings are usually made of the assault.
- The sadistic rapist has no remorse.
- He may attempt to hide his face by wearing a hood or mask.

will usually use a weapon to gain control of the victim while exposing himself to minimum risk of harm or detection. Once the victim is in his control, he will use excessive and brutal force to maintain both psychological and physiological control of her.

The Rapist's Approach

For a more complete profile of the perpetrator, it is important that the investigator document the method of approach used by the attacker. Three such forms of behavior exhibited by rapists are offered by Hazelwood and Burgess:[17]

1. *Con approach.* The victim is approached openly with a subterfuge or "cover." Typically, the attacker is friendly and will offer some type of assistance or will request directions.
2. *Blitz approach.* Immediate physical assault is used to subdue the victim. This approach leaves no opportunity to cope verbally or physically and frequently involves the use of a gag or blindfold.
3. *Surprise approach.* The attacker waits for the victim in a secluded area where he won't be discovered and then approaches on his own volition (e.g., hiding in the backseat of an automobile or stepping out from behind a wall).

Methods of Control

Through the careful interview of the victim, investigators should attempt to determine the method of control used by the attacker. This is a significant component to the profiling process in which similar characteristics might be identified in the examination of other rape offenses. According to Hazelwood and Burgess, the use of force may include four levels of severity:[18]

1. *Minimal force.* Little or no force is used, but minimal slapping may be used to intimidate.
2. *Moderate force.* The repeated hitting or slapping of the victim in a painful manner is accompanied by the use of profanity.
3. *Excessive force.* The victim is beaten on all or most parts of her body.
4. *Brutal force.* Sadistic torture and intentional infliction of physical and emotional pain are employed.

Studies have revealed that rapists reveal a great deal about themselves during the course of the attack through verbal remarks and comments. This makes it extremely important for the investigator to elicit specific information from the victim as to what the attacker said during the assault, specifically, comments regarding demands made of the victim as well as compliments made to the victim during the attack.

Another important step in the investigation is to determine whether or not the attacker stole any items from the victim that might serve as a token or "prize" by which to remember the victim. Such items can be valuable evidence if recovered by police and used as evidence in court.

DISCUSSION QUESTIONS

1. Why does the task of investigating sexual offenses present more hurdles for the criminal investigator than in other areas of criminality?

2. Discuss the problem of date rape and why it is such a difficult crime to investigate.

3. What are the legal elements of rape?

4. Discuss the major points to remember when interviewing a rape victim.

5. What types of evidence should be sought in a rape case?

6. How does the power-reassurance rapist profile differ from that of the anger-retaliatory rapist?

7. Describe physical evidence in rape investigations.

8. Discuss a "typical" rapist and how the actual offender differs from the stereotypic offender.

9. When interviewing a victim of rape, discuss the best initial approach that investigators should use to establish rapport.

10. What are some of the evidentiary concerns that investigators must face when investigating a rape case?

NOTES

1. LANNING, K. W., and R. R. HAZELWOOD (1988, Sept.). The maligned investigator of criminal sexuality. *FBI Law Enforcement Bulletin*, pp. 1–10.

2. See for example, "The Prosecution of Rohypnol and GHB Related Sexual Assaults," The American Prosecutors Research Institute, Alexandria, Virginia, 1999.

3. *People* v. *McCann,* 76 Ill. App. 3rd 184, 186, 394 N.E.2d 1055, 1056 (2d Dist. 1979).

4. MEYER, T. (1984). Date rape: A serious campus problem that few talk about. *Chronicle of Higher Education,* December 5.

5. GRIFFITHS, G. L. (1985, Apr.). The overlooked evidence in rape investigations. *FBI Law Enforcement Bulletin*, pp. 8–15.

6. HAZELWOOD, R. and A. BURGESS (1987). *Practical aspects of rape investigation.* Boca Raton, FL: CRC Press.

7. Ibid.

8. HEISE, L. L. (1993). Reproductive freedom and violence against women: Where are the intersections? *Journal of Law, Medicine & Ethics,* 21(2): 206–216.

9. See, for example, "Drug Facilitated Sexual Assault: Rohypnol and GHB," Training Key #509, International Association of Chiefs of Police, Alexandria, VA, 1999.

10. LEDRAY, LINDA E., R.N., PH.D (1994). *Recovering from rape.* New York, Henry Holt and Company, p. 227.

11. GROTH, A. N., et al. (1977). Rape: Power, anger and sexuality. *American Journal of Psychiatry,* vol. 134: 1239–1243.

12. Ibid.

13. Ibid.

14. Ibid.

15. Ibid.

16. Ibid.

17. HAZELWOOD R. and A. BURGESS (1987). *Practical aspects of rape investigation.*

18. Ibid.

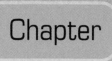
Missing and Abducted Persons

Key Terms

▶ Amber Alert
▶ family abduction
▶ labeling
▶ NCMEC
▶ NISMART
▶ noncustodial parent
▶ nonfamily abduction
▶ runaway or lost child

This chapter will enable you to:

- Understand the complexity of the nation's missing persons problem.

- Discuss the first responder's role in missing persons cases.

- Identify the steps in investigating missing and abducted persons.

- List and discuss the different categories of missing and abducted persons.

- Explain police supervisor responsibilities in missing persons cases.

- Identify guidelines for interviewing suspects in missing persons and abduction cases.

- Understand the investigator's role in missing and abducted persons cases.

INTRODUCTION

Shawn Hornbeck and Ben Ownby disappeared four and a half years and 40 miles apart. Police were stunned to find both boys alive and well in the same suburban St. Louis apartment. The shocking development on January 12, 2007, was viewed as a miracle by residents living in two rural Missouri communities: Richwoods, Missouri, where Shawn was 11 when he disappeared on October 6, 2002, and Beaufort, Missouri 40 miles to the north, where Ben, 13, hadn't been seen since getting off a school bus four days earlier.

A routine search warrant led police to investigate the Kirkwood, Missouri, apartment dweller, Michael Devlin, 41, a manager of a local pizzeria and part-time funeral home worker. Devlin was charged with first-degree kidnapping and held in the Franklin County Jail on $1 million bond.

The key to finding the boys was the spotting of a beat-up white pickup truck by a schoolmate of Ben's who got off the bus at the same time. The friend saw the pickup speeding away about the time Ben vanished from the gravel road near his home. An Amber Alert was promptly issued. The night before the boys were located, Kirkwood, Missouri, police officers were serving a warrant on an apartment complex when they noticed a white Nissan truck matching the description. They contacted the Franklin County Sheriff's Department and determined where the owner of the truck was; then they searched Devlin's home the following day and found the boys.

The two disappearances had similarities. Both boys seemed to vanish without a trace from quiet rural areas. Richwoods is about 50 miles southwest of St. Louis, in Washington County. Beaufort is about 60 miles from the city. Shawn Hornbeck, 15, disappeared from his rural home when he was 11. He went for a bike ride and never returned. His parents, dozens of volunteers, and sniffer dogs searched for weeks. The couple set up a Web site and listened to anyone who offered a tip. In the years since, Shawn's parents, Pam and Craig Akers, devoted themselves to missing child cases. They were reunited with their son in Union, the Franklin County seat where the sheriff's department is located.

Michael Devlin, the 41-year-old man accused of abducting the two Missouri boys, was not one of the usual suspects—and that may have kept police at bay for years. Devlin had no criminal record and no history that thrust him into the legal system and would have put authorities on notice. He was apparently so confident that he could escape detection in suburban Kirkwood that he chatted and joked with police who frequented the pizzeria he managed. Devlin even phoned officers last year, authorities say, to complain that a neighbor had taken his parking space. "He had the whole little town fooled," John Walsh, host of *America's Most Wanted,* said in an interview. "I'd say this is a pretty smart guy." Some of Devlin's neighbors even thought Shawn was his son.

The fact that Devlin could lead a double life and escape the scrutiny of friends, family, and co-workers for so many years has baffled many in the community and led investigators to ponder whether they did enough—or relied too heavily on mistaken assumptions—in looking for Shawn.

In the early days of the investigation of Shawn's disappearance, authorities focused on area residents with records of sexual misconduct involving children. Devlin, however, had little more on his record than a couple of traffic tickets. Police simply didn't have a lead.

Figure 15.1 Abducted boys Shawn Hornbeck (left) and Ben Ownby (below). Both boys were abducted by 41-year-old Michael Devlin and discovered in Devlin's home in January 2007. Devlin was arrested and awaits trial. *Tom Gannam, AP Wide World Photos and Jeff Roberson, AP Wide World Photos*

Standard investigative practice is to look closely at known child predators because child abduction is a crime that is not only compulsive but cyclical. Police don't only want to solve this case but prevent the next one from occurring. Officers in this case questioned whether they missed clues that were in plain sight. The *St. Louis Post-Dispatch* reported that a co-worker of Devlin's at Imo's Pizzeria tipped off police to similarities between Devlin's rusty white pickup truck and the one seen at the site of Ben Ownby's abduction, but the tip was not given top priority because Devlin had no criminal record.

This story illustrates the nature and reality of child abductions and the police response to them. In this case the children were fortunate to be returned unharmed and a suspect captured. This is not true, however, for many of the nation's abductions. This chapter will examine the problem of missing and abducted persons and identify the proper steps for criminal investigators to take in their hunt for the perpetrator.

A LOOK AT THE "BIG PICTURE"

While this chapter addresses missing and abducted persons in general, it will focus primarily on the thousands of children who are discovered missing each year. The magnitude of the missing and abducted problem is complex, multifaceted, and disturbing. For example, there are different types of missing children, including family abductions; endangered runaways; nonfamily abductions; and lost, injured, or otherwise missing children. National estimates for the number of missing children are from incidence studies conducted by the U.S. Department of Justice's Office of Juvenile Justice and Delinquency Prevention.

Over the past 26 years, reports of missing persons have increased sixfold, from roughly 150,000 in 1980 to about 900,000 in 2006.[1] The increase was driven in part by the country's growing population, but the numbers also indicate that law enforcement treats missing persons cases more seriously now. In 2005, an alarming 2,300 Americans were reported missing every day, including both adults and children, but only a fraction of those are what could be characterized as "stereotypical" abductions or kidnappings by a stranger.

For example, the U.S. Justice Department identified 840,279 missing persons cases in 2001. All but about 50,000 were juveniles, classified as anyone younger than 18. The National Center for Missing Adults, in Phoenix, Arizona, consistently tracks about 48,000 "active cases," although that number has increased by nearly 11,000 due to reports of persons missing after the hurricanes of 2006.

Slightly more than half—about 25,500—of the missing are men. About four out of 10 missing adults are white, three of 10 black, and two of 10 Latino. Among missing adults, about one-sixth have psychiatric problems. Young men, people with drug or alcohol addictions, and elderly citizens suffering from dementia make up other significant subgroups of missing adults.

About half of the roughly 800,000 missing juvenile cases in 2005 involved runaways, and another 200,000 were classified as family abductions related to domestic or custody disputes. Only about 100 missing child reports each year fit the profile of a stereotypical abduction by a stranger or vague acquaintance. Two-thirds of those victims are ages 12 to 17, and among those eight out of 10 are white females, according to a Justice Department study. Nearly 90 percent of the abductors are men, and they sexually assault their victims in half of the cases.[2]

With regard to missing children, obtaining an accurate and clear picture of the missing child in America is a difficult task. The complexities of the issue result from the changing definition of what actually constitutes a "missing" or "abducted" child. "Missing" is a term that is widely used in law enforcement, and if a child is missing under virtually any conditions, even if the circumstances are simply a misunderstanding of where the child should be, that incident is counted as a missing child. Parental abductions, which constitute the vast majority of abducted juveniles are, statistically, not as physically harmful to the victim as stranger abductions. Parents in those situations are often involved in a custodial feud with their spouses. The most serious type of abductions, which are classified as "stereotypical kidnappings," tend to be the least common and are often the most dangerous. Over 40 percent of these incidents end with the child's death.

In an early effort to define the missing child problem, the National Incidence Studies of Missing, Abducted, Runaway and Thrownaway Children, known as **NISMART,** initiated a massive research project in 1988. A more recent updated survey was conducted in 1999 and is known as NISMART 2, sponsored by the Department of Justice. As of the preparation of this text, NISMART 2 is the most up-to-date, reliable database on missing children available.[3] In compiling the national data, NISMART expanded the collected information to reflect the population as a whole.

There are three major definitions used in the data to describe the varying circumstances of child abduction. The first is called a nonfamily abduction. NISMART 2 describes this event when "a nonfamily perpetrator takes a child by the use of physical force or threat or detains a child for at least 1 hour in an isolated place without lawful authority." NISMART defines a stereotypical kidnapping as "when a stranger or slight acquaintance perpetrates a nonfamily abduction in which the child is detained overnight, transported at least 50 miles, held for ransom, abducted with the intent to keep the child permanently, or killed." A "family abduction" occurs when "in violation of a custody order a member of the child's family takes or fails to return a child and the child is concealed or transported out of State with the intent to prevent contact."

According to the NISMART survey, more than 203,900 children are abducted by a family member in America each year. The majority of these are abducted by one of their parents during a custodial dispute. These types of incidents usually end with the child returned to the rightful parent and the offender charged with custodial-related offenses. About 46 percent were gone for less than a week. About 21 percent were gone for more than a month. Only 6 percent were not returned to the rightful parent. On occasion, the offender can be charged with kidnapping. Parents who abduct their own children are not usually motivated by violence nor do they have profit as a goal. These incidents are driven by hostility between parents with the innocent child caught in the middle.

The Statistical Breakdown

During the time period studied in the NISMART survey, an estimated 58,200 children were victimized in nonfamily abductions. In these abductions, 53 percent were committed by persons known to the victim, such as a friend, neighbor, or a babysitter. About 75 percent of the perpetrators of nonfamily abductions are male. The victim most often (81 percent) was between the ages of 12 and 17 and most often (65 percent) female. In a finding that conforms with public perception, NISMART found that 71 percent of these abductions occurred outdoors: the street, park, a car, or in a wooded area. Less than 5 percent took place in the victim's own home or yard. The motivations for these abductions were a physical or sexual assault in 77 percent of the cases. The duration of the crime was less than 24 hours in 90 percent of the cases, and the child was returned alive 99 percent of the time.[4]

Profiling the Abductor

A kidnapping is the type of abduction that is most harmful to the child, both psychologically and physically. Many child abductions also involve some type of sexual abuse. An earlier study funded by the Justice Department's Office of Juvenile Justice and Delinquency Prevention (OJJDP) provided additional insight on the child abduction problem. This 1997 survey examined 600 abduction cases across the nation. Findings were very similar to the NISMART project.[5]

In brief, the OJJDP study concluded that the most typical victim in a child abduction murder was an 11-year-old white female from a middle-class neighborhood. This mirrors the NISMART finding that 69 percent of the victims were female and 80 percent were less than 14 years old. The suspect in the case had been arrested for prior offenses against children 53 percent of the time, and the most common crime was sexual in nature. The abductor was usually a white male, single, about 27 years old, either unemployed or worked in unskilled jobs, and lived alone or with parents. NISMART found that the suspect was less than 29 years old in 67 percent of the cases.

At the time of the abduction, the offender had a legitimate reason for being at the scene of the crime. These reasons included: (1) a residence near the site and (2) some type of social activity or work-related duties. Over 57 percent of these types of abductions were considered crimes of opportunity. The method of abduction in 65 percent of the incidents consisted of a sighting, a sudden assault, and a swift abduction. In 53 percent of the incidents, the first contact between victim and suspect took place near the child's home. In 33 percent of the cases, the contact took place less than 200 feet from the home. NISMART concluded that only 5 percent of stranger abductions took place in the victim's home or yard.

The most reliable research available indicates that there are only 100–130 cases of stranger abductions a year in the United States. These events are most frequently committed by males (86 percent) who are between the ages of 20 and 39 (57 percent). Again, the child was taken from an outdoor area in 54 percent of the cases, but in 16 percent of the cases, the victim was abducted from his own yard or home. In the wider category of nonfamily abduction, NISMART found that 71 percent of the victims were taken from an outdoor area. In stereotypical kidnappings, less than 7 percent were taken from a store or mall. Stranger abduction events are usually committed for sexual purposes (49 percent), and in over 40 percent of the cases, the victim was murdered. That is in addition to the 4 percent that have never been found.

The FBI handled 93 cases of stranger abductions cases in 2001. That figure is actually a decrease from years past, especially during the 1980s when the average hovered around 200 incidents a year. Though the victim in most of these cases did not know the suspect, there was previous contact between them prior to the crime. This contact was usually a brief visual observation that took place while the suspect had a legitimate reason for being where he was. Those

A Closer Look
The Case of Elizabeth Smart

In 2002, 14-year-old Elizabeth Smart was abducted at gunpoint from her home in Salt Lake City. After a considerable amount of publicity and a search conducted by literally thousands of police and volunteers, investigators were unable to develop solid leads in the case. It wasn't until Elizabeth's own younger sister recalled a workman who visited the Smart home in 2001 that a suspect was developed.

On March 12, 2003, almost nine months after she was abducted, Brian David Mitchell, 49, was arrested and charged with kidnapping. Elizabeth was found in his custody and safely returned to her parents. During her captivity, she was allegedly sexually assaulted several times. Later, it was discovered that her mother, Lois Smart, had picked up Mitchell off the street in downtown Salt Lake City in 2001 and brought him home to do some minor chores. Mitchell had spent several hours raking leaves and repairing the roof. During that time, he also observed Elizabeth who was home at the time.

The Smart kidnapping emphasizes several characteristics that child abductors seem to have in common. First, they most often have a prior visual sighting of the victim, and the initial contact is frequently made at or near the home. Secondly, the motivation for the crime is often sexual in nature. The victim is usually a female under 14, and the suspect is an unemployed white male with a criminal record. Though the alleged kidnapper, Brian Mitchell, was 20 years older than the NISMART average, he fit the profile reasonably well. Elizabeth Smart could be considered a very lucky victim. That's because females her age, who are abducted under similar circumstances, stand a very good chance of being killed.

reasons included work-related activities, such as a home delivery, a store clerk, a drive-by, in a park, or at a sporting event. In over 85 percent of the cases, the child was kept within 50 miles of the abduction location, and most frequently (28 percent), the victim was held in the home of the suspect.

The duration of a kidnapping episode was usually less than 24 hours (90 percent). Only less than 10 percent lasted longer than one day. Nonfamily abductions showed the same patterns though 30 percent lasted less than even 3 hours. The most dramatic difference between nonfamily abductions and kidnappings was in the treatment of the victim. In 99 percent of nonfamily abductions, the child was returned alive. In kidnappings, a safe return occurred only 57 percent of the time. Ominously, the child suffered a sexual or physical assault in an astounding 86 percent of the stereotypical kidnappings. These findings powerfully emphasize the extreme danger of these events and the urgency of police interaction as soon as possible.

Stereotypical kidnapping, in which a child is abducted and either assaulted or held for ransom, is a crime that first appeared in the United States in the late nineteenth century. During the 1920s, it became entrenched in the public consciousness when a series of child abduction cases terrified parents across the country.

Types of Missing Children Cases

In general, missing children cases fall into three basic categories, nonfamily abduction, family abduction, and runaway (or lost).

The **nonfamily abduction** case, in which a child is removed without authorization from his family by force or trickery, is the most complex and dangerous type of missing child case. In this situation, time is of the essence because the child is considered to be in great danger. Many experts believe that the first few hours after an abduction are the most dangerous for children.

Also included in this category are abductions of newborns and infants from health care facilities, malls, grocery stores, and public transportation facilities, as well as other public places where the mother's or child care provider's attention may be diverted. While the snatching of newborns is not a crime of epidemic proportions, naturally, it causes tremendous trauma for the parents/guardians. The offender almost always is a female and generally does not harm the baby since she usually abducts the child in order to have a baby of her own.

The second type of case is the **family abduction,** which generally occurs in conjunction with divorce and separation. In this type of case, the noncustodial parent removes the child from the care of the custodial parent and may flee to another state or even another country with the child. The child may be at risk with the noncustodial parent. There have been recent cases across the nation in which the child of a family abduction was murdered by the noncustodial parent, who then committed suicide. Family abductions are often very complex cases involving court orders, child protection services, and hidden agendas, as well as raw emotions and sometimes extreme possessiveness toward the children on the part of one or both parents.

The third type of missing child case involves the **runaway or lost child,** who could be in great danger depending on such factors as age, maturity, and intelligence. The voluntary runaway child is the most common missing child case encountered by law enforcement officers.

Abductions via the Internet

Some child abductions have been connected to the Internet as a result of the easy access both child and predator have to this worldwide communications network. Susceptible pre-teens or teens are sometimes lured into false friendships in Internet "chat rooms" and then kidnapped from a prearranged meeting place. In other cases, the abductor may send the child money and a bus ticket to meet in another state. Children and teens who get involved in "chat room" conversations on the Internet have no way to know exactly who they're talking to. One of the many attractions of "chat rooms" is the anonymity they provide. People can be anyone they choose to be online, where real identities are hidden and fictitious names and personalities emerge.

In one case, a preteen boy was lured to San Francisco by an adult male pedophile with a large collection of child pornography. The youth told his friends at school and showed them the bus ticket and money he was sent. His friends revealed this information to the police only after the boy was reported missing. A nationwide search was initiated, and they were questioned.

How do investigators determine if a missing child case involves an Internet lure? A computer in a child's room or home with an Internet connection can steer the investigation in this direction, especially if the parents/guardians reveal that the child spent a lot of time "online" and talked about new friends made via "chat rooms." Another clue is the sudden disappearance of the child for no apparent reason. For example, there was no recent fight between the child and parents, yet the child was gone one day when the parents returned from work. In

Figure 15.2 In September 2006, police arrested Vinson Filyaw in Richland County about 24 hours after rescuing abduction victim Elizabeth Shoaf. Shoaf, who was held captive underground, had sent a text message to her mother on Filyaw's phone while he was asleep. *Kershaw County Sheriff Office, AP Wide World Photos*

Figure 15.3 A hole in the ground where Filyaw kept hostage Elizabeth Shoaf less than one mile from her home. *Jim Davenport, AP Wide World Photos*

Figure 15.4 Trailer where Vinson Filyaw resided. *Mary Ann Chastain, AP Wide World Photos*

a case like this, check to see whether the child took any favorite possessions, a suitcase, duffle bag or backpack, clothes, or money. Missing possessions indicate a runaway, but runaways are not always what they appear to be.

Other clues to the child's disappearance can be found in the computer itself. The computer may yield electronic mail (e-mail) saved on the hard drive, a disk, or a printout. The child may have left notes in schoolbooks that would provide clues, such as the online friend's address, phone number, or e-mail address. Before searching computers for data and evidence, the investigator should consult with the department attorney as well as agency computer specialists since complex investigations involving computer systems and online access services present unique technical, operational, and legal problems.

The Investigative Response

From an investigative standpoint, child kidnapping is one of the most emotionally charged and difficult criminal cases for the law enforcement officer. Time is the merciless enemy. In 1997, the U.S. Office of Juvenile Justice Delinquency and Prevention (OJJDP) reported that most children (74 percent) who are murdered during stranger kidnappings are killed within the first few hours of the event. Therefore it is imperative that investigators utilize every tool available to them including the awesome power of the media.

Amber Alerts, which President George W. Bush signed into law in 2003, provide for blanket media coverage whenever a child is kidnapped. In addition, government funds have been allocated to maintain and improve the national alert network. From the initial responder to each and every member of the investigative team, it is critical that a full agency response be enacted to ensure the safe return of the victim.

The Initial Call for Assistance

The initial response to a missing child call is perhaps the most crucial component of the investigation. The manner in which patrol officers respond to the initial call often determines whether the child is found quickly and returned home safely, remains missing for months or years, or is never found.

In most law enforcement agencies, the patrol officer is the first responder to a missing child call. Therefore, all patrol officers need to be trained to respond to such calls efficiently, compassionately, and professionally—paying particular attention to safeguarding evidence, quickly obtaining as much information as possible about the child and the circumstances, interviewing witnesses, and at the same time calming and reassuring the parents or guardians of the missing child. But before the patrol officer even arrives on the scene, information about the missing child should be relayed from the dispatcher to the responding officers. Dispatch operators, working with a standard list of predetermined questions, should gather pertinent information from the caller and relay it to the responding officers. Once the dispatch operator has calmed the caller, basic facts and information can be gathered to help responding officers, including a brief description of the missing child and information about a possible abductor(s).

Dispatch personnel should, to the degree possible, also provide responding officers with an overview of any agency records concerning the child and family, such as: (1) history of violence or child abuse calls; (2) criminal activities of family members or other persons living at the address (arrests, narcotics, etc.); (3) runaway reports on the child or siblings; and (4) juvenile delinquency reports on the child or siblings. In addition, dispatch personnel should check to determine if there have been recent problems regarding children in the neighborhood. Such information could disclose many things: complaints about prowlers, indecent exposure incidents, attempted abductions, convicted child molesters living in the neighborhood, and the like.

Department policy should provide for an immediate city- or countywide radio alert to all other patrol units and all neighboring law enforcement agencies. Even though such an alert may not contain precise factual information about the missing child or circumstances in this early stage, these immediate radio broadcasts often result in prompt, safe recoveries, particularly when a small child has simply wandered away from home and become lost.

A judgment must be made as to when a person is to be declared as "missing" and the corresponding issue of when a missing persons report should be filed. The responsibility for these determinations lies primarily with knowledgeable reporting parties: persons who are in a position to know the behavioral patterns and character of the individual involved—such as parents, guardians, or close personal friends—and who are also often the best judges of what is highly unusual, irregular, or suspicious behavior with regard to the individual's whereabouts. As such, there should be no mandatory waiting period for filing a missing persons report, and such reports should be allowed to be filed either personally or by telephone. The response by law enforcement includes steps to be taken by the responding officer, the supervisor at the scene, and the case investigator.

RESPONDING OFFICER RESPONSIBILITIES

It is the patrol officer who initially establishes the seriousness of the complaint about a missing child, safeguards the scene, gathers crucial facts, and conducts preliminary interviews of witnesses. For this reason, patrol officers must learn to become as thorough as they can in responding to missing child reports. Assumptions about such cases must be avoided, or officers may overlook crucial information and evidence.

To initiate a successful missing persons investigation, the first responder must focus on quickly gathering factual information and safeguarding potential evidence. This is particularly the case with regard to missing children, whether they may be abducted, runaway, or lost. This may also be true of some elderly persons or others who, because of physical or mental disability or reduced functioning, are not fully capable of taking care of themselves. The elderly, especially those suffering from Alzheimer's disease or similar problems, present specific concerns as the subjects of missing persons reports. Open terrain searches for missing persons in general also require adherence to professionally recognized search management principles. Some of the most widely accepted principles of searching for missing persons are discussed later in this chapter.

The patrol officer who responds to the call is best suited to obtain the details of the initial account, particularly since the officer patrols the area or neighborhood and is likely to notice any unusual activities or suspicious persons. The officer should respond to the call promptly, since the time factor is often crucial, especially in cases involving abductions by strangers.

In 1994, the National Center for Missing and Exploited Children (**NCMEC**) developed a checklist for first responders in missing children cases, listing tasks an officer should complete to ensure a successful investigation.[6] These steps are general, but they do provide a framework for the officer's actions.

The Sixteen Steps of Investigation

Sixteen tasks commonly associated with the responsibilities of the first responder are identified in this chapter. However, it is recognized that in the real world many tasks of first responders, supervisors, and investigators are not distinctly

Figure 15.5 Stephanie Quackenbush stands on the sidewalk in Albany, N.Y., where in 2005 she escaped from a man who tried to abduct her. She later testified at the attacker's trial. *Tim Roske*

or conveniently divided between these respective agency personnel. The following sixteen steps are those that should nominally be taken by officers. It should be understood that not every step may pertain to all situations nor do the steps need to be addressed in the exact order in which they are presented in this book.

Step 1: Interview parents/person who made the initial report to the emergency operations center (EOC).   This interview should be conducted in an area where interruptions are minimal and preferably in private. The purpose of the interview is to obtain a complete description of the missing child, circumstances of how the child came to be missing, and information necessary to make an initial definition and assessment of the type of case. *Case example:* The complainant may be the operator of a preschool who reports that the child was approached by a man whom the child called "Daddy" and the man then put the child in a car and left without speaking to any of the adults at the school. One of the teachers, however, obtained the license tag number of the car. Further questioning of the complainant reveals that the child's parents are divorced and engaged in a bitter custody dispute, although the court has awarded custody to the mother. The officer can make a preliminary assessment that this is a family abduction that may not warrant calling in additional personnel. *Consider another case example:* The mother of a five-year-old girl calls from the mall reporting her daughter missing; the line of questioning and initial actions of the responding officer should be very different from the above since all initial signs point to a possible abduction by a stranger.

Step 2: Verify that the child is in fact missing.   Here the officer needs to make certain that the child cannot be located on the premises or nearby. In the preschool case above, three teachers and 40 children (ranging in age from two through five) saw the missing boy (age three) run and greet his father and then leave in the car. At the flea market, a search of the grounds by security officers failed to turn up the missing five-year-old girl. However, when the patrol officer asked the mother if she had checked her vehicle in the parking lot, the mother said no. The officer went with the mother to the parking lot and found the girl asleep on the back floor of the family van, which had been left unlocked. The little girl said she was tired and went to take a nap without telling her mother because "Mommy was talking to the lady about the furniture, and Mommy told me not to interrupt when grown-ups are talking to each other. So I just came to the van to take a nap." Case closed.

Before beginning an area search, ask those at the scene if a search has already been conducted, and if so, what areas were covered. Officers should never assume that searches conducted, often by distraught parents or others, have been performed in a thorough manner. However, under exigent circumstances, prior search efforts may help officers focus on other alternatives even if their intention is to research those same areas as time permits. Officers should make a quick check of the house and grounds for small children, looking in such places as closets, refrigerators, large boxes and vehicles in garages, storage sheds, under shrubbery, in doghouses, under beds, and behind furniture. The child may have been playing hide-and-seek with an imaginary playmate and fallen asleep. In the case of teenagers overdue home by several hours, the officer should ask the parents if they've checked their answering machine for messages. Perhaps the teenager left a note in the kitchen explaining the absence, and the parents did not find the note. A variety of possible explanations are possible in apparent missing persons cases depending on the circumstances involved, and concerned parents sometimes overlook the obvious.

Step 3: Verify the child's custody status. With divorce so prevalent in the United States and custody battles a common denominator in the lives of many children, the patrol officer should ask the parent if there has been a divorce or separation and, if so, which parent has primary legal custody. If there has been a marital breakup, the officer should raise the issue of a possible abduction of the child by the **noncustodial parent.** Another area of inquiry involves possible emotional problems affecting the child; if the child is taking the parental breakup badly and falsely assuming blame, the child may have run away. All these issues must be explored, no matter how insensitive the questions may seem under the circumstances.

Step 4: Identify the circumstances of the disappearance. Did the child disappear from home or from the residence of a relative or friend? Is the child missing after a visit with a noncustodial parent? Is the child missing from a public place, such as a shopping mall, park, amusement center, or school playground? Was the child seen talking to a stranger? Did the child disappear while the parent/guardian's attention was focused elsewhere, such as paying for a purchase or loading groceries into a vehicle? The NCMEC lists several unusual circumstances that alert the first responding patrol officer to "pull out all the stops" by requesting additional personnel, supervisory and investigative assistance, and any special support units that may be needed, such as K-9 and helicopters. The need for other resources, such as assistance from other law enforcement agencies, fire department search and rescue teams, neighborhood watch teams, and others, can be determined by a field supervisor. Unusual circumstances that may require such additional resources include the following:

- The missing child is 13 years old or younger.
- The missing child is believed to be out of the zone of safety for his or her age and developmental stage.
- The missing child is mentally incapacitated, has attempted or threatened suicide, or has a history of self-destructive behavior.
- The missing child is drug-dependent, including prescribed medication and/or illegal substances, and the dependency is potentially life-threatening.
- The missing child has been absent from home for more than 24 hours before being reported to the police.
- Based on available information, it is believed that the missing child is in the company of adults who could endanger his or her welfare.
- Based on available information, it is determined that the missing child is in a life-threatening situation.
- The absence is inconsistent with the child's established patterns of behavior, and the deviation cannot be readily explained.
- Other circumstances are involved in the disappearance that would cause a reasonable person to conclude that the child should be considered "at risk."

When one or more of these circumstances are present, the patrol officer should take immediate action and call for mobilization of additional resources.

A Closer Look

The Polly Klaas Abduction

On the night of October 1, 1993, 12-year-old Polly Klaas was hosting a slumber party for two of her friends. It was her first sleep-over party ever, and the girls were having a fun time, laughing, hiding under the covers. When Polly went to retrieve pillows from another room, she was confronted by a large-framed man armed with a knife. He threatened to kill the girls if they did not do as he asked.

The man kidnapped Polly and fled the home. Within a few minutes the girls went screaming to Polly's mother. The police quickly responded, and soon, the entire area was filled with cops. Because the girls had gotten a good look at the suspect, police had a detailed description and were able to assemble a composite that was widely publicized. Perhaps no other poster of a kidnap victim and suspect was ever so universally circulated as that of Polly Klaas. She was a beautiful child with long dark hair. Her image was literally everywhere, on television, in supermarkets, gas stations, department stores, even overseas. The search went on for weeks.

A career criminal named Richard Allen Davis, 39, was arrested on November 30 for trespassing on private property on the night of Polly's abduction. A few days later, he confessed to her murder and led police to her body. Davis said he strangled her to prevent her from identifying him. He said that he did not sexually assault Polly, though investigators did not believe him. After a trial, which took place in June 1996, Richard Allen Davis was found guilty of first-degree murder and sentenced to death.

It is always better to overreact when a child's life may be in danger. Resources can be demobilized quickly if it is determined later that they are not needed.

Step 5: Determine when, where, and by whom the missing child was last seen.   For example, if the child disappeared while the parent or guardian was paying for groceries, did any of the cashiers, store employees, or other shoppers see the child leave the store with anyone? If the child disappeared while walking to school, did any residents or delivery persons on the child's route witness the child getting into a vehicle? Interview everyone who may have been in a position to see the child.

Step 6: Interview the individuals who last had contact with the child.   It is especially important to interview the child's friends if the child is a pre-teen or teenager. Friends of older children often know more about the child's attitudes, emotions, and plans than the parents or guardians. Perhaps friends will reveal that the child is having trouble with his father and is staying with another friend. A teacher may reveal that the child's noncustodial parent came to the school to get permission to remove the child from school because the child was being taken to a dental appointment. In the case of a child missing from a public place, it is important to interview those persons operating stores, concessions, or amusements that may have attracted the child's attention, leading the child to wander away from parents or guardians. For example, if a small boy wandered into a video arcade, was given quarters by an adult man to play games, and then left the arcade with the man, the operator of the arcade should be able to provide a description of the circumstances and the suspect, along with time frames.

Step 7: Identify the child's zone of safety for his or her age and developmental stage. Try to determine how far the child could travel from the spot where last seen before he or she would most likely be at risk of being injured or exploited. This perimeter should define the first immediate search zone under many circumstances.

Step 8: Make an initial determination of the type of incident. Based on the available information, determine whether the incident appears to be a nonfamily abduction; family abduction; endangered runaway; or lost, injured, or otherwise missing person. This initial classification will help the officer begin investigative actions. To make the initial classification, the officer should analyze the information already gathered. However, officers must be extremely cautious in **labeling,** or classifying, a missing child case, since the classification process will affect the way in which initial evidence or information is gathered. As the NCMEC advises, even if the initial information suggests a classification into a category considered to be "less urgent," officers should run "parallel investigations" that take all possibilities into account until the case category is clearly determined.

Step 9: Obtain a detailed description of the missing child, suspected abductor(s), vehicles, and the like. If there are several people at the scene, each person should be interviewed separately by the officer to obtain descriptions of a possible suspect and vehicle. Witnesses should not be interviewed in the presence of other witnesses, since there is a tendency on the part of some to "go along"—either consciously or unconsciously with a description given by another witness. As most officers know, the perception and recall of witnesses can be faulty, and when they use one another to fill in missing details in their memory, important details may be lost.

Step 10: Relay detailed descriptive information to the EOC for relay to other law enforcement agencies and information referral sources. Supervisors, in consultation with the public information officer or agency chief executive, may decide at this time to provide descriptive information to the news media to generate assistance from the public in locating the missing child or encouraging any witnesses to come forward.

Step 11: Ensure that any remaining persons at the scene are identified and interviewed and information properly recorded. To aid in this process, if possible, take pictures or videotape everyone present. Note the name, address, and home/business telephone numbers of each person. Determine each person's relationship to the missing child, if any. Note information that each person may have about the child's disappearance. Determine when/where each person last saw the child. Ask each one: "What do you think happened to the child?" Obtain names, addresses, and telephone numbers of the child's friends and other relatives and friends of the family. Friends, relatives, and neighbors may reveal that there are problems in the home, the child is frequently abused (either verbally or physically), the father or "live-in" boyfriend has a "hot temper," or the mother drinks during the day and screams at the kids. This type of sensitive information may be elicited by the officer; the person being interviewed can be assured of privacy and told that the information provided will not be given to family members. Such information can provide important clues to investigators as to the type of case: a homicide by parents or guardians with lies told to police to cover up the crime; a stranger abduction; or a "runaway" or abused child.

Step 12: Continue to update the emergency dispatcher and other appropriate department personnel.   Periodically update the public information officer or department spokesperson. If there is no media relations officer or supervisor on the scene handling these duties, the senior officer at the scene may be asked to provide periodic updates to media personnel. Under such circumstances, the officer must follow the agency's media relations policies and procedures, being careful not to release information that could jeopardize an investigation, falsely accuse individuals, or inadvertently implicate anyone in a crime.

Step 13: Obtain and record permission to search houses or buildings.   This includes any locations where the incident took place or where entry is required to conduct the investigation. To search a house or apartment, obtain the permission of the owner/renter. In the case of a building, such as a shopping mall or store, obtain the manager's permission or the permission of any private security firm working on the premises. Be sure to search any surrounding areas, including vehicles, parking lots, storage sheds, garbage containers, truck trailers at loading docks, warehouse areas behind stores, construction sites, shrubbery, culverts, and other places of concealment.

Even if the child was reported missing from a public place, such as a shopping mall, it is highly advisable to seek permission for a thorough search of the child's home. In some recent cases, the child was murdered in the home, leaving bloodstain evidence, and, after disposing the body, the parents/guardians drove to a public place (mall, gas station, etc.), called the police, and reported that the child had been abducted from that location. By not searching the home, vital evidence of a crime can be lost.

Step 14: Secure and safeguard the crime scene.   This includes securing the area where the incident took place or the location at which the child was last seen as a crime scene in order to safeguard vital evidence. The patrol officer must take control of the immediate area where the incident occurred and establish an appropriate perimeter to avoid destruction of vital evidence.

It is not uncommon for even well-intentioned citizens at a public site to overrun a crime scene, inadvertently destroying or otherwise carrying off such evidence as fibers, hair, cigarette butts, dropped credit card slips and driver's licenses, a weapon, or other possessions with fingerprints. Pedestrian and vehicular traffic at such locations can also destroy any scent trails that may be used by canine teams to track the missing child. Under exigent circumstances and until backup arrives, the patrol officer may obtain assistance from store managers, private security officers, school principals, and other trusted authority figures to block off crime scenes. As soon as possible, backup should be requested to help safeguard a potential crime scene.

At the child's home or crime scene, items of evidential value and other personal effects that may assist in locating the child should be protected and, if appropriate, collected. This includes, but is not limited to, the child's personal articles such as hairbrush, diary, photographs, and items with the child's fingerprints, footprints, or teeth impressions. The contents and appearance of the child's room and residence should be noted. If possible, photographs or videotapes of these areas should be taken.

The child's current bedsheets can be collected, if appropriate, for use by search dog teams and, under some circumstances, may be necessary for later crime laboratory analysis. Recent photos and family videos may also be useful for release to the media if this option becomes necessary. In many cases, widespread use of a child's photo in the media has precipitated telephone tips that have successfully concluded investigations.

The officer should also obtain a set of the child's fingerprints if the parents have had a set prepared as a crime prevention measure. If a fingerprint card is not available, secure items from the child's room that are likely to contain prints, such as a smooth plastic or metal toy, drinking glass, TV remote control, comic books, or game boxes.

Officers should adhere to established department policies and procedures for crime scene processing. However, in addition, when investigating cases of missing children, officers are advised to treat the crime scene processing assignment with a "worst-case scenario" in mind.

Step 15: Obtain photos, videotapes, and any other identifying information on suspects.

In particular, any photos of the suspect should be relayed to the shift commander as soon as possible. In some cases, the first responder may be able to secure photos/videos. For example, store security cameras may provide valuable videotape. In other cases, such as an abduction by a noncustodial parent, the custodial parent or child's school may be able to provide a current photograph, address, place of employment, and other identifying information. Where a license tag number can help identify a suspect, the state department of motor vehicles can generally quickly provide a photo. If the suspect has an arrest record, photos may be available in local, state, or federal law enforcement records systems.

Step 16: Prepare reports and make all required notifications.

Ensure that information about the missing child is entered into the FBI's National Crime Information Center (NCIC) Missing Persons File and that any information on a suspected abductor is entered into the NCIC Wanted Persons File.

The NCMEC recommends that a law enforcement agency take several other steps to publicize the incident, in order to receive tips from the public and obtain help with a widespread search. These measures, which usually are carried out by administrative personnel rather than the first responder/patrol officer, include:

1. Ensure that the details of the case have been reported to the NCMEC.
2. Prepare and update bulletins for local law enforcement agencies, state missing children's clearinghouses, FBI, and other appropriate agencies.
3. Prepare a flyer/bulletin with the child and suspected abductor's photographs and descriptive information. Distribute in appropriate geographical regions.
4. Secure the child's latest medical and dental records. These may be necessary to positively identify the child.
5. Establish a telephone hotline to receive tips and leads from the public.
6. Establish a leads management system to prioritize leads and ensure that each one undergoes a review and follow-up.

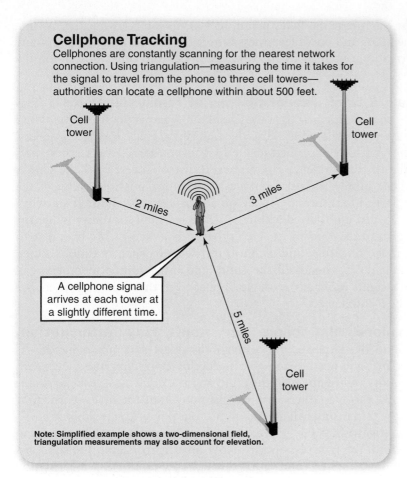

Cellphone Tracking
Cellphones are constantly scanning for the nearest network connection. Using triangulation—measuring the time it takes for the signal to travel from the phone to three cell towers—authorities can locate a cellphone within about 500 feet.

Cell tower

Cell tower

2 miles

3 miles

5 miles

A cellphone signal arrives at each tower at a slightly different time.

Cell tower

Note: Simplified example shows a two-dimensional field, triangulation measurements may also account for elevation.

Figure 15.6   In 2006, 26-year-old Vinson Filyaw abducted 14-year-old Elizabeth Shoaf as she stepped off a school bus. Shoaf was kept in an underground bunker where she text-messaged her mother from Filyaw's cellphone while he slept. Police tracked Filyaw's phone to locate her. Cellphone tracking technology is shown here. *Copyright 2006,* USA Today. *Reprinted with permission.*

THE INVESTIGATOR'S ROLE

Many of the duties of the investigator in a missing/abducted child case are the same as those used in conducting almost any type of investigation. Indeed, some have been referenced in foregoing chapters related to the first responding officer and supervisory responsibilities. However, there are eight basic steps that investigative officers can take to help ensure a successful outcome in a missing/abducted child case. These procedures are geared more toward nonfamily abduction cases and those situations in which a child disappears and could be in danger. Family abduction and runaway (or lost) child investigative procedures are covered in depth in NCMEC's manual.

Step 1: Obtain a detailed briefing from the first responding officer and other on-scene personnel.   The investigator should debrief the first responding officer before conducting any interviews with family members of the missing child or witnesses who may have been identified in the early stages of the case. A thorough debriefing of the first responder will help the investigator analyze the information in order to formulate an approach to upcoming interviews of family members and witnesses.

Step 2: Verify the accuracy of all descriptive information.   The verification process should include all other details developed during the preliminary investigation. At this point the investigator will begin interviewing the missing child's family members and possible witnesses to determine facts and sort out any conflicting information obtained by the first responder and other officers on the scene.

Step 3: Obtain a brief, recent history of family dynamics.   This process will help the investigator hypothesize about various possibilities involving the disappearance of the child. Was the family the truly loving, close-knit family the mother tearfully described to the first responder? Or were there previous police calls to the residence for domestic disturbances? Has the child's school reported the family to social service agencies for possible abuse of the child? Is there a large life insurance policy on a four-year-old child? If so, why? Is the missing little girl an "ugly duckling" with a learning disability while the mother is the glamorous "prom queen" type with a live-in boyfriend who spends all his money on drugs and alcohol? Answers to such questions, often obtained from neighbors, friends of the child, and other family members, can offer invaluable insights to what may have happened to the child and where the child may now be located.

Step 4: Explore the basis for conflicting information. Information offered by witnesses and other individuals may not coincide. As such, the investigator will need to conduct in-depth fact-finding interviews with all witnesses, friends, and relatives of the child and the child's parents/guardians necessary to resolve those conflicts. It is at this point that the investigator may consider asking the parents/guardians to submit to a polygraph examination.

After the investigator has interviewed all relevant persons, it is necessary to meet once again with the first responder, fellow investigators, and the supervising officer to "compare notes" and work through any conflicting information gathered in the course of the investigation. This collaborative process should provide the investigative staff with a solid foundation upon which to structure the future direction of the case.

Step 5: Review and evaluate all available information and evidence.   At this point, an information management system becomes a critical tool in the investigative process. The investigator should designate another investigator, a crime analyst, or a patrol officer to serve as the case information manager, centralizing all data as they are gathered, making comparisons, and keeping track of leads and tips. Appointing one person to be in charge of all information pertaining to the case helps ensure that valuable data will not become misdirected and possibly lost.

Depending on the resources available to the agency, data may be computerized or incorporated into a simple card system, in which facts are indexed for cross-reference and easily available for prompt review. The method of filing does not matter as long as the system works for the investigator in charge of solving the case.

Once the incoming data and evidence have been organized, reviewed, and evaluated, the investigator can develop and execute an investigative follow-up plan and secure necessary additional resources, personnel, and specialized services.

Step 6: Develop an investigative plan for follow-up.   By evaluating evidence and the information gathered from interviews of police officers, witnesses, the child's parents/guardians, and others, the investigator can prepare a follow-up plan which may include the following tasks:

1. Conduct more in-depth interviews with specific people who have been questioned previously.
2. Set up lead-tracking policies and procedures.
3. Gather more complete background information on the missing child, parents/guardians, and possible suspects.
4. Reevaluate the scene and conduct a more detailed search.
5. Canvass the neighborhood to locate potential witnesses and information.
6. Search the child's home even if the child is missing from another location.
7. Obtain search warrants when consent for a search is denied.
8. Administer polygraph examinations to the parents/guardians if officers and investigators suspect they are not telling the truth or something seems awry.
9. Contact social service agencies and the child's school to determine whether the child's family was the subject of abuse investigations or had other problems that may be significant to the progress of the investigation.

Step 7: Determine what additional resources and specialized services are required. At this point, the investigator's assessment of the type of incident (e.g., abducted child, possible abduction, family abduction, lost child, or runaway) should help determine what additional assistance may be needed both from within the department and from outside agencies. For example, the investigator may have been told by a relative of the child that the child's parents appeared in family court to answer child neglect charges. The investigator can save time by asking the police juvenile officer to follow up this lead with the family court and social service agency assigned to the family's case. The juvenile officer could also contact teachers where the missing child attends school and might even interview parents of the child's playmates.

If an abduction is suspected, and it can be assumed that the child may be transported to another jurisdiction, the investigator may want to contact the FBI for help, along with the NCMEC, state police, state missing children clearinghouses, and other law enforcement agencies in the region. An excellent checklist for investigating Internet-related missing children's cases is provided in the NCMEC manual.

Step 8: Execute an investigative follow-up plan. The procedures initiated by the investigator depend on the type of case—runaway, family kidnapping, suspected abduction by a stranger, or a lost child. Though the procedures are similar to those involved in investigating other major cases, investigators should be aware that the missing/abducted child case may bring the added factor of emotional stress and that the degree of stress will vary depending on the circumstances of the case.

THE 2003 CHILD PROTECTION ACT (AMBER ALERTS)

In September 2006, Vinson Filyaw, a 26-year-old unemployed construction worker, approached 14-year-old Elizabeth Shoaf as she stepped off her school bus in Lugoff, South Carolina. Posing as a police officer, Filyaw used handcuffs to restrain Elizabeth and dragged her back to a bunker located near his rural trailer home. Filyaw told Elizabeth that the entrance to the bunker was booby-trapped and warned her that if she tried to escape or if anyone tried to rescue her, a bomb would detonate. While Filyaw had Elizabeth in his custody, he sexually assaulted her.

For ten days family members, police, and volunteers conducted a sweeping search for Elizabeth but found few clues. Elizabeth engineered her own remarkable rescue by snatching Filyaw's cell phone as he slept and sending a text message to her mother describing the location where she was being held. Investigators using cell phone tracking technology traced the call to Filyaw's cell phone. Investigators deducted Elizabeth's kidnapper was, in all likelihood, a known sex offender who was suspected of a sexual assault against a 12-year-old relative.

Using the signal from a nearby cell tower to triangulate her location, authorities began scouring the area and were able to rescue her. Police also seized a cache of pornography, canned goods, cheap generic cigarettes, homemade hand-grenades, and incendiary devices fashioned out of black powder from fireworks. They did not, however, find Filyaw.

After a failed attempt to hijack a car to make his escape, Filyaw was found walking along the side of Interstate 20. He was charged with kidnapping, first degree sexual assault, impersonating a police officer, and possession of incendiary devices.

This case also illustrates the seriousness and reality of child abductions and points to the need for community and police cooperation in the investigative phase. It also shows the importance of Amber Alerts and how they provide much-needed and timely information regarding child abductions.

In April 2003, President George W. Bush signed into law the so-called Child Protection Bill, which encourages states to establish **Amber Alert** systems to quickly post information about child abductions. The measure was hailed as an important milestone in the protection of America's children, because when a child is reported missing, that case becomes a matter of the most intense and focused effort by law enforcement.

The law also enhanced penalties for youth abductions and child sex crimes, boosted funding for missing and exploited children programs, and increased penalties on those convicted of child pornography, including images created digitally.

The Amber Alert system makes use of radio, television, roadside electronic billboards, and emergency broadcast systems to disseminate information about kidnapping suspects and victims soon after the abduction of a child under 18 is reported. In such cases, authorities say, the child could be killed or seriously injured a short time after being kidnapped.

The alerts, named after a 9-year-old Texas girl, Amber Hagerman, who was kidnapped and killed in 1996, are in effect in 41 states at the time of this writing. Amber's mother, Donna Norris, attended the bill-signing ceremony along with the survivors of two high-profile kidnapping cases: Jacqueline Marris and Tamara Brooks, two California teenagers rescued in the first use of the system in that state, and Utah teen Elizabeth Smart, whose father, Ed Smart, called for a national Amber Alert system after her recovery in March 2003.

One of the primary purposes of the new law is to encourage states to develop Amber Alert systems of their own. Attorney General John Ashcroft stated the bills aim to create a "seamless" system across the country. After the signing of the bill, an Amber Alert coordinator was appointed at the Justice

Department to assist states and was designated $10 million for the establishment of the initiative.

INTERVIEWING SUSPECTS IN ABDUCTIONS

Once a suspect has been identified, the investigator must carefully plan an interview to gain as much information as possible without violating the suspect's constitutional rights. A checklist of sample questions to ask a suspect may include:

- What do you think should happen to someone who would do this?
- Have you ever done this before?
- Have you ever thought of doing this before?
- Did you do it?
- Do you know who could have done this?
- Explain to me why . . .
- Do you keep a diary, calendar, notebook, computer? Can I look at it?
- Have you ever been arrested for this type of crime?
- Have you ever been questioned about this type of crime before?
- Do you own, possess, or have access to (items described by witnesses)?
- Do you know this child? His or her family? The family's business?
- Is there any reason why someone would accuse you of this?
- If it becomes necessary, would you . . . (submit to a polygraph, give fingerprints, stand in a lineup)?
- Would you let me search your . . . (car, house, storage locker, other places)?
- How do you react to stress?
- What is your general mode of transportation?
- Do you drive around a lot? Go places unannounced?
- What are your sleeping habits?
- Do you ever lie? If so, how frequently, under what circumstances, and why?

During the interview, treat the subject with consideration but be firm. As soon as the interview begins, size up the subject—is he intelligent, emotional, or very self-assured? Be prepared for the interview by gathering as many facts as possible about the incident before confronting the subject.

As the interview progresses, the effective investigator may obtain more answers by being a good listener—letting the subject talk, not trying to manipulate what the subject is saying. Concentrate on how the subject answers questions as much as what he says. Also watch the subject's body language and facial expressions. Encourage the subject to tell it in his own words, emphasizing that the subject should tell you all the facts. At the same time, do not be visibly shocked by anything the subject says—if an investigator shows shock by facial expressions or a look of disgust, the subject could begin to gain the upper hand in the interview. If necessary, the investigator should be empathetic. Be patient and do not expect to obtain answers to all questions quickly. Ask questions that require more than a yes or no answer. Some examples are:

- Tell me what happened then . . .
- I'd like to hear more about . . .
- And what happened then . . .?

Don't rush the subject; set aside sufficient time for a thorough interview. Be direct and professional—do not make the subject guess what information is needed. Allow the subject to "save face" if embarrassing questions are asked. If the subject feels humiliated, the interview may come to an abrupt halt. Avoid using technical terms or police slang.

As the interview is drawing to a close, try to get the subject to help time-orient the facts, putting them in chronological order. Be aware of what the subject did not say during the interview.

One of the most important procedures to follow throughout the interview is to observe the subject's due process rights (Fourth and Fifth Amendments). Throughout the missing/abducted child investigation, be certain to take all precautions to observe the legal rights of any potential suspects so that a successfully investigated case will not be lost in court.

DISCUSSION QUESTIONS

1. List and discuss the three types of missing persons cases discussed in this chapter.

2. Explain the significance of the NISMART data on abducted children

3. Explain how it can be determined if a missing child case is a result of an Internet lure.

4. List and discuss the duties of a responding officer to a missing person call.

5. List and discuss the steps that a criminal investigator should follow in the investigation of a missing person.

6. Discuss the origin, function, and utility of Amber Alerts.

7. Identify the types of questions that should be asked of a suspect in a child abduction case.

NOTES

1. HAMMER H., D. FINKLEHOR and A. SEDLEK (2002). *Runaway, thrownaway children: National estimates and characteristics.* National Incidence Studies of Missing, Abducted, Runaway, and Throwaway Children Survey, United States Office of Justice Programs, October.
2. Ibid.
3. Ibid.
4. Ibid.
5. FLORES, J. ROBERT (1999). Administrator of Office of Juvenile Justice and Delinquency Prevention. "Non-family Abducted Children: National Estimates and Characteristics."
6. National Center for Missing and Exploited Children (1994). *Missing and abducted children,* pp. 21–25. www.missingkids.com.

Key Terms

► battered child
► battered child syndrome
► child abuse
► child molester
► fixated child molester
► Munchausen syndrome by proxy
► pedophilia
► preferential molester
► regressed child molester
► shaken baby syndrome
► situational molester
► sudden infant death syndrome

This chapter will enable you to:

- Describe the roles of and distinctions between the pedophile and the child molester.

- Understand the problem of child abuse and the investigator's response to the problem.

- Identify various techniques of child molestation investigations.

- Discuss the role of the medical profession in cases involving sexual misconduct with children.

- Identify interview techniques for child victims of sexual misconduct.

- Understand problems associated with placing children on the witness stand in criminal trials.

INTRODUCTION

In March 2004, emergency crews in Crystal Lake, Illinois, responded to a call for assistance at the home of 44-year-old Kathy Leonard. When they arrived, they found Leonard's son, 15-year-old Seamus M. Leonard, who suffered from cerebral palsy, lying dead amidst piles of trash. Emergency personnel commented to local media that the condition of this victim was worse than any victim they had ever seen. McHenry County State's Attorney Gary Pack told *The Crystal Lake Northwest Herald,* "It would bring anyone to tears."

A subsequent autopsy revealed the boy died of pneumonia; malnutrition was listed as a contributing cause. Six other children, ages 3 to 17, who also lived in the home, were placed in protective custody under the State Department of Children and Family Services.

After the discovery, the home was deemed uninhabitable by the city's building department and county health department. Interestingly, case workers from the Illinois Division of Children and Family Services had visited the home in January 2003, one year earlier, following a domestic violence complaint. They claimed that there were no indicators of child neglect during their visit. Leonard was arrested and charged with involuntary manslaughter in the death of her son.

Stories such as this shock the conscience of people around the nation and serve as an ongoing reminder that child neglect and abuse remain the constant concern of a free and civil society.

ABUSE OF CHILDREN

The Leonard case illustrates the complexity of **child abuse** cases. The numbers of child abuse cases, of course, reflect only those cases that come to the attention of the police. It is likely that many more cases exist. Forms of assaults against children can include physical harm, sexual abuse, emotional abuse, and neglect and often include forms of pushing, shoving, slapping, and whipping.

The Scope of the Problem

The problem of child abuse is a considerable public concern and statistics are alarming. For example, in 2006, the National Center for Victims of Violent Crime reported the following:[1]

- An estimated 896,000 children were victims of maltreatment (neglect or abuse).

- Fifty-two percent of child maltreatment victims were girls and 48 percent were boys.

- More than one-half of all child victims were white (54 percent); one-quarter (26 percent) were African-American, and one-tenth (11 percent) were Hispanic. American Indians or Alaska Natives accounted for 2 percent of victims, and Asian-Pacific Islanders accounted for 1 percent of victims.

- Approximately 40 percent of child victims were maltreated solely by their mothers; another 19 percent were maltreated solely by their fathers; 18 percent were abused by both parents. Child victims abused by a non-parental perpetrator accounted for 13 percent of the total.

- The youngest children (from birth through age three) were the most likely to experience recurring maltreatment.

Figure 16.1 Sarah Lunde, 13, was abducted and found dead April 16, 2005. Convicted sex offender, 36-year-old David Onstott, was indicted by a Florida grand jury a month after Lunde's disappearance.
Getty Images, Inc.

- Children abused by someone other than a parent were 16 percent less likely to experience recurrence than children who were abused by their mother.
- Victimization rates are inversely proportional to the age of the child—the older the child, the less likely he or she is to be maltreated.
- In 2002, an estimated 1,400 children died due to child abuse or neglect. Five percent of child molesters released from prison commit a new sex offense within three years of their release.
- Twenty-nine children were murdered by their babysitters in 2003.
- Victims of child abuse comprised 21 percent of the recipients of crime victim compensation in 2003.

Nearly 3 million cases of child abuse and neglect were reported in 1993 according to the National Committee on the Prevention of Child Abuse (NCPCA), a 23 percent increase in only five years. Of these cases, about 1,300 resulted in death. However, these reported cases represent only a portion of all actual instances of child abuse. In addition, the escalation of drug abuse in the United States has added another tragic dimension to the child abuse problem.

Child abuse, in all its varied forms, is a symptom of a pathologic social environment in general and, in particular, a signal of a family in distress. The greater availability of highly addictive and generally more affordable drugs, such as crack cocaine, has added more impact on families with children who are already at risk as well as created additional cases of drug dependency and family crises. The debilitating and all-consuming nature of these drugs directly fuels the environment that fosters child abuse and neglect.

Figure 16.2 Jessica Lunsford, age nine, was abducted and killed in February 2005. *Steve Cannon, AP Wide World Photos*

One of the traditional problems in dealing effectively with child abuse has been the inability of the two lead investigative authorities—social welfare and law enforcement agencies—to work together in a strategic manner. These agencies often work along parallel lines with one another, each addressing its respective component of the same individual or family problem. Obvious reasons for this are based on differences in philosophy and training of personnel as well as the administrative and statutory demands under which they must work. While the duties and responsibilities of these two components cannot and should not join, there are points at which they do intersect.

Once a situation of abuse or neglect has been reported to law enforcement authorities, it has often already reached a point where permanent or irreparable damage has been enacted upon the child. Law enforcement and social welfare agencies share a responsibility in seeing that children do not become the targets of adult violence and parental neglect. Routine sharing of information by these agencies in a strategic manner, where permissible and appropriate, can often prevent child abuse or neglect from taking place. The point at which social welfare problems start to become law enforcement matters often represents a critical juncture for the welfare of the children involved. The key is often to determine the appropriate point for law enforcement intervention. This is generally best performed by pooling the interests and capabilities of welfare officers, law enforcement prosecutors, and relevant others in a team approach to meet the needs of specific cases.

The Nature of Child Abuse

Child abuse is a generic term that incorporates a variety of purposeful acts resulting in child injuries. Probably the most dramatic of these and the most often reported to the police is physical child abuse that results in death or serious injury. However, child abuse is far more pervasive and often more subtle. For example, physical battering may be the result of a parent's momentary fit of anger, or it may be part of an ongoing abusive situation. In the case of sexual abuse situations within families, offenses are more frequently calculated and may form a long-term pattern of sexual abuse. Physical neglect of a child's needs for nourishment or medical care, reckless disregard for his or her safety, and failure to provide food or medical care are all elements of the child abuse and neglect problem.

The physical effects of child abuse are only part of a child's injuries. The psychological and emotional impact of abuse frequently have long-term consequences for the child. Many children blame themselves for the abuse, adopting the feeling that they are bad and deserve the abusive treatment. Others may adopt the long-lasting perception that violence is a natural, even acceptable, component of family life and interpersonal relationships. As a consequence, many abused children carry to the next generation the same type of treatment that they endured. Other children translate physical abuse into later criminal violence. The fact that so many violent offenders have histories of child abuse and neglect is testimony to the fact that child abuse is often an intergenerational phenomenon. As such, it is important not only for the current victim but for future generations to identify child abuse whenever possible and to bring appropriate enforcement and treatment to bear on the problem.

INVESTIGATIVE RESOURCES

The point at which an investigation of child abuse begins depends largely on the reporting party or agency and the degree to which a case of abuse, neglect, or abandonment can be legally established. For example, abused children who require immediate medical attention suggest a point of investigative departure through interviews with medical staff. In most cases, investigation of child abuse will require contact with one or more sources of information depending on the nature of the complaint and the perceived scope of the abuse. Basic types of questions can be identified for conducting interviews with individuals who report child abuse. Such inquiries are generally warranted prior to direct contact with the family and the child.

Other basic types of information available through the police department should also be collected early in the investigation. This includes such information as the existence of criminal records or charges against any members of the family or court protection orders that may have been filed against any family members. Other general sources of investigative information can be gathered from a variety of resources in the community. These are reviewed in the following sections.

Emergency Room Personnel and Medical Examiners

In the worst case scenario—the death of a child—a medical examiner may be the primary source of contact for investigative purposes. Police departments in general and investigative personnel in particular must develop a good working relationship with the medical examiner's office. In these and related circumstances, a collaborative relationship generally proves to be far more productive than either the police or medical personnel working independently. The investigative officer should be present at the autopsy or at the initial examination of the body and should brief the examining physician on the circumstances of the alleged accident if information is available. This also holds true for emergency room physicians who treat a child following a presumed serious but nonfatal accident. In both cases, physical examinations may reveal certain types of injuries that confirm or suggest abuse. These include the following:

1. *External signs.* Some injuries have identifiable patterns that can be linked to specific objects used in an attack. For example, one may be able to identify bite or scratch marks; coat hanger or hot iron impressions; fingertip marks caused by tight gripping; straight, curved, curvilinear, or jagged lesions that may indicate whipping by specifically shaped objects; and scald or peculiar burn marks.

    The location of some injuries is also indicative of abuse. These include injuries to the genitals, buttocks, and rectal areas, as well as trauma to the torso, upper arms, and thighs. These and related injuries are particularly incriminating if they are not accompanied by other relatively common injuries suffered by children, such as skinned knees and bruises to the elbows, shins, and forehead, or by other injuries that would have probably been received as part of the accident. For example, most often children who are involved in accidents also display these signs of typical childhood play. On the other hand, children who are abused may show few or none of these signs and, except for the abusive injuries, may even appear well groomed and dressed.

    There may also be signs of old injuries to various parts of the body that are in different stages of healing. Some children seem to be accident-prone and may accumulate a variety of injuries over time. However, injuries that are not common to childhood and that appear to have been received over a period of time can be signs of a steadily escalating cycle of abuse.

    In all cases of suspected abuse, injuries should be photographed in color in order to assist in establishing the extent of damage and the age of injuries at later trial presentation.

2. *Internal signs.* As noted, some injuries are not characteristic of childhood activities and common accidents. For example, it is very unlikely that pre-toddlers would be able to break a major bone, such as a thigh or upper arm bone, or other smaller bones given the children's lack of mobility and the inherent difficulty in breaking the bones of young children. Some fractures will be apparent externally. Others, particularly older fractures, require radiological examination in order to be identified. The nature of some fractures provides almost indisputable evidence of abuse. These include spiral fractures, indicating vigorous handling, shaking, or twisting, and fractures to the rear and upper part—occipital and varietal bones, respectively—of the skull, suggesting that the child was swung by the feet into a solid object or suffered a blow to the head. Subdural hematomas, without evidence of contusions on the scalp, or skull fractures may suggest violent shaking of an infant, causing whiplash of the child's head and subsequent internal injuries.

Like the emergency room physician, the medical examiner may be confronted by a child whose history, pattern, or extent of injuries does not correlate with the alleged cause of death. Also typical of the abused child is an inordinate parental delay in seeking medical attention, evidence of administration of home remedies for a serious injury, a history of prior visits to different emergency rooms, frequent changes of physicians, any prior diagnosis of "failure to thrive," even multiple emergency room visits with a well child. If any of these situations are encountered, one should consider child abuse as likely.

At the autopsy, there are procedures that should be performed to establish the full scope of current and past injuries to the child, as well as any possible contributing causes of death. A principal purpose of the medical–legal autopsy is to establish a cause of death. However, this is not the only purpose. As one noted pathologist states: "If the purpose of the examination did not extend beyond this (determining the immediate cause of death), much evidence concerning the nature of the perpetrator, the degree of injury, the intervals between episodes of injury, the magnitude of force directed at unexamined portions of the body, and perhaps the presence or absence of underlying natural disease or old trauma which may have contributed to the death may not be revealed."[2] Some medical examiners may feel comfortable with simply establishing a cause of death. However, at trial, they probably would not be able to positively exclude other possible causes of death because of the limited scope of the examination. This factor could compromise the prosecutorial effort. By the same token, the lack of any external trauma does not necessarily mean that the child did not die from abuse. Many fatal internal injuries are not detectable through external examination alone. The importance, therefore, of a detailed and thoroughly documented autopsy cannot be overemphasized in cases of suspected child abuse. Photographic evidence coupled with detailed measurements and laboratory data is essential for both investigation and prosecution.

Based on the judgment of a physician, the diagnosis of one or more of these suspicious injuries may be sufficient evidence to conclude that the child suffered from abuse. These injuries are particularly incriminating when they do not correlate with parental explanations of how they were incurred. This underscores the importance of a close and ongoing communication between police investigating officers and physicians. Examining physicians must be kept informed about the course of the investigation and the types of questions that should be answered as the result of their examination. Children who suffer from physical abuse are termed **battered children** (Figures 16.3 and 16.4). Battered children suffer from a wide array of abuses, including minor assaults to severe beatings, which in some cases cost them their lives. Because of the privacy and nature of the crime, such victims often have nowhere to turn. Child abuse is aggravated by high levels of unemployment, poor parenting skills, stress, marital conflict, and a general lack of information about child development.

As with any assault case, evidence is a primary objective. Bruises, bloody clothes, dramatic changes in a child's behavior, and statements from possible witnesses are all important. Special care must be afforded the interview of a child victim, as children are imaginative and highly susceptible to suggestion. Because of this, the use of specially trained child interviewers is recommended to secure a competent statement from the child victim.

BATTERED CHILD SYNDROME

Battered child syndrome is a tragic and disturbing phenomenon. Unfortunately, it is a crime that is often successfully hidden by its perpetrators. Law enforcement has an important role to play in uncovering cases of battered child syndrome and gathering evidence for successful prosecution. Investigators must have a working knowledge of battered child syndrome and what it means to an

Figure 16.3 Child Victimization Rates by Age Group, 2002. According to this chart, the largest victimized age group is the youngest, with a rate of 16.0 per 1,000 children of the same age group. *U.S. Department of Health & Human Services, Administration for Children and Families [2003]*

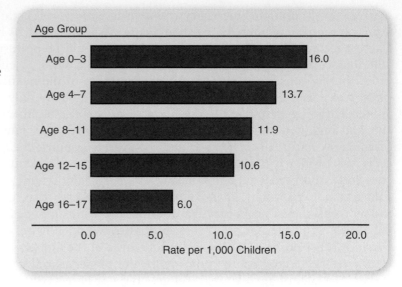

investigation. Battered child syndrome is defined as the collection of injuries sustained by a child as a result of repeated mistreatment or beating. If the child's injuries indicate intentional trauma or appear to be more severe than could reasonably be expected from an accident, battered child syndrome should be suspected. In such cases, an investigator must do more than collect information about the currently reported injury. A full investigation requires interviewing possible witnesses about other injuries that the child may have suffered, obtaining the caretaker's explanation for those injuries, and assessing the conclusions of medical personnel who may have seen the victim before.

The issue of whether information on the victim's prior injuries or medical condition will be admissible at trial should be left up to the prosecutor. However, an investigator's failure to collect such information leaves the prosecutor without one of the most important pieces of corroborative evidence for proving an intentional

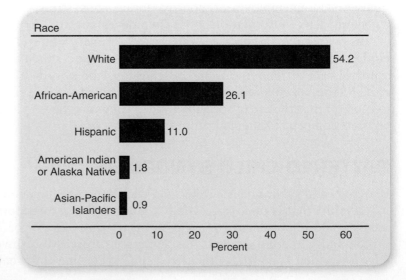

Figure 16.4 Percentage of Child Victims by Race, 2002. This chart shows that one-half of all victims were white (54.2%), one-quarter (26.1%) were African American, and one-tenth (11%) were Hispanic. *U.S. Department of Health and Human Services, Administration for Children and Families [2003]*

act of child abuse. Evidence of past inflicted injuries may also be the only information available to help the prosecutor distinguish between two or more possible perpetrators in the current case and may help refute claims by the child's parents or caretakers that injuries suggestive of physical abuse were caused by an accident.

Recognizing Abuse

There are several signs of abuse that officers can identify while assessing the situation. For example, if the child has an injury that is inconsistent with the explanation given by the parents, abuse might have occurred. If the officer is told that a child's hand was severely scalded in water by "accident," the officer should question why the child didn't take the obvious action of withdrawing his hand. It would be logical to suspect that someone forcibly held the child's hand in the water.

Other injuries can also be good indicators of child abuse (e.g., cigarette burns, bruises, cuts that appear to be nonaccidental in origin). In addition, abused children will sometimes have bite marks appearing on the abdomen, scrotum, and buttocks.[3] Most typically, however, abuse takes the form of severe and numerous beatings going far beyond normal disciplinary measures. Such evidence includes injuries in different stages of healing or complications stemming from old injuries that are not explained sufficiently by the parents.

Taking the Initial Report

State laws generally require certain persons to report instances of child abuse, neglect, or sexual abuse. These persons include school officials, medical personnel, attorneys, social workers, and others. Such reports can be made verbally or in writing to the state department of family or child services, welfare department, the juvenile court, or a local law enforcement agency. Typically, special forms are used for child abuse and molestation cases, and laws require immediate action. Initial child abuse reports are confidential in nature and contain the child's name, address, and age as well as information on the child's parents or legal guardians.

In addition, the name and address of the person suspected of abusing the child are documented as well as the nature of the alleged offense. In the case of an emergency circumstance or one that appears to be life threatening for the child, the police can remove the child from the home provided that the welfare or juvenile justice official taking the report deems it necessary. All allegations will be investigated by local law enforcement.

The Initial Police Response to Child Abuse

The time factor is crucial in the law enforcement response to suspected child abuse. Complaints are sometimes logged during or shortly after a battering incident; therefore, the safety of the child is the utmost priority for the responding officer. Consequently, the responding officer's first task is to get medical attention for the child. In absence of any immediate danger to the child, most state laws require that officers at least attempt to resolve any problems before physically removing the child from the home. In the event that the child is facing imminent danger, of course, removal from the home is appropriate.

The second responsibility of the responding officer is to determine if a crime has, in fact, been committed. If such determination is made, the officer should

> **Justifications for Officers Making an Arrest**
>
> • Injury to the child is severe.
> • Evidence of a serious crime exists.
> • It seems likely that the suspect will flee the scene.
> • There is a disturbance of the peace.
> • The suspect seems to pose a danger to others.

conduct a criminal investigation accordingly, such as identifying evidence. Subsequent to the investigation, it may be necessary to take a suspect into physical custody.

STEPS IN INVESTIGATING BATTERED CHILD SYNDROME

Investigators confronted with the case of possible child abuse or child homicide must overcome the unfortunately frequent societal attitude that babies are less important than adult victims of homicide and that natural parents would never intentionally harm their own children. When battered child syndrome is suspected, the investigator should always:

- Collect information about the "acute" injury that led the person or agency to make the report.
- Conduct interviews with medical personnel who are attending the child.
- Review medical records from a doctor, clinic, or hospital.
- Interview all persons who had access to or custody of the child during a time in which the injury or injuries allegedly occurred. Always interview the caretakers separately—joint interviews can only hurt the investigation.
- Consider any statements the caretakers made to anyone concerning what happened to the child to require medical attention.
- Conduct a thorough investigation of the scene where the child was allegedly hurt.

Interviews with Medical Personnel

It is important for the investigator to contact all medical personnel who had contact with the family, such as doctors, nurses, admitting personnel, emergency medical technicians (EMTs), ambulance drivers, and emergency room personnel.

- Talk with those who provided treatment for the child about the diagnosis and what treatments were used. The attending physician will often be able to express at least an opinion that the caretaker's explanation did not "fit" the severity of the injury. Failure to obtain an opinion from the attending physician should not end the investigation.
- Speak with any specialist who assisted the attending physician.
- Have someone knowledgeable about medical terms translate them into layperson terms so that the exact nature of the injuries is clear.
- Obtain available medical records concerning the injured child's treatment, including records of any prior treatment. (*Note:* If only one caretaker is

suspected of abuse, the nonabusive caretaker may need to sign a release of the records. If both are suspected, most states have provisions that override normal confidentiality rules in the search for evidence of child abuse. Procedures for obtaining these records must be confirmed in each state.)

- Interview the child's pediatrician about the child's general health since birth, and look for a pattern of suspected abusive injuries.

It is absolutely vital that photographs of the child be taken as soon as possible after a child has been brought to the treatment facility. Most clinics and hospitals have established procedures for photographing injuries in obvious cases of abuse, but when the injuries are more subtle, they may overlook the need for photographs. The investigator should make sure that medical personnel take and preserve photographs or that the investigating team takes them.

Other Important Sources of Information

Interview siblings, other relatives, neighbors, family friends, teachers, church associates, and others who may know about a child's health and history. People who surround the child and are part of his or her life are sometimes overlooked as sources of background information for a child abuse or homicide prosecution.

Review EMT records or 9-1-1 dispatch tapes. These records are frequently overlooked but can be valuable sources of information. Families with one or more emergencies may in fact be abusing children and not just be hit by a long streak of "bad luck."

Once the family history is obtained, request any police reports that may be held by law enforcement agencies in the jurisdiction where the family lives. Also check the child welfare agencies' files on the family. Collect additional family history concerning connections between domestic violence and child abuse, substance abuse and child abuse, and other connections, even apparently unrelated arrests or charges. These records may be helpful in piecing together the complicated picture of what happened to the child this time and who was responsible.

Consultation with Experts

Identifying experts is important to the child abuse investigator. If the investigator does not have a basic knowledge of the causes of young children's injuries, experts should be consulted. Attending training conferences can provide the investigator with a great deal of basic knowledge and help establish a network of experts.

Interviews with Caretakers

A major trait of abuse by caretakers is either complete lack of an explanation for critical injuries or explanations that do not account for the severity of the injuries. The investigation must not be dictated solely by caretakers' early explanations, because once they learn their excuses don't match the medical evidence, they will come up with new ones.

In child homicide cases, for example, investigators will learn quickly about "killer couches," "killer stairs," and "killer cribs." Abusers freely use these terms in their explanations of the child's death. However, studies show that children do not die from falls from simple household heights; they usually do not even suffer severe head injuries from such falls.

In nearly every case of actual abuse, caretakers will not be consistent in their explanations of the injuries over time. Sometimes the changes are apparent from statements that abusers have made to others. Additional interviews may be needed to document the changes in explanations and to follow up on additional information that the investigation uncovers.

The Crime Scene Investigation

Caretakers' changes in explanations often mean that investigators must visit the home or the scene of the injury more than once. The ideal time to obtain such evidence is immediately after the child's injury is reported, before the caretakers have an opportunity to tamper with the scene. If the caretakers do not consent to a search of the scene, a search warrant may be necessary. The strongest evidence of the need for a search warrant will be the medical evidence supporting what probably happened to the child and the caretakers' inconsistent or absent accounts of the events.

Whatever explanation caretakers offer for a child's injury or injuries, it is vital that the investigator secure physical evidence. He or she must be thorough in obtaining photographic evidence of the location where the injury took place, as physical evidence and records must be preserved, for example:

- The crib from which the child allegedly fell.
- The child's "environment," including bedding on the bed or in the crib and on other beds in the home.
- Any toys or objects on which the child allegedly landed.
- In cases where the child was apparently burned, a record of any sinks, bathtubs, and pots or pans containing water. In addition to testing the temperature of the standing water, test the temperature of water from the water heater and from each tap. Check the temperature setting of the water heater. This may help disprove an allegation that the child accidentally turned on the hot water. Other sources of heat in the home should be documented, regardless of the caretakers' initial explanation of what burned the child.
- A complete photographic or videotape record of the home or other location in which the injuries allegedly occurred, focusing on areas that the caretakers already have identified as the site of the particular trauma (e.g., stairs, bed or crib, or bathtub).

The investigator should be trained by his or her local crime laboratory personnel on the types of evidence that can and should be processed in preserving these cases:

- If the child suffered apparent cigarette burns, collecting cigarette butts found in the home may facilitate analysis of the burn patterns.
- If the case involves a combination of sexual and physical abuse, collecting the child's clothing and bedding may allow identification of what happened and who was involved.
- If the child shows evidence of bite marks, saliva swabbing should be done to allow positive identification of the biter.
- If the child has suffered a depressed skull fracture, any objects the approximate size of the fracture should be seized for appropriate analysis.

INVESTIGATOR GUIDELINES FOR CHILD HOMICIDE

It is not always readily apparent that the child's death was the result of homicide. In cases such as the following, homicide may be evident:

- It is fairly obvious that the child's death was caused by an abusive injury.

- The person who had custody of the child at the time the abusive injury was inflicted is known. Most infant deaths occur when the baby is in the care of known individuals.

- The injuries themselves are obviously the result of a deliberate intent to do harm, that is, there is really no question that someone abused the child and that the abuse caused the child to die. Such cases include strangulation, beating, severe inflicted burns such as scalding, and the use of a weapon.

Unfortunately, the more carefully planned out a killing is, the less likely a medical explanation for the death will be found. Most injuries resulting from abuse are much more subtle than poisoning, beating, bludgeoning, shooting, or strangulation. Suffocation, for example, often leaves absolutely no medical sign of the cause of death. Most infant deaths are related to head injuries, some of which leave no external sign of trauma.

In case after case of suspicious deaths of children, the caretakers' explanation is: "She fell off the couch (chair, changing table, bed, or down the stairs)." Investigators must be aware that *children do not die from simple falls*. When investigating whether a child's death was a homicide, investigators must ask themselves the following questions:

- How do we find out what actually happened to the child?

- How can we make sure that we're talking to the right expert about what could have caused the child's death?

- How do we know we have talked to everyone who might be able to shed light on a difficult case?

When presented with a child who has died under suspicious circumstances in which there is no obvious sign of abuse, the investigator should ask an experienced pediatrician to help locate a specialist whose medical expertise can help make sense of a confusing picture. However, everyone who handles child fatalities must have a basic understanding of the following conditions: shaken baby syndrome, Munchausen syndrome by proxy, and sudden infant death syndrome (SIDS).

SHAKEN BABY SYNDROME

The classic medical symptoms associated with infant shaking are:

- Retinal hemorrhaging (bleeding in the back of the eyeball), often bilaterally (in both eyes).

- Subdural or subarachnoid hematomas (intracranial bleeding, most often in the upper hemispheres of the brain, caused by the shearing of the blood vessels between the brain and the dura mater of the arachnoid membrane).

- Absence of other external signs of abuse (e.g., bruises), although not always. Symptoms include breathing difficulties, seizures, dilated pupils, lethargy, and unconsciousness.

According to all credible studies in the past several years, retinal hemorrhaging in infants is, for all practical purposes, conclusive evidence of **shaken baby syndrome** in the absence of a good explanation. Good explanations for retinal hemorrhaging include:

- A severe auto accident in which the baby's head either struck something with severe force or was thrown about wildly without restraint during the crash.
- A fall from several stories onto a hard surface, in which case there are usually other signs of trauma, such as skull fractures, swelling, and intracranial collection of blood.

Simple household falls, cardiopulmonary resuscitation (CPR), and tossing a baby in the air in play are not good explanations for retinal hemorrhaging. There simply is not enough force involved in minor falls in play activities to cause retinal hemorrhage or the type of severe life-threatening injuries seen in infants who have been shaken.

In most cases of shaken baby syndrome, there is no skull fracture and no external sign of trauma. The typical explanation given by caretakers is that the baby was "fine" and then suddenly went into respiratory arrest or began having seizures. Both of these conditions are common symptoms of shaken baby syndrome.

The shaking necessary to cause death or severe intracranial injuries is never an unintentional or nonabusive action. Rather, such injuries are caused by a violent, sustained action in which the infant's head, which lacks muscular control, is violently swept forward and backward, hitting the chest and shoulders. The action occurs right in front of the shaker's eyes. Experts say that an observer watching the shaking would describe it as "as hard as the shaker was humanly capable of shaking the baby" or "hard enough that it appeared the baby's head would come off." In almost every case, the baby begins to show symptoms such as seizures or unconsciousness within minutes of the injury being inflicted. The baby may have difficulty breathing, or breathing may stop completely.

Shaken baby syndrome occurs primarily in children 18 months of age or younger. It is most often associated with infants less than a year old, because their necks lack muscle control and their heads are heavier than the rest of their bodies. An infant cannot resist the shaking, but a toddler can, to some extent. Although the collection of injuries associated with shaken baby syndrome is sometimes seen in toddlers, it is rare and is always a sign of extremely violent and severe action against the child.

MUNCHAUSEN SYNDROME BY PROXY

Munchausen syndrome is a psychological disorder in which a patient fabricates symptoms of disease or injury in order to undergo medical tests, hospitalization, or even medical or surgical treatment. To command medical attention, patients with Munchausen syndrome may intentionally injure themselves or induce illness in themselves. In cases of **Munchausen syndrome by proxy,** parents or caretakers suffering from Munchausen syndrome attempts to bring medical attention to themselves by inducing illness in their children. The parent then may try to resuscitate or have paramedics or hospital personnel save the child. The following scenarios are common occurrences in these cases:

- A child's caretaker repeatedly brings the child in for medical care or calls paramedics for alleged problems that cannot be documented medically.

- The child experiences "seizures" or "respiratory arrest" only when the caretaker is there, never in the presence of neutral third parties or in the hospital.

- When the child is hospitalized, the caretaker turns off the life support equipment, causing the child to stop breathing, and then turns everything back on and summons help.

- The caretaker induces illness by introducing a mild irritant or poison into the child's body.

INVESTIGATIVE GUIDELINES

- Consult with all possible experts, including psychologists.

- Exhaust every possible explanation in the cause of the child's illness or death.

- Find out who had exclusive control over the child when the symptoms of the illness began or at the time of the child's death.

- Find out if there is a history of abusive conduct toward this child.

- Find out if the nature of the child's illness or injury allows medical professionals to express an opinion that the child's illness or death was neither accidental nor the result of a natural cause or disease.

- In cases of hospitalization, utilize covert video surveillance to monitor the suspect. Some cases have been solved in this fashion.

- Determine whether the caretaker had any medical training or a history of seeking medical treatment needlessly. Munchausen syndrome by proxy is often a multigenerational condition.

SUDDEN INFANT DEATH SYNDROME

Sudden infant death syndrome (SIDS) is not a positive finding; rather, it is a diagnosis made when there is no other medical explanation for the abrupt death of an apparently healthy infant. When a baby dies from shaking, intracranial injuries, peritonitis (inflammation of the peritoneum, the membrane that lines the abdominal cavity), apparent suffocation, or any other identifiable cause, SIDS is not even considered a possibility. SIDS rarely occurs in infants older than seven months and almost never is an appropriate diagnosis for a child older than 12 months.

SIDS cases must be approached with great sensitivity. However, before SIDS can be determined to be the cause of death, investigators must ensure that every other possible medical explanation has been explored and that there is no evidence of any other natural or accidental cause for a child's death.

An investigator's suspicions should be aroused when multiple alleged SIDS deaths have occurred under the custody of the same caretaker. Statistically, the occurrence of two or three alleged SIDS deaths in the care of the same person strongly suggests that some degree of child abuse was involved. Whenever there is evidence that the child who has died was abused or that other children in the family have been abused, SIDS is not an appropriate finding.

Even when there is no affirmative medical finding of the cause of death, prosecution may still be possible. In some cases, experts can explain what occurs when a child is suffocated and can render a medical opinion that suffocation is one of the ways that someone could cause the child's death without leaving obvious medical signs.

Conclusion

Both the medical and legal professions have made great strides in identifying nonaccidental trauma inflicted on children. This progress accounts for what appears to be an increase in the number of identified child abuse homicides. Sadly, however, there will always be some children who die of abuse that is never discovered. Children deserve investigators' best efforts to turn over every stone in cases involving any suspicion of abuse of children.

SEXUAL ABUSE OF CHILDREN

Another shocking case emerged in December 1995, when an 11-year-old testified that she was molested during sexual orgies supposedly staged by a Pentecostal preacher in Wenatchee, Washington. She also testified that her foster father, who happened to be Detective Bob Perez, lead police investigator in the case, also physically abused her. Prosecutors charged 28 persons in the case, charging that they forced 50 children to have sex with each other and with adults in two sex rings. Nineteen either pleaded guilty or were convicted in the case; only one was acquitted. In yet another case, the Boy Scouts have dismissed over 1,800 scoutmasters suspected of molesting children between 1971 and 1991—some of those dismissed may have moved to other troops to continue their abuse.[4]

In recent years, the problem of child sexual abuse has generated increased attention and is becoming more openly discussed than ever before. For example, in 1992, a former Roman Catholic priest, James Porter, was arrested for sexually abusing as many as 80 children in Massachusetts and two other states during the 1970s. Statistics also point out that child sexual abuse is a growing problem. Although it is difficult to estimate the incidence of child sexual abuse, stories of abuse such as those discussed above illustrate the seriousness of the problem. In one study by Diana Russell, women in the San Francisco area were surveyed and Russell found that 38 percent had experienced intrafamilial or extrafamilial sexual abuse by the time they reached 18.[5] A more recent survey of Minnesota students in grades 6, 9, and 12 revealed that about 2 percent of the males and 7 percent of the females had experienced incest, while 4 percent of males and 13 percent of females had experienced extrafamilial sexual abuse. Although the percentage of abused females is smaller than that found by Russell, research by Glenn Wolfner and Richard Gelles indicates that up to one in five girls suffers sexual abuse.[6]

Although these results are alarming, it is probable that they still underestimate the true incidence of child sexual abuse. It is difficult to get people to respond to questions about child sexual abuse, and many victims either are too young to understand their abuse or have repressed their memory of such incidents. Of course, children may be inhibited because parents are reluctant to admit that abuse occurred. In one study, 57 percent of children referred to a clinic because they had sexually transmitted diseases claimed not to have been molested despite irrefutable evidence.[7]

As with the previous categories of sexual criminal activity, much misunderstanding exists regarding the sexual abuse of children. This category of offense includes:

- *Exploitation.* The use of children for illegal activities such as prostitution and pornography.
- *Incest.* Sexual relations between children and their parents.
- *Child sexual abuse.* The sexual molestation of children, as well as seduction and statutory rape.

The Child Protection Act of 1984 described child pornography as a highly organized business that focused on runaways and homeless youth, and one that operates on a national basis. It provided for increased penalties for adults involved in it and pointed out that such acts are injurious to the physical and emotional well-being of the child. In addition to this act, most states have passed legislation addressing child abuse and the sexual exploitation of children.

The basis of sexual misconduct with children is **pedophilia,** sexual attraction to children. A surprising number of people share this preference, and some are more willing than others to make physical overtures toward satisfying their desires. Surprisingly, there have been groups formed to promote sex with children. Such groups produce manuals and literature to support their perspective and have actually approached legislatures to restructure or eliminate laws governing "age of consent."

One such group, Paedophilia (British spelling), asserts that its members possess a natural sexual attraction toward children and that the attraction is as natural as the attraction of a man to a woman. Indeed, this group even suggests that for some, the sexual attraction to children is as natural as certain people's orientation toward homosexuality or heterosexuality and may therefore be impossible to change. Groups sharing similar goals and desires are:

- The René Guyon Society
- The North American Man/Boy Love Association
- The Pedophile Information Exchange
- The Child Sensuality Circle
- The Pedo-Alert Network
- Lewis Carroll Collectors Guide

All of these groups advocate adult–child sex and the changing of laws that make it a crime.[8] In any case, it is clear that a subculture exists regarding this problem and that a great deal of misunderstanding also exists about how best to deal with the situation. In addition to these organizations, yet another category of child sexual offender exists: the stereotypic child molester or child rapist. Unlike people associated with the above-mentioned organizations, this class of offender will usually conduct deeds individually with the victim.

In any case, the investigation of sexual offenses involving children must be handled carefully through the use of technical investigative techniques and training. Additionally, investigators must have an in-depth understanding of the underground subculture of groups or individuals who exploit children sexually through incest, child pornography, prostitution, and molestation.

The Preliminary Investigation

In the early phase of the investigation, the investigator must collect as much information about the charge as possible. This is typically done by interviews with people who are most closely associated with the child. Assuming that such persons are not suspects in the case, they could provide the investigator with information regarding any abnormalities in a child's physical appearance as well as unusual behaviors and actions by the child. In the event that the person being questioned becomes a suspect, investigators should be careful to avoid accusations or passing judgment. In addition, if during the interview the subject develops into a suspect, the officer must remember to afford the subject all of his or her due process rights under the Fourth, Fifth, and Fourteenth Amendments.

Interviewing the Child Victim

The interview process of the child victim requires patience, practice, and understanding. Several different considerations will determine at what point the interview should occur. These are the child's age and his or her ability to communicate with others and to describe what occurred. Other considerations include the possibility of retaliation by the abuser–molester.

To help ensure that the maximum amount of information is learned from an interview, investigators should take care to see that the child victim is as comfortable as possible. Thus the interview should not be conducted at the police station but at a location with familiar surroundings, such as at a specially designed room located at the juvenile center, a hospital, or a friend's home. Privacy is also an important variable in this regard. Studies show that children need support, so if they request a nonoffending parent or other person present, it should be allowed. In such cases, the parent should not be with the child during

Figure 16.5 Interviews with possible child abuse victims must be conducted with specially trained personnel.

the course of the interview but should be permitted to be nearby (but out of view) in an adjacent room to give the child a sense of security.

Because a child's attention span is short, questions should be clearly spoken and to the point. This technique can be developed only through practice and self-discipline, as interviewers proficient at dealing with adults may not be successful with children. The quality of the child's responses is also a critical consideration. It is therefore important for the interviewer to be able to decipher what the child is trying to say. For example, the child may have different perceptions of words such as *sex, kiss, hug,* and *touch.* The interviewer must learn to ask specific questions regarding what the child means, to avoid confusion later in court. In addition, the interviewer might choose to use anatomically correct dolls to help the child describe exactly what happened, what part of the body was touched, what body part did the touching, and generally what happened.

Techniques for the Child Interview.   The relationship or rapport between the child victim and the investigator is also of great importance. Questions can sometimes be developed through information obtained from the division of child services, welfare office, physician, and so on regarding the parents or legal guardian(s) of the child. Other factors affecting the direction of the interview include the child's:

- Age
- Developmental stage
- Siblings
- Family composition
- Ability to read or write
- Intellectual development (or lack of)

Typically, to best reassure the victim, an interview might begin by the following opening remarks by the officer: "I am a police officer, and let me tell you what police officers do. My job is to talk to children about these things because we want them to stop happening." Interviews should continue with simple questions such as the child's name, age, grade, school, favorite teacher, brothers and sisters, and favorite television shows. The interviewer might also choose to share the names of his or her children. These opening remarks can help the investigator determine the general intelligence and sophistication of the child.

WHAT TO ASK

- *"Who did it?"* Investigators shouldn't expect the child to offer an abundance of information with this initial question, but chances are that the child knows the identity of the abuser. Absent any more definitive information, investigators should at least attempt to learn the relationship of the offender to the child.

- *"What happened? I need to know exactly what the man did. Can you describe what happened? Did he touch you?"* In the case of sexual abuse, the child should also be asked if he or she ever saw the offender's penis. This should, of course, be phrased in the words of the child. Once basic information is learned, the investigator can then inquire about other types of sexual or physical misconduct.

- *"When did it happen?"* Depending on the age of the child victim, details on when the crime occurred may be difficult to obtain. The investigator should attempt to learn how recently the assault occurred and how many times abuse occurred. Generally, the courts have held that information from children under six years of age may not be considered reliable.
- *"Where did it happen?"* Most child sexual and physical abuse occurs in the home. Therefore, questioning should try to determine the room in which it occurred and where the other family members were and what they were doing at the time of the incident(s).
- *"Was there any coercion or enticement?"* This is to determine if any force or pressure was used, either physical or psychological, and how much. In most cases, there is some inducement given the child to keep silent about the incident. Therefore, such questions could include: "Did he tell you not to tell?" "What did he say?" "Did he say something bad would happen to you?" "Did he tell you that you should keep this a secret?"

PHYSICAL EVIDENCE IN CHILD SEXUAL MOLESTATION CASES

- Camera or video equipment used for taking photographic images of the victim engaged in sexual acts with the offender.
- Notebooks, diaries, papers, or anything else linking the offender to the victim.
- Negatives or undeveloped film that would depict the victim (or other juveniles).
- Magazines, books, or movies depicting juveniles in sexual situations.
- Newspapers, magazine clippings, or other publications listing phone numbers with other sexual interests that might tend to identify juveniles involved with the suspect.
- Evidence of occupancy, such as bills, letters, rent receipts, or other mail or correspondence showing that the suspect resides at a particular location or is in control of a particular location.
- Any items of physical evidence belonging to the victim or used by the subject in sexual acts.

Closing the Interview

At the conclusion of the interview, thank and compliment the child on his or her maturity, responsibility, and cooperation. This is not the time to try to make the child promise to testify at a later court date. A later meeting would be a better time to do so because of the child's inability to comprehend what a trial consists of. The parents should then be given honest and straightforward responses as to what the next phase of the investigation will be. During this explanation, it would be helpful to define the steps in the criminal justice process as it pertains to children, as well as the role of the parents. Ask for the parents' cooperation and advise them on whom they can contact if they are in need of help or information.

CHILDREN AS WITNESSES

One of the most compelling reasons why children are such formidable victims is the fact that they may be considered incompetent witnesses in the courtroom. Indeed, many such cases rely heavily on testimony from child victims. If the incident really

> **Characteristics of Child Victims**[10]
>
> • In the 8- to 16-year-old age group
> • Unsupervised
> • From unstable home environment
> • From low- or average-income families
> • Subject to abrupt changes in moods
> • Not necessarily delinquent
> • In possession of more money than normal, new toys, new clothes, etc. (gifts from the molester)
> • Withdrawn from family and friends

happened, the child can be irreparably scarred, but if it didn't, the accusation can ruin the life of the accused. Until about a decade ago, there was little discussion of the possibility of false allegations in child sexual abuse cases. In recent years, however, skepticism has grown, partly because of sophisticated studies showing that witnesses, especially younger ones, can be influenced by the biases of interviewers.

In 1989, the McMartin Preschool case involved nine children who accused staff members at a suburban Los Angeles day care center of wholesale sexual molestation. After what some newspapers called the longest criminal trial ever, charges against the school's founder, Virginia McMartin, and four teachers were dropped. The determination as to whether or not a child should be considered as a competent witness rests with the discretion of the courts. Experienced investigators suggest that children will usually tell the truth to the best of their ability and that when they lie, it is to get out of trouble, not "into" trouble.

Factors considered by the trial judge are the child's age, intelligence, and sense of moral and legal responsibility. A child will be deemed competent to testify if he or she possesses the capacity to observe the events, to recollect and communicate them, and to understand questions and answer intelligently with an understanding of the duty to speak the truth.[9] In short, the child must understand that some form of punishment will result if the truth is not told. In the absence of clear physical evidence such as rectal or vaginal abrasions, it is difficult to distinguish false allegations from truthful ones. Typically, interviewers will have the child demonstrate the abuse incident with an anatomically correct doll. Some courts, however, have ruled them out because they view them as suggestive.

David Raskin, a forensic psychologist at the University of Utah, devised a form of interview designed to show the quality of a child's story. Derived from experimental work done in Germany in the 1950s, the interview allows the child to begin the interview with a free narrative, holding off prompting as long as possible. A series of questions then follows and is succeeded by a validity assessment that looks for shifts of focus, reappearing elements, and digressions. Raskin asserts that when people anchor events in their memory, they are not told in a straightforward manner. Specifically, most people correct themselves, add elements momentarily forgotten, and redescribe the event. The technique is based on the premise that when someone is inventing a story, it is difficult for them to proceed in this fashion.

THE CHILD MOLESTER

Child molesters represent the most common type of pedophile. The term *pedophile* is commonly used by medical treatment and law enforcement and psychology professionals alike and generally refers to one who engages in some form of child sexual exploitation. The specific images of the child molester conjured up by society vary greatly. Such images range from child molesters who coax or pressure their victims into sexual activity to the more violent child rapist who overpowers and threatens his victims, and all variations in between. In reality, the child molester is not a crazed psychopath but more accurately is a product of his or her own emotional immaturity.

Herman Goldstein defines this offender as "a significantly older person who engages in any type of sexual activity with individuals legally defined as children."[11] The term *pedophile* is also associated with *child molester,* although the two terms may not portray the same type of person, that is, a pedophile, one whose sexual orientation is toward children, may harbor thoughts of sexual relations with children but may never act out such fantasies. Conversely, however, it might be a safe assumption to consider most child molesters as pedophiles, as their sexual desires are, indeed, manifested by sexual assault.

In most cases of abuse, only one child and one adult are involved, but cases involving several adults and several children have been reported. For example, a 54-year-old man, who had previously won a community award for his work with youth, was arrested for child molestation involving boys as young as 10 years old. The man would encourage and photograph sexual acts between the boys, such as mutual masturbation and oral and anal sex. He would then have sex with one of them.[12]

A study of 229 convicted child molesters revealed the following information. Nearly 25 percent of their victims were under 6 years of age. An additional 25 percent were ages 6 to 10, and about 50 percent were ages 11 to 13. Fondling of the child was the most common sexual behavior, followed by vaginal and oral–genital contact. Bribery was most often used to gain participation of the victims.[13] Studies have shown that the pedophile has the highest recidivism rate of all sex offenders, approximately 25 percent.[14] Incidents of child molestation are believed to be one of the most underreported types of crime. This can be attributed to several phenomena, including embarrassment on the part of the child, fears of bearing the blame for the incident, a fear of being labeled after the incident is exposed, apprehension about the court process, concern that no one will believe the child victim, and fear of reprisal by the offender.

For investigative purposes, the child molester can be viewed as falling into two distinct typological categories: situational and preferential. The **situational molester** doesn't necessarily suffer from any specified psychological disorder but may commit such crimes because of one of several external factors. These include intoxication, drug abuse, mood or mental conditions, or other social conditions. In contrast, the **preferential molester** has sexual desires focusing on children and is typically suffering from a more identifiable psychological disorder.

Accordingly, studies of child molesters have revealed two psychological types: fixated and regressed.[15] The **fixated child molester** is one whose primary sexual orientation is toward children and whose sociosexual maturation develops as a result of unresolved conflicts in his or her development. With this offender, children have always been the focus of sexual interests, and sexual contacts with age mates have been situational but never preferred. The child molester will probably not be a stranger to the victim, that is, statistics have shown that such offenders are not only commonly known but frequently related to their victims. Examples are:

- A natural parent or other family member, including a stepfather, step-mother, or uncle
- A trusted adult, neighbor, boyfriend, or familiar person
- A remote acquaintance (e.g., co-worker)

The **regressed child molester,** however, represents a clear (but possibly temporary) departure from a primary orientation toward age mates, as the child becomes a substitute for an adult partner. Unlike the fixated offender, regressed child molesters did not previously exhibit preferences for younger persons in their formative years. Rather, when adult relationships develop conflicts and become emotionally unfulfilling, sexual attraction to children emerges.

INVESTIGATING THE MOLESTER

It is important for any investigator to understand, as fully as possible, the methods used by child sex offenders. When an investigator understands the molester's desires and intentions, he or she can more adequately seek out the proper evidence for prosecution. For example, investigations have shown that child molesters frequently collect pornography and child erotica. Such items will aid the prosecution in establishing intent or motive of some offenders. Pornography fuels the desires that they harbor for sexual contact with children.[16] Studies have also shown that child sexual assault is frequently a premeditated act, that is, offenders might only casually consider a particular course of action (fantasizing) without a specific plan or act, or they might take a more overt action in stalking and abducting their victim.

Premeditation and Intent

The circumstances of any given incident can show premeditation on the part of the molester. For example, in one such case, a man boarded a transit bus loaded with children. The offender was then seated next to a young girl approximately 10 years old, and during the bus ride, the man's arm came to rest on the child's inner thigh or upper leg. Subsequent investigation revealed that the same man was frequently among a group of children at the time a local school let out and had no business being there. Here he also used his "hand trick" as was used on the bus.[17]

Types of Pedophile Sexual Offenders

Child Molester (Generally Nonviolent)

- Has access through family, enticement, or deception.
- Lures the child, or tricks the child into sex acts; will sometimes pressure the child into sexual activity.
- Gives gifts or rewards to the child.
- Cautions his or her victims against disclosure.
- Frequently explains that the activity must be kept a "secret" between the offender and the child.
- Gives the child attention, acceptance, recognition in exchange for sex.
- Often targets handicapped children because they are loners.
- May target the child of a single parent who may have no male figure in the immediate family.
- May be a child rapist (forcible).
- Overpowers and controls the child much as do adult rapists.
- Uses physical force or threats.
- Is part of a small minority of sex offenders of children.

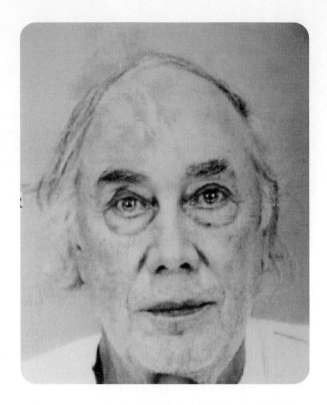

Figure 16.6 Dean Schwartzmiller is thought to have molested as many as 36,000 children over three decades in several states, Mexico, and Brazil. *Santa Clara County Sheriffs Office, AP Wide World Photos*

As this case illustrates, premeditation can be demonstrated through comparing different situations with which the same suspect was involved and establishing an MO. As indicated, investigators should remember that molesters frequent places where there are children in their target group. This will help establish the molester's intent and might also help establish probable cause to stop, detain, identify, and possibly arrest offenders.

Figure 16.7 Two girls, ages 7 and 9, ride their bikes in front of the home of convicted child molester Dean Schwartzmiller, in San Jose, California. *Paul Sakuma, AP Wide World Photos*

DISCUSSION QUESTIONS

1. Discuss the distinctions between child physical and sexual abuse.

2. Describe some of the physical indications of child abuse.

3. Define the term *pedophile,* and discuss how the term relates to sexual misconduct with children.

4. Describe the "typical" child molester and how the actual offender differs from the stereotypic offender.

5. What are the differences between the fixated and the regressed child molester?

6. List and discuss three problems in investigating child molestation cases.

7. When interviewing a child victim of sexual abuse, discuss the best initial approach that investigators should use to establish rapport with the child.

8. What are some of the problems that investigators must face when using a child victim as a witness?

9. List and explain the symptoms of Munchausen syndrome by proxy.

10. Identify types of evidence in shaken baby syndrome cases.

NOTES

1. CHILDREN'S BUREAU. (2004). *Child maltreatment.* Washington, DC: U.S. Department of Health and Human Services. Online: http://www.acf.dhhs.gov/programs/cb/publications/cm02.
2. Ibid.
3. GEBERTH, V. (1990). *Practical homicide investigation,* 2nd ed. New York: Elsevier.
4. GEISSINGER, S. (1993). Boy Scouts dismissed 1,800 suspected molesters from 1971–1991. *Boston Globe,* October 15, p. 3.
5. RUSSELL, D. (1983). The incidence and prevalance of intrafamilial and extrafamilial sexual abuse of female children. *Child Abuse and Neglect,* 7:133–146.
6. WOLFNER, G., and R. GELLES (1993). A profile of violence toward children: A national study. *Child Abuse and Neglect,* 17:144–146.
7. LAWSON, L., and M. CHIFFEN (1992). False negatives in sexual abuse disclosure interviews. *Journal of Interpersonal Violence,* 7:532–542.
8. GOLDSTEIN, H. (1977). *Policing a free society.* Cambridge, MA: Ballinger, p. 1.
9. KLOTTER, J. (1990). *Criminal law,* 3rd ed. Cincinnati, OH: Anderson.
10. ST. LOUIS SCHOOL OF MEDICINE (1991). *Forensic investigation of wrongful death.* St. Louis, MO: St. Louis University Press.
11. GOLDSTEIN (1977). *Policing a free society.*
12. BURGESS, A. W., C. R. HARTMAN, and M. P. MCCAUSLAND (1984). Response pattern in children and adolescents exploited through sex rings and pornography. *American Journal of Psychiatry,* 141:656–662.
13. ERICKSON, W. D., N. H. WALBEK, and R. K. SEELY (1988). Behavior patterns of child molesters. *Archives of Sexual Behavior,* 17:77–86.
14. Ibid.
15. GROTH, A. N., and J. BIRNBAUM (1981). *Men who rape: The psychology of the offender.* New York: Plenum Press.
16. GOLDSTEIN (1977). *Policing a free society.*
17. Ibid.

Part

IV

Property Crimes

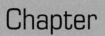

Key Terms

▶ burglary
▶ burglary tools
▶ fence
▶ fungible goods
▶ Neighborhood Watch
▶ proactive patrol
▶ property crime

This chapter will enable you to:

- List the elements of the crime of burglary.
- Describe the various categories of burglaries.
- Discuss the steps in the preliminary investigation of burglaries.
- Consider the various types of evidence required in a burglary case.
- Describe how to trace stolen property.
- Estimate the value of circumstantial evidence in burglaries.
- Comprehend the problem of forgery and fraud.

INTRODUCTION

The crime of **burglary** is generally considered a covert crime in which the criminal works during the nighttime, outside the presence of witnesses. The burglar has often been portrayed in the media as a cunning masked person who is quick to elude police. In actuality, burglars are represented by virtually every creed, gender, and color and may indeed be skillful in their techniques, but they may also be bungling amateurs. In fact, it is estimated that opportunists commit most burglaries. Burglary for the most part is a **property crime.** The crime differs from robbery, as burglars are more concerned with financial gain and less prepared for a violent altercation with the victim. Their goal is to steal as much valuable property as possible and sell what they steal (usually to a fence, who has connections to dispose of the property before police can discover it).

BURGLARY

The Uniform Crime Reports (UCR) Program employs three classifications of burglary: (1) forcible entry, (2) unlawful entry or no force used, and (3) attempted forcible entry. In most jurisdictions, force need not be employed for a crime to be classified as burglary. Unlocked doors and open windows are invitations to burglars, and the crime of burglary consists not so much of a forcible entry as it does the intent of the offender to trespass and steal.

Many people fear nighttime burglary of their residence. They imagine themselves asleep in bed when a stranger breaks into their home, resulting in a violent confrontation. Although such scenarios do occur, daytime burglaries are more common. Many families now have two or more breadwinners, and since children are in school during the day, some homes—and even entire neighborhoods—remain unoccupied during daylight hours. This shift in patterns of social activity has led to growing burglary threats against residences during the daytime.

Trends

In 2005, law enforcement agencies reported an estimated 2,154,126 burglary offenses—a 0.5 percent increase compared with 2004 data. Burglary accounted for 21.2 percent of the estimated number of property crimes committed in 2005. Of all burglary offenses in 2005, 65.8 percent were of residential structures.

Most (62.4%) of residential burglaries in 2005 took place during the day, between 6 A.M. and 6 P.M. The average dollar loss per burglary offense was $1,725. Of nonresidential burglaries, 58.0 percent occurred at night.

Comparative Rates

Burglary Trend

Year	Number of Offenses	Rate per 100,000 Inhabitants
2004	2,144,446	730.3
2005	2,154,126	726.7
Percent change	+0.5	+3.6

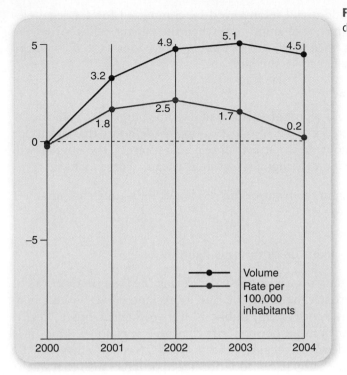

Figure 17.1 Burglary: Percent change. FBI, Crime in the United States, 2006.

Burglary versus Robbery

A distinction should be made between the terms *burglary* and *robbery*, as they are commonly confused. Burglary is considered a property crime in which the thief seeks to avoid direct contact with people during commission of the crime. In addition, locations of burglaries are usually unoccupied homes or businesses where no witnesses are present. The crime of robbery is quite different. Here, the robber chooses to confront his or her victim at a location where witnesses are present. Robbery is therefore classified as a crime against persons. In this chapter, we examine burglary.

Why Criminals Burglarize

Burglary is an appealing alternative to the criminal because it offers a quick opportunity to acquire money or other valuables on short notice. Drug addicts have typically been associated with burglaries because they need a constant source of cash with which to purchase drugs. Some burglars are violent in nature, but experience has shown that they will usually try to avoid confrontations during the commission of their act. In fact, many will actually flee the area when confronted.

Elements of Burglary

Although the elements of the crime are defined by each state's criminal code, many differences exist regarding these laws. Some commonalities, however, are also present and are generally reflected in the elements of the crime.

Burglary is a crime against the dwelling that is violated. Accordingly, no violence need be directed toward any occupants. As a rule, once the burglar is inside the structure, no additional felony need be committed for the legal elements of the crime to be met. Exceptions are when the person believes that the structure he is entering is open to the general public. Decisions as to the validity of this claim are typically left up to the jury.

How a Thief Works

Although many jurisdictions report an increase in daytime burglaries, some occur at night, typically between 7 and 12 P.M. It is during those hours that a burglar becomes most inconspicuous on the street. In selecting a target, the burglar will look for certain things to indicate that a structure is vacant. These include:

- Newspapers collecting in the front of the residence, indicating that no one has been home for a while.
- Empty garage left open.
- House with too many lights on or just one light left on.

When a daytime burglary occurs, it is usually during the time that most people are working. To approach the residence, the more innovative burglar may pose as a salesperson, insurance agent, public utility worker, or other "legitimate" person. This permits him or her to verify that no one is home. Once it is determined that the residence is vacant, either a quick, forceful entry can be made into the house, or the burglar can look for a tree or large bush that might cloak a window, which he or she can then use to enter the house unnoticed by neighbors.

TYPES OF BURGLARIES

Burglaries can be divided into two general categories: residential and commercial. *Residential* burglars may focus on apartments or houses and will usually work the higher-income areas of town. In both cases, the experienced burglar will be familiar with preventive measures employed by residents. Such measures are sometimes easily defeated through knowledge of how they work. For example, an apartment dweller was careful in placing a steel rod in the track of the sliding glass door leading to the patio area before he left town. The burglar, however, simply removed the six screws securing the "nonmovable" piece of glass next to the sliding door, slid the pane of glass to the side, and entered the apartment. Once inside the structure, money is most typically sought, but other valuables might be taken as well.

Warehouses, stores, taverns, and restaurants are all common targets of *commercial* burglaries. Occasionally, employees of companies will be implicated

---

Elements of Burglary

Burglary is committed when a person

- Knowingly breaks or
- Remains in
- A building or structure belonging to another
- For the purpose of committing a crime therein.

in such thefts, as they have direct knowledge of the types of merchandise in stock and locations of cash.

ATM Burglaries

In February 1998, six people in Orlando, Florida, were charged in connection with three ATM (automated teller machine) thefts after a predawn gun battle with police. The suspects were thought to be connected with a Yugoslav–Albanian–Croatian crime ring that targets ATM machines nationwide. In another February 1998 case, three people in Los Angeles were charged with burglarizing seven bank ATMs. In one case, one suspect disabled the alarms in the machines and then destroyed the surveillance tapes while the other two served as lookouts.

Burglaries of automated teller machines (ATMs) are one new form of burglary that is on the increase. The ability of banks to provide increased security measures, along with the proliferation of small freestanding ATMs, has become a concern for criminal investigators. In 1997, there were over 200 ATM burglaries (and attempted burglaries), compared with 70 in 1992. This compares to a reduction of bank robberies, down 13 percent during 1997.[1] Of course, the use of ATMs is also up considerably in recent years. In 1997, there were 11 billion ATM transactions, compared to 4 billion in 1985. The amount stolen from ATMs ranges from $15,000 to $250,000, so the "take" for a successful burglar can be fairly substantial.

TYPES OF BURGLARS

Criminals who commit property crimes can be categorized into one of two groups: amateurs or professionals. Although both pose a problem to society, each group has special characteristics.

The Amateur Burglar

The amateur burglar might travel a broad geographical area in search of the best opportunities for stealing. Many such persons will resort to more personal contact with victims, such as purse snatching, muggings, or even robbery. The amateur thief will sometimes be armed and can pose a serious threat to communities in which he operates.

Juveniles pose another type of amateur thief. Most juveniles are opportunists who search for homes and businesses with unlocked doors or open windows. It is also characteristic of juveniles to resort to needless destruction of property during the commission of their crimes. In one case, three juveniles entered a residence to steal some liquor, but while they were there, they carved their initials in a grand piano, broke record albums in half, and spray-painted obscenities on the walls. The juvenile burglar will sometimes go to the kitchen and consume food from the cabinets or refrigerator during the commission of the crime. In this case, fingerprints may be lifted from the walls, cabinets, and so on for later use in identifying a possible suspect.

The Professional Burglar

The professional thief represents a unique criminal type. Such a person takes a great deal of time in planning a crime to avoid detection and net the greatest

Figure 17.2 Pry marks such as these are often evidence of a forcible entry.

cache of property possible. The "pro" commonly relies on the expert use of tools for entry into otherwise secure structures. He might also consider making a bogus burglary call to another part of town to occupy the local police, thus giving him more freedom in his work. Pros typically drive trucks or vans, which conceal and transport their tools. Fake company names may even be painted on the sides of vehicles to deter suspicion by neighbors.

Figure 17.3 Heel of suspect's shoe, seized as evidence.

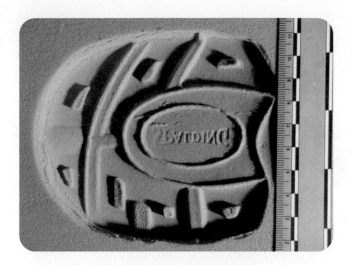

Figure 17.4 Imprint of suspect's shoe heel found at scene of burglary—matching shoe seized in the investigation.

THE PRELIMINARY INVESTIGATION

It is the patrol division that will probably respond first to a burglary call. The first thing officers should do is determine whether a crime is currently in progress. If so, an ample number of officers should be dispatched to prevent the escape of the suspect(s). Officers approaching the burglary location should do so quietly, without warning emergency lights or siren. En route, officers should also be on the lookout for persons fleeing the scene. It is also important for each officer to know exactly which fellow officers are responding to the call. As a rule, the first officer to receive the call will assume responsibility for placement of assisting officers.

After arriving, great care should be taken not to slam car doors, to turn down police radios, and to avoid the jangling of keys while approaching the residence. In addition, officers should approach the residence on both the front and back sides in the event that the suspect attempts to flee.

Indications of Burglary

At the scene, certain reliable indicators that a burglary has been (or is being) committed can be observed (e.g., open doors or windows). Sometimes a burglar who makes his entrance through a window will remove the glass. This makes it difficult

Figure 17.5 Tire track evidence documented and preserved at a burglary scene.

Figure 17.6 Tire matching tire impressions from the scene—Investigators must remember to photograph all tread on the suspect tire in order to capture the section of tread that touched the ground.

for the officer to detect a break-in with only a superficial glance. So when checking glass, the officer should look for a reflection with the use of a flashlight. Sometimes burglaries can be detected by spotting debris on the floor from shelves or counters. Also, debris can be found around desks and cabinets. Other indicators include vehicles parked near the suspect location for no apparent reason or trucks parked close enough to a building to permit access to a roof or to conceal a window or door. In the case of a building burglary, a burglar alarm is another indicator of possible entry. Although wind, stormy conditions, or malfunctions can set off some alarms, the responding officer should not assume anything. Every alarm situation should be responded to as though it were a burglary in progress.

Yet another sign of a burglary in progress is a person serving as a lookout. Lookouts may be on, in, or near buildings, or sitting in cars. Burglars have been known to use such tactics as parking a car a few feet down the street, raising the car's hood, using citizens band walkie-talkies, or just blowing the horn as a signal that police are approaching.

Approach with Caution!

Officers should enter the structure with weapons drawn, using their flashlights for illumination rather than room lights. This is done as a precaution to avoid the forming of silhouettes. In addition, officers should hold flashlights to their

Figure 17.7 Shoe print located at burglary scene.

Figure 17.8 Seized shoe from suspect matching impressions.

sides while flashing them sporadically, to avoid making targets of themselves. Once the location has been secured, or "flushed" for suspects, certain aspects of the scene should be documented.

- Document the time of the call.
- Record details about the type of structure.
- Record and document the method of entry and exit used by the suspect.
- Determine the whereabouts of the owner.
- Log all items of property taken and their original locations.
- Discuss with neighbors whether they noticed anything suspicious.

If no suspects are located in the structure, investigators should follow the preliminary investigation steps outlined in Chapter 3. If suspects are thought to be inside the burglary location, entry should not be considered until sufficient backup has arrived and each officer knows the exact location of other officers at the time of entry.

Physical Evidence

Experience has shown that most burglars are convicted on circumstantial evidence. Therefore, any physical evidence located at the burglary crime scene will be critical to the case. In addition to forensic evidence such as broken glass, tool

Investigative Techniques in Burglary Cases

- Determine the point of entry.
- Check to see if a window or door was forced open.
- What type of tool was used?
- Are there tool marks?
- Is there evidence of lock picks?
- Look for footprints, tire tracks, and so on.
- Look for other trace evidence: cigarette butts, fibers, hair, pieces of broken tools, and so on.
- Sketch the scene.
- Interview victims and witnesses.
- Make a list of property taken (include serial numbers).
- Make a list of all persons on the crime scene.

Figure 17.9 Boltcutters are considered a pinching type of tool and have interactive blades that oppose each other.

marks, and fingerprints at the burglary crime scene, other evidence should also be sought by the investigator. In the case of safe burglaries, safe insulation can be used to link the suspect to the crime scene.

Possession of Burglary Tools

Possession of **burglary tools** is considered a separate felony offense by most jurisdictions. If circumstances surrounding the confiscation of the tools indicate that they were intended for use in a burglary, possession of them is usually sufficient for a conviction, even though a burglary has not yet been committed.

Many legitimate uses, of course, can be found for the preceding tools and materials. The investigating officer should therefore determine if possession of the tools is legitimate and if there is any criminal "intent" present that would support criminal charges. Burglary tools can consist of numerous items.

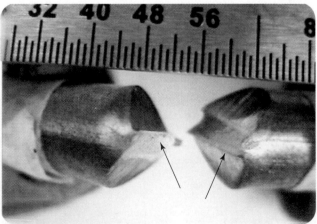

Figure 17.10 A copper wire that was cut by a pair of bolt cutters (right). Notice how the cut is peaked (at the arrows) and not flat. A microphotograph of the copper wires (left). The boltcutters in Figure 17.9 were identified as cutting this copper wire.

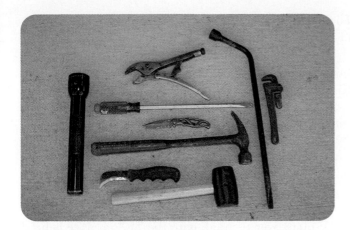

Figure 17.11 Burglary tools.

SAFE BURGLARIES

Although safe burglaries are not the problem they once were, they still occur and pose some unique obstacles to the investigator. Such problems are usually attributed to the fact that many safe burglars use sophisticated tools such as torches, sectional crowbars, and even explosives. A safe can be defined as either a portable or semiportable container that is designed to limit unauthorized entry and is typically opened with a combination lock. Several methods are used by burglars to gain forceful entry into the safe:

- *Peeling or ripping.* These techniques are very similar and represent the most common type of entry into safes. The chisel, sledgehammer, crowbar, and drill are the most commonly used tools for this technique. The peel attack is initiated by producing a hole at the edge of one of the outer steel doorplates. A jimmy is then used to systematically break each spot-weld or rivet used to hold it in place. The plating is bent back, or peeled, to expose

Possession of Burglary Tools

Ronald is standing in an alley behind a store late at night. A police car arrives, and the officers see Ronald. The officers also see a crowbar, a false key, a lock pick, and a force screw near the area where Ronald is standing. In addition, Ronald has no reasonable explanation for standing in the alley. Under these circumstances, Ronald has probably committed the crime of possession of burglary tools. Although many burglary tools can be purchased in hardware stores, investigators must show that the "intent" was present for the suspect to use them in a burglary. For example, the "reputation" or criminal history of the suspect can offer some evidence to show criminal intent to commit the crime.

- Explosives
- Slim jims
- Any instrument designed for cutting or burning or opening containers, such as torches or welders
- Portable key cutters
- Key blanks
- Pry bars
- Bolt cutters
- Explosives or chemicals
- Tension wrenches
- Lock picks

the safe's insulation. The chisel is used to remove the insulation and expose the locking mechanism. That apparatus is then pried loose, and the door is opened.

- *Punching.* The experienced safe burglar can complete a punch attack in just a few seconds. Required tools are a small sledgehammer, a chisel, and a punch or drift pin. Typically, the crime involves a blow from a hammer that disables the combination dial, thus enabling the criminal to remove the dial ring around the clock, breaking it off with a chisel. The drift pin is now used to drive the spindle back into the safe, leaving a broken locking mechanism and hole in the center of the safe door. The door can now be opened.

- *Pulling.* This method, which is most successful on older models of safes, involves the placing of a V-plate over the dial, with the "V" in place behind the dial. The screw bolts are then slowly tightened one at a time until the dial is pulled out.

- *Blasting.* This technique simply involves drilling a hole into the safe close to the locking bar area, placing nitroglycerin on a piece of cotton, and placing the nitro in the hole. When it explodes, the safe is blown open, and entry can be made.

- *Chopping.* A chop attack is a crude method of entry into insulated safes. The safe is simply turned upside down and attacked with an axe or sledgehammer. Once a hole is present, the intruder can reach the contents. Both experienced safe crackers and amateurs use this technique.

Certainly, many safes can be opened easily by the use of a combination, if known by the intruder. This can occur when employees standing near or around the safe write combinations down for future reference. Safes can also be burglarized when found unlocked by the intruder. Indeed, when investigators find a burglarized safe that has not been forced open, it is usually because the perpetrator had knowledge of the combination. Cases such as this often implicate an employee.

TRACING STOLEN PROPERTY

Once a successful burglary has occurred, the thief will probably seek to get rid of the stolen property as soon as possible. To this end, a **fence** is used. The fence is a person who buys and sells stolen property with criminal intent.

The Fence

Fencing operations can range from professional to highly unorganized. For example, a nonprofessional fence might simply take a trunk full of stolen property in his or her vehicle to a location such as a factory parking lot, where workers on break can come for "good deals." The professional fence may operate from an otherwise legitimate business such as a pawnshop or used furniture store. People operating in this fashion don't necessarily consider themselves criminals but yet seldom question the lawful ownership of property they receive. From this fixed location, the fence purchases property on a random basis from thieves in the area. This arrangement tends to foster a degree of dependency between the thief and the fence, each needing the services of the other.

Proving the Receipt of Stolen Property

Establishing proof of a fencing operation is a grueling and time-consuming task. However, it is during the possession and storage of stolen property that a fence is most vulnerable. Although many arrests result from lengthy investigations, many are made when suspected stolen property is identified. This is sometimes necessary when there is a risk of losing the property and confiscation is required. As a first rule of thumb, the property in question must be identified as stolen, a task that is more difficult than it may first seem. For instance, many suspected thieves are in possession of property that bears no identification numbers. Without some type of identification number, positive identification is extremely difficult.

In addition, many companies fail to maintain adequate inventory control. Poorly kept records also make it difficult to trace property even when identification numbers are present. Another category of untraceable goods is **fungible goods,** items such as tools, liquor, and clothing that are indistinguishable from others like them. In the absence of some type of identifying numbers, such items are virtually untraceable. To convict a thief for a property offense in this category, investigators must prove that the suspect received stolen property. Laws addressing stolen property also include possession, concealment, and sale of stolen property. Because evidence in this category is sometimes difficult to obtain, investigators might have to rely on circumstantial evidence for prosecution.

One method of showing possession of stolen property is to locate the property on the premises of the suspect. This finding, however, may not be sufficient to prove "criminal intent." It is helpful to show that the stolen goods are in close proximity with personal goods owned by the suspect. This will avoid the defense that the stolen goods were in the possession of someone else living at the same residence.

Circumstantial Evidence

Other than the evidence discussed previously, investigators might need to rely on circumstantial evidence to prove receipt of stolen property. Such evidence is described as follows:

- Did the suspect pay for the merchandise with a check or cash?
- Was the property purchased for considerably lower than the normal retail price?
- Does the suspect have a receipt for the property?
- Were the stolen items isolated from other items in storage?
- Is there property from several different thefts present at the location?

Once property is retrieved, a determination should be made as to how it got there. The owner of the property should examine it and make a positive identification. In many cases, a secondhand store or pawnshop owner can make a positive identification of a fence.

BURGLARY PREVENTION THROUGH PROACTIVE PATROL

The patrol function of most police departments has undergone substantial change during the last decade. No longer can police patrol in a meaningless, nonproductive pattern. Factors such as vehicle cost and maintenance and officer training expenses have forced this arm of law enforcement to adopt new methods of enforcement.

Closer working relationships have recently developed between the police and the public. Programs such as **Neighborhood Watch** are evidence of this. As a result, merchants and residents have been encouraged to take a more proactive role in detecting and reporting activity that might be criminal in nature. There has been an increasing awareness that although communities would like potential criminals to believe that the police are everywhere (the notion of police omnipresence), in fact, crimes are not repressed or prevented.

Proactive patrol can be an effective tool in burglary prevention as well as that of many other crimes. As Thomas Adams points out, rather than stake out 847 drugstores because there is a drugstore burglar operating in the community, it makes more sense to locate known drugstore burglars and watch them instead.[2] After watching certain known burglars for a period, officers can examine reports of new drugstore burglaries that might have occurred during the time of the surveillance. This will tell the officers that this particular burglar is not the same suspect as the one committing the current rash of burglaries. He is then dropped from the list of burglars under surveillance, and officers proceed to watch other known burglars until the perpetrator is caught. Hence a classic process of elimination occurs through the efficient use of police patrol talents.

DISCUSSION QUESTIONS

1. Discuss the distinction between robbery and burglary.
2. Explain the differences between crimes against property and crimes against persons.
3. List and discuss the elements of the crime of burglary.
4. What characteristics does the house burglar look for in "casing" a neighborhood?
5. Discuss the differences between residential and commercial burglaries.
6. What physical evidence should be considered in investigating a burglary?
7. Describe the procedure for responding to a burglary-in-progress call.
8. Discuss the crime of possession of burglary tools.
9. Discuss the methods that are considered most common in the investigation of safe burglaries.
10. What role does a fence play in the crime of burglary?
11. Describe and discuss the measures for proving the receipt of stolen property.
12. Discuss fungible property and how it relates to the investigation of burglaries.
13. Discuss proactive patrol and how it can be used to combat the crime of burglary.

NOTES

1. LOWRY, T. (1998). Cash machines provide new target for burglars. *USA Today*, March 16, p. 1B.

2. ADAMS, T. (1990). *Police field operations*, 2nd ed. Upper Saddle River, NJ: Prentice Hall.

Key Terms

▶ booster
▶ check kiting
▶ embezzlement
▶ fences
▶ hot list
▶ identity theft
▶ pilferage
▶ plastic worker
▶ shoplifting
▶ snitch

This chapter will enable you to:

- Understand the problems of forgery and fraud.
- Define the various types of embezzlement.
- Describe the methods of check kiting and credit card fraud.
- Understand the problem of shoplifting.

INTRODUCTION

In 2002, 25-year-old Ted Roberts and 22-year-old Tiffany Fowler were arrested in Orlando, Florida, and charged with stealing moon rocks from the Johnson Space Center in Houston, Texas. Roberts had been working as a student intern at the center, and Fowler was a Space Center employee. Officials realized that the lunar samples, along with a number of meteorites, were missing when they discovered that a 600 pound safe had disappeared from the Houston facility. They had been alerted to the loss by messages placed on a Web site run by a mineralogy club in Antwerp, Belgium, offering "priceless Moon rocks collected by Apollo astronauts" for sale for up to $5,000 per gram. Roberts and Fowler were arrested by federal agents pretending to be potential buyers for the moon rocks.

Probably the most commonly committed crime of personal gain is larceny–theft. It is defined as the unlawful taking, carrying, leading, or riding away of property from the possession of another. Larceny–theft is one of the eight Index crimes according to the Uniform Crime Reports. Generally, the two terms are considered synonymous. In some states, criminal law recognizes simple larceny (e.g., shoplifting) and grand larceny (e.g., auto theft). In most cases, what distinguishes one form of larceny from another is the dollar amount of the items stolen. Often, when anything stolen is valued under $200, the charge is simple larceny, while stolen property valued in excess of that figure is grand larceny. As a rule, thefts of any amount are considered larceny. The following offenses are examples of larceny:

- Pocket picking
- Breaking into coin machines
- Purse snatching
- Shoplifting
- Stealing bicycles
- Stealing motor vehicles
- Stealing valuables left in unattended buildings
- Stealing motor vehicle accessories

LARCENY–THEFT OFFENSES

There are many types of larceny–theft offenses, and their rate of occurrence is considerable. A lack of witnesses or other "concrete" evidence makes larceny a difficult crime to solve. Although there are many different types of larceny–theft offenses, in this book we attempt to discuss only a few of the most problematic.

Elements of Larceny–Theft

A person commits the crime of larceny–theft if he or she

- Takes and carries away
- The personal property
- Of another
- Without consent and with the intent to steal.

Comparative Rates

Larceny–Theft Trend

Year	Number of Offenses	Rate per 100,000 Inhabitants
2004	6,947,685	2,365.9
2005	6,776,807	2,342.6
Percent change	−2.3	−3.2

Before the investigator can determine whether a crime has been committed, he or she must understand the legal elements.

In larceny–theft investigations, the state must show that there was a "taking" at least for a brief time and that the defendant had control over the property "of another." The taking must be deliberate and with the intent to steal.

The UCR defines larceny–theft as the unlawful taking, carrying, leading, or riding away of property from the possession or constructive possession of another. It includes crimes such as shoplifting, pocket picking, purse snatching, thefts from motor vehicles, thefts of motor vehicle parts and accessories, and bicycle thefts, in which no use of force, violence, or fraud occurs. In the Uniform Crime Reporting Program, this crime category does not include embezzlement, confidence games, forgery, or worthless checks. Motor vehicle theft is also excluded from this category inasmuch as it is a separate Crime Index offense.

Trends

According to the 2005 Uniform Crime Reports published by the Federal Bureau of Investigation, there were an estimated 6.8 million (6,776,807) larceny–theft offenses nationwide during 2005. From 2004 to 2005 the rate of larceny–thefts declined 3.2 percent, and from 1996 to 2005, the rate declined 23.3 percent.

Two-thirds of all property crimes in 2005 were larceny–thefts. with 2,286.3 larceny–theft offenses per 100,000 inhabitants. The average value for property stolen during the commission of a larceny–theft was $764 per offense.[1]

FORGERY AND FRAUD

Theft crimes in the form of forgery or fraud accounted for 54 percent of the 28,012 white-collar felony dispositions in 1993. In addition, fraud constituted 38 percent and embezzlement made up 8 percent of white-collar dispositions. Fraud cases may be enigmatic in nature. For example, in 1992 physician Cecil Jacobson (the sperm doctor) was convicted of secretly fathering the children of as many as 75 of his patients through artificial insemination. In this case, the federal jury ruled that he wrongfully used his sperm instead of that of anonymous donors to impregnate patients after promising to use donors who resembled their husbands and that he used hormone injections to trick women into thinking they were pregnant and then told them they'd miscarried, ensuring that they would return.

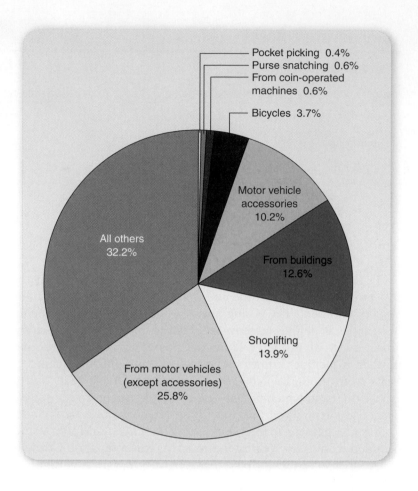

Figure 18.1 Larceny–theft: Percent distribution, 2005. Due to rounding, the percentages may not add up to 100. FBI, Crime in the United States, 2006

Check Fraud

Despite all the talk of electronic banking, one low-tech device is increasingly popular: the checkbook. Just as check writing has boomed, so has check fraud. According to the American Bankers Association, check fraud is a growing concern, costing banks $815 million in 1993, up 43 percent from 1991.[2] In addition to its impact on banks is its effect on consumers. For example, check fraud leads to higher fees for bounced checks, and when a person is a victim of check fraud, dealing with it can impose a severe hardship in reconciling and closing an account and dealing with creditors seeking payment for merchandise purchased with bogus checks. Why is there an increase in check fraud? The American Bankers Association responds with several reasons:

- The proliferation of personal computers and high-quality copiers, which make it easier and less expensive to forge copies of checks.
- Checking account customers who don't safeguard their account numbers.
- Competition for business, which discourages some banks from stepping up procedures to detect and combat fraud because it might inconvenience customers.

Criminals realize that check forgery is not only lucrative, but because it is a nonviolent crime, their chances of being prosecuted are unlikely. Bands of crim-

$40 Million Check Fraud Ring

In April 1996, law enforcement agencies began targeting a group of people who allegedly operated a fraudulent check-cashing scheme in the United States and abroad. On June 12, 2000, nine persons, primarily Nigerian nationals, were arrested in the Los Angeles area for their involvement in a check scheme that involved over $40 million. All of those arrested pleaded guilty. Federal agents identified five of the nine people as the ringleaders of the scheme.

Theft of Credit Cards and Checks

Those involved in this scheme illegally obtained millions of dollars by stealing not only credit cards but also blank and completed checks. The stolen completed checks ranged from roughly $10,000 to over $2 million. Checks addressed to businesses and high-tech customers were stolen by mail carriers with the U.S. Postal Service. Checks were also stolen from company mailrooms before they were sent and after they were received. Usually, the targeted businesses, including Toyota and Disney, were large corporations known to write many checks.

Dozens of companies did not discover the missing money until reviewing their checking records, months after the thefts.

Most of the stolen checks were then given to forgers who prepared them for deposit by changing the payee name and dollar amount of the check. Some checks were deposited after only the endorsements were forged. The altered checks were deposited into accounts in banks and brokerages in the United States, Indonesia, Senegal, Germany, England, and Hong Kong; these accounts were established using false personal or business names. In some instances, account names were established that were similar to the names of the targeted businesses.

With the stolen money in their false accounts, those involved in the scheme wrote checks, purchased cashier's checks, withdrew cash, and transmitted money by wire transfer.

Here's how the scheme worked: A check worth over $160,000 was stolen from a large entertainment company, altered, and deposited into a bank account controlled by one of the defendants. The money in the account was then divided into 33 cashier's checks and distributed to members of the gang.

inals often travel from region to region targeting different banks and payroll accounts. After infiltrating an employer and forging documents, they can walk off with as much as $300,000 per day.

Forgery of a victim's personal check involves acquiring both the check and a form of identification of the victim. He or she must then be able to forge the victim's name on the instrument successfully to the point that it closely resembles the original. In addition to the signature, amounts of checks can sometimes be altered to represent larger amounts. This can be accomplished in several ways. For example, the amount $10 can be altered to read $100 simply by adding a zero onto the designated amount and then altering the written portion of the instrument. Forgery of government checks is another growing problem in many parts of the country. Many such checks, such as welfare and unemployment payments, are mailed in groups, at regular intervals, and are sometimes stolen directly from mailboxes.

Banking institutions often consider the government check as legitimate because of its "official" appearance. Therefore, its legitimacy often goes unquestioned. Once passed, the forged government check may go undetected for months before the crime is discovered. Another method of forgery includes the use of fictitious checks drawn on a nonexistent firm or person. These schemes, called **check kiting,** are commonly encountered by law enforcement authorities. Kiting consists of drawing cash on accounts made up of uncollected funds. By using two different banking institutions, the kiter may use funds from one bank to cover checks drawn on another. Each time the bank pays out funds against the account balance, the kiter has been successful in cheating the bank out of its own funds.

Banks are responding with new methods designed to stop bank fraud. For example, in 1995, the Texas Banking Association began experimenting with a new program where a thumbprint is required from nonaccount holders who wish to cash checks. The thumbprints are kept on file only until the check clears. Pilot programs in Nevada and Arizona have resulted in a 40 to 80 percent reduction in check fraud losses.[3] Other services, such as the Duplex/BEI Check Fraud Prevention Program, aid banks in identifying patterns of criminal behavior to single out suspicious checks before they lose money. For example, a criminal opens an account with a small amount of money and waits a few months to deposit a fraudulent check for $80,000. He then withdraws the money after two business days, knowing that the bank is required to make the money available promptly. By the time the bank finds out that a check is counterfeit, a criminal is already gone with the money.

Investigating Check Forgery

One problem presenting itself in forgery cases is when the victim desires only restitution from the suspect and is unwilling to follow through with prosecution. The posture of the victim must therefore be determined early by the investigating law enforcement agency; otherwise, the police simply become a collection agency for the victim, and much valuable time is lost. To deal with this problem, many law enforcement agencies ask the forgery victims to sign a written agreement in which they agree to prosecute. Failure to sign the agreement would result in future claims of forgery being declined for investigation by the police. Witnesses in a check fraud case may include employees who both accepted and deposited a forged instrument.

A logical first step of the forgery investigation is to interview the person who was the recipient of the bad check: the acceptor. This is probably the most important source of investigative leads. After all, the acceptor is a witness to the crime, and he or she alone can describe the actual circumstances surrounding the crime. The investigator should consider asking the acceptor the following questions:

- What remarks did the suspect make during passing of the check?
- Was the check written or signed in the presence of the acceptor?
- What credentials, if any, were offered as identification?
- What was the suspect's description? (This should include physical, dress, mannerisms, and so on.)
- Was the customer a repeat customer or known to the acceptor?
- What type of transportation was used to and from the institution?

Responses to these inquiries, along with the investigator's personal evaluation of the competency of the acceptor, may help identify the suspect. The depositor is the next player who should be interviewed. This is the actual person whose account was used to draw funds from. The depositor should be asked to examine the forged check for anything that might be observed from it. If the signature on the check is not that of the depositor, a statement to that effect should be made to the investigator. Next, the investigator should inquire as to whether another party was allowed to use the depositor's account.

An affidavit should then be acquired from the depositor along with standards of the depositor's handwriting as it appears on his or her checks. The depositor should be asked how the suspect may have acquired the stolen checks. In the event that the depositor claims that checks were stolen during a burglary, the offense report should be pulled and reviewed. It is in the investigator's interest at this point to identify a possible discrepancy between the statement of the depositor and information from an offense report. Finally, the instrument itself must be secured as evidence and a receipt for it should be issued to the victim.

EMBEZZLEMENT

Embezzlement is a low-profile crime that typically consists of employees of organizations stealing large amounts of money over a long period of time. Embezzlement is also extremely difficult to detect. Those who are successful in the embezzling of funds can cause extensive fiscal damage to victim organizations, frequently resulting in their financial ruin.

The crime of embezzlement is increasing at 15 percent per year and has an estimated annual cost of $4 billion.[4] The number of people arrested for embezzlement, however, has increased 40 percent since 1985, indicating that (1) more employees are willing to steal from their employers, (2) more employers are willing to report instances of embezzlement, or (3) law enforcement officials are more willing to prosecute people involved with the crime of embezzlement.

Embezzlement is usually defined under individual state statutes dealing with grand theft. Generally speaking, however, it can be described as a fraudulent appropriation of property by a person to whom that property has been entrusted. Although the elements of the crime may vary, some common elements can be generalized:

- A trusting relationship exists between the suspect and the victim.
- The perpetrator had lawful possession of the pilfered belongings at some time during the relationship.
- The property was stolen or converted to a form of possession that was contrary to the trust relationship.

Crime Prevention Key: Avoiding Becoming a Victim of Check Fraud

- Don't give your checking account number or the numbers at the bottom of your checks to people you don't know, including people who say they are from your bank. They have no business requesting such information.
- Reveal checking account information only to businesses you know are reputable.
- Guard your checkbook. Report lost or stolen checks immediately.
- Properly store or dispose of canceled checks.
- Report any inquiries or suspicious behavior to your banker, who will take steps to protect your account and to notify authorities.
- Do not leave your automated teller machine receipt at the ATM machine because it contains account information. Dispose of it safely and securely.

- There was criminal intent to deprive the lawful owner of the property either temporarily or permanently.

The element of trust is critical in establishing the crime of embezzlement. For example, a bank teller has the lawful right to handle a bank's cash. Secretly taking quantities of that cash for his or her own personal use, however, is a form of possession that is contrary to the trust relationship with the bank.

Investigating Embezzlement

A primary element of the crime of embezzlement is the element of trust. So, to investigate this type of crime, the investigator must show that the suspect first accepted the property in the scope of employment and then misappropriated it for his or her own use. Intent is relatively easy to demonstrate in these cases, however, as it usually requires some form of concealment or secrecy, such as altering business records. The investigation of embezzlement allegations is a tenacious and time-consuming task because paper trails are sometimes difficult to follow. Yet the investigator must be able to explain fully to a prosecutor, judge, and jury how the crime was committed and offer convincing evidence to support the findings of the case. This task can be especially perplexing when dealing with a company whose record-keeping practices are already haphazard.

Because many embezzlement cases require a degree of accounting expertise, investigators lacking such expertise may become frustrated, and the successful outcome of the case may then be jeopardized. The most common way of overcoming this obstacle is for the investigator to solicit the victim's help in providing technical support during the investigation. Company executives and consultants outside the company are generally willing and able to explain specific accounting processes. Embezzlers usually prefer to steal cash because it is both difficult to trace and easy to conceal. Investigators may, however, find this to be an advantage. For example, if an employee is found to be spending significantly large amounts of cash, he or she might also be hard-pressed to explain the origin of the money.

To seek a complaint, the investigator must put together a complete investigative file on the suspect and all circumstances surrounding the violation. The file should contain the following:

- A complete investigative report that identifies specific funds that were taken without authorization.
- Methods used for the pilfering.
- Photocopies of all checks and related documents pertaining to the theft(s).
- A statement of determination outlining the economic and psychological impact of the crime on its victim.

Categories of Embezzlement

Many different types of embezzlement exist. These will vary depending on the degree of trust that exists between the suspect and victim, but will typically fall into one of several categories discussed below.

Theft of Currency.   The most common form of embezzlement is the theft of cash from a trusted party. Although a serious crime, such thefts are usually for modest amounts of money that may not be considered all that financially damaging to the victim company. Theft schemes most commonly used include:

- Taking cash from the register and then entering a negative of the same amount so that the cash drawer balance agrees with the register tape balance. In the event that the register tape contains many (sometimes hundreds of) entries, the negative balance may be difficult to detect.
- Corporate executives working for lucrative companies that make "cash loans" and fail to pay them back.
- Failing to ring up a sale and taking the cash from the cash drawer for the same amount.
- Sales clerks charging more than the amount on the receipt and pocketing the difference, hoping customers won't notice the difference.

Manipulation of Accounts.   Embezzlement cases in which accounts are manipulated typically involve employees of an accounting department. For example, a typical case would be an accountant who makes payments to a fictitious company for services never rendered or goods never received and then endorses the check for payment. A scheme such as this can result in insurmountable losses for the victim company. Another way to embezzle from records is to manipulate payroll accounts. Typically, this type of case involves entering a bogus employee on the records or failing to remove a former employee from the records. In either case, the suspect intercepts the payroll check, endorses it with the name of the person who is on the records, and cashes it.

Retail Theft.   As indicated, one of the hallmarks of embezzlement is the stealing of merchandise by a company's employees, or **pilferage**. This form of crime is also extremely difficult to detect, and it is difficult to determine the value of goods taken by employees over a period. One estimate is that pilferage accounted for 30 to 75 percent of all shrinkage and amounts to losses of $5 billion to $10 billion annually. According to McCaghy, several different methods are commonly used to steal from employers:[5]

- Factory workers zip up completed garments and take them home.
- Cashiers ring up lower prices on single-item purchases and pocket the difference. Many work with accomplices.
- Clerks do not tag sale merchandise and then sell it at its original price, pocketing the difference.
- Receiving clerks obtain duplicate keys to storage facilities and return after hours to steal.
- Truck drivers make fictitious purchases of fuel and repairs and split the difference with truck-stop owners.
- Some employees simply hide items in garbage pails or incinerators or under trash heaps until they can be retrieved.

Another form of inventory theft is when an inventory clerk writes a receipt for "damaged" goods that are shipped to an accomplice's residence. The goods can then be sold for cash. Because the merchandise was never returned to the manufacturer, the company will probably not detect a problem. The receipt indicating "returned goods" indicates that the goods were damaged; therefore, they will not be included in the victim company's inventory. Many companies consider this type of loss as shrinkage, that is, an unexplained loss.

In a 1983 study of theft in the workplace, John Clark and Richard Hollinger found that 35 percent of employees reported involvement in pilferage.[6] The study indicates that most theft is a result of factors relating to the workplace, such as job dissatisfaction and a general feeling of worker exploitation by employees.

CREDIT CARD FRAUD

In September 1996, 36-year-old Nigerian-born Olushina Adekanbi was arrested on credit card charges. What made this case unusual was the fact that Adekanbi, who also went by over two dozen aliases, had earned the nickname "King of New York" because he ran the largest credit card fraud ring in the United States. The ring was wanted for obtaining at least $650,000 in goods and cash advances, as well as gaining illegal access to credit lines worth an estimated $8 million.[7]

Credit card fraud is a growing problem in the twenty-first century. The worldwide traffic in counterfeit cards costs issuers of plastic $1.6 billion a year in false charges.[8] Although credit cards were designed to provide consumers with convenience and increased purchasing power, the criminal has also identified ways to profit from this financial medium. Records from credit card transactions have provided law enforcement with a twofold benefit: (1) the apprehension of the fraudulent credit card user and (2) accurate records that often point to other crimes.

Millions of credit cards issued by both international and local banking institutions are negotiable instruments that can be used fraudulently to obtain goods and services. All credit cards have one thing in common: They can be used to obtain something of value simply by presenting the card. Therefore, the security of the card is of utmost importance. Many credit card companies go to great lengths to offer cardholders some type of security or "insurance" against unlawful use of the card.

Obtaining Credit Cards

Credit cards are acquired by criminals through a variety of methods, including burglaries, robberies, mailbox thefts, and falsified applications to issuing companies. In addition, pickpockets and muggers may seek credit cards as readily as they seek cash. Waiters and retail clerks have been known to retain credit cards that are forgotten by customers. Such cards are sometimes sold to professional **plastic workers** who have experience in dealing with stolen credit cards.

Using Stolen Credit Cards

Credit card thieves must act quickly to overcome protection systems offered by companies. Techniques used are designed to upset and confuse salesclerks while not attracting attention to the thief. The thief will typically stroll through a store as if he is shopping but is actually evaluating sales personnel. Once he identifies a salesclerk who he feels is easily manipulatable, that person is selected as the target. It is the intent of the thief to manipulate the clerk so that he or she fails to follow the prescribed security measures established by the store.

The floor limit is one primary loophole that is easily exploitable. The conscientious **plastic worker** is careful to purchase items that are under the designated limit, typically $50 to $100. In the event that the thief is using a "hot" card, he must be careful that the clerk doesn't check the **hot list** or cancellation bulletin. Because these lists are so lengthy, clerks frequently fail to check them. This procedure is sometimes overlooked when the thief carefully plans his or her purchase at closing time when employees are rushed to balance their register and go home.

Investigating Credit Card Theft

Police officers investigating lost or stolen credit cards should consult the credit card company for assistance, as many companies employ professional investigators who can offer valuable help in the investigation. Certain types of information are necessary during the credit card investigation that can be acquired with the assistance of the card company's investigator. Such information includes:

- The victim store's name and address.
- The names of the store manager and clerk who were victimized (the clerk may be an excellent witness if he or she observed the signing of the card slip).
- The name of the legitimate cardholder and his or her address and telephone number.
- The facts and circumstances surrounding the theft or loss of the card.
- A detailed description of the item(s) purchased and the amount of the sale.

Once identified, the plastic worker will be charged with each purchase as a separate offense, each of which must be supported by documentation and evidence. Investigations should always include how the credit card was obtained in the first place. Depending on the circumstances, this can constitute a separate offense. For example, the card could have been purchased from a pickpocket. The investigator should learn how, when, and where the card was acquired from its lawful owner.

Decisions to prosecute are usually left up to the office of the prosecutor who functions in the jurisdiction of the victimized merchant. In the event the case does go to court, the lawful owner of the card and experts from the credit card company can testify on behalf of the state.

SHOPLIFTING

Shoplifting is a common form of theft involving the taking of goods from retail stores. In fact, it has grown into one of the biggest concerns in the area of retail business. Statistics bear this out: Shoplifting incidents have grown dramatically in the last 20 years, and some retailers expect an annual increase of from 10 to 15 percent. Some studies have even suggested that one out of every nine retail customers steals from department stores. Moreover, the increasingly popular discount stores such as Wal-Mart, Kmart, and Target employ a minimum of retail sales help and rely heavily on highly visible merchandise displays to attract purchasers.

According to the *Economic Crime Digest*, shoplifting is the form of theft that occurs most frequently in business and accounts for some of the greatest losses: an estimated $16 billion a year. The FBI reports that shoplifting acts number some 1 million yearly and have increased 30 percent since 1985. Because shoplifting is a kind of larceny–theft, it has basically the same elements of larceny–theft as discussed earlier.

Modern retail stores market their wares by allowing potential customers to examine them while on display. Computers may be tinkered with, clothes may be tried on, and television sets may be adjusted to demonstrate the clarity of the picture and the function of other features. The list goes on. Because stores often provide carts for the transportation of goods that the customer may wish to purchase, the courts have held that they have a lawful right to possess those goods for limited purposes. Concealment of goods by customers, however, is not allowed by businesses or the courts. Accordingly, the merchandise is offered for sale and if a customer chooses not to purchase the merchandise, it must be returned to the display shelves in good condition.

Generally speaking, the shoplifter can be characterized as either professional or amateur. The professional shoplifter will steal goods for resale or bartering, whereas the amateur steals merchandise for his or her own use. Records show that the majority of shoplifters fall into the amateur category. The professional shoplifter, however, represents a much greater problem for investigators. It is the professional who will often work in groups of three or four and will often victimize several shopping areas at a time. They are commonly trained on what items to steal, how to conceal them—wearing special clothing to help them conceal merchandise—and where to take the merchandise for resale after the theft.

Figure 18.2 The offense of shoplifting represents a significant percentage of larceny–theft crimes.

Investigations have revealed women who appear to be pregnant but who are wearing a specially made receptacle for small items. In another case, a heavy-set woman had been stealing small television sets by concealing them in a prerigged harness that was located between her legs.

A classic study of shoplifting was conducted by Mary Owen Cameron, who found that about 10 percent of all shoplifters were professionals who derived the majority of their income from shoplifting.[9] Sometimes called boosters or heels, professional shoplifters resell stolen merchandise to pawnshops or fences at usually one-half to one-fourth the original price. According to Cameron's study, most shoplifters are amateur pilferers, called **snitches.** Snitches are usually respectable persons who do not perceive of themselves as thieves, yet are systematic shoplifters who steal merchandise for their own use rather than for resale.

Investigating Shoplifting

One problem with shoplifting is that many customers who observe theft are reluctant to report it to managers or security personnel. Many store employees themselves don't want to get involved with apprehending a suspected shoplifter. In fact, an experiment by Hartmann and his associates found that customers observed only 28 percent of staged shoplifting acts that were designed to get their attention.[10] In addition, only 28 percent of people who said they had observed an incident reported it to store employees. Another study by Blankenburg showed that less than 10 percent of shoplifting was detected by store employees and that customers seemed unwilling to report even severe cases.[11] Even in stores with an announced policy of full reporting and prosecution, only 70 percent of the shoplifting detected by employees was actually reported to managers and only 5 percent was prosecuted. Shoplifting cases can be investigated in one of two ways: reactive or proactive. A *reactive* investigation will include interviews of witnesses, collection of physical evidence, and conducting of other follow-up functions. The *proactive* case will probably be handled by in-house security personnel and will focus on the shoplifter who is caught in the act. In the case of proactive investigation, investigators should follow several rules of thumb:

- Be sure that probable cause exists before restraining a suspect.
- Observe the person concealing store merchandise that has not been paid for, not simply concealing "something" that cannot be positively identified as store merchandise.
- Keep the person under observation.
- Before arresting the person, always ask first for a receipt.

Remember, if the person has not yet walked beyond the last pay station, an arrest may not be lawful or appropriate, but confronting the person may still result in reclaiming of the merchandise. Most shoplifting cases are handled through local police and sheriff's departments and are prosecuted locally as well. When a store is involved with cases such as these, store policy should be considered as well as the opinions of the local prosecuting attorney.

The Growing Problem of Retail Theft. Retail theft cost the industry more than $37 billion in 2005, up from $31 billion in 2003. Retail theft becomes especially problematic during the holiday season when overcrowded

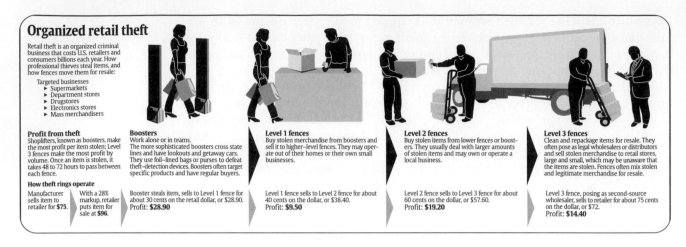

stores make shoplifting more difficult to detect and fraudulent returns easier to conceal. In 2006, it was estimated that retailers expected to lose $3.5 billion due to just fraudulent returns after December's busy holiday season.

Retailers are particularly concerned about gangs that have established supply chains that make organized theft, known as "boosting," too profitable to give up without a fight. For example, a single **booster** operating as part of the gang can steal up to $200,000 worth of merchandise in a weekend. In August 2006, for example, in Ocala, Florida, Beall's cameras caught a gang of exotic dancers that stole approximately $170 worth of goods from the Bradenton store. Apparel from other retailers filled the women's rented SUV. Two of the three women, who worked for an exotic dancing and escort service called Black Xtasy, admitted that they were traveling the state to steal. The suspected leader of the gang had retail theft warrants against her in two other Florida counties.

In another case, Walgreens' Divisional Coordinator for Organized Retail Crime, Jerry Biggs, stated that one group shoplifted from 24 of the drugstores in seven hours. In a videotaped interview with police, shoplifter Jesus Hernandez said he could easily boost $10,000 worth of merchandise in four hours. Fernandez specialized in stealing diabetic test strip packages, which sell for up to $100.

During a typical boosting, one or more gang members distract store clerks while one or two others lift merchandise. Some members stand outside the store doors, ready to signal if police or security officials are coming. Still others are in parking lots ready with getaway cars. The gangs are often armed with knives, guns, and even brass knuckles for fighting off store security personnel.

The thieves typically seem to stay one step ahead of security devices. Even locked glass display cases can be cracked. For example, in 2006, 14 Target stores in California, Illinois, and Colorado were hit by thieves who broke open locked cases, filled carts with iPods, and pushed the carts out the doors. Professional shoplifters usually carry shopping bags lined with foil and duct tape to block the electric current that detects security tags. Some thieves remove security tags and hide merchandise under larger packages.

Some security analysts have suggested that antitheft systems seem to only work against people who don't know how to thwart them. Security personnel for retail stores must be cautious in making apprehensions. This is because retail companies must balance the importance of capturing thieves with possibly upsetting and frustrating paying customers.

Returns are one area where retailers have cracked down in recent years. While some will still give cash for a return without a receipt, many major retailers require receipts. In addition, many retailers are using electronic receipts that track purchases made with a credit card or check. These receipts nearly eliminate the ability to use counterfeit receipts or to return stolen goods. They also use display devices that make it difficult to slide all the items on a hanging rack into a bag, but not too difficult for legitimate customers to use.

The prosecution of retail crime is complicated in part because much of the merchandise stolen doesn't come with serial numbers. That makes it difficult for investigators to identify the merchandise as stolen. Unless merchandise is made under a retailer's private label and the store has alerted police of the theft, police who stop the driver of a car full of stolen items may have difficulty making an arrest and in many cases will not even seize merchandise as evidence.

As illustrated in Figure 18.3, retail theft has become more organized in recent years. Businesses such as supermarkets, department stores, drugstores, electronics stores, and mass merchandisers are frequently the targets for such theft rings. Thieves work closely with **fences** who act on numerous levels to quickly turn over their stolen merchandise and place layers of people between each stolen merchandise transfer.

In short, the criminal world has recognized retail theft is a much more profitable crime than burglary with much less penalty. For example, while larceny overall was down 4.5 percent from 2000 to 2004, shoplifting increased nearly 12 percent, according to the 2005 Uniform Crime Report published by the FBI.[12]

IDENTITY THEFT

In 2000, golfer Tiger Woods discovered that his identity had been stolen and that credit cards taken out in his name had been used to steal $17,000 worth of merchandise, including a 70-inch TV, stereos, and a used luxury car. In 2001, the thief, 30-year-old Anthony Lemar Taylor, who looks nothing like Woods, was convicted of falsely obtaining a driver's license using the name Eldrick T. Woods (Tiger's given name), Wood's social security number, and his birth date. Because Taylor already had 20 previous convictions of all kinds on his record, he was sentenced to 200 years in prison under California's three strikes law. Like Woods, most victims of identity theft do not even know that their identities have been stolen until they receive bills for merchandise they haven't purchased.

Identity theft, which involves obtaining credit, merchandise, or services by fraudulent personal representation, is a special kind of larceny. According to a recent Federal Trade Commission survey, identity theft directly impacts as many as 10 million victims annually, although most do not report the crime. Identity theft became a federal crime in 1998 with the passage of the Identity Theft and Assumption Deterrence Act. The law makes it a crime whenever anyone "knowingly transfers or uses, without lawful authority, a means of identification of another person with the intent to commit, or to aid or abet, any unlawful activity that constitutes a violation of federal law, or that constitutes a felony under any applicable state or local law."[13]

Identity theft is the wrongful use of another's personal information, such as credit card numbers, social security number, and driver's license number, to commit fraud or another form of deception. This is usually done for monetary gain, although there may be other motives.

Identity theft has become a major problem in the United States. The target of identity theft is information that will enable the thief to assume another's identity for a criminal purpose. In the last few years, personal information has become one of the commodities most sought after by criminals in this country and elsewhere. Because it is usually part of a larger criminal enterprise, the theft of personal information is one of the most serious of all crimes. On May 31, 2001, the *Washington Post* reported:

> Some law enforcement officials and regulators say identity theft has become one of their most pressing problems. The federal Office of the Comptroller of the Currency recently estimated that there are half a million victims of identity theft per year in the United States. The Justice Department told Congress last week that Internet fraud, including identity theft, is one of the nation's fastest-growing white-collar crimes. And James G. Huse, Jr., the Social Security Administration's inspector general, testified that the misuse of Social Security numbers in fraudulent activity is "a national crisis."[14]

Although identity theft is in itself a criminal act under both federal and most state laws, the theft is almost always a stepping stone to the commission of other crimes. Typical crimes associated with identity theft include credit card fraud, bank fraud, computer fraud, Internet fraud, fraudulent obtaining of loans, and other schemes designed to enable the perpetrator to profit from the original theft. Often, there are several types of fraud involved in, or resulting from, the initial identity theft. Furthermore, funds obtained illegally as a result of the identity theft and its resultant frauds may be used to finance other types of criminal enterprises, including drug trafficking and other major forms of criminal activity.

The escalation of identity theft in the United States is due in large part to the technology revolution, which has brought the country into the so-called information age. The vastly expanded use of computers to store personal data and the growing use of the Internet have provided criminals with new incentives and new means to steal and misuse personal information. As the use of technology to store and transmit information increases, so too will identity theft. Consequently, identity theft will likely become an even greater problem in the future.

Financial Losses. Accurately defining the financial losses of the vast number of crimes committed by means of identity theft is not possible at this time. Many identity theft crimes are not reported to police, and there is no single source of information on this issue. The U.S. Secret Service, the U.S. Postal Inspection Service, and the FBI are among the principal federal enforcement agencies that share jurisdiction for investigation of these crimes. This does not include the thousands of reports and investigations that are handled by state and local authorities. It is fair to say, however, that the cumulative financial losses from identity theft and the various crimes that feed from it are staggering.

Financial loss statistics generated by investigations handled by the U.S. Secret Service's financial crimes division in fiscal year 2000 reveal total actual losses in closed identity theft cases totaled $248.1 million. However, the potential losses from identity theft cases discovered during the same period are estimated at nearly $1.5 billion. Further, it is calculated that the average actual loss in each closed identity theft case in fiscal year 2000 was $46,119. These figures graphically illustrate the magnitude of the problem caused by identity theft in America today.

Personal Costs.   Perhaps even more tragic than the monetary loss is the personal cost of identity theft. Because identity theft by definition involves the fraudulent obtaining of funds in the name of someone else, the victim of identity theft may sustain not only great financial loss but also severe damage to credit standing, personal reputation, and other vital aspects of the victim's personal life. For example, the victim may suffer garnishments, attachments, civil lawsuits, and other traumatic consequences stemming from the identity theft. In some cases, the victim may be forced into bankruptcy, further damaging his or her reputation and credit. In other instances, the victim may become subject to criminal prosecution because of crimes committed by the perpetrator of the identity theft in the victim's name.

Even if the victim ultimately clears his or her credit records and avoids other personal and financial consequences of identity theft, the physical and mental toll on the victim can be significant. Typically, a victim of identity theft will spend months or years trying to clear his or her credit records. Many hours of difficult and stressful effort are often necessary, because the merchants and institutions that have been defrauded in the victim's name are not easily persuaded that the victim is innocent of any wrongdoing. The frustration and distress engendered by this heavy burden often take a significant toll on the mental well-being and physical health of the victim. And, worst of all perhaps, the victim's efforts to clear him- or herself may be unsuccessful, leaving the victim under a cloud for the rest of his or her life.

Virtually anyone may become the victim of identity theft. Contrary to popular misconception, personal information is not stolen just from the affluent. Persons of even modest means may become victims of identity theft. In the majority of cases, all that is required is good credit, which is what identity thieves use to steal thousands upon thousands of dollars in the name of the victim.

No particular age group is immune from identity theft. Federal Trade Commission (FTC) data indicate that while 6.2 percent of individuals reporting identity theft to the FTC during the period from November 1999 to March 2001 were age 65 or over, the average age of victims was 42 years, and the most commonly reported age was 33 years. Younger Americans may be victimized at a higher rate because they are more likely to use the Internet, which is the primary tool in many identity theft crimes. However, elderly Americans are highly vulnerable to other types of identity theft schemes, particularly the various telephone scams used by perpetrators to acquire personal information.[15] The elderly have always been targeted by perpetrators of fraud and will no doubt continue to be frequent victims.

The victims of identity theft may be residents of almost any geographical area. The FTC reports that between November 1999 and March 2001, complaints of identity theft were received from all 50 states and the District of Columbia. According to the same data, the greatest number of complaints came from California, New York, Texas, and Florida. The highest concentration of complaints per 100,000 people reportedly came from the District of Columbia, Nevada, Arizona, California, and Maryland. The FTC also reports that the cities with the largest number of complaints were New York City, Chicago, Los Angeles, Houston, and Miami, in that order. However, one should not conclude from this that identity theft is confined to any particular city, state, or region. The problem is national in scope, and not even the residents of the smallest locality of the least populous states are safe from it.

Identity Theft Legislation

Identity theft was not a federal crime until Congress passed the Identity Theft and Assumption Deterrence Act of 1998.

> This statute makes it a federal offense when any person knowingly transfers or uses, without lawful authority, a means of identification of another person with the intent to commit, or to aid or abet, any unlawful activity that constitutes a felony under any applicable state or local law.

This crime carries a maximum penalty of 15 years' imprisonment, a fine, and criminal forfeiture of personal property used to commit the offense.

Although this provision specifically targets identity theft, identity theft usually is part of a larger criminal scheme and generally involves other federal statutes, such as statutory prohibitions against credit card fraud, computer fraud, mail fraud,[16] bank fraud, or wire fraud.[17]

In July 2006, the National Conference of State Legislatures reported that all 50 states had passed some form of identity theft legislation. These statutes impose varying penalties for identity theft. Typically, they base these penalties on the dollar amount of loss resulting from the theft: Thefts involving small losses are treated as misdemeanors, while larger monetary losses are usually considered felonies of varying degrees.[18]

Local law enforcement officials should check to determine whether they have such a statute and what that statute provides. Online access to these statutes is available through the Internet.

The Role of the Federal Trade Commission

The Federal Trade Commission (FTC) is the federal government's principal consumer protection agency, with broad jurisdiction extending over nearly the entire economy, including business and consumer transactions on the telephone, the Internet, and elsewhere. The FTC's mandate is to prohibit unfair or deceptive acts or practices and to promote vigorous competition in the marketplace. The FTC act authorizes the commission to halt deception in several ways, including through civil actions filed by its own attorneys in federal district courts. Of particular importance in the realm of identity theft is the fact that the act also gives the FTC jurisdiction over cross-border consumer transactions. Many identity theft enterprises operate outside the borders of the United States.

Of particular importance here are the provisions of the federal Identity Theft and Assumption Deterrence Act of 1998 (18 U.S.C. §1028), which gives the Federal Trade Commission a substantial role in the campaign against identity theft. Under the act, the FTC is empowered to act as a nationwide clearinghouse for information related to identity theft crimes. This is an important aspect of the effort to combat identity theft, for in the past, one of the major factors that hampered detection, investigation, and prosecution of these cases was the lack of any central source of information about identity theft. Identity theft is widespread, and a single identity theft ring may operate over great distances and in many states. Consequently, the availability of a central database is essential to enable law enforcement agencies to identify organized or widespread identity theft operations and facilitate cooperation between appropriate federal and state agencies. Special agents from the federal enforcement branches previously mentioned work closely with the FTC in this regard.

In accordance with the mandate of the Identity Theft and Assumption Deterrence Act of 1998, the Federal Trade Commission has established a number of central resources to provide information to law enforcement agencies about identity theft crimes. The FTC also provides guidance to victims of identity theft in order to help them defend themselves against the effects of this crime.

Types of ID Theft and ID Theft Operations

We have already examined some of the national resources available for combating identity theft and alluded to the types of crimes that are committed as part of identity theft. In this section, we will take a closer look at the various types of identity theft schemes and the nature and modus operandi of the identity theft perpetrators.

As has been noted, the key target of identity theft perpetrators is personal and confidential information of individuals. There are so many methods by which identity thieves may acquire personal information that it is impossible to catalog them all here. However, the following methods are commonly used:

- Stealing wallets and purses containing personal identification, credit cards, and bank cards.

- Stealing mail, including mail containing bank and credit card statements, preapproved credit card offers, telephone calling cards, and tax information.

- Completion of a false change-of-address form to divert the victim's mail to another location.

- Searching trash for personal data (a practice known as dumpster diving) found on such discarded documents as so-called preapproved credit card applications or credit card slips discarded by the victim. To thwart an identity thief who may pick through your trash to capture your personal information, tear or shred your charge receipts, copies of credit applications, insurance forms, bank checks and statements, expired charge cards, and credit offers you get in the mail.

- Obtaining credit reports, often by posing as a landlord, employer, or other person or entity that might have a legitimate need for, and right to, credit information.

- Obtaining personal information at the workplace or through employers of the victim.

- Discovering personal information during physical entries into the victim's home. Such entries may be unlawful, as in burglary, or initially lawful, as when friends, service personnel, or others are invited to enter the home.

- Obtaining personal information from the Internet. This may be information stolen by hackers or freely provided by the victim in the course of making purchases or other contacts. Many victims respond to unsolicited e-mail (spam) that requests personal information.

- Purchasing information from inside sources such as store employees, who may for a price provide identity thieves with information taken from applications for goods, services, or credit. At least one instance has been reported of an employee of a credit bureau collaborating with identity thieves to provide personal information from credit bureau records.

- Pretexting, in which a thief telephones the victim or contacts the victim via Internet and requests that the victim provide personal information. For example, the thief may claim to be from a survey firm and ask for personal data. Another scheme is for the thief to claim that the victim has won a prize or been selected for some special honor or privilege that requires that the victim provide personal information. Still another means of theft is for the perpetrator to call the victim and pretend to have found something thatthe victim has lost and then demand that the victim provide personal information in order to obtain the return of the lost item.

- Shoulder surfing, a practice whereby the thief positions himself or herself near a victim in order to obtain personal information by overhearing the victim or seeing the victim's actions. For example, the thief may stand near a pay telephone in a public place and listen as the victim gives telephone credit card number information or other personal information in the course of making a call. Similarly, thieves may loiter near an automated teller machine (ATM) and visually observe the victim keying in password numbers on the machine.

- Skimming, which is the electronic lifting of the data encoded on a valid credit or ATM card and transferring that data to a counterfeit card. There are many variations of this practice. For example, an identity thief may recruit an employee of a retail store, restaurant, or other retail establishment. The employee is provided with a handheld electronic device that can read data from a person's credit card when the consumer presents it to the employee. The collusive employee then surreptitiously "swipes" the credit card through the handheld "reading" device, which records the electronic data from the card. The employee then returns the device to the thief, and the thief extracts the recorded data from the device.

- Identity thieves may also purchase personal information about potential victims from persons or entities that routinely collect such information. In some instances, these entities may be legitimate, but many times they are criminal enterprises formed for the specific purpose of selling information to thieves.

How Stolen Information Is Used

There are literally hundreds of ways in which identity thieves may use the information they have stolen. The following are just a few examples:

- Once they have a victim's credit card number, thieves may call the victim's credit card issuer and, pretending to be the victim, ask that the mailing address on the account be changed. The thieves then run up high charges on the credit card, and because credit card statements are no longer being sent to the victim's real address, the victim might be unaware of what is happening for weeks or even months.

- These same thieves who have obtained a victim's credit card information may also request that the credit card company send them credit card "checks," which are written for cash just as are bank checks. Again, the charges are unknown to the victim because the credit card statements are no longer coming to the victim's address.

- Having obtained personal information such as name, date of birth, social security number, and so on, the thieves open new credit card accounts in the victim's name and run up charges until the victim becomes aware of the fraud. Similarly, credit accounts may be opened at stores using the victim's identity.

- The thieves open bank accounts in the victim's name and write bad checks on the account.

- The thieves obtain loans, such as real estate, auto, or personal loans, using the victim's identity.

- The thieves counterfeit checks or debit cards and drain the victim's bank accounts of funds.

- The thieves establish services such as utility, telephone, or cell phone service in the victim's name.

- The thieves make long-distance calls using stolen credit card numbers.

- The thieves may obtain other goods and privileges by using the victim's identity and information, either in person, by telephone, or via the Internet.

These are only a few of the numerous schemes that an identity thief may use to obtain money, goods, or services at the expense of the unwitting victim.

Often a web of conspirators ties these individual criminal acts together. Investigation of one individual involved in identity theft therefore often leads to others working together, often in elaborate plots. The following actual case prosecuted in the western district of Washington State illustrates this point:

Between January 27, 1999, and April 14, 2000, a woman and other persons conspired to execute a scheme to defraud several commercial businesses in western Washington and elsewhere, including financial institutions, investment companies, credit card companies, merchant banks, and merchants, and to obtain money and merchandise from these businesses by means of false and fraudulent pretenses.

The conspirators assumed the identities of third persons and fraudulently utilized the social security account numbers and names of these persons. The conspirators then created false identity documents such as state identification cards, driver's licenses, and immigration cards. Using the identities and names of these third persons, the conspirators obtained credit cards and opened banking and investment accounts at numerous locations.

The conspirators also prepared fraudulent and counterfeit checks using the account names and numbers for actual bank accounts. The perpetrators then deposited the counterfeit checks into accounts opened by them, using one of their assumed identities. Shortly thereafter, they would withdraw the funds fraudulently credited to their accounts at the time they deposited the counterfeit checks. Over an eight-month period, counterfeit checks totaling over $1 million were deposited at various banks and investment firms.

In addition, the conspirators purchased legitimate cashier's checks with fraudulently obtained monies and then altered the checks to reflect much higher values than the amounts purchased. Over five months, these transactions accounted for more than $350,000.

The scheme also included telefaxed "letters of authorization" using other identities authorizing wire transfer of funds to co-conspirators, altered credit cards, and related offenses.

Such involved criminal conspiracies begin with, and are perpetuated by, identity theft. The result of all of these schemes may be that bill collectors begin to dun the victim, the victim's credit standing is ruined, and legal procedures may be instituted to collect the fraudulent debts from the victim. Identity thieves may even file for bankruptcy in the victim's name to avoid paying debts incurred while using the victim's personal information or for other reasons, such as to avoid eviction from the house or apartment they have obtained by using the victim's identity.

The Investigative Response

A police department's first step in combating identity theft is to ensure that its personnel have a comprehensive knowledge of what identity theft is, who commits it, and how it is committed. The department's members must be aware of federal, state, and local resources available to assist them in reporting, investigating, and prosecuting identity theft.

Because identity theft so often is a multi-jurisdictional crime, it is necessary for each department to cooperate closely with other agencies in identity theft cases. For example, investigation and prosecution of the illustrative case cited above could not have been successfully undertaken without coordination and cooperation with several federal agencies. The sharing of information about identity theft cases with other agencies is essential as it may lead to not only a successful prosecution of the case in one jurisdiction but concurrent investigation in other areas of the country.

In this regard, it is essential for state and local law enforcement agencies to participate in the Federal Trade Commission's Identity Theft Clearing House. Such participation provides access to extensive information about identity theft activity both nationwide and in the department's own region or state.

Reports of Identity Theft

In the past, police have been slow to respond to reports of identity theft. In some cases, local police departments refused to take complaints about identity theft because the crime was not well understood, or a state statute was lacking, or the department could not identify the venue in which the theft occurred or the perpetrator was operating. This attitude by local police often created great frustration among victims and generated considerable ill will among these victims toward the departments concerned.

Today, identity theft has been identified as a major crime problem in America, and most states now have statutes making it a specific crime. A relative wealth of information and assistance currently exists to deal with identity theft. These and other factors combined make it essential for police departments to respond properly to identity theft complaints, initiate investigations, and prosecute violators where possible. In addition, departments have an obligation to assist the victims through counseling, advice, and referral where reasonable and appropriate. A proper investigative response to identity theft will include the following:

1. *Develop a standardized procedure for taking identity theft reports.* Complaints should be taken by the police department in detail and in a manner consistent with the severity of the crime. Aspects of the online reporting form used by the FTC may be useful as a guide to local law enforcement agencies in their efforts to gather all pertinent information about the crime. Victims should not be brushed off or arbitrarily referred to other agencies as a standard course of action. Thus, departments should NOT merely refer victims to prosecutors' offices or to private attorneys for civil actions. It is the department's obligation to take the complaint and act on it.

2. *Initiate criminal investigations of identity theft reports.* Police should initiate investigation of identity theft reports. Again, identity theft is as much a crime as any other offense and should be treated as such. Unless and until it develops that the complaint is unfounded or for some other reason the department cannot proceed further, identity theft should be aggressively and fully investigated.

3. *Prosecute violators.* Identity thieves should be prosecuted. Identity theft is not just a prank; it is a serious crime and should be prosecuted to the fullest extent of the law. Unfortunately, the maximum penalties for these types of crimes in some states are not sufficient to garner the attention of prosecutors whose caseloads may already be overloaded with other criminal activity. In these states, a long-term effort by local police and prosecutors needs to address this by calls for harsher criminal penalties for identity theft.

4. *Cooperate with other agencies.* Investigations of multi-jurisdictional identity theft schemes may involve a number of agencies. Each police department should cooperate fully with any agency participating in an identity theft case. If it proves impossible to prosecute the identity thief in the department's own jurisdiction, full cooperation should be given to departments in other jurisdictions where there is a greater likelihood of successfully prosecuting the perpetrators.

5. *Assist victims by providing the victims with helpful information.* Victims of identity theft are often unaware of the proper steps to take in order to minimize the damage suffered because of the identity theft and protect themselves against further victimization. Each police department should provide every identity theft complainant with information as to the steps that the victim should take. Much of that information is available through counselors at the FTC. To summarize this and other information, police officers

responding to victims of identity theft and taking crime reports on these matters should keep the following instructions in mind in order to deal most effectively with these crime victims:

- Contact the fraud departments of each of the three credit reporting agencies. Give the agency full details of the theft, including a case number as provided by local police, and request that a fraud alert be placed on your file.

- Request a copy of your credit report, review the report for errors or fraudulent entries, submit any changes necessary, and get a new copy at a later date to ensure that changes or problems have been corrected.

- Contact all credit card companies where you have an account and notify them of the fraud. Close existing accounts and open new accounts with new PIN numbers and passwords.

- Contact banks and financial institutions. To be safe, close accounts and open new accounts with new PINs and passwords. Major check verification companies should also be contacted and asked to notify retailers not to accept your stolen or misappropriated checks. The bank may be able and willing to do this for you. ATM cards that may have been compromised should be canceled and new ones obtained with new PINs and passwords.

- If there is reason to believe that investment or brokerage accounts have been tampered with or otherwise compromised, contact the broker or investment account manager as well as the Securities and Exchange Commission.

- If unauthorized new accounts have been opened through utility or telephone companies or if the victim's own service is being used to make unauthorized calls, contact the utility or service provider immediately. If the companies do not cooperate, contact the state's public utility commission and/or the Federal Communications Commission (FCC).

- If there is reason to believe that the social security number is being misused, this should be reported to the Social Security Administration's fraud hotline. In addition, it is wise to contact the Social Security Administration to verify the accuracy of the earnings reported under the victim's social security number. Request a copy of your social security statement.

- If a driver's license or driver's license number is involved in the identity theft, contact the jurisdiction's department of motor vehicles. The same is true if a nondriver's identity card is involved. If the driver's license number is the same as the victim's social security number, a different number should be substituted.

- If someone has filed bankruptcy in the victim's name, the victim should contact the U.S. Bankruptcy Trustee in the region where the bankruptcy was filed.

- In some instances, the perpetrator of the identity theft may have committed a crime in the victim's name. When this becomes known, the appropriate agencies should be contacted for information as to how the victim's name may be cleared. The procedures for this vary widely among jurisdictions, and it may be necessary for the victim to hire an attorney to accomplish the name-clearing process.

- The victim should contact other police departments where the victim resides or where the identity theft may have taken place. The victim should obtain a copy of the police report regarding the theft from each department to whom the theft has been reported. This is essential, because even if the police do not apprehend the perpetrators, the police report may assist the victim in dealing with creditors during efforts to avoid financial liability for fraudulent actions and to repair the damage done to the victim's credit. The fact that a victim has reported and personally attested to the truth of the allegations in a written police report helps other agencies verify the credibility of the victim and take measures on his or her behalf.

- The victim should contact the Federal Trade Commission via telephone or mail to report the identity theft.[19]

- Because the types of identity theft schemes are so varied, other agencies or entities may need to be contacted. If any agency or entity not otherwise discussed above is involved in some manner, it should be contacted immediately. For example, the Internal Revenue Service (IRS) should be notified if tax issues may be involved.

Many of the reports and requests discussed above may be made initially by telephone. However, all such requests should be followed up in writing, since telephone reports are often insufficient to preserve the victim's legal rights and written reports may be necessary to obtain the cooperation of the entity being contacted.

The telephone numbers, addresses, Web sites, and other appropriate data necessary to enable the victims to contact these various agencies should be kept on file in the police department and made available to them. These addresses, telephone numbers, Web sites, and related information can be found in several current guides for identity theft victims, such as the FTC publication *ID Theft— When Bad Things Happen to Your Good Name*. Police departments should consider maintaining a supply of copies of this or similar publications and distribute them to identity theft complainants for their information and assistance.

It is important that local police departments take a proactive role in the education of the public regarding identity theft and the means of preventing it. Even though no person in the information age can completely control the dissemination of his or her personal information, there are specific steps that everyone can take to minimize exposure to identity theft. Crime prevention units and community policing officers should take advantage of their roles within the community by providing citizens with information that they can use to protect themselves against identity theft. There is considerable literature available, both in printed form and on the Internet, about preventive measures. Officers should be aware of these sources and provide them to citizens whenever possible.[20]

DISCUSSION QUESTIONS

1. Discuss the problems inherent in the investigation of forged government checks.
2. What methods of forgery are considered most common?
3. What types of evidence should be obtained from witnesses in a check-kiting scheme?
4. Define embezzlement and how it relates to criminal investigation.
5. What factors make the investigation of an embezzlement case so difficult?
6. What are the categories of embezzlement, and how are they best investigated?
7. What schemes are most typical in the stealing of currency?
8. Explain some of the methods most commonly used by criminals to avoid detection when using stolen credit cards.
9. What types of information are required, and what steps are necessary in the successful investigation of a stolen credit card?
10. Discuss the elements of the crime of shoplifting.
11. Discuss the ways in which stolen information is used by criminals.
12. Explain the role of the Federal Trade Commission in identity theft investigations.

NOTES

1. FBI, Crime in the United States, 2005 (2005).
2. AMERICAN BANKERS' ASSOCIATION (1994). Report.
3. DUGAS, C. (1995). Check fraud costs banks, consumers. *USA Today,* November 14, p. 4B.
4. BENNETT, W., and K. HESS (2001). *Criminal investigation,* 6th ed. Belmont, CA: Wadsworth.
5. MCCAGHY, C. (1976). *Deviant behavior.* New York: Macmillan, pp. 348–349.
6. CLARK, J., and R. HOLLINGER (1983). Theft in the workplace. *Crime and Justice,* October, pp. 117–118.
7. GREENWALD, J. (1996). Credit where none is due. *Time,* February 19, p. 50.
8. Ibid.
9. CAMERON, M. O. (1983). The scourge of shoplifting. *Criminal Justice Ethics,* Winter–Spring, pp. 3–15.
10. HARTMANN, D., D. GELFAND, B. PAGE, and P. WALKER (1972). Rates of bystander observation and reporting of contrived shoplifting incidents. *Criminology,* vol. 10: 248.
11. BLANKENBURG, E. (1976). The selectivity of legal sanctions: An empirical investigation of shoplifting. *Law and Society Review,* vol. 11: 109–129.
12. O'DONNELL, J. (2006). Stores protect turf from gangs of thieves. *USA Today,* November 17, pp. 1B-2B; FBI, Crime in the United States, 2005.
13. FBI, Crime in the United States 2004.
14. "Identity Thieves Thrive in Information Age," *Washington Post,* May 31, 2001, page A01. Viewed online at http://www.washingtonpost.com.
15. FEDERAL TRADE COMMISSION REPORT. *Identity theft complaint data, figures and trends on identity theft,* November 1999 through March 2001, p. 3.
16. 18 U.S.C. § 1343.
17. 18 U.S.C. § 1344.
18. 18 U.S.C. § 1028.
19. These items are all listed in the FTC publication, *ID Theft—When bad things happen to your good name,* published February 2001.
20. FTC online publications, *Pretexting: Your personal information revealed,* dated January 2001, available at http://www.ftc.gov/bep/conline/pubs/credit/pretext.htm.

Key Terms

▶ carjacking

▶ chop shop

▶ joyriding

▶ National Auto Theft Bureau (NATB)

▶ off-road machinery

▶ salvage switch

▶ stripping operation

▶ tagging

▶ tin trucks

▶ vehicle identification number

This chapter will enable you to:

- Understand the extent of the motor vehicle theft problem.

- Define the elements of the crime of motor vehicle theft.

- List the steps of the preliminary investigation.

- Recognize methods of altering a stolen vehicle.

- Discuss the significance of the vehicle identification number (VIN).

- Describe methods of disguising a stolen vehicle.

- Recognize a stolen vehicle.

- List methods commonly used in motor vehicle fraud.

- Identify techniques of investigation of motorcycle thefts.

INTRODUCTION

Carlos Ponce was one of the longtime leaders of an auto theft ring that operated throughout South Florida and sold stolen cars around the country. Ponce, also known as El Rey de los Carros (King of the Cars), ran an interstate auto theft ring that stole luxury cars in South Florida. The ring renumbered the cars using the vehicle identification number (VIN) identities of other identical "clone" vehicles and then shipped the vehicles to out-of-state buyers using fraudulent Florida titles. The ring was responsible for stealing hundreds of vehicles, worth an estimated $8 million, from South Florida and using an illicit pipeline—maintained in part from inside a federal prison—to ship the vehicles as far as Massachusetts and California. In 2006, a Miami-Dade Police investigation known as Operation Road Runner arrested Ponce and ten of his associates.[1] The Ponce operation illustrates the level of sophistication and organization of some automobile theft operations and reminds us that there are considerable profits for criminals involved in automobile theft.

Since the turn of the century, the advent of the automobile has either directly or indirectly changed the lives of all people. Its impact has inspired both positive and negative uses. Indeed, it has not only enhanced private lives, business, and public-service organizations but has offered criminals innovative ways of transportation to and from their crimes. The value and utility of the motor vehicle have, therefore, become deeply ingrained in today's society.

According to the Uniform Crime Reports, the crime of motor vehicle theft includes trains, airplanes, bulldozers, most farm and construction machinery, ships, boats, and spacecraft. Vehicles that are temporarily taken by individuals who have lawful access to them are not thefts. Consequently, spouses who jointly own all property may drive the family car, even though one spouse may think of the vehicle as his or her exclusive personal property. Because most insurance companies require police reports before they will reimburse car owners for their losses, most occurrences of motor vehicle theft are reported to law enforcement agencies. Some of these reports, however, may be false. People who have damaged their own vehicles in solitary crashes or who have been unable to sell them may try to force insurance companies to "buy" them through reports of theft.

Motor vehicle theft can turn violent, as in cases of carjacking—a crime in which offenders usually force the car's occupants into the street before stealing the vehicle. For example, in February 2000, Christy Robel watched in horror as her six-year-old son, Jake, was dragged to his death after a man jumped behind the wheel of her car and sped off. Robel had left the car running with the boy inside as she made a brief stop at a Kansas City sandwich shop. The carjacker, 35-year-old Kim Davis, tried to push Jake from the car as he made his escape, but the boy became entangled in his seat belt and was dragged for five miles at speeds of more than 80 miles an hour. In October 2001, Davis was convicted of murder and was sentenced to spend the rest of his life in prison without possibility of parole.

According to the FBI, auto theft is an estimated $7 billion business and continues to grow despite a declining theft rate across the United States. For record-keeping purposes, the Uniform Crime Reports defines a motor vehicle as a self-propelled vehicle that runs on the ground and not on rails. This definition includes automobiles, motorcycles, bicycles, trucks, motor scooters, buses, and snowmobiles. Excluded are airplanes, trains, most farm and construction machinery, ships, boats, and spacecraft—whose theft would be considered larceny. Motor vehicles that are taken temporarily by persons having legal access to them are not considered motor vehicle theft.

MOTOR VEHICLE THEFT OFFENSES

The Uniform Crime Reporting (UCR) Program defines motor vehicle theft as the theft or attempted theft of a motor vehicle. This offense includes the stealing of automobiles, trucks, buses, motorcycles, motor scooters, and snowmobiles, among others. The taking of a motor vehicle for temporary use by persons having lawful access is excluded from this definition.

Trends

In 2005, there were an estimated 1.2 million motor vehicle thefts, or approximately 416.7 motor vehicles stolen for every 100,000 inhabitants. Automobiles comprised 73.4 percent of the motor vehicles reported stolen in 2005. The rate of motor vehicle theft decreased 1.1 percent, respectively, when compared with data for 2004.

When considering data for 10 years earlier, the estimated volume and rate of motor vehicle thefts in 2005 decreased 11.4 percent and 20.7 percent, respectively, when compared with estimates for 1996. Property losses due to motor vehicle theft in 2005 was estimated at $7.6 billion, averaging $6,173 per stolen vehicle.

Motor vehicle thefts are common throughout the United States and as a rule require a police report before insurance companies will act on claims. Both police and insurance investigators know that sometimes motor vehicle theft reports are false. Such cases involve persons who attempt to defraud the insurance company or dispose of a vehicle after using it to commit a crime while trying to claim insurance money for it.

Auto theft is big business. Investigations have shown that there are some large organized groups of car thieves that fill orders for contract buyers. Some cars are stolen for shipment out of the country, typically to Mexico. Juveniles often steal cars as a lark or on a dare to joyride. Some thieves intend to keep the car for themselves, while others will sell the stolen car to an associate after disguising the vehicle with new paint, plates, and wheels. Stolen vehicles may even be used in other crimes, such as armed robbery or drive-by shootings. Stolen cars are often involved in hit-and-run accidents, with injuries, leaving the owners to explain their alibis and prove that they didn't cause the incident and then file a false auto theft report to cover it up.

Comparative Rates

Motor Vehicle Theft Trend

Year	Number of Offenses	Rate per 100,000 Inhabitants
2004	1,237,851	421.5
2005	1,235,226	416.7
Percent change	−1.1	−2.2

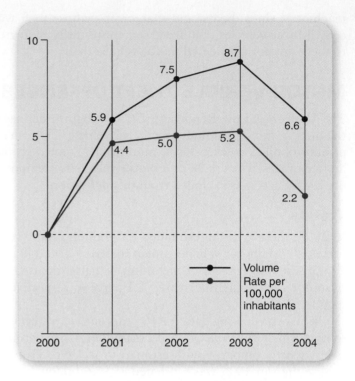

Figure 19.1 Motor vehicle theft: Percent change from 2000. FBI, Crime in the United States, 2005.

Experienced car thieves can steal an automobile in less than a minute. Many crude thieves simply smash the driver's-side window. A majority of stolen cars are taken for the value of their parts. Some of the most frequently stolen types of cars have remained constant over the years, suggesting that they are being stolen for parts. According to insurance companies, a $20,000 stolen vehicle can be stripped and sold into $30,000 worth of parts inventory to unscrupulous scrap and auto-body shops. Stolen cars, vans, trucks, and motorcycles cause economic hardship for victims and increase insurance premiums for law-abiding citizens.

Motor vehicles are stolen from a variety of sources: shopping malls, streets, driveways, parking lots, garages, and car dealerships. Auto theft seems to occur with greater frequency where large groups of cars are parked together for extended periods, such as at airports, shopping centers, colleges, sporting events, fairgrounds, movie complexes, and large apartment complexes.

Motor vehicle thieves target a wide range of popular passenger vehicles, often seeking valuable parts from older model year vehicles for sale on the black market. Their preferred targets for theft vary from one year to the next, but many models remain a constant. For example, the Toyota Camry, Honda Accord, and Ford Taurus are particularly attractive targets, along with sport utility vehicles (SUVs), pickup trucks, and mini-vans, according to a recent study by the National Insurance Crime Bureau (NICB), a not-for-profit insurance organization committed to combating vehicle theft and insurance fraud.

According to the NICB, close to 1.2 million vehicles were stolen in the United States in 2004 alone, and the nine vehicles most frequently reported stolen that year were:[2]

1. 1995 Honda Civic
2. 1989 Toyota Camry

3. 1991 Honda Accord

4. 1994 Dodge Caravan

5. 1994 Chevrolet full-size C/K 1500 Pickup

6. 1997 Ford F150 Series

7. 1990 Acura Integra

8. 1988 Toyota Pickup

9. 1991 Nissan Sentra

High-end cars and trucks are also commonly targeted. Vehicle theft trends change over time and appear to be directly related to the types of vehicles consumers desire. This is reflected in the popularity of stolen SUVs in recent years and is seen in *Forbes* magazine's 10 most commonly stolen luxury vehicles:[3]

1. Cadillac Escalade

2. Hummer H2

3. BMW 7L Series

4. Honda S2000 Convertible

5. Lincoln Navigator

6. Chevrolet Avalanche

7. Mercedes-Benz S-Class

8. Chevrolet Corvette

9. Mercedes-Benz SL-Class Convertible

10. BMW X5

Vehicles are typically taken for their parts, which are no longer manufactured and are too difficult or expensive to obtain. Individual car components in high demand are "tuners" or "street racers," which are often stolen for illegal export to Central and South America or Europe.

To help protect their vehicles, experts recommend that motorists always remove the keys from the ignition and vehicle, lock the doors, close the windows, hide valuable items, park in well-lit areas, and use a combination of antitheft devices. Motorists driving theft-prone vehicles need to take additional steps such as installing a visible deterrent like a steering wheel lock, an alarm, a starter or fuel disabler, and a tracking device.

The crime of **carjacking** remains a public concern. It occurs when the offender forces the driver of an automobile out of the vehicle before stealing it. In one case during July 1991, a 34-year-old woman was accosted by two men who climbed into her BMW and drove off—dragging her for about two miles. Police didn't know if the woman's clothing became entangled or if she hung on to save her 22-month-old daughter. The child, while still strapped to her child-protection seat, was thrown out of the moving vehicle, miraculously escaping injury. The men were later captured by police and charged with kidnapping, robbery, and felony theft.

Historically, many vehicles have been stolen to remove major parts and sell them to salvage yards or repair shops. Today, another criminal goal has captured the attention of law enforcement authorities: vehicles that are stolen and stripped for valuable accessories, such as seats, expensive radios, custom wheels, and tires.

MOTIVATIONS FOR MOTOR VEHICLE THEFT

Let us now take a closer look at the reasons for auto theft: joyriding, theft for resale, transportation for other crimes, and stripping and chop-shop operations. Understanding these will help investigators understand motivations for the crime, which gives the investigator a handle on how to anticipate the instances of this crime as well as how to prevent such activity.

Joyriding

For years, **joyriding** has ranked as the premier criminal motivation for motor vehicle theft, committed primarily by juvenile offenders. Since the mid-1970s, however, the average age of the auto-theft criminal has risen steadily. While typically in the company of friends, the juvenile auto thief steals a car for enjoyment for short periods. When the ride is over, the vehicle is sometimes stripped of certain "resalable" items, such as cellular telephones, radio equipment, and so on. Tracing personal effects left in a vehicle is difficult because frequently the identification numbers of the items have not been prerecorded by the victim.

Theft for Resale

Hard-core criminals have found motor vehicle theft for resale to be highly profitable, with minimal risk. Many methods are used to dispose of stolen vehicles. For example, many are transported to foreign countries for resale. Although this

Figure 19.2 Car thief breaching steering column of vehicle.

Motor Vehicle Theft Facts[4]

- Until recently, vehicle theft statistics reflected a continuing upward trend.
- There were 1,246,096 thefts of motor vehicles in 2002.
- Throughout the nation, a motor vehicle theft occurs every 22 seconds, averaging three every minute.
- 83.5 Percent of motor vehicle thieves are male.
- The average value of theft contents from a motor vehicle is $461.
- Of all motor vehicle thefts, 77 percent are automobiles.
- An average of 14.8 percent of motor vehicle thefts are cleared by arrest.

---

involves elaborate transportation schemes, once the vehicle makes it into the hands of the foreign car buyer, its chances of being recovered are minimal. Included in this category are luxury cars and heavy equipment, both of which will frequently bring much higher illicit prices than the vehicle is actually worth.

Transportation for Other Crimes

In addition to the profit motive, automobiles have been stolen for use in the commission of other crimes. Here, the vehicle may be used either as transportation to and from various crimes or used in the crime itself. This helps insulate the criminal from detection by not having to use his or her own vehicle in the perpetration of the crime. The availability of potential target vehicles and the opportunity to steal them will typically dictate which type of vehicle is chosen. One of the greatest problems in investigating stolen vehicles is the ability of the law enforcement officer to "read" a vehicle properly as one that has been stolen. These identification techniques are discussed in the following sections.

Stripping and Chop-Shop Operations

The high profitability of stolen motor vehicles has created a secondary market of sorts for auto thieves. This market's commodity is the parts of certain stolen autos. The terms **chop shop** and **stripping operations** refer to locations where stolen vehicles are disposed of. In a typical stripping operation, a stolen vehicle is taken to a location, typically a private garage in an unpopulated residential area of town. Such garages are usually rented by people using fictitious names to avoid detection by authorities.

The strip location can sometimes be spotted as buildings with covered windows in areas of frequent deliveries. In addition, people who are seen loading large items into vans in residential garages would be worthy of further investigation. In contrast, chop-shop operations vary in size and represent a growing business in which market entry is fairly easy. Anyone with a truck, garage, backyard, or a piece of secluded land can get into the business.

Although similar to strip locations, chop shops usually involve larger garages and deal in larger quantities of goods. They are sometimes large enough

---

Elements of Motor Vehicle Theft

Most state laws dealing with auto theft address the act of unauthorized use rather than actual "theft" of the vehicle. The elements are typically as follows: A person commits the act of auto theft if he or she:

- Intentionally acquires, drives, or
- Transports a motor vehicle
- Without the consent of the lawful owner.

Figure 19.3 A thief breaking into a car in a parking lot. The criminal act is captured on a video still from a security camera. *Daniel Allan, Getty Images, Inc.—Taxi*

to house both the stolen vehicle and the **tin truck** (the auto parts transport vehicle) inside the building, where detection is much more difficult. Another difference between strip and chop-shop locations is that chop shops will usually remove any identifying numbers from remains of vehicles left behind after the valued parts have been removed. The unused parts are typically dumped in lakes or ponds, or areas outside the location of the chop shop. Many salvage yards readily accept parts from auto thieves. Such parts are easily made part of the existing inventory.

Once inside the garage, the stolen vehicle is disassembled. It is here where the prime body parts are removed. These include bumpers, front-end assemblies, trunk lids, and doors. Interior parts, tires, and radios are also of great value to the thief.

Chop-shop operators use torches, power saws, or other tools to disassemble stolen vehicles. After thieves have stripped the stolen vehicle, the parts are transported in tin trucks, from which the parts are sold to repair shops and salvage yards that use them to repair damaged vehicles. Once an auto has been stripped, the remaining parts are abandoned. Such vehicles are then typically driven or even pushed to a location away from the strip location.

Investigating officers should always remember that victims might be able to recall certain characteristic marks on their stolen vehicle. These markings, which include cigarette burns in the seat, dents on fenders, and so on, might be identifiable once shown to the victim.

THE PRELIMINARY INVESTIGATION

The investigation of a stolen auto typically begins with a report by the victim to the police. As a rule, it is the task of the patrol officer to respond to such complaints and determine the facts and circumstances surrounding the alleged theft. These inquiries should include:

- Where was the vehicle last seen?
- Who was the last person to use the vehicle?
- Were the keys left in the ignition?
- Was the vehicle left unlocked?
- Is the victim in arrears on payments?
- Are others allowed to drive the vehicle?
- Was the vehicle equipped with special equipment, such as special wheels, fog lights, or special sound system?

Answers to these questions allow the officer to determine if a crime has been committed or if another situation is at hand, such as a civil dispute (divorce) or vehicle repossession by a bank or finance company. Other explanations for the disappearance of a vehicle might also exist. For example, the driver might have been intoxicated and may have been involved in a hit-and-run accident. The motor vehicle theft claim might be an effort to cover up the details and avoid suspicion.

True ownership of the vehicle must also be determined early in the investigation. This can be accomplished simply by requesting certain specific information from the victim, such as the title of the vehicle or a copy of the vehicle's insurance policy. Special characteristics of the vehicle should also be noted in the theft report. Details such as cigarette burns on the vehicle's seats, scratches or dents, rusted areas of the vehicle, decals or stickers, and so on will all distinguish the stolen vehicle from others like it on the street.

The Investigative Traffic Stop

Traffic stops are another way in which motor vehicle theft investigations are commonly initiated. Once again, the patrol officer is one of the primary players in this early stage of the investigation. Once a motor vehicle has been observed as being in violation of the law, officers have legal authority to stop it. In most cases,

Figure 19.4 A police officer examines the stolen car that jumped the curb, striking pedestrians, in the East Village section of New York. *Adam Nadel, AP Wide World Photos*

law enforcement officers will focus their attention on the motor vehicle's license plates. These will typically only provide officers with the information they are seeking regarding the registrant of the vehicle. In this situation, such limited information from the license plates includes the fact that the license plates are not stolen and that the owner's name and address match the registration.

It is here, however, that the motor vehicle thief may slip past the watchful eye of the patrol officer. Indeed, the officer making the stop should take time to record and check the validity of the VIN. In almost all cases, this will reveal whether or not the vehicle is properly registered or even stolen. Police officers must therefore have sufficient knowledge about the construction of the VIN to avoid common errors in recording and identifying it.

Professional motor vehicle thieves have practiced several methods of theft. Although complex to the inexperienced thief, these methods are commonly used in organized theft rings. Theft methods most commonly employed include altering the VIN, **tagging,** or altering title documents, modifying body parts of a stolen vehicle, and dismantling the vehicle for sale or exchange of parts.

THE VEHICLE IDENTIFICATION NUMBER

The **vehicle identification number** (VIN) is as unique to a motor vehicle as a fingerprint is to a human being. It has no resemblance to other numbers commonly dealt with in criminal investigation, such as one's social security number or date of birth. Instead, it is assigned to the vehicle by the manufacturer at the time of production and is designed to distinguish each vehicle from all others. The primary purpose of the VIN is for identification and registration.

Figure 19.5 Photo of typical vehicle identification number (VIN) located on dashboard of vehicle.

History of the VIN

Before 1968, VIN locations varied from manufacturer to manufacturer depending on the make of the vehicle. Since then, however, all American-made automobiles are assembled with the VIN plate visible through the windshield on the driver's side of the automobile. It can also be found on a federal safety certification label located on the driver's door or the driver's doorpost.

Exceptions to typical VIN locations are those of certain luxury automobiles that have their VINs affixed to the left-side windshield post. Any alteration of the VIN should be grounds for a more complete inspection of the vehicle. Before 1981, manufacturers' VIN numbering systems varied. In fact, manufacturers used slightly different systems of VIN numbering. Since then, however, the standard 17-character VIN was adopted, requiring all vehicles manufactured in the United States to have the standardized VIN.

How the VIN Works

The VIN consists of a combination of letters and numbers. To the average car owner, these combinations would mean very little, but to the criminal investigator, they are invaluable in identifying a stolen motor vehicle. To understand the VIN better, let's look closer at the function of each digit of the 17 numbers. For illustration sake, we consider the following VIN:

1J3CJ45A0CR335521

The numbers and letters represent the following information:

1	Nation of origin
J	Name of the manufacturer (e.g., General Motors, Honda)
3	Specific make of the vehicle (e.g., Buick)
C	Type of restraint system
J45	Car line series and body type
A	Engine description
0	Check digit
C	Model year
R	Assembly plant location
3 3 5 5 2 1	Sequential production numbers

With the exception of the check digit, one can easily see the function of each of these characters. The ninth character is called the check digit. It may be a number or a letter; however, it is derived mathematically from the other characters in the VIN to reveal coding and recording errors. Beginning in 1968, U.S. automobile manufacturers have placed a portion of the VIN on other areas of the vehicle, such as the engine and the transmission.

The Altered VIN

Because many vehicles are stolen for the sole purpose of resale, many methods are employed by the thief to disguise the true identity of the car. In fact, all outward appearances would indicate that the vehicle is legitimate, so once the VIN has been accomplished, it can then be sold to an unsuspecting customer.

Figure 19.6 Photo of vehicle identification number (VIN) located on the doorjamb of vehicle.

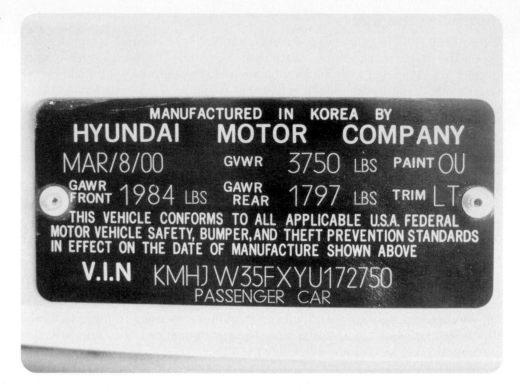

DISGUISING THE STOLEN VEHICLE

One common way of disguising a vehicle is to change the VIN and alter the documents that coincide with the VIN (i.e., tagging). Other ways in which a vehicle's true identity can be altered include the salvage switch, a modified VIN, or a bogus VIN.

The Salvage Switch Method

The **salvage switch** involves the thief purchasing a wrecked vehicle that is unrepairable strictly for its certificate of title and for the vehicle identification number. The purchase can be made from an individual or an insurance company, but typically is made from a wrecking or salvage yard. The vehicle must have both a VIN plate and documents to support ownership of the vehicle. Next, the thief steals a similar type of vehicle, removes its VIN tag, and replaces it with the salvaged vehicle's VIN. Any other numbers are either altered or removed from the vehicle. It is then sold to either an innocent buyer or to a person who may well suspect the validity of the transaction but participates anyway because of a favorable price.

The Modified VIN Technique

Another method of disguising a stolen vehicle is to replace the original VIN with a phony one. This can be done in several ways. One way is to use a simple label maker, which can easily be purchased at hardware stores. The VIN is then stamped on a label. Next, it is spray painted with flat black paint and placed over the original VIN. Other identifying numbers on the vehicle are either removed or altered. Vehicles tagged in this fashion should be fairly easily detected by observant investigators through observing size, texture, and the size of the numbers of the tag. Another way that thieves have attempted to alter VINs is to remove the original VIN, alter it, and replace it on the vehicle. Again, this method is usually detected by the trained investigator but may appear legitimate to the untrained eye.

The Bogus VIN

Still another method is to construct a completely bogus VIN that closely resembles the original. Many criminals will attempt to steal blank VIN tags, which are then stamped with numbers and placed on vehicles. This is where the ninth digit of the VIN, the check digit, is beneficial in determining the authenticity of the tag.

Since 1970, American-made vehicles have also displayed a federal safety certification label on the driver's door or the driver's doorpost. This label also displays the VIN for the vehicle and should match the VIN tag on the vehicle's dash. To dispose of the vehicle after it has been tagged, the auto thief adopts several methods. For example, in the salvage operation, the title will typically be placed in the fictitious name before sale. In instances in which the VIN has been altered or manufactured by the thief, phony title documents can then be prepared to match the bogus VIN. In other cases, title documents may not even exist, only the registration of the vehicle. In such cases, buyers who might suspect that the car is of suspicious origin might continue with the transaction because of a low sale price. Such sales are typically conducted in cash, at the thief's request.

THE RIP-OFF

Typically, vehicles are stolen because of carelessness on the part of the owner—drivers who leave their keys in an unattended car or motorists who leave their cars running while they enter an establishment for a short period. Vehicle thieves commonly watch these locations to wait for the most opportune time to make their steal.

When keys are not left in the ignition, many thieves have traditionally resorted to entry techniques ranging from the classic "smash-and-grab" technique to unobtrusive use of a screwdriver and flat iron. Today, entry into vehicles is becoming more innovative. One such innovation includes the use of porcelain chips broken from spark plugs. This technique involves attaching the chips to a wire, string, or other handle, and simply hitting them against the vehicle glass for quick entry. This method reduces time, noise, and chances of detection but may leave microscopic fragments of glass on the intruder's clothing.[5] These fragments are excellent evidence and hopefully can be located shortly after the theft by seizing the suspect's clothing for examination.

Another technique commonly used by thieves is to observe or "case" a parking lot where cars are parked while people are at work. In this case, the thief has several hours' leeway from the time the vehicle is stolen to the time the theft is discovered. Thus the vehicle may be transported far from the theft location by the time of discovery.

Many motorists invest in antitheft devices in their vehicles. Although many of these devices have proved to be effective, thieves have learned methods of defeating them in many cases. The level of expertise in disabling an antitheft device depends on several variables: the thieves' degree of mechanical experience,

Figure 19.7 The vehicle safety inspection (top) and vehicle registration (below) stickers will also provide identifying numbers and investigative leads.

the quality and effectiveness of the device, and the location of the vehicle when stolen.

TOOLS OF THE TRADE

Vehicles are obtained by many different means by professional thieves. For example, tow trucks are often used to transport a vehicle desired by the vehicle thief. Other common methods are the use of public parking facilities, such as mall parking lots and car rental lots. In these instances, all vehicles are prime targets especially if they are left with keys in the ignition. Entry into a vehicle can be accomplished using several tools. Professional thieves become proficient in the use of these tools and employ them in a manner in which little, if any, damage is done to the exterior of the vehicle, which could easily be noticed.

Many tools that thieves commonly use also have a legitimate function, which is, however, put to a sinister use by the criminal. When means are devised to counter or deter motor vehicle thefts, criminals inevitably devise methods with which to defeat these means.

RECOGNIZING THE STOLEN VEHICLE

As much as routine plays an important role in many aspects of criminal investigation, recognizing a stolen or "hot" auto is a task for which there is no set method. Indeed, the desire to identify stolen automobiles is always present within the law enforcement community; however, the expertise typically is not. Recognition of a stolen vehicle requires attention to detail. These details must then be evaluated properly so that appropriate action can be taken. No single point may identify a stolen auto as stolen, but subtle signals, typically in the form of circumstances, will alert officers to the presence of a stolen vehicle:

- *Missing locks.* If vehicle locks are observed missing, further investigation might be warranted. Certainly, a former victim might be driving his or her vehicle, but the driver might also be the thief.

- *Vehicles parked away from main flow of traffic.* Vehicles such as these could be stolen vehicles that were abandoned after serving a thief's purpose. Such an area could also be a drop location where the vehicle could be picked up and taken to a strip location or chop shop. If located, the vehicle should be photographed and searched for evidence such as personal papers or documents left behind by the thieves.

- *Accumulation of dirt or old parking tickets.* Vehicles so distinguished might also be stolen vehicles that have been dumped.

- *Missing license plates or parts.* This may also be an indicator that the vehicle has been abandoned.

- *License plates or lack of license plates.* This is usually one of the first tip-offs to a stolen vehicle. A simple piece of carefully placed tape can quickly alter the appearance of a number on a license plate. In addition, dirty plates on a clean car or clean plates on a dirty car both indicate that plates have been switched. Further, a vehicle may have only one plate when two are required, or plates may be attached in a hurried manner, such as with wire or string.

In addition to the preceding signals, investigating officers should look for anything unusual about the driver of the vehicle or the vehicle itself. Officers

> **Motor Vehicle Theft: Tools of the Trade**
>
> - *Slim jim.* This is a thin, easily obtainable piece of metal or aluminum, notched at both ends. This tool enables easy entry by the thief, who slides the tool in the small crevice between the door and the door frame. Once the lock is manipulated, the door is easily opened.
> - *Slide hammer.* This tool is also referred to as a dent puller or slam puller. Once the thief removes the lock cap of the ignition, the slam puller is inserted by screwing the tip into the keyway. Force is then applied to the slide mechanism, away from the steering column, and the lock is removed. The vehicle can then be started by inserting a screwdriver, which is twisted just like a car key.
> - *Ignition extractor.* The lock cap is removed upon getting into the vehicle. The extractor is attached and turned to remove the lock. The vehicle can then easily be started with a screwdriver.
> - *Force tool.* The force tool is placed over the lock and tapped after removal of the lock cap, the ratchet is turned, thus destroying the locking mechanism.
> - *Key cutter, codebook, and blank keys.* These tools enable entry into a single-key vehicle and are widely used. A door lock is pulled, and the code number from that lock can be obtained and a new key made. This gives the thief a new key that he can use at a time of his choosing.

should also be prepared to ask certain questions of the driver of the vehicle, if available. Questions officers should ask themselves include:

- Does the driver match the vehicle?
- Is the driver familiar with the operation of the vehicle?
- Can the driver (once away from the car) estimate the approximate mileage of the vehicle?
- Can the driver state when and where the last servicing was performed? (The answer can be compared to the "lube" sticker on the doorjamb.)
- Can the driver state what the license plate is on the vehicle?
- Can the driver answer questions based on information from the registration of the vehicle?
- Are the keys used by the driver actually intended for the vehicle in question? Are they made from original manufacturer blanks?

THE USEFULNESS OF ALARMS

These days, more and more people are installing car alarms to protect their automobiles. Since peaking in 1991 at 1.66 million, the number of stolen vehicles has dropped each year, to approximately 1.45 million in 1995.[6] Experts have observed that auto-theft season typically runs from April to August, and there is no indication that this trend will change in the near future. A 1995 Gallup poll made some interesting observations:

- Six percent of motorists say they sometimes leave their keys in the ignition, down from 11 percent just one year earlier.
- Twenty-one percent sometimes leave their car door unlocked, down from 31 percent in 1994.

Another variable that can be attributed to the reduction of car thefts is the widespread installation of high-quality car alarms. Many new cars and trucks come factory-equipped with alarms thought to be effective in deterring theft. For example, the BMW antitheft system has reduced thefts by 80 percent. The system relies on an ignition key with a computer chip. The key interfaces with a computer chip inside the ignition to start the car, so using a duplicated key won't work. After-market alarms are also gaining popularity as a preventive measure. Motorists can purchase devices that prevent a vehicle from being started unless a hidden switch is flipped. The switch controls fuel flow to the engine or current from the battery. Another type of antitheft device uses a radio transmitter to tell police where to find a vehicle once it is stolen. As of the time of preparation of this book, that device is available in large metropolitan areas in 11 states. Another device uses satellite technology to intercept a stolen vehicle. Once a victim realizes that his or her car has been stolen, they call an "800" number, and the alarm company sends a signal to a satellite that activates the vehicle's flashers and sounds an ear-piercing alarm. The vehicle's whereabouts can also be tracked via satellite.

CARJACKING

In the early 1990s, a new form of auto theft began to emerge—carjacking. **Carjacking** is defined by the U.S. Department of Justice as "completed or attempted robbery of a motor vehicle by a stranger to the victim."[7]

A carjacking typically consists of a single gunman placing a pistol to the head of an unsuspecting driver at locations such as stoplights, garages, fast-food restaurants, gas stations, and parking lots. Another common technique is the so-called bump and run, where the thief stages a minor rear-end collision. When the driver exits his or her vehicle to inspect the damage, one thief holds up the occupant(s) while, often, another drives their vehicle.

According to the Bureau of Justice Statistics, an average of about 49,000 completed or attempted nonfatal carjackings took place each year in the United States between 1992 and 1996. In about half of those incidents, the offender was successful in taking the victim's vehicle. In addition, about 27 homicides by strangers each year involve automobile theft. Some of these may have been

Figure 19.8 Carjacking, depicted here, is also a form of robbery and is one method used by criminals to acquire a desired vehicle. *Jack Star, Getty Images, Inc. PhotoDisc*

> **Prevention Key: Auto Theft**
>
> - Never leave your car running and unattended, even to dash into a business.
> - Never leave your keys in the car or ignition, even inside a locked garage.
> - Always roll up your windows and lock the car, even if it is in front of your home.
> - Never leave valuables in plain view, even if your car is locked. Put them in the trunk out of sight.
> - Always park in a high-traffic, well-lighted area, if possible.
> - Install a mechanical device that locks to the steering wheel column or brake to prevent the wheel from being turned more than a few degrees. Commonly called clubs, collars, or J-bars, these devices can act as a highly visible physical deterrent if installed properly.
> - Investigate the purchase of an auto security system if you live in a high-theft area or drive a theft-prone vehicle.
> - Display an alarm decal near the door handle.
> - If you park in a fee garage, take the pay ticket with you. It's the thief's ticket out of the garage, too. If you use valet parking, leave just the ignition key with the attendant. Make sure no identifying information is attached to the key. Do the same when you take your car for repairs.
> - Carry your driver's license, registration, and insurance card with you. Don't leave personal identification documents or credit cards in your vehicle.

carjackings. Other statistics about carjackings include: about seven of ten completed carjackings involve firearms; most carjackings did not result in injury to the victims; a majority of carjackings were committed at night.[8]

Drivers should copy their license plate and vehicle identification numbers (VIN) on a card and keep them with their driver's license. If a vehicle is stolen, police will need this information promptly. Most carjackers are between 15 and 23 years of age and are often seeking a car to help them commit other crimes. Investigators have known that auto alarms or antitheft devices installed in vehicles might simply encourage the amateur thief to resort to robbing the motorist at gunpoint instead of stealing the vehicle discreetly. Increased security, such as closed-circuit TV around other common robbery targets such as convenience stores, might also encourage robbers to resort to carjacking. In addition, police reports have noted the drug addict seems to be taking more risks than traditional car thieves. Vehicles targeted for carjacking include luxury models, starting at $40,000, which are then either exported for profit or "chopped" up for parts as discussed earlier in this chapter. In the latter case, a stolen car that has been chopped will usually net the thief anywhere from two to three times the vehicle's original price.

THEFT OF OFF-ROAD MACHINERY

Theft of machinery such as bulldozers, tractors, wheel loaders, and excavators has also emerged as a profitable enterprise for criminals. Estimates of the profits of stolen farm and construction equipment are well over $1 billion annually.[9] The theft problem is intensified by the fact that there is no standardized system for identifying off-road construction and farm equipment. Unlike automobiles, which have vehicle identification numbers, **off-road machinery** is not marked with a universal identification number system. Rather, each manufacturer has its own method of marking its vehicles. This results in great difficulty in identifying off-road machinery.

Compounding the problem is the fact that there is considerable difficulty establishing proof of ownership of off-road equipment. This is because off-road machinery is not sold with vehicle titles and is not registered in the same fashion

> **Prevention Key: Carjacking**
>
> • Lock car doors.
> • If someone approaches your car, carefully drive away.
> • Be aware of your surroundings.
> • While driving, stay in the center lane; don't get blocked into the curb lane.
> • If confronted by a carjacker, don't resist.
> • The greatest protection is staying alert!

as are automobiles. The National Auto Theft Bureau (NATB) has implemented a national database that helps combat this problem. The database, called the North American Theft Information System (NATIS), operates 24 hours a day, seven days a week, and cross-indexes product identification numbers with unique numbers on principal component parts such as engines and transmissions.

MOTOR VEHICLE FRAUD

The problem of motor vehicle fraud is also growing nationwide. For example, in 1989 the NATB estimated that 15 percent of all vehicles reported stolen were fraudulent claims. The person who commits motor vehicle fraud does so with a clear profit motive and will usually attempt to collect payment through her or his insurance company. The problem is compounded by the notion that many people have the attitude that fraud is only an insurance problem and doesn't really hurt anyone. Some feel that after paying insurance premiums for years they are entitled to get a return on their money. Indeed, many expenses are ultimately incurred in the detection, apprehension, prosecution, and incarceration of offenders.

Methods of Fraud

Although many methods of motor vehicle fraud exist, the most common is to alter the vehicle's identity by changing the VIN plate and reregistering the car. A second common method is the *owner give-up:* This term applies when the owner conspires with a third party, typically for a fee, to have the vehicle disposed of so that the owner can collect the insurance money. Reasons for motor vehicle fraud include:

- Desire for immediate cash
- End of costly repair bills
- Avoidance of hassle of selling
- Breaking of car lease

Many theft reports also include nonexistent vehicle contents such as camera equipment, furs, golf clubs, and so on. Here, the greedy thief attempts to "sweeten the pot" and increase her or his criminal profits.

STOLEN MOTORCYCLES

The rate of recovery for stolen automobiles has been much higher than that for stolen motorcycles. This indicates that expertise and proficiency in investigating motorcycle thefts require special training. The average police officer tends to overlook the problem of motorcycle thefts because he doesn't know what specifically to look for.

Perhaps one of the most commonly overlooked areas in motorcycle thefts is the manner in which they are identified. There are more than 70 different brands of motorcycles sold in the United States. Many of these manufacturers use different numbering systems. This creates confusion for police officers during investigations.

A second reason why motorcycle thefts are on the increase is because of inadequate registration procedures. Too commonly, motorcycles are registered by engine number rather than frame number. One basic problem in this area is when the model designator is omitted from registration. When this occurs, several motorcycles can be registered using the same VIN.

The Motorcycle VIN

The VIN on a motorcycle is possibly of greater value in identifying stolen motorcycles than stolen automobiles. Because parts on motorcycles are commonly replaced and exchanged, sometimes the only remaining identifier on the motorcycle is the VIN. As indicated, VINs are located on parts of the motorcycle for the same purpose as for other motor vehicles. As a rule, the VIN is dye-stamped into the steel frame of the motorcycle, although locations will vary from one manufacturer to another. For the most part, the VIN can be found on the right and left sides of the motorcycle's headstock or engine cradle. In addition, most manufacturers place a serial number on the engine case. This is a different number from the VIN and should be so noted by investigators. As with automobiles, a federal safety certification sticker can reveal valuable information about the motorcycle, such as the month and year the bike was manufactured. As with the VIN, this sticker is located on the left or right side of the headstock or engine cradle.

Methods of Motorcycle Theft

As with automobiles, different techniques are used to steal motorcycles. For example, the thief may obtain a lock number from the ignition, go to a dealer and report that his key was lost or stolen, and give the lock number. A key can be made from the lock number given by the thief, providing him with a way to start the motorcycle and drive away at his leisure. Some motorcycles are obtained by the thief acquiring a fake driver's license and going to a motorcycle dealer for a test drive. The dealer might hold the driver's license as security while the thief is out on a test drive—the thief, of course, doesn't return. In other cases, trucks are used to transport the stolen motorcycles to safety. Even if front fork locks are used as antitheft devices, two or three thieves may easily pick up the motorcycle and place it into the truck for transportation. This technique is commonly employed by gangs who "shop" for unattended motorcycles.

THE NATIONAL AUTO THEFT BUREAU (NATB)

The **National Auto Theft Bureau** (**NATB**) is a nonprofit private crime prevention agency underwritten by more than 600 property-casualty insurance companies. The Chicago-based organization was established to aid law enforcement and insurance investigators in investigations and prosecutions of vehicle crimes such as vehicle theft, vehicle arson, and vehicle fraud. The NATB maintains district offices throughout the United States, Mexico, and Canada, and publishes an annual manual for the identification of stolen automobiles. In addition, the NATB's role is to implement policies for the prevention of vehicle theft. To aid the investigator, the NATB publishes passenger identification manuals that interpret characters in the vehicle's VIN.

DISCUSSION QUESTIONS

1. List and discuss the various criminal motivations for motor vehicle theft.

2. What is the first thing a responding officer must do in investigating a claim of auto theft? What other inquiries should the officer make of the victim?

3. Explain the VIN and its role in criminal investigation of motor vehicle theft.

4. Define and discuss the practice of tagging stolen motor vehicles.

5. Identify and discuss entry techniques that are most commonly used by motor vehicle thieves.

6. List and explain the various tools that criminals most commonly use in the theft of motor vehicles.

7. What characteristics should the investigator look for in recognizing a stolen vehicle?

8. Describe how a chop-shop operation works and how it can be detected by investigators.

9. Discuss how the act of motor vehicle fraud is committed.

10. To what extent does the investigation of stolen motorcycles differ from the investigation of other motor vehicle thefts?

NOTES

1. State of Florida Attorney General's Web site: www.myfloridalegal.com (August 14, 2006).
2. National Insurance Crime Bureau (2005, Nov. 7). Hot wheels: Do you know where your car is?
3. As reported by CCC Information Services on MSN Autos at www.msn.com.
4. FBI (2003). Crime in America, 2002. *Uniform Crime Reports.* Washington, DC: U.S. Government Printing Office.
5. Ferguson, B. E. (1990, Sept.). Porcelain chips: An auto theft innovation. *Law and Order,* pp. 154–155.
6. Eldridge, E. (1996). Car security systems rob thieves of opportunity. *USA Today,* May 23, p. 1B.
7. Klaus, P. (1999). *Carjacking in the United States, 1992–1996.* Washington, DC: U.S. Department of Justice, Bureau of Justice Statistics.
8. Ibid.
9. National Auto Theft Bureau (1989). *Annual report.* Palos Hills, IL: NATB.
10. Ibid.

Key Terms

▶ alligatoring
▶ booby trap
▶ fire triangle
▶ olfactory senses
▶ paper trail
▶ plant
▶ point of origin
▶ span of the fire
▶ trailer

This chapter will enable you to:

- Understand the scope of the problem of arson.

- Learn the elements of the crime of arson.

- Appreciate the relationship between police and fire investigators.

- Learn techniques of arson investigation.

- Conduct the preliminary investigation in arson cases.

- Ascertain the role of the insurance industry in arson investigations.

- Learn how to investigate bombs and bombers.

- Understand searching techniques for bombs and booby traps.

INTRODUCTION

Perhaps one of the oldest known crimes is the act of arson. It creates a severe threat to human life and costs society billions of dollars per year. Although arson can be defined as the malicious or fraudulent burning of property, it can also be considered a crime against both persons and property. Furthermore, it receives little media attention and is difficult to investigate because evidence is difficult to locate and criminal intent is difficult to prove. Unlike other "sensational" media events such as murder cases and drug raids, arson is generally considered a low-priority crime even by law enforcement agencies. Several explanations can be cited for this:

- Arson is a time-consuming and difficult crime to investigate.
- There is much misunderstanding about the motives behind the crime of arson.
- Few arson cases lead to arrests, and less than 20 percent of arrests result in convictions.
- Arson used to be classified as a property crime rather than a crime of violence, as it is today.

ARSON OFFENSES

The Uniform Crime Reporting (UCR) Program defines arson as any willful or malicious burning or attempt to burn, with or without intent to defraud, a dwelling house, public building, motor vehicle or aircraft, personal property of another, etc. Only fires determined through investigation to have been willfully or maliciously set are classified as arsons. Fires of suspicious or unknown origins are excluded from this category.

Trends

In 2005, the FBI reported 67,504 arson offenses in the United States. Arsons involving structures (residential, storage, public, etc.) accounted for 43.6 percent of the total number while mobile property was involved in 29.0 percent of arsons. The rest were arsons of other types of property. The average value loss per arson offense was $14,910 in 2005, and arsons of industrial and manufacturing structures resulted in the highest average dollar losses (an average of $356,324 per arson). On a positive note, in 2005, arson offenses declined 2.7 percent when compared to arson data from 2004.

The United States has one of the highest fire death rates in the industrialized world. According to a 1998 publication by the National Fire Protection Association, the U.S. fire death rate was 14.9 deaths per million population. Between 1994 and 1998, an average of 4,400 Americans lost their lives and another 25,100 were injured annually as the result of fire.[1] Furthermore, about 100 firefighters are killed each year in duty-related incidents. Each year, fire kills more Americans than all natural disasters combined.[2]

National statistics show that "when measured on a cost per incident basis, arson is the most expensive crime committed." The high cost and widespread misunderstanding associated with the crime of arson can be attributed to several factors, which include:

- A lack of public education concerning the problem of arson.
- A reluctance on the part of prosecutors to file arson cases that rely on circumstantial evidence.
- Quick payments on fire losses by insurance companies.
- A lack of adequate training for investigators.

Many arson crime scenes are not recognized or treated as such, and much evidence is destroyed. Despite the fact that many of the preceding considerations are no longer considered as great a problem as they used to be, arson still accounts for substantial losses to victims. For example, property losses alone are estimated at $5 billion annually in addition to the estimated 1,000 lives claimed by arsonists each year.[3]

Because valuable evidence is sometimes destroyed during a blaze, it is often difficult to determine that arson was committed. Other complicating factors include the fact that there are few, if any, witnesses to the crime, physical evidence is difficult to locate, and if the crime is executed properly, it is difficult to determine the fire's point of origin. Finally, often it is the victim of the fire who ends up being the perpetrator of the crime. For these reasons, arson investigation is one of the more difficult crimes to solve.

ELEMENTS OF ARSON

As with all crimes, the elements must be established before a criminal charge can be levied against the suspect. As with most other crimes, the elements of arson differ from one state to the next, but some commonalties do exist.

Legal Categories

Arson is also legally characterized by two distinct categories: aggravated arson and simple arson. *Aggravated arson* is the deliberate burning of property while creating an imminent danger to human life or risking great bodily harm. *Simple arson,* a lesser offense, is the burning of property that does not result in such a risk to human life. In addition to aggravated and simple arson, most states have recognized that attempted arson is also punishable under law.

THE POLICE AND FIRE ALLIANCE

Once a fire is determined to have a suspicious origin, investigators from the local fire and police departments as well as the victim's insurance company will become involved with the case. Problems and confusion will sometimes unfold if investigators from these agencies fail to understand differences in their roles. The traditional role of the fire department is to investigate every fire for cause and origin. Accordingly, 80 percent of the fire protection in the United States is provided by volunteer fire departments.[4] To this end, firefighters are usually trained in the suppression of fire rather than its investigation.

When suspicious fires are discovered, however, it is generally while it is being extinguished. So what, then, is the role of the firefighter? As a rule, it is threefold: (1) to extinguish the fire, (2) to investigate the origin of the fire, and (3) to "detect" the possibility of arson but not to investigate arson. Few fire departments have legal authority to investigate arson fires, although their assistance in such an investigation is not disputed.

When the fire investigation becomes a question of who committed the crime, the matter then becomes a law enforcement concern. This is critical because once it is determined that law enforcement should take over the investigation, fire investigators should yield the crime scene to the arson investigators and respond to them in an adjunct role. Immediate obeyance of this principle will minimize confusion and duplication of efforts at the crime scene.

The police investigator has a statutory role in investigating the arson, as it is a violation of state or federal law. The principal goal of the police investigation in an arson case is to identify the perpetrator(s) of the crime and to identify and secure sufficient evidence to prosecute and convict.

Finally, the role of the insurance investigator is to make a determination as to whether or not the insurance company owes payment for the fire loss. The insurance investigator is not a law enforcement officer. Their authority to investigate is specified in the insured's contract. This contract refers to many of the provisions of the 1943 New York Standard Policy, which sets forth conditions subscribed to by the insured in the event of a loss.[5] In kind, most insurance companies state that coverage is void if the company's investigation proves arson or fraud.

ARSON INVESTIGATIVE TECHNIQUES

The act of arson has been described as a stealthy, cowardly crime that, by its very nature, leaves very little direct evidence as to the identity of the arsonist. Many arsonists, however, fail to cover their tracks adequately and may therefore leave some type of evidence behind. For example, in many commercial arsons, the suspect leaves a **paper trail** that investigators can follow. This includes financial records, inflated insurance coverage, little or no inventory, and excessive debts. In an ideal situation, the arsonist will either be convicted, through the use of well-documented motives and opportunity, or might be willing to cooperate with authorities in identifying accomplices, motives, and prior victims.

THE PRELIMINARY INVESTIGATION OF ARSON

The preliminary investigation of arson begins basically like many other crimes, with a thorough examination of the crime scene. Arson does not have an immediate corpus delicti. It is, therefore, the responsibility of the investigator to prove that a specific fire did occur and that it was ignited deliberately. To accomplish this, both direct and circumstantial evidence can be used to show that the fire was ignited. Such evidence, however, may not reveal the opportunity or motive of the fire setter. As with most crimes, motive is important, but the key responsibility of the arson investigator is to connect the suspect with the crime scene regardless of motive.

Elements of Arson
A person knowingly damages a building or property of another, by
• Starting a fire or explosion, or • Procuring or causing such property to be burned.

Shattering glass, splitting brick, and shredding human flesh, the explosion engulfed the New Woman All Women Health Care clinic in Birmingham, Alabama, on January 20, 1996. In an instant, an off-duty city police officer lay dead and a nurse severely injured. With a crude-but-lethal mix of dynamite and nails, the mysterious antiabortion clinic terrorist had struck again.

But this time, witnesses spotted a truck near the clinic and had the presence of mind to get the license number. Police quickly identified the vehicle owner—a 32-year-old former U.S. Army demolitions man who lived in a remote area at the western end of the state. The chase would wind across some of the country's most rugged and foreboding terrain as well as back in time. Rudolph's bombs had a signature in the nails they used. That signature and other clues allowed authorities to tie Rudolph to several bombings in the Atlanta area, including the knapsack bomb detonated in the midst of the 1996 Olympics in Atlanta's Centennial Park.

In the wake of the Birmingham clinic blast, a team of hunters located Rudolph's abandoned and mired-in-the-mud truck in the thick woods some eight miles from his last known residence, a trailer near the rural town of Murphy in northwestern North Carolina. The $275-per-month abode had been hastily abandoned; the lights were still on and the front door was ajar.

The Telltale Nails

The FBI seized nails and other materials from a nearby shed. The nails were reported to be similar to those used in the shrapnel charge of the Olympic Park bombing. Although there was no witness that could place Rudolph in Atlanta on the day of that bombing, forensic evidence—the unique properties of the metal components of the pipe bomb that tore through the Olympic Park—linked the suspect to the bomb. Meanwhile, remnants of steel plates used to direct the force of the blast in the devices in both the Centennial Park and Atlanta-area abortion clinic bombings were traced to Franklin, North Carolina. A steel plant there fashions 1/8-inch-thick steel plating. A known friend of Rudolph's works in the plant.

By early October 1998, the Justice Department was ready to formally charge the itinerant carpenter and outdoorsman with the Olympic bombing and the other bombings in the Atlanta area. The problem was that he had disappeared into North Carolina's Nantahala Mountains, a wilderness region he had roamed throughout his life. Part of the reason for announcing the formal charges was reportedly to discourage people from thinking of Rudolph as a wrongly pursued scapegoat. From the earliest days of the chase, it was suspected that the fugitive was receiving aid and assistance from some local residents. But the mystery of where Eric Robert Rudolph was hiding was perhaps less vexing than the more fundamental mystery of exactly who he really is.

The North Carolina mountains where Rudolph spent most of his life are home to the "Christian Identity" movement. Adherents of this cult are reported to believe that the white race is God's chosen. They are also militantly opposed to abortion and homosexuality, and in some cases are reportedly rabidly anti-Semitic.

After at least three of the Atlanta-area bombings to which Rudolph had been connected, Reuters and the *Atlanta Journal and Constitution* received letters from the "Army of God" claiming credit for the blasts. The Rudolph family was reported to have once lived nearby the underground bunker headquarters of one of the local leaders of the Christian Identity movement. In 1984, Eric and his brother Daniel were reported to have lived with their mother in a community of white separatists deep in the Missouri Ozarks.

That brother—Daniel Rudolph—had demonstrated a particularly disturbing form of antigovernment fanaticism. In March 1998, shortly after Eric became infamous as the Birmingham bombing suspect, Daniel—apparently with forethought—sliced his hand off with a power saw in the garage of his home near Charleston, South Carolina. Taping the disfigurement on a home video, he stared into the lens of the rolling camera and said simply, "This is for the FBI and the media." The hand was later recovered from the garage and reattached.

Available information suggests that in 1996 Eric Rudolph was going through some sort of life change. Two months before the bombing in Centennial Olympic Park, and calling himself "Bob Randolph," Rudolph sold his inherited home in Nantahala near Murphy, North Carolina, netting $65,000. He was also in the process of slowly making himself disappear.

According to the few people who crossed his path during this period of frequent moves in and around the Murphy area, Rudolph stopped seeing family and friends, even telling casual acquaintances that his family was dead. The man, described most often as quiet, polite, and handsome, lived last in a trailer near Murphy where he paid his rent, food, and fuel bills in cash.

Friends and acquaintances of that time recalled little about the reclusive man, except that he had nothing to say about abortion or the antigovernment sentiments that were popular among some of the locals. His only displayed bias was against the transplanted Floridians, whom he called "Floridiots," whose presence seemed to irritate him. Not surprisingly, these same folks were shocked when "Bob Randolph" became the celebrated target of a nationwide manhunt that sent hundreds of FBI, ATF, and other law enforcement officials to scour the North Carolina mountains. They had been searching ever since.

Finally, in May 2003, despite thousands of hours spent by experienced federal, state, and local police, rookie police officer Jeffery Postell spotted and arrested Rudolph near a grocery store in Murphy, North Carolina.

Identify the Point of Origin

The first step in an arson investigation is to determine the fire's **point of origin.** This may be the most critical phase of the investigation, which includes the ruling out of natural or accidental causes. The materials used in the setting of the fire, along with the type of material being burned, may show a distinct burn pattern. Hence it is important to identify the point at which the fire originated, for it is here that most of the physical evidence can be located indicating a fire of incendiary nature. The fire's point of origin may be determined in several ways. The questioning of witnesses could reveal the necessary information. In addition, an inspection of the ruins at the fire scene might reveal valuable evidence.

Search for Flammable Liquids

A search for liquid accelerants should be conducted at all arson crime scenes. The identification of liquid accelerants can generally be used to trace the fire's point of origin successfully. Detecting the odor of such accelerants may be the investigator's first clue. It is important, therefore, for investigators to be timely in their arrival at the crime scene because such odors dissipate quickly. One technique to detect the presence of flammable liquids is to place suspected residue in water and look for a thin film to float in the surface of the water. The formation of this film is reasonable grounds for suspecting that flammable liquids are present.

Observe the Span of the Fire

Determining the time **span of the fire** is also of paramount importance. Although the majority of evidence collection is conducted at the crime scene, much can be learned simply by observing the fire. Specifically, physical characteristics of the fire such as smoke, direction, flames, and distance of travel are important. Immediately after the fire is extinguished, samples of debris should be collected that might have been the material used for starting the fire. When the rubble is being cleaned up, investigators should be present to observe any additional evidence that might be uncovered.

Photograph the Scene

Complete photographs of the structure should be taken to help preserve the crime scene for the courtroom. This makes a "record" of the condition of the scene at the time the fire was extinguished. When taking photos, the investigator should focus on the location of rags, large amounts of paper, cans, or empty receptacles that might have been used in setting the fire.

Identify Plants or Trailers

Finally, identifying the areas of **plants** (preparations used to set the fire) and **trailers** (materials used to spread the fire) can reveal important clues to the investigator.

- *Plants:* preparations used to set the fire. These include newspapers, rags, and other flammable waste material.
- *Trailers:* materials used in spreading the fire. These include gunpowder, rags soaked in flammable liquid, and flammable liquids such as gasoline, kerosene, and alcohol.

Some arsonists prefer to use delayed timing devices to allow a time lag between the setting up of the arson and the fire's outbreak. To this end, mechanical devices and chemicals are commonly employed. Such devices may well be intact when probing the crime scene for evidence.

Question Witnesses

Witnesses also play an important role in determining causes of the fire and possible suspects. Questions to be asked of the witnesses include:

- Who are you, and why were you present at the fire?
- What attracted your attention to the fire?

The witnesses' observations of the intensity, color, and direction of the fire may also prove to be of great value. Certainly, the observations of witnesses should only be viewed as information to give the investigator a lead as to where to begin looking for evidence. The actual point of origin, of course, must be determined by a thorough examination of the premises.

Observe Alligatoring

The term **alligatoring** refers to the pattern of crevices formed by the burning of a wooden structure. Resembling the skin of an alligator, this pattern reveals a minimum amount of charring, with alligatoring in large segments, when a fire is extinguished rapidly. As the fire continues to burn, the alligatoring will become smaller, with charring becoming deeper.

Figure 20.1 The alligatoring effect results from the charring of wood, which gives it the appearance of alligator skin. *Evidence Photograhers International Council, Sanford Weiss*

In a fire crime scene, liquids tend to flow downward and pool around fixed objects such as furniture. Their trails, however, are relatively easy to trace and provide the investigator with good evidence. An accelerant such as gasoline, kerosene, or alcohol can be traced from the point it was spilled to the lowest point of flow. At times, unburned amounts of these liquids may be found at low points, where the heat was not intense enough for ignition.

Other Clues

Many things can indicate that a fire of suspicious origin was arson. In one example, many fires were set at the scene, but evidence showed that each was set independently, with no proof of spontaneous combustion. Other clues include:

- *Flames.* The color of the flame is noteworthy in the early phases of a fire. For instance, a blue-orange flame represents burning alcohol. Certainly, if this material is not normally stored on the premises, one could assume that it was used as the accelerant in the fire. Information as to the description of the fire can be gained from witnesses who arrived on the scene before investigators.

- *Smoke.* As indicated earlier, smoke can also be of value in determining what substance was used to start a fire. If smoke can be observed at the beginning of a fire, before spreading to other parts of a structure, its color should be noted. For example, black smoke indicates that the material is made with a petroleum base. White smoke, conversely, indicates that vegetable matter is burning, such as straw or hay. If the structure is completely engulfed in flames, it will be difficult to make determinations as to what materials are being burned.

- *Size of the fire.* Depending on certain factors, such as the time element of the fire, the size of the fire might give investigators information to determine an act of arson. For example, structures that are engulfed in flames in a short period might indicate arson. Fire investigators recognize that fires of "natural" origin burn in a definable pattern. Therefore, fires burning quickly or in a direction that is not logical will indicate that an accelerant has been used. Factors to aid the investigator in determining the "normal" course or pattern for a fire should consider such variables as ventilation and contents of the structure.

- *Odors.* Distinguishable odors can be emitted from certain types of fires that might indicate a specific fire starter, such as kerosene, gasoline, and alcohol. These materials ensure that a fire will erupt, and arsonists expect any evidence of these accelerants to be destroyed in the fire. Investigators should, therefore, try to detect any odors by using their own **olfactory senses.**

MOTIVATIONS OF THE ARSONIST

As a defense attorney once said, "It is not a crime to have a motive." Indeed, when an investigator is successful in the collection of evidence to show the insured's participation in the crime, along with evidence of a motive showing arson as a reasonable alternative for the arsonist, a prosecutable case may have been developed. Once it has been determined that the fire was of incendiary

Types of Evidence in Arson Cases

- *Evidence of incendiary origin.* The basic type of evidence in this category is physical evidence (e.g., laboratory analysis of fire debris), expert observation of burn patterns and fire characteristics, and negative corpus evidence (e.g., elimination of accidental causes).
- *Evidence of motive.* In fraud cases, this can involve complex analysis of financial and property records. Here, a distinction can be made between evidence of a general hostility (e.g., a previous argument) and specific hostility (e.g., threats to burn). In addition, motive can be important in cases involving a pyromaniac and vandalism, which are frequently irrational acts.
- *Evidence linking a suspect to the commission of arson.* Direct linkage, such as eyewitness testimony or a confession, is clearly preferable to circumstantial linkage, which simply reflects opportunity.

origin, possible motives must be examined to help identify the suspect. Motives for arson include profit, revenge, vandalism, crime concealment, and pyromania.

Arson for Profit

This category represents an estimated one-half of all fire-related property damage in the United States, and the corresponding increase in the number of arsons reported to officials in recent years.[7] The typical arson-for-profit criminal is the businessperson who sets fire to his or her business or hires a professional arsonist to do the task. Traditionally, this category of arson has posed relatively low risk and high profit for the criminal and has virtually become a business in and of itself.

Economic gain from this type of arson may be either direct or indirect. For example, a home or business owner will see a direct financial gain when the insurance company pays the claim. In comparison, an employee in a warehouse who starts a fire and readily extinguishes it might benefit from a raise or promotion for his or her quick and "responsible" response and effort in saving the business. As indicated earlier, insurance fraud is a common motive for arson, perhaps one of the most frequent. A common method of insurance-related fraud is the purchasing of old run-down buildings in inner-city areas. Over a period of several months, shrewd businesspersons then sell and resell the property.

Each of these transactions raises the value of the property, at least on paper. The properties are then insured for the highest possible dollar amount. Sometimes the target of the arsonist is not the building itself but what it contains. A computer dealer, for example, might remove any valuable computers and software from his

A Closer Look

Understanding Fire Behavior[6]

In one ATF (Alcohol, Tobacco, and Firearms) case, there were two eyewitnesses who saw the two owners exiting the building while splashing liquid. One of the witnesses mentioned this to one of the firefighters during the fire, who suggested that she tell her story to one of the detectives. As sometimes happens, the witness chose not to bother and left the scene. Fortunately, when the detectives went to reinterview the witnesses in the case, both were able to remember that they saw two men setting the fire. Therefore, it pays to reinterview witnesses.

or her business and leave behind computers and software that are outdated or in which they have invested too much money. Once the fire destroys the building, the arsonist simply claims the insurance coverage that covered the burned stock and realizes a "market" return on the stock.

Not all arson-for-profit crimes focus on businesses or are perpetuated by people in big business. Indeed, high car payments or excessive mechanical difficulties with an automobile may compel the ordinary citizen to commit automobile arson to collect on the insurance. This type of criminal activity has resulted in an estimated 1,500 automobile arsons each year.[8]

Arson for profit can take many forms, so in all circumstances the conditions surrounding suspicious fires must be investigated thoroughly for possible motives. These motives should include the possibility that arson was used to cover up another crime, such as homicide or burglary.

Arson for Revenge

A high percentage of arsons are attributed to revenge, jealousy, and spite. People committing such acts are usually adults who target both individuals and property. Offenders include jilted lovers in personal relationships, disgruntled employees, feuding neighbors, persons who were cheated in business and personal transactions, and persons motivated by racial prejudice. From an investigative standpoint, once revenge has been identified as a possible motive in a fire, the list of suspects can be narrowed greatly. From here, care should be exercised in interview and interrogation techniques to extract sufficient and pertinent information.

Arson for Vandalism

Not much planning or preparation is required for a fire designated as vandalism. In addition, readily available materials are commonly used by the arsonist. As we discuss later, about 95 percent of the arsons for vandalism are caused by juveniles, owing in large part to peer pressure. Statistics show that most violators in this category are lower-class youths who choose to commit the crime in the morning or early afternoon.

Motives in this category differ from case to case but include vandalism and revenge. Typically, however, the motive is profit. Indeed, people who have been unable to contract a professional arsonist have been known to hire juveniles to commit such acts. Certainly, the juvenile fire starter will work for much less than the professional "torch."

Children of many ages have experimented with fire out of curiosity. Some, according to theorists, are abused children and set fires as a call for help. Juvenile fire-setter programs have sprung up around the country to identify these problem children and to deal with their underlying problems.

Evidence of Planning or Pre-knowledge

- Removing items of value from the crime scene before a fire.
- Making off-the-cuff remarks or jokes about burning the structure before the fire.
- Increasing insurance coverage or obtaining coverage for the first time before the fire.
- Making unusual changes in business practices just before the fire (e.g., closing earlier or later, having different people lock up).
- Taking obvious actions designed to avoid suspicion, such as booking for banquets that the insured has no intention of carrying out, filing for bankruptcy, and so on.

Arson for Crime Concealment

It is common for some criminals to try to cover up their crimes through the use of a fire. Murders, burglaries, and other crimes have been concealed through the employment of this method. Fire investigators must consider this as an alternative motive for all fires.

Pyromania

A pyromaniac is a person who is a compulsive fire starter. This person is motivated by several aspects of the fire-setting experience. For example, some experts claim that the pyromaniac gains sexual stimulation by starting and viewing a fire. In addition, excitation is achieved by the crowds that gather and the emergency vehicles that converge on the scene. Pyromaniacs are impulsive fire setters; their acts are seldom planned. Investigators can only examine the routes or paths that the fires seem to establish. Investigations have revealed that the pyromaniac may have a sordid past, which includes being abused as a child, bedwetting, and cruelty to animals.

SERIAL FIRE SETTERS

Serial criminals of any type pose great concerns for communities and law enforcement officials alike. The serial arsonist can be defined as one who sets fires repeatedly. This criminal, however, is at somewhat of an advantage because expertise in fire investigations is not as common as in other crimes. The FBI's National Center for the Analysis of Violent Crime (NCAVC) has conducted research in this area and has concluded that compulsive fire setting can be classified as mass, spree, and serial.

A Closer Look

Arson for Revenge[9]

Jane (not her real name) is a 27-year-old white female, well-groomed and friendly. Her records indicate below-average intelligence. She was arrested in 1984 and charged with several counts of arson. This was her first incarceration. She set a fire to a vacant farmhouse in 1980, amounting to $30,000 in damages; a barn in 1984, resulting in a $150,000 loss; and a corncrib in 1984, worth $10,800. The fires were revenge-motivated according to Jane, who claims that she set fire to the barn because she claimed the owner would not give her some kittens.

　　The corncrib fire was a result of a long-standing grudge against its owner, who years earlier had removed Jane from the school bus she was driving because of her bad language and behavior. Jane indicates that she was under medication for a heart ailment. While growing up she had constant conflicts with her parents, whom she claimed abused her emotionally and physically. Jane stated that she also had been raped at age 18 by her father and brother. As with many arsonists, Jane reports problems establishing and maintaining relationships. While incarcerated, Jane had numerous run-ins with corrections officials for minor nuisance offenses. She is presently in a halfway facility, working on her high school equivalency diploma and holding down a part-time job. Her caseworker feels that Jane will be released sometime soon.

- A *mass arsonist* sets three or more fires at the same location.
- *Spree arsonists* set fires at three or more separate locations, with no cooling-off period between them.
- The *serial arsonist* sets three or more separate fires with a definite cooling-off period between them. This period may last for days, weeks, or months.

PROFILING THE FIRE STARTER

The investigator, once identifying a possible motive, may wonder to what extent the fire starter shows a propensity for violence. Surprisingly, David Berkowitz, the "Son of Sam" mass murderer who terrorized New York in 1976 by killing five people and wounding seven others, reported to the police that he was personally responsible for setting more than 2,000 fires from 1974 to 1977.[10] Police reports also showed that Berkowitz set these fires in cars, dumpsters, brush, and vacant and unoccupied stores. In addition, police seized notepads bearing handprinted notes by Berkowitz that gave details on 1,411 fires for the years of 1974, 1975, and 1977, including the date and time of the fire, street, type of weather, and the fire department code, indicating the type of responding apparatus and property burned. The following questions are therefore raised:

- Does Berkowitz typify the fire starter?
- Are arsonists homicidal?
- Do they keep meticulous diaries of their fires?

According to James in his article "Psychological Motives for Arson," gender, age, education, intellectual level, or economic status does not in any way limit the possibility that a person will engage in arson.[11] On the other hand,

Figure 20.2 Scene of a suspect fire with a burned-out, collapsed garage in Laguna Beach, California. Crime scenes such as these are extremely difficult to investigate. *Jonathan Nourok, PhotoEdit Inc.*

Problems in Arson Investigation

- Locating witnesses.
- Locating and preserving physical evidence.
- Determining whether the victim is also the suspect.
- Coordinating the investigation among police, fire, and insurance agents.
- Determining if the fire was arson or had some other cause.

---

from a study of large samples it does appear that, statistically, persons of certain ages and with certain characteristics are more apt to set fires than are others.

THE ROLE OF THE INSURANCE INDUSTRY

Because of the severe financial strain arson has placed on the insurance industry, insurance companies are becoming more involved with investigations involving arson. Insurance carriers are usually more than willing to assist local law enforcement and fire officials during the course of an investigation. In fact, independent information offered by an insurance company might prove to be highly valuable in discovering motives and suspects for a crime. Indeed, the crime of arson is one that permits the investigator to work hand in hand with the "victim." In addition, many insurance carriers might even offer financial assistance to fire investigators. This may come in the form of providing heavy machinery for aid in processing the crime scene or by bringing in experts in arson investigations to aid local investigators in the investigation.

Insurance company assistance can come in many other forms, such as providing local investigators with financial audits and income tax returns; such information may not be readily available to the local investigator. To protect insurance companies from civil recourse in disclosing some of the information discussed previously, many states have passed laws granting limited civil immunity to insurance companies that assist local arson investigators during the course of an ongoing investigation. This contributes to an increased flow of information from insurance companies to local investigators, which increases the chance of an eventual prosecution of the arsonist and subsequent relief from civil claims liability for the insurance company.

Characteristics of the Fire Setter[12]

- *Age:* typically around 17 years of age.
- *Gender:* usually male.
- *Race:* predominantly white.
- *Intelligence:* research indicates that fire setters are often mentally deficient.
- *Academic performance:* most have a history of poor academic performance.
- *Rearing environment:* most appear to come from unstable home environments within lower socioeconomic groups.
- *Social relationships:* typically experience difficulties in relationships.
- *Sexual disturbance:* usually associated with sexual perversion; fire setting tends to serve as a sexual substitute.
- *Motive:* revenge most typically the underlying motive.

PROSECUTION OF ARSON CASES

There exists an old adage: "Without the **fire triangle**—heat, fuel, and oxygen—there can be no fire." Similarly, the successful prosecution of an arson case must include a triangle consisting of police detectives, fire investigators, and a prosecutor. Sadly, in many parts of the United States, prosecution of arson crimes may never occur. Some reasons include: (1) There is no one qualified or trained to conduct the investigation; (2) the time required for a thorough arson investigation by police or fire authorities is not available; and (3) prosecuting attorneys are reluctant to file and pursue prosecution. The third reason is the most prevalent, as arson cases are difficult to prosecute.

Prosecution of an arson case is time-consuming and requires expertise. Courts have ruled that circumstantial evidence, the most common type of evidence in an arson case, has the same probative value as direct evidence, but it is up to the prosecution to weave the web of circumstantiality.[13] Many prosecutors find this an intimidating and unrewarding task.

A good arson investigator begins with the notion that he or she must collect sufficient circumstantial evidence to convince a jury that the suspect committed the crime. Statistics reveal that most successful arson prosecutors rely on circumstantial evidence.

Proving the arson case "beyond a reasonable doubt" through the use of circumstantial evidence is difficult but not impossible. Prosecutors are frequently reluctant to proceed with charges in an arson case because evidence is fragmented and circumstantial. The trained investigator, however, knows what evidence to look for and is aware of the amount of evidence sufficient to remove reasonable doubt from the minds of prospective jurors.

BOMBING INCIDENTS

Even though this section addresses bomb investigations, a brief opening discussion about terrorism is prudent as a number of terrorist organizations in the twenty-first century have utilized bombs in various forms. The World Trade Center and Pentagon terrorist attacks of September 11, 2001, marked a dramatic escalation in a trend toward more destructive terrorist attacks which began in the 1980s. Until the September 11 attack, the October 23, 1983, truck bombings of U.S. and French military barracks in Beirut, Lebanon, which claimed a total of 295 lives, stood as the most deadly act of terrorism. The attacks of September 11 produced casualty figures more than ten times higher than those of the 1983 barracks attacks.

Evidence for Arson Prosecution

- *Evidence of participation.* This might be the disabling of a fire alarm or rearranging combustibles at a fire's location.
- *Exclusive access.* If firefighters are required to use force to gain entrance into a structure, the arsonist would have difficulty doing the same to set the fire. This indicates the complicity of the business owner in locking up the structure.
- *Motive.* Establishment of a motive is one critical element in showing jurors a suspect's criminal intent.
- *False statements.* A convincing element in an arson prosecution is the "victim's" false statements to the investigators.

The September 11 attack also reflected a trend toward more indiscriminate targeting among international terrorists. The vast majority of the more than 3,000 victims of the attack were civilians. In addition, the attack represented the first known case of suicide attacks carried out by international terrorists in the United States. The September 11 attack also marked the first successful act of international terrorism in the United States since the vehicle bombing of the World Trade Center in February 1993.

Today, the most serious international terrorist threat to U.S. interests stems from Sunni Islamic extremists, such as Osama Bin Laden and individuals affiliated with his Al-Qaeda organization. Al-Qaeda leaders, including Osama Bin Laden, had been harbored in Afghanistan since 1996 by the extremist Islamic regime of the Taliban. Despite recent military setbacks suffered by the Taliban and the apparent death of Al-Qaeda operational commander Mohamed Atef resulting from a U.S. bombing raid, Al-Qaeda is considered a capable terrorist network. The network's willingness and capability to inflict large-scale violence and destruction against U.S. persons and interests—as it demonstrated with the September 11 attack, the bombing of the *U.S.S. Cole* in October 2000, and the bombings of two U.S. embassies in east Africa in August 1998, among other plots—make it a clear and imminent threat to the United States and pose a number of unique challenges for criminal investigators.

Individuals who have been investigated for possible terrorist links include Richard Reid and Zacarias Moussaoui. Let's now consider investigative leads as well as evidence developed against these terrorist suspects to illustrate.

On December 22, 2001, Richard C. Reid was arrested after a flight attendant on American Airlines Flight 63 observed him attempting apparently to ignite an improvised explosive in his sneakers while on board a Paris-to-Miami flight. Aided by passengers, attendants overpowered and subdued Reid, and the flight was diverted to Logan International Airport in Boston. Evidence strongly suggests that Reid, who was traveling on a valid British passport, was affiliated with the Al-Qaeda network. Reid was indicted on nine counts, including placing an explosive device on an aircraft and attempted murder. The FBI investigation has determined that the explosives in Reid's shoes, if detonated in certain areas of the passenger cabin, could have blown a hole in the fuselage of the aircraft.

Investigators also learned that Reid and another subject, Zacarias Moussaoui, were known associates. Moussaoui came to the attention of the FBI while taking flight-training classes in Minnesota in August 2001. Moussaoui had paid over $8,000 in cash for flight simulator lessons on a 747-400, which far exceeded his training level as a pilot. Moussaoui showed unusual interest in the instructor's comment that airplane cabin doors could not be opened during flight. In addition, his flight instructor was concerned that Moussaoui expressed interest only in learning how to take off and land the 747-400. In preparation for high-fidelity simulator training, he expressed strong interest in "piloting" a simulated flight from London's Heathrow Airport to John F. Kennedy Airport in New York. When the instructor took his concerns to the FBI, Moussaoui was interviewed by Special Agents from the FBI and the U.S. Immigration and Naturalization Service (INS). He was determined to be an INS overstay and was detained by the INS on August 16, 2001. Following his detention, Moussaoui refused to allow a search to be conducted of his possessions, including a laptop computer and a computer disc. Attempts were made to obtain authority to conduct a search of this computer. However, due to the lack of probable cause and

A Closer Look

Arson and Trace Evidence[14]

In California in early 1989, a pipe bomb that had been placed on a vehicle exploded, killing the driver. An investigation by the ATF, the Rialto, California, Police Department, and San Bernardino Sheriff's Department ensued. Evidence recovered at the scene was forwarded to the ATF laboratory for examination. Intact powder particles found at the end caps of the bomb enabled chemists to identify the type and brand of powder used. A subsequent search of the suspect's residence uncovered a can of smokeless powder identical to the powder identified. Additional evidence recovered during the search linked the suspect to the bombing, for which he was arrested and tried on state murder charges.

lack of predication, neither a criminal nor intelligence search could be conducted. Following the September 11 attack, a criminal search of the computer was conducted. Nothing was located that connected Moussaoui with the events of September 11; however, information about crop-dusting was located on the computer. As a result, crop-dusting operations in the United States were grounded briefly on two occasions in September 2001. On December 11, 2001, the United States District Court for the Eastern District of Virginia indicted Moussaoui on six counts of conspiracy for his role in the events of September 11, 2001.

What Is a Bomb?

Bombs can be constructed to look like almost anything and can be placed or delivered in any number of ways. Bombs are often made out of common household items regularly found in the kitchen, garage, or under the sink. The easiest bomb to construct is the pipe bomb, which is often packed with screws and nails which act as projectiles, similar to a hand grenade. These are materials that the bomber relies on, in part, to help conceal his or her identity. Because they are usually homemade, these bombs are limited in their design only by the imagination of the bomber. So when searching for a bomb, the investigator should simply look for anything that appears unusual.

Statistics show that the use of bombs by drug traffickers is becoming more common. In 1990, the ATF reported an increase of 1,000 percent between 1987 and 1989. These included 126 bombings around the country.

In addition to drug traffickers, in 1990 the ATF showed an increase in mail bombs. The mail bomber attempts to gain from violence and intimidation what he or she fails to attain peacefully. Such devices are typically sent by "hate" or special-interest groups representing a particular lifestyle or belief, or protesting certain laws. During 1990, for example, mail bombs killed a federal judge and a city alderman.

Teen Bombings

A disturbing trend across the nation is the growing number of teenagers who have been linked with bombing incidents. Many techniques of how to construct a bomb cheaply have been learned through the Internet. Experts theorize that

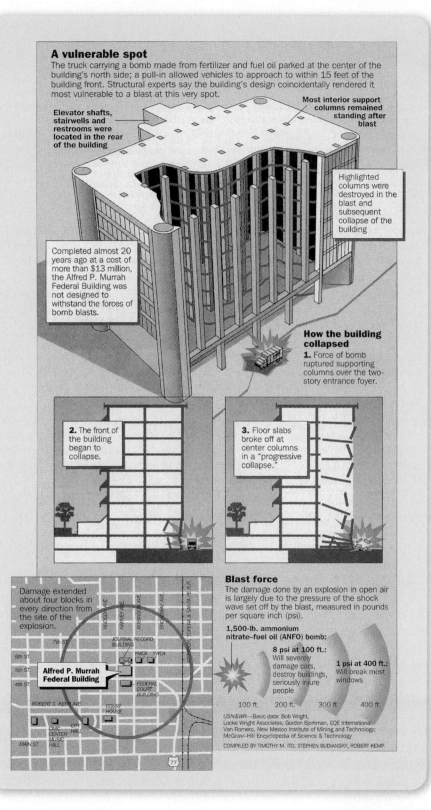

A Closer Look
The Case Against the Unabomber

Ted Kaczynski, a math professor-turned-hermit, was charged with four of the 16 bombings linked to the Unabomber and faced the death penalty if convicted. After his arrest, he initially pleaded innocent of the charges and was remanded to the Sacramento, California, jail. Following his arrest, Kaczynski's Montana cabin was searched by federal agents, who found, among other things, a bomb (which they exploded safely), the original antitechnology manuscript, and his secret identification number. Under law the prosecution must also provide the defense with any evidence it has which might show that the accused is innocent. Here is what prosecutors filed in federal court:

- Investigators found a deposit credited to Kaczynski's account at Western Federal Savings in Helena, Montana, on December 11, 1985, the same day that he was alleged to have planted his first fatal bomb 900 miles away in Sacramento. But the deposit slip was actually dated December 9.

- The Bureau of Alcohol, Tobacco, and Firearms determined that a bomb placed at the University of Utah in October 1981 was a hoax. What prosecutors failed to say was that the FBI and postal inspectors disagreed. Also, in a letter to the *New York Times,* the Unabomber described that bomb as a botched operation.

- Crime scene investigators found in excess of 20 latent fingerprints, some of which were identified and some which were not, and none of which were Kaczynski's fingerprints. But the Unabomber's letter boasted about using gloves to avoid the fingerprints.

- In earlier affidavits, FBI analysts had pointed to scores of similarities between Kaczynski's writings and the Unabomber's manifesto and letters, including similarly misspelled words. But in a later filing, prosecutors suggested that defense attorneys talk to a political science professor at Brigham Young University concerning his work on the Unabomber case.

In December 1997, Kaczynski admitted to the FBI that he was in fact the Unabomber and agreed to a plea bargain, pleading guilty to two counts of murder in exchange for a life sentence without the possibility of parole.

well-publicized bombing incidents such as the Oklahoma City bombing and the Unabomber saga have stimulated interest among teenagers in bomb making.[15] It is unclear whether teen bombers are really interested in hurting anyone, or just intrigued by their ability to manufacture a bomb. How-to information is also readily available in bomb-making manuals such as the *Anarchist's Cookbook* and the *Poor Man's James Bond.* These manuals have also been found online.

The Internet has given teens a way to communicate with like-minded youths who may also be curious about bomb building. In 1996, a Montgomery County, Maryland, neighbor who suspected that illegal drugs were being shipped to teenagers at a vacant house tipped the police, who found bomb-making ingredients and plans for making a bomb. In a better known case, Harvey "Buddy" Waldron, a Washington State football player, was killed in an explosion in Pullman, Washington, in 1993 when he and a teammate assembled an 8-inch pipe bomb, wired to a clock, that they had planned to detonate in a wheat field. To combat the spread of bombings, in 1996 the state of Georgia enacted the first comprehensive antibomb law which includes penalties for both teens and adults.

INVESTIGATING THE BOMB THREAT

Bomb threats are delivered in a variety of ways, but most are telephoned in to the target. Occasionally, these calls are through a third party. Sometimes a threat is communicated through writing and recording. There are two general explanations as to why bombers communicate a bomb threat:

1. The caller has definite knowledge or believes that an explosive or incendiary bomb has been or will be placed, and he or she wants to minimize personal injury or property damage. The caller may be the person who placed the device or someone who has become aware of such information.

2. The caller wants to create an atmosphere of anxiety and panic that will, in turn, result in a disruption of normal activities at the facility where the device is supposedly placed.

Whatever the reason, there will certainly be a reaction to it. Through proper planning, however, the wide variety of uncontrollable reactions can be minimized. The bomb threat caller is the best source of information about a bomb. When a bomb threat is called in, the following steps should be implemented:

- Keep the caller on the line as long as possible.
- Ask him or her to repeat the message and record every word spoken by the person.
- Ask the caller the location of the bomb and the time of detonation of the device.
- Inform the caller that the building is occupied and the detonation of a bomb could kill or injure innocent people.
- Pay particular attention to background noise such as motors running, music playing, or any other noise that may give a clue as to the location of the caller.
- Listen closely to the voice (male or female), voice quality (calm or excited), accents, and speech impediments.
- Interview the person who received the call for the preceding information.

The Written Bomb Threat

When a written threat is received, all materials should be saved, including envelopes and containers. Remember that paper is an excellent preservative of latent fingerprints. In addition, handwriting, typewriting, and postal markings can provide good investigative leads. Therefore, once the message is recognized as a bomb threat, further handling of the material should be minimized and it should be stored in a safe place.

Booby Traps

The use of bombs and **booby traps** has also become of particular concern to drug enforcement officials over the years. Many drug manufacturers have learned the skills of protecting their marijuana plots or chemical laboratories with such devices. The booby trap provides low-cost protection to the illegal drug operation and is designed to serve any of three purposes.

1. To warn the suspect of any intruders by the sound of explosive devices.
2. To deny any intruder or police access to the inhabited area by injuring or killing them.
3. To slow down police pursuit in a raid situation by injuring or killing officers.

If explosives are located, officers should never attempt to dismantle or defuse them unless they have received technical training in bomb disposal. Instead, they should be sufficiently trained to identify such devices so that (1) they can be avoided, and (2) properly trained personnel can be notified.

Explosive booby traps are activated by numerous methods, including remote control, manual control, or activation by the victim (usually, a trip wire or hidden pressure plates installed in the ground). Booby traps can be placed either outside or inside the suspect's residence, and their design is limited only by the imagination of the criminal. For example, one exterior trap is called the mouse trap because it literally employs a mouse trap that is used as a firing pin for a shotgun shell that is also attached to the trap. The trap can be affixed to trees or fence posts and can either maim or kill the intruder. An example of an indoor trap is the magazine bomb. This device consists of a magazine that has had a portion of the inner pages removed to conceal a hidden mouse trap. Once the magazine is opened, the trap detonates a blasting cap.

Safety Precautions

In raid or search situations in which explosive devices are expected to be encountered, investigators should be accompanied by an explosives expert. This person can be used to inform officers of what type of device is at hand and how best to proceed safely with the raid. Other precautions include the following:

- Only one officer at a time should approach the suspected booby trap.
- When trip wires are located, both ends of the wire should be checked (some devices use more than one trip wire).
- Wires that appear to be electric should not be cut.
- Be aware of fuses or obvious means of detonation (i.e., mercury fuses).
- No containers should be opened without a thorough examination.

No single strategy exists to safeguard officers adequately from all hazards posed by booby traps or explosives. Each case is different and should be evaluated individually, with consideration given to the number of possible suspects (and their backgrounds) and the location of the raid. In any case, keen observation and prudent judgment are still the best investigative precautions.

BOMB SEARCH TECHNIQUES

The following room search technique is based on the use of a two-person searching team. There are many minor variations possible in searching a room. The following contains only the basic techniques. When the two-person search team enters the room to be searched, they should first move to various parts of

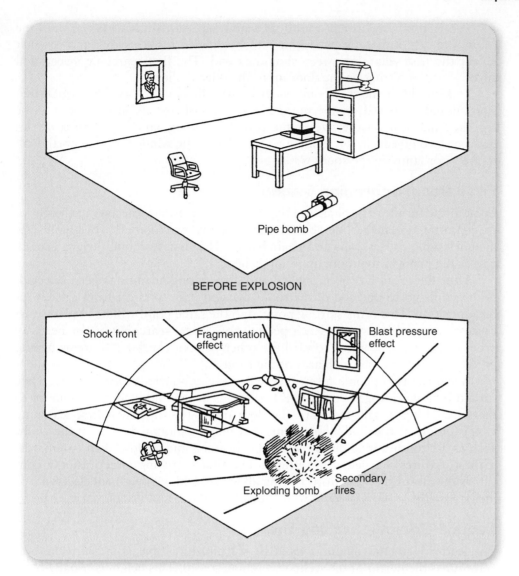

the room and stand quietly with their eyes closed and listen for a clockwork device. Frequently, a clockwork mechanism can be quickly detected without use of special equipment. Even if no clockwork mechanism is detected, the team is now aware of the background noise level within the room itself.

Background noise or transferred sound is always disturbing during a building search. If a ticking sound is heard but cannot be located, one might become unnerved. The ticking sound may come from an unbalanced air conditioner fan several floors away or from a dripping sink down the hall.

Sound will transfer through air-conditioning ducts, along water pipes, and through walls. One of the most difficult buildings to search is one that has steam or hot water heat. This type of building will constantly thump, crack, chatter, and tick due to the movement of the steam or hot water through the pipes and the expansion and contraction of the pipes. Background noise may also include outside traffic sounds, rain, and wind.

The lead investigator of the room searching team should look around the room and determine how the room is to be divided for searching and to what height the first searching sweep should extend. The first searching sweep will cover all items resting on the floor up to the selected height.

You should divide the room into two virtually equal parts. This equal division should be based on the number and type of objects in the room to be searched and not on the size of the room. An imaginary line is then drawn between two objects in the room (e.g., the edge of the window on the north wall to the floor lamp on the south wall).

First Room-Searching Sweep

Look at the furniture or objects in the room and determine the average height of the majority of items resting on the floor. In an average room, this height usually includes table or desktops and chair backs. The first searching height usually covers the items in the room up to hip height.

After the room has been divided and a searching height has been selected, both people go to one end of the room division line and start from a back-to-back position. This is the starting point, and the same point will be used on each successive searching sweep. Each person now starts searching his or her way around the room, working toward the other person, checking all items resting on the floor around the wall area of the room.

When the two people meet, they will have completed a *wall sweep*. They should then work together and check all items in the middle of the room up to the selected hip height, including the floor under the rugs. This first searching sweep should also include those items that may be mounted on or in the walls, such as air-conditioning ducts, baseboard heaters, and built-in wall cupboards, if these fixtures are below hip height. The first searching sweep usually consumes the most time and effort. During all the searching sweeps, an electronic or medical stethoscope is used on walls, furniture items, and floors.

Second Room-Searching Sweep

The lead investigator again looks at the furniture or objects in the room and determines the height of the second searching sweep. This height is usually from the hip to the chin or top of the head. The two persons return to the starting point and repeat the searching technique at the second selected searching height. This sweep usually covers pictures hanging on the walls, built-in bookcases, and tall table lamps.

Third Room-Searching Sweep

When the second searching sweep is completed, the lead investigator again determines the next searching height, usually from the chin or the top of the head up to the ceiling. The third sweep is then made. This sweep usually covers high-mounted air-conditioning ducts and hanging light fixtures.

Fourth Room-Searching Sweep

If the room has a false or suspended ceiling, the fourth sweep involves investigation of this area. Check flush or ceiling-mounted light fixtures, air-conditioning or ventilation ducts, sound or speaker systems, electrical wiring, and structural frame members. Have a sign or marker indicating "Search Completed" posted conspicuously in the area. Place a piece of colored cellophane tape across the door and doorjamb approximately 2 feet above floor level if the use of signs is not practical.

The room searching technique can be expanded. The same basic technique can be applied to search any enclosed area. Encourage the use of common sense or logic in searching. For example, if a guest speaker at a convention has been threatened, common sense would indicate searching the speaker's platform and microphones first, but always return to the searching technique. Do not rely on random or spot-checking of only logical target areas, as the bomber may not be a logical person.

In conclusion, the following steps should be taken in order to search a room:

1. Divide the area and select a search height.
2. Start from the bottom and work up.
3. Start back-to-back and work toward each other.
4. Go around the walls and proceed toward the center of the room.

WHEN A BOMB IS FOUND

It is important to stress that personnel involved in a search be instructed that their only mission is to search for and report suspicious objects. Under no circumstances should officers attempt to move, jar, or touch a suspicious object or anything attached to it. The actual removal of the bomb should be left to professional bomb disposal personnel. Once the suspected bomb is located, the following procedures should be followed: Report the location and description of the object to the supervisor or command center. Fire department and rescue personnel should also be notified and placed on standby. If necessary, sandbags or mattresses (never metal shields) should be placed around the suspicious object. Do not attempt to cover the object. Instead, you should:

- Identify the danger area, and block it off with a "clear zone" of at least 300 feet, including floors below and above the object.
- Be sure that all doors and windows are open, to minimize primary damage from the blast and secondary damage from fragmentation.
- Evacuate the building.
- Do not permit reentry into the building until the device has been removed or disarmed and the building is declared safe for reentry.

Handling the Media

It is important that all inquiries from the news media be directed to one person who is designated as spokesperson. All other persons should be instructed not to discuss the situation with outsiders, especially the news media. The purpose of this provision is to furnish the news media with accurate information and to see that additional bomb threat calls are not precipitated by irresponsible statements from uninformed sources.

DISCUSSION QUESTIONS

1. Discuss the reasons why arson is considered a low-priority crime.

2. Discuss and compare the relationship between fire and police departments and the insurance companies that represent victims of arson.

3. Discuss the main things to remember in the preliminary investigation of the suspected arson.

4. What significance does a fire's point of origin have regarding the investigation of a suspected arson fire?

5. Explain the three sides of the fire triangle.

6. List and discuss the various clues that flames and smoke can offer the investigator in the arson investigation.

7. What types of evidence are necessary in the successful prosecution of an arson case?

8. Discuss the searching sweep methods that should be employed when attempting to locate a bomb or booby trap.

9. Explain the safety precautions that should be observed in searching for a booby trap.

10. Explain procedures to follow in the event that an explosive device is discovered.

NOTES

1. NATIONAL FIRE PROTECTION ASSOCIATION (1998). *Fire loss in the United States, 1987–1996*, 11th ed. Boston: NFPA.
2. Ibid.
3. WOODFORK, W. G. (1990, Dec.). Not just a fire department problem. *Police Chief*, p. 28.
4. O'CONNER, J. J. (1987). *Practical fire and arson investigation*. New York: Elsevier.
5. GOODNIGHT, K. M. (1990, Dec.). Arson for profit: The insurance investigation. *Police Chief*, p. 53.
6. HART, F. (1990, Dec.). The arson equation: Arson + circumstantial evidence = conviction. *Police Chief*, p. 34.
7. O'CONNER (1987). *Practical fire and arson investigation*.
8. Ibid.
9. ICOVE, D. J. (1990, Dec.). Serial arsonists: An introduction. *Police Chief*, p. 46.
10. RIDER, A. O. (1980, June–Aug.). The firesetter: A psychological profile. *FBI Law Enforcement Bulletin*, p. 9.
11. JAMES, J. (1965, Mar.). Psychological motives for arson. *Popular Government*, p. 24.
12. RIDER (1980). The firesetter.
13. HART (1990). The arson equation.
14. HARNETT, D. M. (1990, Apr.). Bombing and arson investigations enhanced by advances in ATF labs. *Police Chief*, pp. 20, 24, 26, 28.
15. FRANKEL and FIELDS (1996). New teen fad.

Vice Crimes and Related Offenses

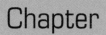

 **Drug Offenses**

Key Terms

▶ crack
▶ crystal meth
▶ date rape drug
▶ dependence
▶ designer drug
▶ drug courier profile
▶ flashback
▶ freebase
▶ pharmaceutical diversion
▶ scammer
▶ tolerance
▶ undercover

This chapter will enable you to:

• Understand the hazards of drug abuse.

• Learn the various characteristics of drug abuse.

• List the categories of drug dependence.

• Describe the most common drugs of abuse.

• Learn the provisions of the federal Controlled Substances Act.

• Initiate drug investigations.

• Understand the trends in drug abuse prevention.

INTRODUCTION

Over the years, the scope of the drug problem has expanded to the point where an estimated two out of every three crimes committed are a result of some type of substance abuse (Figures 21.1 and 21.2). Drugs such as marijuana, cocaine, heroin, PCP (phencyclidine), LSD (lysergic acid diethylamide), methamphetamine, and designer drugs are representative of the most popular substances of abuse in the United States and, consequently, account for much of the nation's crime.

Because of the widespread nature of the problem in both the political and social arenas, policy makers are at a crossroads as to what to do about it. Drug crimes, for example, are generated from two general areas: drug users (both addicts and recreational users) and drug sellers (independent and organized factions). Therefore, the supply-and-demand argument is debated as police continue to concentrate on the arrest of dealers or users. In either case, police authorities are duty bound to enforce existing drug control laws vigorously on both local and national levels. Although much media attention has been given to drug control in recent years, law enforcement's drug control mission has been well under way since early in the twentieth century. It was during that period that one of the first major drug laws was passed by Congress: the 1914 Harrison Narcotic Act.[1]

Enforcement of this act required federal agents to arrest and interrogate suspects, search and seize contraband, and infiltrate criminal organizations through undercover techniques. Such duties represent only a few investigative responsibilities in this complex area. Many techniques have evolved since then: some more traditional, some controversial. In this chapter, we examine the many areas of concern for the criminal investigator in investigating drug offenses.

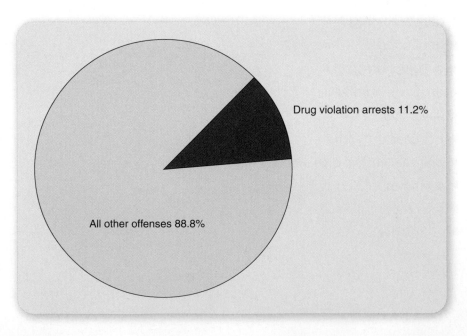

Figure 21.1 Drug violation arrests accounted for 11 percent of all arrests in 2002. National Drug Control Strategy (2004). The White House Office of National Drug Control Policy, Washington, D.C., March

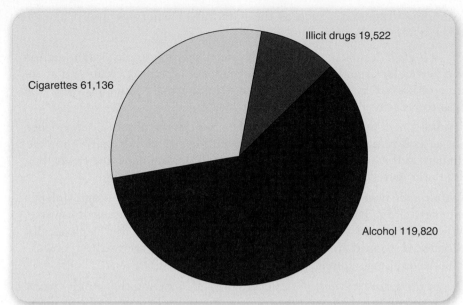

Illicit drugs 19,522

Cigarettes 61,136

Alcohol 119,820

Figure 21.2 Treatment of illicit drugs, alcohol, and cigarettes. Current users by substance (in thousands). *National Drug Council Strategy (2004). The White House Office of National Drug Control Policy, Washington, D.C., March.*

PRINCIPAL DRUGS OF ABUSE

For the criminal investigator to be prepared best for his or her duties in drug enforcement, a certain understanding of the specific drugs of abuse is necessary. Because of the growing problem of drug abuse in the United States, much information about drug effects has surfaced in recent years. Accordingly, dealing with drug abuse requires a broad understanding of the most common drugs of abuse and how they affect public health and safety.

Characteristics of Drugs

To begin our understanding of drugs, we should consider that all drugs, whether legal or not, fall into one of five categories:

1. Cannabis
2. Narcotics
3. Stimulants
4. Hallucinogens
5. Depressants

Each of these categories, discussed in upcoming sections, represents the overall effects common with drugs associated within it.

Another element that makes a drug particularly menacing to society and that is considered in determining the degree of its legal use is its **dependence** factor. The drug's level of dependence will fuel a user's desire to consume more of it. Once the use-to-abuse cycle is under way, drug habits may cost the user as much as $400 per day.

Dependence manifests itself in two distinct ways: physical and psychological. Drug users may experience only psychological dependence on drugs, but some drugs produce both physical and psychological dependence, making them more dangerous. There are other danger factors that one should consider when understanding drug abuse, such as the withdrawal syndrome and drug synergism. These four terms are discussed next.

- *Physiological dependence.* This term refers basically to physical addiction to a particular drug. Physiological dependence on a drug creates an alteration of normal body functions which necessitate continued presence of a drug to prevent the withdrawal syndrome.

- *Psychological dependence.* This usually precedes the physical dependence phase, as it refers to one's "desire" to continue use of a drug. Physiological changes in the body do not occur with psychological dependence, as the drug user merely "thinks" that he or she needs the drug.

- *Withdrawal syndrome.* This term is closely related to physiological dependence on a drug. The withdrawal syndrome is basically a series of adverse physical symptoms that appear when a drug to which a user is physically addicted is stopped abruptly or severely reduced. Withdrawal symptoms include vomiting, nausea, sweating, convulsions, and fever.

- *Drug synergism.* A synergy is a severe physical reaction that results when a user ingests more than one type of drug at a time. This typically occurs in a "party" situation when users experiment with more than one type of drug. This is a common cause of overdose that could result in coma, cardiac arrest, or even death.[2]

Cannabis

Although considered a mild hallucinogen, marijuana falls into its own category: cannabis (*Cannabis sativa*). It is the most commonly abused cannabis product and grows in almost all parts of the world. History has shown that this plant has been cultivated throughout time to make rope from its tough fiber. Cannabis products include:

- Marijuana   • Hashish   • Hashish oil

Each produces basically the same intoxicating effect, but hashish and hashish oil are more concentrated. Marijuana products are usually smoked in the form of loosely rolled cigarettes or "joints" and are used in conjunction with other types of drugs. When smoked, the THC (tetrahydrocannabinol) is absorbed into the lining of the lungs and is passed into the bloodstream. Its effects are felt almost instantly and will reach their peak in 10 to 30 minutes. Marijuana users remain under the influence of the drug for up to four hours.

Marijuana.   Growers of marijuana cultivate the plant for the flowering tops, which produce high concentrations of the mind-altering substance THC. Accordingly, it is the high THC concentration in the plant that is sought by marijuana consumers. Marijuana was first regulated in 1937 with the passage of the Marijuana Tax Act. Today, although some states have chosen to decriminalize the drug, it is still basically illegal to one extent or another. The effects of marijuana are somewhat difficult to articulate, as different users are affected in different ways. Frequently, the effects of marijuana depend on the user's experience and expectations as well as on the activity of the drug itself. In low doses, restlessness and a sense of well-being are experienced. This is followed by a feeling of relaxation and sometimes hunger pangs, especially for sweets. High doses may result in image distortion, a loss of personal identity, and possible hallucinations.

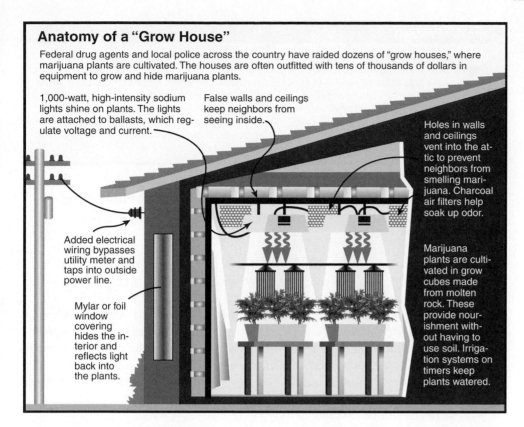

Anatomy of a "Grow House"

Federal drug agents and local police across the country have raided dozens of "grow houses," where marijuana plants are cultivated. The houses are often outfitted with tens of thousands of dollars in equipment to grow and hide marijuana plants.

1,000-watt, high-intensity sodium lights shine on plants. The lights are attached to ballasts, which regulate voltage and current.

False walls and ceilings keep neighbors from seeing inside.

Holes in walls and ceilings vent into the attic to prevent neighbors from smelling marijuana. Charcoal air filters help soak up odor.

Added electrical wiring bypasses utility meter and taps into outside power line.

Mylar or foil window covering hides the interior and reflects light back into the plants.

Marijuana plants are cultivated in grow cubes made from molten rock. These provide nourishment without having to use soil. Irrigation systems on timers keep plants watered.

Figure 21.3 Home grown marijuana can be a simple or complicated process. This figure depicts the complexities of a high-tech "grow house." *USA Today. February 7, 2007. Reprinted with permission.*

Marijuana "Grow Houses."   As of 2006, marijuana cultivators have increasingly begun to conceal their growing operation by making use of "grow houses." The grow house has proven to be a predominantly suburban phenomenon. For example, in December 2006, the Drug Enforcement Administration reported that over 10,000 plants were seized in a four-bedroom house in Derry, New Hampshire. In California, such operations have grown considerably.

Growers have been known to pay as much as $750,000 in new subdivisions and typically obtain 100% financing and putting no money down. Interiors are then gutted to make use of every available square foot for growing apparatuses, and the plants themselves. Irrigation systems with timing devices are also commonly installed and operated using water tanks, pumps, generators, and power packs. To avoid suspicion resulting from large power usage, growers have been known to by-pass an electric company's utility meter and create their own circuit boxes. Grow houses are typically unoccupied.

As a rule, criminal investigators will need a search warrant for entry into a grow house. Seizure of equipment, plants, and establishment of residency however, can provide the basis for an arrest and prosecution under applicable state or federal law.

Narcotics

In medical parlance, narcotics are opium and opium derivatives or their synthetic substitutes. Narcotic drugs are essential in the practice of medicine, as they are the most effective drugs for the relief of pain. For the most part, legally manufactured narcotics are administered orally or injected. Their illicit counterparts (e.g., heroin) may also be sniffed or smoked. Drugs in the narcotic category include:

Cannabis Products

- *Marijuana.* This is the most widely used of the cannabis family. It is a tobaccolike substance produced by the drying of leaves and the flowering tops of the plant.
- *Hashish.* Hashish, or "hash," consists of the drug-rich resinous secretions of the cannabis plant, which are collected, dried, and then compressed into cakes or cookielike sheets that are usually smoked in pipes. The average THC content is 6 percent.
- *Hashish oil.* Hash oil is produced by a process of repeated extraction of cannabis plant material that yields a dark syruplike liquid. The liquid is then placed in or on conventional cigarettes and smoked. The average THC content is 20 percent.

- Opium
- Diacetylmorphine (heroin)
- Codeine
- Meperidine (Demerol)
- Hydromorphone (Dilaudid)

Those who use narcotics initially desire the euphoric dreamlike effects of the drug. Drugs falling into this category, however, are extremely physically addicting, and users may find dependency difficult to cure.

The withdrawal syndrome is also commonly associated with this class of drugs. In addition, continued use of narcotics produces tolerance. As **tolerance** develops, users find that they require greater and greater doses of the drug to feel its effects. This, of course, increases the user's propensity for overdose. Narcotic drugs produce pinpoint pupils, reduced vision, drowsiness, and decreased physical activity.

These drugs can be divided into two categories:

1. *Natural origin narcotics.* Organic narcotics are derived from the opium poppy (*Papaver somniferum*), which is cultivated in such countries as Hungary, Turkey, India, Burma, China, Lebanon, Pakistan, Afghanistan, Laos, and Mexico. The milky fluid that is extracted from the poppy plant is raw opium gum base and is very addictive. It is this raw base that is further refined to produce such drugs as opium, heroin, morphine, and codeine. Of these, heroin is the most widely abused narcotic of natural origin in the United States.[3]

2. *Synthetic narcotics.* In contrast to narcotics of natural origin, synthetic narcotics are produced entirely in the laboratory. Researchers have attempted to develop a narcotic drug that offers the analgesic properties of morphine without the dangerous side effects of tolerance and physical dependence. The most common types of synthetic narcotics include meperidine (Demerol), methadone, and hydromorphone (Dilaudid). Because these (and others) are produced by legitimate pharmaceutical manufacturers, diversion of them onto the street is a growing problem. This results from pharmacy robberies and burglaries as well as unscrupulous physicians, nurses, and other medical practitioners who either desire profit or have personal drug problems.

Heroin.   The abuse of heroin (diacetylmorphine) occurs in virtually all parts of the world. It appears on American streets in both white and brown powder form and is most widely abused in the inner cities. First-time users of heroin are lured to the drug for its euphoric effects, but because of its addictive qualities, physical addiction develops rapidly after regular use.

Heroin is diluted by the addition of milk sugar or baking soda. Accordingly, pure heroin is rarely sold on the street. In some cases, the user sniffs heroin, but

Figure 21.4 Self-administering illicit drugs through injection is fraught with danger of infection or overdose. *Getty Images, Inc.*

generally it is injected. Injection methods include skin popping (under the skin) and mainlining (intravenous). Because needles and syringes are commonly shared between intravenous drug users, the instance of infection with the AIDS virus is high among heroin addicts. Another form of heroin is called black tar heroin. Surfacing in the western states in the mid-1980s, it is produced crudely in Mexico and resembles roofing tar or coal.

There are an estimated 500,000 addicts in the United States. Organized crime syndicates from the United States, Latin America, and southeastern and southwestern Asia strive for control of this lucrative illicit market.

Stimulants

Drugs falling in the stimulant category do so because they literally stimulate the central nervous system and give the user a feeling of alertness. With this category of drugs, the use-to-abuse cycle often begins with users who work more than one job or need to stay alert for long periods. Such abusers may take "uppers" in the morning to get going and then take "downers" at night to sleep. Included in this category of abusers are over-the-road truck drivers, college students, entertainers, and so on. Stimulant drugs include nicotine, caffeine, amphetamine, methamphetamine, and cocaine.

Nicotine, found most commonly in tobacco, is the most prevalent stimulant, followed closely by caffeine, an active ingredient in coffee, tea, and many soft drinks. When used in moderation, these drugs relieve feelings of exhaustion and fatigue and have become an accepted part of our culture. The most dangerous stimulants, however, also possess a dependence-forming quality and are available only by prescription. These include cocaine, amphetamine, methamphetamine, methylphenidate (Ritalin), and phenmetrazine (Preludin).

Tolerance to stimulants develops rapidly, and users may ingest increasingly larger doses of the drug. Once the abuse cycle becomes chronic, users may become affected by the following displays of behavior: teeth grinding, touching

---

Commonly Abused Narcotics

- *Opium:* the raw milky liquid extract from the opium poppy plant. Raw opium is commonly abused in the areas of southeastern and southwestern Asia and is most commonly smoked in "gum" form.
- *Morphine:* the principal constituent of opium, considered one of the most effective drugs for the relief of pain. It is marketed in the form of white crystals, hypodermic tablets, and injectable preparations.
- *Heroin:* available in brown or white powder and most commonly injected. Heroin is highly addictive and usually sold with a street purity of 5 percent.
- *Codeine:* an alkaloid found in raw opium but most commonly produced from morphine. Compared with morphine, codeine produces less analgesia, sedation, and respiratory depression. It is most typically found in prescription cough medicines.
- *Hydromorphone (Dilaudid):* a synthetic narcotic analgesic marketed in both tablet and injectable form. This drug is more sedating than morphine and is considered to be up to eight times as potent. It is most commonly obtained by addicts through fraudulent prescriptions.

---

and picking of the face, performing the same task over and over, suspiciousness, and even paranoia.

Cocaine.   Cocaine (*Erthroxylon coca*) is a stimulant that has achieved the highest degree of notoriety. Cocaine is the most potent stimulant of natural origin and is made from extracting coca base from coca leaves, which grow almost exclusively in South America. Cocaine, first isolated in 1844, was most commonly used as an anesthetic in eye surgery. Later, it became useful as an anesthetic in nose and throat surgery because of its ability to anesthetize tissue while restricting bleeding. Today, because of the dangers associated with cocaine, many other safer drugs are used for these purposes. Cocaine is distributed in both a white powder or a solid form called **crack.** Accordingly, the drug is administered by snorting, injection, or smoking in **freebase** form. It is commonly adulterated by adding lactose, baking soda, mannitol, or other anesthetics, such as lidocaine. In its freebase form, crack is converted to the form of small chips, resembling soap or paint chips, sometimes called rocks. After heating the drug in a pipe, the vapors are then inhaled. Effects last only eight to 10 minutes and are usually followed by a sudden "crash," which leads to additional doses.

The process for conversion from powdered cocaine to crack is relatively simple. Cocaine hydrochloric acid (powder) is mixed with baking soda and water and is then heated. This produces a product that is "cracked" into small pieces that are ready to be sold. Other cocaine sensations include euphoria, increased alertness, and shortness of breath. Because of the intensity of its pleasurable effects, it has the potential for extraordinary psychic dependency. Those under the influence show signs of congestion, similar to those of the common cold.

Once dependency develops, users may experience anxiety, paranoia, restlessness, extreme irritability, and even tactile hallucinations. Extreme use of cocaine can result in seizures and death from respiratory failure, stroke, cardiac arrest, or cerebral hemorrhage. Complicating matters further, there is yet no treatment for cocaine overdose. Nor does tolerance develop to the toxic effects of cocaine. Indeed, studies in the late 1980s revealed that repeated use of cocaine actually lowers the dose at which toxicity occurs.

Methamphetamine.   Methamphetamine, or "meth," is a dangerous, sometimes lethal and unpredictable drug. Meth is also known as speed, ice, and crystal. Like cocaine, meth is a potent central nervous system stimulant. Meth represents the fastest-growing drug threat in the United States today. Meth can be smoked, snorted, injected, or taken orally, and its appearance varies depending on how it is used. Typically, it is a white, odorless, bitter-tasting powder that easily dissolves in water. Another common form of the drug is crystal meth, or ice, named for its appearance (that of clear, large chunky crystals resembling rock candy). **Crystal meth** is smoked in a manner similar to crack cocaine, and about 10 to 15 "hits" can be obtained from a single gram of the substance. Users have referred to smoking ice as a "cool" smoke, while the smoking of crack is a "hot" smoke. The euphoric effect of smoking ice lasts longer than that of smoking crack.[4]

Methamphetamine use increases heart rate, blood pressure, body temperature, and rate of breathing, and it frequently results in violent behavior in users. Meth also dilates the pupils and produces temporary hyperactivity, euphoria, a sense of increased energy, and tremors. High doses or chronic use have been associated with increased nervousness, irritability, and paranoia. Withdrawal from high doses produces severe depression.

Chronic abuse produces a psychosis similar to schizophrenia and is characterized by paranoia, picking at the skin, self-absorption, and auditory and visual hallucinations. Violent and erratic behavior is frequently seen among chronic, high-dose methamphetamine abusers. The most dangerous stage of the binge cycle is known as tweaking. Typically, during this stage, the abuser has not slept

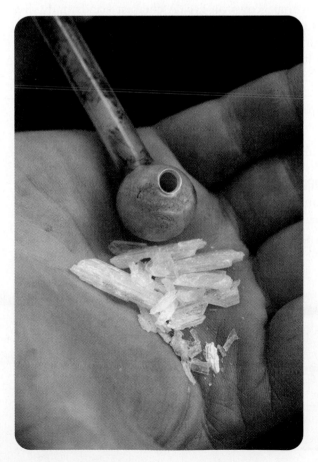

Figure 21.5 Close-up of methamphetamine crystals and crack pipe held in the palm of a drug user's soiled hand. *Robin Nelson, PhotoEdit Inc.*

in three to 15 days and is irritable and paranoid. The tweaker has an intense craving for more meth; however, no dosage will help re-create the euphoric high. This causes frustration and leads to unpredictability and a potential for violence.

Hallucinogens

Hallucinogenic drugs, produced both organically and synthetically, create a sense of distorted perceptions in the user. Generally, they act on the central nervous system by creating sensations such as excitation, euphoric mood changes, and sometimes extreme depression. Of particular mention, those under the influence of hallucinogens experience an altered sense of direction, space, and time. Users sometimes claim to be able to "see" sounds and "hear" colors. Hallucinogens include LSD, Ecstasy (MDMA), peyote, and psilocybin mushrooms.

Hallucinogens are distinct from the other categories of drugs in that long after they are expelled from the body, the user may still experience flashbacks. A **flashback** is a temporary reoccurrence of a psychedelic experience. This could be described as the overintensification of a particular color, the perceived movement of a stationary object, or the mistaking of one object for another.

The abuse of hallucinogens has seen varied levels of popularity over the years. They reached their peak in the late 1960s and early 1970s, but have become popular numerous times since then. The most popular forms of hallucinogens are LSD, PCP, psilocybin, and peyote.

LSD. LSD (lysergic acid diethylamide) was developed in Germany in 1938 from the ergot fungus, a fungus that grows on rye. A chemist accidentally discovered its effects in 1943 and reported that he saw a stream of fantastic colors and extraordinary vividness. Since then it has been used to study causes of mental illness because of its similarity to certain chemicals found in the brain. Today, LSD, or acid, is found in several street forms: tablets, thin squares of gelatin (also called windowpanes), or impregnated paper (also called blotter). Blotter acid is distinguishable by unique artwork, frequently depicting cartoon characters, printed on the paper.

PCP. Phencyclidine was developed in 1959 as a general anesthetic, but because of its adverse effects, its use on humans was discontinued. It later became commercially available for use as a veterinary medicine. In 1978, phencyclidine was rescheduled from Schedule III to Schedule II because of public protests about its dangers. (See section "The 1970 Controlled Substances Act" for more on classification of drugs.) PCP is also sold on the street by other names, such as angel dust, wack, water, juice, and rocket fuel. It is manufactured

Commonly Abused Stimulants

- *Cocaine:* the most potent stimulant known. Primarily an illicit product coming from South America available on U.S. streets in both powder and freebase (crack) form. Cocaine is highly addictive and is ingested by smoking (freebasing), injection, or snorting.
- *Amphetamine:* developed at the turn of the century; used legally to treat narcolepsy and obesity. Amphetamines are produced both legitimately and clandestinely and may be found on the street in tablet, injectable, or powdered form.
- *Phenmetrazine (Preludin):* synthetic stimulant similar to amphetamine that is commonly diverted from legal channels onto the street. Abuse generally involves the dissolving of tablets into a liquid solution and injecting with syringes.

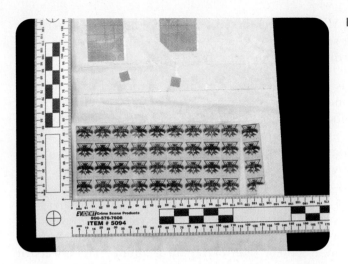

Figure 21.6 LSD "blotter acid."

in illicit laboratories in both powder and liquid form and is usually ingested by smoking or inhalation. PCP produces varying effects on different users. For example, a moderate amount produces a sense of detachment, distance, and estrangement from surroundings. Heavier doses are associated with severer reactions. Specifically, users experience a blank stare, rapid eye movements, acute anxiety, and extreme paranoia. Perhaps the most devastating effect is the user's sense of strength and invulnerability. Recent research has shown that such reactions may develop after only one dose of the drug, making PCP one of the most dangerous of illicit substances.

Depressants

Drugs falling within the depressant category are potentially addictive in both the psychological and physical sense. Depressants act on the central nervous system, but when taken as prescribed may help to relieve anxiety, irritability, and tension and to induce sleep. When taken in excess, however, depressants affect the user much like alcohol. Specifically, when taken in smaller doses, they produce feelings of intoxication and euphoria. Depressant drugs include barbiturates and benzodiazepines (tranquilizers).

Tolerance with depressant drugs develops rapidly, thus closing the gap between an intoxicating and lethal dose. Some depressant abusers have exceeded their prescribed doses up to 20 times, resulting in an increase in their dependence on the drug. In the drug abuse world, depressant abuse sometimes occurs because users are trying to counter or "come down" from the effects of stimulants. In addition, many overdoses are attributed to the deadly mixing of alcohol and depressants, or synergism.

Barbiturates.   Barbiturates are the depressants most frequently prescribed and are used primarily as sedatives for their calming effects or to induce sleep. Of the hundreds of barbituric acid derivatives that have synthesized over the years, only about 15 are currently in use.

Barbiturates are classified as ultrashort, short, intermediate, and long-lasting. Of these, the most commonly abused are the short acting and intermediate acting, which include such drugs as phenobarbital (Nembutal), secobarbital (Seconal), and amobarbital (Amytal). Small doses of barbiturates tend to calm the nerves and even cause sleep. Commonly, a feeling of excitement will preempt these more relaxed feelings. When doses increase, however, users risk more serious consequences, such as coma and death from respiratory arrest and cardiovascular complications.

Rohypnol.   Rohypnol is a brand name for flunitrazepam and is commonly known as ruffies. Rohypnol has never been approved for medical use in the United States; therefore, doctors cannot prescribe it and pharmacists cannot sell it. However, it is legally prescribed in over 50 other countries and is widely available in Mexico, Colombia, and Europe, where it is used for the treatment of insomnia and as a preanesthetic. Therefore, it was placed into Schedule IV of the Controlled Substances Act in 1984 due to international treaty obligations. Like similar drugs (such as Valium, Librium, Xanax, and Halcion), Rohypnol's pharmacological effects include sedation, muscle relaxation, reduction in anxiety, and prevention of convulsions. However, its sedative effects are approximately seven to 10 times more potent than diazepam (Valium). The effects of Rohypnol appear approximately 15 to 20 minutes after administration and last approximately four to six hours. Some residual effects can be found 12 hours or more after administration.

Rohypnol causes partial amnesia; users are unable to remember certain events that they experienced while under the influence of the drug. This effect is particularly dangerous when flunitrazepam is used to aid in the commission of sexual assault; victims may not be able to clearly recall the assault, the assailant, or the events surrounding the assault.

It is difficult to estimate just how many Rohypnol-facilitated rapes have occurred in the United States. Very often, biological samples are taken from the victim at a time when the effects of the drug have already passed and only residual amounts remain in the bodily fluids. These residual amounts are difficult, if not impossible, to detect using standard screening assays available in the United States. If exposure to Rohypnol is to be detected at all, urine samples need to be collected within 72 hours and subjected to sensitive analytical tests. The problem is compounded by the onset of amnesia after ingestion of the drug, which causes the victim to be uncertain about the facts surrounding the rape. This uncertainty may lead to critical delays or even reluctance to report a rape and to provide appropriate biological samples for toxicology testing.

While Rohypnol has become widely known for its use as a **date rape drug,** it is abused more frequently for other reasons. It is abused by high school students,

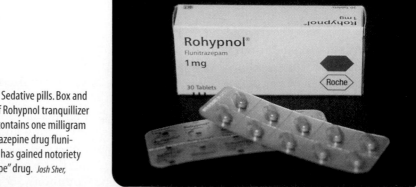

Figure 21.7 Sedative pills. Box and blister packs of Rohypnol tranquillizer pills. Each pill contains one milligram of the benzodiazepine drug flunitrazepam. This has gained notoriety as the "date rape" drug. *Josh Sher, PhotoEdit Inc.*

college students, street gang members, rave party attendees, and heroin and cocaine abusers to produce profound intoxication, boost the high of heroin, and modulate the effects of cocaine. The drug is usually consumed orally, is often combined with alcohol, and is abused by crushing tablets and snorting the powder.

Gamma Hydroxybutyrate (GHB).   γ-Hydroxybutyrate (GHB), known as liquid X, Georgia home boy, goop, gamma-oh, and grievous bodily harm, is a central nervous system depressant abused for its ability to produce euphoric and hallucinatory states and its alleged ability to release a growth hormone and stimulate muscle growth.

Although GHB was originally considered a safe and "natural" food supplement and was sold in health food stores, the medical community soon became aware that it caused overdoses and other health problems. GHB can produce drowsiness, dizziness, nausea, unconsciousness, seizures, severe respiratory depression, and coma. GHB can be found in liquid form or as a white powder material. It is taken orally and is frequently combined with alcohol. Abusers include high school and college students and rave party attendees who use GHB for its intoxicating effects. Some bodybuilders also abuse GHB for its alleged anabolic effects.

Like Rohypnol, several cases have documented the use of GHB to incapacitate women for the commission of sexual assault. In 1990, the Food and Drug Administration (FDA) issued an advisory declaring GHB unsafe and illicit except under FDA-approved, physician-supervised protocols. In March 2000, GHB was placed in Schedule I of the Controlled Substances Act.

Designer Drugs

The term **designer drug** has been coined to refer to a class of drugs that are specifically designed to emulate controlled substances. Illegal chemists intent on circumventing drug regulations have become adept in creating such substances. Designer drugs include:

- Ecstasy (MDMA)
- China white (fentanyl)

One of the more infamous designer drugs is Ecstasy (also called Adam and Eve or XTC), a combination of synthetic mescaline and amphetamine that possesses a hallucinogenic effect. It is also called MDMA (for 3,4-methylene dioxymethamphetamine). Although controlled by the Drug Enforcement Administration (DEA) in 1985, this drug still remains fairly popular on the illicit drug scene. Another successful designer drug is china white heroin. This drug, which is not actually heroin at all, may be thousands of times more powerful than heroin. But from a user's viewpoint, fentanyl and heroin are functionally interchangeable. Fentanyl can be packed like heroin and "cut" with the same diluents. Side effects, however, seem to be much more severe than with heroin. Indeed, Parkinson's disease is a common result of its use.

THE GENERAL STRUCTURE OF DRUG LAWS

As with all criminal violations, drug investigators must familiarize themselves with the law in order to make prosecutable cases. Laws governing illicit drugs appear in virtually all levels of government. Accordingly, drug penalties under different levels of government will also vary from one jurisdiction to the next. Generally, criminal law considers several categories of illegal behavior regarding drug abuse:

- *Possession.* Possession usually manifests itself in one of two ways: (1) actual physical custody of the drugs, or (2) constructive possession. The latter requires the subject to have knowledge of the presence of the substance and the power and intent to control use of the drug.
- *Distribution.* The charge of drug distribution is of a more serious nature than possession and is most commonly imposed for any exchange of illegal drugs between two or more persons. Exchanges also include drug sales, passing drugs to another, or delivering an illicit drug whether or not for sale or profit.
- *Manufacturing.* Criminal charges can also be assessed for producing illicit drugs. Drugs such as LSD, methamphetamine, fentanyl, and PCP are more typically products of illicit drug labs. Most criminal laws also include as manufacturing the growing of cannabis (marijuana) or conversion of one drug to another, such as cocaine to crack. As drug distribution networks become larger and more sophisticated, more powerful laws may be needed for successful prosecution. Laws such as RICO, CCE, and conspiracy statutes better enable prosecutors to attack the management figures of drug-dealing organizations.

THE 1970 CONTROLLED SUBSTANCES ACT

The Controlled Substances Act (CSA) has been the legal foundation of the federal government's battle against illicit drug abuse since its implementation in 1970. This comprehensive law includes numerous laws dealing with manufacturing, distribution, and possession of dangerous drugs. The CSA basically took all drugs considered dangerous under existing federal law and placed them into one of five schedules. The placement of a drug under any particular category was based on its medical use, potential for abuse, and safety or propensity for dependence. Under this act, drugs can be added, removed, or rescheduled at the initiation of the Department of Health and Human Services, by the DEA, or by the petition of any interested person (i.e., a drug manufacturer, medical association, pharmacy association, public interest group, state or local agency, or individual citizen).

The point of concern in changing a drug's status is whether it has a potential for abuse. If a drug does not have a potential for abuse, it cannot be controlled. Unfortunately, the term *potential for abuse* is not clearly defined under the CSA and therefore has many different interpretations. Generally, however, the following items have determined whether or not a drug has a potential for abuse:

- There is evidence that people are taking the drug(s) containing such a substance in amounts sufficient to create a hazard to their health or to the safety of other people or the community.
- There is sufficient diversion of the drug(s) from legitimate drug channels.
- People are taking the drug(s) containing such a substance on their own initiative rather than on the basis of medical advice from a practitioner licensed by law to administer such drugs in the course of his or her professional practice.

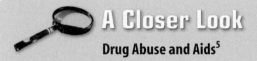

A Closer Look

Drug Abuse and Aids[5]

Needle Sharing

Among intravenous (IV) drug users, transmission of the AIDS virus most often occurs by sharing needles, syringes, or other "works." Small amounts of contaminated blood left in the equipment can carry the virus from user to user. IV drug users who frequent "shooting galleries"—where paraphernalia is passed among several people—are at especially high risk for AIDS. But needle sharing of any sort (at parties, for example) can transmit the virus, and National Institute of Drug Abuse (NIDA) experts note that almost all IV drug users share needles at one time or another. Because not every IV drug user will enter treatment and because some must wait to be treated, IV users in many cities are being taught to flush their "works" with bleach before they inject. Used correctly, bleach can destroy virus left in the equipment.

Sexual Transmission

IV drug users also get AIDS through unprotected sex with someone who is infected. In addition, the AIDS virus can be sexually transmitted from infected IV drug users to persons who do not use drugs. Data from the Centers for Disease Control (CDC) show that IV drug use is associated with the increased spread of AIDS in the heterosexual population. For example, of all women reported to have AIDS, 49 percent were IV drug users, while another 30 percent, non-IV drug users themselves, were sexual partners of IV drug users. Infected women who become pregnant can pass the AIDS virus to their babies. About 70 percent of all children born with AIDS have a mother or father who "shot" drugs.

Non-IV Drug Use and AIDS

Sexual activity has also been reported as a means of AIDS transmission among those who use non-IV drugs such as crack or marijuana. Many people, especially women, addicted to crack (or other substances) go broke supporting their habit and turn to trading sex for drugs. Another link between substance abuse and AIDS is when people using alcohol and drugs relax their restraints and caution regarding sexual behavior. People who normally practice safe sex may neglect to do so while "under the influence."

- The drug(s) containing such a substance are new drugs so related in their action to the drug(s) already listed as having potential for abuse.

INITIATING DRUG CASES

Because of ongoing public concern about drug abuse and violent crime, drug investigations have become a mainstay in many law enforcement agencies. Goals of drug investigation are to:

- Identify and locate known or suspected drug sellers.
- Understand the different types of drugs available on the street, their prices, and packaging methods.
- Identify locations of frequent drug abuse activity.
- Collect evidence on those involved in drug trafficking.

- Reduce the availability of drugs through the aggressive apprehension of drug users and sellers.

The planning and initiation phase of a drug case involves several steps which usually begin with the receipt and verification of information. It is in this early phase when investigators learn of suspected criminal activity through various sources of information. Great discretion is required here because not every source of information is reliable. Information sources include:

- Other law enforcement agencies (e.g., police departments, sheriff's departments, federal agencies).
- Other units within the police department (e.g., prostitution and vice divisions, the patrol division).
- "Unofficial" information from other officers within the department.
- Other criminal justice agencies (e.g., probation and parole, the courts).
- Information provided by good citizens.

CONFIDENTIAL INFORMANTS

Planning drug investigations through the use of informant information is one of the most common avenues in which drug cases are initiated. Ironically, such information may prove to be extremely valuable or extremely worthless, and investigators must determine its reliability early in the investigation so that costly time is not wasted. Once information is received, the investigator must make an effort, independent of the initial source, to verify it. This is generally accomplished by one of three basic methods: surveillance, the development of an informant, and use of specific sources outside the investigator's agency.

CASE PLANNING

Drug cases will frequently net suspects from all walks of society: from the old to the young, the very rich to the very poor, the meek to the violent. Over the years, thousands of drug cases have endured the scrutiny of many a prosecutor, defense attorney, and court of law. Therefore, investigative methods have been somewhat refined over the years, thus dictating that drug enforcement is not an area for trial-and-error tactics. Drug arrests and raids also typically draw media attention, and investigative methods and techniques might fall under close scrutiny. The drug case might also ultimately employ the use of sophisticated federal laws such as conspiracy, the Racketeer Influenced and Corrupt Organizations (RICO) Act, and the Continuing Criminal Enterprise (CCE) Act. Implementation of these laws may not be apparent early in the investigation, as drug investigations will typically gain momentum over time. Accordingly, investigators should plan their cases carefully and thoroughly in anticipation of their use.

The target of the investigation will usually determine the level of involvement of the law enforcement agency. One important planning element is the extent of violations being committed by the target individual. The investigator should establish:

Drug Schedules Under the Controlled Substance Act (CSA)

Schedule I

The drug or other substance has a high potential for abuse. The drug or other substance has no currently accepted medical use in treatment in the United States. There is a lack of accepted safety for use of the drug under medical supervision.

Examples: heroin, LSD, marijuana, peyote, methaqualone

Schedule II

The drug or other substance has a high potential for abuse. The drug or other substance has a currently accepted medical use in treatment in the United States or a currently accepted medical use with severe restrictions. Abuse of the drug or other substance may lead to severe psychological or physical dependence.

Examples: amphetamines, some morphine derivatives, cocaine, phencyclidine (PCP)

Schedule III

The drug or other substance has a potential for abuse less than the drugs or other substances in Schedules I and II. The drug or other substance has a currently accepted medical use in treatment in the United States. Abuse of the drug or other substance may lead to moderate or low physical dependence or high psychological dependence.

Examples: some barbiturates, some opium derivatives, glutethimide

Schedule IV

The drug or other substance has a low potential for abuse relative to the drugs or other substances in Schedule III. The drug or other substance has a currently accepted medical use in treatment in the United States. Abuse of the drug or other substance may lead to limited physical dependence or psychological dependence relative to the drugs or other substances in Schedule III.

Examples: chloral hydrate, tranquilizers, some stimulants and depressants

Schedule V

The drug or other substance has a low potential for abuse relative to the drugs or other substances in Schedule IV. The drug or other substance has a currently accepted medical use in treatment in the United States. Abuse of the drug or other substance may lead to limited physical dependence or psychological dependence relative to the drugs or other substances in Schedule IV.

Examples: some extracts of opium, some extracts of morphine, some derivatives of codeine. Since passing of the CSA, most states have adopted state versions of the law, which typically include a localized model of the five federal schedules. This allows prosecutors to file charges under either federal or state criminal justice systems, depending on the type of crime committed and the desired result of the criminal prosecution.

- Whether the person is a drug user or drug dealer.
- If he or she is a dealer, whether the level is wholesale or retail.
- Any other crimes that the target person is responsible for or involved in (e.g., assault, robbery, murder).
- Whether the target can be used to reach others in the drug organization.

Other considerations are also determined by the level of involvement of the target individual. One of the most critical is the arrest strategy to be used. This consideration examines the use of a particular type of drug buy (buy-bust or buy-walk). This determination rests on whether or not the suspect is being considered for later use as an informant. Departmental factors also play a significant role in drug case planning. Obviously, some law enforcement agencies have more resources than others, but certain critical factors should be considered. Investigative resources to consider are:

- *Personnel.* Drug investigations require a sizable commitment of human resources, in particular, sworn personnel. Multiple officers are required during **undercover** operations, raids, and surveillance operations.
- *Money.* As with many police operations, money is always an issue. Drug investigations, however, require large amounts of cash for drug transactions between undercover agents and suspects, as well as for overtime, investigative expense, and equipment.
- *Equipment.* Drug investigations are becoming more and more technical with the introduction of high-technology equipment. Most equipment of this nature is typically used for surveillance operations, but investigators must be aware of what type of equipment is available and which is best suited for his or her agency's mission.

The resources cited earlier represent only a few of the most critical. Others include legal assistance, which should be a required ingredient in any drug investigation. Drug laws are becoming more complex in nature, thereby increasing the opportunities for investigators to make "technical" mistakes during their investigations. If there is any legal question in the mind of the investigator, he or she should always consult a knowledgeable prosecutor for advice before proceeding.

The list of potential informational resources is limited only by the investigator's imagination. The investigator should always keep in mind that information on just about everyone is available somewhere.

INVESTIGATION OF AN ILLEGAL DRUG LABORATORY

The investigation of illicit drug laboratories usually begins with a base of criminal intelligence information. Such information can be acquired through many sources, including other law enforcement agencies or criminal informants. Other than the preceding sources of information, the drug laboratory can be discovered by other means. For example, an abundance of a drug such as methamphetamine or PCP that is selling at an unusually low price might indicate a laboratory nearby. Once officers suspect an illicit drug lab, the following investigative steps should be considered:

- Check with the local utility companies to see if unusually large amounts of electricity are being used.
- Verify who is receiving mail at the suspect residence by checking with U.S. postal officials in the area.
- Conduct a criminal background investigation on each suspect.
- Survey the suspect location for evidence of exhaust fans used for ventilation.
- Be aware of any unusual odors in the area indicating the presence of a lab.
- Acquire a court order for the telephone tolls of the suspect's phone to reveal associates.

After the preliminary information has been acquired and verified, a second phase of the investigation should be conducted. This phase is designed to give information to the investigator of much greater depth to prepare for possible search warrants, undercover surveillance, or raids. The investigator should:

A Closer Look
Becoming a DEA Diversion Investigator (DI)

A Diversion Investigator (DI) is a specialist responsible for addressing the problem of controlled pharmaceutical and regulated chemical diversion from their legitimate channels in which they are manufactured, distributed and dispensed. The DI aids pharmaceutical and chemical industries in complying with the CSA and other pertinent acts, as well as international treaties and conventions. DIs investigate and uncover suspected sources of diversion and take appropriate criminal, civil, or administrative actions. In order to accomplish this mission, a wide range of work activities is employed. One activity, for example, is the scheduled investigation of registered handlers of controlled substances. These investigations serve to deter diversion through evaluation of the registrants' record-keeping procedures, security safeguards, and general compliance with the CSA and implementing regulations. Legitimate handlers of controlled substances who are subject to investigation are drug manufacturers, distributors, importers and exporters, and narcotic-treatment programs. Recently, there has been a push to investigate the diversion of controlled substances via the Internet. The rapidly changing environment and the increased diversion of controlled substances using the Internet has created the need for programs to target these sources of diversion.

Frequently, DIs are involved in investigations aimed at serious violators of controlled substance laws and regulations. These registrant violators have a documented or suspected history of drug and chemical diversion to illicit markets. DIs collect and analyze information developed during their investigation and consult with supervisory personnel to determine if criminal prosecution is warranted. DIs also work closely with DEA Special Agents and state and local law enforcement officers to provide assistance in making undercover purchases and executing search warrants. DIs work closely with attorneys for the DEA, the United States Attorneys Office, and state and local prosecutors. DIs are frequently required to testify about the results of their investigations in criminal trials, Grand Jury proceedings, and administrative hearings.

The job of a DEA Diversion Investigator involves maintaining contact with all levels of the dug and chemical registrant population. DIs will often answer questions from registrants concerning their responsibilities under the CSA.

Qualifications

General: Candidates must be a U.S. Citizen and possess a valid driver's license.

Physical: Candidates are required to obtain a medical examination to determine physical and mental fitness and must be free of any impairment which would interfere with normal work performance. Distant vision should be 20/40 (uncorrected or corrected with glasses or contact lenses). Near vision should be 20/25 and must be sufficient to read Jaegar Type #2 at 14 inches (glasses or contact lenses permitted). Depth perception and ability to distinguish shades of color (color plate test) is essential. Candidates must be able to hear conversational voices at a distance of 20 feet with both ears. The use of a hearing aid is permissible.

Education: Candidates must have a bachelor's degree (any major) and meet one of the following Superior Academic Achievement Provisions: a grade-point average of "B" (GPA of 2.95 or higher) for all completed undergraduate courses. A grade-point average of "B+" (GPA of 3.5 or higher) for all courses in major field of study or rank in the upper third of class in the college, university, or major subdivision.

Experience: One year of specialized experience equivalent to the next lowest grade level or an equivalent combination of education and experience.

(*continued*)

A Closer Look

Becoming a DEA Diversion Investigator (*continued*)

Special Skills: In addition to the minimal qualifications, credit may be given to those individuals who possess one or more of the following special skills:

- Investigative experience
- Proficiency in a foreign language
- Accounting experience or degree
- Chemistry experience or degree
- Pharmacology/pharmacist experience or degree
- Computer skills/experience
- Military service
- Law enforcement experience or degree

- Determine the number of inhabitants of the lab.
- Learn the identity of the inhabitants.
- Learn if any weapons are present at the lab location.
- Determine if any security measures have been taken by the suspects (e.g., guard dogs, booby traps).
- Attempt to determine the stage of the cooking process. (Is there any finished product available to seize?)
- Determine what chemicals are being used in the drug lab. These may serve as precursors, solvents, or reagents in the synthesis process. In addition, chemicals may be corrosive or even explosive in nature. For example, methamphetamine and PCP laboratories require large amounts of ether, which is extremely unstable and poses an imminent danger to anyone present on the scene.

THE DRUG RAID

Drug raids have proved to be one of the most dangerous aspects of the drug enforcement function and require careful development of raid skills by drug investigators. Improper planning and the failure to identify the many situations that can be presented during a raid can embarrass and draw much public ridicule to the department.

Purpose of the Raid

The word *raid* tends to conjure up many different mental images. Within the context of drug enforcement, a raid can be defined as "intrusion into a building or locality for lawful purposes." These purposes are typically the arrest of a suspect, the recovery of stolen property, or the seizure of drug evidence. Because drug evidence can easily be destroyed, it is important that the raid be a surprise to the suspect(s) before they can destroy the evidence. It is also important for the investigator to have an idea of what kind of drug is being sought and where it might be hidden in the raid location. Knowledge of the layout of the location is also important for the safety of the raid team.

Team Personnel

Because of overlapping jurisdictions in drug investigations, it is common for raid teams to be made up of officers from several departments. At times, the multi-jurisdictional composition of the raid team can pose unique problems in planning and executing the raid. Accordingly, it must be determined early which agency will have primary responsibility for the raid. The additional agencies simply support the lead agency in the drug raid effort.

The raid should also be under the authority of one investigator commonly known as the commander. This officer is responsible for the entire raid planning and execution. Clearly, the raid commander should strive to ensure that the police have superiority of personnel over the opposition. Personnel in a drug raid serve four functions:

1. Perimeter units make up the largest number of personnel. It is their main charge to seal the outer boundary of the raid area. This protects against curious onlookers who might hamper the operation.

2. The cover unit has the task of capturing the criminal if he or she breaks away from the apprehending unit.

3. The apprehending unit (also called the entry unit) enters the location and places the suspect in custody. It is this unit that is exposed to the greatest amount of danger.

4. The support or search unit serves as a reinforcement detail to the apprehending unit. This unit is also responsible for conducting a thorough, systematic search of the location.

A composition of the support team should provide the following:

- A tape recorder to make a log of all events in the raid.
- A photographer to assist the recorder.
- An evidence collector or property custodian to receive, assemble, and tag all goods or properties seized and properly identify persons arrested.

Preraid Planning

Operational planning of the raid should be kept to the immediate members of the raid team. All the activities that precede the raid culminate in the preraid briefing of raid personnel. At the preraid meeting, the following activities should be carried out:

- The raid commander must be identified.
- All team members must be familiar with one another.
- A mock-up diagram should be made to show team members their tasks in the operation.

- All suspects should be clearly identified.
- Raid officers should know the nature of the evidence in the case.
- Detailed descriptions of automobiles should be disseminated to team members.
- Information on timing should be specific.
- Because most raids are pursuant to a search warrant, all team members should be aware of who is in possession of the warrant.
- Postentry assignments should be given, which include custody of prisoners, custody of evidence, and custody and handling of seized vehicles.

Raid Execution

While the preraid plan is still fresh in the minds of team members, the raid should begin. In the early phase of the raid execution, all team members should assemble at a meeting point in close proximity to the raid location. The meeting point can be a school, warehouse, and so on. All outside contact such as telephone calls should be restricted and monitored closely by the raid commander.

At the meeting point, any last-minute updating should be discussed and related problems resolved. The perimeter team members should proceed to their assigned locations to seal off the area. Next, the cover and entry detail should move directly into the target location, being as covert as possible. The cover detail should then proceed with their assigned duties. These include:

- Cover all escape routes.
- Set up observation posts of the location.
- Prevent anyone from leaving or entering the location.
- Locate any person who might disclose the team's presence to the suspects.

Several strategies are available to the entry unit. These include (1) warning the suspect that the raid is imminent, (2) the tactic of surprise, or (3) the tactic of subterfuge, such as an officer posing as delivery person. Once inside, all occupants should be rounded up and detained until a determination can be made as

Figure 21.8 Search warrant briefing.

Operation Speedball

The king of the road in motorcycles is the world-renowned Harley-Davidson. It's the choice of many bikers, but apparently a requirement for membership in the infamous Outlaws Motorcycle Club of North Carolina, a notorious motorcycle gang that originated nearly 30 years ago. Another requirement? Only white males need apply.

The Outlaws is one of the largest and most violent motorcycle gangs in the United States. It's composed of 36 chapters throughout the United States and has a following in Canada, Europe, and Australia. These bikers have done more than gone for Sunday afternoon rides on the interstate, though—their activities have included drug trafficking, racketeering, acts of violence, and property crimes. However, a successful local–state–federal investigation entitled Operation Speedball spiked the gang's activities and dismantled its entire operation.

Who Are These Guys?

The Outlaws gang based its operations in Charlotte and Lexington, North Carolina, where it controlled a major drug distribution network using the U.S. mail and Western Union. Its drug operations included cocaine, marijuana, and methamphetamines. Gang members also owned and controlled two motorcycle chop shops where dozens of bikes were illegally obtained, chopped (disassembled), and then sold as parts to other bikers for profit.

The gang's insignia is a skull crossed with two pistons, popularized by Marlon Brando in the film *The Wild One*. Its mottoes, "God forgives, Outlaws don't" and "Snitches are a dying breed," were a big deterrent to getting witnesses to come forth and testify against members. From a law enforcement perspective, the Outlaws Motorcycle Club was not an easy group to infiltrate—its members were highly suspicious of any outsiders they met through business. In one instance, a couple of aspiring bikers wanted to be part of the gang's drug distribution operation run out of a topless nightclub. Unfortunately, the bikers' eagerness sent the wrong signal—the Outlaws suspected them of being "narcs" (they weren't). Gang members locked the doors to the club and beat the Outlaw wannabees into extended hospital stays.

Another instance involved two young African-American men who wandered into an Outlaws motorcycle parts shop/tattoo parlor to get tattoos. One of the young men already had the word "Outlaw" tattooed on him. The letter-stenciled design was similar to the club's symbol—gang members in the shop took offense at the tattoo and declared they would "beat" the tattoo off the guy. Both men were severely beaten.

Law enforcement, however, was finally able to infiltrate the group. The four-year investigation, which began in 1995, was spearheaded by the FBI Charlotte Office and the Charlotte–Mecklenburg Police Department. Many investigative techniques were used during this investigation. With all that hard evidence against the Outlaws, the efforts of the law enforcement joint task force culminated in Operation Speedball, to put a halt to the gang's activities. The search warrants resulted in the recovery of over 100 firearms, five pounds of methamphetamine, drug records, drug ledgers, several motorcycles, motorcycle parts, and other contraband. Then the arrests began.

To date, Operation Speedball has led to 33 arrests; 22 federal felony convictions on racketeering, firearms, and drug distribution charges; and seizures, forfeitures, and recoveries of stolen motorcycles, stolen parts, and property totaling in excess of $817,000. This case marked the first use of the RICO statute against a criminal enterprise in the Western District of North Carolina.

It was also the first time the Outlaws Motorcycle Club sent up the white flag in unison—most of them pleaded guilty. The investigation also led to the indictment and conviction of eight members of a Mexican drug trafficking organization that was supplying the Outlaws with methamphetamine.

---

to who should be arrested. Then the processing of the scene occurs with the recording and tagging of evidence and photographing the scene. As soon as possible after the raid, there should be a briefing of the team members. This should include notes of their observations and subsequent completion of all reports to the commander.

Figure 21.9 Tactical team serving a high-risk search warrant while utilizing a "flash-bang" diversionary device.

REVERSE STING DRUG OPERATIONS

The reverse sting narcotic sale is one in which undercover investigators, posing as dealers, sell large quantities of narcotics to known traffickers (also see Chapter 7 on undercover operations and surveillance). These types of operations have proven successful in penetrating otherwise untouchable drug markets. The same reverse sting techniques can also be used against drug consumers on the street.

Street-level reverse sting operations can be used whenever any type of controlled substance is being sold in a high-traffic environment. However, police agencies have found it particularly effective in dealing with rock cocaine sales. Rock cocaine, or crack, has become the drug of choice and a serious crime problem on the streets of many American towns and cities.

Planning the Reverse Sting

The "rock reverse" is almost always set up on the street in an area generally occupied by large numbers of street dealers or directly in front of a known crack house.

The operation is dangerous for undercover officers and takedown officers so it is important that personnel be selected carefully for this assignment. All weapons that may be used in the operation should be thoroughly inspected, and officers assigned should wear soft body armor, as they should during all assignments.

Reverse sting operations are manpower-intensive. The reverse sting operation discussed here requires between 20 and 25 officers in order to be conducted safely and efficiently. While this is a considerable expenditure in manpower, the operation can be justified based on the large number of arrests that can be made and the positive impact this has on the community. Additionally, considerable amounts of property and assets may be forfeited to the jurisdiction as a result of these operations.

Manpower Considerations

Three undercover investigators should be designated to perform the principal street sales assignments. Each officer should be dressed in a manner characteristic of the local dealers. Primary undercover officer "A" is responsible for making the drug sale while undercover officers "B" and "C" position themselves within 200 feet of officer "A" on each side. Vehicle assignments are as follows:

- *Vehicle 1* is the principal vehicle used to accommodate officers making the arrest. Ideally, this vehicle should be an inconspicuous panel or step van without rear or side windows and with double folding side doors. Five officers should be assigned to this vehicle, three of whom should be uniformed and the remaining two wearing reflective raid jackets. Three of these officers should be designated to employ weapons during the arrest and the other two assigned to searching and handcuffing the arrestees.

- *Vehicles 2 and 3* are designated as blockade cars. These should be unmarked inconspicuous sedans or other vehicles with two undercover officers assigned to each. Parked about 100 feet on each side of the van, these vehicles are pulled up to a position to block the suspect's vehicle at the time of the arrest or takedown.

- *Vehicle 4* should be a surveillance van with audio/video and night vision capabilities. The surveillance van is stationary and is placed undercover within 100 feet of the primary undercover officer (A).

- *Vehicles 5 and 6* are marked units with two uniformed officers in each. These vehicles are assigned locations just outside the takedown area and are meant to provide additional coverage should suspects flee the area.

In addition to these assignments, a prisoner transportation van should be stationed just outside the operations area to insure expeditious handling of arrestees (see Figure 21.10).

Conducting the Sting

The primary takedown vehicle must be in close proximity to the primary undercover officer as rapid response is essential in making the arrest. There must also be an appropriate place to locate the surveillance van so that it will be inconspicuous and provide for good audiovisual coverage. In some cases, officers may choose to conduct surveillance from a building location directly opposite the takedown area rather than use a van.

Once the operational area has been identified, diagrams of the neighborhood should be developed. These diagrams should include all relevant buildings and features and identify the position of all police vehicles and personnel to be deployed in the operational area. The diagram should be used during the personnel briefings to walk through the entire operation. If feasible, it is preferred that the entire operation be practiced in a nonpublic area just prior to being employed in the target area.

The reverse sting requires that a quantity of crack cocaine be packaged for sale. A court order may be required for use of this or other contraband from police property control. Preferably, the crack that is used in the sale should be laboratory tested.

Each cocaine rock should be sealed in clear plastic tape, a plastic bag, balloon, or other means. The method for sealing the rock should correspond with the method popularly used in a given area. The plastic bag or other method also allows the cocaine to be marked and discourages suspects from attempting to swallow the evidence.

Figure 21.10 Locations of officers and police vehicles in a reverse sting operation.

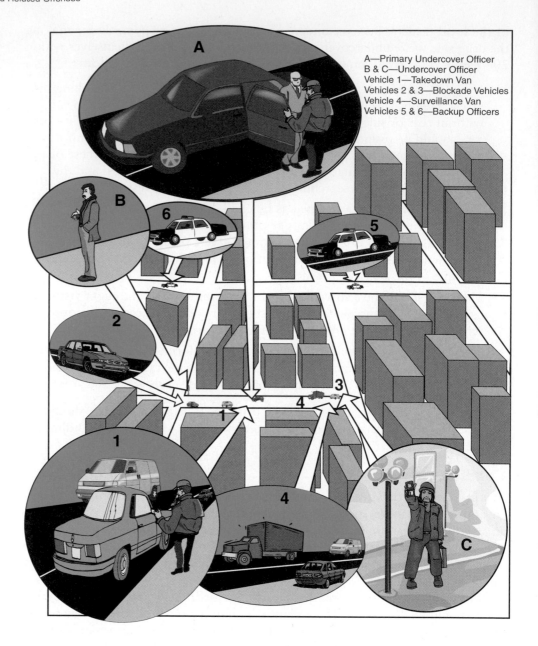

A—Primary Undercover Officer
B & C—Undercover Officer
Vehicle 1—Takedown Van
Vehicles 2 & 3—Blockade Vehicles
Vehicle 4—Surveillance Van
Vehicles 5 & 6—Backup Officers

Prior to sealing the crack, a piece may also be broken off from each rock and stored in evidence, a measure that helps in prosecuting buyers who manage to swallow or otherwise dispose of the evidence during their arrest. It should be noted that if the suspect swallows the cocaine, he should be immediately transported to an emergency medical facility. A potentially lethal overdose can thus be avoided.

Approximately 20 minutes prior to the operation, marked police vehicles with uniformed officers should be sent into the target area in order to disperse any actual drug dealers. While in the area, these officers should also make contact with the citizens and request that they and their children stay out of the operational area. Most citizens will comply, particularly in view of the fact that their neighborhood may have been overrun by the drug dealers for some time.

The primary undercover officer is responsible for selling the rocks while the two other undercover officers direct potential customers to him and provide backup protection. If the operation lasts for an extended period of time, these three officers should rotate assignments.

The primary undercover officer should be positioned directly opposite the takedown van so that takedown officers will be in position almost immediately following their exit from the vehicle. The primary undercover officer should also be wired with a body transmitter so that the transaction can be recorded verbatim. The transmitter also serves as a backup safety device so problems that may develop can be overheard by the officer in the surveillance van.

The undercover officer who is responsible for the sale has the major responsibility for ensuring that an "entrapment" situation is not created by what he or she says or does. The guidelines for the operation developed with the local prosecutor must be specific in terms of the types of language and actions that can be used to establish contact and a dialogue with potential buyers.

Typical guidelines for reverse sting operations instruct undercover officers to stand alongside the street in the target area and act in a manner generally characteristic of local street dealers. Officers are told to ask (after first being approached by a suspect) general questions such as "What do you want?" or "What are you looking for?" After the customer states that he is looking for crack, the officer is free to negotiate a price and conclude the sale.

Through the careful development of an acceptable dialogue between the undercover officer and customer, the danger of entrapment is virtually eliminated. Predisposition of the suspect to commit the crime can easily be shown through audio and video recordings of the incident. The suspect can be seen on videotape slowly driving into an area frequented by crack cocaine dealers. The suspect can be heard asking the undercover detective for cocaine. Predisposition can also generally be established by prior arrest records for drug offenses or by the presence of drug paraphernalia that may be found in the suspect's vehicle.

It should also be noted that in most cases it is necessary that the suspect actually take possession of the cocaine before he can be arrested and charged with possession. Examining the cocaine prior to purchase does not normally constitute possession.

Some agencies use prearranged signals between the undercover officer and the takedown team to initiate the arrest when the transaction is complete. A discrete signal, such as scratching one's face or another movement, is most useful if a body transmitter is *not* used by the undercover officer. If the transmitter is used in conjunction with visual surveillance, however, the officer conducting the surveillance should order the takedown. This latter approach is preferable for two reasons:

1. Police officers involved in undercover drug sales have been robbed of their drugs at gunpoint.
2. Some drug buyers, particularly those who have been arrested in stings on prior occasions, can readily detect commonly used police signals.

Once the takedown command is given, the officers from the van should exit the vehicle, announce that they are police, and establish a good field of fire that will not jeopardize the undercover officer or other police personnel. Speed in making the takedown is essential. It is far more likely that control and compliance of suspects can be established if officers deploy rapidly and thwart any attempts of the suspect to flee or otherwise react.

As officers exit the van for the takedown, the blocking vehicles should move into positions that will reduce the likelihood of an attempted escape. Officers in the blocking vehicles can also serve as backup to those in the van.

Once all suspects are in custody, a prisoner van can be summoned and other personnel can drive the suspect's vehicle to the impoundment area.

PHARMACEUTICAL DIVERSION

As we see from our earlier discussion, many potent and addictive drugs are manufactured legally for legitimate medical treatment. The availability of these medications has created a relatively new type of criminality: **pharmaceutical diversion.** Criminal investigations into this type of activity, also called compliance investigations, have revealed widespread diversion of drugs by health care professionals and street criminals alike.

Diversion by Legal Registrants

There are many restraints under the Controlled Substances Act (CSA) for those handling controlled substances. In addition to federal law, most states have adopted laws similar to the CSA to give a more localized means of controlling diversion activities. As the law is structured now, all medical professionals who are required to handle controlled substances must register with the DEA and obtain a registration number that is unique to them. Legal registrants of pharmaceutical drugs include:

- Importers
- Exporters
- Manufacturers
- Wholesalers
- Hospitals
- Pharmacies
- Physicians
- Nurses
- Drug researchers

Under law, anytime that drugs are purchased by a registrant, the assigned number must be made available to the supplier. This creates an audit trail for investigators in the event that a registrant is suspected of diverting drugs.

Diversion Tactics

Since the passage of the Controlled Substances Act, both legitimate and illegal drug markets have become more sophisticated. Advancement in cancer treatment research has produced powerful painkillers that addicts have learned can substitute for heroin. Legitimate manufacturers now market popular "mood enhancement" drugs, which have potential for abuse.

Today's drug buyer has learned that it is safer to obtain brand-name drugs that have been diverted onto the street than it is to deal with the drug peddler who is dealing an unknown product from a clandestine laboratory. Drugs purchased from a clandestine laboratory cannot allow the buyer to know what kind of poison is before him or if he will be ripped off with a no-impact placebo. On the other hand, when purchasing diverted drugs, the drug buyer has the assurance of a clearly identifiable, marked product coded by a manufacturer who prepared the dose under rigid guidelines enforced by U.S. government inspectors.

Availability of diverted drugs is also a factor in their increased usage. Unlike substances such as heroin and cocaine, diverted pharmaceuticals are produced within the United States and are not subject to the periodic shortages that affect smuggled products—the product is available at virtually every street-corner pharmacy in the country. The problem of the addict or the drug seller is reduced to how to divert the drug onto the street.

Drug diversion tactics may be classified under five general headings: wholesale-level diversions, illegal sales by medical practitioners, theft, fraud, and forgeries.

- *Wholesale-level diversion,* such as large-scale theft or fraud from the manufacturer or distributor, is minimal at the present time because of strict, enforceable controls that have been legislated for this level of the drug distribution system. The DEA reports few diversion incidents at this level, but a simple comparison of the number of incidents may be somewhat misleading, since one diversion incident at the wholesale level—such as a hijacking of a major drug shipment—can place thousands of illegal doses on the streets. Nonetheless, wholesale-level distribution is believed to be adequately controlled by existing laws and investigative techniques.

- *Illegal sale by medical practitioners* accounts for the largest current volume of diverted drugs. Illegal sales may originate with doctors, pharmacists, or employees at hospitals. The person responsible for the diversion may attempt to cover his tracks with a fraudulent paper trail of some kind, or may seek to confuse investigators by destroying part of the legitimate paper trail. The existence of required reports and records, however, constitutes an important part of any investigation of the medical practitioner.

- *Theft as a diversion tactic* is reported to be on the increase. This category includes burglary of storage facilities, armed robbery of pharmacies and doctors' offices, pilferage, and employee theft at both hospitals and pharmacies. According to DEA statistics, theft of legally manufacturered pharmaceuticals accounts for nearly 300 million illegal doses reaching the streets per year. It should be noted that reports of theft or burglary are also used by doctors and pharmacists to account for inventory shortages or to explain missing reports and drugs that were dispensed illegally.

- *Fraudulent schemes* to fool a doctor or pharmacist into prescribing drugs produce an unknown quantity of diverted drugs that is presumed to be large. Frauds are perpetrated by persons who obtain drugs for their own use and persons who either sell the prescribed drugs or turn them over to a criminal employer who sells them elsewhere. The scale of such frauds varies from the individual addict who supplies himself to well-organized activities that utilize paid "patients" to obtain prescriptions and paid "runners" to fill prescriptions at various pharmacies throughout a city.

- *Prescription forgery* as a classification includes consideration of counterfeit, and altered and forged prescriptions. Many forgeries are carried out with the knowledge of either the physician or the dispensing pharmacist, although some forgeries have been shown to originate with the pharmacist to disguise the loss of drugs that were illegally sold. The exact volume of drugs diverted by prescription forgery is unknown but is presumed to be significant.

Drugs obtained with forged prescriptions can be sold on the street at inflated prices. For example, the painkiller Dilaudid, prescribed frequently for cancer patients, is known on the street as "drug store heroin." The pharmacist pays about $.30 per tablet for the substance and may market at three times that for prescription sales to legitimate customers. A tablet of Dilaudid can be sold on the street to heroin addicts for $50, which explains the incentive for prescription forgery.

Physician Investigations

It is somewhat shocking to realize that doctors are as corruptible as any other human being. They prescribe illegally for many reasons: They may want money, sex, security, or escape, just like everybody else does; the doctor may be an addict or an alcoholic, his practice may be slipping as he grows old or senile, he may have become hardened and bitter due to personal failures. Doctors are people, and the DEA estimates that approximately 2 percent of them are engaged in illegal drug traffic. Such so-called script doctors write prescriptions for controlled substances for a fee without properly examining or diagnosing the patient.

Over the past decade, several investigative programs conducted by the DEA have confirmed that medical practitioners (doctors and pharmacists) are the major sources of diverted drugs.

Doctors Who Divert Drugs

Generally, four types of doctors are involved in the diversion of pharmaceutical drugs.

1. *Dishonest:* A dishonest doctor makes a profit from the illegal sale of pharmaceutical drugs, or may be involved in cases where prescriptions are given to suspects for the purpose of unlawfully distributing illicit drugs.

2. *Impaired:* Some physicians use drugs both on and off the job. Drug dependency may develop for a number of reasons: marital problems, stress on the job, and recreational use. The recidivism rate, however, is generally low for those who are treated properly and on a timely basis.

3. *Dated:* A doctor who has been in practice for a number of years may be willing to indiscriminately hand out drugs to anyone who has an apparent legitimate need for medication. Doctors who fall into this category are not necessarily criminals but more likely are set in their ways and unwilling to conform to new rules and regulations.

Examples of Drug Diversion by Doctors

1. A physician writes a prescription in a patient's name, picks up the drugs personally, and tells the pharmacist he or she will take it to the patient.
2. A physician sends a patient to the pharmacy to have a prescription filled but requires the patient bring the drugs back to his or her office. Only part of the drug is administered and the physician keeps the rest.
3. A physician writes a prescription in the name of a family member and then picks up and uses the drugs.
4. A physician writes a prescription in his or her own name at various pharmacies at the same time.
5. A physician self-administers injectable drugs taken from nurses' stations, hospital emergency rooms, or hospital pharmacies.
6. A physician orders drugs from several pharmacies at the same time, using official DEA order forms, while also ordering the same drugs from a mail-order drug company.
7. A physician obtains drug samples and self-administers them.

4. *Gullible:* This physician is not cautious enough to recognize a scam. Although possibly an otherwise competent doctor, he or she will easily fall victim to professional patients.

A number of investigative responses have emerged over the years to deal with the diversion problem. The most effective response combines the strength of each investigative approach. Statistical data collected and analyzed by DEA identifies pharmacies and/or doctors who are prescribing or dispensing abnormally large quantities of drugs. DEA or other narcotics specialists in the state may provide guidance with respect to elements of proof required to convict under specific laws. Ultimately, however, the classic "doctor bust" is the result of one or more undercover drug buys, usually by a police officer who obtains controlled drugs.

For example, it became known (from a report made by a uniformed patrol officer) that a doctor who resided in an old hotel was prescribing drugs for a fee. An investigator visited the doctor and explained that he was a truck driver and wanted 100 Ritalin tablets, a stimulant that is sometimes prescribed for weight reduction. The prescription was written without a physical examination although the detective was not overweight. Another investigator called on the doctor, again describing himself as a trucker, and received 200 Preludin tablets, stimulants that are also prescribed for the treatment of obesity. The investigator, who was in excellent physical condition, asked the physician if an examination was necessary. The doctor replied, "No. You look okay to me." The doctor was an alcoholic with a failed practice who supported himself by writing prescriptions for anyone who would pay the fee.

Doctors also provide drugs for sex. For example, a woman who wanted help kicking her addiction told police officers about a doctor who had been supplying her with drugs in return for sex. In this investigation, the officers decided to obtain evidence against the doctor by having the complainant record the transaction. The woman went to the doctor's office with a recording device. After a preliminary conversation about nonexistent medical symptoms, the woman offered to perform oral sex in return for 30 Preludin pills. The doctor agreed. The difficult problem with this technique is a claim of entrapment as a legal defense. This type of investigation must be carefully constructed.

The doctor who provides drugs for sex may take elaborate precautions, perhaps because he perceives discovery in this relationship more threatening to his family life than if he had taken money as payment. An investigation similar to the one described above involved a woman who attempted to acquire prescription drugs in return for sex, uncovered the following precautions. Acting as an informant for the police, the woman had to fill out a medical complaint form in the doctor's waiting room in order to see him in his examination room. As soon as the woman was alone with the doctor, she offered to have sex with him in return for prescription drugs that she intended to sell. The doctor refused her request. As a result, the doctor made a notation on the woman's medical form, which was filed by his nurse. It read: "Patient has no illness. She offered to pay $50 for speed (amphetamine). Told her that it was impossible and discouraged her from returning to this office."

Actually, the doctor had told the woman to return to his office the next day, when his nurse would not be working. The woman returned, had sex with the doctor, and received her prescription.

The doctor who prescribes drugs may be an elderly practitioner who is losing his practice to younger competition. Responding to reports that one elderly doctor was providing drug prescriptions irresponsibly, an investigator visited the doctor's office, which was located in his home. During a preliminary conversation that remained largely social, the doctor appeared to be mentally confused, perhaps senile. The prescription for the requested drugs was then written by the doctor's wife without the benefit of physical examination or direction from the doctor.

It is not uncommon for a medical practice (at least the prescription-writing function) to be taken over by a family member, a nurse, or a paid assistant when the doctor becomes incompetent due to age or illness. Abuse of the prescription-writing power sometimes follows.

Nurses Who Divert Drugs

Diversion problems also involve nurses. A distinction needs to be made between diversion drugs for resale and diversion because of personal addiction. Both present unique problems, and may require different solutions. Studies have shown that of those nurses who are diverting drugs, more are physically addicted than are selling drugs for profit. This distinction may affect the manner in which an investigation is approached and how the suspect is dealt with.

Drug Theft

Most health care institutions experience some degree of diversion, and generally the employees are the culprits. Those employees most likely involved with drugs are those who have access—physicians, nurses, pharmacists, and other employees. The most commonly diverted drugs are Valium, morphine, Demerol, Tylenol III with codeine, Percodan, Percocet, and Ritalin. The type of user and the opportunities available will have a bearing on whether tablets, capsules, or injectable substances are preferred. Diversion may occur in many different areas of the health care facility, but it will most commonly take place at the hospital pharmacy, the nursing station, or the recovery floor.

Substituting Drugs

If outright theft is not considered safe by the violator, he or she may substitute a noncontrolled drug for a controlled drug. Drug substitution may be accomplished, for instance, by appearing to inject a patient with a prescribed

Recognizing the Drug-Impaired Health Care Worker

Drug abusers often exhibit aberrant behavior. Certain signs and symptoms may indicate a drug addiction problem in a health care professional. Telltale signs include:

- Work absenteeism—absences without notification and an excessive number of sick days used.
- Frequent disappearances from the work site, long unexplained absences, improbable excuses, and frequent or long trips to the bathroom or stockroom where drugs are kept.
- Excessive amounts of time spent near where drugs are stored. Volunteering for overtime and being at work when not scheduled to be there.
- Unreliability in keeping appointments and meeting deadlines.
- Work performance that alternates between periods of high and low productivity and that may suffer from mistakes made due to inattention, poor judgment, and bad decisions.
- Confusion, memory loss, and difficulty concentrating or recalling details and instructions. Ordinary tasks require greater effort and consume more time.
- Interpersonal relations with colleagues, staff, and patients suffer. Rarely admits errors or accepts blame for errors or oversights.
- Heavy "wastage" of drugs.
- Sloppy recordkeeping, suspect ledger entries, and drug shortages.
- Inappropriate prescriptions for large narcotic doses.
- Insistence on personal administration of injected narcotics to patients.
- Progressive deterioration in personal appearance and hygiene.
- Uncharacteristic deterioration of handwriting and charting.
- Wearing long sleeves when inappropriate.
- Personality change—mood swings, anxiety, depression, lack of impulse control, suicidal thoughts or gestures.
- Patient and staff complaints about health care provider's changing attitude/behavior.
- Increasing personal and professional isolation.

medication while in fact a worthless substance may be used in its place. This may cause the patient to suffer and could result in medical setbacks.

Substitutions are commonly carried out through "charting" (backdating patients' charts to show that drugs were administered, which were in fact stolen) or forging other nurses' names. To avoid the possibility of substitution, two nurses should be required to obtain drugs needed on the floor. This would add a check-and-balance to prevent one of them diverting the drugs.

Diversion by Street Criminals

Finally, the scope of the diversion problem extends to the street, where criminals called **scammers,** or professional patients fraudulently attempt to obtain prescriptions for controlled drugs. Physicians are the most likely target of the scammer, for it is he or she who can write prescriptions or literally give away certain drugs. The pharmacist is the second-most likely target of the scammer, who might attempt to "pass" a forged prescription. Hundreds of schemes have been revealed over the years in which scammers have tried to dupe medical care professionals out of drugs. Such cases include those who have a legitimate ailment (e.g., a toothache) and who travel from one doctor to another trying to obtain prescriptions for pain medication.

Another common scam involves the criminal who takes a legitimately written prescription and alters the quantity of the prescribed drug (provided that it is not written out in longhand). In this case, a quantity marked "10" might be altered to form a "40," and a quantity of "5" may be altered to form a "25." Once obtained, the drugs are usually sold on the street for many times their worth.

EXTRAORDINARY DRUG ENFORCEMENT TECHNIQUES

The scourge of illicit drugs across the United States in the past two decades has resulted in vigorous enforcement of many drug control laws. Along with such aggressive enforcement of traditional drug laws (i.e., distribution, possession, and manufacturing of drugs) comes a wave of nontraditional techniques. The use of nontraditional drug control measures has resulted from criminals who, through expensive attorneys, vast experience in drug trafficking, and common sense, have learned to avoid detection. Since the late 1980s, such control tactics have resulted in convictions of drug dealers, raids, curfews, random searches, and the forfeiture of property. Such measures have not only become more and more popular with the police and the general public but they have enjoyed broad support from the courts. Proponents of unconventional enforcement techniques argue that such measures are necessary to combat the violence and social degradation that accompany drug abuse. Conversely, some civil libertarians claim that such techniques only tend to erode basic rights such as the safeguard against unreasonable search and seizure. Let's now take a look at a couple of the most commonly used nontraditional drug enforcement techniques.

Drug Courier Profiling

Since 1985, the DEA has employed a tactic that has since been called a **drug courier profile** (known as Operation Pipeline). Basically, it involves agents observing suspected drug traffickers and developing a pattern of behavior typical of those who use commercial airlines or public highways for drug trafficking. The profiling technique originated with law enforcement officers stationed at airports looking for people paying for plane tickets with cash, using an alias, boarding long flights without checking luggage, and staying briefly in distant cities known to be drug-source cities.

Because these actions can also be innocent, the practice has drawn criticism from civil libertarians. They claim that profiling is a shortcut to establishing the level of suspicion required by the Constitution before the police can interfere with a person's liberty. Most lower courts have responded by upholding the practice because of earlier Supreme Court decisions that permit the use of a "totality of the circumstances" approach to brief detentions by police.

In a precedent-setting decision by the Supreme Court, the technique of drug courier profiling was upheld. The drug decision, *United States* v. *Sokolow* (1989), was written by Judge William H. Rehnquist which overruled an earlier decision by the U.S. Court of Appeals in California. In the earlier decision, the court ruled that a brief detention by drug agents of a passenger at Honolulu International Airport was unconstitutional. In his opinion, Chief Rehnquist described evidence available to the agents in what he called "a typical attempt to smuggle drugs through one of the nation's airports." Rehnquist added that "any one of these factors is not by itself proof of any illegal conduct and is quite consistent with innocent travel. But we think taken together they amount to reasonable suspicion."

The agents detained the man long enough to let a trained dog sniff his luggage, and then they found several pounds of cocaine in his shoulder bag. When they stopped him, the agents knew little about him except that he had paid $2,100 for tickets from a roll of $20 bills; had just made a round-trip flight from Honolulu to Miami; stayed in Miami less than 48 hours with no checked luggage; looked

Basic Principles of Drug Courier Profile Use

1. *Drug courier profiles may be used only as a basis for further investigation. Such profiles do not, standing alone, justify an arrest.*
   This principle has been made clear by the courts. Any attempt to arrest a drug courier based solely on the use of the courier profile will almost certainly result in all evidence being suppressed and the criminal charge being dismissed. In addition, the officers and agencies involved may face a very real threat of civil liability as a result of their actions.[7]

2. *The factors which make up the elements of a drug courier profile may, however, under certain circumstances justify an "investigative stop."*
   United States v. *Sokolow* and other court decisions have held that it is not the drug courier profile in itself but the facts and circumstances known to the officers at the time they decide to make an investigative stop that determine whether or not the stop was valid. If, under the totality of the circumstances, the officer's suspicion was reasonable, the stop is valid. The fact that the behavioral characteristics of the suspect which aroused the officer's suspicion happened to appear on a "profile" is irrelevant. It is the circumstances that determine a reasonable suspicion, not the existence or absence of a formal "profile."
   Therefore, the profile can be used only as a starting point: <u>All</u> of the circumstances of the case must be considered, not just the items appearing in the profile.
   Even though the profile may certainly be used, it must not be applied in a mechanical, unthinking manner. The officer must consider the profile items in connection with the particular circumstances existing at the time and place. However, the officer may evaluate the circumstances in light of his or her own experience. Conduct seemingly innocent may, when viewed as a whole, reasonably appear suspicious to an officer who is familiar with the practices of drug smugglers and the methods used by them to avoid detection.[8]

3. *The officer must be able to articulate the factors that led the officer to form a reasonable suspicion of the person stopped.*
   Unless the involved officer can successfully explain to the court the factors that justified the stop, the stop will be held invalid and any subsequent arrest, search, or seizure will likely be invalidated, too. It doesn't do any good to say to the court "I just had a feeling that something was wrong." The officer must be able to list and explain the specific and particular observations which led the officer to conclude that the person in question might be a drug courier. The ability of the officer to state and explain his or her decision in clear, concrete terms can "and often does" make the difference between winning and losing a case of this type. Therefore:

4. *Know not only what factors are included in the profile but also why they are included.*
   Because the unthinking, mechanical employment of a profile has been disapproved by the courts, the officer must be able to demonstrate to the court that the use of the profile was made intelligently and with an understanding of the meaning of the profile factors.[9]

5. *Where possible, try to identify for the court factors in addition to those listed in the profile that contributed to the overall decision to detain the suspect.*
   This will help demonstrate to the court that the use of the profile was not mechanical and unthinking.

6. *Limit detention of the suspect to the minimum necessary to obtain further information.*
   Even if the initial detention is valid, if you hold the suspect for too long or otherwise exceed the balance of "reasonable" detention, the case may be thrown out by the courts. If the initial detention produces additional grounds for suspicion, the detention may be extended, but after a reasonable time, the officers must make the decision to arrest or release the suspect. This is particularly sensitive when the suspect has been removed to a private room for questioning.

7. *If the suspect has not yet been arrested, obtain either a valid consent or a search warrant before searching the suspect's luggage or automobile.*
   Because of the limitations imposed by *Terry* v. *Ohio,* do not permit a complete search of person, luggage, or automobile of the detained suspect unless an arrest has been made or probable cause for such a search has arisen. It will be necessary to have either the suspect's consent or a warrant before anything more than the *Terry* "frisk" can be conducted. Therefore, if the valid consent to search the suspect's luggage or automobile cannot be obtained and there is not yet probable cause for an arrest and/or a complete search, get a search warrant before searching luggage or vehicles. If the foregoing principles are observed, the use of drug courier profiles will be both proper and effective.

nervous; and had used a name that did not match the name under which his telephone number was listed. The man, Andrew Sokolow, was eventually convicted on federal drug charges. The issue was whether the factors matching Sokolow to a drug courier profile were sufficient to justify his stop and subsequent search without a warrant. The Court held that the stop was within the law.

In the Supreme Court's opinion, certain facts of the *Sokolow* case were pointed out, including Sokolow's attire of a black jumpsuit with gold jewelry and the roll of $20 bills appearing to contain a total of $4,000. Chief Justice Rehnquist also remarked "while the trip from Honolulu to Miami, standing alone, is not a cause of any sort of suspicion, there was more: Surely few residents of Honolulu travel from that city for 20 hours to spend only 48 hours in Miami during the month of July." Airport detentions have now expanded to the highways where the DEA's Operation Pipeline identifies vehicles and their occupants who seem to "fit" a certain set of criteria common to those who transport drugs or drug money across the country. Although practices such as drug courier profiling remain controversial, there seems to be growing support in the law enforcement community, the public sector, and the courts for innovative drug control stratagems such as these.

Asset Forfeiture

Because of the increasingly high profits of the drug trade, the practice of asset forfeiture has become an essential tool in drug control. Generally, the theory behind asset forfeiture is to take the profit out of illicit drug sales by seizing money or property that was either used to facilitate a drug crime or acquired with illicit drug revenues. Today, in addition to federal forfeiture laws, most state laws also provide for seizure of assets in drug cases. Although federal seizure laws have been used effectively since the late-1960s, the locus for forfeiture on the federal level is now the 1984 Comprehensive Crime Control Act (CCCA), which provides a revised civil provision for asset forfeiture. A unique aspect of this act is that it specifically recognizes the important role played by local and state law enforcement in drug control. Therefore, included in the act is a provision that enables federal and local law enforcement agencies to work together in facilitating the seizure of property. This can be accomplished on the federal level even though a federal agency was not involved directly in the investigation. The following types of property may be seized under federal forfeiture laws:

- All controlled substances.
- Raw materials and equipment used to manufacture controlled substances.
- Property used as a container for controlled substances.
- Vehicles, boats, and aircraft to transport materials used in violation of the CSA.
- All money, negotiable instruments, securities, or other things of value exchanged for controlled substances; all proceeds traceable to such an exchange.
- Real property and any improvements thereon used or intended to be used to commit or facilitate a violation of the CSA.

Under the 1984 act, the Attorney General or a designee can make an "equitable" transfer of the forfeited property so as to reflect the contribution of the state or local agency that participated in any of the facts that led to the seizure of the property. Under these circumstances, all agencies—federal, state, and local—benefit.

DISCUSSION QUESTIONS

1. List and discuss the five categories of drugs.

2. Discuss the main drugs of abuse produced by the cannabis plant.

3. The term *narcotics* relates to a category of drugs that are distinguished in what fashion?

4. How do drugs in the stimulant category differ from narcotic drugs?

5. Describe the hallucinogenic category of drugs. Give examples.

6. Explain how drug cases are initiated and developed.

7. Discuss the legal basis for an entrapment defense.

8. Explain the various drug-buy operations most commonly used in undercover operations.

9. Explain the term *pharmaceutical diversion.*

10. What role does the seizing of a drug suspect's assets play in drug control?

NOTES

1. LYMAN, M., and G. POTTER (2002). *Drugs in society: Causes, concepts and control,* 4th ed. Cincinnati, OH: Anderson.
2. Ibid.
3. DRUG ENFORCEMENT ADMINISTRATION. www.usdoj.gov/dea.
4. DRUG ENFORCEMENT ADMINISTRATION. www.usdoj.gov/dea. (December 2000).
5. U.S. DRUG ENFORCEMENT ADMINISTRATION (1988). *Drugs of abuse.* Washington, DC: U.S. Government Printing Office.
6. DRUG ENFORCEMENT ADMINISTRATION. www.deadiversion.usdoj .gov/career/di_invest.htm.
7. DRUG ENFORCEMENT ADMINISTRATION. www.usdoj.gov/dea.
8. Ibid.
9. Ibid.

Key Terms

▶ Bank Secrecy Act
▶ churning
▶ computer virus
▶ confidence game
▶ cybercrime
▶ cyber-extortion
▶ data diddling
▶ hacker
▶ hardware
▶ masquerading
▶ pigeon drop
▶ pyramid scheme
▶ scanning
▶ smurfing
▶ software
▶ Trojan horse

This chapter will enable you to:

- Understand the various types of white-collar crime.
- Understand the problem of money-laundering investigations.
- List the various techniques used by organized crime to launder money.
- Learn the different types of confidence games and how they are committed.
- Know the history and nature of computer crimes.
- Know what evidence to look for in the investigation of computer crimes.
- Understand the profile of the computer crime suspect.

INTRODUCTION

In the 1930s, criminologist Edwin Sutherland first coined the phrase *white-collar crime* to describe the criminal activities of the rich and powerful. He defined white-collar crime as "a crime committed by a person of respectability and high social status in the course of his occupation." Historically, law enforcement has paid little attention to the phenomenon of white-collar crime. In the past, even when a conviction did occur, offenders would typically get off with little more than a small fine and admonition by the court. Let's now consider the impact of white-collar crime by looking at the Martin Frankel embezzlement case.

Neighbors knew there was something strange going on in 44-year-old Martin Frankel's sprawling stone mansion well before firefighters found piles of documents burning in two fireplaces and the rest of the 12-room house ransacked and empty. There had been an all-day, late-night parade of limousines and leased Mercedes; armed guards, surveillance cameras, and spotlights; and the suicide of a young New York woman found hanged in a nearby house leased by Frankel. Then there was Frankel himself: a reclusive man who bought one, then another, $3 million estate on a secluded cul-de-sac in Greenwich, Connecticut's backcountry neighborhood, paying cash for both.

In May 1999, Frankel vanished along with hundreds of millions of dollars in insurance company money. He left behind a smoldering to-do list that included "launder money" and astrological charts asking, "Will I go to prison?" Among receipts found in the mansion was one for $10 million paid to a Los Angeles diamond broker.

The Frankel case was complicated to say the least. Upon his disappearance, police investigators began sorting out the clues that suggested billions of dollars in fraud. Those clues led to places such as the Vatican, a dozen Bible Belt insurance companies, and even past and present Justice Department officials.

Federal investigators uncovered an unlicensed brokerage operation on Frankel's Greenwich estates that siphoned investment money from a dozen insurance companies in Mississippi, Oklahoma, Tennessee, Missouri, and Arkansas. The companies were placed in state receivership because they could not account for the millions of dollars invested with Frankel's Liberty National Securities Inc., a firm not licensed by the Securities and Exchange Commission. Frankel systematically drained these assets through various financial accounts and transferred them into accounts outside the United States under his control. State regulators claimed that at least $218 million was missing, while another estimate was as high as $915 million. Also missing was as much as $1.98 billion from the St. Francis of Assisi Foundation, a charitable organization that Frankel established in the Virgin Islands.

The scale of Frankel's operation was apparent by 1997, when Greenwich police went to interview him about the hanging of a 22-year-old woman living in a home Frankel rented for $15,000 a month. The interview took place in an office-type room with numerous computer monitors displaying information from various financial markets. The death was ruled a suicide and the police went away. But when police returned one month later to investigate a fire, they found 80 computers, computer servers, and a sophisticated fiber-optic network tied to securities information services. It was a well thought-out con.

But Frankel had even bigger plans. He established the Assisi Foundation in August 1998 and recruited the help of prominent people, including Thomas Bolan, a New York lawyer, and two priests, the Reverend Peter Jacobs and Monsignor

Emilio Colagiovanni. But the operation began to crumble when Mississippi and Tennessee regulators became concerned about the money flow from local insurance companies to Frankel's unlicensed investment firm. Once initial inquiries were made, Frankel's Greenwich neighbors saw moving vans at his mansion.[1]

The Frankel case was closed with his arrest on September 6, 1999, at a luxury hotel in Hamburg, Germany. Frankel's arrest stemmed from an anonymous tip.[2]

DEFINING WHITE-COLLAR CRIME

According to the Bureau of Journal Statistics (BJS), white-collar crime is not an official crime category, but it represents a unique area of criminality that differs from other categories of criminality, such as violence and property crime. White-collar crime is a somewhat generic term meaning different things to different people. Although white-collar offenses are less visible than crimes such as burglary and robbery, their overall economic impact may be considerably greater. The appropriate definition of white-collar crime has long been a matter of dispute among criminal justice practitioners. A particular point of contention is whether it is defined by the nature of the offense or by the status, profession, or skills of the offender.

In an effort to understand this criminal phenomenon better, the *Dictionary of Criminal Justice Data Terminology* offers the following definition of white-collar crime: "non-violent crime for financial gain committed by means of deception by persons whose occupational status is entrepreneurial, professional or semi-professional, and utilizing their special occupational skills and opportunities." Simply put, white-collar crime could be explained as "nonviolent crime committed for financial gain and accomplished by means of deception."[3] Some of the most notable white-collar crimes are insider trading, money laundering, confidence games, and computer crime.

CORPORATE CRIME

In 1995, American Airlines loaded nine times the legal limit of a dangerous and unstable substance called Dioxital on a Mexico-to-Miami flight. The shipper told the airline the product's name but didn't think it was hazardous. Employees didn't check into it further even though airline procedures require them to do so when they receive cargo with a chemical product name. Only when the 100-pound barrel fell off a forklift and caught fire while being unloaded at Miami did American employees realize the danger.

Against the orders of fire officials, the airline kept the barrel at the airport for three years, eventually shipping it to a Wichita chemical plant for disposal after a federal investigation began. While airline officials claimed that they never put passengers in danger, federal investigators disagreed, for it was the same compound that in 1996 was blamed for the cargo fire that crashed a ValuJet DC-9 into the Florida Everglades near Miami, killing all 110 aboard.[4] Had the 100-pound barrel fallen over in the air, instead of on the ground, a similar catastrophe could have occurred with the American Airlines flight. The airline pleaded guilty of a criminal charge and paid an $8 million fine, making it the first major airline to gain a criminal record for its handling of hazardous materials.

As the U.S. population grows, as technology expands, and as world travel becomes an increasingly common occurrence, the opportunities for corporate

America to become more powerful is more and more likely. Accordingly, corporate opportunities for profit and expediency may be pursued at the cost of safety and fairness. Cases such as the American Airlines one were almost commonplace in the 1990s, and they raised questions about how such incidents can be avoided in the twenty-first century. Let's now consider other high-profile cases of alleged corporate crime.

In 1999, an antitrust suit was brought against Microsoft by the Justice Department, which claimed, among other things, that by giving away their Internet browser, Microsoft was unfairly putting their competition out of business.

One of the most widely publicized corporate crimes of the twentieth century was the 1996 case involving the Archer Daniels Midland Company (ADM). Caught in a Justice Department sting, ADM—the world's largest grain processor—pleaded guilty to charges of price-fixing for two products: lysine (a feed product for livestock) and citric acid (used in soft drinks and detergents). As a result, ADM was fined over $100 million, and its Asian co-conspirators paid $100 million to settle civil suits brought by shareholders and customers.[5]

Ironically, ADM's stock actually jumped; Wall Street considered the judgments and fines to be bargains because the company cheated customers out of more than $170 million. Along with the low fine, ADM was also given what is known as a sweetheart deal. In exchange for pleading guilty, the company was granted immunity against charges of price-fixing in the sale of high-fructose corn syrup, which along with the corn-derived fuel ethanol is ADM's leading product.

Scandals within the insurance industry also permeated news reports in the late-1990s. One such case involved Metropolitan Life when it was fined $20 million in 1993 for cheating its customers. Two years later, the nation's largest insurance company, Prudential, outdistanced the Metropolitan case by being fined $35 million.[6]

After an 18-month investigation, a task force of insurance regulators from 30 states concluded that for 13 years Prudential salespeople nationwide practiced a deception called **churning**, often with the knowledge and approval of management officials—often up to the level of vice presidents. Some salespeople were even promoted after their successes at conning their customers. Churning is the practice of convincing customers to use the cash value of old insurance policies to pay premiums on new, more expensive policies.[7] Some 10 million customers were not warned that the premiums of the new policy would probably eat up any equity they had accrued, leaving them with policies they couldn't afford and consequently with no insurance coverage. As a result of the Prudential case, numerous other insurance companies were sued for identical or similar conduct.

In the meantime, many other high-visibility corporate crimes have become a mainstay of criminal justice. Those stories that make their way to the attention of the American people display a panorama of civil, criminal, and social antics and greed by corporate executives who often shape our lives.

MONEY LAUNDERING

The mere existence of large profits earned in the illicit drug trade illustrates the ability of large-scale drug traffickers to launder billions of dollars every year. Investigations have revealed that such laundering activities commonly use the services of many Fortune 500 companies.

The Martha Stewart Securities Case

One of the high-profile white collar crime cases in 2004 was the arrest and prosecution of Martha Stewart, former CEO of Martha Stewart Living. Stewart avoided a loss of about $51,000 by selling nearly 4,000 shares of ImClone Systems stock on December 27, 2001, rather than the next trading day, when the stock tumbled after regulators rejected the company's application for a key cancer drug. Ironically, Erbitux, the ImClone drug at the heart of the scandal, was approved by regulators in February 2004 to treat certain forms of cancer.

Prosecutors argued that Stewart sold her ImClone stock only after her broker, Peter Bacanovic, told his assistant to tip her off that ImClone founder Sam Waksal was trying to sell. Stewart and Bacanovic had told investigators they had an arrangement to sell once the stock fell to $60. The government's star witness in the case, Douglas Faneuil, Bacanovic's former assistant, testified that his boss ordered him to pass the inside tip about ImClone to Stewart.

On March 5, 2004, a jury found Stewart guilty on four counts of obstructing justice and lying to investigators. Peter Bacanovic was also found guilty on four of the five charges against him. Each of them faced up to five years in prison and $250,000 in fines for each count.

In contrast to the Martha Stewart securities conviction in 2004, other CEOs have also recently been arrested and charged with a number of different white-collar crimes. For example, Dennis Kozlowski and Mark Swartz were charged with embezzling Tyco of $600 million; John Rigas and his sons were charged with stealing millions from Adelphia, the cable company Rigas founded; and the collapse of Enron and WorldCom led to billions of dollars in losses for investors and costs thousands their jobs.

Figure 22.1 Martha Stewart, former Director and Chief Creative Officer of Martha Stewart Living Omnimedia (MSLO), was convicted in March 2004 of insider trading.
Source: Peter Morgan, Reuters, Corbis-NY

The History of Money Laundering

The practice of money laundering began in Switzerland during the 1930s as concerned Europeans began funneling their capital beyond the clutches of Hitler's Third Reich. In time, Switzerland's infamous numbered accounts became an enormously profitable business. Today, Swiss bank secrecy laws have been relaxed because of numerous criminal cases involving money laundering. Criminals are therefore seeking other financial havens in which to deposit their ill-gotten gains. The flooding of entire regions with drug money is one of the more sinister and surreptitious types of drug-related crime. The term *flooding*, tracked by the regional Federal Reserve Banks, seems to describe this phenomenon with great precision.

In 1985, another scandal surfaced involving the prestigious First National Bank of Boston. In this case, federal prosecutors charged that the bank was making unreported cash shipments of $1.2 million. It would receive $529,000 in small bills and send $690,000 in bills of $100 or more. The bank was fined $500,000 for violating federal reporting requirements under the **Bank Secrecy Act** (BSA). In 1991, a New York State grand jury indicted the London-based Bank of Credit and Commerce International (BCCI) and its two principal officers for fraud, bribery, money laundering, and grand larceny after a two-year investigation. BCCI had looted depositors out of more than $5 billion, which was called "the largest bank fraud in history." In this case, bank officials knowingly made billions of dollars in loans to confederates who had no intention of repayment.

Combating the Money Laundering Problem

It's ironic that the very institutions that could do the most to stop money laundering seem to have the least incentive to do so. For example, the basic fee for recycling money of a suspicious origin averages 4 percent, whereas the rate for drug cash and other "hot" money may range from 7 to 10 percent. Perhaps one could inquire why the investment of drug money in legitimate businesses should be cause for concern. Considered very narrowly, the influx of large amounts of cash has provided some short-term financial benefits for Latin American debtor nations as well as domestic beneficiaries of illegal drug money.

It cannot be overemphasized, however, that this flood of money is not only a consequence of the drug problem but a major problem in its own right. For example, the money that enters the local economy is a primary cause of inflation. Even the banks that stand to gain from accommodating drug traffickers ultimately bear the costs of any losses that drug-related transactions generate. Part of the problem the United States has regarding money laundering activities is that U.S. drug users are primarily consumers rather than producers of drugs. Additionally, the United States is used as a repository for large amounts of drug proceeds.

Most drug profits are funneled to upper echelon members of drug cartels rather than the low-level producers and growers. Therefore, it is because of the tremendous profits of drug trafficking organizations that new members are constantly being lured into this illicit business. Unfortunately, profits are also so large that any losses, owing to forfeitures by the government, can usually be easily absorbed through future illicit dealings, making it unlikely that drug organizations will actually be put out of business.

Presumably, dealers consider that the risk of imprisonment or loss of assets is a mere risk of conducting business. Therefore, if we assume that the motivation behind the illicit drug trade is profit, we should conclude that government action against such a lucrative class of crime must include an attack against the proceeds of that criminal act. The success enjoyed by drug traffickers poses somewhat of a dilemma for them: how to reduce the likelihood of detection and subsequent asset seizure by law enforcement officials. This is accomplished by a criminal technique known as money laundering in which illegal cash proceeds are made to appear legitimate or the sources of illegal proceeds are disguised. As money laundering laws become more and more effective against the leaders of drug organizations, the risk of detection of such leaders is more likely.

The money laundering process can take many forms, including (1) simply merging illicit money with a legitimate cash source, which usually uses a business that generates large amounts of cash; and (2) using sophisticated international money laundering techniques (discussed next). The goal of the financial investigation is to reduce the rewards achieved through drug trafficking and therefore immobilize drug trafficking organizations.

Techniques of Money Laundering

On November 6, 1995, U.S. Customs agents intercepted $11 million in cash in Tampa, Florida. The money was soon linked to a money laundering operation spearheaded by the Cali cartel in Colombia. As astonishing as it sounds, this seizure is just one of many like it, where millions of dollars generated by organized crime enterprises are seized by authorities each year.

According to the U.S. Congress' Office of Technology Assessment (1995), money generated by organized crime and other profit-motivated crime in the United States is estimated at $300 billion annually. Syndicates earn huge profits on the illegal goods and services they sell to the public and through their extortionary relations with the business world. Much of this profit is in the form of cash, and virtually all of it must be converted to legitimate forms before it can be invested or spent. Drug traffickers and other racketeers who accumulate large cash inventories face serious risks of confiscation and punishment if considerable unexplained hoards of cash are discovered. For these criminals to enjoy the fruits of their illegal enterprises, they must first convert those cash proceeds to a medium that is both easier than cash to use in everyday commerce and that avoids pointing, even indirectly, to the illegal activity that produced it.

Money laundering conceals the source of the illegal money and gives that money a legitimate history and paper trail. Despite extensive media saturation on the topic, our knowledge of the money laundering problem remains limited. Estimates of how much money is laundered are virtually impossible to make with any precision. The President's Commission on Organized Crime estimated that billions of dollars in illegal drug profits are laundered in the United States each year. The commission further asserted that between $5 billion and $15 billion of those drug profits are laundered through international financial channels.[8]

Illegal drug transactions are usually cash transactions, commonly using large amounts of currency to pay off the various actors in each drug deal and to purchase sophisticated equipment. It is important for the trafficker to legitimize his or her cash proceeds in a fashion that permits the trafficker to spend it wherever and whenever he or she desires without, conversely, attracting suspicion. Obviously, the trafficker could choose to store the cash in a strongbox or wall safe, but such methods would not be plausible for the trafficker who generates hundreds of thousands or even millions of dollars in illegal cash each year. To combat this technique, the Treasury Department implemented the Currency Transaction Report (CTR), requiring banks to report cash transactions of $10,000 or more. In 1989, the U.S. government processed an estimated 7,000,000 CTRs, compared with an estimated 100,000 ten years earlier. Traffickers quickly circumvented this requirement by developing such activities as corrupting bank employees.

The many different techniques for laundering illicit proceeds are limited only by a trafficker's imagination and cunningness. An entire "wash cycle"—to transform small denominations of currency to businesses, money market deposits, or real estate—may take as little as 48 hours.

The method chosen by any given trafficker will no doubt reflect his or her own situation and any unique circumstances involved. Money laundering techniques illustrate the ingenuity of the drug trafficker in hiding millions (and even billions) of dollars of illicitly gained revenues. Money laundering techniques include bank methods, smurfing, currency exchanges, double invoicing, and acquisition of financial institutions.

Bank Methods.   The most common methods for laundering money are called bank methods. In this basic technique, the traffickers take their cash to a bank and conduct several transactions that usually involve trading currency of small denominations for larger ones. This is done for obvious portability purposes. It is also common for cash to be exchanged for Treasury bills, bank drafts, letters of credit, traveler's checks, or other monetary instruments.

During the early-1980s in Miami (considered the hub of the cocaine banking business in the United States), large daily shipments of currency would arrive and be deposited in numerous accounts, but they would then be disbursed immediately through the writing of checks payable to true or nominee names. Ultimately, these funds were deposited in other domestic accounts in the same or different banks or wire transferred to offshore bank accounts in foreign countries with strict bank secrecy laws.

Ironically, there is no requirement to report these transactions because the BSA's reporting requirements don't pertain to interbank transfers. Therefore, the biggest problem posed to the traffickers is the initial depositing of the currency into the banks. Once funds are deposited, a trafficker can communicate with the bank through a fax machine or personal computer and literally route funds all over the world without ever coming face-to-face or even speaking with a banker. One method of conducting mass deposits, called **smurfing**, first appeared during the mid-1980s and is discussed next.

Smurfing.   A trafficker provides several individuals, or smurfs, with cash from drug sales (Figure 22.2). Each smurf goes to different banks and purchases cashier's checks in denominations of less than $10,000, thus bypassing the reporting requirement. The smurfs then turn the checks over to a second person, who facilitates their subsequent deposit into domestic banks or transports them physically to banks in Panama or Colombia. In some instances, the monetary instruments are premarked "for deposit only," making them nonnegotiable to the courier.

Currency Exchanges.   Traffickers may also use either money exchanges or brokerage houses for facilitating movement of their money. Foreign currency exchanges are frequently set up as storefronts that deal regularly in large cash transactions. In using the exchange, the trafficker can avoid using traditional banking institutions and therefore avoid risky reporting requirements. Banks traditionally deal with exchange companies and customarily don't question large transactions from them. The currency exchange business can also move money in other ways for the trafficker. In particular, money sent to other jurisdictions in payment for foreign drug shipments is common. Using a dummy corporation, a trafficker will sometimes contact his or her lawyer and request that the lawyer accept a huge deposit into the lawyer's foreign account. The lawyer will then wire the money directly into the dummy account, where it remains unsuspected.

Double Invoicing.   Double invoicing is yet another popular method of hiding illicit financial gains. In this technique, a company orders merchandise from a foreign subsidiary at an inflated price. The difference between the inflated price and the actual price is deposited by the subsidiary in a special offshore

Figure 22.2 Smurfing chart.

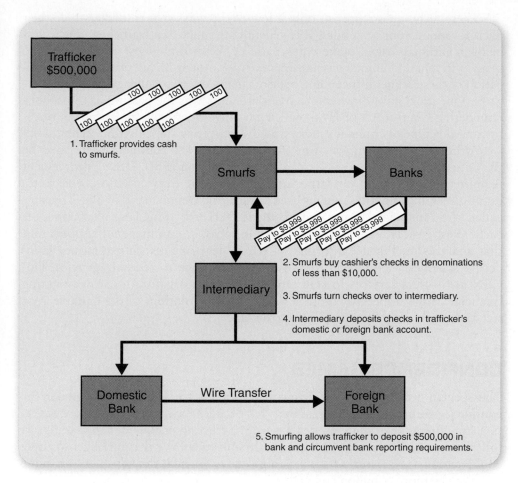

account. Occasionally, the same technique is employed in reverse: The company sells merchandise at an artificially low price, and the difference between the two prices is deposited in a secret foreign bank account maintained by the company.

Acquisition of Financial Institutions. This fifth money laundering method, possibly the most difficult to detect, simply involves acquiring a domestic or international financial institution. By controlling an entire institution, traffickers can go far beyond the immediate aim of concealing illicit earnings. They effectively take over part of the local banking system and divert it to their own needs. Such operations, which have been identified in South Florida and southern California, enable traffickers to manipulate correspondent banking relations, make overnight deposits, arrange Eurodollar loans, and take advantage of the abuse list (customers exempted from cash-reporting requirements).

The Smurfing Process

1. Trafficker provides cash to smurfs.
2. Smurfs buy cashier's checks in denominations under $10,000.
3. Smurfs then turn checks over to an intermediary.
4. Intermediary deposits checks in trafficker's domestic or foreign bank account.
5. Smurfing allows trafficker to deposit $500,000 in bank and circumvent bank reporting requirements.

These techniques represent only a few of the ways that traffickers hide their illicit revenues from drug sales. It is generally thought that traffickers, regardless of their national origin, make regular use of these techniques. The fact that so many different and unique mechanisms exist for money laundering makes investigation of these crimes difficult and presents many unique challenges to the investigator. One great aid to law enforcement attempts was the passing of the Money Laundering Control Act of 1986, which gave investigators more latitude in investigating this type of criminal activity and in uncovering these myriad techniques.

Although investigations of money laundering are routinely performed by such agencies as the Federal Bureau of Investigation (FBI), Drug Enforcement Administration (DEA), and the Internal Revenue Service (IRS), a recently established investigative unit housed under the Department of the Treasury called the Financial Crimes Enforcement Network (FinCEN) also conducts such investigations. FinCEN, established in 1990, is a multiagency support unit that analyzes intelligence information which develops suspects in money laundering schemes. In addition to providing assistance to federal agencies, FinCEN also offers services to state and local police organizations investigating financial crimes, especially those associated with violations of the Bank Secrecy Act and the Money Laundering Control Act.

CONFIDENCE GAMES

The spectrum of white-collar crime also extends to the timeless scam of the **confidence game** (or "con"). Criminals for decades have practiced the art of getting something for nothing by stealing from a trusting person. When reading the following con-artist scams, it might be difficult to believe that intelligent people could actually fall victim to such manipulation. Indeed, they do. Let's examine some of the more common con games.

The Pigeon Drop

Probably the most practiced confidence game of all time, the **pigeon drop** comes in many varieties. In this scam, a lot of losers pay a few winners. Although these scams are conducted in different ways, most seem to follow the basic pattern. Here's how it works: Con man 1 finds a wallet, purse, attaché case, or even a paper bag apparently filled with money. An unsuspecting victim standing nearby witnesses the discovery. At that time, con man 2 appears and claims that he is entitled to a share of the loot just as much as the other.

It should occur to the victim at this point that he or she should share in the proceeds. An argument then breaks out about whether they should divide the money immediately or check it out to see if it is stolen. Con man 1 says his "boss" has police "connections" and can check. A quick phone call is then made by con man 1 who then says that the money was probably dropped by some drug dealer or big-time gambler and that they should divide it between them.

The boss offers to hold the money until all three can produce a substantial amount of their own money to show that they are acting in good faith and can be trusted to keep the secret. Con man 2, apparently determined not to be cut out of the deal, produces a large sum of money on the spot to prove his reliability. Con man 1 and the victim then hurry off to get their part of the money. When the victim returns and hands over his share, it is the last he or she sees of the cons or the boss.

The key to the success of this scam is the powerful acting between the cons—in particular, the bickering between the two men that makes the victim feel that he or she will be left out unless they abide by the conditions of the agreement. The reliability of the boss is the convincer (sometimes this character portrays a police detective). The amount of money in question is always so great that the victim wants to believe.

The Bank Examiner Scheme

In this scam, con artists pose as FBI agents, bank examiners, police officers, detectives, or bank officials. The victim is then contacted by them pretending to need help in conducting an investigation. The con asks the victim to verify their present balance, which is, say, $5,000. After doing so, the victim is advised that the bank's records reflect a lesser amount (e.g., $3,000), and it is suggested that someone might be tampering with the account.

Con man 1 instructs the victim to meet him at the bank, and con man 2 remains in the neighborhood and observes the victim leaving. After arriving at the bank, con man 1 meets the victim and accompanies him or her to the teller, where the money is withdrawn. During this process, the victim is told that one of the tellers might be the thief and not to act nervous. After the withdrawal, con man 1 advises the victim just to hang on to the money until the bank contacts them.

Later that day, con man 2 goes to the home of the victim and explains that a sting operation will occur to apprehend the suspect teller and that the victim should now give the money to con man 2 so that he can redeposit it at the "suspect" teller's window. Con man 2 then uses the victim's phone to call "the bank" and speak with con man 1. The victim is then allowed to speak to con man 1, who reassures the victim that the money will be kept safe. As a valued bank customer and upstanding citizen, the victim complies, and the money and the cons are never seen again.

The Pyramid "Get Rich Quick" Scheme

"Earn thousands the easy way. A small investment could earn you $100,000 in less than a year!" Among the oldest con games, pyramid rackets have been used to swindle millions of dollars annually, employing everything from dollar bills to chain letters to more sophisticated schemes that sell franchises to unsuspecting persons who then must sell more franchises to more victims, and so on.

Theoretically, **pyramid schemes** can continue indefinitely, but actually "bubble" and soon collapse because of the sheer numbers involved. A typical operation swept California during the 1970s. In the scheme, two players paid an entry fee of $1,000 apiece. Half this amount, $500, went to the top of the pyramid while the remaining $500 from each of the two new players went to the player who recruited them. So the first player got his or her money back and then waited to move up another rung on the pyramid as each of the two new players each recruited two more players so that they could also recover their initial $1,000 investment. As each step of the pyramid was mounted, the initial player moved from rung 16, to rung 8, to rung 4, to rung 2, and finally to rung 1. After reaching the top rung, the player received the money that accumulated at the top for him: $16,000.

Although it may seem fairly easy for new players to induce two new players to the scheme, the numbers become astronomical. Essentially, each player on rung 16 creates two entirely new pyramids, and the progression gets bigger and

A Ponzi Scheme[9]

The Ponzi scheme struck again, this time by a French businessman seeking fame and fortune in the United States. What made this case a little different, though, was the fact that the victims of the scam fought back—and to a certain extent succeeded—in getting back their hard-earned money.

What Is a Ponzi Scheme?

A *Ponzi scheme* is a type of investment fraud wherein the operator promises high dividends or financial returns that are not expected from traditional investments. Instead of investing victims' funds, the operator pays the original investors "dividends" using the money that subsequent investors give. The scheme generally falls apart when the operator flees with all the proceeds or when a sufficient number of new investors cannot be found to allow the continued payment of "dividends."

The Ponzi scheme was named after Charles Ponzi of Boston, Massachusetts, who operated an investment scheme in the early twentieth century. He guaranteed investors a large return on their investments but ultimately could not pay the dividends. Ponzi was found guilty of mail fraud and imprisoned for five years.

Modern Example of a Ponzi Scheme

In 1984, Jean Claude LeRoyer, 54 years old with a history of criminal activity, began the Metro Display Company, with the idea of selling bus-stop shelters with advertising space throughout southern California. He pitched his plan to individual investors and soon received about $48 million from them. The majority of LeRoyer's investors were retirees on fixed incomes who were hoping the investment could better their financial futures.

The advertised investment strategy was as follows: LeRoyer claimed that an investor could buy a bus-stop shelter for about $10,000. He promised each investor $170 in monthly dividend payments and that Metro Display would buy back the shelter from the investor for their initial $10,000 investment after five years. The company also pledged to give investors a 20 percent share of that shelter's advertising revenue for the following five years. This process, according to LeRoyer, would double an investor's original investment. Sound too good to be true? It was.

By 1991, Metro Display had become one of the largest and fastest-growing public bus-stop shelter firms in southern California. The company owned 2,600 shelters in more than 60 cities and counties in southern California and southern Nevada. However, LeRoyer quickly began losing control of his investment scheme. Over 1,600 shelters remained to be built, and other financial problems were beginning to mount. LeRoyer failed to advise his investors, among other things, that 25 percent of their investments were being used to pay sales commissions and that funds from new investors were used to cover the monthly payments due longtime investors. He claimed he was selling ads in the shelters for about $1,000 a month per shelter when actually the price was closer to $200. In addition, only 10 to 15 percent of the shelters carried paying ads, not the 85 percent that

bigger. For example, there are 16 players on the bottom rung, and it takes 32 new players to get them to advance to the next rung. Each of these 32 players must now recruit two new players, bringing the number to 64 total. Those 64 must now recruit two new players, each totaling 128 people. The total then jumps to 256, at which time the original 16 players have reached the top of the pyramid. However, for the players on the next rung, 512 players are needed for them to advance to the next rung. For the next group, the required number is 1,024, and so on. The California pyramid scam finally died out as cons were unable to attract enough gullible people to keep it alive.

Travel Scams

"Dear Consumer: You have just won a free vacation for five days and four nights in the Bahamas. Just call this 800 number for details." Postcards with messages such as these are becoming more common throughout the United States. The way this scam works is that when the victim calls the number, she is told that she will

LeRoyer had claimed. Business grew dismal, new investor funds trickled to a halt, and longtime investors clamored to get their monies back from LeRoyer's collapsing business.

The Securities and Exchange Commission (SEC) was alerted. The SEC froze the sale of any additional shelters and called on the U.S. Attorney's Office, the Internal Revenue Service (IRS), and the FBI office in Los Angeles to form a special task force for a securities investigation of Metro Display, which had garnered a lot of attention with its irregular business transactions.

The FBI executed six search warrants and confiscated computers and files from Metro Display's offices and from both LeRoyer's office and home. The FBI also investigated criminal misrepresentations and fraud by wire deals by the company's salespeople. The files revealed that in the first six months of 1991, Metro Display recorded losses of more than $7 million. The files also showed that LeRoyer and his wife, Karen, had diverted more than $800,000 from the bus-stop shelter business to make improvements on their luxurious home. The LeRoyers also paid hefty amounts of money to relatives employed in the business.

Because of LeRoyer's diversion of funds from the business, the SEC filed a financial fraud and misappropriated funds lawsuit against LeRoyer. He, in turn, filed for bankruptcy and removed himself from control of Metro Display. However, he did continue to serve the company in a lesser capacity.

In October 1996, LeRoyer pleaded guilty to filing false tax reports and to six charges of mail fraud, the mail fraud charge being from his use of mail to further his scheme. He was sentenced to 46 months in jail and was ordered to pay restitution to his victims.

The company's chief financial officer also pleaded guilty and was sentenced to one year in prison. Karen LeRoyer, the firm's former bookkeeper, pleaded guilty to three counts of filing false tax reports. She was sentenced to five months in jail for her role in the investment scheme, but the presiding judge placed her on probation so that she could look after the couple's newly adopted eight-year-old daughter.

Three of Metro Display's salespeople were indicted for their parts in the scheme. During their six-week trial held late in the summer of 1998, prosecutors used 36 witnesses and 350 document exhibits (selected from the more than 2,500 documents seized) to demonstrate the salespeoples' involvement in the fraudulent activity. All three were convicted and received prison terms ranging from three to seven years.

Investors were only able to get back less than half of their original investments. About 200 Metro Display investors, many of them retirees, did not want to take their losses lying down. They formed a group to try to get the company back on sound financial ground in the hopes of ultimately selling it in order to recoup their losses. Investors, mostly volunteers, did everything from answering phones to selling ads. Slowly, Metro Display emerged from bankruptcy and was sold. Generally, investors in Ponzi schemes lose much of their invested monies.

receive a package in the mail detailing the vacation offer. The operator then asks the victim for her credit card number, telling her that a small service charge will be made to her account if she accepts the vacation offer. The victim is assured, however, that she will have a review period to decide if she wants the package before her account is billed for the service charge. The company is slow in sending the vacation package materials, and when it does arrive, the review period, according to the company, has already expired. The company then quickly bills the victim's credit card for hundreds of dollars for its "service fee."

Home Repair Scams

The home repair scam begins with a worker who goes door-to-door offering repair services for a modest fee. Services include driveway repair, roof repair, and so on. Scammers accept money for repair jobs that they never finish, or fail to honor warranties on home improvement projects. One such scam is the asphalt scam. Here, the worker offers to use the remaining asphalt from one job to repave a second driveway. More often than not, the worker either starts the job and then claims it will cost hundreds or thousands of dollars more to complete, or he will just lay black paint instead of asphalt on the driveway and leave town with the victim's money.

Elderly people are prime targets for such scams because many own their own homes, and many of those are older homes. Many such homes actually are in need of repairs, and the crafty con artist looks for this. The criminal will generally ask for a large down payment before he begins the work, and there have been cases in which the worker will accompany the victim to the bank to withdraw the money. The con will sometimes use the obituaries to seek out elderly persons living alone. The con then claims to be a building or health inspector who is there to check out the furnace. Once in the basement, they either cause damage or claim that a health or safety threat exists. Then they demand money from the victim for either repairs or reassembly.

Contest Cons

Contest cons usually begin by sending a computerized "personal" letter to the victim stating that he or she has just won a new car, a diamond necklace, a food processor, and so on. All the victim needs to do to collect the prize is visit a time-share resort. If the victim does so, however, he or she will be subjected to high-pressure sales tactics to buy one of the units. Then when prizes are given, they are usually cheap imitations of the real thing. Letters of this sort may appear urgent and may represent companies with names that resemble official organizations.

The Magazine Subscription Scam

The magazine subscription scam begins with a phone call asking the victim if he or she would like to receive five magazines for two years at no cost. The offer is that all the victim has to pay is a nominal fee, say $1.75 per week, as a service charge. The caller will then request the victim's charge card number. Victims may find that they are charged several hundred dollars of fees that are unwarranted. The scammers are so slick that consumers are unaware that they have purchased magazines until they receive the bill. Some salespeople avoid identifying themselves as magazine subscription salespeople or with the name of their company. Others encourage consumers to make purchases without giving the total costs, or ask the consumer for a credit card number for "verification" purposes and then use the number to charge for unwanted subscriptions.

Because crime scenes are virtually nonexistent in cases involving fraud and confidence games, investigators should focus on learning as much as possible about the victim and those who are responsible for the crime. In addition, records and documents should be identified and examined for possible clues as to the identity of the perpetrators. Investigative efforts to identify suspects in the case are often handicapped by the victim's inability to remember details about the swindler(s).

COMPUTER CRIME

On the morning of May 4, 2000, a computer virus called the "love bug" made its way around the world in a matter of hours, causing an estimated $10 billion damage (Figure 22.3). The virus originated in the Philippines, where two

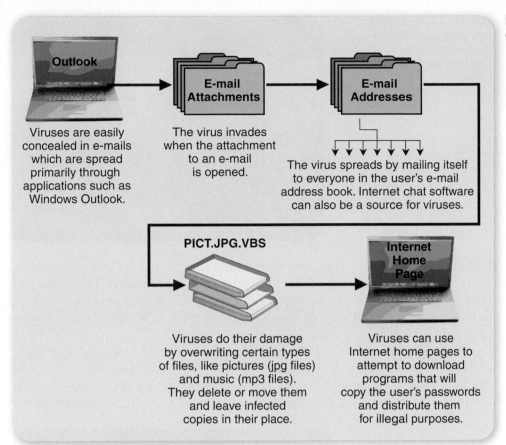

Figure 22.3 The anatomy of a computer virus.

suspects, Onel de Guzman and his friend, Michael Buen, both 23 years old, were arrested.[10] Experts were astonished that the two suspects were such "average computer enthusiasts" and how simple the virus was for them to create. Once they had developed the virus, they hacked their way into four accounts with the Sky Internet ISP (Internet service provider) to release the virus. The ISP was able to trace the bug to the phone number for de Guzman's apartment.

The structure of the virus was simple. For example, it was designed to go into Microsoft's Outlook, find all the victim's addresses there, and resend itself to all of those addresses. Computer experts reported that it took less than 20 lines of code to accomplish that. Corporations and other business entities moved quickly by shutting down e-mail servers and warning workers. Within half a day, antidotes were available. But by then the love bug had already been a sensation, interrupting work for millions of people.

In the twenty-first century, a new form of criminality is upon us, creating untold options for criminal entrepreneurs and new challenges for police. With the personal computer now in many households, and mainframe computers acting as the epicenter of almost all Fortune 500 companies, the problem of computer crime, or **cybercrime,** is now a mainstream social problem. According to one definition, cybercrime is "the destruction, theft or unauthorized use, modification, or copying of information, programs, services, equipment or communication networks."[11]

For obvious reasons, cybercrime has had a relatively short history. Although electronic crime has been somewhat of a problem for the past three decades, it

Figure 22.4 Inside a computer: investigators must have knowledge of the proper components of a computer to know whether it might produce evidence.

wasn't until the 1970s that a new term entered the public lexicon—**hacker.** Early hackers began using school computers for a number of misdeeds—the least of which was altering grades. By the end of the decade, modems (devices linking computers to telephone lines) and computerized bulletin board services emerged.

While the first generation of hackers during the 1980s seemed more mischievous than criminal, their emergence was the predecessor for a far more insidious type of computer crime. Many large corporate computers are now "hacked" not as a prank, but as a target of large-scale theft. Indeed, computers

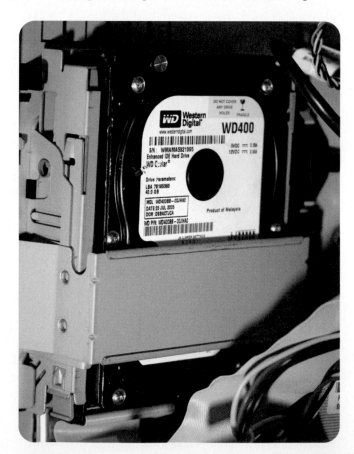

Figure 22.5 This seized computer's hard drive is thought to contain evidence, including e-mail conversations and business records.

have provided opportunistic criminals with a new genre in which to ply their crimes, and many of today's criminals are quite computer literate. One early example of cybercrime involves the planting of an unauthorized program known as a Trojan horse, which automatically transfers money to an illegal account whenever a legal transaction is made. To many thieves and hackers, this was akin to striking pure gold.

Computer criminals today have posed as financial advisers or licensed brokers on the Internet and solicited investments in fictitious mutual funds.[12] In some cases, they have attempted to extort money from their victims. In one of the biggest cases of **cyber-extortion,** a computer hacker stole credit card numbers from an online music retailer, CD Universe, and released thousands of them on a Web site when the company refused to pay $100,000 ransom. In January 2000, the *New York Times* reported that the hacker claimed to have taken the numbers of 300,000 CD Universe customers. The hacker turned out to be a 19-year-old from Russia going by the name of Maxim.[13]

Defining Computer Crime

As indicated, many different types of crimes are committed through illegal use of the computer. Computer crime, however, is not well understood in the criminal justice community partially because of its newness on the criminal frontier and the level of competency required for many such offenses. Other factors also contribute to confusion about the crime, such as media sensationalizing of events involving computers. Because of this, a consensus of the definition of computer crime is difficult to obtain.

According to the National Institute of Justice (NIJ), state and federal criminal codes contain more than 50 different definitions of computer crime, each somewhat different from the other. For the sake of simplicity, let's define computer crimes as violations of criminal law that require a knowledge of computers for their perpetration.

Internal computer crimes are alterations to computer programs that result in the performance of unauthorized functions within a computer program. Such crimes have been around for years and have acquired names such as Trojan horses, logic bombs, and trap doors to indicate different programming techniques designed to carry out the unauthorized functions.

The Nature of the Crime

Computer crime is difficult, if not impossible, to detect. According to the FBI, it is believed to cost private and public businesses anywhere from $40 billion to $100 billion yearly. The gradual evolution of occupations in this field has created new opportunities for criminals, who benefit as computer programmers, operators, tape librarians, and electronic engineers. Here, criminality is removed from the street and resides in the privacy of the homes of computer criminals, many of which have raised flooring, lowered ceilings, flashing lights, and air-conditioning motors. Hence methods of crime have changed. A new computer jargon has now developed that has identified automated criminal methods such as data diddling, Trojan horses, logic bombs, salami techniques, superzapping, scavenging, data leakage, and asynchronous attacks.

Targets or victims of computer crime have also taken on a nontypical effigy. For example, electronic transactions and money, as well as paper and plastic money (credit cards), are typical targets for automated loss. Financial transactions are typically conducted over telephone lines where money is debited and credited inside computers. In essence, the computer has become the vault for the business community. Physical assets such as warehouse inventories and materials leaving factories are also tracked through the use of computers. The timing of computer crimes also differs greatly from traditional crimes. From a traditional standpoint, most crimes are measured in minutes, hours, or even days. In contrast, some computer crimes are measured in milliseconds (as little as 0.003 of a second).

Another atypical dimension to computer crime is that geographical constraints do not hinder the computer criminal, as with many other types of crime. A telephone with an attached computer terminal (modem) in one country can easily be used to engage in a crime in a different nation. All of these factors and more should be considered in dealing with the problem of computer crimes.

Computer Crime Investigations

Computer crime investigations are dynamic in nature. Therefore, their detection and investigation differ in several respects from the investigation of other more traditional crimes. These differences include:

- Physical evidence in computer crimes is different from that in traditional crimes.
- The volume of evidence encountered can be burdensome.
- Offenders can commit their crimes with ease.
- Offenders can destroy evidence with ease.

Such investigations require a greater amount of technical expertise by investigators and prosecutors. Despite the contrasts cited earlier, certain approaches of the computer crime investigation remain consistent. For example, such investigations generally require a considerable investment of time, sometimes taking from one month to a full year in duration. This is due, in part, to the fact that identification and analysis of data are necessary to organize information for complicated search warrants. In addition, the investigation of computer crime requires interaction between investigators and victims. The victims, because of their knowledge of computer systems, can aid the investigator in providing technical expertise.

Another commonality in computer crime investigations is that they are largely investigative in nature (i.e., standard investigative procedures can be employed): an estimated 90 percent traditional police work and 10 percent technical skill.[14]

Yet another distinguishing attribute of computer crime investigations is that they are typically proactive in nature. Proactive initiatives include the monitoring of electronic bulletin boards and regular contact with local schools and businesses to help prevent and detect possible crimes with computers.

Classification of Computer Crimes

Because computers have been used in almost all types of crimes, classification will extend beyond the simple category of white-collar crime. The computer crime involves the use of both computer hardware and software. **Hardware** is generally considered the physical computer itself and any peripherals associated with it, such as printers, telephone modems, external disk drives, and so on. **Software,** conversely, refers to the medium on which information is stored (e.g., computer tapes and floppy disks).

During the mid-1970s, the federal government attempted to amend the U.S. Criminal Code to make crimes of unauthorized acts in, around, and with the use of computers. In 1986, President Reagan authorized another law, outlawing the illegal use of computers: the Electronic Communications Privacy Act. This law basically prohibits eavesdropping on electronic mail, conversations on cellular phones, video conference calls, and computer-to-computer transactions.

In recent years, four main categories of computer crime have been identified:

1. The introduction of fraudulent records or data into a computer system.
2. Unauthorized use of computer-related facilities.
3. The alteration or destruction of information or files.
4. The stealing, whether by electronic means or otherwise, of money, financial instruments, property, services, or valuable data.

Computer crime has also been classified by the types of information loss, including modification, destruction, disclosure, and use or denial of use. These violations can involve changing information, prohibiting access to information, and removing or copying it wrongfully.

Typical Forms of Computer Crimes

Many computer crimes take the form of traditional crimes. They may, however, also concern special crimes in which the computer is the primary tool of the criminal of such crimes. These crimes have been labeled according to their criminal function and include computer hacking, scanning, masquerading, false data entry, Trojan horses, computer viruses, and others.

Computer Hacking.   In its most favorable use, the term *computer hacker* signifies a compulsive computer programmer who explores, tests, and pushes the computer to its limits, regardless of its consequences. In reality, it can involve the destruction of valuable data, resulting in massive costs. According to a report issued by the NIJ, the typical computer hacker is a juvenile possessing a home computer with a telephone modem who uses electronic bulletin boards for a variety of illegal purposes. Such criminals may become involved in crimes such as credit card fraud and using unauthorized numbers to arrange mail-order purchases to vacant homes where the delivery can be intercepted and kept.

Scanning.   Scanning is the process of presenting sequentially changing information to an automated system to identify those items receiving a positive response. The method typically is used to identify telephone numbers that access computers, user identifications, passwords that facilitate access to computers, and credit card numbers that are used illegally for purchasing merchandise or services through telemarketing. Many computer systems can deter scanners by limiting the number of access attempts and therefore create a long delay designed to discourage the scanning process.

Masquerading.   Masquerading is the most common activity of computer system intruders. It is also one of the most difficult to prove once the case goes to trial. It is the process of one person assuming the identity of an authorized computer user by acquiring items, knowledge, or characteristics. For one to have physical access to a computer terminal or system, many such systems require that the user enter a specified identifier such as a security code or password. Anyone possessing the correct security code or password can masquerade as another person.

An example of a clever masquerade occurred when a young man posed as a magazine writer and called on a telephone company, indicating that he was writing an article on the computer system used by the phone company. The conversation revealed a detailed briefing on all of the computer facilities and applications systems. As a result, the perpetrator was able to steal more than $1 million worth of telephone equipment from the company.

Evidence showing the act of masquerading is difficult to obtain. When an intrusion occurs, the investigator must obtain evidence identifying the masquerader at a terminal as performing the acts producing the events in the computer. This task is especially difficult when network-weaving connections through several switched telephone systems interfere with tracing devices (e.g., pen registers and dialed number recorders).

False Data Entry (Data Diddling).   The false data entry type of computer crime is usually the simplest, safest, and most commonly used method. It involves changing data before or during their input to computers. Generally, anybody associated with or having access to the process of recording, encoding, examining, checking, converting, updating, or transforming data that ultimately are entered in a computer can change these data.

A typical example of a false data entry, or **data diddling,** is the case of a timekeeping clerk who filled out data forms of hours worked by 300 employees in a railroad company department. He noticed that all data on the forms entered into the timekeeping and payroll system on the computer included both the name and employee number of each worker. However, the computer used only employee numbers for processing. He also noticed that outside the computer, all manual processing and control were based only on employee names, because nobody identified people by their numbers.

He took advantage of this situation by filling out forms for overtime hours worked, using the names of employees who frequently worked overtime, but entering his own employee number. The scheme was successful for years until detected by an auditor examining W-2s, who noticed the clerk's unusually high annual income. A subsequent examination of the timekeeping computer files and data forms and a discussion with the clerk's supervisor revealed the source of the income.

Trojan Horses.   The **Trojan horse** method is the secret placement or alteration of computer instructions so that the computer will tell a second computer how to perform illegal functions. It is unique in that it will usually also allow the victim computer to perform most or all of the functions for its originally intended purposes. The Trojan horse program is also the primary method used for inserting instructions for other abusive acts, such as logic bombs, salami attacks, and viruses.

In 1981, one Trojan horse technique, the electronic letter bomb attack, received considerable news media attention because its use would have made most computers with terminal-to-terminal communication vulnerable to compromise. The attack method consisted of sending messages to other terminals with embedded control characters ending with the send-line or the block-mode control command. When the messages reach the intelligent terminals, the send line or block control command is sensed, and the entire message is sent back to the computer for execution of the embedded control character commands as though they came from the victim at the receiving terminal with all of his or her computer access authority.

Many local police computers are linked with state and national crime information networks. The Trojan horse technique can be prevented in two ways. First, send-line or block-mode types of commands can be removed from all terminals allowed access to the computer. Next, a logic filter can be placed in the computer to prevent all control character commands from being sent in terminal-to-terminal messages. Trojan horses can be detected by comparing a copy of the operational program under suspicion with a master or other copy known to be free of unauthorized changes. Second, the suspect program can be tested with a wide range of data that might expose the purpose of the Trojan horse.

Computer Viruses.   A **computer virus** is a set of computer instructions that reproduces itself in computer programs when they are executed within unauthorized programs. The program may be inserted through a special program designed for that purpose or through use of a Trojan horse—hidden instructions inserted into a computer program that the victim uses. Then the virus multiplies itself into other programs when they are executed, creating new viruses. Such programs can lie dormant in computer systems for weeks or even months and may infect entire computer networks, rendering them useless. Although the first three cases of computer viruses were reported in November 1987, hundreds of subsequent cases have since appeared in various academic and research cultures. Some cases have emerged as a result of disgruntled employees of computer program manufacturers who have contaminated products during delivery to customers.

Investigators should first interview the victims to identify the nature of the suspected attack. They should then use the necessary tools (not resident system utilities) to examine the contents after a suspected event.

Superzapping.   This superzapping technique stems from Superzapper, a macro or utility program used in most IBM mainframe computer centers as a systems tool. Most computer centers have a secure operating mode that requires a "break-glass-in-case-of-emergency" program that will bypass all controls to disclose any of the contents of the computer. Illegal use of the Superzapper program enables thieves, for example, to tinker with the program so that checks can be issued to their private accounts.

Salami Techniques.   The salami technique is an automated form of the Trojan horse method where small amounts of assets (i.e., money) are taken from specified accounts or sources and where the whole appears to be unaffected. In this way, over time, a substantial amount of money can be diverted to the thief's personal account while going undetected.

Trap Doors.   A trap door is a technique in which programmers insert debugging aids that break security codes in the computer and then insert an additional code of their own. This enables entry into the program for such purposes as false data entry.

Logic Bombs.   A logic bomb is a set of instructions inserted in a computer program that looks for specific errors in a computer's normal functioning. Once identified, the logic bomb kicks into action and exploits the error identified. The end result is the victim computer reacting in certain ways that might result in crashing of the program.

Asynchronous Attacks.   Many computer functions rely on the asynchronous functioning of a computer to complete certain functions, such as calling for the output of certain reports in a predesignated order. Frequently, many such functions are programmed into the computer at once. The asynchronous attack confuses the computer system, making it unable to differentiate one job from another.

Computer Program Piracy.   Piracy is the unauthorized copying and use of computer programs in violation of copyright and trade secret laws.

Automatic Teller Machine Frauds

Most states that have a computer crime statute include a provision for fraudulent use of ATMs. Typically, the ATM fraud involves persons with legitimate bank accounts who made fraudulent deposits (e.g., depositing empty envelopes) and then withdrew money from those accounts based on those deposits. Although most banks now use cameras to photograph customers, cases are difficult to make because suspects are difficult to locate. [*Note:* ATMs are also becoming targets of theft by criminals who simply steal the entire ATM machine. This decreases their risk of being shot while committing the crime, and often enables them to steal more money than in other types of commercial robberies.])

The Preliminary Investigation of Computer Crimes

As with any preliminary investigation, each department's standard operating procedure should be followed regarding dealing with victims, evidence, and suspects. Investigators should remember that computer crimes will involve persons who communicate in a language that may be difficult to understand. Because of this, a computer expert should be identified to assist him or her in the course of the investigation. Indeed, it is imperative that every aspect of the investigation be fully understood throughout the inquiry.

The degree of cooperation by the victim will also vary from one investigation to the next. Precluding the possibility that the victim is also a suspect in the case, it is imperative that they understand that maximum cooperation is required to achieve both positive results and to avoid wasting much valuable time. Another problem encountered in computer crime cases is that often midway through the investigation, the victim will decide to settle for restitution and not pursue the prosecution further. Therefore, investigators should be assured by the victim that they will see the case through to the end and be willing to testify in court.

Jurisdiction is another important variable to consider early in the investigation of computer crimes. Often, a suspect computer will have been used in facilitating a crime in another jurisdiction because of complex computer networking. It is necessary, therefore, to determine what federal, state, or local laws might apply to the type of computer crime committed.

Evidence Considerations

As in the preparation of any case for criminal prosecution, the collection and preservation of evidence are critical elements (Figure 22.6). Experience has shown that the most typical defense ploy in a computer crime case is to attack the admissibility of evidence seized. Such attacks often result in the suppression of evidence that might otherwise easily incriminate the suspect.

Obtaining Computer Crime Evidence. It is fairly easy to obtain documents in computer crime cases, as such documents are easily identified by noncomputer experts. These include computer manuals, program documentation, logs, data and program input forms, and computer-printed forms. Ascertaining whether they are complete, originals, or copies can be determined by document custodians.

Requesting specific program documentation may require assistance and knowledge of computer concepts to determine the extent and types of documentation required. In addition, taking possession of other computer media may be more complicated. Magnetic tapes and diskettes, for example, are usually labeled externally. Additionally, a large tape or disk file may reside on more than one reel or cartridge. In this case, assistance may be needed to check the contents of a tape or disk by using a comparable computer. The search for information inside a computer is usually highly complex and will probably require the aid of an expert. Preparing a search warrant for this task will also require expert advice. In both cases, expert advice can come from the following sources:

- Systems analysts
- Programmers who wrote the programs
- Staff who prepared the data in computer-readable form
- Tape librarians
- Electronic maintenance engineers who maintain the hardware

Advice and help from such people will aid the investigator in his or her role in the investigation. Once the case goes to court, the same people can offer expert testimony to establish the integrity and reliability of the evidence seized.

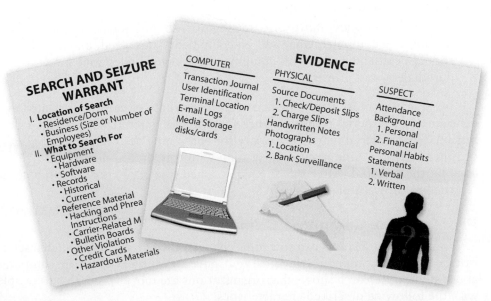

Figure 22.6 Computer evidence.
From National Institute of Justice, Research in Brief: Computer Crime, *U.S. Government Printing Office, Washington, DC, 2004*

Examining Evidence for Criminal Content. Computers can maintain an extremely large amount of information in a small amount of space. A floppy disk is small enough to fit inside a pocket and can easily be hidden in books or taped to the bottom of a keyboard. A floppy can hold more than enough information to make a case by providing direct evidence or direction to evidence.

If there is printer activity, this information can require a great deal of time to sort through. It is important not to blindly push this potential evidence aside; doing so may very well cost a case. Buried deep inside the amount of paper could be the secret bank account number where the suspects have hidden their assets or their list of past, present, and future victims for rape and murder.[15]

Preserving Computer Crime Evidence. Determing if the evidence can be collected and preserved for future analysis is not as easy as it sounds. Investigators must check their warrants constantly for what they can and cannot seize. If something is found that is needed but is not covered in a search warrant, the wording must be amended before seizure of that item can proceed. Seizing materials not included in a search warrant could cost an investigator the success of an entire investigation.

Some types of computer evidence require special care and attention. Because of this, storage areas must be controlled and special care must be given to protect the evidence from physical damage. Certain care measures are required for the most common types of computer evidence:

- *Magnetic tape and disks.* Handle with care. This type of evidence is also easily destroyed by exposure to magnetic fields such as stereo speakers and printers.

- *Printed computer listings.* No restrictions on storage are required for paper printouts of computerized data except that they should not be stored in direct sunlight. This practice will reduce the chance of fading.

- *Computer.* All types of computers are sensitive—be careful. Even when a computer is turned off, disruption by moving can occur. If there is a hard drive, it should be "parked" before being moved, to avoid destroying information contained on the disk.

- *Additional computer hardware.* Investigators should document the configuration of a computer, what add-on equipment is involved, and how it should be disconnected. This equipment can include telephone modems, autodialers, and printers.

Investigators must also remember that the owners of computer-related evidence may have special problems when the evidence is removed from their possession. Such material may be necessary for continuing their legitimate business or other activities. One manner of dealing with this situation is to arrange for copying the material. After this is accomplished, the copy, not the original, is returned to the rightful owner.

Profile of the Computer Criminal

Computer crimes suspects can sometimes be identified on the basis of characteristics of known computer criminals who have been interviewed in computer abuse studies. Research shows that organizations are more vulnerable to people with the following described characteristics:

- *Age.* Most perpetrators are young and were educated in colleges and universities where computer attacks are common and sometimes condoned as "educational activity."

- *Skills and knowledge.* Most suspects will be among the most skilled and higher-performing technologists. This is seen, in particular, in organizations in which a worker is overqualified for the work that he or she is doing.

- *Positions of trust.* In most cases, perpetrators perform their acts while working at their jobs. Investigators should anticipate that vulnerabilities identified will usually result in the most qualified person taking advantage of them.

- *Assistance.* Perpetrators in many types of computer crime have been known to need assistance. This is because computer crimes require more knowledge and access than one person usually possesses.

- *Differential association.* Frequently, people working together may encourage each other to engage in unauthorized acts that escalate into serious crimes.

- *Robin Hood syndrome.* Most computer crime perpetrators interviewed in the study differentiated between harming people and organizations, the latter of which was easily condoned. In addition, they rationalized that they were only harming a computer and not causing any loss to people or organizations.

Interviewing the Computer Crime Suspect

To investigate computer crime, investigators should have a thorough understanding of the damage that a suspect can do in the computing facility. For example, if an employee believes that he or she is a suspect, the employee may have the means to go into the computer system and destroy valuable evidence, even after the crime has been committed. In addition, logic bombs could be inserted into the computer to render the system dysfunctional. In all cases, suspects should be restricted from access to the computer system once becoming a suspect except under strictly supervised conditions.

In addition, a criminal background check should be performed on both the suspect and victim. This is particularly important in computer crime cases because most employers fail to do this. Many suspects will voluntarily talk with investigators, as they may feel that their actions might be unethical or immoral but not criminal in nature.

DISCUSSION QUESTIONS

1. List and discuss the five most common techniques used by traffickers to launder illicitly gained drug currency.

2. What is meant by the term *confidence game*?

3. Explain the details of the pigeon drop scam and why it is used so widely.

4. Why do so many people fall victim to scams?

5. List and discuss the types of crimes, both traditional and nontraditional, that are facilitated through the use of computers.

6. Discuss the crime and consequences of introducing a computer virus into a computer system.

7. Discuss the steps that investigators should consider during the preliminary investigation phase of the computer crime investigation.

8. What role does the victim play during investigation of a computer crime?

9. List and discuss the primary types of computer crime evidence and how it should be collected and preserved.

10. In a computer crime, why is it important for investigators to move quickly in the investigation once a suspect has been developed?

NOTES

1. BAYLES, F. (1999). Man, millions vanish in Greenwich, Conn. *USA Today,* June 29, p. 4A.
2. BLOCK, S. (1999). Fugitive goes from high life to prison cell. *USA Today,* September 7, p. 3A.
3. U.S. BUREAU OF JUSTICE STATISTICS (1986, Nov.). National Institute of Justice, The impact of white collar crime in America. *Research in Brief,* Washington, DC: U.S. Department of Justice.
4. ADAMS, M. (2000). Careless cargo. *USA Today.* January 26, p. 1B.
5. SHERRILL, R. (1997, Apr. 7). A year in corporate crime. *The Nation,* pp. 11–12.
6. Ibid.
7. Ibid.
8. PRESIDENT'S COMMISSION ON ORGANIZED CRIME (1984). *The impact.* Washington, DC: U.S. Government Printing Office.
9. FBI (2000). www.fbi.gov.
10. MANEY, K., and P. MCMAHON (2000). "Love bug" virus created in ordinary petri dish. *USA Today,* May 15, pp. 1A–2A.
11. PERRY, R. (1986). *Computer crime.* New York: Franklin Watts.
12. ROSNOFF, S. M., et al. (1998). *Profit without honor.* Upper Saddle River, NJ: Prentice Hall.
13. Hacker's ransom. (2000). *USA Today,* January 11, p. 3A.
14. NATIONAL INSTITUTE OF JUSTICE (1989, June). National Institute of Justice, *Research in brief,* Washington, DC: U.S. Department of Justice.
15. CLARK, F., and K. DILIBERTO (1996). *Investigating computer crime.* Boca Raton, FL: CRC Press.

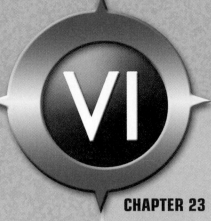

VI

Prosecution

CHAPTER 23 ▶ Preparation for Court

Key Terms

▶ credibility

▶ cross-examination

▶ demeanor

▶ direct examination

▶ expert witness

▶ pretrial conference

▶ testimony

This chapter will enable you to:

• Learn the role of pretrial procedures in prosecution of the defendant.

• Understand how the criminal trial process operates.

• Consider the characteristics of the jury in a criminal trial.

• List the functions of the opening and closing arguments.

• Evaluate the differences between direct and cross-examination.

• Learn how the investigator prepares for court.

• Understand the techniques most commonly used by defense attorneys to discredit an investigator's testimony.

• Learn the importance of good courtroom demeanor when testifying in court.

• Understand the role of the expert witness in a criminal prosecution.

INTRODUCTION

Not all criminal cases go to trial. In fact, most are settled outside the courtroom through the plea-bargaining process. For those cases that make it to the trial stage, however, it is imperative that the evidence be well organized and that the investigator, who is essentially the "star witness," be prepared to give skilled courtroom testimony in the case. As we have discussed throughout the book, the admissibility of evidence in court is the compelling reason for investigators to follow closely the correct procedures in evidence collection. Once investigators are satisfied that the evidence has been collected appropriately, the question of how best to present the evidence to the judge and jurors is addressed. For such a critical task, the role of the investigator in the courtroom is not always understood by all investigators. After all, police officers spend most of their time on the street and not in the courtroom. In this chapter, we examine several critical aspects of the courtroom process and how this important criminal justice function interacts with the duties of the criminal investigator.

PREPARING FOR TRIAL

The importance of proper trial preparation cannot be overemphasized. In some instances, officers are overly casual about their prospective trial appearances. This often results in them appearing in court unprepared to testify effectively. The following principles should be understood and observed by officers in efforts to adequately prepare for court presentation.

First, officers should cooperate fully with prosecutors in the preparation of trial testimony and other evidence (see Figure 23.1). Requests from the prosecutor's office should be complied with in all respects where possible. If for some reason the request cannot be fulfilled, the prosecutor's office should be made aware of the problem and alternate plans mutually agreed upon. Sometimes poor relations between the prosecutor's office and the police department cause a lack of communication or cooperation between these agencies. Such problems benefit no one but the criminals being brought to trial. Police agency managers must make it clear to all police officers that full and willing cooperation with prosecutors is expected by the department. Political feuds, "turf wars," personality conflicts, and the like cannot be tolerated. If a problem arises, it should be resolved quickly and without regard to who was right and who was wrong, and steps should be taken by the department to minimize the possibility of the same problem arising again in the future.

One of the typical areas of conflict between prosecutors and police revolves around the issue of when a case presented by the police will be brought to trial by the prosecutor's office. When the prosecutor declines to prosecute or a pretrial plea bargain is arranged that appears to be excessively favorable to the defendant, it is sometimes difficult for police officers who have labored on the case to understand why the matter is not being carried forward to trial. Police resentment toward the prosecutor's office is frequently the result. Officers must understand that the prosecutor's job is a difficult one, and that sometimes hard decisions have to be made, decisions that may be unpopular with the police and others. For example, the heavy workload burdening the average prosecutor's office and the lack of adequate manpower to deal with that workload sometimes limit the number of cases that can be brought to trial. The result may be

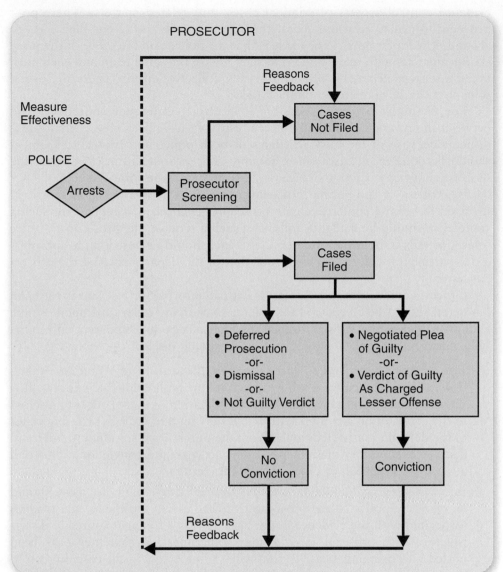

Figure 23.1 Diagram of the relationship between police and prosecutors.

plea bargains or a decision not to go to trial on minor cases or on those cases that appear to the prosecutor to be weak or to have technical problems that may make a successful trial result doubtful. The prosecutors are in the best position to judge the strength of the case and the probability of conviction, and officers should be sufficiently well versed in the rules of evidence and the realities of the criminal justice system to accept the prosecutor's decision without resentment or recrimination. Blaming the prosecutor for the shortcomings of the judicial process is counterproductive and should be avoided.

This is not to say that all prosecutors are blameless where difficult working relationships develop between their office and the police. Prosecutors often share in the problem by not providing appropriate and timely feedback to police personnel on case progress and decisions, failing to brief officers adequately prior to trial, failing to work cooperatively with officers responsible for the evidence control aspects of criminal cases, and related matters. Where poor prosecutor–police relations exist, there is generally sufficient blame to go around. The larger point to be made is that the police and the office of the prosecutor must come to understand that they are on the same team and each must take those steps necessary to maximize their collective efforts. There are several steps that can be taken to accomplish this.

For example, wherever possible, a **pretrial conference** should be held between the prosecutor and all officers testifying in a given case. Often this is difficult because of the busy schedules of both police and prosecutors, but it should be done in all cases where feasible and without fail in cases involving serious crimes or in those in which the testimony may be complicated.[1]

Regardless of the normal procedure, in any case in which police officers involved feel that a conference with prosecutors is needed, a request for such a conference should be made. If, following such a request, the prosecutor's office refuses or fails to hold the conference, this fact should be noted in the appropriate departmental records for the protection of the department and the officers concerned.

Officers should provide prosecutors with all information relevant to the case. No detail should be considered too minor, since many cases turn upon minute factual or legal points, the significance of which may become apparent only in the full context of the trial. In particular, officers should disclose the following:

1. *Information beneficial to the defendant (disclosure of exculpatory evidence).* The prosecution's job is to convict the guilty, not the innocent. It is therefore the ethical as well as the legal obligation of every officer to disclose to the prosecution any information that may tend to establish the innocence of the defendant as well as guilt. From the purely legal standpoint, failure to disclose exculpatory matters may lead to a wrongful conviction, a mistrial, a reversal on appeal, or other unfavorable results.

2. *Information revealing flaws in the prosecution's case.* Full disclosure should be made by police to the prosecutor's office of any problems that may be associated with the evidence in the case. This is a frequent source of dissatisfaction with prosecutors, who may sometimes feel that they have been misled into bringing a case to trial when some defect in the case, known to the police but unknown to the prosecutors, makes conviction unlikely. For example, if an officer knows or suspects that a search was or may have been unlawful or an arrest invalid, the problem should be disclosed to the prosecutor, either in the written report, during the pretrial conference, or by other means. This is not an easy thing for an officer to do, especially if the defect is due to some error on the part of the officer, but candor is vital, however painful or embarrassing it may be. In many instances, the prosecutor who is aware of such a problem may be able to deal with it effectively at the trial, avoiding adverse consequences from the defect. By contrast, when such a defect surfaces unexpectedly during the trial, the prosecutor is often powerless to save the situation, with resultant embarrassment for all concerned. Advance disclosure, however painful, greatly minimizes the potential ill effects of flaws in any case.

3. *Familiarity with the rules of evidence.* Officers should be familiar with the basic rules of evidence applicable to the court in which the trial is to be held. Although dealing with evidentiary questions at the trial is the province of

the prosecutor and such questions will ultimately be decided by the trial judge, an understanding of the applicable rules of admissibility will assist police in several ways, including the following:

- It will enable officers to identify, and discuss with prosecutors, possible flaws in the case prior to the trial date.
- It will help officers prepare and give their testimony, since fundamental errors (such as testifying in a form that will render the testimony inadmissible hearsay) can be avoided.
- It will help officers to understand the reasons behind a prosecutor's strategy in the trial of a given case, and will also help them to accept the decision without resentment when a prosecutor decides not to take a case to trial because of evidentiary problems.

Prior to the trial date, officers should review carefully all reports and other documents relevant to the case to ensure that the officers are completely familiar with all of the pertinent facts. The more complex the case, the more important this step becomes. Nothing destroys the chances of a conviction more quickly than a police officer on the witness stand who is visibly unfamiliar with the facts and whose testimony is thus lame, incomplete, and generally lacking in credibility to the jury.

4. *Notes and reports in the courtroom.* In many instances, officers may wish to carry reports or other documents into the courtroom for reference while they are testifying. In some types of cases, particularly traffic cases, this is routine in many courts. However, in any case in which the use by police officers of notes, reports, or other items to refresh memory is not automatic or routine in that particular court, the officer should discuss with the prosecutor in advance of the court date the necessity for, and the desirability of, carrying such aids with the officer to the witness stand. Although rules of evidence vary in different courts, in general anything that the officer uses while on the witness stand to refresh memory may be seen by the defense attorneys and may be used by them to cross-examine the officer or otherwise to attack the prosecution's case. Thus, the decision to take such items into the courtroom for use during testimony is not a matter to be taken lightly, and it should be discussed fully with the prosecutor prior to the trial whenever possible.

5. *Physical evidence.* Procedures for getting evidence and related materials to court vary among jurisdictions. In some cases, the prosecutor's office may take custody of evidence that is planned for introduction in court in a pending trial and make arrangements for its availability at trial. In other instances, it falls upon the police department to ensure that evidence requested by the prosecutor is available in court in accordance with established schedules provided by the prosecutor. Whatever the arrangement, police should provide any assistance requested by, or necessary to, the prosecution to ensure that all of the physical evidence pertinent to the case will be available at the time of trial. This includes, for example, transporting exhibits to the courtroom and ensuring the availability of any supporting documentation (e.g., chain-of-evidence receipts) that may be needed. Laboratory certificates or other forensic reports that may be required in connection with the case should also be ready for presentation.

6. *Witnesses.* Failure of witnesses to appear at trial is a recurrent problem and one that often results in dismissal of criminal charges against defendants or failure of the prosecution's case. Officers should provide prosecutors with assistance as needed in ensuring that witnesses will be present and ready to testify on the day of the trial. The extent of this assistance will depend on local practice and any requests that may be made by the prosecutor's office in a specific case. In some jurisdictions, for example, victim and witness advocates are available to assist in this effort. Ideally, the prosecutor's office might fulfill most or all of these functions, but caseloads and lack of manpower often make it impossible for the prosecutor to interview witnesses adequately in advance of the trial. In addition, the police officer has usually dealt personally with the witness(es) during the investigative stage of the case and may therefore be the person best able to work with the witness in the trial phase and to make certain that the witness is ready, willing, and able to testify as planned. Therefore, unless local practice or a specific request dictates otherwise, officers should be prepared to ensure that witnesses:

   • Have been informed of the date, time, and place of trial;

   • Have transportation to the place of trial;

   • Have been adequately informed of what is expected of them during testimony;

   • Have been advised to respond truthfully to questions posed to them on the stand;

   • Have been advised to state facts and not to offer personal opinions or conjecture while on the stand unless requested to do so by the prosecutor; and

   • Have been briefed on any other matters that will enable the witness to testify in a timely and effective manner.[2]

Police officers should also ascertain whether the witnesses have any questions regarding the trial, whether regarding legal matters or other aspects of the witnesses' appearance in court. Questions that the officer cannot readily and fully answer should be referred to the prosecutor for clarification and the clarification transmitted to the witness.

7. *Communication with defense attorneys.* Defense attorneys will frequently attempt to interview police officers about a case in the hope of developing information that will enable them to achieve a favorable result for their clients. There should be no communication between officers and defense attorneys regarding pending criminal cases without the express approval of the prosecutor's office.[3]

8. *Testifying for the defendant.* On some occasions, the defense attorney may summon a police officer as a witness on the defendant's behalf. This places the police officer in an extremely awkward position. The generally accepted practice is that "officers shall not testify for a defendant in any criminal case without being legally summoned to appear, prior knowledge of the agency chief executive, and written authorization of the prosecutor's office." However, it should be pointed out that regardless of department policy or any other factor, if the officer is subpoenaed by the defense and the subpoena is not quashed, the officer is obligated to appear and testify. Any officer receiving such a subpoena should immediately notify the officer's

supervisor (or other designated department official) and the prosecutor's office.

Going to Court

Before actually attending the criminal court proceeding, officers should ready themselves for the situation. One of the first steps is for the officer to prepare himself or herself psychologically, by strengthening feelings of confidence and self-assurance. Officers should also realize that as witnesses, they are also on display, as they are when on duty. It is a simple fact that the general public expects more stringent behavior from a law enforcement officer than from an average citizen. As a result, the following steps should be followed before entering a courtroom:

- Know which courtroom you'll be testifying in. If you are unfamiliar with the particular courthouse or courtroom, check it out before the trial so that you will know your way around.

- Do not discuss anything about the case in public or where your conversation might be overheard. Anyone could be a juror or defense witness.

- Treat people with respect, as if they were the judge or a juror. Your professionalism, politeness, and courtesy will be noted and remembered, especially by those who see you in court in an official capacity.

- Do not discuss your personal life, official business, biases, prejudices, likes and dislikes, or controversial subjects in public, for the same reasons as listed above. You might impress a judge, juror, or witness the wrong way.

- Judges and attorneys have little patience with officers appearing in court late, so be on time. Know when you will be expected to testify.

- Dress appropriately. Look businesslike and official. If in uniform, it should be neat, clean, and complete. If not in uniform, a sport coat and slacks are as appropriate as a business suit.

- Avoid contact with the defense counsel and any defense witnesses before the trial. Assume that they will try to get you to say something about the case to their advantage.

These suggestions, in addition to the pretrial conference, will prepare an officer well for the courtroom experience. Above all, however, officers are expected to tell the truth.

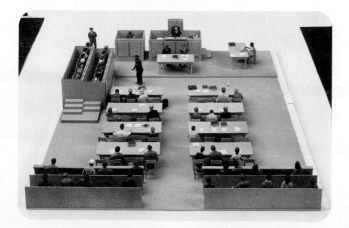

Figure 23.2 A model of a courtroom. *Steve Gorton, © Dorling Kindersley*

THE INVESTIGATOR AS A PROFESSIONAL WITNESS

The **testimony** given by the investigator is a crucial part of any criminal trial. An experienced and knowledgeable witness can make the job of the prosecutor and subsequent conviction of the defendant much easier. Conversely, a witness who is disorganized, unkempt, and unclear in thought can inadvertently sabotage even the best of criminal cases.

Preparing for Court

The best way for investigators to prepare for trial is not to wait for one or two days before trial to get organized, but to keep the rules of evidence in mind from the beginning of the investigation through its closure (months, even years in some cases). In addition, the investigator should be sure to meet with the prosecutor sometime before trial for the pretrial conference. The officer should check all personal reports and notes pertaining to the case and be sure that he or she has sufficient information to respond to the anticipated "who, what, when, where, why, and how" questions.

Reviewing Evidence and Reports

Before the trial, the investigator should go back over his or her list of evidence and be sure that all is accounted for and easily identifiable. The chain of custody should also be reexamined to be sure that all necessary persons who were involved with the evidence will be available if needed to testify in court. The investigator should also consider how the evidence will be transported to court and who will maintain possession of it once the court proceeding is under way. In the case of drug or forensic evidence, it is likely that the police chemist will already have custody and transport it to court. The investigator, however, might be required to locate and transport other items in evidence, such as written statements, cassettes or videotapes of transactions and statements, or photographs. All such evidence should be closely reviewed by the officer before trial.

Because the investigator may not testify solely from notes and reports, they should be reviewed before the trial. Although lawful and appropriate to do so, the defense attorney may inquire of the officer on the witness stand whether this was done before trial and may even attempt to take custody of the report to place into evidence under the "past recollection recorded" exception to the

Figure 23.3 Prosecutor examining criminal investigator.

hearsay rule. If the defense attorney gains access to the official report of the investigator, the report will be used to attack the **credibility** of the investigator. One typical defense ploy is to attack the credibility of the officer by highlighting any inconsistencies between the testimony given by the officer and what is reflected in the official report. An inconsistency can be just about anything but includes both facts testified to that differ from the report or a seemingly important fact in the report that the witness failed to mention in his or her testimony.

In the event that this occurs, it is usually a better idea to acknowledge the discrepancy and not become defensive about it. The prosecutor can then decide whether or not to "clean up" the problem through additional questioning if it appears to be of any consequence to the prosecution's strategy.

Credibility as a Witness

Other than the technique cited earlier, defense attorneys will use other means to attack an officer's credibility. This is usually accomplished through attempting to demonstrate the officer's bias, or that he or she is lying. Bias can be raised in many different circumstances. For example, the defense attorney can try to convince the jury that the officer is just trying to protect his or her "conviction" record by embellishing his or her answers to make the suspect look more guilty, thus resulting in a conviction.

In addition, racial bias can sometimes be argued if the defendant is a minority and a different ethnic background from the officer. In this case, the officer must testify only to the facts of the case that indicate guilt of the defendant, not on stereotypic perceptions of the defendant's racial or ethnic group. Credibility can also be attacked on the basis of the officer's reputation for truthfulness. This is most typically used against undercover officers, who are required to work proactively and assume a false identity (e.g., a cover story and an assumed name). It is common for the attorney to have the officer affirm that he or she was required to "lie" while working undercover and then turn around and try to convince the jury that the officer is a liar by nature. If successful, the defense can argue that the investigator's testimony is not credible.

Appearance in Court

If for any reason it appears that the officer will be late in appearing for a court date, or will be unable to appear at all at the specified time, he or she must notify the court as soon as possible. The notification should include the officer's name, the defendant's name, the court in which the appearance is scheduled (including the name of the presiding judge if known), and the reason for the absence or tardiness. When absence or tardiness occurs, the matter should be reviewed by the officer's supervisor or other designated department official. If the reasons are inadequate, the matter may be referred for disciplinary action.

Some fail to appreciate the importance of the officer's physical appearance and personal conduct while the officer is testifying in court. In reality, these matters are of the greatest possible significance and literally can make or break a case. In this regard, there are several matters that officers should know when appearing in court.

Officers should dress appropriately when testifying in court. The International Association of Chiefs of Police (IACP) states that officers' personal appearance in court should "conform to the highest professional police standards." Uniformed personnel should wear the departmental uniform approved for such appearances; detectives and other plainclothes personnel should conform to their departmental dress standards for courtroom testimony.[5] Whether the officer is in uniform or in civilian dress, the clothing should be neat and clean, shoes should be shined, and similar matters attended to. This is not just a matter of departmental pride; psychological studies reveal that jurors frequently give less credibility to the testimony of witnesses who are dressed sloppily. This is why exceptional care is taken by defense attorneys in dressing their clients (particularly in high-profile cases) in the most appropriate clothing. If the officer is in civilian clothes, conservative dress is normally appropriate. Extreme styles of clothing may prove distracting to the jurors, causing them to pay less attention to the substance of the officer's testimony and even in some cases arousing hostility toward the officer. Although the investigator may wear faded blue jeans when on duty, it is important for him or her to dress more formally for court. Some disagreement exists in this area, as some think that the witness's choice of clothing should coincide with the atmosphere of the community. Others believe that a uniformed officer should wear plain clothes in court to avoid the authoritarian appearance depicted by the uniform.

The foregoing are general rules only; departmental guidelines regarding courtroom attire should be followed at all times. This includes specific courtroom regulations regarding the carrying of firearms in the courtroom.

Courtroom Demeanor

The investigator should also remember that a certain amount of theatrics also plays a role in a trial. Both the judge and jury will be watching the investigator's **demeanor** closely as well as listening to what he or she has to say. First impressions can make a difference. Juries expect a certain type of person as a police witness. They expect that an organized, intelligent, serious, no-nonsense kind of person will be representing the government. There are times, however, when witnesses may reveal a sense of humor, and the jury can be impressed. Such displays of humor in the courtroom should not be directed toward anyone in particular and should be made with caution so as not to offend any member of the jury.

TESTIFYING IN COURT

The manner in which an officer testifies may be as important as the content of the testimony. An officer's conduct on the stand often determines the degree of credibility that will be given to the officer's statements by the jury. Thus, the demeanor of the officer on the stand may be critical to the outcome of the case. Officers should remember that a trial is an adversarial proceeding and that defense attorneys will not hesitate to take advantage of any shortcomings displayed by the officer while on the witness stand. Therefore, officers must keep several principles in mind while testifying in court, including the following:

1. *Confine the testimony to known facts.* Officers should normally restrict their statements to those that are personally known by them to be the truth. If the officer is making a statement based on information or belief only, that should be made clear in the testimony. Defense attorneys are skilled at finding discrepancies in an officer's testimony and employing those discrepancies to the detriment of the officer and the prosecution's case.

2. *Avoid expressing opinions or conclusions except when these are specifically authorized by the rules of evidence.* Police officers normally testify as "lay witnesses," meaning that they should state only facts and not express opinions or engage in conjecture or speculation. In some specific instances, lay witnesses are permitted to express opinions, and this applies to police officers as well as to any other witness. However, officers should not offer opinions or conclusions on **direct examination** unless an opinion or conclusion has been specifically solicited by the prosecutor. Officers should avoid expressing opinions during **cross-examination** by the defense attorney; when the defense attempts to get an officer to express an opinion, it is usually with the intent of employing that opinion to embarrass the officer and discredit the officer's testimony. If the defense attorney on cross-examination asks the officer to express an opinion, the officer should delay answering to allow the prosecution an opportunity to object.

3. *Do not volunteer information.* Officers should respond only to the question asked. They should not volunteer information over and above the minimum required to answer the question posed. There are two reasons for this.

   First, if the officer is testifying on direct examination, the prosecutor is intentionally attempting to place specific facts before the jury in a predetermined order. If the officer volunteers information that has not been requested, this may disrupt the prosecution's presentation of the case.[6] It may also provide the defense with an unexpected windfall that the defense can exploit to the benefit of the defendant and the detriment of the prosecution.

   Second, if the officer is testifying on cross-examination, the defense attorney may be deliberately attempting to manipulate the officer to volunteer something that the defense can use to discredit the officer and/or the prosecution's case. Defense attorneys are skilled in this technique. Therefore, on cross-examination the officer should respond only to the question asked to avoid giving the defense an opening that may prove fatal to the prosecution.

4. *Speak calmly and audibly in a natural voice.* Always speak in a calm tone of voice. Keep the voice at its normal pitch; do not attempt to alter the natural voice, as this causes stress and will be sensed by the jury.

   Speak in a tone of voice that is clearly audible to the jurors. Officers must remember that it is the jury that will decide the case, and jurors will not be persuaded by testimony they cannot hear. Studies indicate that where jurors have difficulty hearing and/or understanding the witnesses' testimony, their attention span becomes limited, they lose interest in the witness, and the witness's evidence is therefore wasted. This does not mean that the witness should shout when on the witness stand, but particularly in courtrooms where microphones are not employed, testifying officers should make certain that they speak at a level that will make their words audible to the jury without requiring the jurors to strain to hear what is being said.

5. *Use plain, easily understood terms.* The officer must testify in plain, easily understood language. If the jury does not understand the words being used, the testimony will be unpersuasive. Officers should avoid using police terminology or slang; such terms will confuse many jurors and may convey an adverse impression of the witness. This is a common error among police officers inexperienced in courtroom testimony, and it should be avoided.

   If technical terms are used, they should be explained in a straightforward manner, without any hint of condescension. Jurors, like anyone else, do not like to be patronized or talked down to.

6. *Maintain self-control.* During the stress of a courtroom appearance, it is often difficult for a witness to retain his or her composure. This is particularly true when a defense attorney is deliberately attempting to goad the witness which is an all-too-common tactic. However, keeping one's self-control is vital on the witness stand, whatever the provocation.

   There is an old saying that "he who loses his temper loses the battle." This applies in the courtroom, too. The witness who loses his or her temper on the witness stand makes the defense attorney's whole day. Studies indicate that when any witness becomes visibly angry or otherwise loses composure, the jurors tend to lose respect for that witness and thereafter give that witness's testimony less weight. This is particularly true for police witnesses. Jurors apparently feel that a police officer who cannot retain self-control is not a credible witness—or a good police officer.

   One aspect of retaining self-control is remaining courteous on the stand. It is only human to feel the need to make a sharp or sarcastic retort to some insulting question or comment by the defense attorney, but to do so plays into the defense's hands. Courteous replies to discourteous questions enhance a police officer's status with the jury and defeat the defense attorney's purpose of discrediting the officer.

   The ability to maintain self-control and a courteous manner in difficult situations is an important tool for a police officer in any situation. It is the mark of a true law enforcement professional, and this is so regardless of whether the officer is in the courtroom or on the street. If the officer behaves in a professional manner on the witness stand, the prosecution's case is materially enhanced and the chances of a conviction are increased accordingly.

THE ROLE OF THE EXPERT WITNESS

Prosecutors may locate an officer with extensive experience in a given area and qualify him or her as an **expert witness.** This often strengthens the prosecution's case and paves the way for testimony by other witnesses. Once the officer is designated by the court as an expert, conclusions may be drawn and they may give their personal opinion as to the facts and circumstances surrounding the case. The expert witness is one whose knowledge exceeds the knowledge of anyone

A Closer Look

How Reliable Is Eyewitness Testimony?[7]

One August night in Altoona, Iowa, the local McDonald's was filled with customers when a man with a gun in his pocket walked in, looking for cash. He slipped a note to the night manager, who led him to the office, opened the safe, pulled out money, and gave it to him. Before the police arrived, the gunman fled through a rear door, commandeered a car from a drive-through lane, ordered the driver out at gunpoint, and sped away.

Initial descriptions were contradictory, the defense lawyer would later argue, but with the help of McDonald's employees, the artist rendered a composite drawing, which led to a photographic lineup and eventually the arrest of Terry Eugene Schultz. Several eyewitnesses said Schultz was the gunman, and he was convicted and sentenced to 25 years in prison—based solely on eyewitness testimony. Powerful, indeed, but no physical evidence tied Schultz to the crime, and his girlfriend insisted that he'd been with her at the time. So, how accurate are eyewitness identifications?

Some experts say "not very." Now there's mounting evidence through DNA science that innocent people have been convicted as the result of faulty identifications. DNA evidence has already freed scores of convicts, and more could be in line if recommendations proposed in September 1999 by the National Commission on the Future of DNA Evidence become a reality. It's difficult to estimate just how many cases of mistaken identity occur, but in 2007, the Innocence Project concluded that over 75 percent of the more than 192 wrongful convictions in the United States involved mistaken identification.

Increasingly, courts are allowing experts to tell juries that eyewitness identifications are sometimes more convincing than they are reliable and that juries should be especially wary when certain problematic factors exist. Mistakes are more likely, for example, when the witness and suspect are of different races, especially when the witness is white and the suspect is black. We also now know that extreme stress, especially when violence or the threat of violence exists, interferes with recall.

Another problem that researchers found is that viewing a composite drawing or lineup can change witnesses' memories of an event. That is, a witness viewing a photo array may pick out a photo that resembles the culprit but isn't. But from that point, the photo becomes part of the witness's memory of the culprit. It is difficult, if not impossible, to quantify the overall reliability of stranger-to-stranger identifications, say experts. In some cases, experts estimate that the chance of faulty identification is as high as 20 percent.

As for Terry Schultz, his case—the McDonald's robbery in 1998—became the vehicle for the Iowa Supreme Court to reverse its own precedent. Citing the wealth of new research on memory, the court reversed his conviction and said that Schultz should be allowed to present such evidence at retrial. However, at retrial, even with new expert testimony, the defense would have to overcome several eyewitnesses' testimony. Schultz, who had already spent two years in prison, didn't want to risk more. He pleaded guilty to lesser charges and received a probated sentence. But other Iowa defendants have used the experts that the Schultz case made possible. Des Moines prosecutors claim, however, that they have seen little difference in trial outcomes.

with a moderate education or experience in the field. Qualifications for the expert witness to establish when on the witness stand include the following:

- Name
- Occupation (and how long)
- Department (and how long)
- Specialized experience (e.g., drug enforcement and how long)
- Officer's training
- Number of training course hours
- Number of similar investigations in which the officer has participated
- Number of arrests made in this type of investigation
- Past experience as an expert witness (and how many court appearances)

At the end of the questioning, the judge will excuse the witness. Officers must remember that the eyes of the jury are still watching and making judgments; therefore, when exiting, witnesses should refrain from staring, smiling, or showing any emotion toward anyone in the courtroom.

SUMMARY

The investigator's appearance on the witness stand is a key part of most criminal prosecutions. Investigators who know how to be good witnesses enhance the prosecution's case; therefore, common sense necessitates that all departments have a policy that provides officers with guidance as to how to be good witnesses. This is also an appropriate and important subject for inclusion in the police academy curriculum and in roll call or in-service training classes where mock trials can be employed to give officers practical experience in courtroom testimony. Being a good witness includes cooperating with prosecutors to the fullest possible extent; arriving at the place of trial in a timely manner; being thoroughly prepared to testify; presenting a good appearance on the stand; and maintaining a calm, controlled, courteous, and professional attitude while testifying.

DISCUSSION QUESTIONS

1. By the time a case goes to trial, what pretrial procedures have already been concluded? Discuss the various phases of a criminal trial.

2. Under what set of circumstances are jurors selected for trial?

3. Explain the distinction between direct examination and cross-examination.

4. Discuss some of the most important things for a witness to remember before testifying at a jury trial.

5. What are the things that the investigator must do to best prepare for a jury trial?

6. Explain the players and the purpose of the pretrial conference.

7. In what ways can defense attorneys attack an officer's credibility in court?

8. Explain what is meant by an officer's courtroom demeanor and how the officer can leave the best positive impression.

9. Describe the procedure for qualifying an officer as an expert witness.

NOTES

1. INTERNATIONAL ASSOCIATION OF CHIEFS OF POLICE (IACP). *Court appearance.* Model Policy Center (1998).
2. Ibid.
3. Ibid.
4. WOOLNER, A. (1999). Courts eye the problems of eyewitness identifications. *USA Today,* September 29, p. 15A.
5. INTERNATIONAL ASSOCIATION OF CHIEFS OF POLICE (IACP). *Testifying in Court.* Model Policy Center (1996).
6. Ibid.
7. U.S. DEPARTMENT OF JUSTICE (1987, Aug.). National Institute of Justice, *Research in brief,* Washington, DC: U.S. Department of Justice.

Appendix  A

▶ Physical Evidence

The impact that a single piece of evidence can have in court is considerable. In maximizing the effectiveness of this evidence, correct collection and preservation techniques must be utilized by the investigator. By following the suggestions presented below, the investigator diminishes the possibility that his or her evidence will become contaminated or damaged, thus elevating its importance to the investigation.

COLLECTION AND PRESERVATION

It is important that each item submitted as evidence be sealed with tamperproof evidence tape, dated, initialed, and labeled as to its contents and its association with the victim or suspect. Evidence stained with bodily fluids (e.g., blood, semen) must be air-dried prior to packaging and submission to the laboratory. Package and seal all items separately in breathable, nonplastic (e.g., paper), loose-fitting containers. Packages should not be tightly bound; the criminalists must return items to containers, which must be resealed following examinations.

Tips for Packaging Evidence in the Proper Manner

1. Always submit a completed laboratory analysis request with each case. Use more than one if necessary.
2. Latent evidence submission envelopes should be used only with ten-print cards or latent-print cards. Other types of packaging should be used for nonprint evidence.
3. Do not package weapons with items of clothing or drug paraphernalia. (Firearms will probably be checked immediately to make certain that they are unloaded.)
4. Always package urine separately from blood. Leave expansion room in urine containers; they will be stored in a freezer.
5. Always package tubes of blood separately from clothing. Clothing will be stored in a freezer; whole blood is placed in a refrigerator.
6. Sexual assault kits should never be packaged with clothing. The kits contain whole blood and should be stored in a refrigerator.
7. Whole blood should always be packaged separately from drug-related items.
8. Never package items for prints with items for serology, trace, firearms identification, and so on.
9. Do not submit open liquor containers to the lab. All containers should be capped and sealed.
10. Evidence stained with bodily fluids (e.g., blood, semen) must be air-dried prior to packaging and submission to the laboratory.
11. Do not submit syringes with uncapped needles or knives or razor blades without protective coverings.
12. Do not submit wet or moist marijuana in plastic bags to the lab; air-dry before submitting.
13. Do not submit drug paraphernalia or miscellaneous items that do not need to be analyzed.

Serology/DNA Analysis

Bodily fluid stains are valuable evidence that can be used to associate a suspect with the crime or to eliminate him or her from consideration. For instance, the presence of seminal stains is confirmation that a sexual act has occurred.

Blood.   When materials stained with blood are to be sent to the laboratory:

- Air-dry the stained material on a piece of clean paper placed in a ventilated area. Place the dried material in a paper bag; label with your initials, the date, and an exhibit number; and seal the bag.
- Any debris that falls from the material onto the paper during the drying process should also be placed in a metal pillbox, labeled, and sealed. If you must fold the material, protect the stained area with a piece of paper.
- Wrap each bloodstained item separately, after drying. Do not package items when they are still moist. Allow them to dry thoroughly. Package items from the victim(s) and suspect(s) into separate containers.
- Collect in a purple-capped Vacutainer a comparison blood standard from each person directly involved in the incident. Freeze or refrigerate dried specimens until ready for transport to the laboratory.

When items stained with blood cannot be sent to the laboratory:

- Always scrape dried blood from an object if possible. Using a clean knife or razor blade, scrape the dried blood into a paper fold and place in an envelope.
- If scraping is not possible, moisten a cotton swab with just enough water to make the tip damp. Do not saturate the swab completely with water. Rub the stained area with the swab to pick up the blood. Keep the blood as concentrated as possible on the tip of the swab. Air-dry the swab and place in an envelope or small paper bag.
- Large fabric items with bloodstains may be processed by cutting out the stained area and sending the cutting to the laboratory. Written notes and/or photographs detailing the location and condition of the stain should be taken before the cutting(s) is removed. Place the cutting(s) in an envelope or paper bag.
- When a puddle of blood is available, soak up the moist blood with cotton swabs. Air-dry the swabs before placing them in an envelope or small paper bag.
- Label all containers with your initials, the date, and the exhibit number, and seal them.
- If scrapings were taken, package and preserve the razor blade used.
- Collect a comparison blood standard from each person directly involved in the incident.
- Freeze or refrigerate dried specimens until ready for transport to the laboratory.

COMPARISON STANDARD FOR BLOOD.   Obtain the standard by having a medical examiner or other qualified person collect at least 5 cubic centimeters of blood from the victim and all suspects. Use purple-capped Vacutainer tubes for the collection of whole blood. Label each tube with the donor's name, the physician's name, and other relevant information. Refrigerate the tubes until ready for transport to the laboratory. Do not freeze whole-blood samples.

Semen.   Air-dry the stained material on a piece of clean paper placed in a ventilated area. Condoms to be submitted should be frozen as soon as possible after collection. Stained areas on large items or items that cannot be sent to the laboratory may be cut out and submitted. Place the dried material in a paper bag, label with your initials, the date, and an exhibit number, and seal the bag. If you must fold the material, protect the stained area with a piece of paper. Wrap each stained item separately.

Do not package items when they are still moist; allow them to dry thoroughly. Obtain a victim sexual assault kit and a suspect sexual assault kit (one per suspect), and follow the instructions provided with the kit. Label kits with initials, date, and exhibit number, and seal them. Refrigerate kits until ready for transport to the laboratory. Freeze or refrigerate dried specimens until ready for transport to the laboratory. Sexual assault kits can be obtained from your local crime laboratory.

Saliva.   Air-dry the stained material on a piece of clean paper placed in a ventilated area. Place the dried material in a paper bag, label with your initials, the date, and an exhibit number, and seal the bag. If you must fold the material, protect the stained area with a piece of paper. Wrap each stained area separately. Do not package items when they are still moist; allow them to dry thoroughly. Collect a comparison standard. Freeze or refrigerate dried specimens until ready for transport to the laboratory.

COMPARISON STANDARD FOR SALIVA.   Obtain saliva samples from victim and suspect, waiting 30 minutes if a person has eaten or been smoking. Have the person spit on a piece of clean cotton cloth about 1 square inch in size. Outline stain arcas with a pencil, air-dry, and place samples in separate envelopes. Freeze or refrigerate dried specimens until ready for transport to the laboratory. Obtain a comparison blood standard as described in the preceding section.

Accelerants and Explosives

Evidence in bomb and arson cases is difficult to find because of its small size, because of the presence of a large amount of debris, and because potentially useful evidence is often washed away when a fire is extinguished. For this reason, great care must be used in the collection and preservation of such evidence.

Arson Debris.   Porous substances absorb liquid accelerants readily and therefore make good debris for laboratory testing. Consider carpeting, carpet padding, wood, and clothing or cloth products when collecting debris. Collect fire debris in unused metal paint cans or plastic bags approved for fire debris (e.g., nylon or Kapak bags). Submit liquids in their original containers if they can be sealed properly.

Explosive Debris.   Collect any items that may have been part of the explosive device. Collect items that were impacted directly by fragments of the explosive device. If explosive residues are found on these items, the type of explosive used may be determined. Package the items in plastic bags or metal containers.

Explosive Substances and Devices.   Any undetonated explosive device must be deactivated before it is submitted to the laboratory. If the device is to be processed for latent fingerprints, package and label accordingly.

Fingerprints

Generally, latent fingerprints on nonporous materials deteriorate rapidly upon prolonged exposure to high temperature and humidity; consequently, items should be processed and/or forwarded to a laboratory as soon as possible. With the assistance of the Automated Fingerprint Identification System (AFIS), we are now able to search the entire fingerprint file; we do not need a suspect. A thorough file search can be made only if correct processing procedures are followed to obtain the best latent print evidence.

On Absorbent Materials.   Place paper or other absorbent material in a plastic bag or cellophane protector. Do not handle the material with your fingers. Do not attempt to develop latent fingerprints on absorbent surfaces yourself. Label the bag or protector with your initials, the date, and an exhibit number. Collect a comparison standard.

On Hard Surfaces.   Dust plastic cards, metal plates, glass bottles, or other hard-surfaced objects for latent fingerprints. Remove developed prints with lifting tape and place the tape on a 3″ x 5″-inch card that contrasts in color with the dusting powder used. Mark the card with your initials, the date, and an exhibit number, place it in an envelope, and seal the envelope.

On Soft Surfaces.   Carefully remove putty, caulking compound, or other soft material bearing visible fingerprint impressions. Leave as much excess material surrounding the fingerprint as possible. Glue the mass of material to a stiff section of cardboard that is marked with your initials, the date, and an exhibit number. Tape a protective cover over the specimen. A paper cup or baby food jar is useful for this purpose. Do not touch or otherwise distort the fingerprint. Collect a comparison standard.

COMPARISON STANDARD FOR FINGERPRINTS.   Collect and identify fingerprints of suspects and other persons under investigation who may have touched an object. Place fingerprint records in a stiff envelope to protect them from being bent. Seal the envelope and label it with your initials, the date, and an exhibit number.

Inked Prints.   Enclose all inked prints for comparison, and designate either on the print or in a cover letter whether prints are for elimination or are of the suspect. If latent prints are reported as palm prints, palm prints should also be submitted to the laboratory.

Packing of Evidence.   Use ingenuity to construct special containers to protect latent print–bearing surfaces. Never place cotton or cloth next to latent impressions. Any amount of paper or cardboard specimens may be placed in one wrapper. Hard-surfaced latent print–bearing objects should never come in contact with another surface (paper sacks, plastic bags, etc.).

Identification.   There is no set requirement of latent print size for a positive identification, and there is no specific number of characteristics required to effect an identification. As a general rule, if the investigator develops an area that appears to have several ridges, regardless of the size of the area, it should be lifted, marked, and submitted to the laboratory.

Firearms and Ammunition

Firearms leave unique markings on bullets and cartridge cases as well as detectable residues on shooters' hands.

Gunshot Residue Kits. The discharge of a firearm can deposit gunshot residues on any object in close proximity to the firearm and, sometimes, at a considerable distance downrange. Gunshot residue kits may be used to test the residue levels deposited on hands. Crime labs are usually capable of analyzing two different types of gunshot residue kits:

1. An A.A. kit consists of five cotton swabs with a bottle of dilute nitric acid and is analyzed using an atomic absorption spectrophotometer.
2. A SEM/EDX kit consists of two adhesive-coated aluminum stubs and is analyzed using a scanning electron microscope equipped with an x-ray dispersive detector.

Each kit contains specific instructions for its use and also a request for certain information in regard to the shooting incident. Be sure to include the type of weapon, ammunition, and time interval until collection of the kit. Kits are to be used as soon as possible after a shooting incident and before hands are cleaned or processed in any other way. An A.A. kit should not be used if the time interval until the collection of the kit exceeds six hours for an active person.

When shooting distance information is requested, submit the victim's clothing with the bullet hole, along with the firearm and ammunition used. If the clothing is bloody, air-dry completely and package in a paper bag. If the victim was not clothed over the area of the wound, take close-up photographs of the wound and remember to include a scale in the photographs. Gunshot residue kits can be obtained from the crime laboratory.

Handguns and Shoulder Arms. Never insert anything into the barrel of a firearm. All firearms should be unloaded prior to submission to the laboratory. Process the firearm for fingerprints if necessary. Take notes describing the position of any expended cartridge cases or live cartridges in the cylinder of the revolver. If pertinent to an investigation, make notes on a safety's position, hammer position, and so on. Remove the cartridge magazine from any semiautomatic firearm and process the exterior for fingerprints if necessary. Cartridge magazines can be placed in separate containers and submitted along with the firearms in a larger container. Attach an identification tag to the firearm that describes the item, the serial number, the case number, chain of custody, and other pertinent details.

Handguns should be submitted in plastic bags, paper bags, or boxes. If handguns are to be processed for fingerprints or serology, do not submit them in plastic bags. Shoulder arms are generally larger items and cannot always be submitted in containers.

Serial Number Restoration. If a firearm's serial number has been obliterated, make an identifying mark on it for future identification. The obliterated area can be restored in the laboratory using one of several methods.

Expended Bullets, Cartridge Cases, and Shotgun Shells.   After recovering an expended ammunition component, it should be placed in a sturdy/unbreakable container such as a small box or metal canister. Bullets that are removed at an autopsy should be washed in warm running water (if not for trace or serology examinations), wrapped in tissue or similar material, and put in an appropriate container.

Do not scratch the sides or bearing surface of a bullet when it is being removed from an object. The base or nose of a bullet can be scribed for identification purposes. Do not scratch or scribe the headstamp area or primer of a cartridge case or shotgun shell. If a casing or shotgun shell must be marked for identification, do so on or near the open mouth area.

Expended ammunition components should be separated and packaged in separate containers. The component's location, case number, and related information can be labeled on the outside of the container. Each container should be sealed with tamperproof evidence tape prior to submission to the laboratory.

Food and Drug Specimens

Since food and drug specimens exhibit a wide variety of identifiable characteristics, they may corroborate other evidence or link a suspect with a crime scene. When handling this evidence, it is important to prevent contamination among the specimens or from other sources. Do not package too much evidence into a container, as that could cause a break in the container with a loss of integrity of the evidence. Also, do not completely cover the evidence container with evidence tape, as this could prevent the container from being adequately sealed later.

Liquids.   Try to collect a minimum of 4 ounces of a specimen using a leakproof container. Seal the container with adhesive tape, and label it with your initials, the date, and an exhibit number. If the container used is glass or has a glass stopper, mark it as fragile. Collect a comparison standard of the same brand and concentration, especially when tampering of medical, food, or other commercial products is suspected. Submit unknown and comparison liquid samples to the laboratory.

Plant Material.   Without heating, dry the sample thoroughly in a secure area by spreading it on clean paper for at least 24 hours. After the sample has dried, place in a pillbox, vial, or other container, and secure with adhesive tape. Do not mix samples. Package each separately to avoid mixing during mailing. Label the outside of the container with your initials, the date, and an exhibit number. Collect a comparison standard. If wet plant material is collected in evidence containers (especially plastic bags), it will mold and degrade to the point where positive test results may not be obtained. These molds are also hazardous to your health.

When numerous plants, bales, or bundles of plant material are seized, submit to the laboratory only representative samples of plant material from these items. Photograph the entire number of original evidence items with a ruler as scale, and weigh them. In a large drug seizure, do not submit the entire amount of evidence to the laboratory. A lab will not have sufficient evidence locker space for all drug seizures. Also, small amounts of drugs submitted to a laboratory allow for quicker testing.

Powders and Solids.   Place powders and solids in a container such as a pillbox, plastic vial, or pharmacy fold. Seal the container and label with your initials, the date, and an exhibit number. Refrigerate samples as needed. Do not add preservatives to solid food samples. Collect a comparison standard.

Tablets and Capsules.   Place tablets and capsules in a container such as a pillbox or plastic vial. Seal the container and label with your initials, the date, and an exhibit number. Collect a comparison standard.

COMPARISON STANDARD FOR LIQUIDS, POWDERS, SOLIDS, PLANT MATERIAL, TABLETS, AND CAPSULES.   Collect comparison standards for food, liquids, plant material, tablets, and capsules (in cases such as unattended death and suspected poisoning). When collecting standards, search the refrigerator, cupboards, and storage places for similar material, particularly that which is labeled. Do not remove these samples from their original containers; seal them in clean (sterile if possible) second containers. Refrigerate samples as necessary to retard further growth of microorganisms and deterioration. Expedite their delivery to a forensic laboratory.

Comparison standards for drugs should be collected in the manner described above. When collecting standards, collect any containers displaying prescription labels. Do not remove pills, capsules, powders, or liquids from their original containers; seal them in clean second containers and label them. Never mix specimens regardless of the proximity to the scene or their similarity in appearance.

Glass

All glass except small fragments might contain latent fingerprints and should be handled accordingly. Where glass fragments might be present on clothing, shoes, tools, or other objects, the articles should be submitted to the laboratory as soon as possible.

Large Fragments.   Dust large fragments for latent fingerprints and submit prints. Protect thin protruding edges of fragments against damage by embedding them in modeling clay, putty, or a similar substance. Avoid chipping the fragments. Use tweezers or similar tools to collect glass. Exercise care in protecting the edges, and avoid scratching the surface. Place adhesive tape on each piece for identification. Place your initials and the date on the tape.

Wrap each piece separately in cotton, place in a sturdy box with a tight-fitting lid, and seal and label each package with your initials, the date, and an exhibit number. Package questioned pieces of glass separately from known pieces. If you are submitting glass for the purpose of determining the direction of a bullet's impact or for other fracture analysis, mark surfaces with tape indicating whether the glass was found outside or inside the building. Similarly, mark glass taken from a window frame to indicate which side was facing out. Collect a comparison standard.

Small Fragments.   Examine articles of clothing and shoes for the presence of small glass fragments. Use tweezers or similar tools to collect glass. Use care in protecting the edges, and avoid scratching the surface. Wrap each article of clothing containing fragments separately in clean paper or plastic bags. Package any questioned pieces of glass separately from known pieces. Seal each bag, and label each with your initials, the date, and specimen information.

Place shoes and other solid objects in separate containers such as shoeboxes. Tape each object to the bottom of containers to prevent rattling. Do not pack articles containing microscopic fragments in cotton or other soft protective materials. Seal each package completely, making sure that there are no holes through which glass fragments might be lost. Place loose glass fragments in pillboxes or plastic or glass vials, and seal them tightly. Place cotton in the container to prevent rattling and chipping during transit. Do not use envelopes as containers. Label everything with your initials, the date, and specimen information. Collect a comparison standard.

COMPARISON STANDARD FOR GLASS.   Always collect glass standards from an area as near as possible to the point of impact. Collect samples that are at least the size of a quarter, and wrap each comparison sample according to appropriate procedures.

Hairs and Fibers

In crimes involving physical contact, particles are often transferred among the victim, suspect, and weapon or other objects. Hairs and fibers are among the most common evidentiary items and can be extremely valuable to an investigation. When submitting hair and fiber evidence, be specific as to their source and association to the victim or suspect. Good evidence containers are a paper fold, pillbox, or tape lift. Each container used should be enclosed within an outside envelope.

Collection of Unknowns.   If hairs or fibers are observed, remove them from the surface with clean tweezers. On suitable surfaces, a tape lift using wide transparent adhesive tape is an excellent procedure.

Collection of Knowns.   Of the various hair regions on the human body, only head hair and pubic hair are considered suitable for comparison purposes.

HEAD HAIR STANDARDS.   Pull 40 to 50 hairs from all over the head, taking approximately 10 hairs each from the top front, top back, back of head, right side, and left side.

PUBIC HAIR STANDARDS.   Pull approximately 25 hairs representative of the pubic region. Hair standards should be packaged in paper folds and enclosed in an outer envelope.

Impressions

Impressions made by footwear, tires, and tools can easily be destroyed during a preliminary crime scene search. To prevent inadvertent loss of such evidence, one of the earliest concerns of any crime scene investigation should be the security of the scene and the collection and preservation of impressions. Impressions should be photographed properly prior to attempting lifts or casting.

Footwear and Tire Impressions.   Photograph each impression with a ruled scale next to it. Photograph the impression from directly above (use of a tripod is highly recommended). Photographs should be taken while a detached flash is held low and to the side of the impression. Each impression should be flashed from four different sides. Black-and-white film gives the best quality photographs for comparison purposes. Photographs of impressions for comparisons should be blown up to a 1:1 scale prior to submission to the laboratory.

After photographing an impression, a lift may be attempted if a residue impression is on a hard surface that cannot be submitted to the laboratory. Adhesive lifters, gelatin lifters, or electrostatic lifting techniques may be utilized. Residue impressions are delicate in nature and can easily be destroyed by improper handling.

Casting techniques should be practiced prior to crime scene utilization. Dental stone or die stone casting material is recommended for the casting of three-dimensional impressions. (The use of plaster of paris for casting of impressions is discouraged.)

Approximately 12 ounces of water should be added to and mixed with 2 pounds of dental stone or die stone. This amount is generally sufficient to prepare casting material for a footwear impression. A 1-gallon plastic Ziploc bag containing premeasured casting material is ideal for the mixing and casting process. A 12-ounce beverage container can be utilized for measuring the water. Additional casting material will need to be mixed for larger impressions such as tire impressions. Prepare the dental/die stone materials into a pancake batter–like consistency in a plastic Ziploc bag.

Pour the solution off the side of the impression, not directly onto or into it. Allow the casting material to flow into the impression. A tongue depressor can be used gently to help the casting material flow over the entire impression. When the dental or die stone has set, place your initials, date, and case-identifying information into the back of the cast.

When submitting a cast to the laboratory, place it in a sturdy box or similar container with sufficient cushioning material (e.g., Styrofoam peanuts or scrap newspaper). If more than one cast is submitted, put each cast in its own box or container. Do not remove the dirt or debris adhering to a cast, footwear, or tire. Each container should be sealed with tamperproof evidence tape prior to submission to the laboratory.

Tool Marks. Do not insert a suspect tool into a tool mark. Whenever possible, preserve tool marks as you find them and submit the intact object bearing the questioned tool marks to the laboratory. If it is not possible to submit the object, remove the portion or section of the object bearing the tool mark. Before a portion or section of a large item is removed, photograph the entire item with the inclusion of a ruled scale. Also take close-up photographs of the questioned tool marks with the inclusion of a ruled scale for reference.

If an item cannot be submitted, a Mikrosil or silicon typecast of the tool mark(s) should be made and submitted to the laboratory for comparison. Tools, casts of tool marks, and so on should be submitted individually in separate containers. Information pertinent to an investigation should be labeled on the outside of the containers. Each container should be sealed with tamperproof evidence tape prior to submission to the laboratory.

Paint

Paint evidence can be in the form of liquid, chips, or smears. A dried paint specimen should be collected in a paper fold, placed in an outer envelope, and marked clearly as to its source. Any questioned paint specimen should also have a known paint standard submitted. Package separately for comparison purposes.

Liquid Paints. Specimens of liquid paint should be submitted in original containers whenever possible.

Questioned Documents

Questioned documents contain a wide variety of identifiable characteristics that can be used to corroborate other evidence and associate a suspect with a crime. Similarly, these can be used by a laboratory to clear a suspect of a crime in certain instances.

Charred Documents. A thin but strong section of cardboard can be inserted gently under charred debris. Thick, firm cotton batting is then placed on a flat surface, with the charred paper deposited onto the batting. Place in a crushproof container; label with your initials, the date, and an exhibit number; and seal. Mark the container "Fragile" in a conspicuous spot.

Crumpled Documents. Do not unfold a crumpled document, but enclose in a crushproof container. Label with your initials, the date, and an exhibit number, and seal. Mark the container "Fragile" in a conspicuous spot.

Intact Documents. Whenever possible, submit the original document rather than a photograph, photostat, or other type of copy. Handle the document carefully; preserve latent fingerprints, using tweezers or gloves as necessary. When identification is necessary, mark in a noncritical area of the document. Use a medium different from that used on the document (e.g., use pencil when the document is in ink). Do not use staples or pins on documents, and do not fold documents. Place them in a protective covering such as an envelope or cover with plastic. Seal and label with your initials, the date, and an exhibit number. Collect a comparison standard.

COMPARISON STANDARD FOR QUESTIONED DOCUMENTS. Standards for questioned documents are not the questioned documents themselves but facsimiles or replicas of handwriting, typewriter print, or ink visible on questioned document(s) that might have been made by the maker(s) of the original document.

Adequate Exemplars. Remember that unlike fingerprints, handwriting and hand printing will change over a period of time and can easily be disguised. Each of us has a normal range of variation in our writing. To make a proper comparison, the examiner must determine the range of variation in each suspect's writing. It is impossible to say whether this range will be shown in 6, 16, or 60 samples. Handwriting (cursive) cannot be compared with hand printing. Age, gender, and writing hand cannot be determined conclusively. About the best that we can do in these areas is make an educated guess.

Don't use a single sheet of paper or a single-page exemplar. To get an adequate sample of writing or printing from a person, it is much better to use several, perhaps 20 or 30, single pieces of paper as your exemplar. Using paper that is about the same size and texture as the document in question is suggested. Always try to duplicate the conditions under which the questioned items were prepared.

GUIDELINES FOR OBTAINING KNOWN HANDWRITING EXEMPLARS. The following guidelines may be used to obtain known handwriting and/or hand printing exemplars from a person:

- Reproduce the original conditions as nearly as possible with respect to text speed, slant, size of paper, size of writing, type of writing instrument, and so on.
- Obtain samples from dictation until it is believed that normal writing has been produced (the number of samples necessary cannot be determined in advance).
- Do not allow the writer to see either the original document in question or a photograph thereof.
- Remove each sample from the sight of the writer as soon as it is completed.

- Do not give instructions in spelling, punctuation, or arrangement.
- Use the same writing media, such as type and size of paper, writing instruments, and printed forms such as checks or notes.
- Obtain the full text of the questioned writing in word-for-word order at least once, if possible. Signatures and less extensive writing should be prepared several times, each time on a different piece of paper. In hand-printing cases, both uppercase (capital) and lowercase samples should be obtained.
- In forgery cases, the laboratory should also be furnished with genuine signatures of the person whose name has been forged.
- Obtain samples of supplementary writings such as sketches, drawings, and manner of addressing an envelope.
- The writer should sign and date each page.
- Witness each sample with date and initials (or name).
- Consider furnishing undictated specimens to supplement the dictated specimens.
- Obtain and submit original documents when possible.
- Familiarize yourself with all aspects of the questioned document involved in a case. Furnish copies of the documents to assist other officers when they are requested to obtain known writing.

Typewriter Examples.   Collect specimens of typewriting from the typewriter believed to have been used, and submit them to a document analyst. When obtaining these examples, use the typewriter in the condition in which it is found (i.e., the same ribbon). Type the text of the questioned material three times, once through carbon paper with the ribbon adjustment set on "stencil." On each specimen record the brand name, model number, and serial number of the typewriter that was used.

Place specimens in a plastic or reinforced envelope. Do not fold. Label with your initials, the date, and an exhibit number. Film-type ribbon cartridges and correction tapes should also be collected and submitted for examination.

Ink Examples.   Collect samples of unquestioned documents that contain the type of ink used in the questioned document. If you are unsure whether the ink on the standard is the same as that on the questioned document, submit samples of all available inks that might have been used. If samples of fluid ink are available, place the bottles containing the ink in a suitable container that is labeled with your initials, the date, and an exhibit number. Label the container as fragile and submit to the laboratory.

Indented Writings.   Loose papers and writing pads should be collected for possible writing and typing impression restoration.

Soil

The success of soil comparisons depends mainly on the quality of the samples collected. Soils located on the sides of suspect shoes are most suitable for soil comparisons. Consider the nature of the crime scene. Is it conducive to the transfer of soil onto a shoe (e.g., a paved parking lot compared to an open field)? Soil standards from the scene should consist of an area approximately 6 inches square by 1/4 inch deep. Plastic bags or metal cans are good containers for soil samples.

Toxicology

Blood Alcohol Determinations. Whole blood is the best body fluid for alcohol testing. Urine is not a reliable specimen for accurate determination of a blood alcohol level. Blood should be collected in a sterile gray stopper blood collection tube that contains the additives sodium fluoride (NaF) and potassium oxalate (KOx). These additives are required to preserve a blood sample for alcohol testing. A new sterile needle must be used as well as a nonalcoholic skin cleanser. Preserve the needle cover or wrapper bearing the word sterile as well as the package from the skin cleanser. These are needed in court to prove that legal collection requirements were followed. Do not preserve the needle itself.

After the blood is collected, mix the blood and the additives in the tube by gently inverting the tube at least 15 to 20 times. This will prevent the blood from clotting. Mark the tube with the person's name and any other pertinent case information. One tube of blood (5 to 10 milliliters) is sufficient for alcohol testing. Do not freeze the blood sample. Protect the blood from extreme heat. Do not store the blood sample in a hot car during the summer.

Toluene/Solvent Abuse and Glue Sniffing. When glue sniffing or other solvent abuse is suspected, collect a blood sample as described above for alcohol testing. Toluene and other solvents cannot be detected reliably in urine samples.

Drug Testing. Urine is the specimen of choice for drug testing. Many more positives are found in urine than in blood. Drug tests on their own will not establish impairment at the time of arrest since different drugs take differing amounts of time to be excreted in the urine. The officer's observations relating to the person's degree of impairment will be very important in establishing intoxication.

Urine collection must be observed to prevent the person from adulterating the sample. An officer of the same gender as the person should accompany the person into the stall and actually observe the urine flowing into the cup. At least 50 milliliters of urine should be collected if possible. If the person cannot provide sufficient urine, have the person drink some water and wait 15 minutes to try again. Once the urine is collected, the sample should be marked with the person's name and sealed. The specimen cup should then be placed in a leakproof plastic bag. If the urine sample cannot be delivered to the laboratory within 24 hours of collection, the urine must be refrigerated. This is a legal requirement. For long-term storage (more than a day), the urine sample should be frozen.

Blood can also be tested for drugs. However, drugs do not remain in the bloodstream for long periods of time. Some drugs may be detectable in blood only for a couple of hours or less. Also, drugs have much lower concentrations in blood than in urine. For these reasons, urine is the preferred specimen for drug testing. If blood is submitted to the laboratory for drug testing, it should be collected in the same manner as for alcohol testing. At least two tubes of blood (20 milliliters) should be collected if a drug test is requested. When submitting evidence for drug testing, indicate which drugs are suspected.

Carbon Monoxide. If carbon monoxide poisoning is suspected, collect a blood sample in the same manner as for alcohol testing.

Safety Considerations. Assume that all samples are infected with something. Wash your hands after handling blood tubes or urine samples. Package all samples in a way that will contain leakage. Notify the laboratory if you believe that a suspect is infected with any disease.

Miscellaneous

Items such as cigarette butts, tobacco, jewelry, magnetic tape recordings, or writing instruments can all serve as evidence to connect a suspect to a crime. Each item, either through its use or basic structure, can provide a unique, identifiable characteristic. For instance, tape recordings of anonymous voices received as part of a threat prior to a bombing or extortion may be identified with known voices of a suspect through voiceprint analysis, provided that care is exercised during the recording of questions and known voices.

Cigarette Butts and Tobacco.   Pick up a cigarette butt on a piece of paper or with tweezers and place in a pillbox. Do not handle the cigarette butt directly with your hands. Mark a label with your initials, the date, and an exhibit number as well as where the object was found. Place the label on the container and seal. Empty tobacco material from pipes or clothes pockets into a pillbox. Mark and seal as above.

COMPARISON STANDARD FOR CIGARETTE BUTTS AND TOBACCO.   No comparison standard of the cigarette material need be collected. If serological testing is desired, however, collect saliva standards from both victims and suspects.

Jewelry.   Handle with tweezers or cloth gloves. Dust for fingerprints and place in a suitable crushproof container. If the composition of precious metals such as gold, silver, or platinum must be determined to prove common origin, send appropriate metal samples for comparison purposes. Label each sample container by writing on it in ink your initials, the date, and an exhibit number. Collect a comparison standard.

COMPARISON STANDARD FOR JEWELRY.   When possible, submit comparison samples of jewelry along with any questioned samples. The origin of some stolen jewelry may be traced to a particular jewelry store by analyzing the adhesive used to glue a precious stone to its setting. Known samples of the adhesive used by the jeweler should be submitted to compare with questioned samples. Place samples in crushproof containers and seal them.

Small Objects.   At each crime scene, search for small objects such as burned matches, fragments of glass, broken fingernails, and cigarette butts. Follow known procedures for each item. If you do not have specific directions for an item of evidence, place it in a crushproof container without touching it directly with your fingers. Seal and identify the container by writing on it in ink your initials, the date, and an exhibit number. Collect a comparison standard whenever possible.

COMPARISON STANDARD FOR SMALL OBJECTS.   Comparison samples of small objects or items found in the possession of a suspect or in his or her belongings should be submitted so that a comparison with items found at the crime scene can be made. Package and identify comparison samples.

Writing Instruments.   Handle with tweezers or cloth gloves, being careful not to smudge fingerprints. Dust for and collect fingerprints. Look for and submit instruments bearing teeth marks. Place the instrument in a suitable crushproof container and identify the container by writing on it in ink your initials, the date, and an exhibit number. Collect a comparison standard.

Collect any writing instruments found in the possession of a suspect or in his or her belongings in the manner described above. Package and identify comparison samples as described above.

Appendix B

Cases

Aguilar v. Texas, 378 U.S. 108 (1964)
Alabama v. White, 496 U.S. 325 (1990)
Arizona v. Evans, 514 U.S. 1 (1995)
Arizona v. Hicks, 480 U.S. 321 (1987)
Arenson v. Jackson, 97 Misc. 606, 162 N.Y.S. (1916)
Ashcraft v. Tennessee, 322 U.S. 143 , 64 S.Ct. 921 (1944)
Barnett v. State, 104 Ohio St. 298, 135 N.E. (1922).
Berkemer v. McCarty, 486 U.S. 420 (1984)
Brinegar v. United States, 338 U.S. 160, 69 S.Ct. (1949)
Brown v. Mississippi, 297 U.S. 278 (1936)
Bumper v. North Carolina, 391 U.S. 543 (1968)
California v. Acevedo, 500 U.S. 565 (1991)
California v. Hodari, 499 U.S. 62 (1991)
California v. Prysock, 451 U.S. 1301 (1981)
Carroll v. United States, 267 U.S. 132 (1925)
Chambers v. Maroney, 399 U.S. 42 (1970)
Cheadle v. Barwell, 95 Mont. 299 1933)
Chimel v. California, 395 U.S. 752 (1969)
Coolidge v. New Hampshire, 403 U.S. 443 (1971)
County of Riverside v. McLaughlin, 500 U.S. 413 (1991),
Cupp v. Murphy, 412 U.S. 291 93 S.Ct. 200 (1973)
Davis v. United States, 512 U.S. 452 (1994)
Draper v. United States, 358 U.S. 307, 79 S.Ct. (1959)
Edwards v. Arizona, 451 U.S. 477 (1981)
Escobedo v. Illinois, 378 U.S. 478 (1964)
Florida v. Andrews, 1987
Florida v. Bostick, 501 U.S. 429 (1991)
Florida v. Jimeno, 499 U.S. 934 (1991)
Florida, v. Royer, 460 U.S. 491 (1983)
Frye v. United States, 54 App. D.C. 46, 293 (1923)
Funk v. United States, 290 U.S. 371 (1933)
Gilbert v. California, 388 U.S. 263 (1967)
Graham v. Connor, 490 U.S. 396 (1989)
Hampton v. United States, 425 U.S. 484 (1976)
Harris v. United States, 390 U.S. 234 (1968)
Hayes v. Florida, 470 U.S. 811 (1985)
Horton v. California, 496 U.S. 128 (1990)
Illinois v. Gates, 462 U.S. 213 (1983)
Illinois v. Rodriguez, 497 U.S. 177 (1990)
Illinois v. Wardlow, (528 U.S. 119 (2000)
Katz v. United States, 389 U.S. 347 (1967)

Ker v. *California*, 374 U.S. 23 (1963)
Mallory v. *United States*, 354 U.S. 449 (1957)
Mapp v. *Ohio*, 367 U.S. 643 (1961)
Maryland v. *Buie*, 494 U.S. 325 (1990)
Massachusetts v. *Sheppard*, 468 U.S. 981 (1984)
McCray v. *Illinois*, 386 U.S. 300 (1967)
McNabb v. *United States*, 318 U.S. 332 (1943)
Minnesota v. *Murphy*, 405 U.S. 420, 104 S. Ct. (1984)
Minnesota v. *Olson*, 495 U.S. 91 (1989)
Miranda v. *Arizona*, 384 U.S. 436 (1966)
Michigan v. *Tyler*, 436 U.S. 499 (1978)
Mincey v. *Arizona*, 437 U.S. 385 (1978)
Minnick v. *Mississippi*, 498 U.S. 146 (1990)
Naler v. *State*, 148 So. 880, 25 (1933)
New York v. *Quarles*, 467 U.S. 649 (1984)
New York v. *Belton*, 453 U.S. 454 (1981)
Nix v. *Williams*, 467 U.S. 431 (1984)
Oliver v. *United States*, 466 U.S. 170 (1984)
Oregon v. *Bradshaw*, 462 U.S. 1039 (1983)
Oregon v. *Elstad*, 470 U.S. 298 (1985)
Payton v. *New York*, 455 U.S. 573 (1980)
Pennsylvania v. *Labron*, 518 U.S. 938 (1996)
People v. *Forts*, 18 N.C. [2nd] 31 (1933)
People v. *Olivo*, 52 N.Y.2d 309 (1981)
Petit v. *Campbell*, 149 S.W.2d 633, 635, 636 (1941)
Rhode Island v. *Innis*, 446 U.S. 291 (1980)
Roviaro v. *United States*, 353 U.S. 53 (1957)
Schmerber v. *California*, 384 U.S. 757 (1966)
Schneckloth v. *Bustamonte*, 412 U.S. 218 (1973)
Sherman v. *United States*, 356 U.S. 369 (1958)
Silverthorne Lumber Co. v. *U.S.*, 251 U.S. 385 (1920)
Spinelli v. *United States*, 393 U.S. 410 (1969)
Stansbury v. *California*, 511 U.S. 318 (1994)
State v. *Bohner*, 210 Wis. 651, 246 N.W. 314 (1933)
State v. *Fournier*, 376 U.S. 575, 589 (1964)
Tennessee v. *Garner*, 471 U.S. 1 (1985)
Terry v. *Ohio*, 392 U.S. 1 (1968)
Texas v. *Brown*, 460 U.S. 730 (1983)
United States v. *Ash Jr.*, 413 U.S. 300 (1973)
United States v. *Chadwick*, 433 U.S. 1 (1977)
Department of Justice v. *Landano*, 508 U.S. 165 (1993)
United States v. *Dunn*, 480 U.S. 294 (1987)
United States v. *Grubbs*, 547 U.S. __, __, (2006)
United States v. *Henry*, 259 F.2d 725 7th Cir. (1958)
United States v. *Irizarry*, 341 F.3d 273, 306 (2003)
United States v. *Leon*, 468, U.S. 897 (1984)
United States v. *Ross*, 456 U.S. 798 (1982)
United States v. *Sokolow*, 109 S. Ct. 1581 (1989)
United States v. *Wade*, 388 U.S. 218 (1967)
Warden v. *Hayden*, 387 U.S. 294 (1967)
Weeks v. *United States*, 232 U.S. 383 (1914)
Wilson v. *Arkansas*, 514 U.S. 927 (1995)
Wong Sun v. *United States*, 371 U.S. 471 (1963)
Wyoming v. *Houghton*, 526 U.S. 295 (1999)

▶ Glossary

A

Abductive reasoning. The process of proposing a likely explanation for an event that must be tested.

Acquaintance stalking. When a stalker and victim know each other casually.

Actus reus. Latin for "the criminal act itself."

Admission. A self-incriminating statement made by a suspect that falls short of an acknowledgment of guilt.

Affidavit. A legal document that presents facts that the officer believes constitute probable cause to justify the issuance of a warrant.

AFIS system. The automated fingerprint identification system.

Aggravated assault. A personal crime where there is a high probability of death; serious, permanent disfigurement; permanent or protracted loss or impairment of the function of any body member or organ; or other severe bodily harm.

Alligatoring. The pattern of crevices formed by the burning of a wooden structure.

Amber Alert. A system that quickly posts information about child abductions.

Analysis. A scientific examination.

Anger-retaliatory rapist. A person who vents his anger and frustration toward the opposite sex by punishing them.

Arrest. The act of a police officer taking a person into custody after making a determination that he or she has violated a law.

Arson. The malicious or fraudulent burning of property.

Assault. To intentionally put someone in fear of immediate battery or to threaten someone while having the apparent ability to carry out that threat.

Associative evidence. Evidence that links a suspect with a crime.

Autoerotic death. Death induced by solo sexual activity in which the participant incorporates the use of self-induced bondage and a ligature to reduce the flow of oxygen while attempting to achieve orgasm through masturbation.

B

Ballistics. The science of tracking the path of a bullet.

Bank robbery. The unlawful taking of money or other assets from a bank through the use of face-to-face contact between suspect and victims.

Bank Secrecy Act. A federal law passed in 1970 to require reporting of large-scale case transactions.

Baseline technique. Crime scene measuring technique in which a line is drawn between two known points.

Battered child syndrome. A clinical term referring to the collection of injuries sustained by a child as a result of repeated mistreatment or beating.

Battered children. Children who suffer from physical abuse.

Battery. An intentional nonconsensual bodily contact that a reasonable person would consider harmful.

Bertillon system. An early criminal identification/classification system based on the idea that certain aspects of the human body, such as skeletal size, ear shape, and eye color, remained the same after a person had reached full physical maturity. It used a combination of photographs with standardized physical measurements.

Best evidence rule. A legal doctrine of evidence that says that no evidence will be admissible in court if it is secondary in nature.

Beyond a reasonable doubt. The standard of proof in a criminal case in which the deciders of fact are entirely satisfied that the defendant is guilty as charged.

Bill of Rights. A constitutional doctrine granting individual freedoms.

Binding material. Material used to incapacitate a victim during the course of a robbery.

Bobbies. London Metropolitan Police Department officers were dubbed bobbies after the department's founder, Home Secretary Sir Robert Peel.

Booby traps. Deadly and dangerous devices used to warn the suspect of any intruders by the sound of explosive devices.

Bookmaking. A type of gambling that usually involves taking bets on sporting events.

Boosters. Professional shoplifters who resell stolen merchandise to pawn shops or fences at usually one-half to one-fourth the original price.

Bow Street Runners. A group of English crime fighters formed by Henry Fielding during the eighteenth century.

Burden of proof. The duty to establish the validity or factuality of the charge against a person.

Burglary. A covert crime in which the criminal works during the nighttime, outside the presence of witnesses.

Burglary tools. Any instrument designed for unlawfully entering a structure.

Burn. A term used in undercover operations when an undercover agent is identified by a criminal suspect.

Buy-bust. When an undercover agent makes a purchase of illicit narcotics and the suspect is immediately arrested.

Buy-walk. When an undercover agent makes a purchase of illicit narcotics and the suspect is allowed to leave for the purposes of continuing the investigation.

C

Carjacking. When an armed robber forces the driver of an automobile out of the vehicle before stealing it.

Carroll Doctrine. A legal principle that enables officers to search an automobile without a search warrant provided that they have probable cause to believe it contains contraband and that the vehicle is mobile.

Chain of custody. Documentation of all who handle evidence in a criminal case.

Check kiting. Drawing cash on accounts made up of uncollected funds.

Child abuse. The physical, sexual, or emotional abuse of children.

Child molester. One who engages in some form of child sexual exploitation.

Chop shop. A secret location where auto thieves dismantle stolen vehicles for the purpose of selling the parts.

Churning. The practice of convincing insurance customers to use the cash value of old insurance policies to pay premiums on new, more expensive policies.

Circumstantial evidence. Evidence that tends to incriminate a person without offering positive proof.

Closed files. Intelligence files that are maintained apart from criminal investigation files to prevent unauthorized inspection of data.

Coercion. The use or threat of illegal physical means to induce a suspect to make an admission or confession.

Collation. The process of comparing texts carefully to clarify or give meaning to information.

Commercial robbery. Robbery of stores and businesses located close to major thoroughfares such as main streets, highways, and interstates.

Composite. A freehand drawing of a suspected criminal.

Computer crime. A violation of criminal law that requires some knowledge of computers for perpetration.

Computer virus. A set of illegal computer instructions designed to ruin computer hardware and/or software while reproducing itself in the computer program when it is executed.

Confession. Direct acknowledgment by the suspect of his or her guilt in the commission of a specific crime or as an integral part of a specific crime.

Confidence game. The criminal practice of gaining the confidence of a would-be victim for the sole purpose of swindling money from them.

Consent search. When police gain permission to search without a warrant.

Conspiracy. An agreement between two or more persons to commit a criminal act, accompanied by the commission of at least one overt act in furtherance of the crime.

Constable. A term given to peace officers during the early formation of policing in England.

Contamination of evidence. The act of adversely affecting evidence by allowing it to be tampered with or by not protecting the chain of custody.

Coordinate method. Measuring an object from two fixed points of reference.

Corpus delicti evidence. Evidence that establishes that a crime has been committed.

Cover story. The fictitious story contrived by the undercover investigator to explain his presence as a drug buyer to criminal suspects.

Covert information collection. A clandestine process of data collection on criminal acts that have not yet occurred but for which the investigator must prepare.

Crack. A freebase form of cocaine.

Credibility. One's ability to be believed.

Crime. Any act prohibited under criminal law that is punishable by a fine, imprisonment, or death.

Crime scene. The location where the crime took place.

Criminal intelligence. Documented information regarding past, present, or future criminal activity.

Cross-examination. A legal line of questioning in a criminal trial designed to weaken or discredit any testimony given during direct examination.

Cross-projection method. Used in indoor crime scenes, it is basically a top-down view of the crime scene where the walls of the room have been "folded" down to reveal locations of bullet holes, blood-spatter evidence, and so on.

Crystal meth. A potent form of methamphetamine.

CSA. Controlled Substances Act of 1970.

Custodial interrogation. A process of questioning a suspect when his or her liberty has been restricted to a degree that is associated with arrest.

Cybercrime. The destruction, theft or unauthorized use, modification, or copying of information, programs, services, equipment or communication networks.

Cyber-extortion. When a computer criminal extorts money from a victim.

Cyberstalking. Preying on a victim through his or her computer.

D

D.A.R.E. Drug Abuse Resistance Education prevention program.

Data diddling. False data entry.

Data mining. The process of generating computer models to predict a terrorist's actions.

Date rape. Rape which occurs when victims and offenders are acquainted before the crime is committed.

Date rape drug. Another term for the drug Rohypnol.

Deadly force. Actions of police officers that result in the killing of a person.

Deductive reasoning. The ability to draw conclusions based on critical thinking.

Deep cover. Working undercover for extended periods of time.

Demeanor. One's persona and how one is perceived.

Demonstrative evidence. Evidence used to clarify an issue rather than to prove something.

Dependence. The degree of an illegal and addicting drug's legal use.

Deoxyribonucleic acid. DNA is the genetic material used in criminal investigations.

Designer drugs. A class of illicit drugs that are specifically designed to emulate controlled substances.

Detention. Something less than an arrest but more than a consensual encounter.

Digital imaging. Generally referring to photographs taken with a digital camera and stored on digital media.

Direct examination. A courtroom procedure whereby a witness is asked what he or she knows about an alleged offense, and a brief explanation as to how he or she personally observed or knew about the incident.

Dissemination. The phase of the intelligence process whereby information is shared with other law enforcement agencies.

Diversion. The trafficking of pharmaceutical drugs to the street from normal, legal channels.

DNA technology.   The science of identifying the genetic facsimile, or "blueprint," of any particular organism in every cell within each human body.

Drug courier profile.   The practice of observing suspected drug traffickers to develop a pattern of behavior that would constitute legal cause for a stop and search by police.

Drug Enforcement Administration.   Established in 1973, the DEA is the only federal investigative body whose sole duty it is to enforce federal drug laws in the United States.

Due process.   The essential elements of fairness under the law, ensuring that no person is deprived of life, liberty, or property without notice of charges, assistance from legal counsel, a hearing, and a chance to confront one's accusers.

Duress.   The imposition of restrictions on physical behavior such as prolonged interrogation and deprivation of water, food, or sleep.

Dying declaration.   A statement given by a dying person that implicates the killer. The legal requirements of a dying declaration are that the victim must be rational and competent and must ultimately die of the wounds.

E

Electronic evidence.   Information and data of investigative value that is stored in or transmitted by an electronic device.

Elements of a crime.   The legal characteristics of a crime.

Embezzlement.   A low-profile crime consisting of employees who steal large amounts of money over long periods of time.

Entrapment.   When an undercover officer convinces a criminal suspect to commit a crime he or she was not predisposed to commit.

Evidence.   A statement, object, or other item bearing on or establishing the point in question in a court of law.

Exclusionary rule.   The legal rule that excludes evidence that has been determined to have been obtained illegally.

Exemplars.   Samples, as of a suspect's handwriting.

Exhibitionism.   A sexual abnormality where the offender receives sexual gratification through revealing his/her genitals to the opposite sex.

Exigent circumstances.   Circumstances whereby a search may be legally conducted without a warrant.

Expert Systems.   A process of utilizing artificial intelligence by computers to make inferences based on available information and to draw conclusions or make recommendations to the systems operators.

Expert witness.   One whose knowledge exceeds the knowledge of anyone with a moderate education or experience in the field.

F

Family abduction.   Abductions related to domestic or custody disputes.

Federal Bureau of Investigation.   Established in 1924 as the primary federal investigative bureau within the U.S. Department of Justice.

Federal Bureau of Narcotics.   One of the first federal investigative bureaus, established in 1930 to combat drug trafficking.

Felony.   A category of crime which is of a more serious nature than a misdemeanor, usually punishable by more than one year in prison up to the death penalty.

Fence.   A person who buys and sells stolen property with criminal intent.

Fetish.   A psychological disorder in which a person has a sexual attraction to a nonsexual item.

Field interview.   Interviewing technique used when patrol officers happen on people or circumstances that appear suspicious but when there is not sufficient cause for arrest.

Field notes.   An investigator's most personal and readily available record of the crime scene search.

Field operations.   The wide array of police patrol duties.

Finished sketches.   A completed crime scene sketch drawn to scale.

Fire triangle.   What a fire needs to burn: heat, fuel, and oxygen.

Fixated child molester.   One whose primary sexual orientation is toward children and whose sociosexual maturation develops as a result of unresolved conflicts in his or her development.

Fixed surveillance.   Observing from a stationary location.

Flashback.   A temporary reoccurrence from a psychedelic experience.

Flash description.   An emergency radio broadcast generally made by the first officer to reach a crime scene, to other officers in the area, in which descriptions of the suspect and his or her vehicle are communicated.

Fleeing-felon rule.   A legal doctrine, no longer in effect, allowing police officers to shoot suspected felons.

Flowcharting.   An informational tracking system that demonstrates a chain of events or activities over a period of time.

Follow-up investigation.   A continuing phase of the investigation, in which information that is learned in the preliminary investigation is added to or built on.

Forensic dentistry.   Scientific examination of dental records.

Forward-looking infrared.   A surveillance technology that measures radiant energy in the radiant heat portion and display readings as thermographs.

Freebase.   A method of ingesting cocaine in a purified form.

Frye test.   A legal standard used to determine the admissibility of scientific evidence.

Fungible goods.   Items such as tools, liquor, and clothing that are indistinguishable from others like them.

G

Gambling.   The wagering of money or other valuables on the outcome of a game or event.

GPS.   Global Positioning Satellite.

H

Hacker.   A computer programmer who explores, tests, and pushes the computer to its limits, regardless of the consequences.

Hardware.   The physical computer and any peripherals associated with it, such as printers, telephone modems, and external disk drives.

Hearsay evidence.   Second-party statements offered to the court by a person who did not originate the statement.

Herschel, William.   A pioneer in the mid-nineteenth century in the use of fingerprinting for purposes of identification.

Homicide. The unlawful killing of one human being by another.

Hoover, J. Edgar. Director of the FBI for almost 50 years.

Hot list. A cancellation bulletin for stolen credit cards.

I

Identi-kit. A computer-generated composite of a suspected criminal.

Incest. Sexual relations between children and their parents.

Inevitable discovery doctrine. A legal doctrine stating that illegally seized evidence is admissible in court provided that eventually it would have been discovered anyway.

Informant. Anyone who provides information of an investigative nature to law enforcement authorities.

Inside team. A surveillance team responsible for briefing officers concerning their actions if a crime occurs.

Intelligence gathering. The covert process of gathering information on criminal activity.

Interrogation. The systematic questioning of a person suspected of involvement in a crime for the purpose of obtaining a confession.

Interview. A relatively formal conversation conducted for the purpose of obtaining information.

Intimate or former intimate stalking. When a stalker and victim were married or divorced, current or former lovers, serious or casual sexual partners, or former sexual partners.

J

Joyriding. When a juvenile auto thief steals a car for enjoyment for short periods of time.

Judicial notice. The admissibility of certain facts without the necessity of introducing evidence.

L

Labeling. Classifying a missing child case.

Latent evidence. Evidence that is not readily visible to the naked eye.

Latent fingerprints. Fingerprints that are nonvisible unless developed through a fingerprint lifting process.

Lineup. The police practice of allowing witnesses or victims to view several suspects for identification purposes.

Link analysis. A charting technique designed to show relationships between individuals and organizations using a graphic visual design.

Lividity. A bloodstain on the body of a deceased person.

Loansharking. Usurious loans made to people for exorbitant interest rates, whose payment is enforced by the use of violence.

M

Manslaughter. The deliberate killing of another person, characterized by either voluntary or involuntary classifications.

Markers. Items placed in crime scene photos that call attention to specific objects or enable the viewer of the photo to get a sense of the size of the object or the distance between objects.

Masquerading.   The process of one person assuming the identity of an authorized computer user by acquiring items, knowledge, or characteristics.

Mass murder.   The commission of four or more murders in a single incident within a short span of time.

Material evidence.   Evidence shown to be important enough to influence the outcome of a criminal case.

Medical examiner.   Public official who makes official determination of cause and time of death in wrongful death cases.

Mens rea.   Latin term meaning "guilty mind," or criminal intent.

Methods of operation.   The behavior of the criminal during the commission of the crime.

***Miranda* warning.**   The legal guidelines to protect the rights of the accused were defined further by the Supreme Court in such cases as *Miranda*.

Misdemeanor.   A less serious crime than a felony, usually punishable by less than 1 year in the county jail and/or a fine.

M.O.   The method of operation used by a criminal to commit a crime.

Mobile surveillance.   Observing a criminal suspect from a moving vehicle.

Money laundering.   A process where illegally earned cash is made to appear legitimate or the sources of the cash are disguised.

Motion.   A written request (also called a petition) or an oral request made to the court anytime before, during, or after court proceedings.

Motivations.   Reasons why someone does something.

Münchhausen syndrome by proxy.   A clinical term referring to when a parent or caretaker attempts to bring medical attention to themselves by inducing illness in their children.

Murder.   The purposeful, premeditated, and unlawful taking of human life by another person.

N

NATB.   National Auto Theft Bureau.

NCAVC.   National Center for the Analysis of Violent Crime.

NCIC.   National Crime Information Center.

NCMEC.   National Center for Missing and Exploited Children.

Neighborhood canvass.   A door-to-door search of the area of a crime to identify witnesses.

Neighborhood Watch.   A program whereby merchants and residents are encouraged to take a more proactive role in detecting and reporting activity that might be criminal in nature.

NISMART.   National Incidence Studies for Missing, Abducted, Runaway and Thrownaway Children.

Noncustodial parent.   A parent who does not have legal custody of a child.

Nonfamily abduction.   When a child is removed from his family through force or trickery.

O

Objection.   A protest to the judge regarding the "form" of the question being asked of the witness.

Obsessive-compulsive behavior.   A psychological disorder referring to a compulsion in certain people to involve themselves in specific types of behavior.

Off-road machinery. Machinery such as bulldozers, tractors, wheel loaders, and excavators.

Olfactory. Pertaining to smell. A distinguishable odor may indicate a specific type of crime.

Open files. Criminal information developed for the purpose of eventually making an arrest and gaining a conviction in a court of law.

Outside team. The arrest team in a surveillance.

Overt information collection. A method of collecting information involving personal interaction with individuals, many of whom are witnesses to crimes, victims of crimes, or the suspects themselves.

P

Paper trail. Evidence in an arson case that shows motive. This includes financial records, inflated insurance coverage, little or no inventory, and excessive debts.

Pedophilia. The basis of sexual misconduct with children.

Peel, Sir Robert. The founder of the London Metropolitan Police Department during the early nineteenth century.

Penal code. Each state's criminal statutes.

Personality profile. A means of identifying the type of person responsible for a particular crime. This is accomplished by identifying psychological and social characteristics surrounding the crime as well as the manner in that it was committed.

Pharmaceutical diversion. The act of diverting controlled drugs from legitimate channels.

Physical evidence. Any type of evidence having shape, size, or dimension.

Physiological addiction. An alteration of normal body functions that necessitates the continued presence of a drug in order to prevent the withdrawal syndrome.

Pigeon drop. A commonly used confidence game.

Pilferage. The stealing of merchandise.

Pinkerton, Allan. The founder of the Pinkerton National Detective Agency in 1850.

Pinkerton National Detective Agency. Founded by Allan Pinkerton in 1850, this was one of the first criminal investigation bodies to exist in the United States.

Plain-view doctrine. A legal doctrine whereby police officers have the opportunity to confiscate evidence, without a warrant, based on what they find in plain view and open to public inspection.

Plants. Preparations used to set an arson fire.

Plastic fingerprints. A fingerprint impression left when a person presses against a plastic material such as putty, wax, or tar.

Plastic workers. White-collar criminals who have experience in dealing with stolen credit cards.

Point of origin. The location on an arson scene where the fire originated.

Polygraph. A mechanical device designed to aid investigators in obtaining information.

Polymerase chain reaction (PCR). A process in which DNA strips can be rapidly reproduced for scientific analysis.

Postmortem lividity. A purplish coloration of the skin of a deceased person.

Power-assertive rapist. A rapist type who attempts to demonstrate his manhood to the victim through sexual assault.

Preferential molester. A child molester who has sexual desires focusing on children and is typically suffering from a more identifiable psychological disorder.

Preliminary investigation. A term referring to the early stages of crime scene processing, usually conducted by the first officer on the crime scene.

Premeditation. Planning beforehand that shows intent to commit a criminal act.

Preponderance of the evidence. The standard of proof used in a civil matter which says that the accused is at fault if he or she contributed more than 50 percent to the cause of the dispute.

Pretrial conference. A meeting between the prosecutor and the investigator at which the prosecution strategy to a criminal case is discussed.

Preventive response. Prevention through deterrence is sometimes achieved by arresting the criminal and by aggressive prosecution.

Prima facie evidence. Evidence established by law that proves a fact in dispute.

Primary physical aggressor. If the police have sufficient reason to believe that a person, within the proceding four hours, committed an active domestic violence or spousal battery, the officer is required to arrest a person. This person is known as the primary physical aggressor.

Private eye. A term referring to a private investigator.

Privileged communications rule. A legal ruling that says that certain statements are inadmissible if stated by people in certain relationships, e.g., husband and wife.

Proactive patrol. An effective police patrol tool to prevent burglary as well as many other crimes.

Proactive response. An investigative approach to crime solving where criminal activity is investigated before it occurs.

Probable cause. The minimum amount of information necessary to cause a reasonable person to believe that a crime has been or is being committed by a particular person.

Profile. A method used to identify an offender's motivations.

Prohibition. Lasting from 1920 to 1933, the period in which the manufacture, sale, and consumption of alcoholic beverages was outlawed.

Proof. The end or net result of the evidence collection process.

Property crime. A type of crime whereby the criminal is more concerned with financial gain and less prepared for a violent altercation with the victim.

Protection orders. A legal document that orders one person to stay away from another.

Psychological dependence. Feeling that a drug is necessary to one's well-being.

Pyramid scheme. A commonly used confidence game.

Pyromaniac. A person with a psychological disorder where sexual gratification is obtained through the setting of fires.

R

Rape. Unlawful sexual intercourse, achieved through force and without consent.

Reactive response. An approach to crime solving that addresses crimes that have already occurred, such as murder, robbery, and burglary.

Reasonable force.   The amount of force that is considered reasonable to capture or subdue a criminal suspect.

Reasonable grounds.   Reasonable grounds for an arrest usually depend on the facts and circumstances surrounding the specific case.

Regressed child molester.   A child molester who views the victim as a substitute for an adult partner.

Relational databases.   Databases that permit fast and easy sorting of large records.

Relevancy test.   Permits, in a court of law, the admission of relevant evidence that is helpful to the trier of fact.

Relevant evidence.   Evidence that is considered logical or rational.

Res geste evidence.   Unplanned and spontaneous statements made by persons present at a crime scene.

Residential robbery.   Robbery when an armed intruder breaks into the home and holds residents at gun- or knifepoint.

Resistance.   A term referring to physical or psychological unwillingness to comply.

RICO Act.   The 1970 Racketeering Influenced and Corrupt Organizations Act.

Rigor mortis.   The process of stiffening or contraction of the muscles of a deceased person after vital functions cease.

RISS projects.   Programs of the federal Regional Information Sharing System.

Rogues' gallery.   A compilation of descriptions, methods of operation, hiding places, and the names of associates of known criminals in the 1850s.

Rough sketch.   The initial crime scene sketch drawn by officers on the crime scene.

Runaway or lost child.   A category of missing children that is the most commonly encountered by law enforcement.

S

Salvage switch.   When a car thief purchases a wrecked vehicle that is unrepairable, strictly for its certificate of title and for the vehicle identification number.

Scammers.   Criminals who defraud; for example, attempt to obtain prescriptions for controlled drugs.

Scanning.   A procedure used in computer crime whereby the criminal presents sequentially changing information to an automated system to identify those items receiving a positive response.

Scene-conscious.   When the crime scene investigator becomes aware of the crime scene situation and is prepared to take certain immediate actions.

School robberies.   Instances of petty extortion or "shakedowns" of students and teachers in public schools.

Scope of the search.   An officer's authority to search incident to an arrest.

Scotland Yard.   One of the first criminal investigative bodies originally formed in England in the mid-nineteenth century.

Search warrant.   A legal document enabling a police officer to search.

Search warrant return.   An itemized inventory of all property and material seized by officers at the location of the search.

Seed money.   Money required to initiate an undercover drug transaction.

Self-defense.   To protect oneself from harm.

Sensational murder.   A series or group of murders that arouse the interest of the general public.

Serial murder.   A sequence of murders where there is a time break between victims of two days to several months.

Serology.   The scientific analysis of blood.

Shaken baby syndrome.   A medical term for murder of infants who are violently shaken.

Shoplifting.   A common form of theft involving the taking of goods from retail stores.

Simple assault.   Threats by one person to cause bodily harm or death to another or purposely inflicting bodily harm on another.

Situational molester.   Child molesters who commit such crimes because of one of several external factors. These include intoxication, drug abuse, mood or mental conditions, or other social conditions.

Smash-and-grab robbery.   A type of robbery whereby the robbers approach a car, break the window, and hold up the driver at gunpoint.

Smurfing.   When money launderers go to different banks and purchase cashier's checks in denominations of less than $10,000 for the purpose of bypassing the reporting requirement.

Snitches.   Amateur pilferers who are usually respectable persons who do not perceive of themselves as thieves yet are systematic shoplifters who steal merchandise for their own use rather than for resale.

Software.   The medium on which information is stored, such as computer tapes and floppy disks.

Span of the fire.   Physical characteristics of an arson fire such as smoke, direction, flames, and distance of travel.

Spree.   Numerous acts occurring in a short span of time.

Stakeout.   Another term for stationary or fixed surveillance.

Stationary surveillance.   Another term for fixed surveillance or stakeout.

Stranger stalking.   When the stalker and victim do not know each other.

Strategic intelligence.   Information that provides the investigator with information as to the capabilities and intentions of target subjects.

Street robbery.   Robbery committed on public streets and alleyways.

Stripping operation.   A criminal endeavor where stolen vehicles are disposed of.

Stop and frisk.   Term referring to an officer stopping and searching a person for weapons.

Substantive due process.   A concept of criminal law that determines whether a statute is fair and reasonable.

Sudden infant death syndrome (SIDS).   A diagnosis made when there is no other medical explanation for the abrupt death of an apparently healthy infant.

Suicide.   The deliberate taking of one's own life.

Support officer.   A surveillance officer, sometimes called an intelligence, cover, or tactical officer, who works in plainclothes and who works with the undercover unit but not in an undercover capacity.

Surveillance.   Surreptitious observation.

Synergism.   A severe physical reaction that results when a user ingests more than one type of a drug at a time.

T

Tactical intelligence. Information that furnishes the police agency with specifics about individuals, organizations, and different types of criminal activity.

Tagging. A process of altering title documents for stolen automobiles.

Terry **doctrine.** A legal principle which states that the police have the authority to detain a person even without probable cause if the person is believed to have committed a crime.

Testimony. A statement made in response to a question or a series of questions.

Texas Rangers. One of the earliest law enforcement and criminal investigative units; formed in Texas before Texas became a state.

Thermal imaging. Using technology to identify heat sources that might reveal criminal activity.

Thief catchers. Thief catchers were recruited from the riffraff of the streets to aid law enforcement officials in locating criminals during the European Industrial Revolution.

Tin trucks. A truck used to transport parts of a stolen vehicle.

Tolerance. A physical condition that develops when a person needs increasing doses of a drug in order to experience its initial effects.

Tort. A personal wrong committed by one person against another.

Trace evidence. A minute or even microscopic fragment of matter such as hair or fiber that is not immediately detectable by the naked eye.

Trailers. Materials used in spreading an arson fire.

Transfer of evidence theory. The theory that whenever two objects meet, some evidence, however microscopic, may remain to demonstrate that the encounter did occur.

Triangulation method. A bird's-eye view of the crime scene, utilizing fixed objects from which to measure.

Triggering Condition. The anticipated future event giving rise to probable cause to search.

Trojan horse. A criminal computer program that automatically transfers money to an illegal account whenever a legal transaction is made.

U

Undercover officer. When a police officer poses as a criminal in order to gain evidence for criminal prosecution.

V

Vehicle identification number (VIN). A 17-digit number assigned to the vehicle by the manufacturer at the time of production designed to distinguish each vehicle from all others.

Vertical integration. The ability of a criminal group to control both the manufacture and wholesale distribution of illicit drugs.

VI-CAP. Violent Criminal Apprehension Program; operated by the FBI.

Vice. Generally associated with organized crime, vice crimes are the supplying of illegal goods and services.

Victimless crime. Most typically, a vice crime where all parties of the criminal act are willing participants.

Visible fingerprints.   A type of fingerprint left at a crime scene that results from being adulterated with some foreign matter, such as blood, flour, or oil.

Voyeur.   A person with a psychological abnormality whereby sexual gratification is obtained by secretly observing people who are engaged in sexual activity.

W

White-collar crime.   A nonviolent crime committed for financial gain and accomplished by means of deception.

Withdrawal symptoms.   A series of symptoms that appear when a drug to which a user is physically addicted is stopped abruptly or severely reduced.

WITSEC Program.   The federal witness security program operated by the U.S. Marshals Service.

Z

Zone search method.   A searching technique; also known as the quadrant method.

▶ Index